# ODD GODS

# ODD GODS

*New Religions &
the Cult Controversy*

EDITED BY JAMES R. LEWIS

## Prometheus Books

59 John Glenn Drive
Amherst, New York 14228-2197

Grateful acknowledgment is made to L. Ron Hubbard Library for permission to reproduce the photograph of L. Ron Hubbard in the photo insert.

Published 2001 by Prometheus Books

Inquiries should be addressed to
Prometheus Books
59 John Glenn Drive
Amherst, New York 14228–2197
VOICE: 716–691–0133, ext. 207
FAX: 716–564–2711
WWW.PROMETHEUSBOOKS.COM

05 04 03 02 01     5 4 3 2 1

Library of Congress Cataloging-in-Publication Data

Odd gods : new religions and the "cult" controversy / [edited by] James R. Lewis.
    p. cm.
   Includes bibliographical references and index.
   ISBN 1–57392–842–9 (hardcover : alk. paper)
   1. Sects—United States. 2. Cults—United States. 3. United States—Religion.
I. Lewis, James R.

BL2525 .O33 2000
291—dc21

                                    00–045843

Printed in the United States of America on acid-free paper

# CONTENTS

# PREFACE

The cult controversy is one of those issues that periodically explodes into public consciousness, dominates the TV networks and newspapers for a time, and then disappears as reporters turn their collective attention toward newer, fresher scandals and disasters. The impression this sporadic coverage has created in the public consciousness is that our society is filled with innumerable weird groups capable of breaking out into some form of sociopathic behavior at any moment. This picture is deeply flawed. In the first few chapters of the present text, I hope to supply some of the pieces missing from this skewed image.

Scholars have studied this conflict since the 1970s. Their collective findings produce a picture of the controversy profoundly at odds with popular stereotypes. While I have attempted to allow competing points of view to find expression in the following pages, my orientation to the issue derives from the consensus viewpoint of mainstream academic.

Chapter 1 presents an overview of the controversy. The two major competing points of view are delineated, particularly with respect to the brainwashing debate. This chapter also provides some historical background, a brief overview of the role of the media, an analysis of what people find attractive about membership in minority religions, and a discussion of the characteristics of truly dangerous groups.

Because of church-state separation issues, the primary battleground for the controversy has been the courts. Chapter 2 surveys the history of this conflict. A number of recent decisions have defeated the "cultic mind control" argument in the courts and eviscerated the anticult movement.

Despite a stereotype that portrays all controversial religions as being more or less similar, the groups that have been attacked as "cults" are actually quite diverse. Chapters 3 through 19 present an overview of many of the groups and movements that have been involved in the cult conflict.

# ACKNOWLEDGMENTS

In compiling a book of this sort, one always incurs innumerable debts. This is especially the case with the present book, parts of which have been adapted from prior publications. Specifically, chapters 1 and 2 have been adapted from chapters 1 and 4 of my earlier book, *Cults in America*. I would like to thank ABC-Clio, and especially Todd Hallman, for permission to draw material from that volume. Also, most of the information on specific groups found in chapters 3 through 19 is based on entries originally published in my *Encyclopedia of Cults, Sects, and New Religions*. I am indebted to Prometheus Books, and especially to Steven Mitchell, for allowing me to adapt that material for the present volume. I would also like to acknowledge Mr. Mitchell's considerable assistance with bringing the present project to fruition.

Many thanks are due the contributors, most of whom are prominent scholars in this field. The present volume is much richer because of their careful research and thoughtful observations. Scholars who composed specific sections are acknowledged by name in bylines. I would also like to thank the many other, unnamed writers whose work is reflected in the present volume. In particular, toward the end of composing the *Encyclopedia*, copies of relevant entries were sent to most of the existing religious organizations covered in the following pages. These groups often responded by returning updated information, sometimes in the form of completely rewritten entries. When the new data could be smoothly integrated into what had already been written, I added the update. Many thanks to these unnamed researchers/writers!

# *1* OVERVIEW

## A TALE OF TWO NEW RELIGIONS

T he cult controversy is a complex social issue that has engendered an emotional and often mean-spirited debate. At the center of this debate are a wide variety of diverse groups that often have little in common. While some are political organizations or psychological movements, the great majority are religious groups. Most embrace belief systems at odds with the Judeo-Christian mainline, although some are quite orthodox. Also, while they are usually relatively small, new organizations, almost all have roots in older, larger traditions. The one trait these groups share is that they are controversial. Decades of social conflict have left their impress on the term "cult," which, to the general public, indicates a religious group that is false, dangerous, or otherwise *bad*.

The sharpness of the cult controversy has tended to polarize participants into extreme positions, making it difficult to find a middle ground from which to approach the issue. Hence, rather than tackling the problem directly, it might well repay our efforts to work our way into the debate indirectly, through the stories of two contrasting religious groups that will serve to highlight some of the dilemmas associated with the cult controversy.

In the following sections, the story of Heaven's Gate, the UFO group that committed suicide in 1997, will be used to exemplify the concerns that "anticultists" bring to the controversy. The Island Pond raid—involving the Twelve Tribes, a less well-known Christian group—will, on the other hand, be used to exemplify the concerns of religious libertarians.

## Heaven's Gate

*Getting off the Planet*

On March 26, 1997, the bodies of thirty-nine men and women were found in a posh mansion outside San Diego, all victims of a mass suicide. Messages left by the group indicate that they believed they were stepping out of their "physical containers" in order to ascend to a UFO that was arriving in the wake of the Hale-Bopp comet. They also asserted that this comet, or parts of it, would subsequently crash into the earth and cause widespread destruction. In a taped message, their leader further noted that our calendars were off—that the year 1997 was really the year 2000, as if everyone was in agreement that the world would end precisely two millennia after the time of Jesus.

Heaven's Gate—formerly known as Human Individual Metamorphosis (HIM)—originally made headlines in September 1975 when, following a public lecture in Waldport, Oregon, over thirty people vanished overnight. This disappearance became the occasion for a media event. For the next several months, reporters generated story after story about glassy-eyed cult groupies abandoning the everyday lives to follow the strange couple who alternately referred to themselves as "Bo and Peep," "the Two," "Do and Ti," and other bizarre monikers.

Bo and Peep founded one of the most unusual flying saucer religions ever to emerge out of the occult-metaphysical subculture. Bo (Marshall Herff Applewhite) and Peep (Bonnie Lu Nettles) met in 1972. In 1973, they had an experience which convinced them that they were the two witnesses mentioned in Revelation 11 who would be martyred and then resurrected three and a half days later—an event they later referred to as the Demonstration. Preaching an unusual synthesis of occult spirituality and UFO soteriology, they began recruiting in new age circles in the spring of 1975. Followers were required to abandon friends and family, detach themselves completely from human emotions as well as material possessions, and focus exclusively on perfecting themselves in preparation for a physical transition (i.e., beaming up) to the next kingdom (in the form of a flying saucer)—a metamorphosis that would be facilitated by ufonauts.

As an unusually fascinating form of rejected knowledge that mainstream scientists tend to classify as paranormal anyway, UFOs have attracted considerable interest within the occult-metaphysical subculture. Almost from the beginning, however, this subculture had transformed flying saucers and their presumed extraterrestrial pilots into spiritual beings who had come to earth to help us along the path. To accomplish the transformation of E.T.s into wise, esoteric beings, "ufonauts" were assimilated into earlier models of spiritual sages, particularly the so-called ascended masters.

The concept of ascended masters or the Great White Brotherhood was codified within Theosophy by Helena Petrovna Blavatsky in the 1880s, and from there has been derived by the various religious groups that descend from the Theosophical Society. Many people in the New Age movement believe that such masters guide the spiritual progress of humanity. The equation of ascended masters with ufonauts seems to have developed out of an earlier idea, which was that at least some of the masters were from other planets in our solar system, such as Venus.

Even much "secular" thinking about UFOs embodies quasi-religious themes, such as the crypto-religious notion that the world is on the verge of destruction and that ufonauts are somehow going to rescue humanity— either by forcibly preventing a nuclear Armageddon or by taking select members of the human race to another planet to preserve the species. The psychologist Carl Jung was referring to the latter portrayal of ufonauts when he called them "technological angels." Jung interpreted the phenomenon of flying saucers—which often appear in the form of circular disks—as mandala symbols, reflecting the human mind's desire for stability in a confused world. From a depth psychological point of view, it is thus no coincidence that the chariots of the gods should manifest in the form of a circle, which is a symbol of wholeness.

But if UFOs are the chariots of the gods, then why don't the Space Brothers just land and communicate their ideas to humanity in person? The same question has sometimes been asked with respect to the Great White Brotherhood. One of the salient characteristics of the ascended masters was that they preferred to communicate their occult teachings through the medium of telepathic messages sent to select individuals. These chosen vessels then relayed the masters' messages to the larger public, either vocally in a form of mediumship later called "channeling" or in written form via a process usually referred to as automatic writing. Because the ascended masters are the primary model for the Space Brothers, it comes as no surprise that later-day UFO prophets should employ the same methods for communicating the wisdom of the ufonauts to the larger public.

Applewhite—the son of a Presbyterian minister, who himself had aspired to a ministerial career—supplied some distinctly Christian elements to his and Nettles's theological synthesis. Of particular importance was the notion of physical resurrection: In the early phase of their movement, Applewhite and Nettles taught that the goal of the process they were teaching their followers was to prepare them to be physically taken aboard the spacecraft where they would enter a cocoonlike state, eventually being reborn in a transformed physical body.

The notion of resurrection is central to chapter 11 of the Book of Revelation, the biblical passage Applewhite and Nettles came to view as describing their particular ministry. This chapter recounts the story of two prophets who will be slain. Then, three and a half days later, they will be resurrected and taken up in a cloud:

> At the end of the three days and a half the breath of life from God came into them; and they stood up on their feet to the terror of all who saw it. Then a loud voice was heard speaking to them from heaven, which said, "Come up here!" And they went up to heaven in a cloud, in full view of their enemies. At that same moment there was a violent earthquake. (Rev. 11:11–13)

In the early phase of their movement, Applewhite and Nettles prophesied that they would soon be assassinated. Using the above passage as a script for future events, they further predicted that they would be resurrected three and a half days later and taken up into a flying saucer. The Two asserted that this event—which, as was said earlier, they termed *The Demonstration*—would prove the truth of their teachings. As for their followers, they taught that Heaven was the literal, physical heavens, and those few people chosen to depart with the Two would, after their physical transformation, become crew members aboard UFOs.

While the basic teachings seem to have remained constant, the details of their ideology were flexible enough to undergo modification over time. For example, in the early days, Applewhite and Nettles taught their followers that they were extraterrestrial beings. However, after the notion of walk-ins became popular within the New Age subculture, the Two changed their tune and began describing themselves as extraterrestrial walk-ins.

Another notion the Two picked up from the metaphysical subculture of their day was the ancient astronaut hypothesis. The term "ancient astronauts" is used to refer to various forms of the concept that ufonauts visited our planet in the distant past. The basic idea that many, if not all of the powerful sky gods of traditional religions were really extraterrestrial visitors intervening in human history has been around for many decades. However, it was not until a series of books about the "chariots of the gods" authored by Erich van Däniken in the 1970s that this notion was popularized.

One aspect of the ancient astronaut hypothesis is the idea that the contemporary human race is the offspring of a union between aliens and native terrestrials. In a somewhat different version of the same idea, ancient ufonauts stimulated the evolution of our apelike forebears to produce present-day humanity. Our space "fathers" have subsequently been watching over us, and will, according to some new age notions, return to mingle with their distant offspring during the imminent new age.

Applewhite and Nettles taught a slightly modified version of the ancient astronaut hypothesis: Aliens planted the seeds of current humanity millions of years ago, and have come to reap the harvest of their work in the form of spiritual evolved individuals who will join the ranks of flying saucer crews. Only a select few members of humanity will be chosen to advance to this transhuman state. The rest will be left to wallow in the spiritually poisoned atmosphere of a corrupt world.

Applewhite would later teach that after the elect had been picked up by the space brothers, the planet would be engulfed in cataclysmic destruction. When, in 1993, under the name of Total Overcomers Anonymous, the group ran an advertisement in *USA Today*, their portrayal of the post-rapture world was far more apocalyptic than Applewhite and Nettles had taught in the seventies:

> The Earth's present "civilization" is about to be recycled—"spaded under." Its inhabitants are refusing to evolve. The "weeds" have taken over the garden and disturbed its usefulness beyond repair.

For followers of the Two, the focus of day-to-day existence was to follow a disciplined regime referred to as the overcoming process or, simply, the process. The goal of this process was to overcome human weaknesses—a goal not dissimilar to the goal of certain spiritual practices followed by more mainstream monastic communities.

The group developed quietly until the media interest evoked in the wake of the Waldport, Oregon, meeting. They subsequently canceled a planned meeting in Chicago, and split the group into a number of autonomous "families" consisting of a dozen or more individuals. Another change was the subsequent announcement that the *Demonstration* had been canceled because their followers had not been making rapid enough progress in the overcoming process. Rather than focusing on the time when they would be taken up by the saucers, they must concentrate on their own development.

The seminomadic period ended within a few years when two followers inherited a total of approximately $300,000. They then rented houses, initially in Denver and later in the Dallas-Fort Worth area. Each house, which they called a "craft," had the windows covered to prevent the neighbors from watching their activities. Followers adhered to a strict routine. Immersed in the intensity of their structured lifestyle, the teachings of the Two became more and more real to members.

The group's strict segregation from society was suddenly altered in 1983 when many followers visited their families on Mother's Day. However, these members dropped out of contact as soon as they left. It was during these visits that they communicated to their families that they were learning computer technology. Another change took place in 1985, when

Nettles died of cancer. The group surfaced again in 1994 when, thinking the lift-off would begin in a year or two, they held another series of public meetings. It was as part of this new cycle of missionary activity that the *USA Today* ad appeared.

Details about how the group came to attach apocalyptic significance to the Hale-Bopp Comet are tantalizingly scanty. For whatever reason, someone outside the group had come to the conclusion that a giant UFO was coming to earth, "hidden" in the wake of Hale-Bopp. This individual then placed his opinion on the Internet. When Heaven's Gate retrieved this information, Applewhite took it as an indication that the long awaited pick-up of his group by aliens was finally about to take place. The decision that the time had come to make their final exit could not have been made more than a few weeks before the mass suicide.

The idea that the group might depart via suicide had emerged in Applewhite's thinking only within the last few years. The earlier idea—an idea that had set Heaven's Gate apart from everyone else—was that group of individuals selected to move to the next level would bodily ascend to the saucers in a kind of "technological rapture." Applewhite may have begun to rethink his theology after his beloved partner died because, in order to be reunited with Nettles, her spirit would have to acquire a new body aboard the spacecraft. While the death of Nettles may or may not have been the decisive influence, he later adopted the view that Heaven's Gate would ascend together spiritually rather than physically.

*The Anti-Cult Movement: A Response*
*to the Anti-Social Actions of Extreme Groups*

The deaths of Heaven's Gate members was, at the time of this writing, the latest in a series of dramatic incidents involving members of minority religions. Other incidents include the Jonestown murder/suicides (1978), the ATF/FBI raid on the Branch Davidian community (1993), the Solar Temple suicides (1994), and the Tokyo subway poison gas attack (1995). In the wake of these events, the mass media sought out a variety of "cult experts" in an effort to make sense of seemingly irrational behavior. Most of these experts offered the public an explanation in terms of the notion of cultic mind control, colloquially known as "brainwashing." The seemingly crazy actions of "cult" members were not difficult to explain, this group of experts claimed, as long as one understands that megalomaniacal cult leaders like Applewhite are able to control the thought processes of their followers: Under the influence of mind control, cult members are capable of anything because they have given up their wills to the leader.

According to spokespeople for cult "watchdog" groups, our society is populated by hundreds—perhaps even thousands—of cult groups, many of which are capable of extreme actions. Beyond mind control and the imputation of sinister motives to the leader, standard accusations leveled against minority religions unfortunate enough to be labeled *cults* include deceptive recruiting practices, financial and sexual exploitation, food and sleep deprivation of members, various forms of illegal activities, child abuse, ritual abuse, and so forth. Because of the interest the mass media have taken in this issue, this stereotype has become widely accepted in contemporary society.

Putting aside the problematic notion of "cultic brainwashing" for the moment, there are or have been groups for which some of these accusations are or were appropriate. In particular, children have been abused within a few religious communities. Members of certain organizations have been financially and/or sexually exploited by the leadership. A handful of minority religions have taken the law into their own hands. And at least one group consciously deceived potential recruits by systematically hiding their identity until after workshop attendees had become de facto members.

There are, however, obvious dangers in unreflectively applying the cult stereotype to every religious group that strikes one as strange or different. The situation is not unlike that of viewing a race or an ethnicity in terms of a generalization derived from the minority group's least reputable members. The types of problems that can be generated by jumping to the conclusion that unusual religious communities must be guilty of misdeeds simply because hostile former members level accusations against them are well exemplified in the raid against the Northeast Kingdom.

## Northeast Kingdom

*The Island Pond Raid*

In the wee hours of the early morning on June 22, 1984, the residents in the small village of Island Pond, Vermont, awoke to a literal governmental invasion of their community. With no advance warning or notice, more than 150 law enforcement officers and agents from various state agencies stormed the twenty or so homes where the members of the Twelve Tribes (then known as the Northeast Kingdom Community Church) lived, arresting more than 100 adults and 112 children.

What was so unusual about this church? How did the State of Vermont become so entangled in the controversy surrounding this community that they acted precipitously, without first conducting a thorough investigation— actions for which they were later forced to apologize? How did a small, peaceable Christian sect become a major target for such radical activities?

The Twelve Tribes began in the foothills of Tennessee around 1972, when an independent fundamentalist preacher, Elbert Eugene Spriggs, built a loyal following of believers into a model New Testament community church. Spriggs called his group the Light Brigade and he spent most of his early ministry pulling drug addicts and alcoholics off the streets of Chattanooga. Later, the name was changed to the Vine Christian Community Church and the ministry spread into surrounding communities.

The church members separated themselves from worldly pursuits and materialistic gains, supporting themselves with homegrown foods and necessities which they also sold to local area residents. One of the mainstays of financial support has been their delicatessen and take out shop, which features natural foods. The church has always attracted the attention of the local residents, but most of them accepted the group as "different, but nice folks." At first glance, the members of the church remind you of the Amish church members. The women wear kerchiefs on their heads, long dresses, little or no make-up, and the men usually wear beards, long hair, and overalls.

The Tennessee community grew to more than four hundred residents and became a very successful example of the "community paradigms" which dotted the countryside during the early seventies and eighties. There was never any violence and very few confrontations with anyone outside of the community. There were a few marital disputes, but only a small number of divorces compared to a typical church of similar size. One of the few problems to surface during the Tennessee years lit the match for the attacks which have followed them for the past fifteen or more years.

Clifford Daniels, a young man with a history of personal problems, joined the community and soon rose to a leadership position managing one of the business interests of the community. Problems developed with the church elders when Daniels "borrowed" some of the business funds and a church vehicle without authority. When the indiscretion was discovered and he appeared before the church Board of Elders, he became violent and attempted to attack one of the leaders with a tire iron.

He was banished from the community. Seeking revenge, Daniels fell in with another former resident of the area, Ted Patrick. Patrick had migrated to southern California, but was still active in the Tennessee foothills where his family and friends continued to live. It was the mid-1970s, and Patrick had gained some notoriety among a growing number of anticult activists as a "deprogrammer"—a term he coined to give credibility to his kidnapping and abductions of young people from religious groups. Borrowing from the brainwashing techniques used by the communists on the American prisoners of war, Patrick's exploits were quickly giving him wide recognition among concerned relatives of adult children who had joined the religious versions of the hippie revolution. Many were more than willing to hire him to return their adult "children" to their control.

Daniels became a good team member for Patrick. The members of Spriggs's quaint community church provided excellent potential for Patrick's deprogramming-for-hire enterprise. Daniels was an eager student, and soon became an independent deprogrammer on his own. By 1984, he was kidnaping twenty to thirty people a given year from a variety of local churches. Throughout his career, Daniels's favorite target has always remained the Northeast Kingdom Church. In spite of the publicity stirred up by Patrick and Daniels against the church to support their kidnapping activities, the church continued to grow and prosper.

In 1976, the church had an opportunity to move onto land they had acquired in northern Vermont. It offered the perfect haven for their lifestyle and the vision which Spriggs saw for his church. The move provided even more fuel for the anticult activists whose numbers had also increased significantly.

Former members who had been deprogrammed by Patrick, Daniels, and other deprogrammers had jumped on the lucrative circuit. Local anticult contacts throughout the country were prompting uneasy relatives to "rescue" their adult offspring with the deprogrammer's expert services, even if it meant that they returned to a life of drugs and purposelessness. Many of the kidnapping incidents were perpetrated by the deprogrammers as a means to gain custody of children who were still in the church when one of the parents had left or were previously deprogrammed.

Some of these would end up in court where the noncustodial parent would seek a new custody hearing by injecting stories by deprogrammed former members about child abuse. A campaign of letters and charges to various officials continued in order to build their cases. At one point, several families were even charged with truancy for failing to send their children to a public school instead of home schooling or because their children were in the church school. The charges were always dropped for lack of evidence.

The fact that they were dropped never troubled their antagonists. The publicity surrounding the charges and the documents alleging the charges proved sufficient documentation to use for more attacks. At the height of his notoriety in the mid-seventies, Patrick traveled the country meeting with local anticult activists and training new converts to become deprogrammers. Long before Spriggs contemplated his move to the New England countryside, Patrick had planted his seeds of destruction.

Patrick joined forces with a local New England activist who owned a remote farm in upper New York state, and the hide-a-way provided Patrick and other deprogrammers with a perfect "safe-house" to keep their kidnap victims while they attempted to convince them to forsake their religious beliefs. Patrick eventually gathered a number of like-minded individuals together in the New England area and helped found the formal organization that became the Citizens Freedom Foundation (later changing its name to the Cult Awareness Network). All of these organizations were interlocked with overlapping board members, leaders, and deprogrammers who functioned as conduits for the deprogramming network.

Although numerous members of these organizations have been arrested, charged, and often convicted for crimes involving their attacks against local churches and religious groups, they have been able to maintain an air of respectability that has gleaned support for their activities. There are many sociological reasons for this phenomenon, but their best ally has always been the natural tendency of people to fear the unknown and the unusual.

The Cult Awareness Network, with the help of New England deprogrammer Galen Kelly, eagerly picked up the campaign against the church from Tennessee. Vermont is a largely rural state, and the Vermonters seemed eager to accept the wild accusations and charges levied against these "strangers" from Tennessee. An article in the *Vermont Magazine* (March, 1991) makes the point very well:

> For the residents of Island Pond, it was watching out for children that proved the greatest challenge to their intolerance of newcomers. It was one thing to wake up and find a couple of hundred New Testament zealots had come to town from heaven knows where. It was another to learn that they had given up all their earthly possessions to join the church—a vow of poverty—and held all things in common, and lived, ate and worked together. It was still another that they criticized much of American culture as corrupt and all other Christian denominations as misguided. It was yet another to see that they drew members from among the young, the transient, the dissatisfied and the burned out. Worse, they looked like hippies.

Jumping on these prejudices, the network of deprogrammers, anticult activists, and deprogrammed former members relentlessly pursued a campaign against the church. The campaign included town hall meetings where lurid stories of abuse and wild allegations of killing babies were proffered with vivid details. Letters of protest and allegations of abuse flooded the offices of the Department of Social Services, the Department of Education, the congressmen, the senators, the governor, and every law enforcement agency that could be found. Even Immigration, the Internal Revenue Service, and state departments were petitioned.

The allegations and protests were peppered with supposed "atrocities" from other states which involved "similar" local churches that had to be addressed by government officials. The charges were embellished with overtones drawn from publicity surrounding the Jonestown incident. Finally, Governor Richard Snelling and Attorney General John Easton were convinced that there were enough allegations and testimonies to take serious action against the community of believers. The anti-Northeast Kingdom Community campaign was working. Kelly and company were actually invited to tag along for the raid on the community at Island Pond.

At 6:30 A.M. on Friday, June 22, 1984, a caravan of state police officers, social service workers, sheriff deputies, and an assortment of other officials swooped down on the residents and arrested 110 adults and took 112 children of all ages into custody. They loaded the 222 men, women, and children into separate buses, separating crying children from their distraught and bewildered parents with little or no explanations. A local resident later recalled, "It was awful. It was just like Vietnam!"

While the Northeast Kingdom Community were huddled in a gymnasium which served as a makeshift detention center, the State Attorney requested a blanket detention order from the District Court in order that a full-scale investigation could be conducted on the incarcerated residents. The judge refused. The court held that "the state failed to present any specific evidence of abuse," and ordered all of the children to be released. After a thorough examination by the social service case workers, no evidence of any abuse of any kind could be found.

The event, however, served the purposes of the Cult Awareness Network. The raid made headlines in news media across the nation. As usual, the fact that the children were all returned, the parents released, and no charges ever filed for lack of evidence barely rated a back-page mention. Deprogrammers still kidnap children as well as adults from the Northeast Kingdom Community. Some have been taken to courts in other states and custody given to the noncustodial parent and others have been returned by the courts. The deprogrammers get paid for their services either way.

The children at Island Pond have been investigated by every agency possible, and the church has never been charged with abuse. News reporters have visited the community and found only fresh, happy, well-adjusted children who are growing up to be responsible, mature adults with deep religious convictions. The ministry of Eugene Spriggs continues to grow. Currently, there are expressions of the home base church in Vermont which are now located in areas throughout the world and in a number of cities throughout America.

—*GEORGE ROBERTSON*

*Religious Libertarianism: A Response to the Persecution of Minority Religions*

It is the concern generated by incidents such as the Northeast Kingdom raid that has led to the emergence of an alternate school of opinion opposed to the "anticult" perspective. This opposing group is comprised of a diverse group of religions, religious liberty organizations, and scholars of minority religions. While not seeking to defend organizations like Heaven's Gate, this school of thought asserts that the extreme actions of a few groups should not be taken as representative of all minority religions, any more than the criminal tendencies of a handful of members of certain racial minorities should be imputed to the race as a whole. Individuals associated with this opposition group see themselves as defending religious liberty.

Because the word "cult" has acquired negative connotations, the people and organizations who defend minority religions do not call themselves the "procult movement," and, further, would not accept the label "cult apologists" with which anticultists seek to stigmatize them. In fact, this opposition group would reject the use of the term "cult" altogether, instead referring to such organizations as new religious movements (the preferred term among academics), alternative religions, nontraditional religions, or minority religions. Recognizing the term's problematic status, *cult* will be avoided when referring to a specific religion throughout this book. It is, nevertheless, still useful to talk about the *cult controversy*, and, where appropriate, "cult" will be utilized when discussing the stereotype associated with minority religions more generally.

At the broadest level, the anticult movement in North America can be subdivided into two wings, consisting of secular anticultists and conservative Christian anticultists. While these two wings share certain traits and in the past have occasionally cooperated with each other, the target of much Christian anticultism is a minority religion's deviation from traditional doctrine—a concern most secular anticultists do not share. Also, Christian anticultists tend not to be involved in the controversial practice of deprogramming—one of the hallmarks of the secular anticult movement. When discussing the anticult movement, the present book will be referring to the secular wing of this movement, unless otherwise noted.

As with other social conflicts, opponents in the cult controversy have become polarized into extreme positions. Many anticultists have come to adopt an attitude of suspicion toward a broad spectrum of religions, ready to portray almost any unusual group as a potential Heaven's Gate, and almost any charismatic religious leader as a potential David Koresh. Defenders of the rights of minority religions, on the other hand, have tended to downplay all issues except the issue of religious liberty. The result of this polarization is an ongoing and frequently bitter debate which periodically finds expression in books, articles, court cases, and, more recently, in official reports issued by European governments.

While the contemporary controversy has certain unique aspects, it is, in many ways, an extension of historically earlier religious conflicts. As a way of providing a background for our discussion of the cult controversy, we will look briefly at the anti-Catholic and anti-Mormon movements of the nineteenth century.

## RELIGIOUS PERSECUTION IN
## NINETEENTH-CENTURY AMERICA

On the evening of July 28, 1834, Edward Cutter, a resident of Charlestown, Massachusetts, was startled by the sudden appearance of an hysterical woman at his doorstep. She was clad only in a nightgown, and delirious from a combination of stress, high fever, and the sweltering heat of a Boston summer. Elizabeth Harrison's closely cut hair indicated that she was a resident of Mount Benedict, the nearby Ursuline convent. A nun of some thirteen years as well as an accomplished music teacher at the convent school, Harrison had undergone a partial breakdown as a result of overwork. Not knowing quite what to do, Cutter took her to a friend's place in nearby Cambridge. As soon as the delirium passed, she returned to the convent.

The news of this unusual but otherwise minor incident somehow filtered out into the surrounding Protestant community—a community hostile to the Catholic presence. While contemporary Americans accept Catholicism as a natural part of the religious landscape, in the early nineteenth century, "Popery" (or "Papism" as it was popularly referred to) was an object of contempt, not unlike the way "Moonies" are regarded in the late twentieth century. The nunnery itself—a newly built structure directly across from Bunker Hill—attracted attention comparable to the attention a Hare Krishna temple would draw if it were to spring up overnight in rural Nebraska. In the words of Louise Whitney who, at the time, was a student at the nunnery school, "The whole establishment was as foreign as the soil whereon it stood, as if, like Aladdin's Palace, it had been wafted from Europe by the power of a magician" (Whitney 1969)

Harrison's story became hopelessly warped and exaggerated into a sensationalistic tale in which pursuing Catholics recaptured an escaping nun and compelled her to return to the convent against her will. Evidently, the news media of the nineteenth century was as irresponsible as the mass media of our own century when covering exotic religions. Within a short period of time, the rumors became quite exaggerated: The nuns, it was said, had not only driven the American lady to madness, but had incarcerated her. Following her escape attempt, they had then, with the approval of the bishop, actually tortured her to death.

Certain particulars of this rumor seemed to follow the plot of a tale that was being circulated at the time by another "escaped nun" from the Ursuline convent, and it is reasonably certain that the Harrison tale was shaped, to a greater or lesser extent, by the Rebecca Theresa Reed story. Reed, who had worked at the convent for a few months as a servant, had, for several years, been propagating the story (later published as *Six Months in a Convent*) that she had aspired to be a nun, but "escaped" from the convent after witnessing unspeakable immorality. One of the focal themes of the anti-Catholic literature of the time was the abuse of young females in catholic nunneries. The Reed story and the Harrison rumor appeared to reinforce each other as well as to give substance to Protestant fears about what was going on behind the benign public face of the local nunnery.

In the midst of this potentially explosive state of affairs, the famous minister Lyman Beecher blew into town, and on Sunday, August 10, delivered an impassioned anti-Catholic sermon in three different churches on the same day. This sermon, published later as a *Plea for the West,* pictured Catholics as being in a state of mental bondage—a "brainwashed" state, in the idiom of the late twentieth century:

> If they dared to think for themselves, the contrast of protestant independence with their thraldom would awaken the desire for equal privileges and put an end to arbitrary clerical dominion over trembling superstitious minds. (Beecher 1835)

Although the oft-repeated charge that Beecher was directly responsible for ensuing events is unlikely, his stormy denunciations of Rome could not have helped the situation.

Afraid of what might happen if they did not act, city officials inspected Mt. Benedict the next afternoon. They were given a complete tour by Elizabeth Harrison, the very nun who was being featured as a tormented prisoner. Finding nothing amiss, they returned home to compose a report that was to appear in the next morning's paper.

However, around eight o'clock that evening—only a few hours after the selectmen had left—a mob arrived in front of the Ursuline convent and demanded that they be shown the nun whom they supposed was being held there against her will. Rather than attempting to reason with them, the mother superior gave in to feelings of exasperation. Indignant that a mob of workingmen should issue demands after having just proved Mt. Benedict's innocence to city officials, she responded with threats of her own, such as, "the Bishop has twenty thousand Irishmen at his command in Boston, and they will whip you all into the sea!" This unwise response only infuriated the crowd who, after a short delay, began to force their way in. Nuns and schoolgirls fled into the back garden, and eventually escaped through a wall-like back fence with the aid of their neighbor, Mr. Cutter. It is unlikely that the schoolgirls, many of whom were from Protestant homes, would have been hurt by the attackers, but some of the nuns, and particularly the mother superior, might well have come to harm.

The assault on the convent was motivated, in part, by the misguided but nevertheless genuine desire to free "imprisoned" inmates. The genuineness of this motivation is evident in many different places in extant documents. It is particularly clear that the mob's initial purpose was to release Elizabeth Harrison, who they still imagined was being held against her will. The rescue operation, however, quickly degenerated into a riot. After failing to discover dungeons and engines of torture, the mob began to run through the abandoned nunnery, looting and destroying as they went. The convent was finally torched, and, intoxicated by the boldness of their actions as well as by rum, the mob turned to the looting and destruction of surrounding buildings. The bishop's house and library were put to flame. The mausoleum in the school's garden was broken into, its coffins opened, and the remains of the dead mutilated. Fire-fighting teams from Charlestown and from the surrounding communities appeared, but were turned back by the crowd.

The following evening the mob returned and burned down fences, trees, and everything else they could find on the grounds. Only the presence of troops guarding Edward Cutter's home kept them from destroying a nearby Catholic church. For the rest of the week, nightfall found club-wielding mobs roaming the streets looking for trouble. The last act of destruction occurred on Friday night when a shack that served as a home to thirty-five Irish laborers was torched.

Although the public's first reactions to the incident were shock and outrage, prevailing anti-Catholic feelings quickly overcame this initial response. While some Protestants expressed outrage over the convent burning, for many others the event was an inspiration for stepped up anti-Catholic activity. For example, within a week of the Charlestown incident, two new anti-Catholic newspapers began publication: *Downfall of Babylon* (Philadelphia) and *The American Protestant Vindicator* (New York).

Of the thirteen persons indicted for arson, all were eventually released, acquitted, or pardoned. The state was empowered to reimburse victims for loss of property due to civil disorders, but public opinion frustrated every effort of the Ursulines to recover their losses. The nuns themselves eventually moved to Canada.

Although immigrant and native-born laborers had scuffled with each other for years, the burning of the Ursuline convent was the first major act of violence in a long series of incidents that were to reach a peak in the Philadelphia riots of 1844. The anti-Catholic crusade did not, however, really die down until after the nation's passions had been redirected into the slavery issue and the Civil War.

When we look back on certain themes in nineteenth century anti-Catholic literature from the perspective of the late twentieth century, it becomes clear that the Catholic church was portrayed in much the same way as "cults" are portrayed in the present period. Convent schools like the one in Charlestown were, for example, often viewed as covert tools ("cult front groups") for converting unwitting non-Catholics. Anti-Catholics explained the conversion of these young Protestant women in terms of flattery and devious indoctrination designed to influence impressionable young ladies to take the veil. In the words of Edith O'Gorman, another ex-nun and author of the anti-Catholic potboiler *Convent Life Unveiled*:

> My confessor flattered me in my delusion, telling me that the Lord had endowed my soul with His highest gifts, and He had designed me from all eternity to become a great saint. . . . At the same time he urged me to hasten my entrance into a Convent, because, if I delayed long in the world, God would withdraw from me those heavenly gifts. As a natural consequence of these false teachings, I soon became puffed up with my own self-righteousness, and was led to regard myself as better than others. (O'Gorman 1881)

Once inside the convent, inmates were convinced to remain by subtle, psychological pressure, such as fear of hell and the belief that any doubts were inspired by Satan. Reed described this "Catholic mind control" in the following words:

> The Bishop said the Devil would assail me, as he did Saint Theresa, and make me think I ought to go back to the world; and make me offers of worldly pleasures, and promise me happiness. In order to prevent this, I must watch and pray all the time, and banish entirely worldly thoughts from my mind. (Reed 1834)

This passage could easily have been taken from a contemporary account of cult "brainwashing."

Although anti-Catholicism was a major phenomenon of nineteenth-century American life, we have conveniently forgotten this ignoble chapter in our national life because it does not accord well with our self-image as tolerant lovers of freedom. Catholics were, however, not the only religious group to be vigorously persecuted in North America. In the colonial period, Quakers were regularly hung in Puritan Boston. In the late nineteenth century, the U.S. government forbade American Indians from practicing their traditional religions, and divided up the reservations among the various denominations in an effort to Christianize them. The prohibition against traditional Indian religions was not overturned until the 1930s.

Among the candidates for the title of most-persecuted religious group in American history, one of the most deserving is the Church of Jesus Christ of Latter-day Saints, popularly called Mormons. In addition to their founder-prophet being murdered by a mob (after he had given himself up peacefully to authorities), the Mormons have the distinction of being the only religious group in American history to be the subject of an openly declared extermination campaign: In Missouri in 1838, then governor Liburn W. Boggs declared that "the Mormons must be treated as enemies, and must be exterminated or driven from the State if necessary, for the public peace." The militia was called up to enforce this declaration. Among other atrocities, the Militia raided Haun's Mill, a small Mormon settlement near Far West, Missouri, on October 30, killing seventeen men, women, and children. Twelve others were wounded, some of whom died later. An old man who was wounded and lying on the ground was shot through the heart, and then his body hacked and mutilated. A young boy of nine, found hiding in a blacksmith shop, was shot in the head with the comment, "Nits will make lice."

The Church of Jesus Christ of Latter-day Saints, like the Catholic Church, became the subject of numerous atrocity tales built around the same themes of captivity and abuse. In anti-Mormon literature, polygamous wives played essentially the same role that nuns played in anti-Catholic literature, and apostate (and pseudoapostate) Mormon females composed similar captivity narratives. However, a certain conceptual problem emerged in Mormon apostate stories: How could one make the case for a state of bondage in a situation where the alleged captive was apparently free to walk out at any time? Nunneries could be portrayed as prisons, but Mormon women were obviously not so confined. Thus, in addition to the "deluded follower" theme used to characterize Catholic bondage, one finds the first theory of "hypnotic mind control" in anti-Mormon literature. For example, in the totally fabricated apostate tale, *Female Life Among the Mormons,* Maria Ward described her "capture" in terms of mesmerism (the original term for hypnosis, also termed "animal magnetism"):

> At the time I was wholly unacquainted with the doctrine of magnetic influence; but I soon became aware of some unaccountable power exercised over me by my fellow traveller. His presence seemed an irresistible fascination. His glittering eyes were fixed on mine; his breath fanned my cheek; I felt bewildered and intoxicated, and partially lost the sense of consciousness, and the power of motion . . . I became immediately sensible of some unaccountable influence drawing my sympathies toward him. In vain I struggled to break the spell. I was like a fluttering bird before the gaze of a serpent-charmer. (Ward 1855)

The Mormon apostate tales, like the Catholic apostate stories, were loosely connected accounts of one sensationalistic atrocity after another, containing many crudely crafted descriptions of violence. The violence in anti-Mormon tales was often quite vivid. For example, in the totally fictional apostate tale, *Boadicea; The Mormon Wife,* Alfreda Eva Bell describes the following cold-hearted murder:

> "Will you go with me?" asked he. "No," answered the dying woman. "Then you are done for," said Yale; and deliberately, before my very eyes, in spite

of my wild screams for his mercy, he fired at her and scattered her brains over the floor. (Bell 1855)

Like sensationalistic anti-Catholic stories, anti-Mormon tales were capable of evoking violent, vigilante-style activity—as is evident in such events as the murder of Joseph Smith—and governmental intervention—as witnessed by such actions as the 1857 invasion of Utah by federal troops.

Contemporary anticult literature bears, as has already been indicated, certain similarities to nineteenth century anti-Catholic and anti-Mormon tales. In the contemporary period, however, the notion of brainwashing or cult mind control has become the center—rather than a subsidiary theme—in the debate over stigmatized religious groups. The link with notions from earlier eras is quite evident, especially in more popular tales. For example, compare the following passage from Chris Edwards's *Crazy for God* (Edwards is an ex-member of the Unification Church) with the description of Mormon mesmerism cited earlier:

> She took my hand and looked me straight in the eyes. As her wide eyes gazed into mine, I felt myself rapidly losing control, being drawn to her by a strange and frightening force. I had never felt such mysterious power radiate from a human being before . . . touching something within me that undermined thought itself. (Edwards 1979)

Although the stage settings are different, the plot has not changed. Like their nineteenth-century counterparts, former members of minority religions recount the same stories of deception and exploitation, which in turn evoke public outrange.

## EMERGENCE OF THE CONTEMPORARY CULT CONTROVERSY AND THE "BRAINWASHING" DEBATE

### Cultic Mind Control

Shifting our attention back to the present, the origins of the contemporary cult controversy can be traced to the early 1970s. In that period, many new religions were arising out of the ashes of the counterculture to become successor movements to the youth movement of the 1960s. Unable to comprehend the appeal of these religions, observers concluded that the founder-leaders of such groups has discovered a special form of social control which enabled them to recruit their followers in nonordinary ways, and, more particularly, to short-circuit their rational, questioning minds by keeping them locked in special trance states. A handful of professionals, mostly psychologists and psychiatrists associated with the anticult movement, attempted to provide scientific grounding for this notion of cultic brainwashing/mind control.

No serious observer would disagree that there are genuine issues of abuse, exploitation, and undue influence associated with at least some minority religions. Serious discussions and analyses of such abuses were, however, overshadowed almost from the very beginning when the debate over new religions came to focus on the notion of cultic mind control. Rather than viewing the social pressures found in minority religions as extensions of garden-variety forms of social influence, anticult professionals argued for the existence of a unique form of influence confined to "cult" subcultures. Viewing this argument as a form of special pleading with potentially grave implications for religious liberty, other professionals—particularly sociologists of religion—focussed their scholarly responses to the cult controversy on a critique of cultic mind control. By the mid-seventies, battle lines had been drawn and the debate would rage back and forth over the same ground for the next two decades.

Since the beginning of the debate, mainstream scholars have been steadily churning out studies directly relevant to the cult controversy. With respect to the mind control accusation that is at the core of the cult stereotype, the operative question that social scientists have asked is: How does one distinguish cultic brainwashing from other forms of social influence like advertising, military training, or even the normal socialization routines of the public schools? Some anticultists have theorized that members of minority religions are trapped in a kind of ongoing, quasi-hypnotic state, while others assert that the ability of cult members to process certain kinds of information has "snapped."

The problem with these and similar theories is that if cultic influences actually overrode the brain's ability to logically process information, then individuals suffering from cultic influences should perform poorly on I.Q. tests or, at the very least, manifest pathological symptoms when they take standardized tests of mental health—and when tested, they do not. If anything, such empirical studies indicate that members of new religious movements are actually smarter and healthier than the average member of mainstream American society (e.g., Sowards et al. 1994).

Other kinds of studies also fail to support the view that new religions rely upon nonordinary forms of social influence to gain and retain members. For example, if new religions possessed powerful techniques of mind control that effectively overrode a potential convert's free will, then everyone—or at least a large percentage—of attendees at recruiting seminars should be unable to avoid conversion. However, sociologist Eileen Barker, in her important study, *The Making of a Moonie,* found that only a small percentage of the people attending seminars sponsored by the Unification Church—an organization which many people regard as the evil cult *par excellence*—eventually joined. Furthermore, of those who joined, more than half dropped out within the first year of their membership. In another important study, Canadian psychiatrist Saul Levine found that, out of a sample of over 800 people who had joined controversial religious groups, more than 80 percent dropped out within two years of membership. These are not the kind of statistics one would anticipate in groups wielding powerful techniques of mind control.

In the face of these and other empirical studies, social scientists have asked further questions: Given the lack of empirical support, where does the brainwashing notion originate? What is the real nature of the conflict that the "cult" stereotype obfuscates? The general conclusion of sociologists (as analyzed, for example, in David Bromley and Anson Shupe's book-length study, *Strange Gods: The Great American Cult Scare*) is that the principal source of the controversy is a parent-child conflict in which parents fail to understand the choices of their adult children, and attempt to reassert parental control by marshalling the forces of public opinion against the religious bodies to which their offspring have converted.

This core conflict is then exacerbated by mass media that are less interested in truth than in printing exciting stories about weird cults that trap their members and keep them in psychological bondage with exotic techniques of "mind control." Also, once an industry is established that generates enormous profits through the "rescue" of entrapped "cult" members (i.e., deprogramming), special interest groups are created that have a vested interest in promoting the most negative stereotypes of alternative religions. These special interest groups add further fuel to the parent-child conflict by scaring parents with horrific stories of what will happen to their adult child if they fail to have her or him deprogrammed. In this manner, many otherwise reasonable and well-meaning parents are recruited into the controversy.

## Deprogramming and the Anticult Movement

The contemporary anticult movement emerged, as noted above, in the early seventies, shortly after the rash of new religions that arose in the wake of the collapse of the counterculture of the 1960s. Opposition to minority religions initially organized itself around deprogrammers—individuals who forcibly abducted individuals from nontraditional religions. In the heyday of deprogramming, "cult" members were snatched off the street and locked up in houses or motel rooms. Relatives and deprogrammers then attempted to demonstrate the falseness of the individual's newfound religion in an effort to convince her or him to defect.

Deprogramming began more or less accidentally when a son and a nephew of Theodore (Ted) Patrick Jr. considered joining the Children of God, a "Jesus Freak" organization. In 1971, Patrick was then-Governor Ronald Reagan's special Representative for Community Relations in southern California, working as a kind of ombudsman. On the fourth of July, he and his family were staying at a hotel on Mission Beach in San Diego. When his son Michael and a nephew failed to return from a fireworks display, he decided to call the police. They showed up as he was dialing, but he was struck by what seemed to be a strange look on Michael's face. They then related an encounter with the Children of God (COG). Alarmed at first, Patrick and his family gradually forgot about the incident.

In his job as ombudsman, however, he began to hear other complaints about the Children of God. One person of particular importance at this early stage of development was William Rambur of Chula Vista, California. His daughter dropped out of school in order to move to a COG ranch in Thurber, Texas. Unable to persuade her to leave the group, he began a personal crusade to warn other parents about the danger of COG. Eventually he linked up with Ted Patrick, and together they formed the first anticult organization. The name of this group, The Parent's Committee to Free Our Children from the Children of God, was later shortened to Free the Children of God, and popularly referred to as FREECOG.

Increasingly frustrated by the authorities' refusal to do anything about COG, Patrick began to consider more desperate approaches. As he studied the matter, he found that kidnapping charges would be difficult if not impossible to make stick if parents were involved at every stage of such an operation. In cooperation with distraught parents, he then commenced to experiment with the tactic of abducting "cult" members bodily, locking them up, questioning their religious choices, and trying to convince them that they had been brainwashed and manipulated by their "cult." In 50 percent or more of the cases, they abandoned their new faith. Thus, the practice of "deprogramming" was born.

Initially, Patrick did not pursue deprogramming for personal enrichment. Gradually, however, he found the demand high enough that he could turn his attention to kidnapping "cult" members on a full-time basis. The father of a new profession, he began to require compensation for his time. In response to critics, Patrick has soft-pedaled deprogramming by asserting that "all he does is talk to people." But in his popular book, *Let Our Children Go,* it is described as follows:

> Deprogramming is the term, and it may be said to involve kidnapping at the very least, quite often assault and battery, almost invariably conspiracy to commit a crime, and illegal restraint. (Patrick 1976)

While Patrick has often denied or downplayed the brutality of his work, in the same book he provides an interesting statement that contradicts his benign picture of deprogramming:

> I believe firmly that the Lord helps those who help themselves—and a few little things like karate, Mace, and handcuffs can come in handy from time to time. (Patrick 1976)

Other anticult organizations began springing up, with Citizen's Freedom Foundation (later renamed Cult Awareness Network) becoming the national umbrella group. The support of deprogramming by anticult organizations evoked some of their most severe criticisms. As early as 1974, for example, the National Council of Churches passed a strong resolution against the practice. Deprogrammers also made the mistake of diversifying their kidnapping activities to include Evangelical Christians. This move provoked the wrath of Christian anticultists who, by the late seventies and early eighties, were withdrawing from their alliance with secular anticultists. For example, Walter Martin, the most prominent Christian anticultist, writing in 1980, asserted that:

> I cannot stand behind such practices. It is true that cultists have been blinded by the "god of this age," but it is also true that they have the right to make up their own minds, and we should not stoop to un-Christian tactics to accomplish God's ends. (Martin 1980)

These and other criticisms influenced the secular anticult movement to rethink their stance on deprogramming. In 1981, for example, Citizen's Freedom Foundation (CFF) issued a statement which read, in part, that "CFF does not support, condone, or recommend kidnapping or holding a person against his will." CFF did, however, continue to voice support for voluntary deprogramming (i.e., counseling situations where "cult" members are free to break off the conversation and leave at any time), usually referred to as "exit counseling."

The vast majority of deprogrammers have little or no background in psychological counseling. Often their only qualification is that they are themselves deprogrammed ex-cult members. While advocates claim that deprogramming does nothing more than reawaken cult members' capacity for rational thought, an examination of the actual process reveals that the core technique of deprogramming involves directly assaulting a person's belief system. The deprogramming process consists of the following:

1. A breakdown in insulation from the outside world, accomplished by physically removing the member from her or his group.

2. A highlighting of the inconsistencies between group ideals and the actions of leaders, as well as internal inconsistencies *within* the group's belief system.
3. The pull of family ties. Deprogrammings are almost invariably paid for by other family members who then participate in the faith-breaking sessions.
4. The presentation of an alternative belief system. Deprogrammers often attempt to convert deprogrammees to conventional religion or, more often, to some highly secular version of the American Way of Life.
5. Offering an alternative explanation for the individual's recruitment and membership—the familiar deception/mind control ideology.

These five factors effectively disrupt the plausibility of the deprogrammee's religious beliefs. Success is not, however, guaranteed, as the high failure rate of deprogramming—between a third to a half return to their respective movements—demonstrates.

Deprogrammed former members of minority religions provide one of the keys to understanding the contemporary cult controversy. Groups opposed to such religions base much if not all of their attack on the testimony of former members who relate tale after tale of manipulation and abuse. Ex-members who have "actually been there," and who have supposedly witnessed all of the horrors about which outsiders can only fantasize, provide the cult stereotype with its most important source of empirical evidence. These narratives, anticultists would have the public believe, give us insights into the real nature and purpose of "cults," belying the benefic image minority religions project to the world.

However, empirical studies contrasting the attitudes of former members who left their movements voluntarily with former members who had been deprogrammed reveal a systematic difference which calls the objectivity of such testimony into question. It was found that most voluntary defectors were ambivalent or even positive about their former religion, often characterizing their membership period as a beneficial learning experience. In sharp contrast, people who had been involuntarily removed described their membership and their former religion in terms of the popular negative stereotype of "cults." The conclusion to be drawn from these findings is that deprogramming is *not* the therapeutic intervention it has been portrayed, but is, rather, an intensive indoctrination process in which the abductee's religious faith is systematically destroyed and replaced with anticult ideology. While this does not mean that there is nothing to be criticized in certain minority religions, a careful consideration of this finding should cause any thinking person to hesitate before accepting the more extreme accusations proffered by anticultists.

Thus, the ex-members who tell their tales of woe before the public by the anticult movement have been carefully selected. While few if any apostates are ever completely objective about their former religion, ex-members who have been intensively "counseled" by anticultists—especially those who have been kidnapped out of their religion—should be especially suspect as being less than neutral witnesses. By relying upon this subset of ex-members, the anticult movement involves itself in a hermeneutic circle. In other words, rather than forming generalizations based on a broad range of data, the anticult movement generates its own data by imposing its brainwashing ideology on a select number of individual cases (deprogrammees), and then "discovers" evidence for its ideology in the testimony of these same individuals. Anticultists depend upon this subset of former members for the ultimate proof of their accusations.

In addition to shaping public opinion by recounting stereotyped atrocity tales, deprogrammees feed into the cult controversy in a number of other ways: In a variety of different court battles, ex-members recruited by anticultists provide negative testimony against their former movements, such as in child custody cases where one of the parents is a "cult" member, and in cases where governmental agencies need evidence for "cult" violations of various governmental regulations. The testimony of a deprogrammed Branch Davidian was, for example, part of the evidence used to obtain a search warrant before the assault on the Davidian community. And finally, at the level of basic research, these former members are interviewed in pseudoscientific surveys designed to substantiate such claims as that brainwashing techniques induce mental illness in their members, and that child abuse is widespread in alternative religious groups.

## STEREOTYPES AND PUBLIC PERCEPTIONS OF THE CULT ISSUE

### Stereotyping Cults

Several decades ago, sociologist Tom Robbins observed that if someone at a previously unknown vegetarian community died from being squashed by a giant cabbage, tomorrow's headline news story—splashed sensationally across the front page—would be a report on an act of "cult" violence. The incident would also immediately become fodder for the propaganda mill of anticult organizations, and be used as an example of "what these awful groups are capable of." This hypothetical community, which, prior to the death, had never been considered "cultic," would then be mentioned in all future discussions of *evil cults*.

Robbins's observation seemed particularly appropriate in the wake of the Mt. Carmel fiasco. Prior to the ATF attack, the Branch Davidians had been a little-noticed group on the outskirts of Waco. Although some of the people familiar with the community had found it to be somewhat eccentric, it was rarely mentioned in the same breath as Moonies, Hare Krishnas, and so forth. In the wake of the tragedy, however, the Branch Davidians were transformed overnight into *the* paradigmatic *evil cult.*

The "reasoning" at work here is the same illogic of stereotyping from which many minorities have suffered:

A Black man raped a woman? Therefore all Black men are rapists.

A Jew cheated a neighbor? Therefore all Jews are cheaters.

A homosexual molested a little boy? Therefore all homosexuals are pedophiles.

A nontraditional religious group in the boondocks of Texas shot four lawmen? Therefore all nontraditional religions are violent cults.

And so forth and so on. We immediately recognize these biased stereotypes for what they are when applied to racial, ethnic, and sexual lifestyle minorities, but fail to recognize similarly demeaning stereotypes when applied nontraditional religions.

What is a stereotype? Stereotypes are generalizations about other groups of people, but they are a peculiar type of generalization. Stereotypes portray certain, most often derogatory, traits as being characteristic of a whole group of people, and then explain or excuse social problems in light of these traits. Stereotypes are also usually held rigidly, in that we tend to ignore or to dismiss evidence that flies in the face of our generalization. Such rigidity indicates that our stereotype in some way protects our self-esteem or shields us from facing some unpleasant fact. Thus, the stereotype of certain races as "lazy," for example, simultaneously boasts the self-esteem of society's dominant racial group as well as blinds one to the inequalities of existing social arrangements. It is relatively easy to perceive that most generalizations about "cults" are little more than negative stereotypes, but what are the social forces that make such stereotypes about nontraditional religions peculiarly attractive to contemporary society?

One of the more widely accepted dictums of sociology is that societies need enemies, particularly societies that are going through a disturbing period of change. External threats provide motivation for people to overcome internal divisiveness in order to work together as a unit. Having an enemy one can portray as evil and perverse also provides support for the normative values and institutions of one's society: "They" are communists;

"we" are capitalists. "They" are totalitarian; "we" are democratic. And so forth and so on.

One of the more interesting corollaries of this general line of thinking is that in situations where external enemies no longer threaten, a society will find groups or individuals within itself that it can construe as threatening and evil. Such enemies become particularly important to communities passing through a crisis in which fundamental values are being called into question; in the words of Albert Bergesen, from his important study, *The Sacred and the Subversive,* "a community will commence to ritually persecute imaginary enemies—conduct a witchhunt—to manufacture moral deviants as a means of ritually reaffirming the group's problematical values and collective purposes." This notion has been effectively supported by certain social historical studies. For example, in an interesting and creative study of New England witchcraft, *Entertaining Satan,* John Demos demonstrated that the persecution and execution of "witches"—usually unsocial, crabby little old ladies—abated during periods of war, and reappeared after peace had returned. This sheds light on our current social situation.

As a potent international threat, communism has largely disappeared. The only significant remaining communist power is Red China, and the Red Chinese are more interested in cooperating with the West than in challenging it. Other threats, such as Iraq, flare up and pass rather quickly. The lack of pressing external enemies in combination with our current, ongoing social crisis would lead the sociologically informed observer to anticipate that our culture will seek out groups within society to take the place of the "commies."

Unless there are groups that are consciously antisocial or criminal like the Mafia or like gangs, the deviations from the norm that a community chooses to perceive as threatening are somewhat arbitrary. The people that our culture have traditionally construed as "deviants" have been racial (e.g., Blacks), ethnic (e.g., Jews), and sexual (e.g., homosexuals) minorities. In recent years, however, it has become socially unacceptable to persecute these traditional groups, at least in the overt manner in which they have been attacked in the past. This leaves few groups of any significant size to persecute. One of the few minorities that liberals have been slow to defend are nontraditional religions. This is due to a number of different factors, including the resistance of traditionally conservative religions to liberal change.

Groups of people experienced as threatening frequently become screens onto which a society projects its anxieties. If, for example, a culture is troubled by sexual issues (as is often the case), then its enemies are perceived as perverse, sexually deviant, and so on. Racial minorities, who have often been viewed as "loose" and sexually aggressive, have suffered from this projection. This was also a dominant theme in nineteenth-century anti-Catholic and anti-Mormon literature. Contemporary "cults," of course, suffer from the same projection.

In the classical formulation of psychological projection, Freud, who was especially concerned with sex and violence, viewed projection as a defense mechanism against unacceptable inner urges. Thus, in a society with strict sexual mores, an individual constantly keeping a lid on his desires might perceive rather ordinary dancing, let us say, as sexually suggestive. Becoming enraged at such "loose" behavior, he might then attempt to lead a movement to have all of the dance halls in town closed down. It should be clear that this hypothetical individual's *inner* struggle is being "projected" outward to provide a script for an *outer* struggle (i.e., internally he is repressing his desires while symbolically battling the same desires in the outer world). The same process is at work in the collective mind of society, perceiving marginal groups as sexually deviant. For instance, the stereotype of the sexually abusive "cult" leader, routinely forcing devotees to satisfy his or her sexual whims, perfectly captures the fantasy of many members of our society who desire to sexually control any person he or she wishes.

The same kind of thing happens with repressed aggressive urges. We live in a society with strict sanctions against overt violence; simultaneously, violence is glorified in the entertainment media. This sets up a cultural contradiction that is projected onto enemies and deviant groups, with the result that minorities are often perceived as violent and belligerent. This accusation is also regularly projected onto nontraditional religions. In particular, the radical actions of a tiny handful of alternative religions is mistakenly taken to indicate a widespread tendency among all such groups.

We can generalize beyond Freudian psychology's emphasis on sex and aggression to see that many other cultural anxieties/contradictions are projected onto minority groups. For instance, our society gives us contradictory messages about the relative importance of money and possessions. On the one hand we are taught that economic pursuits are supposed to be secondary to social and spiritual activities. On the other, we receive many messages from the surrounding society that the single-minded pursuit of wealth is the be-all and end-all of life. This self-contradiction is projected onto alternative religions, as represented in the stereotype of the money-hungry "cult" leader who demands that her or his followers lead lives of poverty while the leader wallows in riches.

Similarly, the accusation of child abuse and contemporary society's seeming obsession with child abuse flows out of another cultural contradiction. Our cultural heritage as well as many modern psychologists hold out the ideal of a child who is constantly under the wing of a loving parent, usually the mother. Current economic conditions, however, often require both parents to work full time, which usually entails leaving young children in the care of strangers. This results in a good deal of guilt, which is easily displaced onto such "deviant" groups as nontraditional religions.

Like the accusation of violence, the radical actions of a tiny handful of alternative religions that have abused children is mistakenly taken to indicate a widespread tendency among all such groups. Despite the outcry against the Branch Davidians, for example, our best current information is that, while strict, the Davidians did *not* abuse their children. However, the readiness of people to buy into the stereotype of child-abusing cultists convicted David Koresh and sentenced him to death before he was able to receive a fair hearing.

One of the more important cultural contradictions that gets projected onto alternative religions is tied up in the brainwashing/mind control notion that is the core accusation leveled against such groups. Discourse that glorifies American society usually does so in terms of a rhetoric of liberty and freedom. However, while holding liberty as an ideal, we experience a social environment that is often quite restrictive. Most citizens work as employees in highly disciplined jobs where the only real freedom is the freedom to quit. Also, we are bombarded by advertising designed to influence our decisions and even to create new needs. Our frustration with these forms of influence and control is easily displaced and projected onto the separated societies of alternative religions, where the seemingly restricted flow of information offers a distorted reflection of the situation we experience as members of the dominant society.

The components of the "cult" stereotype that have been enumerated above, and others that could be mentioned, explain certain themes in anticult discourse as well as why this stereotype is attractive to members of present-day society. Without this preexisting disposition to construe nontraditional religions negatively, the anticult movement would have little or no social influence. However, while the anticult movement has relatively little direct social power, the stereotype it has helped to shape has taken on a life of its own, independent of organized anticultism.

## Self-Fulfilling Stereotypes

Once a stereotype is in place, a variety of different kinds of studies have shown that it becomes self-fulfilling and self-reinforcing. Thus, in a study by Mark Snyder and Seymour Uranowitz, as reported in Paula Rothenberg's *Racism and Sexism,* students were asked to read a short biography about Betty K., a fictitious woman. Her life story was constructed so that it would fulfill certain stereotypes of both heterosexuals and lesbians. In Snyder's words, "Betty, we wrote, never had a steady boyfriend in high school, but did go out on dates. And although we gave her a steady boyfriend in college, we specified that he was more of a close friend than anything else." A week later, they told some of the students that Betty was currently living with her husband, and another group of students that she was living with another woman in a lesbian relationship. When subsequently requested to answer a series of questions about Betty, they found a marked tendency on the part of students to reconstruct her biography so as to conform to stereotypes about either heterosexuality or homosexuality, depending on the information they had received.

> Those who believed that Betty was a lesbian remembered that Betty had never had a steady boyfriend in high school, but tended to neglect the fact that she had gone out on many dates in college. Those who believed that Betty was now a heterosexual, tended to remember that she had formed a steady relationship with a man in college, but tended to ignore the fact that this relationship was more of a friendship than a romance.

More directly relevant to the case at hand is an important article by Jeffrey E. Pfeifer, "The Psychological Framing of Cults," reporting the results of a similar study which compared responses to a biography in which a fictitious student, Bill, dropped out of college to enter a Catholic seminary, join the Marines, or join the Moonies. The short biography incorporated elements of indoctrination often attributed to "cults," such as:

> While at the facility, Bill is not allowed very much contact with his friends or family and he notices that he is seldom left alone. He also notices that he never seems to be able to talk to the other four people who signed up for the program and that is continually surrounded by [Moonies, Marines, Priests] who make him feel guilty if he questions any of their actions or beliefs.

When given a choice of describing Bill's indoctrination experience, subjects who thought Bill had joined the Catholic priesthood most often labeled his indoctrination "resocialization"; those who were told that he had joined the Marines most frequently labeled the process "conversion"; and those who were under the impression that he had become a Moonie applied the label "brainwashing." On various other questions regarding the desirability and fairness of the indoctrination process, subjects who were told that Bill had joined the Moonies consistently evaluated his experience more negatively than subjects who were under the impression that Bill had joined either the Marines or a priestly order.

The implications of this research for the cult controversy is that the minority religions lose their chance for a fair hearing as soon as the label "cult" is applied. After that, the mass media selectively seeks out and presents information about the group that fits the stereotype. In the Branch Davidian case, it was only a matter of time before the media had completely "demonized" Koresh and his followers.

## Cults and the Media

Less than a week after the ATF attack on the Branch Davidian community, the Rev. Mike Evans, who in 1986 had published a popular book about the end of the world, publicly pronounced that David Koresh was demon-possessed. The Waco confrontation had already begun to settle into the routine of an uneventful standoff, and the media was searching around for colorful news—hence the decision to feature a story on the Texas evangelist. "Satan is alive and well on planet earth," claimed Evans in the words of a popular book title. "The spirit that is in Koresh and his followers needs to be exorcised."

He offered his services to the authorities: "If it would save innocent lives, I would be willing to go in there one on one with him and cast that demon out." While he said that he "would prefer going in there and laying hands on him and rebuking the demons in him," Brother Evans also noted that the next best thing to a personal exorcism would be to repeat a prayer through a loudspeaker, "rebuking the demon spirits in Koresh and commanding them to come out in the name of Jesus. Turn it up so loud that Koresh will not have a moment of rest 24 hours a day."

Perhaps taking their cue from pastor Evans, it was not long afterwards that the FBI initiated an harassment campaign against Mt. Carmel. However, rather than attempting to exorcise Koresh, the FBI seemed intent on feeding his demon. Instead of prayers, authorities broadcast, among other sound tracks, Nancy Sinatra music, the sound of a dentist's drill, and the cries of rabbits being tortured to death. (One wonders what kind of tape library stocks rabbit murder sounds—or were the fuzzy cottontails slain at the behest of the FBI and custom-taped for the occasion?) It is difficult to understand what this audio assault and the accompanying light show could have accomplished, except to increase the level of paranoia among the Davidians.

The fact that the media saw fit to give sideshows like Rev. Evans that sprung up around the Davidian siege as much coverage as the siege itself reflects a salient characteristic of the contemporary news media, which is that—because of the intense competition among different news agencies—the media seeks to *entertain* consumers of news, sometimes at the cost of *informing* them. The same drive to increase viewer/reader ratings is evident in the media portrayal of the Branch Davidians. While Rev. Evans had recommended casting out demons, and while the FBI tried to provoke Koresh's inner devils, the media took a somewhat different approach and proceeded to demonize the Davidian leader. In addition to the usual generic accusations about evil cult leaders and ad nauseam comparisons with Jim Jones, reporters dutifully repeated every slanderous remark made about Koresh and the Davidians, whatever the source. Clearly the intention was to appeal to readers/viewers with sensationalism rather than to produce a balanced picture of the Branch Davidians.

More generally, the journalistic penchant for sensationalism has been a decisive factor in promoting the stereotype of "evil cults" to the larger society. The mass media is not, of course, motivated primarily by the quest for truth, although some reporters have more integrity than others. Instead, the mainstream media is driven by market forces and by the necessity of competing with other newspapers, other TV news shows, and so forth.

This is not to say that reporters necessarily lie or fabricate their stories. Rather, in the case of New Religious Movements (NRMs), news people tend to accentuate those facets of "cults" that seem to be strange, exploitative, dangerous, totalitarian, sensational, and the like because such portrayals titillate consumers of news. This kind of reporting contributes to the perpetuation of the cult stereotype. In the words of British sociologist James Beckford:

> Journalists need no other reason for writing about any particular NRM except that it is counted as a cult. This categorization is sufficient to justify a story, especially if the story illustrates many of the other components which conventionally make up the "cult" category. This puts pressure on journalists to find more and more evidence which conforms with the categorical image of cults and therefore confirms the idea that a NRM is newsworthy to the extent that it does match the category. It is no part of conventional journalistic practice to look for stories about NRMs which do *not* conform to the category of cult. (Beckford 1994)

Another important factor is the marked tendency of the mass media to report on a phenomenon only when it results in conflicts and problems. To again cite from Beckford's important paper, "The Media and New Religious Movements,"

> NRMs are only newsworthy when a problem occurs. Scandals, atrocities, spectacular failures, "tug-of-love" stories, defections, exposés, outrageous conduct—these are the main criteria of NRMs' newsworthiness. . . . And, of course, the unspectacular, non-sensational NRMs are permanently invisible in journalists' accounts. (Beckford 1994)

The different media vary somewhat in their tendency to produce imbalanced reports. TV news programs such as *Inside Edition* and *20/20* that have to compete with prime-time TV programming tend to be the most imbalanced. Rather than attempting to produce programs that examine the complex ramifications of issues, news shows usually present melodramas in which guys in white hats are shown locked in conflict with other guys in black hats. On the opposite extreme are the major newspapers, such as the

*Los Angeles Times* and the *Washington Post,* which tend to do the best job of attempting to present balanced articles on controversial subjects. Such "balance," however, usually only means finding the space for opposing views. The journalist appears to be objective when her or his story is two-sided rather than one-sided. The news magazines such as *Time* and *Newsweek* tend to fall somewhere in between.

One of the more unusual aspects of the Waco standoff was the decision of NBC to create a "docudrama" about the Branch Davidians and the events leading up to the original ATF assault *before* the siege ended. The title of this made-for-TV movie, *Ambush in Waco,* seemed to evoke images from the quasi-mythical past of frontier Texas, when sinister savages ambushed noble lawmen. Television, as we have already mentioned, is the least suitable medium for coming to grips with complex moral issues. In the case of *Ambush in Waco,* the ATF agents were dressed in white hats and David Koresh in a black hat. It was, as might be expected, a shallow, rambling production built around a disconnected framework of the most slanderous accusations leveled against Koresh. The ATF was completely whitewashed as a group of noble-minded public servants—not a single question was raised about the propriety of the ATF's actions. The filming of *Ambush* was still in process when the FBI attacked Mt. Carmel. Appealing to the public hunger for sensationalism and violence, the docudrama was a smashing success.

The collapse of the distinction between dramatic time and real time in this and other productions represents a disturbing trend. One can well imagine the creation of a "quickie" docudrama on a sensationalistic murder in which the murder suspect is convicted on TV—but who later turns out to be innocent. It has become increasingly clear that something like this was the case with the Davidians (i.e., a TV conviction), but the "evidence"—as presented in *Ambush in Waco*—has helped to blind the public to the possibility that Koresh and company could have been innocent. Instead, *Ambush* merely reinforced the news media's demonization of the Branch Davidians, and helped to make the final holocaust of Mt. Carmel more acceptable to Americans.

In an important article on the docudrama trend, "From Headline to Prime Time" (published in *TV Guide*), David Shaw observes that "Fact based movies are suddenly the Hula-Hoop, the skateboard, the nintendo of the '90s." He further points out that most such movies are based on disasters, and notes that "the instant dramatization of real tragedy has become a kind of video fast food, drama McNuggets." Shaw's conclusion is worth citing at length:

> Using the powerful and intimate medium of television to pander to the viewer's base instincts is not new, but this rush to do so is the latest step down a very dangerous road. Where will it all end? Will the next David

Koresh be able to sit in his compound and watch his own dramatized death on television—and maybe figure out how to kill the cops instead? . . . Will producers decide that, rather than risk waiting until dramatic events actually take place before they begin costly bidding wars for the dramatic rights of the players, they should open negotiations with soldiers of fortune, jilted lovers, and putative terrorists *before* they do their dastardly deeds . . . perhaps even suggesting a traumatic twist or two in the ultimate execution to jack up the asking price?

## THE APPEAL OF NEW RELIGIONS

Up to this point, the discussion has been focused on the cult *controversy*, and on how that controversy has been misperceived and misrepresented. We now want to turn our attention to understanding the sources of spiritual innovation as well as understanding the appeal of new religions. In successive sections we will examine the real issues—and, in some cases, the real dangers—associated with certain minority religious groups.

There have been a variety of historical periods during which religious innovation has flourished. In the West, there was a proliferation of new religions in the late classical period, as well as in the wake of the Reformation. In the United States, historians have noted a recurring pattern of religious awakenings, beginning with the Great Awakening of the 1740s.

The most general observation we can make is that periods of renewed spiritual activity occur in the wake of disruptive social and economic changes: The established vision of "how things work" no longer seems to apply, and people begin searching for new visions. In previous cycles of American religious experimentation, innovative forms of Protestantism often formed the basis for these new visions. As revivalist fervor died down, new or reinvigorated Protestant denominations became the pillars of a new cultural hegemony.

The most recent period of American religious innovation occurred in the decades following the demise of the 1960s counterculture. However, unlike previous cycles of revival, the religious explosion that occurred in the 1970s and 1980s has not provided a basis for a new spiritual and cultural synthesis. While there has been a growth in conservative Protestant denominations during this period (a growth parallel to the pattern of earlier Awakenings), there has also been a marked growth in "metaphysical" religion. The most visible manifestation of this latter strand of spirituality has been the New Age movement, which offers a vision of the world fundamentally different from that of traditional Christianity. Thus, during this most recent cycle of religious enthusiasm, Protestantism has failed to reestablish its traditional hegemony over American culture.

Other factors inhibiting the formation of a new cultural synthesis have been the growing power of secularization and the influx of new immigrants from non-Protestant (and even non-Christian) countries. In the West's new, pluralistic society, Hindus, Buddhists, Muslims, and so forth represent a growing segment of the culture—a segment for whom neither Protestantism nor the New Age exercises much appeal. Also, a trend toward secularization that was set in motion in the preceding century has shaped yet another important segment of contemporary society, one alienated from religion altogether.

Lacking the power to generate a new basis for cultural synthesis, the current proliferation of new religious movements cannot help but strike the casual observer as a negative phase of contemporary life—a factor contributing to the disintegration of modern life. However, it is the very disconnectedness of the contemporary experience that contributes to the attraction of nonmainstream religions. This "something" is that many alternative religions hold out the possibility of life-transforming experiences—experiences that, to a greater or lesser extent, help one to drop the burden of the past and be reborn into a new and more whole life.

The mainstream Protestant denominations—Methodists, Baptists, and Presbyterians—once offered the seeker life-transforming experiences in the context of revivals and camp meetings. But as these religious bodies settled down into comfortable accommodation with the surrounding (largely secular) society, they lost their intensity. One result of this accommodation was that revivals and camp meetings—and the accompanying intense religious experiences—were relegated to a quaint and mildly embarrassing chapter in denominational histories.

Those of us who are happily adjusted to the social-cultural mainstream often have a difficult time understanding intense religiosity. Academics have not been exempt from this tendency. An earlier generation of sociologists of religion, seemingly obsessed with the issue of conversion to non-mainstream "sect" groups, gave excessive attention to explaining why individuals could become involved in such bizarre churches.

If, however, rather than dwelling on strange externals, we change our point of focus and attempt to really look at what might attract someone to an alternative religion, such involvement is not really difficult to understand. Is the attraction of transformational experiences, for example, really so hard to comprehend? What if we actually could let go of the burden of our past and be reborn as new people? Such transformation may or may not be attainable, but the attractiveness of the possibility is certainly understandable. Many nonmainstream religions—conservative Christian sects included—hold out the promise of such life-changing experiences.

Many people become involved in a religious group in the wake of a spiritual experience. This factor was particularly emphasized in older academic literature about religious conversion. In this body of literature, the suddenness of the experience is stressed. The implicit or explicit paradigm is the Damascus Road experience, in which the apostle Paul was knocked off his horse by a bolt out of the blue, confronted by Jesus, and converted on the spot. Contemporary studies have found, however, that it rarely works that way. Rather, in most cases, individuals just gradually "drift" into a religious group until they cross a barely perceptible line between outsider and insider, undergoing a series of "miniconversions" en route.

Religious experience is, however, only one aspect of the spiritual life, and only one of the factors that attract individuals to deeper religious involvement. Among the many approaches to religious studies, one of the older, yet still useful, scholarly analyses was articulated by the influential historian of religion, Joachim Wach. The primary core of religion, according to Wach, is religious experience. Religious experience, in turn, is expressed in at least three ways:

In a community (church, ashram, etc.)

In a doctrine (theology, worldview, ideology)

In a "cultus" (ritual, ceremony, gathering)

Wach's analysis should give us a basic feel for the fundamental constituents of religion. In outline form, these constituents are:

Spiritual experience

Community

Doctrine/idea system

Gatherings/rites

Each of these four components shed light on how individuals become involved in religious groups. We have already discussed the role of spiritual experiences. Often it is the community dimension of any religious group that is the key element in initially attracting new members. We live in a society that would have been an alien world to our ancestors. Surrounded by masses of people, we rarely know the names of our closest neighbors. In traditional societies, by way of contrast, everyone in a particular village knew everyone else, and took care of everyone else: If, for instance, you saw someone have an accident, you didn't call 911; instead, you ran over and helped out as best you could. Some churches and most alternative religions recreate this kind of community—a community comparable to an extended family.

The family metaphor is particularly apt. In modern society, our families are not the close emotional units they were in traditional societies. A small religious group many times recreates the sense of belonging to a family. If one has never experienced the closeness of a traditional family, it is easy to understand how the sense of belonging to a family unit would be attractive, and even healing.

Something similar can be said about worldviews. In a traditional society, beliefs about the ultimate nature of the universe are largely taken for granted. In contemporary society, by way of contrast, nothing can be taken for granted except death and taxes. We are taught to be "nice" by our school system, but this moral teaching is not grounded in an ultimate source of value. We are also instructed in the basic skills necessary to operate in society, but public school teachers are quiet about the greater questions of death, purpose, and the meaning of life.

We may place a positive or a negative evaluation on this relativistic education, but in any case we have to acknowledge that our culture's ambiguous approach to socialization departs radically from the socialization strategies of earlier societies. Our choices are always varying shades of grey, rather than black and white/good and bad. The results of this ambiguity may be liberating to some people, but to others it is confusing. Without some kind of ultimate grounding, this is necessarily the case.

Nontraditional religions are often criticized for offering their followers the "easy" answers that come with black-and-white thinking. However, to many of the people who belong to such religions, the seeming narrowness of such thinking can be a liberating experience: Once one has stable criteria for what is good and true, this clarity and stability can then free one to go about the business of working, loving, and living life without debilitating anxieties about transcendent meaning and value. This is not, of course, to advocate a rigid belief system, but rather to point out why such a system is attractive without depreciating adherents as being somehow weak or defective.

In summary, we may say that people join alternate religions for the same sorts of reasons one would join any other religion, namely, fellowship, a satisfying belief system, and so forth. When these needs are no longer being fulfilled in an acceptable manner, people leave, much as one would leave an unsatisfying marriage.

## SOCIAL INFLUENCE IN GENUINELY DANGEROUS RELIGIONS

### The Nature of "Cultic" Influence

While we can dismiss the notion of a unique form of influence exerted by minority religions over their followers, it is nevertheless still clear that the members of any group—particularly a tightly knit spiritual community—experience various forms of social influence. Social pressure, conformity, and attitude change are bread-and-butter issues for social psychology, and small group dynamics are ideal situations in which to study such processes. However, the "garden variety" group influences examined by social psychologists rarely find their way into the "cult" debate. On the one hand, they do not serve the purposes of anticultists who are intent on making the case for "cultic mind control." On the other hand, defenders of religious liberty are so focused on demonstrating the presence of free will among members of controversial religions that they tend to gloss over the question of the other, less noble social dynamics found within such groups.

In approaching these dynamics, it should initially be noted that somewhat different factors are involved in *recruitment* as opposed to the ongoing *maintenance* of commitment to a group of any type. Proponents of the brainwashing theory have tended to ignore this particular distinction. At an earlier stage of the cult controversy, anticultists, particularly deprogrammers, tended to portray recruitment as a kind of "spot hypnosis" that was able to override the will of the recruit. This perspective ignored the obvious, which was that not everyone was susceptible to proselytizers—indicating that factors other than an irresistible hypnosis technique were at work in the recruiting situation. In particular, more objective observers noted that the great majority of individuals who joined high demand religions were unattached young people—people with few responsibilities and who were thus relatively free to experiment with an alternative lifestyle.

Another point infrequently emphasized in anticult literature is that comparatively few nontraditional religions are as demanding as the Moonies or the Hare Krishna movement. In fact, the great majority of religions stigmatized as "cults" are more like mainstream churches and synagogues in that they do not require members to leave their families or their jobs and move into an isolated communal facility. Recruitment to such groups thus tends to take place quite differently—through family, friend, and employment networks—and more gradually than the "Pied Piper" syndrome that is a cornerstone of the stereotype of cult recruitment.

As has already been indicated in previous sections, it does not require a great leap of the imagination to understand the initial attraction of becoming a member of such communities. Intensive religious groups provide participants with a ready-made fellowship, a stable worldview, and clear ethical guidelines that sharply contrast with the ambivalence and ambiguity of life in contemporary mass society.

Once one joins a religious group, the ordinary forces of social conformity come into play to further socialize the recruit into the mores of her or his new community. In a classic study of the sociology of knowledge, *The Social Construction of Reality*, Peter L. Berger and Thomas Lockman make the case that the plausibility of any given idea is dependent upon the people one is in conversation with on a day-to-day basis. Thus, if all of one's acquaintances are Republicans, even someone who had previously been a Democrat tends to "convert" to Republicanism, and vice versa. Similarly, the notion that Rev. Moon might be the new messiah seems silly to non-Moonies. But if one was to live in a community in which all of one's conversation partners held this belief, it would not be long before one would begin to entertain the idea as a plausible option.

The motive in such situations is the natural human desire to be accepted, and the socially learned value of not wanting to disagree with others. These motives can actually alter the manner in which we perceive the world, as demonstrated in a classic experiment by social psychologist designed by Solomon Asch. In the Asch experiment, a subject was asked to judge which of three sample lines a given line was closest to in length. Unknown to the subject, however, the other seven people in the room were only pretending to be experimental subjects. Instead, they had been instructed to falsely identify a different line—one that was obviously unequal in length. When it came the subject's turn—who was always the last person to speak—he or she was thus faced with the dilemma of listening to his own senses or to the group judgment. A full 80 percent of the subjects in Asch's original experiment were influenced by the group to go against the evidence of their senses at least some of the time.

If the social forces influencing people to conform can have this high success rate with a group of strangers, imagine how such forces must be amplified within a group of friends—or, to take the case at hand, within a closeknit religious fellowship. It should not be too difficult to perceive how the desire to conform, in combination with the ongoing conversation that gives a belief system much of its plausibility, influences group members to become convinced of ideas that seem odd or nutty to outsiders. Clearly, it is unnecessary to posit a special form of social influence conforming to the popular notion of "cultic brainwashing" in order to explain such behavior.

In most cases, the results of these forces of social influence are benign. There are, however, situations in which the very same forces can be put to socially undesirable ends. In a different series of experiments, psychologist Stanley Milgram demonstrated how, in the right circumstances, ordinary individuals could be manipulated into obeying orders to torture and even kill other human beings. (No one was actually harmed; instead, experimental subjects were tricked into believing they had murdered someone.) While the implications of these experiments are frightening, at the same time they shed light on such apparently crazy acts as the Jonestown and the Heaven's Gate suicides: Under the right circumstances, people can be led to undertake extreme actions—even mass suicide. Once again, it should be noted that it is unnecessary to invoke ad hoc notions of cult mind control to explain such events.

If, however, the forms of social influence at work within minority religions are not distinctive enough to allow one to distinguish a dangerous group from a healthy group on the basis of socialization routines, then, How can we distinguish the Solar Temples, Jonestowns, and Heaven's Gates from benign religious organizations? While any simple criterion for making such a distinction is likely impossible, there are, nevertheless, a few guidelines that could function as "early warning signs" for a religion that has gone or is going "bad."

## "Cults" or Bad Religion?

While the majority of minority religions are innocuous, many have been involved in social conflicts. A handful of these conflicts have made national and even international headlines, from the siege of the Branch Davidian community to the group suicide of Heaven's Gate members. One consequence of these highly publicized incidents is that they have served to reinforce unreflective stereotypes about "cults" and "cult leaders" that are appropriate for some—but certainly not the majority of—minority religions. Unfortunately, such stereotyped information is often the only "data" readily available to the media and law enforcement at the onset of such conflicts.

Putting aside the technical discourse of sociologists, in ordinary language people talk as if there is an objective category of groups called "cults" that can be distinguished from genuine religions. In this commonly accepted view, cults are by definition socially dangerous false religions, led by cynical cult leaders who exploit followers for their own gain.

This stereotype is, however, deeply flawed, and for more than one reason. In the first place, as we have already seen, "cult" is a socially negotiated label that often means little more than a religion one dislikes for some reason. To certain conservative Christians, for example, a "cult" is any religion that departs from a certain traditional interpretation of scripture. Alternately, ultraconservative Christians who take a strictly fundamentalist approach to scripture often appear "cult-like" to many mainline Christians. In other words, one person's cult is another person's religion.

In the second place, the founders of new groups are—despite whatever personal flaws some might have—almost always sincerely religious. Part of the problem here is that most people unreflectively assume that religion is always something "good." If, therefore, a given religious body does something "bad," then ipso facto it must not be a "real" religion. Instead, it must be a false religion, created for no other reason than the founder/leader's personal gain. This attitude is, however, naive. The ancient Aztecs, to take an extreme example, regularly tortured and sacrificed other human beings as part of their religious rites. These practices were, in fact, a central aspect of the Aztec religion. But, however much we might be able to explain and even to understand why the Aztecs engaged in such practices, no contemporary person would defend these rites as "good."

The proper question to ask, then, is not whether some particular group is or is not a cult (in the sense of a "false religion"), but, rather, whether or not the social-psychological dynamics within a particular religion are potentially dangerous to its members and/or to the larger society. Unfortunately, once we get beyond such actions as torturing and murdering other human beings, the criteria for what one regards as harmful can be quite subjective. It has been seriously asserted, for example, that requiring "cult" members to be celibate and to follow vegetarian diets are harmful practices. Similarly, requiring followers to engage in several hours of meditation per day plus discouraging the questioning of "cult" doctrine have often been portrayed as parts of a group's "brainwashing" regime designed to damage one's ability to reason properly.

Once again, the problem with such criteria is that they are naive. If celibacy was harmful, for example, then how does one explain the lack of more-than-ordinary pathology among monks and nuns? Also, if certain mental practices actually damaged the brain, then why do members of intensive religious groups perform so well on I.Q. tests and other measures of individual reasoning ability? Such critical criteria also reflect an abysmal ignorance of traditional religious practices: Many traditional religions have promoted celibacy, restricted diets, prescribed lengthy prayers and meditations, discouraged the questioning of group ideology, and so on. Clearly, if one wants to delineate serious criteria for determining "bad religion," then one must avoid focusing on traits that embody more than the observer's ethnocentric attitudes.

To begin with, making a radical lifestyle change as part of joining a religious group should not, in itself, be taken to indicate that the individual has therefore become involved in something harmful. Friends and family members may feel that an individual is making a mistake to quit a job or to drop out of school—actions that, by the way, *very few* contemporary new religions would actively encourage—but a free society means nothing if one is not also free to make mistakes.

If one wishes to develop objective criteria for distinguishing harmful or potentially harmful religious organizations from harmless religions, one needs to place oneself in the position of a public policy maker. From this perspective, religions that should raise the most concern are those groups that tangibly, physically harm members and/or nonmembers, or engage in other antisocial/illegal acts. However, a public policy maker might well respond that this post facto criterion is too little too late, and that what is needed are criteria that could act as early warning signs—criteria indicating that a previously innocuous group is potentially "going bad." In the following discussion we will make a stab at developing such criteria, with the caveat that the presence of the less serious factors listed below in any given group does not automatically mean they are on the verge of becoming the next Heaven's Gate.

## Early Warning Signs

As part of this discussion, we shall be referring to a few false criteria for distinguishing a healthy from an unhealthy religion. In the first place, the mere fact that a group is headed up by a charismatic leader does not automatically raise a red flag. This is because new religions are much like new businesses: New businesses are almost always the manifestation of the vision and work of a single entrepreneur. In contrast, few if any successful businesses are the outgrowth of the work of a committee.

Also, to found a religion, a leader usually makes some sort of claim to a special insight or to a special revelation that legitimates both the new religion and the leader's right to lead. The founder may even claim to be prophet, messiah, or avatar. While many critics of alternative religions have asserted that the assumption of such authority is in itself a danger sign, too many objectively harmless groups have come into being with the leader asserting divine authority for such claims to be meaningful danger signs.

Far more important than one's claim to authority is what one does with the authority once he or she attracts followers who choose to recognize it. A minister or guru who focusses her or his pronouncements on the interpretation of scripture or on other matters having to do with religion proper is far less problematic than a leader who takes it upon her- or himself to make decisions in the personal lives of individual parishioners, such as dictating (as opposed to suggesting) who and when one will marry. The line between *advising* and *ordering* others with respect to their personal lives can, however, be quite thin. A useful criterion for determining whether or not this line has been crossed is to examine what happens when one acts against the guru's advice in such matters: If one can respectfully disagree without suffering negative consequences as a result, then the leadership dynamics within the group are healthy with respect to authority issues.

One of the clearest signs that leaders are overstepping their proper sphere of authority is when they articulate certain ethical guidelines that everyone must follow *except for* the guru or minister. This is especially the case with a differential sexual ethic that restricts the sexual activity of followers but allows leaders to initiate liaisons with whomever they choose.

Perhaps the most serious danger sign is when a religious group places itself above the law, although there are some nuances that make this point trickier than it might first appear. All of us, in some sphere of life, place ourselves above the law, if only when we go a few miles per hour over the speed limit or fudge a few figures on our income tax returns. Also, when push comes to shove, almost every religion in the world would be willing to assert that divine law takes precedence over human law—should they ever come into conflict. Hence a group that, for example, solicits donations in an area where soliciting is forbidden should not, on that basis alone, be viewed as danger to society. Exceptions should also be made for groups or individuals who make a very public protest against certain laws judged as immoral, as when a conscientious objector goes to jail rather than be drafted into the military.

On the other hand, it should be clear that a group leader who consistently violates serious laws has developed a rationale that could easily be used to legitimate more serious antisocial acts. Examples that come readily to mind are Marshall Herff Applewhite, founder/leader of Heaven's Gate, who regularly ducked out on motel bills and who was once even arrested for stealing a rental car, and Swami Kirtananda, founder of the New Vrindavan community, who was caught authorizing the stealing of computer software before being arrested for ordering the murder of a community critic. Documentable child abuse and other illegalities committed within the organization are also covered by this criterion.

Another misconceived criterion is perceiving groups as dangerous because of apocalyptic theologies. Almost every religion in the larger Judeo-Christian-Islamic tradition has an apocalyptic theology, even the traditional peace churches that forbid members from participating in the military. Thus, contrary to the assertions of some contemporary critics of religion, having an apocalyptic theology does not, in itself, raise a red flag. This is because in most apocalyptic scenarios it is God and his angels who fight the final battle, not flesh-and-blood human beings. The human role is spiritual, and the "saved" fight a spiritual war, not a literal, physical war.

An apocalyptic theology is only dangerous when individual followers believe they are going to be called upon to be foot soldiers in God's army, and prepare themselves by stocking up on weapons and ammunition. Groups that come to mind here are some of the Identity Christian churches who see themselves as preparing to fight a literal war with God's enemies. On the other hand, a community's possession of firearms—in the absence of such a theology of physical confrontation—is probably not dangerous, if no other danger signs are present. If the simple possession of firearms by members was a significant danger sign, then the Southern Baptist Convention would be the most dangerous "cult" in the nation.

Another false yet frequently voiced criterion is that religious groups are dangerous which see only themselves as saved and the rest of the world as damned. Like apocalypticism, this trait is far too widespread among traditional religions to constitute an authentic danger sign. A more meaningful characteristic should be how a religion actually treats nonmembers.

Another criterion is a group's relative isolation. This trait is somewhat more complex than the others we have examined. On the one hand, there are abundant examples of traditional religions establishing communities or monastic centers apart from the larger society that have posed no danger to anyone. On the other hand, some of the worst abuses have taken place in the segregated (usually communal) subsocieties of certain minority religions. From the suicidal violence of People's Temple to the externally directed violence of certain Identity Christian groups, it was the social dynamics found in an isolated or semi-isolated community that allowed such extreme actions to be contemplated.

In order to flag this characteristic while simultaneously avoiding stigmatizing every religion that sets up a segregated society as being potentially dangerous, it might be best to invert this trait and state it as a counterindicator. In other words, rather than asserting that any religion with a partially isolated community is potentially dangerous, let us instead assert that the relative *lack* of such boundaries indicates that the group in question is almost certainly *not* dangerous.

A final early warning sign is a group's readiness to deceive outsiders (and, to a lesser extent, the systematic deception of insiders). Some critics have said that a recruiter who invites a potential convert to a dinner without mentioning that the event is being sponsored by such-and-such church is deceptive. Others have criticized religions possessing a hierarchial system of knowledge to which only initiates are privy. These kinds of criticisms are silly. When a guru publicly asserts that his organization does not own any guns and police later find a small arsenal in his basement, *that's* deception.

To summarize, the traits we designated above as "early warning signs of 'bad religion'" are:

1. The organization is willing to place itself above the law. With the exceptions noted earlier, this is probably the most important characteristic.
2. The leadership dictates (rather than suggests) important personal (as opposed to spiritual) details of followers' lives, such as whom to marry, what to study in college, etc.

3. The leader sets forth ethical guidelines members must follow but from which the leader is exempt.
4. The group is preparing to fight a literal, physical Armageddon against other human beings.
5. The leader regularly makes public assertions that he or she knows are false and/or the group has a policy of routinely deceiving outsiders.

Finally, we noted that, while many benign religions constitute semisegregated communities, socially dangerous religions are almost always isolated or partially isolated from the larger society.

These five traits are about as close as one can get to legitimate, objective criteria for judging whether or not a given religious organization is going—or has gone—"bad." With the exception of placing the group's actions above the law, none of these characteristics, taken by itself, is necessarily cause for alarm. On the other hand, a group possessing more than one or two of the above traits might well bear closer scrutiny. As a corollary to this line of analysis, minority religions possessing none of the above traits are, from a public policy standpoint, almost certainly harmless.

# 2 COURT DECISIONS, LEGISLATION, AND GOVERNMENTAL ACTIONS

*Michael Homer and James R. Lewis*

**B**eyond the limited domain struggles that have taken place around deprogrammings, the principal arenas within which the cult controversy has been fought are the courts and the media (the "court" of popular opinion). Perhaps paradoxically, the anticult movement has suffered defeat in the courts but has been victorious in the media. The current state of affairs is comparable to the situation the civil rights movement found itself during its heyday: While going from victory to victory in the courts, in popular opinion Blacks were still viewed as second class citizens, particularly in the deep South.

One of the principal reasons why minority religions have had such success in the legal arena is that the courts have been compelled to treat such groups seriously as *religions,* entitled to all of the rights and privileges normally accorded mainstream denominations. Critics of new religions would like to draw a sharp line between religions and cults, and treat cults as pseudoreligious organizations. The courts, however, are unable to approach such groups differently as long as group members manifest sincerity in their religious beliefs.

This situation explains why none of the legislative efforts to regulate new religious movements have been successful. For example, the New York state legislature once tried to enact a law that would have made starting a pseudoreligion a felony, but it failed to pass because—among other factors—it lacked an objective criterion for distinguishing false from true religions. Without a truly neutral standard, any such law violates the establishment clause of the First Amendment. It is, in fact, the separation of church and state mandated by the First Amendment that has discouraged legislation in this area. This has left the courts to bear the burden of adjudicating the controversy, making an overview of the relevant legal activity far more lengthy and involved than with most other public issues.

Because cases involving contemporary minority religions are often argued in terms of religious liberty issues, earlier religious liberty decisions are directly relevant to the present controversy. While anticultists have accused cults of "hiding behind the First Amendment," they have been largely unsuccessful at persuading the legal system to set aside First Amendment concerns when dealing with controversial minority religions. The necessity of taking cults seriously as "real" religions explains why it is necessary to refer back to earlier legal decisions involving Mormons, Jehovah's Witnesses, and others.

The following discussion begins with an overview of court cases and legislation not dealing explicitly with contemporary "cult" groups, but nevertheless relevant to the controversy because of the religious liberty issue. This will be followed by an examination of the first important "new religion" cases prior to the emergence of the cult controversy as an important public issue. In addition to the initial efforts of governmental bodies to regulate minority religions by passing new laws, deprogrammers and their clients began using conservatorship laws to legitimize their kidnapping activities. While initially experiencing some limited success, in the long run this strategy was defeated in the courts.

Following the demise of the conservatorship tactic, torts by ex-members claiming damage at the hands of their former religions became the chief strategy by which to weaken controversial minority religions. Once again this tactic initially had a few notable successes, only to be ultimately frustrated by the defeat of coercive persuasion/"brainwashing" theory in the courts. Of the other legal arenas in which the cult controversy has been fought, perhaps the most important has been the sensitive issue of child abuse/child custody. Other areas have been zoning, solicitation, and taxation issues.

For a long time, it seemed that the new religions and their enemies were more or less evenly matched in the courts, although the balance of power would periodically swing one way or the other. This situation changed dramatically in the mid to late nineties with the decisive defeat of the "brainwashing" notion in the courts, and with the declaration of bankruptcy by the largest anticult organization in the United States.

## RELEVANT COURT DECISIONS NOT DIRECTLY INVOLVING CONTEMPORARY NEW RELIGIONS

### Mormon Polygamy Cases

Religious beliefs are fully protected under the First Amendment to the Constitution. However, it has become a well-recognized principle of constitutional law that religious conduct may be circumscribed. In *Cantwell* v. *Connecticut* (discussed below), for instance, the United States Supreme Court acknowledged that religious conduct "remains subject to regulation for the protection of society."

According to the Court, religious practices may be regulated even at the expense of religious freedom. This view dates back to the time of Thomas Jefferson, who proposed legislation in the Virginia House of Delegates recognizing that government may "interfere when [religious] principles break out into overt acts against peace and good order" (quoted in the *Reynolds* v. *United States* decision). This governmental interference includes allowing for recovery to those who suffer harm as a result of tortious conduct by another. Religious organizations are not exempt from liability for tortious conduct.

Because of the First Amendment, religious liberty cases are almost by definition Supreme Court cases. The first Supreme Court decision having a direct bearing on the contemporary debate over cults was the 1878 case, *Reynolds* v. *United States*. Lurid stories about the plural wife practices of the Church of Jesus Christ of Latter-day Saints had titillated other Americans for over three decades—stories implying that Mormon polygamy was a thinly veiled excuse for sexual indulgence. As a consequence, Congress legislated against plural marriage as a form of bigamy in the *Revised Statutes of the United States*, sect. 5352:

> Every person having a husband or wife living, who marries another, whether married or single, in a Territory, or other place over which the United States have exclusive jurisdiction, is guilty of bigamy, and shall be punished by a fine of not more than $500, and by imprisonment for a term of not more than five years.

George Reynolds was a member of the LDS Church convicted under this statute. Reynolds asserted that, because plural marriage was prescribed by his religion, that his conviction was a violation of the free exercise of religion provision of the First Amendment.

In 1878 this case was considered by the Supreme Court. When Chief Justice Morrison Waite wrote the Court's decision, he was aware that history was being made: This was the first judicial effort to interpret the meaning of the "free exercise of religion." Justice Waite's decision cited, among other things, contemporaneous scholarly opinion that polygamy was detrimental to a free society, and concluded that in the First Amendment:

> Congress was deprived of all legislative power over mere opinion, but was left free to reach actions which were in violation of social duties or subversive of good order.

In other words, while Congress cannot prescribe laws against what one may *believe* ("opinion"), it may legislate against *actions* harmful to society—such as the plural wife system was judged to be.

This decision was amplified in a second LDS case, *Davis* v. *Beason*, decided by the Supreme Court in 1889. Samuel D. Davis had had his voter registration in Idaho rescinded merely for belonging to the Mormon church. Davis argued his case, like Reynolds, on the free-exercise provision of the First Amendment. Associate Justice Stephen Field wrote the court's decision, asserting, like Waite had before him, that not every action prescribed by a religion can be protected by the First Amendment:

> History discloses the fact that the necessity of human sacrifices, upon special occasions, had been a tenet of many sects. Should a sect of [this kind] ever find its way into this country, swift punishment would follow the carrying into effect of its doctrines, and no heed would be given to the pretence that, as religious beliefs, their supporters could be protected in their exercise by the Constitution of the United States.

Finally, in the decision to two other LDS cases, Justice Joseph Bradley responded to the free exercise of religion argument by noting that "no doubt the Thugs of India imagined that their belief in the right of assassination was a religious belief." (Bradley wrote a joint decision for the Supreme Court in *Mormon Church* v. *United States* and *Romney* v. *United States*.)

Following *Reynolds* and the other LDS decisions, the standards for measuring the harmfulness of religious conduct have been based on socially accepted, traditional notions of religious practice. Because the practice of polygamy was offensive to the notions of traditional religious institutions and because the court in *Reynolds* assumed that there were innocent victims who suffered harm from such conduct the religious practice was not allowed to continue.

In *Reynolds*, the Court relied on various excerpts from writings by Thomas Jefferson, one of the proponents of the free exercise clause. Jefferson believed that "religion is a matter which lies solely between man and his God; . . . that the legislative powers of the government reach actions only, and not opinions" and that government may not opine on the validity of a religion but may only regulate actions that are in violation of social duties or subversive of good order.

The court in *Reynolds* deferred to contemporary social norms and opinions concerning polygamy and found that it was an odious practice and void under the common law. The Supreme Court upheld the trial court's jury instructions, which reminded the jury of the evil consequences that were supposed to flow from plural marriages. Those "evil consequences" were the subject of numerous books and articles published by anti-Mormons during the second half of the nineteenth century as well as congressional testimony. Thus, the *Reynolds* decision reflects the willingness of the highest court to adopt a standard consistent with majoritarian social norms to the detriment of minority religious practices.

Together, *Reynolds, Davis,* et al., involving the most despised "new religion" of the day, all asserted the absolute right of the government to regulate religious activity. Although, in hindsight, these specific decisions may appear contrary to the spirit of the free exercise clause, at the same time they articulate the obvious point that not every activity deserves the protection of the First Amendment merely because it has a religious basis. In the context of the contemporary cult controversy, anticult spokespersons have sometimes referred back to the belief-action dichotomy laid out in *Reynolds* v. *U.S.* The *Reynolds* decision was not, however, the final word on the meaning of the free exercise provision.

## Jehovah's Witnesses Cases

The Jehovah's Witnesses were the most controversial new religion of the mid-twentieth century. Like the LDS, the Witnesses remain the focus of much contemporary Christian anticultism because of perceived doctrinal deviations from the Evangelical mainstream. The group's aggressive proselytizing in combination with members' refusal to participate in such nationalistic activities as saluting the flag led to persecution and arrests. In response, the Witnesses formed a legal wing for the express purpose of challenging these arrests on First Amendment grounds.

The first important Supreme Court victory for the Jehovah Witnesses was the 1938 case of *Lovell* v. *City of Griffin.* The Supreme Court's decision in this case overturned the conviction of a Witness for distributing literature without a permit. The permit ordinance, however, left too much to the discretion of the relevant city official, making it unconstitutional on the basis of the *free speech* (as opposed to the freedom of religion) provision of the First Amendment.

The freedom of religion clause was brought into play two years later in another significant Supreme Court victory for the Witnesses, *Cantwell* v. *Connecticut*—a case that extended the freedom of religion provision of the federal constitution to the states, and which served to call into the question the 1887 *Reynolds* decision giving government the power to regulate religious actions. *Cantwell's* departure from the LDS cases is reflected in the decision composed by Associate Justice Owen Roberts:

> The Amendment embraces two concepts—freedom to believe and freedom to act. The first is absolute but, in the nature of things, the second cannot be. Conduct remains subject to regulation for the protection of society. The freedom to act must have appropriate definition to preserve the enforcement of that protection. In every case the power to regulate must be so exercised as not, in attaining a permissible end, unduly to infringe the protected freedom.

The *Cantwell* decision was reinforced by further cases decided three years later. In 1943, four cases involving the right of Jehovah's Witnesses to canvass door-to-door reached the high court. Three were decided in favor of the Witnesses (*Jones* v. *Oplika, Murdock* v. *Pennsylvania,* and *Martin* v. *Struthers*). The fourth case (*Douglas* v. *Jeannette*) was decided against the Witnesses, but on technical grounds. Associate Justice William O. Douglas wrote the Court's decision in *Jones* and *Murdock,* referring to the tradition of itinerant evangelism as support for the argument that the solicitation activity of Witnesses was a religious activity, and thus protected by the First Amendment.

Another case involving the refusal of Witnesses to salute the flag, *West Virginia State Board of Education* v. *Barnette,* was decided the same year. *Barnette* was decided in favor of the Jehovah's Witnesses, overturning a related Supreme Court decision, *Minersville School District* v. *Gobitis,* made against the Witnesses in 1940. The decision in *Barnette* was made on free exercise of religion rather than free speech grounds.

## The Sherbert-Yoder Test

In 1963, the high court decided *Sherbert* v. *Verner,* a key case for what would become known as the "Sherbert-Yoder Test" for deciding free exercise of religion cases. In this case, the Supreme Court decided in favor of a Seventh-day Adventist who had been denied unemployment benefits because she had not been able to accept employment requiring work on Saturday. *Wisconsin* v. *Yoder,* decided six years later, concluded that a state law mandating high school education was an excessive burden on the Amish religion.

Without going into all of the details of these cases, the resulting Sherbert-Yoder Test sets forth criteria for adjudicating conflicts between the interest of the state and the dictates of a religion. These criteria have been summarized by William C. Shepherd as follows:

1. Are the religious beliefs in question sincerely held?
2. Are the religious practices under review germane to the religious belief system?
3. Would carrying out the state's wishes constitute a substantial infringement on the religious practice?
4. Is the interest of the state compelling? Does the religious practice perpetuate some grave abuse of a statutory provision or obligation?
5. Are there alternative means of regulation by which the state's interest is served but the free exercise of religion is less burdened?

(Shepherd 1985)

The Sherbert-Yoder test has become the definitive standard for deciding cases involving the free exercise of religion. It would be the crucial criterion for determining the outcome of later cases involving new religious movements.

To get a sense of the importance of the Sherbert-Yoder test, we might look briefly at a few of decisions made prior to and after *Sherbert*. In 1949 in *Bunn* v. *North Carolina*, for example, a lower court ruled that public safety outweighed the concern for the free exercise of religion involving the handling of poisonous snakes. The U.S. Supreme Court dismissed the appeal without comment. Only two years before *Sherbert*, in *Braunfeld* v. *Brown*, the Supreme Court decided against Orthodox Jewish merchants protesting Pennsylvania laws requiring them to close their stores on Sunday.

In 1981, the Supreme court ruled on *Thomas* v. *Review Board*. In this case, a Witness who had quit his job rather than work in an armaments factory and been denied unemployment benefits. The court decided in favor of the Jehovah's Witnesses, echoing the decision in *Sherbert*. This case is important as the first major case after *Yoder* to be decided according to the Sherbert-Yoder Test.

The Sherbert-Yoder Test was the standard until the 1990 case of *Employment Division* v. *Smith*. In this decision, the Supreme Court ruled against the right of Native American Church members to use peyote. The case evoked outrage from church-state scholars and others, who characterized the decision as supplanting religious sincerity with the values of the majority as the standard for determining which religious acts merit the protection of the free exercise clause of the First Amendment.

Reacting to the Supreme Court's decision in *Employment Division* v. *Smith*, a broad coalition of religious groups supported and pushed through the Religious Freedom Restoration Act (RFRA), a legislative measure intended to reestablish Sherbert-Yoder standards for the free exercise of religion. RFRA was overwhelmingly endorsed by both houses of Congress.

## EARLIEST CASES INVOLVING
## CONTEMPORARY NEW RELIGIONS

## The Ballard Decision

Prior to the emergence of the modern cult controversy and even prior to the formulation of *Sherbert* v. *Verner*, there was one extremely important Supreme Court case involving a contemporary new religion. This 1944 case, *United States* v. *Ballard*, focused on the belief system of "I AM" Activity, a neo-Theosophical group from which a whole family of other groups—including Church Universal and Triumphant—traces its roots. The case was built around the charge of mail fraud, based on the "ridiculous" nature of the group's beliefs. In the words of Justice Jackson who wrote the dissenting opinion in *United States* v. *Ballard*:

> Scores of sects flourish in this country by teaching what to me are queer notions. It is plain that there is wide variety in American religious taste. The Ballards are not alone in catering to it with a pretty dubious product.
> The chief wrong which false prophets do to their following is not financial. The collections aggregate a tempting total, but individual payments are not ruinous. I doubt if the vigilance of the law is equal to making money stick by over-credulous people. But the real harm is on the mental and spiritual plane. There are those who hunger and thirst after higher values which they feel wanting in their humdrum lives. They live in mental confusion or moral anarchy and seek vaguely for truth and beauty and moral support. When they are deluded and then disillusioned, cynicism and confusion follow. The wrong of these things, as I see it, is not in the money the victims part with half so much as in the mental and spiritual poison they get.

The founder of the movement, Guy Ballard, had long been interested in occultism and Theosophy. He married Edna Wheeler in 1916, and together they founded the "I AM" Activity in the 1930s. Ballard's revelations from Saint-Germain were spread during the lectures of the Ballards, who traveled in the 1930s as "Accredited Messengers" of the Masters. Further messages from the ascended masters, especially from Saint-Germain and the Master Jesus, were sometimes produced in public or private.

Saint-Germain and Jesus were considered the mediators between the "I AM Presence" and humans. The Ascended Masters were at one time all human beings who were able to transcend the physical world through the purification of their lives. The goal of human life is represented by ascension. In 1938, the "I AM" Activity was said to have been given a dispensation according to which persons who had devoted themselves so much to the movement that they had not given all they might to personal purification, could upon normal death ascend from the after-earth state without reembodiment.

The "I AM" Activity worked publicly from 1937 to 1940 to establish a group of devoted followers numbering over one million. With the death of Guy Ballard on December 29, 1939, the movement began to decline. Edna Ballard claimed that her husband had become an ascended master. However, the fact that Guy Ballard had experienced a physical death rather than bodily ascension threatened the movement's credibility. The following year a sensational trial of the leaders of the movement took place, after some members of Ballard's personal staff accused the Ballards of obtaining money under fraudulent pretenses.

The indictment was voided in 1944 by the Supreme Court with a landmark decision on religious liberty. Justice Douglas, in stating the prevailing opinion, wrote:

> Heresy trials are foreign to our Constitution. Men may believe what they cannot prove. They may not be put to the proof of their religious doctrines or beliefs. Religious experiences which are as real as life to some may be incomprehensible to others. Yet the fact that they may be beyond the ken of mortals does not mean that they can be made suspect before the law. . . . If one could be sent to jail because a jury in a hostile environment found one's teachings false, little indeed would be left of religious freedom. . . . The religious views espoused by respondents might seem incredible, if not preposterous, to most people. But if those doctrines are subject to trial before a jury charged with finding their truth or falsity, then the same can be done with the religious beliefs of any sect. When the triers of fact undertake that task, they enter a forbidden domain.

## Founding Church of Scientology v. United States

What the Jehovah's Witnesses were to the mid-twentieth century, the Church of Scientology became to the latter part of the century. Like the Witnesses, Scientology early set up a strong legal wing that litigated for religious rights as well as for human rights more generally. One of the first new religions to be embroiled in controversy, Scientology would prevail in most of its legal suits and eventually play a major role in eviscerating the Cult Awareness Network, the most important anticult group in the United States.

The Church of Scientology was one of the genuinely new religions to originate in the United States in the twentieth century. The Church was founded by L. Ron Hubbard, a talented writer and adventurer with a consuming interest in the human mind. By 1950 Hubbard had completed enough of his research to write *Dianetics, the Modern Science of Mental Health*, which quickly became a bestseller. In 1951 he announced that the "applied religious philosophy" of Scientology had been born.

Auditing, Scientology's core technique, consists of guiding someone through various mental processes in order to first free the individual of the effects of the "reactive mind," and then to fully realize the spiritual nature of the person. Electrical devices called E-Meters, which rely upon the same basic technology as lie detectors, are used to help the auditor discover emotionally loaded memories. When the individual is freed from the effects of the reactive mind, she or he is said to have achieved the state of "Clear."

Somewhat naively, Hubbard contacted the medical and the psychiatric associations, explaining the significance of his discoveries for mental and physical health, and asking that the AMA and the APA investigate his new technique. Instead of taking this offer seriously, these associations responded by attacking him. The subsequent popular success of Dianetics did nothing to improve the image of Hubbard in the minds of the medical-psychiatric establishment, and was likely instrumental in prompting the FDA raid against the church.

On January 4, 1963, the Founding Church of Scientology in Washington, D.C., was raided by United States marshals and deputized longshoremen with drawn guns, acting in behalf of the Food and Drug Administration (FDA). Five thousand volumes of church scriptures, twenty thousand booklets, and one hundred E-Meters were seized. It took eight years of litigation to finally obtain the return of the materials. Finally, in 1971, the U.S. District Court for the District of Columbia issued the *Founding Church of Scientology* v. *United States* decision. The Food and Drug Administration was ordered to return the books and E-Meters that had been taken in the 1963 raid. In its decision, the court recognized the church's constitutional right to protection from the government's excessive entanglement with religion.

## DEPROGRAMMING IN COURT

The cult controversy proper did not get under way until after the collapse of the sixties counterculture. Rather than re-engaging with mainstream society, many former counterculturists continued their quest for an alternative lifestyle in a wide variety of religions. Hence the membership of many unusual religious groups that had existed quietly on the margins of American society suddenly exploded into public view.

In many cases, friends and family of cult members found it difficult to believe that, without coercion and brainwashing, loved ones could choose to embrace something that they find offensive. They saw "deprogramming" as the natural antidote to this mental programming or brainwashing. By attempting to deprogram the church member, friends and family believed they were helping the member recognize the wrongfulness of his or her choices.

When a person is targeted for deprogramming, he or she is enticed away from the organization or is actually kidnapped and taken to a remote place. While at the remote location, the person is subjected to intensive discussions in which he or she is presented with the "truth" about the religious organization, its tenets and leaders. The process is intense and stressful. Numerous "anticult" organizations promoted kidnapping and deprogramming of church members who had been "deprived of their free will."

These deprogramming activities invade the civil rights of members and deprive the members of choice in their affiliations. Deprogramming also exploits family ties and may further the destruction of family relations. Family members are often the instigators of the kidnapping and deprogramming, and the deprogrammers are the facilitators. In addition to deprogrammers, bodyguards are sometimes hired to prevent the member from escaping. The fact that family members are generally involved makes prosecution of the perpetrators difficult. The state has been reluctant to prosecute a family member for kidnapping. If family members are not prosecuted, judges and juries appear reluctant to convict others who become involved at the request of the family members, the instigators. Further, family members often refuse to testify against the perpetrators, making it virtually impossible to convict.

In deprogramming cases, there is generally testimony by former members. This testimony is filled with a high level of hostility, which increases the prejudice of the judge and jury. The testimony of former members also tends to confuse the legal issues with religious questions. This entanglement of legal and religious issues often confuses the judge and jury and results in placing the religious practices of the church on trial.

In the case of LaVerne Collins (now LaVerne Macchio), a member of Church Universal and Triumphant, LaVerne's mother and sister decided to "rescue" LaVerne from the church because they believed the church was seriously damaging LaVerne and her family. Family members hired deprogrammers and bodyguards to kidnap and deprogram Ms. Collins. At the time of her abduction, LaVerne was thirty-nine years old and the mother and primary caretaker of four children ranging in age from three to fourteen. She was a part-time school teacher and had resided in the same house in Ada County, Idaho, for fifteen years. LaVerne was missing for several days, and there was concern in the community for her safety.

After LaVerne's escape from the deprogrammers, charges were filed against LaVerne's mother and sister, the deprogrammers, and the bodyguards for kidnapping and false imprisonment. Later, at LaVerne's request, all charges against family members were dropped. As a result, the deprogrammers were acquitted. The bodyguards, who were to be tried separately, reached an unusual plea bargain with prosecutors: They would enter guilty pleas on either a felony kidnapping charge or a misdemeanor false imprisonment charge, depending on the outcome of an appeal challenging the judge's ruling to allow the deprogrammers the use of the "necessity defense" at their trial.

When authorities have attempted to resist efforts to kidnap and deprogram members of religious groups by prosecuting those involved, defendants have often been able to assert successfully the defenses of necessity and "choice of evils." The necessity defense has been a major factor in the acquittal of the deprogrammers. The jury appeared to accept the contention that the illegal actions of the defendants were necessary to protect the victim from her own choices and that the church was the greater evil—a view reflecting traditional prejudices.

One element that must be proved under the necessity defense is that there was imminent danger requiring the kidnapping. The standards for determining the nature of the danger and its imminence are colored by the fear and mistrust many have of nontraditional religions. The courts have had difficulty establishing an objective standard by which to measure the danger or threat to the deprogramee. When the "choice of evils" defense is raised, courts have often allowed the jury to consider evidence concerning the supposed evils associated with the church's religious practices.

There is a long line of cases in the area of deprogramming. *People* v. *Brandyberry*, for example, involved a member of the Unification Church who was kidnapped and held in captivity for several days in an attempt to deprogram her. The trial court balanced the "method of cult indoctrination" and of "coercive persuasion" against the evils of abduction and of forced deprogramming to justify kidnapping; however, the court of appeals evaluated only the imminence of grave injury to the victim. The court of appeals acknowledged that to proceed in the manner permitted by the trial court would invite the jury to "consider the morality and desirability of church doctrine and practices rather than whether in fact the victim was threatened by the prospect of a grave or imminent injury."

The trial judge in *Brandyberry* relied on a decision from the Minnesota Supreme Court, *Peterson* v. *Sorlien*, 299 N.W. 2d 123 (Minn. 1980), *cert. denied*, 450 U.S. 1031 (1981). The *Sorlien* court allowed parents to deprogram their child without fear of civil liability when the parents reasonably believed that the child was being unduly influenced by the religion and that the child had lost his or her capacity to reason.

Another common issue raised in deprogramming cases is that of involuntary treatment. Deprogrammers have sought orders requiring involuntary treatment for those who have been deprived of their free will and coercively persuaded to join a new religion. They argue that these individuals must be subject to involuntary treatment because they have lost their capacity to reason by virtue of the controlled environment and brainwashing to which they have been subjected. The control of the environment includes control over eating, sleeping, and other basics of life. Most courts have been reluctant to order such involuntary treatment. However, when courts permit the necessity or "choice of evils" defense, an individual's rights under the free exercise clause and right to be free from compulsory medical treatment are often abused.

Victims of deprogramming have also brought civil actions against kidnappers and deprogrammers. These actions have included claims for violations of civil rights, intentional infliction of emotional distress, conspiracy, and false imprisonment. These actions have had mixed results, but generally the cause of action has been allowed. In fact, one appeals court recognized that deprogrammers practice patterns of coercion similar to those alleged against the church (just as many anticult organizations have all of the essential characteristics of the "cults" they attack). However, in most cases, when civil claims are brought against deprogrammers or family members, the defendants try to make the religious practices of the church the focus of the trial. The defenses of necessity and "choice of evils" allows the trier of fact to review the religious organization's practices, and the degree to which those practices comport with the trier of fact's values may affect the outcome of the case.

## LEGISLATIVE EFFORTS AND CONSERVATORSHIP CASES

### Attempting to Legislate Against Cults

In the early years of the cult controversy, parents concerned about the religious choices of their adult children lobbied various legislatures. A number of states established committees and hearings to investigate the cult menace. Some resolutions were passed, but legislative bodies were ultimately unable to act against minority religions because of the church/state separation issue. The strongest effort ever made by a U.S. legislature was New York State Assembly Bill AB9566-A, which would have made "Promoting a Pseudo-Religious Cult" a felony, introduced by Robert C. Wertz on October 5, 1977:

> A person is guilty of promoting a pseudo-religious cult when he knowingly organizes or maintains an organization into which other persons are induced to join or participate in through the use of mind control methods, hypnosis, brainwashing techniques or other systematic forms of indoctrination in which the members or participants of such organization engage in soliciting funds primarily for the benefit of such organization or its leaders and are not permitted to travel or communicate with anyone

outside such organization unless another member or participant of such organization is present.

A number of different groups, including the American Civil Liberties Union, lobbied heavily against the bill and it was ultimately defeated.

## Efforts to Amend Conservatorship Laws

Failing to win the support of legislatures, some parents of cult members turned to more desperate measures in the form of the vigilante actions of deprogrammers. To protect themselves, it was sometimes possible to use existing conservatorship laws to legitimize their kidnapping activities. Conservatorships were originally designed to protect very elderly or very disturbed people from being unfairly taken advantage of. Such individuals are reduced to the legal status of children, unable to do such things as independently enter into contracts.

In some early cult conservatorship cases, psychiatrists sympathetic to the plight of concerned parents signed conservatorship orders without ever meeting the adult child—feeling that mere membership in a group like the Hare Krishna movement or the Unification Church was sufficient evidence for declaring her or him incompetent. After this practice was challenged, anticultists pushed for amended conservatorship laws that would de facto legitimate deprogramming. Once again, such an amendment almost succeeded in the state of New York, where it was defeated only because the governor vetoed it. This measure was introduced on March 25, 1980, as 11122-A. The flavor of this proposed amendment is captured in its first section, "Persons for whom a temporary conservator may be appointed":

> The supreme court and the county courts outside the city of New York, shall have the power to appoint one or more temporary conservators of the persons and the property of any person over fifteen years of age, upon showing that such person for whom the temporary conservator is to be appointed have become closely and regularly associated with a group which practices the use of deception in the recruitment of members and which engages in systematic food or sleep deprivation or isolation from family or unusually long work schedules and that such person for whom the temporary conservator is to be appointed has undergone a sudden and radical change in behavior, lifestyle, habits and attitudes, and has become unable to care for his welfare and that his judgment has become impaired to the extent that he is unable to understand the need for such care.

## The Faithful Five/Faithless Four Case

The primary conservatorship decision involving a stigmatized minority religion was *Katz v. Superior Court* (73 Cal. App. 3d 952, 141 Cal. Rptr. 234, 1977), also referred to as the "Faithful Five/Faithless Four" case. *Katz* was initially decided in favor of parents seeking conservatorships for their five adult offspring who were members of the Unification Church—only to have the appeals court overturn the decision almost immediately. Four out of five of these individuals left the Church anyway, hence the unusual nickname for this case.

*Katz* was set in motion when the parents approached a California superior court for thirty-day conservatorships for their adult children. The goal was to forcibly incarcerate the five "Moonies" in the Freedom Ranch Rehabilitation Center, a deprogramming facility run by the Freedom of Thought Foundation of Tucson, Arizona. The parents contended that conservatorships were necessary because of their offsprings' "mental illness or weakness and unsound mind" and propensity "to be deceived by artful and designing persons." The parents' counsel further argued that the five had been victims of "psychological kidnapping."

One expert witness in the case, psychiatrist Samuel Benson, described the putative victims as suffering from a wide variety of pathological symptoms, including: "memory impairment," "short attention spans and a decreased ability to concentrate," "limited ability toward abstractions," "defensive attitudes toward id urges," and "various degrees of regression and childlike attitudes." Benson further contended that these symptoms were the direct result of "coercive persuasion"—aka "brainwashing"—techniques, as reflected in literature on former Korean War and Vietnam War POWs.

Despite counter-testimony by the five Unificationists and their own psychological/psychiatric consultants, and despite the obvious constitutional issues which should have been taken into account, the judge decided for the parents, declaring that:

> We're talking about the very essence of life here, mother, father and children. There's nothing closer in our civilization. This is the essence of civilization.

When some of the conservatees petitioned the order, a California appellate court heard their appeal. The court of appeals found the conservatorship statute unconstitutionally vague:

> In the field of beliefs, and particularly religious tenets, it is difficult, if not impossible to establish a universal truth against which deceit and imposition can be measured.

The appellate court also pointed out that there had been no demonstrated emergency as the conservatorship law required. In the absence of demonstrable physical deprivation, the equal protection and due process of law forbid involuntary confinement:

> If there is coercive persuasion or brainwashing which requires treatment, the existence of such a mental disability and the necessity of legal control over the mentally disabled person for the purpose of treatment should be ascertained after compliance with the protection of civil liberties provided by the Welfare and Institutions Code. To do less is to license kidnapping for the purpose of thought control.

Finally and perhaps most importantly, the court of appeals held that the conservatorship orders had violated the Unificationists' rights to freedom of association and freedom of religion. The beliefs and behaviors used as criteria to determine the pathological state of the alleged victims (and to become the targets of the "treatment" to be administered at the Freedom Ranch Rehabilitation Center) were those that stemmed from religious conviction—precisely the arena into which the court system was forbidden to inquire. Hence, "in the absence of such actions as render the adult believer himself gravely disabled," state processes "cannot be used to deprive the believer of his freedom of action and to subject him to involuntary treatment."

The *Katz* decision did not immediately stop other parents from applying for temporary conservatorships for their adult children. There were also ongoing efforts to amend conservatorship laws so as to target members of minority religions. Retrospectively, however, it is evident that *Katz* marked an important watershed, after which the conservatorship tactic went into a gradual decline and eventually died out.

## EX-MEMBER LAWSUITS AGAINST MINORITY RELIGIONS

The issue of conservatorships for members of controversial religions was eventually completely eclipsed by tort cases brought by ex-members against their former religious group. Because the Constitution does not protect all religiously motivated conduct, courts have come to award damages to individuals who claim to have incurred personal injury because of their religious affiliation. Underlying the rationale for such decisions is the traditional notion that religion should benefit and improve one's life and well-being. When religious beliefs and practices do not fulfill these expectations but instead subject a person to personal harm, those beliefs and practices become suspect and generally open to scrutiny by the courts.

Unfortunately, the willingness of courts to examine nontraditional religious practices in light of mainstream traditions often leads to religion-bashing in the judicial forum. Nontraditional beliefs are often found offensive only because of fear and misinformation. Since the emergence of the cult controversy, many minority religious groups have been accused of brainwashing or coercive persuasion. It is claimed that these religious practices subject the individual to a controlled environment in which individuals lose their capacity to reason and think for themselves.

In the early nineties, a judge considered religious practices when sentencing an individual who had pled guilty to charges of murder for hire and conspiracy to tamper with a federal witness. The court sentenced Richard LeBaron to five years for killing a man and his daughter at point-blank range because he had been "brainwashed" by a church to which he had belonged since he was a child. The court believed that because of this brainwashing, LeBaron had lost his capacity to reason and think for himself while committing the crimes, that his thoughts were coerced and not his own, and that he was not totally responsible for his choices and actions.

Religious practices that are assumed to extinguish the individual's capacity to reason and consent foster suspicion and leave the religious organization open to harassment and liability. The courts may, and often do, consider the religious beliefs and practices of nontraditional churches in the context of civil and criminal litigation. Since religious freedom is not absolute, as long as the courts are convinced that certain religious practices cause harm to society or individual church members, all religions will be subject to scrutiny and regulation by the courts and government. When children are involved, the scrutiny is even more exacting. Although the First Amendment was meant to protect individual rights, the courts' willingness to delve into religious beliefs and practices affecting a variety of areas has at times resulted in inflaming juries against nontraditional religious practices, which can ultimately tip the scales of justice against the interests of the church. This has particularly been the case in civil suits.

Religious groups, both traditional and nontraditional, have been named in suits for intentional infliction of emotional distress and liability for "outrageous conduct" through spiritual counseling. When counseling by clergy goes awry, the minister or pastor becomes subject to litigation for intentional infliction of emotional distress. The emotional distress arises from beratement for sinful conduct and the member's perception that the pastor's counseling is malicious and intended to demean. A variety of different minority religions have been besieged with lawsuits by ex-members for personal injury claims ranging from fraud to intentional infliction of emotional distress.

In his recent book, *Understanding New Religious Movements*, John Saliba points out that contemporary minority religions have been taken to court for a wide variety of different reasons:

1. the mental distress and psychological damage they have caused;
2. kidnapping and brainwashing young adults, thus forcing them to become members;
3. the corruption of minors;
4. sexual servitude;
5. defamation;
6. alienation of affections;
7. wanton misconduct and outrageous acts;
8. harassment; and
9. wrongful death.

Decisions in such cases have varied so widely that general conclusions are difficult to draw. All of the better known and many of the lesser known new religions have been involved in such cases. The *Molko-Leal* case will be examined in the present section because of its significance for later developments in the cult controversy. The *Mull* case will be examined partially because of its influence on a later tax case, and partially because the present writer has more direct familiarity with Church Universal and Triumphant than he does with certain other religious movements.

## The *Mull* Case

In one prominent case, Gregory Mull, a San Francisco building designer, became a member of Church Universal and Triumphant in 1974 at the age of fifty-seven. He relocated to the Los Angeles area in 1979 and became employed at the church's Malibu headquarters doing design work.

The church loaned Mull a total of $37,000 during the time he was relocating, for which Mull signed two promissory notes. His tenure on church staff lasted about eight months; then he resigned from the organization over a dispute involving repayment of the notes. The church filed an action against Mull in 1981 for repayment of the $37,000; Mull counterclaimed for fraud, duress, undue influence, involuntary servitude, assault, extortion, intentional infliction of emotional distress and quantum merit, seeking total damages of $253 million. The case was tried in 1986 in Los Angeles Superior Court.

Mull claimed at trial that he was a victim of church mind control and that when he signed the notes, he lacked the legal capacity to do so. He also claimed, in the alternative, that church officials unduly pressured him through psychological and emotional manipulation to sign the notes.

Mull asserted that while he was on staff he was physically debilitated by decreeing (a form of church prayer), a vegetarian diet, and various health practices, such as fasting and enemas. Mull also claimed that, subsequent to his resignation, he had been assaulted at a church event and that church officials had publicly disclosed private facts causing him personal suffering. Finally, he claimed that for his design services while he served on staff, he should be compensated at $2 million.

At the four-week jury trial, the judge allocated one day to evidence involving the promissory notes and the remainder to testimony on a variety of church practices and beliefs. The testimony by numerous expert witnesses, appearing for both sides, and by both present and ex-church members covered reincarnation, the ascended masters, and the church founder's role as a prophet of God, with each side alternately supporting and ridiculing same. The claims of involuntary servitude and extortion were dismissed before trial. The jury gave a general verdict on all of the remaining claims, finding against the church and its leader, Elizabeth Clare Prophet, for $1.5 million in compensatory and punitive damages.

The results in *Mull* are not particularly surprising given the plaintiff's emotionally charged claims and the willingness of the court to allow evidence which was not relevant to his claims but which the appeals court also ruled was not prejudicial. Given this atmosphere, it was unwise, in hindsight, for the Church to have initiated the action to collect the value of the promissory notes from Mull. The case has probably made the church more willing to compromise on subsequent claims.

Not all such cases have been decided in favor of plaintiffs. William Purcell, another ex-member of Church Universal and Triumphant, also brought an action against the church and its leaders, claiming fraud, clerical malpractice, psychological malpractice, cancellation of written instruments, involuntary servitude, intentional infliction of emotional distress, and seeking the imposition of a constructive trust. When Purcell filed his suit in 1984, he sought the return of contributions that he had made, claiming that he had made the contributions based on false representations by the defendants. The action was dismissed in 1986 on summary judgment in favor of the church and its leaders.

## *Molko and Leal* v. *Unification Church*

David Molko and Tracey Leal had been members of the Unification Church for approximately six months when they were kidnapped and deprogrammed. Not long after forsaking their new religion, they sued the church for fraud, intentional infliction of emotional distress, and false imprisonment. They also sought the return of $6,000 worth of donations and payment for the work they did while members. The Unification Church counter-charged that the psychological harm Molko and Leal had experienced was caused by deprogramming procedures rather than by church-related activities.

This case dragged on for years. In the first round, charges against the

Unification Church were dismissed in 1986. Then, three years later after a number of appeals, the case was finally cleared for trial by the California supreme courts. For a number of different reasons, this case was finally settled out of court in November of 1989.

This case is particularly important because of an amicus brief initially filed on behalf of the Unification Church by the American Psychological Association and a number of individual scholars. Margaret Singer, one of the expert witnesses in this case, and Richard Ofshe would later sue the APA et al., citing this amicus brief as the basis for an accusation of a conspiracy against them.

## CHILD ABUSE AND GOVERNMENT INTERVENTION INTO NONTRADITIONAL RELIGIONS

### Child Abuse

On the morning of Sunday, July 26, 1953, a force of one hundred twenty Arizona peace officers, together with one hundred news reporters, drove across unpaved roads to the Mormon fundamentalist community of Short Creek, Arizona, to arrest thirty-six men, eighty-six women, and pick up two hundred sixty-three children. It was a sneak attack and was compared by one Associated Press reporter to "a military assault on an enemy position." Sect members were clearly out numbered as there were two officers for every home in the community. Although the element of surprise was not completely successful, the officers arrested most of the targeted men and women. The Arizona governor announced on the radio that the purpose of the raid was "to protect the lives and futures of two hundred sixty-three children" and that the religious community was "the foulest conspiracy you could imagine" which was "dedicated to the production of white slaves." Apparently, some officials in the Mormon Church (which had only abandoned polygamy itself fifty years earlier) not only applauded the raid, but may also have provided relevant information to the police and other civil authorities.

Shortly after the raid, the mothers and children were bused to Phoenix where they were initially kept in a crowded rest home and were told they would remain there for up to a month before being placed in permanent foster homes. Eventually, juvenile hearings were held in Arizona state courts which resulted in the placement of most of the children in foster homes around Arizona, often accompanied by their mothers. Then in March 1955, an Arizona Superior Court judge ordered that all of the children be restored to their families, which brought an end to Arizona's efforts to segregate children from fundamentalist parents.

One of the primary reasons the "raid" on plural marriage communities and the subsequent efforts of Arizona and Utah officials to separate parents from their children failed was because state officials eventually recognized that polygamist family ties were so strong that all attempts to punish the practice of polygamous marriage, perpetuated by the parents, through their children, would be counterproductive, and that it would not be in the best interests of the children to be separated from their parents, since there was no evidence of child molestation or deviant sexual activities involving the children.

The Short Creek raid bears certain strong parallels with the Northeast Kingdom raid described in the opening sections of this book. In both cases, governmental authorities intervened directly in the affairs of stigmatized religious communities from the high moral ground of protecting children from abuse, only to discover that no such abuse was occurring—except in the imaginations of community critics. Much the same thing happened at Waco, but with far more tragic circumstances.

Although child abuse is technically the jurisdiction of the state rather than the federal government, concern that the Davidian children were being abused was one of the principal reasons cited by authorities as justification for both the initial ATF attack and for the concluding FBI assault. On April 21, White House spokesperson George Stephanopoulos, defending the holocaust, asserted that there "is absolutely no question that there's overwhelming evidence of child abuse in the Waco compound." This was a very odd line of defense, as if the assertion that the Davidians practiced such abuse justified gassing and incinerating the entire community.

However, on the very day of Stephanopoulos's remarks, the Justice Department publicly acknowledged that they had no solid evidence of child abuse—only *speculation* by mental health professions who had been studying Koresh from a distance. Also on the same day, 1,100 pages of unsealed documents relevant to the case were released. These included only two allegations of child abuse by disgruntled former members. Otherwise nothing else was reported, certainly nothing like credible evidence.

Certainly during the siege itself, the FBI showed little regard for the children. The weird light and sound show, which included recordings of dentists' drills and dying rabbits, would hardly have promoted any child's sense of well-being. Deteriorating sanitary conditions, caused by decaying bodies and the buildup of sewage, were also given as a justification for attacking Mt. Carmel on April 19. The Attorney General told Larry King on national television that she feared that "if I delayed, without sanitation or toilets there . . . I could go in there in two months and find children dead from any number of things."

The Texas Department of Human Services had investigated Mt. Carmel on child abuse allegations on at least three different occasions. No credible evidence for such accusations was found. The same can be said for the twenty-one children released from Mt. Carmel between the ATF raid and the FBI assault—no hard evidence of child abuse. On March 5, Janice Caldwell, director of the Texas Department of Protective and Regulatory Services, stated that "they're in remarkably good shape considering what they have been through. No signs of physical abuse have been found." The March 6 edition of the *Houston Post* noted that "all the youths appear to be in good condition psychologically and physically." In the same article, a social worker asserted that "the children are remarkably well-educated."

The lack of any solid evidence for Davidian child abuse probably explains the reason why the Attorney General and the FBI dropped this explanation as soon as reporters began to raise questions about specific evidence for abuse. Retrospectively, it is clear that the charge of child abuse leveled against the Davidians was little more than a pretext that legitimated the drastic actions of April 19, 1993.

Child abuse is one of those issues like AIDS and the plight of the homeless which has been uppermost in the public consciousness during the last decade or so. As a consequence, accusations of child abuse are more effective at attracting attention than other kinds of charges, particularly if the media can be persuaded to pick up the story. Although one of the principles of our legal system is that a person is innocent until proven guilty, the mass media presents its information so that merely reporting sensationalistic accusations is often sufficient to convict the accused in the mind of the general public.

What this means for nontraditional religions accused of child abuse is that such groups lose their chance for a fair hearing as soon as the media labels them "cults." Cults are, by definition, abusive, so to assert that such-and-such a "cult group" is *non*-abusive sounds like a contradiction in terms. Thus, simply succeeding in getting the cult label to stick to any given religious community—whether the community be the Branch Davidians, the Northeast Kingdom Community, or the Short Creek polygamists—is to succeed in convicting the group in the popular imagination.

One of the earliest cases involving children in a religious setting was *Prince* v. *Massachusetts* (1944). Ms. Prince, a Jehovah's Witness, was the custodian of her nine-year-old niece. She was convicted of violating state child-labor laws for taking her niece with her to sell religious literature. The United States Supreme Court upheld her conviction. It stated that "the family itself is not beyond regulation in the public interest, as against a claim of religious liberty. . . . [N]either rights of religion nor rights of parenthood are beyond limitation."

The state has an interest in protecting juveniles under its traditional role as *parens patriae* (literally, "parent of the country," referring to the state's sovereign role as guardian of persons under legal disability). The state's interest is in restricting any conduct that is harmful to the child.

"The state has a wide range of power for limiting parental freedom and authority in things affecting the child's welfare; . . . this includes, to some extent, matters of conscience and religious conviction." The court indicated that parents could become martyrs if they wanted to, but they did not have the right to make martyrs of their children and subject them to emotional, psychological, or physical injury. The court left no doubt that if a judge perceives that a religious practice or religious belief may be harmful to a child, the court can and will restrict the religious conduct.

While the accusation of child abuse has often been used to stigmatize unpopular religious groups, there are other situations of child endangerment where the concern of the state to protect children is more legitimate. Courts have even, at times, restricted the religious practices and beliefs of parents when it is believed that those practices and beliefs harm the child.

In a California case, *Walker* v. *Superior Court,* a court allowed the prosecution of a mother on charges of involuntary manslaughter and felony child endangerment because the mother had not sought medical treatment for her daughter when the daughter was dying of acute meningitis. Although certain statutes allowed parents to seek spiritual treatment of children, when the life of the child was seriously threatened, "the right of a parent to rely exclusively on prayer must yield." The court had little tolerance for religious practices and beliefs when the parent endangered the child's life by pursuing his or her own religious interests and not placing the general welfare of the child paramount. Prayer treatment was accommodated only as long as there was no serious risk of harm or danger to the child's life. When a child's life is threatened, religious beliefs take a second seat. The California court quoted the United States Supreme Court in *Prince* v. *Massachusetts*: "The right to practice religion freely does not include liberty to expose the community or child to communicable disease or the latter to ill health or death." When the religious beliefs and practices of parents interfere with the general welfare of a child, the courts show no reluctance to interfere.

In another example of this pattern, a jury in Minneapolis recently reviewed the religious practices of the Christian Scientists. An eleven-year-old boy with diabetes died because his mother would not seek treatment because of her religious beliefs. After the child died, the father brought suit and obtained a $14.2 million jury verdict against the church and his ex-wife. The trend in society today is to protect children. When the life of a child is weighed in the balance against the religious freedom of a parent, society tips the scales in favor of the child.

## Child Custody Cases

Religious practices and beliefs have also become the subject of child custody cases where nonmembers attempt to highlight nontraditional aspects of a spouse's or ex-spouse's religion to obtain custody of a minor child. Nonmembers seek to show that the religion deviates from social normalcy and, therefore, adversely affects the child's behavior. It is argued that the church's influence is mentally, physically, and emotionally detrimental to the child's well-being. Nonmembers have been successful when the court determines that the practices complained of are not merely religious but are detrimental practices that harm the child.

In a Kentucky custody case, Melanie Pleasant-Topel was allowed to retain custody of her minor son, Sean Pleasant, but was given strict guidelines by the court as to the religious practices of the Church Universal and Triumphant to which she could expose her son. For example, she was required to follow what American society dictates as a normal and appropriate diet, rather than a vegetarian or nontraditional diet (which the church does not require in any event). She was also required to send him to the school he had been attending rather than to a church school. However, to the extent the custodial member parent raised the child within the framework the court determined normal, the court did not interfere with the custody.

In another case in which a member of Church Universal and Triumphant was involved, the church and its practices were central to the action. The mother, Charlene Viau, had been a member of Church Universal and Triumphant for approximately eleven years. Although the father contended the church was an "armed camp" and raised serious concerns that the church environment would be harmful to the child, the court awarded custody of the minor child to the mother, finding that there was no reasonable likelihood of future impairment to the minor child.

Another child custody action involving this church occurred in Indiana. The court found that the influence of Church Universal and Triumphant would be harmful and detrimental to the children and that the mother's association with the church demonstrated her poor judgment and inability to properly raise the children. Custody of the children was given to the father.

While these results seem contradictory, individual facts and circumstances often dictate results. Unfortunately, all the relevant circumstances are not always apparent from court records. In other cases, decisions are often result-oriented, and their stated rationale may be misleading. Nevertheless, certain basic principles are almost universally recognized in these types of cases.

In New Mexico, a father who was a devout Sikh in Yogi Bhajan's Sikh Dharma organization sought to change the custody of his children. Until their divorce, both parents had actively practiced the Sikh religion as brought to this country by Yogi Bhajan, and involved their children in the religion. Following her remarriage, the custodial mother withdrew from the Sikh religion and discouraged her children from participating in it. The father wanted his children raised in the Sikh religion and sought to modify the custody order to give him custody of the children so that he could control their religious upbringing. The court noted that the paramount concern was the general welfare of the children. The court also recognized that religious restrictions on visitation "have been upheld where evidence of physical or emotional harm to the child has been substantial." The courts have not hesitated to interfere when it is shown that the child suffers anxiety and other emotional distress because of the religious differences of his parents.

In an action in Tennessee to modify visitation, the court noted that the general trend in custody cases is to not allow religious beliefs to be controlling: "The law tolerates and even encourages, up to a point, the child's exposure to the religious influences of both parents even if they are divided in their faiths." Courts will generally not interfere with the religious training a noncustodial parent gives his or her children absent "a clear and affirmative showing that these activities and expressions of belief are harmful to the child." However, courts will not allow conflicting beliefs of parents to cause the children emotional harm; the paramount interest of the court is the general welfare of the child.

Many child custody cases exemplify how the cult stereotype may be used as an ideological resource in specific social conflicts. There is enough ambiguity in the "cult" label to make its application in particular cases a matter of negotiation. Occasions for such negotiation arise in the context of social conflicts. For individuals or groups locked in certain kinds of struggles with members of minority religions, the "cult" stereotype represents a potent ideological resource which—if they are successful in making the label stick—marshals public opinion against their opponent, potentially tipping the balance of power in their favor.

The stigma of the "cult" stereotype has been particularly effective in more than a few child custody cases, in which one parent's membership in a minority religion is portrayed as indicative of her or his unworthiness as a parent. For such "limited domain" legal conflicts, it is difficult to deploy the stereotype unless there is some larger, earlier conflict that led to press coverage in which the particular minority religion in question was labeled a "cult." Lacking earlier "bad press," the cult label can still sometimes be made to stick on the basis of testimony by disgruntled former members.

For the most part, individuals involved in such relatively limited conflicts do not become full-time "anticult" crusaders. While they may enter into a relationship with the anticult movement, they normally drift away from this involvement within a short time after the termination of their particular struggle. Also, if anticult rhetoric fails to accomplish their end, but some other tool works in their particular conflict, they are usually quite ready to dispose of the cult stereotype and adopt an entirely different angle of attack.

One case in which the employment of the cult stereotype was clearly opportunistic involved a mother's association with the Movement of Spiritual Inner Awareness (MSIA). Her affiliation was effectively used against her by her ex-husband in a dispute involving their mutual offspring. In this particular case, a divorced mother petitioned the court to permit her to relocate in order to take a position in an MSIA-inspired organization offering human potential seminars. The ex-husband argued that he did not want his son involved in a "cult," and dragged up old rumors about MSIA and its founder in an effort to prevent his ex-wife from leaving the state. Perceiving that not only would she have a difficult time winning her case, but also that her husband might undertake further actions that could result in her son being taken from her, she dropped the case.

What is especially ironic about this case is that for several decades the father has been deeply involved in est—a human potentials group that has very frequently (far more frequently than MSIA) been labeled a "cult." As someone whose participation in est has likely sensitized him to the cult controversy, the ex-husband's utilization of the stereotype is clearly little more than a tactic intended to win support for his side of the case, rather than a reflection of deeply held views about the dangers of sinister "cults." The chances of this gentleman becoming a full-time anticult crusader are nil. Here it is clear that the cult stereotype is an ideological resource, deployed without a deep investment in the stereotype per se.

## TAX CASES

Churches act as fiduciaries, enter into contracts, purchase property, and otherwise conduct business within the communities where they are located. Churches expose themselves to tax liability when their conduct is not purely religious. Scrutiny becomes particularly focused on churches when they are the recipients of gifts, devises or other transfers of property, or are otherwise benefitted. There have been a number of IRS cases involving minority religions in which the Internal Revenue Service has revoked the tax-exempt status of controversial new religions, often at the prompting of enemies of the particular religion involved.

In 1985, for example, the Way International's tax-exempt status was revoked following allegations of partisan political involvement and certain business activities at its New Knoxville headquarters. The ruling was reversed by the Supreme Court in 1990. Most recently, in 1993, the IRS ceased all litigation and recognized Scientology as a legitimate religious organization. This followed years of contentious litigation between the agency and the Church of Scientology.

## Church Universal and Triumphant

We have already had occasion to refer to the Church Universal and Triumphant (C.U.T.) in earlier sections. C.U.T. is a Montana-based New Age church led by Elizabeth Clare Prophet. An indirect spin-off of the "I AM" Religious Activity that grew quietly in its early years, by the late 1980s it had become *the* most controversial new religion in North America in terms of negative media coverage.

Founded as the Summit Lighthouse by Mark L. Prophet in 1958, Elizabeth took over his role as the primary mouthpiece for the Masters after Mark's death in 1973. The group moved to Montana in 1986. Much of the church's negative media coverage derived from incidents clustered around its extensive fallout shelters and its preparations for the possibility of a nuclear attack against the United States. At one point in the construction, for instance, fuel stored in several underground tanks (which were sold to the church in defective condition) ruptured and spilled gas and diesel oil into the water table. In 1990, members from around the world gathered in Montana because of the predicted possibility of an atomic holocaust—a gathering that would have gone all but unnoticed had not a local paper painted it in sinister colors and broadcast the news through the AP wire service to the world.

On the heels of this extensive publicity, Church Universal and Triumphant had its tax exempt status revoked in October 1992. The revocation followed an inquiry which began in 1989 under the Church Audit Procedures Act. Three reasons were given for the revocation: The church was alleged to be involved to an excessive degree in nonexempt commercial activities, it had made an allegedly improper payment on behalf of a church official as part of a court judgment (in the *Mull* case, discussed on p. 74), and it had allegedly been involved at an official level in a scheme by two church employees to illegally purchase weapons. The IRS claimed Church Universal and Triumphant owed back taxes on business income, employment taxes, and excise taxes.

The church strongly disputed all three reasons given for the revocation, filing a declaratory judgment action to reverse the IRS decision. The church and the IRS entered into extensive settlement negotiations, and the court extended various pretrial hearing dates to accommodate the negotiations. In taking its action against the church, the IRS was clearly influenced by negative publicity, including coverage from the Gregory Mull case, investigative articles in the *Bozeman Daily Chronicle* discussing Church

Universal and Triumphant operations, an ex-member's claim that the
Church Universal and Triumphant supported international rebel groups,
the appearance of Elizabeth Clare Prophet's daughter on the *Oprah Winfrey
Show* and discussions of alleged church money given to another daughter,
a Montana newspaper article about gun ownership by Church Universal
and Triumphant members, and the guilty pleas of Vernon Hamilton and
Edward Francis to charges that they had illegally purchased weapons.

Initially, the focus of the IRS investigation appeared to be limited to
the church's potential liability for unrelated business income tax; the
church's tax-exempt status was secondary. However, the information
gleaned from newspapers, particularly the illegal gun purchases by Mr.
Hamilton and Mr. Francis, changed the focus to the tax-exempt status of
the church. There were, however, irregularities in the agency's investigation that led to a compromise agreement in mid 1994—a compromise that
included restoring the church's status as a charitable organization.

## Rev. Sun Myung Moon's Income Tax Evasion Case

The Unification Church (UC), formally the Holy Spirit Association for the
Unification of World Christianity, has been one of the most controversial
new religions in late twentieth-century North America. We have already
noted a number of cases above in which the UC has been involved. Derided
in the West as "the Moonies," the UC is an international messianic religious
movement led by the Reverend Sun Myung Moon, a Korean national. While
polemical opponents have identified any number of departures from Christian orthodoxy, the major novelty is the explicitness with which the present
is identified as the time of the Christ's Second Advent.

After the departure of the Children of God (later known as the
Family) from the United States in the mid-1970s, the Unification Church
became the most controversial religion on the American scene. This was
in part due to the activities of the UC itself, which attracted attention by
staging major rallies across the nation in 1976. The California branch of
the church was also involved in a deceptive recruiting operation that made
the cult stereotype seem particularly applicable. Perhaps most importantly,
however, the leadership of the anticult movement made a conscious choice
to focus attention on the Unification Church. The strategy was that, if the
government could be moved to act against the UC, this would establish a
precedent which could then be turned against other minority religions.
However, as we have noted, anticultists were largely unsuccessful in evoked
governmental action.

One of the few areas in which the assault on this religion was successful
was in a tax case involving the founder, Rev. Sun Myung Moon. In 1982,
Rev. Moon was convicted and jailed on tax evasion charges for failure to

pay a purported tax liability of $7,300 over a three year period. This liability came about as a result of a church checking account that had been opened in Rev. Moon's name by early missionaries in New York rather than as a result of an intentional action on his part. It should also be noted that having a church account in the name of the pastor is a common practice in such denominations as the Baptist Church. This case was regarded by most jurists, civil libertarians, and religious leaders as biased and an intrusion on essential religious freedoms, and the Unification Church decried the case as religious persecution.

The case briefly made headlines, and the anticult movement congratulated itself on finally having achieved a victory in the area of invoking a governmental response. In the long run, however, the results of the case were ambivalent. Clergymen from a wide variety of different congregations came to Rev. Moon's defense, including such national figures as Jerry Fallwell. The UC thus acquired contacts and allies it could never have hoped to have made without the case.

Like many other Christian denominations, the Unification Church embraced a theology of redemptive suffering that could speak directly to the conviction and incarceration of the church's founder. Accepting this turn of events as divinely ordained, Rev. Moon also stood up well under the conditions of his imprisonment, which were certainly more tolerable than the persecution he had suffered under the North Koreans in the fifties. In the end, the UC probably emerged stronger than it had been prior to the case.

## ZONING AND SOLICITATION

Minority religions have also encountered less momentous problems with local ordinances governing zoning and solicitation. These cases have had ambivalent results. To cite just a few solicitation cases that made it all the way to the Supreme Court, in 1981 in *Heffron* v. *International Society for Krishna Consciousness*, the high court supported the state's right to require solicitors—including members of the Hare Krishna movement—to be confined to a booth rather than to wander about at the state fair. However, the very next year in *Larson* v. *Valente*, the Supreme Court decided in favor of the Unification Church against a solicitation law that, it was clear, targeted new religious groups.

Zoning has also been an arena in which minority religions have had to contend with prejudice against "cults." Residents generally resent any "invasion" into their neighborhood that disturbs in any way the status quo of the neighborhood. People purchase homes in certain neighborhoods specifically relying on the zoning codes and the general tenor of the neighborhood and are suspicious of new groups using property in the neighborhood for other, nontraditional purposes.

## Church Universal and Triumphant

The Church Universal and Triumphant has encountered several zoning problems over the years. One high-profile case involved its purchase of a large mansion in Minneapolis in an area which was zoned for single-family residential dwellings but which also allowed for usage by churches and religious organizations. The property and building purchased by the church had previously been used as a duplex. Church Universal and Triumphant proposed to use the building for worship services and as a religious community residence and Teaching Center.

As soon as the church purchase was completed, the homeowners in the area expressed concern about the church's being located in the area. The residents did not understand the religion, particularly since the church and its tenets did not fit into the traditional religious mold. The residents encouraged and then joined a suit by the city of Minneapolis to stop the church from using the property, claiming it offered insufficient parking and the church's religious community and center did not constitute a valid accessory use. In Minnesota, a church sanctuary as well as a monastery and rectory can be situated in a single-family residential zoning area. The court found that the Teaching Center qualified as a church monastery or rectory and that the church was in "substantial compliance" with the zoning code's parking requirements. The Minnesota Supreme Court affirmed this decision.

The hostility encountered by Church Universal and Triumphant in Minneapolis is not unique. When the Church of Jesus Christ of Latter-day Saints ("Mormons") tried to purchase property in Seattle and Portland to construct temples for worship by its members, strong sentiments were expressed in opposition to the church. A comparable situation has generated a long-running conflict with respect to a retreat facility established by the Church of the Movement for Inner Spiritual Awareness.

## The Movement for Spiritual Inner Awareness

In the mountains overlooking Santa Barbara, California, the Institute for Individual and World Peace (an organization founded by John-Roger, founder-leader of the Movement for Spiritual Inner Awareness) purchased some property—later named Windermere—for the purpose of building a peace retreat facility. Bordered on one side by a national forest, the property is also directly adjacent to a semirural neighborhood populated by individuals who moved away from the city for the purpose of enjoying country living. Some of these people viewed their new neighbors with concern. When they heard about plans to build a facility that, they imagined, would attract large numbers of outsiders from the Los Angeles area who, they imagined, would disturb their peaceful rural setting, some were upset. Eventually some neighbors organized the Cielo Preservation Organization (named after the main road in the area) to oppose the construction of the retreat—construction which cannot proceed without approval from the county.

Not long after a negative article about MSIA appeared in the *Los Angeles Times*, almost everyone in the neighborhood received a copy. This slanted article immediately became a centerpiece in some of the neighbors' opposition to IIWP's retreat plans. By 1994, the *Times* report had been superseded by the considerable publicity Arianna Huffington's MSIA connections were generating in the southern California media. Thus, in a December 1994 article in the local Santa Barbara paper on the conflict between Windermere and the neighborhood, Huffington and her "cult" connections are brought up and discussed near the beginning of the article:

> His [John-Roger's] teachings drew national attention during this year's California Senate race between incumbent Diane Feinstein and Rep. Michael Huffington because the Montecito congressman's wife, Arianna, had ties to the John-Roger organization, which some critics claim is a cult. Arianna Huffington has said it is not a cult, and described her past connection with MSIA as a casual one.

Despite the cautious wording of this passage, the net effect of mentioning such accusations is that otherwise uninformed readers may conclude that the "cult" label is probably appropriate for MSIA, thus influencing them to side with the retreat's opponents.

This labeling enterprise has been highly successful in generating anti-IIWP/anti-MSIA sentiment in Santa Barbara county. The point here, however, is that the Cielo Preservation Organization is less concerned about the ranch owners' religious persuasion than about preventing, in the words of a local organizer, hordes of "L.A. cowboys" from invading the area, thus spoiling their rural privacy. The claim that the Windermere Ranch is populated by "weird cultists" is simply one among many accusations hurled at IIWP in an all-out effort to short-circuit their retreat plans rather than representing a deep commitment to the anticult position.

## LIBEL CASES

Considering the often highly charged remarks that have been hurled back and forth in this controversy, it is surprising that there have been so few libel cases. These few cases have, however, been significant. Overseas, there was a long-running libel case in England that the Unification Church had brought against the *Daily Mail.* This case was eventually decided in favor of the newspaper. Perhaps the most significant "cult" libel case in the United States was in 1985 when the Local Church won a libel case against authors who had accused the church of being a "destructive cult."

## The Local Church Libel Case

The Local Church, also known as the Little Flock, was founded in the 1920s in China by Ni Shutsu, popularly known as Watchman Nee. Accused of being a spy for the Americans and the Nationalist government, he was sent to prison in 1952, where he died twenty years later. Among Nee's followers was Witness Lee, founder and elder of the church at Chefoo. The movement spread around the Pacific Basin, and was brought to the West Coast of the United States by migrating members. Lee himself moved to the United States, where he founded Living Stream Ministry, and has led the spread of the Local Church.

While highly orthodox in doctrine, Lee brought innovation to the church by introducing a number of theological emphases as well as new practices such as "pray reading," and "calling upon the name of the Lord." "Pray reading" is a devotional practice using the words of Scripture as the words of prayer. During this practice, which is supposed to allow the Scripture to impart an experience of the presence of God in the person praying, people repeat words and phrases from the Scripture over and over, often interjecting words of praise and thanksgiving. "Calling upon the name of the Lord," on the other hand, represents an invocation of God by the repetition of phrases such as "O Lord Jesus." Both these practices have been subjects of controversy.

A controversy emerged in the 1970s between the Local Church and some members of the larger Evangelical Christian community who regarded the innovations of Lee as departing from acceptable Evangelical thought. This controversy culminated in a series of legal actions in the mid-1980s. A number of anticult writers accused the Local Church of heresy and attacked its unique forms of Christian piety. The lawsuits instituted by the Local Church brought retractions and apologies from all organizations except the Spiritual Counterfeits Project, a Christian anticult group which had published the book *The God-Men,* attacking the church. This case went to trial, and in 1985 a financial settlement was ordered against the Spiritual Counterfeits Project, which was driven to bankruptcy in the face of an $11 million judgment.

The Local Church case sent a chill through the ranks of people who regularly wrote on the cult controversy. Subsequently, writers moved away from referring to a wide variety of minority religions by name, and instead shifted to writing about "cults" in general. The only groups it was safe to name were religions that had been decimated or eliminated by violence, such as the People's Temple.

## Cynthia Kisser v. the Church of Scientology

In 1990, Michael Rokos, then president of the Cult Awareness Network (CAN), resigned when it was discovered that he had been arrested several years earlier for propositioning a young policeman who had been posing as an teenager. After Cynthia Kisser, CAN's executive director, took over the day-to-day running of the organization, members of some of the groups attacked by CAN began investigating her background in hopes of finding a similar skeleton in the closet. Eventually they discovered that Kisser had worked briefly as a topless dancer in the 1970s.

While topless dancing is nowhere near as serious of an act (many people would not even consider it immoral) as propositioning underage boys, critics—including Heber Jentzsch, President of the Church of Scientology, International—seized upon this item of information and hurled it at CAN in an effort to discredit the organization. Kisser responded by suing Jentzsch and the Church of Scientology for defamation of character in 1992. She filed two suits, one in federal court and one in state court. Both were dismissed, the first in 1994, the second in 1995. Kisser's appeal met a similar fate.

In dismissing her federal case, U.S. District Judge James B. Zagel remarked:

> Statements charging Kisser with exposing her breasts in public for remuneration could affect the public's assessment of her as a critic of religious cults. Some might regard such activity as the symptom of a character so deeply flawed that they could expect other symptoms, such as untruthfulness. Some who regard topless dancing as base, immoral or sinful . . . might consider a former topless dancer less likely to understand, appreciate or fairly judge the motives and practices of organizations claiming spiritual inspiration and purpose, or their members' lifestyles.

Zagel further noted that Kisser did not "offer any clear and convincing evidence showing a reckless disregard for the truth," as required by law. Not long after the federal case had been decided, her state case was dismissed with prejudice. Kisser's appeal of the federal decision was finally dismissed in 1997. These defeats took place around the same time that the Cult Awareness Network itself was being dismantled in the courts, in what must stand as the worst losing streak in the anticult movement's short history.

## THE DEFEAT OF ANTICULTISM IN THE COURTS

For many years the legal struggle between minority religions and their critics went back and forth in the courts, so that, throughout the 1980s, it appeared to longtime observers as though the conflict had reached a kind of stasis. It was thus somewhat surprising when, in the 1990s, the scale tipped decisively in favor of the new religious movements. The defeat of anticultism in the courts took place in two distinct arenas: First, mind control/coercive persuasion/brainwashing was rejected as a theory that could have a bearing on the outcome of any legal case. Second, the Cult Awareness Network was sued out of existence in the wake of a deprogramming-related lawsuit. Subsequently, the Cult Awareness Network (CAN) name, mailing address, and phone number were purchased by the Church of Scientology.

### The Fishman Decision

For many years, Dr. Margaret Singer, a clinical psychologist, had been the most weighty expert witness in court cases involving the notion of coercive persuasion, popularly known as "brainwashing." Part of her legitimacy as an expert derived from her association with other psychological researchers who had examined American soldiers released from POW camps following the Korean War. Singer had testified in such prominent cases as *Katz, Mull,* and *Molko-Leal,* to name just a few.

Her demise as an expert witness began, ironically, with an effort of Singer and some of her colleagues to legitimize the anticult position on mind control within the psychological profession. This group had formed a task force on "deceptive and indirect methods of persuasion and control" within the American Psychological Association (APA). This task force submitted its report to the Board of Social and Ethical Responsibility for Psychology of the APA. The report was rejected by the Board in May of 1987, with the statement that "in general, the report lacks the scientific rigor and evenhanded critical approach needed for APA imprimatur." Task force members were explicitly warned not to imply that the APA in any way supported the position the report put forward.

The other document that would be brought forward to discredit Singer was an amicus brief filed by the APA and twenty-three scholars in support of the Unification Church in the *Molko-Leal* case. Singer had already testified in this case, and the foreword to the amicus brief cast a harshly critical comment in Singer's direction: "APA believes that this commitment to advancing the appropriate use of psychological testimony in the courts carries with it a concomitant duty to be vigilant against those who would use purportedly expert testimony lacking scientific and methodological rigor." The wording at the end of this statement clearly echoes the decision of the APA board to reject to task force report, although this brief had been filed *before* the report had been rejected.

These two rejections subsequently led to the rejection of Singer as an expert witness in a series of cases, culminating in *U.S. v. Fishman* in 1990. Stephen Fishman had argued that his criminal behavior, mail fraud, had been caused by the Church of Scientology's mind control/thought reform techniques to which he had been subjected. U.S. District Court Judge D. Lowell Jensen reviewed the scientific status of Singer's theories—as well as the related ideas of sociologist Richard Ofshe, whom the defense had also called as an expert witness—in some detail. Ofshe was rejected out of hand as an expert witness. Singer, on the other hand, could testify as a mental health professional, on the condition that she *not* "support her opinion with testimony that involves thought reform, because the Court finds that her views on thought reform, like Dr. Ofshe's, are not generally accepted within the scientific community." This turns out to be a benchmark decision, which is subsequently used to disqualify Singer and Ofshe from testifying in other cult cases.

Singer and Ofshe then sued the APA and the ASA, alleging that these two organizations had conspired with twelve individual scholars to discredit them. On August 9, 1993, a federal judge threw their suit out of court. They refiled an almost identical suit in state court in California, but this new suit was thrown out in June 1994. Upon appeal, the case was dismissed with prejudice. With this last dismissal, "cultic mind control" was finally demolished in the courts.

## The Scott Case and the Demise of the Cult Awareness Network

For many years, the Church of Scientology had invested its legal resources into fighting various governmental agencies—most recently, a host of cases involving the Internal Revenue Service. In 1993, the IRS halted all Scientology-related litigation and extended unqualified recognition to the church and its various affiliated organizations. This action had many different spin-off effects, including the freeing of Scientology's legal resources to fight other enemies. It was thus almost inevitable that the church would turn its big guns on the Cult Awareness Network.

Despite public statements to the contrary, CAN regularly referred worried parents to vigilante deprogrammers. It was in this practice that Scientology found the weak point which eventually brought the organization down. In a criminal case in the state of Washington, deprogrammer Rick Ross and his associates had been referred to the mother of Jason Scott by the Cult Awareness Network. Scott, a member of a Pentecostal church, had been handcuffed, silenced with duct tape across his mouth, abducted, and forcibly held against his will for days in a failed attempt to destroy his beliefs. The Church of Scientology supported this case in a number of ways, such as by supplying witnesses against Ross and CAN.

When the criminal case failed to convict Ross, the Church helped Scott file a civil suit against his kidnappers and the Cult Awareness Network. The jury in this new case found the conduct of some of the defendants "so outrageous in character and so extreme in degree as to go beyond all possible bounds of decency . . . atrocious and utterly intolerable in a civilized community," and approved a $4.875 million verdict against Ross and CAN. When the defendants moved to have the verdict set aside as "unreasonable," U.S. District Judge John Coughenour denied the motion, stating:

> The court notes each of the defendants' seeming incapability of appreciating the maliciousness of their conduct towards Mr. Scott. . . . Thus, the large award given by the jury against both CAN and Mr. Ross seems reasonably necessary to enforce the jury's determination on the oppressiveness of the defendants' actions and deter similar conduct in the future.

The Cult Awareness Network initially filed for bankruptcy under Chapter 11, hoping to continue its operations. However, CAN was finally forced to file Chapter 7 bankruptcy in June 1996. When CAN's resources were auctioned to raise money for the settlement, the Church of Scientology purchased the Cult Awareness Network name, phone number, and post office box address.

# 3

# THE CHRISTIAN
# TRADITION

The United States is home to a greater diversity of religions than any other country in the world. Long a refuge for groups escaping religious persecution, this country attracted independent sectarians from all over the world. Although every major tradition in the world can now be found here, the United States' historical background makes Christian organizations—particularly Protestant groups—the dominant structures on the religious landscape. For a number of different reasons, Protestant Christianity is particularly prone to schisms. The present chapter will provide an overview of these internal schismatic factors as well as an introduction to some of the movements that have contributed to the splintering of existing denominations into new sects.

Ever since Martin Luther articulated the doctrine of *sola scriptura* ("scripture only") as the sole principle of religious authority, variant interpretations of the Bible have been central to the formation of new Christian groups. For Christians, the Bible refers to the Hebrew Bible (called the Old Testament [OT] by Christians) plus an additional collection of documents called the New Testament (NT). The word "Bible" simply means *book*, from the same root as the term *bibliography*. The word *testament*, on the other hand, means to bear witness, from the same root as *testimony*.

The Judeo-Christian Bible is a complex document that is regarded by the faithful as a more or less direct revelation from God. For traditional Protestants, the Bible is the only criterion for proper belief and practice. Since the advent of Protestantism in the sixteenth century, new understandings of the Bible have played a significant role in the emergence of new Christian sects. Only rarely have Protestant sects emerged with new scriptures supplementing the Judeo-Christian Bible.

Both the Old Testament and the New Testament represent collections of materials that have been selected out of a larger possible set of documents. The commonly accepted selection is referred to as the canon (Greek for *measuring rod*) or as canonical scriptures. In contrast to a scriptural tradition like Buddhism which is open to new additions, the Jewish and Christian communities reject additions to their scriptures, and thus have what are called *closed* canons. The specific contents of the Jewish and the Christian canons were determined at rather late dates, about 90 C.E. (C.E. means "Common Era," the secular equivalent of A.D.) for Judaism and about 400 C.E. for Christianity.

The Bible is central to Judaism and Christianity because it is regarded as containing a record of God's revelations to, and dealings with, humanity. It is, in effect, a witness or "testament" to this ongoing relationship. A central motif through which this relationship has been understood from the earliest times is that of a covenant or *contract*. In Hebrew scriptures, God is portrayed as offering a special relationship with his chosen people through a contract that specifies the terms of this relationship. The details of this contract have been modified and expanded from time to time, in a series of covenants with Noah, Abraham, and Moses. The most well-known of these contracts is God's agreement with Moses on Mt. Sinai, a covenant that involved, among other things, the Ten Commandments.

As in ordinary, worldly contracts, the divine covenant contains various stipulations (God's commandments) that humans must live up to in order to obligate God to fulfil his end of the bargain. These stipulations assume their most complex form in Jewish religious law. Many biblical stories recount Israel's deviation from God's commandments, the subsequent withdrawal of God's protection, and the punishment of Israel for these deviations through invasions and other disasters. When Israel repents and returns to the law, God's favor is restored and, subsequently, Israel returns to stability and prosperity.

Christianity began life as a Jewish sect. Far from attempting to found a new religion, the first Christians viewed themselves as Jews following the teachings of the Jewish Messiah. It was only later, after many non-Jews converted, that Christianity became a religion distinct from Judaism. Although Christianity shares much with Judaism, these two faiths differ significantly with respect to such fundamental issues as God's relationship with humanity.

In the Christian understanding of covenant theology, God offers humanity a new contract—a new testament—as revealed in the person and teaching of Jesus. In this new covenant, humanity is no longer obligated to carry out the details of the Jewish law. Unlike previous covenants, the new covenant focuses on the eternal fate of individuals rather than the worldly fate of the nation of Israel. Also, rather than being offered only to Jews, the new contract is offered to humanity as a whole. Individual salvation and the question of how that salvation can be achieved is a dominant theme of traditional Christianity.

Salvation, according to this tradition, is necessary because otherwise the individual is condemned to spend eternity in hell, a place of eternal punishment (though some religious bodies view the unredeemed human being as suffering the less horrific fate of being blotted out into nothingness). Born into sin, the sentence of eternal damnation is the fate of every person unless she or he is saved from this fate by being "born again" through faith in Jesus Christ. All other doctrines are built around a warning of condemnation and a message of redemption. As the core doctrine, it would be natural that arguments over soteriology (one's theory of redemption) would lead to religious schisms. Disagreement over competing notions of salvation led to the split between Catholicism and Protestantism.

Given the stark contrast between heaven and hell as eternal abodes of the soul, serious thinkers have had to grapple with the question of what happens to people who, while not saints, nevertheless are generally good people who have never committed any major sins in their lives. Reflection on this problem led to the development of purgatory, an intermediate realm between heaven and hell. In purgatory, souls are tortured for their sins, but are eventually released and allowed to enter heaven.

According to the Christian tradition as it had developed up to the time of Martin Luther (regarded as the founder of Protestantism), the sacraments (e.g., baptism, communion, etc.) of the church were salvific— meaning that they contributed to the individual's salvation. For baptized Christians, participation in the sacraments was viewed as shortening the time one spent in purgatory. The variable length of time one spent in purgatory was thus a way of "quantifying" salvation, so that better people suffered for shorter periods in purgatory than moral slackers.

The church also cautiously adopted the idea that the prayers and other actions of the living could shorten the time the deceased spent in purgatory. It was specifically this doctrine of the role the living could play to rescue souls from purgatory that set the stage for the Protestant Reformation.

To raise money for the facade of St. Peter's in Rome, certain officials of the church sold "indulgences" which, it was advertised, could free souls from purgatory. While the actual nature of what was being promised was more complex than this, some less-than-scrupulous indulgence salesmen presented the arrangement in an oversimplified manner. The Reformation began as a protest against such a simplified view of release from purgatory. Because purgatory had been the bone of contention, Protestants later rejected the doctrine of purgatory and everything connected with it. Salvation once again boiled down to a stark choice between heaven and hell—a salvation that could be accomplished solely by the individual's faith, entirely independent of the sacraments of the church.

The doctrine of salvation continued to play a role in the ongoing generation of new Christian sects within Protestantism. One of the points on which most Christians differ from other religious traditions is on the importance of correct doctrine (orthodoxy) in assuring one's salvation. In most other religious traditions, moral actions and the correct performance of religious rituals (orthopraxis) are the key requirements for being a good Jew, Hindu, or whatever. By stressing the centrality of correct doctrine in assuring salvation, Protestant Christianity opened the door for disagreement and schism.

Within most strands of the Protestant tradition, the only criterion for correct belief and practice is the Bible. Another principle of the Protestant movement was the Priesthood of all Believers, meaning that no specially consecrated priesthood was necessary to ensure salvation. Hence, no group of individuals was designated as more qualified to interpret the Bible than anyone else. Thus, people could study the Bible and come up with new understandings of the meaning of certain sections of scripture— new understandings that potentially formed the basis of new sects. This, in fact, is precisely what occurred, and Protestantism began splintering into distinct sects and denominations almost as soon as it had split with the Catholic Church—a splintering process that continues to this day.

From a certain perspective, one might think that Christians would eject the old covenant record from their scriptures. However, while certain sections of Jewish scriptures were regarded as having been superseded by the Christian revelation, the early Christian community still judged the Old Testament as instructive for its revelation of God's nature and will for humanity. It was thus retained as part of Christian scriptures.

While many conservative Christians have claimed that the Bible is completely consistent, and have further asserted that the meaning of the Biblical message is "obvious," there is, in point of fact, enough diversity within the scriptures to permit many different understandings about the nature of God and his will for humanity. The wide variety of Christian sects claiming to be biblically based should be evidence enough that the Bible is capable of being differently understood by equally sincere Christians. Disagreement over the meaning of particular passages, or emphasizing certain parts of scripture over certain other sections, can lead to denominational splits and to the formation of new sects.

The emergence of Protestantism is a case in point. Martin Luther, who constantly doubted his salvation, was reading the Bible one day when he chanced across the passage, "He who through faith is righteous shall live" (Romans 1:17). Luther, who was a New Testament scholar, had probably read this same passage hundreds of times before, but on this particular day

Father David, founder of the Family (aka the Children of God).
(*Courtesy World Services*)

Young members of the Family performing a sackcloth vigil. (*Courtesy World Services*)

Author and colleague with devotees of Krishna.

Adi Da Samraj and devotees. (*Courtesy Adidam*)

Subramuniyaswami (right center, wearing a mala of Rudraksha beads in his hair)
with members of his monastic community, the Saiva Siddhanta Church.
(*Courtesy Saiva Siddhanta Church*)

Donald Walters, founder of Ananda Village. (*Courtesy Ananda Village*)

Swami Vivekananda, one of the earliest and most influential teachers to spread Hinduism to the West. (*Courtesy American Religion Collection*)

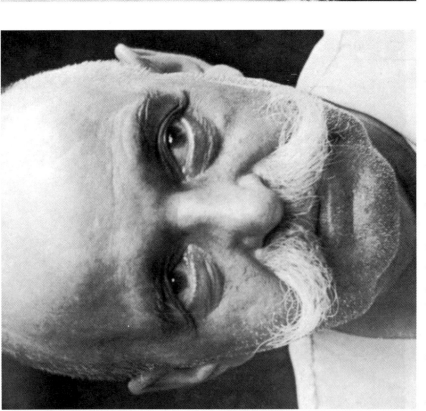

Georgei Ivanovitch Gurdjieff, an influential early twentieth-century Sufi teacher. (*Courtesy American Religion Collection*)

Transcendental Meditation claims to be able to teach meditators to levitate. (*Courtesy AUM Shinrikyo*)

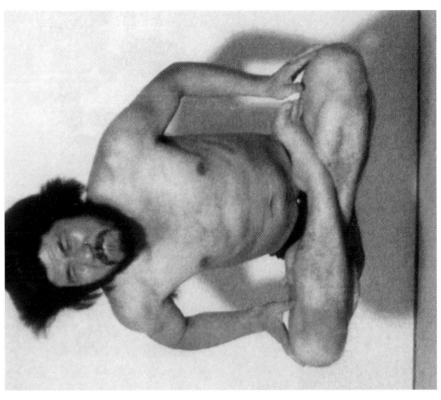

Paramahansa Yogananda, founder of the Self-Realization Fellowship. (*Courtesy Self-Realization Fellowship*)

John Roger Hinkins, founder of the Movement of Spiritual Inner Awareness. (*Courtesy Movement of Spiritual Inner Awareness*)

Shoko Askara, founder of AUM Shinrikyo. (*Courtesy AUM Shinrikyo*)

Sri Harold Klemp, current leader of Eckankar. (*Courtesy Eckankar*)

Paul Twitchell, founder of Eckankar. (*Courtesy Eckankar*)

American members of Sikh Dharma at a communal meal.
(*Courtesy Richard Rosenkrantz*)

American members of Sikh Dharma at a religious gathering.
(*Courtesy Richard Rosenkrantz*)

it leapt out at him with new meaning: The individual need not become righteous in order to deserve salvation; rather, it was faith alone that made one
"righteous" enough to be saved. It was Luther's new understanding of scripture—reinterpreted through that one passage—which led him to oppose
the practice of selling indulgences, and which inadvertently set off a chain
of events leading to the Protestant Reformation. Similar reinterpretations of
scripture have played a role in the formation of other new sects.

Like Luther, founders of new Christian groups do not usually think of
themselves as having "reinterpreted" the Bible. Rather, they feel that they
have discovered some part of the original meaning of scripture that other
readers have somehow missed or not fully understood. The ideal of most
new sects is to restore the church to the way it was in biblical times. This
was clearly Martin Luther's ideal: The church, Luther felt, had become
corrupted by Roman paganism. Thus, the goal of the Reformation was not
to start a "new" religion, but to cleanse Christianity and restore it to its
original purity. This pattern of rejecting what becomes viewed as corruptions and returning to the pure biblical model is a basic dynamic in the
formation of most Christian sects.

One should also note that the series of successive revelations characteristic of biblical covenant theology practically begs the question of newer
covenants: Why not further revelations? Why not a New New Testament
that supersedes both the Old and the New Testaments? God has been
adjusting the terms of the divine-human contract for thousands of years,
so why should he stop with Jesus' revelation? The dynamic potency of
covenant theology for legitimating newer revelations has manifested in
such diverse new religious movements as Islam (an offshoot of the Judeo-
Christian tradition whose "Newer Testament" is the Koran) and Mormonism (whose New New Testament is the *Book of Mormon*). Thus the
Bible, either through new interpretations or through the potential
dynamism of biblical covenant theology, is an important source of—or an
important aspect in the formation of—new religious sects.

One of the other factors contributing to the formation of new Christian sects is the tension between faith and works. According to the apostle
Paul, Christ's death on the cross freed humanity from the burden of
having to obey Jewish religious law in order to gain salvation. Instead, all
one needed to do was to accept, in faith, Jesus Christ as one's Lord and
Savior. Salvation, in other words, is not dependent on either "being good"
or on doing good actions. If, however, salvation is not dependent upon
morality, then to what extent, if any, should we feel bound by the con-
straints of morality and religious law?

If we press this conundrum to one extreme, we get antinomianism,
namely, the position that our actions should be bound by no laws of
morality or religion at all. Pressed to the other extreme, this dilemma

results in legalism, meaning that we are required to adhere rigidly to every rule or risk loosing our salvation. Legalists have often been accused of preaching a doctrine of salvation by works—the idea that we earn our salvation by doing good actions rather than by faith. While no Protestant Christian would acknowledge that they propagate a "works gospel," this accusation has commonly been used to legitimate the formation of new churches. On the other hand, the loosening of moral requirements in established denominations has regularly led to new sects which have broken away to form stricter religious bodies.

Yet another factor in the formation of new Christian bodies is the impact of what has been referred to as *modernism*. Since the rise of science and other forces set in motion after the collapse of feudalism, a significant sector of Western culture has emerged that has developed independently of the influence of traditional religion. The secularizing impact of modernism has often clashed with traditional religious ideas—in conflicts over everything from the truth of the theory of evolution to the undesirability of the secular entertainment industry. By the late nineteenth century, many of the major Protestant denominations were adapting to the rise of modernism by remolding their theology in the light of science and other secular philosophies. These denominational bodies also became increasingly tolerant of their members being engaged in activities and forms of entertainment that an earlier generation of religious leaders would have regarded as sinful.

In response to modernism, many religious bodies split into liberal and conservative wings. The most significant early twentieth-century reaction to modernism was the fundamentalist movement. While fundamentalism has become a watered-down term which can be used to refer to almost any form of traditional religiosity, *fundamentalism* originally referred to a conservative Christian intellectual movement that articulated the "fundamentals" of the Christian faith. The original fundamentalists viewed themselves as opposing the tendency of modernists to adapt religion to secular culture, which they saw as watering down the truth. Many contemporary, conservative Christian religious bodies would adhere to the doctrines of the fundamentalist movement, although, because it has become a term of derision and contempt, they are often reluctant to claim the label "fundamentalist." A more neutral label that many such denominational bodies would accept is "evangelical."

**FUNDAMENTALIST MOVEMENT.** The Independent Fundamentalist movement is characterized by an intense effort to thoroughly revive primitive Christianity. The movement attempts to recreate the Apostolic church by intense concentration on the Bible, and by the adoption of a biblical lifestyle, theology, and ecclesiology.

The movement was begun in England in the 1820s by John Nelson Darby

(1800–1882), an Anglican priest ordained in 1826. He rejected the idea of a state church, and when he withdrew from the Anglican Church in 1827 he began to pursue a nondenominational approach to church life. He began establishing fellowship groups of Christians who agreed with his view that the true church is a temporary structure composed of individual believers.

When he became interested in eschatology, Darby created a system of thought known as dispensationalism, which is a view of the Bible as a history of God's dealing with people in terms of various periods—dispensations—of history. His system had seven basic dispensations:

1. Paradise to the flood
2. Noah
3. Abraham
4. Israel, divided into three subperiods: under the law, under the priesthood, and under the kings
5. Gentiles
6. The Spirit
7. The fullness of time

Darby also believed that people could be divided into three groups: the Jews, the Church of God or Christians, and the Gentiles (all non-Christians who were not Jews).

Since Darby's discussion of the present and future was somewhat vague, his system was refined by his theological successors, such as C. I. Scofield and Harry A. Ironside. The new system, that has become the basis for most modern discussions of dispensational schemes, includes the following dispensations:

1. Innocence, from creation to the fall of Adam
2. Conscience, from the fall to the flood
3. Government, from Noah to Abraham
4. Promise, from Abraham to Moses
5. Law, from Moses to Jesus
6. Grace, from the cross to the second coming
7. Personal reign of Christ, from the second coming to and including eternity

Darby's rejection of denominated, primarily state-church, Christianity led to his second key idea, that is ecclesiology. He asserted that anyone seeking the interests of any particular denomination has to be considered an enemy of the work of the Holy Spirit. According to Darby, unity is to be found in the Unity of the Spirit, and can be perfected in spiritual persons. A number of churches adopted Darby's ecclesiology, and they generally have a statement of belief in the spiritual unity of believers in Jesus Christ.

Other central issues of Darby's thought were common to the orthodox Protestantism of the Reformation, such as belief in God, the Trinity, the divinity of Christ, the person and work of the Holy Spirit, the Bible as the word of God, and the necessity of man's repentance, forgiveness, and salvation. Although he never developed an expectancy of Christ's imminent return, Darby believed in the approaching end of the age, and prominent in his dispensational scheme is the particular form of eschatology known as premillenialism.

Darby's followers accepted no authority except his "charismatic" leadership, and the gospel assembly became the central building block among them. The group never accepted any name, although it was often referred to as Church of God as well as Brethren. Among the main activities of the Brethren were the teaching of the Bible, the preaching of the gospel, and the publication of pamphlets and tracts. Bible reading constituted a major new form that evolved out of the Reading Meeting of the British Brethren, where students used to gather in a home in order to search the Scripture.

Within the growing movement—known as the Plymouth Brethren from the name of the English town where the most prominent assembly of the movement was held—a separation began to appear in the 1840s when Benjamin W. Newton and Darby began to differ on eschatology and ecclesiology. The controversy that followed the accusations against Newton for holding a heretical Christology led to the permanent division of the movement into the "Open" Brethren and the "Exclusive" Brethren. While the Exclusive Brethren believe in receiving no one at the Lord's table who is not a true Christian in the fullest sense, the Open Brethren receive all believers as true Christians.

Darby's movement produced a massive body of literature that soon attracted a large segment of conservative Christianity, and in the 1880s and 1890s the thought of the movement became institutionalized in many Bible colleges, such as Moody Bible Institute in Chicago. Among the books that increased the popularity of Darby's thought were *Jesus Is Coming*, by William E. Blackstone, and the *Scofield Reference Bible*, by C. I. Scofield, which has become the cardinal work in the movement as well as the standard by which to judge the dispensational movement.

The *Scofield Reference Bible* has led to growth in orthodox dispensationalism, and it has inspired a number of leaders, such as J. C. O'Hair, to launch new teaching. Two English scholars, in particular, produced a major deviation from Darby's scheme. Ethelbert W. Bullinger and Charles Welch asserted that the dispensation of grace begins with the cross, the resurrection, and Pentecost, and ends with the second coming of Christ. Bullinger also divided this period into two dispensations. One covers the era of the Apostolic church, beginning with Pentecost and closing with the end of the ministry of the apostles and Paul.

During the twentieth century, Darby's followers remained in the conservative wing of the movement; however, various groups began to form in the 1920s as a result of doctrinal disputes. The discovery of the dispensational theology of Darby by clergy and laymen of American Protestant churches led to the formation of Fundamentalism as a movement within American Christianity. This movement can be dated from 1910. In America, people accepted Darby's ideas without leaving their own church to join the Brethren. Among the most prominent members of the movement was evangelist Dwight L. Moody. Annual meetings were organized became the Niagara Conference on Prophecy from 1883, when they were moved to Niagara-on-the-Lake, Ontario. In 1890 the Niagara Conference adopted a fourteen-point creedal statement that set forth the movement's priorities. Most importantly, it included a Calvinist theological emphasis on human depravity and salvation by the blood of Christ. Furthermore, the five *fundamentals* were considered to be:

1. The inspiration and infallibility of the Bible
2. The deity of Christ
3. The substitutionary atonement of Christ's death
4. The literal resurrection of Christ from the dead
5. The literal return of Christ in the Second Advent

These points became the crucial issues in the 1920s modernist-fundamentalist controversy. Modernist thinking was characterized by a theology accepting the theory of evolution and higher biblical criticism, the study of the Bible in the light of the findings of secular historians and archeologists. As a result of the controversy, fundamentalism has become split into two parties: one emphasizing separation from all apostasy and from particular forms of evil, such as communism, and a second one, known as Neo-evangelicalism, emphasizing a conservative theology.

Among the major debates that led to the formation of new groups was the controversy concerning Bullinger's teachings contained in his book *How to Enjoy the Bible*, in which his desire for symmetry and mathematical order influenced his interpretation of the Scriptures considerably. Among his beliefs, shared by his follower Charles H. Welch, were *annihilationism*, the belief that the wicked are destroyed instead of existing in eternal torment, *soul-sleep*, the idea that the soul exists in an unconscious state from death to the resurrection of the body, and the belief that the Lord's Supper is not to be observed in the post-Acts church. The views of Bullinger spread in America in the 1920s through some advocates such as Pastor J. C. O'Hair who, believing that the church influenced by Paul's later epistles is the church existing in the dispensation of grace, founded a group known as the Grace Gospel Movement.

**PENTECOSTALISM.** Pentecostalism is a large and diverse movement of Protestant Christian enthusiasm which emphasizes the supernatural "gifts of the Holy Spirit" and especially glossolalia or "speaking in tongues." The hallmark of the movement is belief that this experience of ecstatic spiritual utterance is the sine qua non or "initial physical evidence" of the baptism of the Holy Spirit, a second step in Christian initiation after conversion.

Pentecostalism is a distinctly twentieth-century phenomenon with roots in the nineteenth-century holiness revivals. During the twentieth century it grew from only a few thousand scattered adherents to millions of members in several denominations. Some observers of world Christianity aver that it is the fastest growing Christian movement in Latin America and Africa. However, North America seems to be its home and there it has become established as a part of the religious landscape. Those once considered "holy rollers" are at the end of the twentieth century joining the mainstream.

According to Pentecostal legend, the movement began at the moment of the century's turn. On New Year's Eve, 1900, a student named Agnes Ozman spoke in tongues during an all night prayer vigil at Charles Parham's tiny Bible college in Topeka, Kansas. The college and its founder were independents on the fringe of the larger holiness movement—a radical Wesleyan movement which emphasized emotional conversion, sanctification (holiness of life), and a "deeper" or "higher" spiritual life marked by a "filling of the Holy Spirit" after the model of the day of Pentecost (Acts 2). Miss Ozman was not the first person to speak in tongues, but she is claimed by Pentecostals as the first person in modern history whose gift of glossolalia was recognized as the evidence of the baptism in the Holy Spirit.

Parham's students fanned out from Topeka to all parts of the United States preaching this new gospel of Holy Spirit baptism accompanied by speaking in tongues. They proclaimed a "latter rain" of spiritual gifts as promised on the Old Testament book of Joel and partially fulfilled on the day of Pentecost. For them, this outpouring of ecstatic and supernatural gifts and experiences was proof that Christ's second coming was near and that God was raising up a new movement of Christians to prepare the world for his advent.

A second major event in Pentecostal history was the Azusa Street Revival, which began under an African-American Pentecostal preacher named William Seymour in 1906 in Los Angeles, California. This extremely emotional revival lasted for over one thousand days with services held daily in an old livery stable converted into a storefront mission. During those three years numerous emissaries of the new movement travelled to major cities as well as to small towns and rural areas establishing Pentecostal missions. Most early converts were Christians already ripened for this new revival by the holiness movement. Most were also economically marginalized and relatively uneducated.

By 1905 or 1906 there may have been as many as twenty-five thousand full-fledged Pentecostal adherents scattered across North America in several thousand storefront missions. These early Pentecostals eschewed formal liturgy, theology, and "worldliness." By the latter they meant entertainment, apparel, language, and possessions, which were heavily influenced by the post–Civil War secularization of American society. In many ways, these Pentecostals were at one with their Wesleyan holiness and other conservative Protestant cousins in holding to a basically Puritan lifestyle and code of conduct. Even "conspicuous consumption" (spending money on luxuries) was often condemned as sinful.

Soon after the turn of the century, several holiness associations of churches formally embraced the new Pentecostal message and experience. Most of these were in the South and several were primarily African American. The earliest Pentecostal denomination was perhaps the mostly black Church of God in Christ. An already existing, mostly white holiness denomination known as the Pentecostal Church of the Nazarene faced a dilemma. With the word "Pentecostal" in their name would they embrace the new Pentecostal distinctive of speaking in tongues? The decision was that they would not and the word was dropped from the denomination's name. It became simply the Church of the Nazarene. Other holiness denominations and associations of churches faced similar decisions and some embraced the attitude toward tongues-speaking expressed by Christian and Missionary Alliance founder A. B. Simpson: "Forbid not, seek not." Others took an adamant stance against glossolalia.

In 1914 a convention of Pentecostal ministers was held in Hot Springs, Arkansas. Out of this came a new denomination destined to be one of the largest Pentecostal organizations of churches—The Assemblies of God. The "Assemblies" or "AG" established its world headquarters in Springfield, Missouri, and slowly absorbed numerous independent missions, churches and tiny Pentecostal denominations. By the 1980s, the AG could credibly claim to be the fastest-growing major denomination in the United States with over one million members.

Perhaps the most famous and influential Pentecostal leader was a woman—Aimee Semple McPherson. Sister Aimee, as she was known to her followers, built a large Pentecostal church in Los Angeles known as Angeles Temple and went on to found a Pentecostal denomination known as the Church of the Foursquare Gospel or simply the Foursquare Churches. The "Foursquare" refers to four distinctives of the Pentecostal message preached by Mrs. McPherson: salvation, healing, baptism in the Holy Spirit, and the second coming of Jesus Christ. Throughout the 1920s and 1930s the ministry of Mrs. McPherson expanded nationwide with numerous tent crusades, open-air healing meetings attended by thousands, a radio station, and publications. She was also often the center of media attention because of her flamboyant personality and alleged scandals. Numerous Pentecostal organizations spun off from her ministry. Mrs. McPherson died in 1945.

The Second World War marked a turning point in the history of Pentecostalism. To a large extent it had been a loose network of semi-independent churches, ministries, evangelists, and parachurch organizations. Before the war most Pentecostals strongly criticized identification with the values and goals of secular society ("middle-class values") and avoided ecumenical cooperation and formal church hierarchy. They saw themselves as a latter-day remnant raised up by God to warn society of impending doom and the need to come apart and be separate. They reveled in their special status as a religious minority and relished moderate persecution. Women and persons of color played major roles in Pentecostal life. Worship was often extremely emotional, emphasizing ecstatic experiences of supernatural healing, vocal prophecies, speaking in tongues, and open weeping by congregants and ministers alike.

After the Second World War, Pentecostalism began to change. With some notable exceptions they embarked upon a search for respectability and acceptance—if not by secular society at least by the conservative Protestant establishment. Many Pentecostal leaders encouraged a softening of their distinctives—especially the so-called wildfire of spiritual emotion that was an expected part of revivals. During the 1940s and 1950s, several Pentecostal denominations sought for and gained admission to the newly forming National Association of Evangelicals—an ecumenical umbrella organization of conservative Protestant denominations. Also during the same era Pentecostals began establishing colleges which sought formal accreditation and a few trusted leaders earned seminary degrees. Postwar upward mobility affected second and third generation Pentecostal members and "conspicuous consumption" dropped from the catalogue of Pentecostal sins.

As already noted, the defining tenet of classical Pentecostalism is speaking in tongues as the "initial physical evidence of the baptism of the Holy Spirit." Without this dinstinctive belief Pentecostalism would be little different from the rest of evangelical Protestant Christianity.

Pentecostals believe in common with other evangelical Christians that initiation into authentic Christianity involves a conversion experience sometimes known as being "born again." Baptism is usually performed only on people mature enough to express faith in Jesus Christ as Lord and Savior. Immersion is the normative mode. A few Pentecostals practice baptism by effusion or sprinkling. Pentecostals stress the present operation of the supernatural power of the Holy Spirit through gifts and "anointings." These include healing by laying on of hands and prophecy. Most Pentecostals believe in a premillenial second coming of Christ in the near future.

Pentecostals claim to believe in the sole authority of the Bible for

Christian faith and practice. More mainline conservative Protestants some-times question whether in fact Pentecostals add supernatural messages such as interpretations of tongues and prophecy to the Bible as authorita-tive for faith and practice. According to their offical statements of faith, however, Pentecostals do believe in the unique inspiration and authority of the Bible over even prophecies.

All Pentecostals distinguish between conversion and baptism in the Holy Spirit. The first event is for forgiveness of sins and reconciliation with God and is by grace through faith alone. The second experience is subse-quent to conversion and is for "enduement with power" for Christian living. This distinction is based on patterns discerned in the book of the Acts of the Apostles in the New Testament. Some non-Pentecostal Chris-tians agree that there is such a subsequent and separate experience avail-able to all true believers. However, only Pentecostals insist that this second experience is always accompanied by speaking in tongues. Pentecostals also claim that speaking in tongues, once received as a sign-gift from the Holy Spirit, becomes a regular part of a believer's spiritual life—a "prayer language" of a higher sort.

Early in Pentecostal history a rift developed between those who believed in the classical doctrine of the Trinity (God as one divine sub-stance eternally existing as three persons) and those who rejected it in favor of a version of the ancient heresy of "modalism" or "Sabellianism." The latter group which organized as the United Pentecostal Church calls itself "Jesus Only" or "Oneness" Pentecostalism. They believe that water baptism is necessary for salvation and only valid when performed "in the name of Jesus." The vast majority of Pentecostals reject Oneness Pente-costals as heretics and vice versa.

Another doctrinal debate arose early in Pentecostal history around the issue of sanctification. As already noted, most early Pentecostals were pre-viously followers of the "holiness movement" and believed that entire san-tification is possible for true Christian believers. Other Pentecostals, more influenced theologically by Baptists than by Wesleyans, rejected entire sanctification or perfection in favor of a progressive view. Classical Pente-costalism is divided by this line. The Assemblies of God, Church of the Foursquare Gospel, Open Bible Standard Churches, and other mostly Northern denominations reject entire sanctification and hold to a two-step model of Christian initiation: conversion and baptism in the Holy Spirit for power for Christian service. The Church of God (Cleveland, Ten-nessee), the Pentecostal Holiness Church, the Church of God in Christ, and other mostly Southern Pentecostal denominations believe in entire sanctification (Christian perfection in holiness) and affirm a three-step model of Christian initiation: conversion, baptism in the Holy Spirit, and sanctification. These two camps accept one another in fellowship.

The largest and most influential North American Pentecostal denominations have already been mentioned. In addition there are numerous smaller denominations many of which are regional. Thousands of independent Pentecostal congregations exist across America. This situation makes it almost impossible to come up with reliable statistics. An educated guess places the total constituent membership of Pentecostal churches in the United States near the end of the twentieth century between five and ten million. (This number would include the many independent charismatic churches which have no links to the historic or "classical" Pentecostal movement but have been started by individuals influenced by television evangelists.)

A cooperative fellowship of Pentecostal denominations exists. It is the Pentecostal Fellowship of North America, founded in Des Moines, Iowa, in 1947. In the 1990s it consisted of about twenty-five distinct white Pentecostal denominations, most of which affirm the classical Pentecostal tenet of speaking in tongues as the evidence of Holy Spirit baptism. In 1994 this umbrella organization is considering reorganization for the purpose of becoming racially inclusive.

There are no major Pentecostal-wide publications. However, most Pentecostal denominations have their own magazines and the PFNA (mentioned above) publishes a regular newsletter. The most widely distributed and read Pentecostal publication is the Assemblies of God periodical *The Pentecostal Evangel.* Many independent Pentecostal evangelists and ministries also publish magazines.

A number of stable Pentecostal institutions of higher education exist in North America. The Assemblies of God owns and operates several Bible colleges and liberal arts colleges. Two are in the headquarters city of Springfield, Missouri: Central Bible College and Evangel College. Other Pentecostal colleges include Lee College in Cleveland, Tennessee; Eugene Bible College in Oregon; and Southern California College in Costa Mesa. In the late 1960s, independent healing evangelist Oral Roberts established Oral Roberts University in Tulsa, Oklahoma, which quickly drew Pentecostal students from all over the world. However, ORU and Roberts himself are not classically Pentecostal but rather belong in the category of neo-Pentecostal or charismatic.

Pentecostals have been reluctant to establish universities or seminaries. The Church of God in Christ operates a seminary named after its founder, Charles Mason, in Atlanta. The Assemblies of God founded a seminary in their headquarters building in Springfield, Missouri in the early 1970s. To a very large extent, Pentecostal students who wanted theological training on the graduate level have had to attend evangelical seminaries such as Fuller Seminary in Pasadena, California. They have often then found themselves shunned by Pentecostal leaders who tend to be somewhat skeptical of the value of higher education.

During the 1980s and 1990s, the media focused a great deal of negative attention on certain television evangelists of questionable ethics and morals who had tenuous ties to Pentecostalism. Among the most notorious were Jim Bakker, founder of the "PTL" organization, and Jimmy Swaggert of Baton Rouge, Louisiana. Both had national television shows and elaborate offshoots such as a Bible college, retreat center and theme park, and musical production studios. Their downfalls created some public hostility toward Pentecostals since both of these men were associated with the Assemblies of God.

Within Pentecostalism some debate continues regarding the exact nature of speaking in tongues as evidence of the baptism of the Holy Spirit. Some leaders continue to insist on the traditional language of "initial physical evidence," which implies that one cannot be fully Spirit-filled without speaking in tongues, while others are willing to soften such language in order to accomodate evangelicals such as Billy Graham who claims to be Spirit-filled but never to have spoken in tongues. For more and more Pentecostals speaking in tongues should be seen as the normative sign of Spirit baptism but not as the absolutely definitive and necessary physical evidence.

*—ROGER E. OLSON*

**CHARISMATIC MOVEMENT.** The charismatic movement represents a branch of the larger Pentecostal Christian tradition, which is based on the experience of being filled with the Holy Spirit. It focuses upon miracles, signs, wonders, and the so-called gifts of the Spirit, such as glossolalia, faith healing, and exorcism. The word "pentecostal" stems from the biblical account of the day of Pentecost, during which the Holy Spirit descended upon the first Christians, whereas "charismatic" derives from the Greek term *charism,* which means supernatural gifts of the Spirit.

An intermittent history of charismatic practices can be traced among sectarians like the Montanists, Anabaptists, Camisards, Shakers, Irvingites, Mormons, and a number of nineteenth-century Holiness groups. The twentieth-century Pentecostal and charismatic movements mark the restoration of the charismata, which ceased in the main body of the church soon after the apostolic age. Pentecostals believe that the experience of Spirit baptism and the practice of the gifts of the Spirit that occurred on the day of Pentecost were meant to be normative in the life of the church and of each believer.

The major concern for Pentecostalism is experience rather than doctrine. Spirit baptism and the practice represent the only elements on which there is unanimity. Most American Pentecostals adopt the major tenets of fundamentalism, and believe that the initial evidence of Spirit baptism is always glossolalia, whereas other Pentecostals claim that it may be evidenced by any one of the charismata.

The worship service constitutes the heart of Pentecostalism. Pentecostal worship originally included speaking in tongues, prophesying, healings, exorcisms, hand-clapping, uncoordinated praying aloud, running, jumping, falling, dancing in the Spirit, crying, and shouting. These practices are still in evidence among ethnic minorities in North America and Europe, throughout sub-Saharan Africa, Latin America, and parts of Asia. However, for all Penetcostals, worship constitutes the recapturing of awe, wonder, and joy in the immediate experience of the Holy Spirit.

The Pentecostal movement traces its origins to the United States where it emerged as a protest against the increasing formalism, modernism, and middle-class character of mainstream denominations. American Pentecostalism represented an amalgam of extremist Wesleyan and Keswick views on premillennialism, dispensationalism, faith healing and the Baptism in the Spirit as an enduement of miraculous power. Early American Pentecostalism was characterized by ascetism, and prohibitionism against tobacco, alcohol, dancing, gambling, movies, coffee, tea, cosmetics, and jewelry. Its followers opposed all man-made organizations, and called only for spiritual unity based on Spirit baptism. American Pentecostal denominations were at first separatist toward each other as well as toward non-Pentecostal churches. This isolationism came to an end in 1943 when a number of Pentecostal denominations joined the National Association of Evangelicals.

Pentecostals can be distinguished in three main groupings: (1) classical Pentecostals, whose origins can be traced back to the Pentecostal revival in the United States at the beginning of this century; (2) charismatics, whose origins date back to the Pentecostal revival within the non-Pentecostal Christian communions in the United States during the 1960s; and (3) those who hold the fundamental beliefs and practices of Pentecostalism, although some of their beliefs are considered heretical or non-Christian by the other two major groupings. The latter grouping is concentrated in Africa, Latin America, and Asia.

The charismatic or Neo-Pentecostal movement emerged in the 1960s in nearly all the Protestant denominations, the Roman Catholic Church, and in Eastern Orthodox communions as a result of the interest in Pentecostalism that emerged after the so-called Deliverance, or Healing Revival occurred in the late 1940s. This was led by a group of faith-healing evangelists who reemphasized the charismata, and who attracted multitudes of non-Pentecostals. In 1951 Pentecostal Demos Shakarian was encouraged to found the Full Gospel Business Men's Fellowship, International (FGBMFI) in order to provide support for the healers. This organization organized several luncheon and dinner meetings in luxury hotels all over the country, which attracted many new converts to the charismatic movement. FGBMFI thus represented a bridge from the Deliverance revival to the charismatic revival.

In 1961, the pastor of an Episcopal church in Van Nuys, California, named Dennis Bennet, claimed that he had received the baptism in the Spirit, and that he had spoken in tongues. A charismatic revival among Protestant denominations emerged after this event, and was promoted by FGBMFI. Charismatics were at first accused of being schismatic and fanatical, but they eventually proved otherwise. During their meetings, which were marked by restraint, they were very careful not to challenge the doctrines and practices of their denominations.

Charismatic practices emerged also among Roman Catholics. In 1967 Roman Catholic students and faculty at Duquesne, Notre Dame, and Michigan State universities became involved with the charismatic movement. A number of prayer groups and conferences were organized, and the movement grew rapidly, soon surpassing its Protestant counterpart. Among its adherents were many religious and bishops, and one cardinal, Leon Joseph Cardinal Suenens of Belgium.

The charismatics have rejected almost all of the Holiness and fundamentalist heritage of the Pentecostal movement. They have focused on integrating the experience of Spirit baptism and the practice of charismata into the traditional beliefs and practices of their respective churches without altering them. Some charismatics view Spirit baptism as a distinct act of grace, whereas many Protestant and Roman Catholic charismatics consider it as a renewal or actualization of the baptism in the Spirit, received by all Christians in water baptism or conversion. Many Protestant charismatics hold the initial evidence of speaking in tongues, whereas other Protestant and all Roman Catholic charismatics reject it.

**CHRISTIAN IDENTITY.** The Christian Identity movement is an American offshoot of an older religious movement, "British-Israelism" (also known as "Anglo-Israelism"). Christian Identity doctrine crystallized in the mid- and late-1940s and by the 1970s had become an important element in the belief system of racists on the extreme political right.

British-Israelism, from which Christian Identity emerged, developed in Victorian England, the heir to a long tradition that linked British destiny with the Biblical Israelites. In an 1840 set of lectures, John Wilson argued that the British peoples were actually the descendants of the migrating "ten lost tribes" who had forgotten their true "identity." As developed by subsequent writers, British-Israelism posited a revisionist history of Britain and the ancient world, and identified England as a divine instrument for the fulfillment of God's purposes.

While Anglo-Israelism never developed into a denomination, it did become an organized social movement. In the hands of talented propagandists, such as Edward Hine (1825–1891), it secured a following and developed an organizational framework, initially in England, and then in Canada and the United States. Hine's missionary activities in North America between 1884 and 1888 solidified its presence, particularly in the Northeast.

Hine worked in conjunction with the movement's main American expositor, C. A. L. Totten (1851–1908), whose voluminous writings spread British-Israel teachings up to World War I. In his and Hine's view, America and Great Britain constituted the descendants of Ephraim and Manasseh, the tribes deemed central to the fulfillment of the divine design in history.

Like his English colleagues, Totten had no interest in challenging the political status quo, which British-Israelites saw as divinely ordained. Less politically circumspect positions would have to await the tumultuous environment of the Depression era.

By the late 1920s the American branch of British-Israelism had passed into the hands of a Massachusetts lawyer and indefatigable organizer, Howard Rand (1889–1991). Rand brought American British-Israelites under the umbrella of a new organization, the Anglo-Saxon Federation of America. His colleague in this enterprise was Henry Ford's publicist, William J. Cameron. Together, they linked the Anglo-Saxon Federation with explicitly right-wing political agendas. Rand cultivated contacts with extreme conservatives, while Cameron was already well known as the former editor of the Dearborn *Independent,* the most notorious anti-Semitic publication in America. During the 1930s, Rand and Cameron succeeded in diffusing British-Israel ideas widely, while demonstrating their compatibility with right-wing political positions.

With the end of the Second World War, the stage was set for the emergence of Christian Identity doctrine in Southern California. Southern California had absorbed a number of British-Israel influences during earlier decades. It was the site of active branches of the Anglo-Saxon Federation; a center of activity by Pentacostalists, whose leadership had been influenced by Totten's writings; and touched by the ideas of an unusually anti-Semitic group of British-Israelites based in Vancouver, British Columbia.

The key figures in the emergence of Christian Identity—Bertrand Comparet, William Potter Gale, and preeminently, Wesley Swift—were all associates of Gerald L. K. Smith, based in Los Angeles, was the most widely known anti-Semitic agitator of the 1940s and served as the center of an informal national network of those on the extreme right. Comparet served as his attorney, while Swift was a principal organizer for Smith's Christian Nationalist Crusade. Swift and Gale, and to a lesser extent Comparet, combined British-Israel ideas with a wide range of other concepts, drawn from evangelical religion, occultism, and right-wing politics. All three maintained dual agendas, engaged in sermonizing, church organizing, and religious writing, while simultaneously participating in political activities directed against such adversaries as Jews, nonwhites, the United Nations, and the Internal Revenue Service.

As the 1960s ended, however, the dominance of the first generation of Identity preachers waned. Wesley Swift died in 1970, Bertrand Comparet in 1983, and William Potter Gale in 1988 (just before a jail sentence was to begin for his antitax activities). While the movement had neither a formal leadership structure nor a mechanism for designating succession, a new generation of major figures began to appear in the 1970s, such as Richard Girnt Butler (first in California, then in Idaho), Dan Gayman in Missouri, James K. Warner (first in California, then in Louisiana), and Pete Peters (in Colorado).

Neither British-Israelism nor Christian Identity established machinery to define orthodoxy and heresy. Hence beliefs ascribed to both groups here constitute dominant tendencies, subject to variation according to the whims and preferences of individual believers.

Christian Identity theology is built around three central beliefs: The Israelite ancestry of "Aryans"; the imminence of the "last days" of history; and the Satanic paternity of Jews.

From British-Israelism, Christian Identity took the idea of a link between Biblical Israelites and persons of northwestern European background. However, they have modified the linkage in two significant respects. First, they claim descent not simply from the "ten lost tribes" of legend but from all the Israelite tribes. Second, where British-Israelism generally spoke of linkages between Israelites and various nationalities or ethnic groups, Christian Identity is much more prone to address the issue in racial terms. The latter-day Israelites are, therefore, identified as "whites" or "Aryans." While submerged motifs of racial superiority were present in British-Israelism, with its claim to demonstrate the Anglo-Saxons' right to rule, racial themes are now overtly stated.

The second major feature—Christian Identity's millennialism—also echoes older themes, for Anglo-Israelites expressed the common evangelical Protestant concern to pinpoint the arrival of the climax of history. Millennialism, however, has become far more significant for Identity believers. They are best classified as premillennialist, but post-tribulationist. That is, they believe the millennial rule of the saved will follow rather than precede the Second Coming. However, unlike most Protestant fundamentalists, they reject the concept of a "rapture," in which the saved will be lifted off the earth before the period of violence (the "Tribulation") that climaxes in Armageddon. Instead, Identity followers believe they must survive a period of violence and persecution under the Anti-Christ, a time they often characterize in terms of race war.

Identity's most distinctive theological hallmark, however, is its view of Jewish origins. Most British-Israelites regarded Jews as descendants of the tribe of Judah, hence merely one component of "all-Israel." Over time, and markedly after the end of the British mandate over Palestine, British-Israel writers began to suggest that Jews had forfeited their place in the economy of salvation through intermarriages with heathen peoples, from the Canaanites and Edomites, to the medieval Khazars. Building upon this, Christian Identity radically delegitimized Jews by asserting that they are not part Israel but are instead the direct, biological descendants of Satan. They advance a myth of the Fall in which original sin consists of a sexual coupling between Eve and Satan or his humanoid instrument, begetting Cain, whom they call the first Jew. Hence in addition to more traditional anti-Semitic motifs, Christian Identity adds a link with primal evil.

Like Anglo-Israelism, Christian Identity did not develop along denominational or sectarian lines. It consists of dozens, perhaps hundreds, of small independent churches, Bible study groups, and ministries conducted through publications, cassettes, or radio programs. While some ministers have sought ascendancy within the movement at various times, such claims are ultimately dependent upon whatever personal allegiance they can command.

In the absence of any overarching organizational structure, variations in doctrine or associated political positions cannot be resolved. Indeed, even the existing relatively small congregations are subject to frequent splits and defections. For this reason, there are no reliable estimates of the movement's size. In addition to the organizational factor that makes the collection of membership data impossible, the stigmatizing nature of Identity religious beliefs and political positions gives the movement a semi-clandestine character. Estimates of its size have ranged from a low of two thousand to a high of fifty thousand to one hundred thousand. As in most such cases, the lowest and highest figures are almost certainly incorrect.

Identity's religious beliefs have led a number of believers into highly controversial, sometimes violent, political affiliations. These flow primarily from the tendency to divide the world between "Aryan Israelites" and non-whites (in Identity's eyes Jews are, by definition, nonwhite). This racial theology has led to strong overlaps between Identity and elements of the white supremacist extreme right. Some racist groups are direct outgrowths of Identity churches. Thus, Aryan Nations in Hayden Lake, Idaho, is the political arm of the Church of Jesus Christ-Christian. Some initially non-Identity racist organizations have embraced Identity beliefs, notably substantial segments of the Ku Klux Klan. Finally, some extreme right-wing organizations not primarily racist have attracted large numbers of Identity adherents (e.g., Posse Comitatus groups). In short, Identity overlaps upon a complex, chaotic mix of extremist organizations, directly affecting the ideology of some while modifying others indirectly.

By defining the world in racial terms, Identity creates a Manichean universe in which the chosen few battle against the evil world that surrounds them. In political terms, this vision of cosmic combat leads many Identity believers to identify state and national governments with the Jewish conspiracy and the forces of Anti-Christ. While the expression of this antipathy is most often limited to the written and spoken word, it has sometimes erupted into acts of open defiance. Identity believers have been prominent in resistance to the collection of income tax, for which some have been prosecuted. They have also been involved in confrontations with authority that threatened or resulted in violence.

In 1983, confrontations between law enforcement authorities and a North Dakota Posse Comitatus leader and Identity believer, Gordon Kahl, resulted in the deaths of two federal marshals. In 1985, federal law enforcement authorities besieged and captured the commune of a heavily armed paramilitary Identity group in Arkansas, the Covenant, Sword and Arm of the Lord, with no loss of life. In 1983 and 1984, an insurgent group of racial separatists known as the Order or the Silent Brotherhood engaged in a wave of crimes, mostly in the West, preparatory to the launching of attacks on the federal government. Half of its forty members were Identity believers. Between 1984 and 1986 the members of the order were captured and tried (its leader, Robert Matthews, was killed in a shootout with the FBI), and with the organization's demise, the level of Identity-related violence dropped substantially. Nonetheless, because the movement is fragmented, the possibility of violent episodes in the future cannot be ruled out.

*—MICHAEL BARKUN*

**OLD CATHOLICS.** Among the divisions experienceed by the Western liturgical tradition, is the split that developed in Port-Royal, France, in the seventeenth century. The split arose among members of a mystical movement focused on the Dutch theologian Cornelius Jansen (1585–1638), and were popularly known as Jansenists. Believing that the human will was not free and that redemption was limited only to few individuals, Jansenists were condemned by the pope and opposed by the Jesuits. They were variously accused of being Protestants, as well as heretics, whereas they accused the Jesuits of despotism and laxity in doctrine and discipline. In the face of the persecution initiated by the Jesuits, the Jansenists lost power, and many of them moved to Holland, in the territory of Utrecht.

Utrecht's bishop, Peter Codde, refused to condemn the Jansenists when the pope asked him to do so, and for this reason he was accused of Jansenism by the rival party behind Theodore De Cock, who was eventually banished from Holland by the government for various reasons. Codde, on the other hand, was deposed by the pope, and Utrecht remained without episcopal functionaries, as well as without ordinations and confirmations.

This problem was alleviated in 1719 by the bishop Dominique Marie Varlet's stop in Amsterdam, who confirmed more than six hundred children. However, these confirmations led to his suspension from office, and to his eventual return to Amsterdam, where he settled. Varlet consecrated a new archbishop of Utrecht, Cornelius van Steenoven, who was followed by Cornelius Wuytiers. The dividing line between the Church of Utrecht, known as the Old Catholic Church, and Rome continued for about 150 years.

The Old Catholic movement's history can be traced officially from the 1870s and the reaction to the declaration of papal infallability and primacy at the First Vatican Council, which pushed a large number of Roman Catholic priests and laymen to join the Church of Utrecht. Many who belonged to the upper middle class were strongly influenced by secularism and nationalism. A congress of about three hundred opponents to the pope was organized in Munich, Germany, where the Old Catholic Church was organized along national lines. A similar congress was organized in Cologne in 1872. In 1874 a constitution recognizing national autonomy and establishing an international Synod of Bishops was adopted. In Prussia and Baden, they were granted a subsidy and a share of Catholic Church property by the government. In Switzerland, they were more influenced by secularism and theological liberalism than the Old Catholics of Germany, but they did not gain following.

The Declaration of Utrecht (1889) represents the doctrinal basis for the Old Catholic community. According to this document, the Old Catholics accept the decrees of the first eight ecumenical councils. Sacred Scripture and tradition are considered their sources of revelation, although the Old Catholics do not place the deuterocanonical books of the Old Testament on parity with the others. Also, their notion of tradition differs from the Roman Catholic one. They reject the treasury of merits, indulgences, venerations of saints, images, and relics, as well as Mary's Immaculate Conception, Assumption, and position as mediatrix of all graces. The Old Catholics forbid private Masses, and permit the reception of the Eucharist under one or both species. Also, auricular confession is not obligatory, and sins can be confessed before the congregation or a priest. They abolished such practices as clerical celibacy, pilgrimages, processions, the rosary, and scapular. Their liturgy resembles the Roman Catholic one, and is celebrated in the vernacular. Also, their liturgical vestments resemble the Roman Catholic ones.

There were many similarities bewteen the Old Catholic Church and the Anglican Church. Intercommunion with Old Catholics and Anglicans was admitted by the Polish National Catholic Church, which originated from cultural xenophobia and Polish Nationalism, and which subscribed to the

Declaration of Utrecht. A schism occurred because of the inability to acco-modate to a non-Polish priesthood, and a schismatic church was established in 1897 in Scranton, Pennsylvania, where a number of earlier Polish dissi-dent groups where absorbed under the jurisdiction of Francis Hodur.

The Old Catholic Church was marked by an antiauthoritarian char-acter, and most of its bishops have been self-appointed, and pressed for recognition of orders while keeping independence of jurisdiction. Some have also sought recognition by bishops of the Eastern Orthoox Church, and when this has occurred, the variation in ritual and doc-trine increased considerably.

The Old Catholic Church also came to America, although a chaotic episcopal scene emerged, as many bishops claim dioceses that exist only on paper, and various ordinations are attributed to bishops whose existence cannot be verified. Most American Old Catholics derived from two lines of succession, those of Joseph Rene Vilatte and Arnold Harris Mathew. There is also another faction derived from miscellaneous Eastern and Western orders which was led by Hugh George de Willmott Newman. While Euro-pean Old Catholic churches entered in full communion with the Church of England, American churches remained considerably autonomous.

Arnold Harris Mathew (1852–1919), who began his career as a Roman Catholic priest, eventually entered into communion with the Church of England for a period after which, however, he made peace with Rome, and became a layman and author. His work includes a collaboration with H. C. Lea in the third edition of the *History of Sacerdotal Celibacy in the Christian Church*, published early in this century. In September 1907 he began to cor-respond with the Swiss Old Catholic Bishop Eduard Herzog, and later with Bishop J. J. Van Theil of Haarlem. In these letters he suggested the orga-nization of an Old Catholic church in England. Under the guidance of Father Richard O'Halloran, who was leader of a group of disgrunted ex-Catholics, he became bishop of the Old Catholics in England, although he did not have valid orders. The problem was solved in 1908 when he was consecrated in Utrecht by the Archbishop, although the Anglicans protested. When he returned to England, no following was waiting for him as a bishop because O'Halloran had lied to him, so he decided to resign with a letter to the archbishop of Uthrecth. But his resignations were refused, and he eventually declared his independence from Utrecht after secretly consecrating two ex-Roman Catholic priests as bishops without informing Utrecht. He built a small church and died in poverty in 1919.

Mathew was responsible for the development of Old Catholicism in America, as a result of his consecration of Prince de Landas Berghes et de Rache, Duc de St. Winock on June 28, 1913. De Landas Berghes, who was supposed to set up an independent church in Austria, established Mathew's succession in the United States where he moved after he was prevented from returning to Austria from England because of World War I. When in America, and before his submission to Rome in 1919, he consecrated as bishops Fathers W. H. Francis Brothers and Henry Carfora, the originators of most Old Catholic bodies in America.

Joseph Rene Vilatte, however, can be considered the first man to bring Old Catholicism to America. He believed both Roman Catholic and Protestant positions invalid. He preached Old Roman Catholic doctrines in the 1880s among French and Belgian immigrants in Wisconsin. After his success in Wisconsin, he was ordained by Bishop Herzog. He eventually obtained consecration as archbishop of the Archdiocese of America in 1892 from Archbishop Alvarez of Ceylon.

He returned to Roman Catholicism for a short time in 1899–1900, and for the next twenty years operated as an archbishop for the American Catholic Church from which, however, he was eventually removed bacause the Syro-Jacobite Church of Malabar refused to recognize his various consecrations. He again returned to the Roman Catholic Church in 1925. After his death, the American Catholic Church was taken over by bishops with theosophical leanings.

Hugh George de Willmott Newman (1905– ) can be considered the most original bishop in the Old Catholic movement. He is known for introducing the practice among the autonomous bishops of seeking numerous reconsecrations. He was convinced that the reconsecrations could legitimize an otherwise inconsiderable ecclesiastical juristiction through the embodiment of a wide variety of lines of apostolic succession, that could lead to the formation of the ecumenical church. He was first consecrated in 1944 by Dr. William Bernard Crow, deriving his orders from Luis Mariano Soares of the small Syro-Chaldean church in India, Ceylon, Socotra, and Messina. He also received no less than nine additional consecrations in the next ten years. During these reconsecrations he usually reconsecrated the other bishop, in order to pass along the apostolic lineage that he had just received. Newman consecrated W. D. de Ortega Maxey of the Apostolic Episcopal Church, who established an American branch of Newman's Catholicate of the West, and became the main source for American bishops to receive Newman's lineage.

The independent Old Catholic jurisdictions in America base their story on the search for legitimacy through ever more valid consecrations. This practice is founded on the tradition, typical of episcopal churches, of establishing legitimacy by tracing the line of succession from the original twelve Apostles. In order to be validly consecrated and to be able to validly ordain priests, a bishop must himself be consecrated by a validly consecrated bishop. The practice of receiving multiple consecrations has become increasingly popular for independent bishops, and it has become particularly common after changing fidelity to a different jurisdiction.

A complex mixing of liturgies has been initiated by the importing of Eastern orders into Western churches, and through the combining of Western and Eastern lineages in bishops such as Newman. A number of different liturgies, such as Roman, Anglican, Eastern, or even theosophical, have often been adopted by the independent jurisdictions, no matter the practices of the body from which they received their apostolic succession. Some other independent jurisdictions, on the other hand, have written their own liturgy. Determinations about the liturgies that a congregation may use represent one of the few decisions that the bishop can make, since American jurisdictions are usually very small, with an unpaid clergy and property owned by the congregation. Having an unpaid clergy was a practice introduced by Bishop Mathew. Since they have no financial attachment to any particular jurisdiction, priests and bishops frequently leave at will. Because of this practice, the Old Catholic Church has split up into more than one hundred different jurisdictions, and the problem of straightening out the line of succession has been made extremely complicated by the continuous flux within the jurisdictions. An effort to solve this problem has been made by H. R. T. Branweth, Peter Anson, and Arthur C. Piepkorn, and continued in recent years by Karl Pruter, Bertil Persson, and Alan Bain.

A new set of independent Catholic jurisdictions has emerged since the Roman Catholic Church's Second Vatican Council and the adoption of the new liturgy for the mass. The new jurisdictions have an allegiance to the Latin liturgy and numerous other practices that have been abandoned by the post-Vatican church. While some of these jurisdictions receive Old Catholic orders for their bishops, others wait for some kind of recognition from Rome. An example of the latter jurisdiction is represented by the followers of Swiss Archbishop Lefebvre. The Archbishop Lefebvre broke with Rome because its recognition never occurred, and consecrated four bishops who were destined to carry on his work. Another example is represented by Vietnamese Archbishop Ngo-Dinh-Thuc, who had previously consecrated bishops for an equally conservative Latin Rite Catholic Church. The possibilities of reconciliation with Rome seem quite small.

# 4 MILLERISM AND THE ADVENTIST TRADITION

**A**dventism shares many of its theological perspectives with other Christian denominations. There is general agreement with respect to doctrines concerning the Bible, God, Christ, and the sacraments. Its Baptist origins are reflected in the idea of ordinances—instead of sacraments—baptism by immersion, and the practice of foot washing. Sabbatarianism was transmitted directly by the Seventh-day Baptists. However, from an eschatological point of view, the Adventists went far beyond the Baptists in their theology by asserting that the end of the world was imminent.

The American millennial movement began in New York under the impetus of the Baptist layman William Miller who, after being a Deist, became involved with the study of the Bible. He became more and more convinced that he was living near the end of his age and that he had to preach about it. He began preaching in several cities, and he published his first work—a series of sixteen articles—in the *Vermont Telegraph* in 1832.

After the Baptists gave him a license to preach in September 1833, Miller dedicated ten years of his life preaching and teaching his message of the imminent return of Jesus. He also published his lectures in his first book, *Evidences from Scripture and History of the Second Coming of Christ about the Year 1843: Exhibited in a Course of Lectures*, which greatly stimulated the movement.

Central to Miller's belief was the conviction that, from the study of Daniel and Revelation, he had deciphered the chronology concerning the end of the age. He claimed that the end of the seventy weeks mentioned in Daniel 19:24 was 33 C.E., at the cross of Jesus, and the beginning was, therefore, 457 B.C.E. His view, sustained by several figures, also included 1843 as the year of the cleansing of the sanctuary. Miller published his chronology of prophetic history that covered the Old Testament period and showed that 1843 was the end of the sixth millenium since creation in a number of books.

Among several others who began to join Miller was Joshua Himes, who invited Miller to preach in his Boston church, and who started to publish the movement's first periodical, *Signs of the Times*, in 1840. The first conference of the growing movement was held on October 13, 1840, at Charon Street Church in Boston. Several leaders attended it, among whom were Josiah Litch, Joseph Bates, and Henry Dana Ward.

After the Boston conference, which was very successful, other conferences on Miller's message, known as "the midnight cry," were held in other cities. However, the movement began to face opposition by established denominations, which began to counteract Miller's influence. Several ministers and laymen were expelled from formerly cooperative churches, and a series of articles against Millerism were published in the *New York Christian Advocate* of 1843.

The first camp meeting of the movement was held at East Kingston, New Hampshire, in 1843. In November of the same year the second periodical, *The Midnight Cry*, was begun. During the same period, Miller also perfected his view concerning the second coming that, according to his new stance, would occur somewhere between March 21, 1843, and March 21, 1844. Although a large comet as well as other spectacular phenomena appeared in the sky in the late February, the second coming did not occur.

The outburst of increased opposition of the churches, as well as the lack of prior religious connection from which disappointed Adventists could gain nourishment, led Charles Fitch to start the "come out" movement. Although Fitch was opposed by Miller, many believers in Christ's imminent return started to "come out" of their denominational churches and form their own churches.

Soon new adjustments in Miller's chronology were made by Samuel S. Snow, who looked to October 22, 1844, as the real date of return. But again, nothing happened, and a "great disappointment" arose leaving the movement in chaos. Miller eventually retired from active leadership in the movement, while the believers were organized into a number of denominational bodies.

Among the main options open to followers of Miller after the great disappointment of 1844 were generally the disbanding of the group and a return to preexcitement existence, as well as the process, known as spiritualization, of claiming that the prophecy, as a visible historical event, was in error, and that it had to be reinterpreted as an invisible, spiritual event. Other followers, on the other hand, decided to return to the original source of revelation, and seek a new date. Few groups lasted beyond the projected dates.

**SEVENTH-DAY ADVENTIST CHURCH.** Not all of Miller's followers felt downhearted. One, Ellen G. White, received a vision in which the Adventists, as Miller's folowers had come to be known, traveling straight to heaven. White, her husband, James, and others began meeting in Washington, New Hampshire, and soon many were hailing Ellen White as a messenger endued with special gifts by the Holy Spirit. Working with a member of her group, Hiram Edson, the idea developed that Miller was not wrong about the occurrence of an eschatologically significant event, but that he was wrong about the nature of the event. Jesus did not return to earth in 1844, but he did begin the cleansing of the heavenly sanctuary (Hebrews 8:1–2).

By 1850 the Whites were making the initial efforts at unifying the disparate branches of Adventists. To that end they began publishing a journal, the *Review and Herald.* They moved to Battle Creek, Michigan, in 1855, and by 1863 had sufficiently organized the network of Sabbatarian adventists to organize the Seventh-day Adventist Church. At the time the formal organization occurred, there were some 3,500 members in 125 congregations.

Many of the Adevntists' beliefs are taken over from the Baptist roots of the early members. Some teachings of American Methodism also filtered into the group. Thus, they are trinitarians who attest to salvation by Christ through his atoning work on the cross. They also insist on the Bible as the rule of faith and practice baptism by immersion. The Sabbatarian teachings of the Old Testament are accepted, as are many of the dietary regulations. Members are also forbidden to use tobacco or alcohol. Although the insistence on White's status as a prophet is maintained, the church has shied away from specific predictions since the days of Miller and White.

The church has a largely democratic structure of local conferences composed of local churches which vote to elect representatives to regional and general conferences that meet every five years. The church has an active publishing arm (three publishing houses in Idaho, Nebraska, and Maryland) and an aggressive policy of overseas missions that carries on work in 185 countries. The church operates a dozen colleges and universities as well as secondary and primary educational facilties. The membership is just under 700,000 in the United States and over 5,000,000 worldwide.

**JEHOVAH'S WITNESSES.** Another small group to survive the Great Disappointment led by Jonas Wendell projected a new date in 1874. Disappointed followers spiritualized the 1874 date and projected yet another date in 1914.

Charles Taze Russell (1852–1916), who had joined Wendell's group, soon disagreed on the manner of Christ's return, and in 1876 was instrumental in restarting the publication of the suspended *Herald of the Morning,* and coauthoring *Three Worlds or Plan of Redemption.* Russell rejected a belief in hell as a place of eternal torment. He also believed that the Greek word *parousia* meant presence, and he was convinced that, in 1874, the Lord's "presence" had begun. Finally Russell believed that because of Adam, all were born without the right to live, whereas because of Jesus, all have inherited sin cancelled, so that all people were guaranteed a second chance which would be offered during the millenium, that is, Christ's reign on earth with his saints for one thousand years. Among Russell's beliefs was also the denial of certain orthodox ideas such as the Trinity.

Other Adventists such as J. H. Paton, A. P. Adams, and A. D. Jones joined Russell, and this coalition lasted until 1878 when the prophecy of the second coming in the month of April was disconfirmed. Russell, Paton, and Jones began *Zion's Watch Tower and Herald of Christ's Presence.* The first issue in 1879 marks the beginning of Russell's movement known as the "Millenial Dawn Bible Students."

Zion's Watch Tower Tract Society was set up in 1881, and in 1886 the first of six volumes of *Studies in the Scripture* appeared. Titled *The Plan of the Ages,* it provided the substantial ideological base of Russell's thought. According to Russell, history could be divided into a number of eras. The first dispensation was from Adam to the flood, whereas the patriarchal age was followed by the Jewish age, which lasted until Christ's death. The gospel age of 1845 years ended in 1874, which marked the dawning of the millenial age and which would begin with a "harvest period" or millenial dawn period of forty years (1874–1914) marked by a return of the Jews to Palestine and the gradual overthrow of the Gentile nations. The climax would be in 1914, characterized by the glorification of the saints, the establishment of God's direct rule on earth, and the restoration of man to perfection on earth. Since this apocalyptic date coincided with World War I, it was viewed by Russell's followers as a cause for great hope, whereas the war was interpreted as God's direct intervention in the affairs of man, as well as a signal of the beginning of the end of the world.

Another element in Russell's thought was his doctrine of the future church, according to which the church consisted of 144,000 saints from the time of Christ to 1914, who would receive the ultimate reward of becoming "priests and kings in heaven," whereas others would make up a class of heavenly servants termed "the great company." After his death, Russell's ideas became the subject of much controversy, which led, in the next decade, to the rise of power of Judge J. F. Rutherford, and the emergence of Jehovah's Witnesses.

The Sacred Name Movement, which is often thought of as the "Elijah Message"—a reference to Elijah's words in 1 Kings 18:36 which extol Yahweh as the Elohim of Israel—began as a result of the conviction of several believers that God's name is an important doctrinal consideration. This issue was raised forcefully in the 1920s by the International Bible Students, who were on their way to becoming the Jehovah's Witnesses. In the twentieth century, many scholars began to assert that "Yahveh" was the correct pronounciation of the "YHWH," the spelling of God's name in Hebrew, and by the mid-1930s several members and ministers of the Church of God, Seventh-Day, such as Elder J. D. Bagwell, began to use the "sacred name" and to promote the cause actively. The Faith Bible and Tract Society was organized in 1938, and in the same period the Assembly of Yahweh Beth Israel was also formed. The *Faith* magazine, which supported the Old Testament festivals as being contemporarily valid, represented a fundamental force in spreading the Sacred Name movement. Its editor, Elder C. O. Dodd, gradually began to use "Jehovah," then "Jahoveh," "Yahovah," "Yahvah," and "Yahweh." A number of assemblies, which were formed in the 1940s following the Adventist and Old Testament emphases, eventually became substantial movements that are still in existence as primary religious bodies.

**DAVIDIAN SEVENTH-DAY ADVENTISTS.** The Davidian Seventh-day Adventists are a small Adventist reform movement whose founder was Victor T. Houteff. Originally known as the Shepherd's Rod, the group adopted the Davidian name in 1942. In the late 1950s the group split. The two major successors are the General Association of Davidian Seventh-day Adventists and the Branch Davidians.

Victor T. Houteff was a Bulgarian immigrant who settled in Milwaukee in 1907. He moved to Illinois and converted to Seventh-day Adventist teaching in 1918. His thought matured when he was serving as assistant Sabbath day superintendent at the Olympic Exposition Park Seventh-day Adventist Church. He presented his ideas in weekly lessons, and began publishing his interpretations in 1930 in the form of pocket-sized tracts under the title *Shepherd's Rod*. He drew the title from Micah 6:9 ("Hear ye the rod"). Houteff believed that the leaders of the General Conference had led the denomination astray and that his teaching was the truth. General Conference Seventh-day Adventists viewed him as a zealous reformer and tried to dissuade members from following him. He argued that he was trying to call the church to reform. He did not want to walk away from the denomination: His entire message was addressed to Adventists only. The General Conference disfellowshipped him in 1930, but he spent the remainder of his life trying to reform the mother church.

Houteff and his loyal following looked for a new site. He said that the phrase from Isaiah "in the midst of the land" led him to believe that the New Israel would be located in the central United States. He had already experienced the cold winters of Illinois; he and two followers, therefore, scouted several sites in Texas. Furthermore, he believed that this location would facilitate distribution of his tracts. Thus, three principle reasons—biblical, economic, and propagandizing—drew him to central Texas. He wanted to establish a community uninfluenced by the temptations of city life and therefore bought property outside the city limits, near Waco, Texas. He named the place Mt. Carmel. In the fall of 1935—at the end of a summer of migration—thirty-five faithful gathered to begin life together. Their numbers would soon grow to between sixty and seventy. Their chief task was to operate a printing press which produced vast quantities of tracts, setting forth Houteff's ideas and distributing his message throughout the worldwide Adventist community.

The community faced a serious crisis in 1942. The Adventist tradition had always embraced a conscientious objector status during war, and Houteff shared this belief. He was willing for his young followers to serve the country through hospital work but appealed to the Draft Board for exemptions from bearing arms. His petition was denied. He therefore changed the name of his group to Davidian Seventh-day Adventists, thereby bringing them under the umbrella of a denominational name with a well-established tradition of conscientious objection.

Houteff died in 1955. His death devastated the community. They had relied on him for leadership and had believed that he would inaugurate the new age through the teachings set forth in his publications. Moreover, he was to be the "Elijah" who would announce the second advent. His wife Florence succeeded him.

Waco residential development grew in the direction of old Mt. Carmel, and in 1957 Florence sold the site and bought rural property ten miles east of Waco. Florence made a fateful decision. Whereas Victor's teaching had all pointed toward signs of the new age, she actually set the date for April 22, 1959. The mass mailings from Mt. Carmel carried the prediction and called for the faithful to gather at New Mt. Carmel in March, 1959. People sold houses and businesses in California, Washington, Canada, South Carolina, and elsewhere to gather for the great event. By mid-April, eight hundred to nine hundred people had gathered to await a sign of the beginning of the end: Restoration of the true church, a war in the mid-East, or the establishment of a Davidic kingdom in Israel. Just as the Millerites experienced their Great Disappointment in 1844, so now the Davidians had a disappointment to deal with in their history.

Despite the 1959 Disappointment, the Davidians have survived. They have divided into several autonomous communities, which are scattered throughout the United States (New York, South Carolina, Missouri, and Texas) and the Carribean. In 1992 a group of Jamaican Davidians purchased a vacated Presbyterian church on the site of the original Mount Carmel in Waco, where they have once again established a printing press in order to distribute Houteff's message. Meanwhile, in 1955, after the death of Houteff, Ben Roden had organized an alternative group—the Branch Davidians. This group flourished in the wake of the 1959 fiasco, and contended for the new Mt. Carmel property. They remained there under the leadership of the Rodens—Ben (1955–78), Lois (1978–85), and George (1985–87)–and Vernon Howell (1987–93), who took the name David Koresh. Despite a disastrous fire in 1993 in which eighty-one of them perished, the Branch Davidians returned to the site in September, 1994.

The Davidians draw deeply from the Judeo-Christian tradition as articulated by the Seventh-day Adventists, including the second advent of Christ, Sabbath worship and dietary regulations. Many of the Davidians did not eat meat, but often did use milk and dairy products. The seventh-day tradition teaches that the Ten Commandments were nowhere abrogated in scripture. Instead, the church made the mistake of shifting to Sunday. Part of the Adventist message is to call all Christians back to observing the fourth commandment. But the central message is the imminent return of Christ. This doctrine gained intense interest and wide following in the 1840s when William Miller predicted its literal fulfillment for 1844; Ellen White reinterpreted the message and provided the foundation for a viable denomination.

Houteff's fascination with the return of Christ led him to search for the time that it would occur and to prepare the church for the event. The imminent return of Christ was the all-consuming idea of his life and of the Davidian experience. Houteff believed that events in history provided signs of the end of time predicted in the Bible. The scriptures therefore held the key to knowing the future—if the code could be deciphered. Houteff spent countless hours reading the prophets, Daniel and Revelation, and the works of Ellen White in order to match current developments in society and the church with Biblical warnings and predictions. He used the analogy of a scroll being unrolled and new passages being read; he argued that through his teachings God was revealing "present truth" never before known. He did not set the date of the new age, but he created a logo for the movement which was a picture of a clock set near 11:00; according to his conviction, humanity was in its last hour.

Not only must one search for the truth about the future; one must prepare for the great event. But in Houteff's view, the great event could never take place, given the condition of the church. Adventism had fallen prey to worldliness: Members were devoting themselves to movies and parties and adopting worldly dress. Houteff was particularly hard on ministers and those who trained them because they relied on their formal education rather than on true knowledge of prophecy. He called them blind leaders of the blind. He likened the Seventh-day Adventist church to the lukewarm Laodiceans described in the third chapter of Revelation. The only hope was to send a message of reform to the church and work for 144,000 elect (about half of the Seventh-day population when he announced his message) who would come out of the compromised church and follow his leadership. Christ's church must be pure before Christ will return.

The Davidians set an example for all Adventists. They lived simply, set apart from the world. They did not intermarry with non-Davidians; several divorced, choosing commitment to belief over devotion to spouse. Davidians were not allowed to play miniature golf, go to movies, or engage in competitive activities. Women's dress lengths and hair styles were regulated.

Houteff wrote *The Leviticus of the Davidians*, the constitution of the group. Houteff was president, his wife was secretary, and his mother-in-law was treasurer. Houteff held veto power over all decisions in the community. A former member described his personality as domineering. But the chief source of his authority was the belief of the community that he was a prophet who was revealing new truths to them. It was this belief which inspired the community to work sacrificially for their common goal. This precedent was critical for the Davidian tradition. They would henceforth always defer to their leaders who assumed the role of a prophet or messiah who interpreted scriptural text to the community.

Despite organizing in the midst of the Depression, the community succeeded in meeting its basic needs. They grew food, and built housing, dining, and meeting facilities which they connected with an underground network of tunnels. They built a dam and created a water supply system. They brought electricity and a telephone into the community and had selected newspaper articles read aloud during meals. The Davidians created their own school, but were especially concerned that members have useful skills. All of the children were expected to work and were taught trades. Several of the adults took jobs away from the community to provide cash. The Davidians even created their own monetary system (of paper bills and cardboard coins), which could be used only at Mt. Carmel.

The economy was not an end in itself. The Davidians worked hard, but they devoted much energy and time to regular worship on Friday and Saturday. In addition, they observed daily morning devotions. Each evening Houteff provided detailed exegesis of biblical passages. In this setting, his purpose was primarily instructional. He continuously elucidated the text to his followers.

The Mount Carmel community supported sixty to seventy followers for a generation. Davidians worked to increase their following in Adventist churches. The gathering of about nine hundred followers in 1959 is a measure of its size and influence among Adventists.

Houteff's plan was to produce tracts in the hundreds of thousands, locate Adventists and disseminate his ideas in print. He therefore worked out his exegetical studies, secured assistance in polishing his English, and published his ideas. The focal point of the community became the press. The other activities supported the publication of Houteff's message. The tracts were pocket-sized, 70 to 120 pages long, and were illustrated. Houteff was prolific. The *Shepherd's Rod* conveyed his original ideas, and he produced hundreds of additional pages of biblical exegesis. The *Symbolic Code* is equally extensive. Its earliest issues were filled with reports of people convinced by the Davidian message. Houteff's writings remain a powerful legacy in the Davidian community.

The Davidians created mailing lists, set forth their ideas in Sabbath schools and camps, and in the mid-1950s bought a fleet of cars to facilitate their outreach effort. They converted people from diverse ethnic and national origins. The tracts were produced almost exclusively in English, however, and converts were therefore English-speaking.

The Davidians at old Mt. Carmel are still reprinting the Houteff tracts in their original format, and the Salem Davidians have recently published two massive volumes of reprinted materials under the titles *The Shepherd's Rod Series* (1990) and *The Symbolic Code Series* (1992). Current Davidians are divided, but they all appeal to Houteff; his writings assure his position as the key figure in the movement.

The Davidians are no strangers to controversy. Much of the opposition they have faced has come from the Seventh-day Adventist General Conference. Houteff's ideas were reviewed after he began his teaching in 1929 and the church disfellowshipped him in 1930. He continued to try to persuade Adventists to hear his message. Other denominations would not have the framework of interpretation to follow his arguments. His entire message was directed to Adventists. When it was clear that he was officially rejected, he wrote repeatedly in his tracts that readers must make up their own minds—as followers of Luther and other reformers were compelled to do—and not to listen to Adventist preachers who were deceiving them. In the early and mid-1950s, Houteff organized a particularly aggressive missionary campaign. The General Conference of Seventh-day Adventists Committee on Defense Literature therefore turned its attention to him and produced *Some Teachings of the Shepherd's Rod Explained* (1956). And again, following the failed prediction of 1959 the Research Committee of the General Conference of Seventh-day Adventists produced another critique of the group in *Report of a Meeting Between a Group of Shepherd's Rod Leaders and a Group of General Conference Ministers* (1960).

Houteff's presence held the Davidians together, but when he died in 1955 Ben Roden emerged as leader of a new wing which he called the Branch Davidians. Florence Houteff's failed prediction discredited her leadership, and she resigned. The Davidians temporarily dissolved their organization, but splinter groups arose in the early 1960s, seeking control of the land and claiming leadership of the movement. Davidians and Branch Davidians persist today. They both find their common roots in the classic era of Victor and Florence Houteff, 1929–1959.

*—WILLIAM L. PITTS*

**BRANCH SEVENTH-DAY ADVENTISTS.** The Branch SDAs were one of several splinters which broke with the main body of Davidic SDAs following Victor Houteff's death. The name comes from Benjamin Roden's warning to "get off the dead Rod and move into a living Branch." This faction rejected Florence Houteff as leader or prophet. In 1958, Benjamin Roden and his wife Lois visited Israel, established a commune, occupied the site briefly and urged followers to consider relocating there. The commune there soon failed.

Florence Houteff, despite strong internal opposition from Davidian leaders, prophesied that on April 22, 1959, God would directly intervene in Palestine and remove both Jews and Arabs in preparation for the establishment of the Davidic empire. Davidians believed that only God's chosen faithful would avoid being destroyed at the time the new kingdom was established. Many members believed that Victor Houteff would be resurrected at this time to assume leadership of the city of God. Due to the prophecy, group membership swelled to 1,500. Between 500 and 1,000 believers sold their homes and possessions and moved to Waco in 1959 in anticipation of the end of time.

When Mrs. Houteff's prophecy did not come about, widespread disillusionment occurred among the members. The faithful began to scatter and form splinter groups. Many of Florence Houteff's former followers joined the Branch SDAs. The remaining association divided into two groups, one led by Florence Houteff and the other led by editor M. J. Bingham, which strongly opposed Houteff's prophetic speculations. A year later only fifty members remained at Mt. Carmel.

The same year that Florence Houteff's prophecy failed, Vernon Howell (who would later change his name to David Koresh) was born to a single mother in Houston, Texas. He lived with his grandmother during the first five years of this life until his mother remarried. Continuous academic problems apparently created by a learning disability troubled his early school years.

Pressure from the Bingham faction of the church led to Mrs. Houteff's decision to discontinue her leadership of the association in December of 1961. The leaders and members who desired to continue the association reorganized in 1961 in Los Angeles, taking the name Davidian Seventh-day Adventist Association. They moved to Riverside, California, where they remained until 1970.

In 1962 Florence Houteff stunned her few remaining followers with the announcement that her teachings contained errors. Shortly after this announcement she closed the new center, declared the Davidic SDAs dissolved, moved away, and sold most of the Mt. Carmel property. Florence Houteff's failed prophecy presented Benjamin Roden with another opportunity to lead the church. Within a short time, the fifty-seven-year-old Roden won the loyalty of most of the remaining Davidians, gained legal control over the remaining seventy-seven acres of Mt. Carmel property and renamed the group the General Association of Davidian Seventh-day Adventists (GADSA). Roden saw his mission as creating a Christlike moral character in the ranks of the faithful. He taught that the Second Coming would occur soon after the members had attained sufficient moral rectitude.

In 1970 one segment of the Davidians in Riverside, California, moved to Missouri as the Davidian Seventh-day Adventist Association and another moved to Salem, South Carolina, as the General Association of Davidian Seventh-day Adventists. The 549-acre tract in Missouri contains an administration building, an apartment complex, several houses, a printing plant, a 300-seat auditorium, a cafeteria complex, and a ministerial school.

Also in, 1970 Benjamin Roden announced a spiritual vision of the beginning of the rule of God on earth and announced himself the successor to the biblical King David. He granted the power to name the successor to GADSA leadership in the chairman of the executive council, a position Roden himself held, and he installed his son George as second in command and heir apparent.

Meanwhile, Vernon Howell dropped out of high school in 1974 before completing the tenth grade. His passions as a teenager were playing guitar and studying the Bible. He memorized long sections of the New Testament, preaching to anyone who would listen. In the years that followed, he held a succession of short-term, menial jobs, devoting most of his attention to playing the guitar and restoring cars.

Benjamin Roden's wife Lois began having spiritual visions in 1977. She first announced that the Holy Spirit was in fact female and then elaborated on this vision, asserting that God is both male and female and that at the second coming the Messiah would assume female form. Later she founded a magazine, *Shekinah*, as a vehicle for her theological views. This publication continues today as the periodical of the Branch SDAs. Soon after her vision she began intensive scriptural study and subsequently was awarded GADSA ministerial credentials.

On October 22, 1978, Benjamin Roden died. Lois Roden quickly laid claim to GADSA leadership. However, a substantial proportion of GADSA members defected as a result of political infighting and Lois's controversial theological doctrines. George Roden was determined to regain what he believed to be his rightful position as leader of GADSA. He unsuccessfully appealed to Mt. Carmel residents and the courts. The feud between mother and son became so bitter that Lois Roden finally obtained a court order barring George from the Mt. Carmel property.

In 1979, Vernon Howell began participating in study sessions at a Seventh-day Adventist Church in Tyler, Texas, that his mother attended. There was a succession of incidents in which he announced that God intended for him to marry the pastor's daughter, continually preached his own version of SDA theology to other church members, and took over the pulpit to propound his own theological views.

Howell learned of the Branch Davidians from an SDA friend and began working as a handyman at Mt. Carmel in 1981. He became a favorite of sixty-seven-year-old Lois Roden. Rumors began circulating that the two were lovers. The relationship elevated Howell's status with the group and gained for Lois Roden an ally in her struggle with her son. Vernon Howell and George Roden competed for power, both claiming divine inspiration and revelations.

Vernon Howell was finally disfellowshipped by the Seventh-day Adventist Church in 1983. Lois Roden attempted to resolve the power struggle between her son and Vernon Howell by naming Howell as her successor and inviting Branch Davidian adherents to come to Mt. Carmel to listen to his teachings and prophecies. Howell was able to attract young adults to the group due to his own youthful demeanor and his musical and automotive interests. This was something that the Rodens had been unable to do. Converts point to Howell's biblical knowledge more than any other single factor in explaining their own attraction to the Branch Davidians.

In 1984 Vernon Howell married fourteen-year-old Rachael Jones, whose father Perry Jones was one of the most senior and respected members of the Davidian community, having been an early and loyal follower of Benjamin and Lois Roden. Over the next five years the couple gave birth to a son, Cyrus, and a daughter, Star.

The Branch Davidians recruited both nationally and internationally, travelling to Hawaii, Canada, England, Israel, and Australia. Efforts at street recruiting had been unsuccessful, so the recruitment campaigns continued to target current or former Seventh-day Adventists. Branch Davidians were willing to disrupt church services to gain a hearing for their messages. Those converted were usually disfellowshipped by the SDA. The recruitment campaigns yielded several dozen converts and created an international, interracial community of about one hundred at Mt. Carmel.

George Roden organized and won an election for the presidency of the Branch Davidians in 1985, after which he ousted Howell and his followers at gunpoint from Mt. Carmel and renamed the community Rodenville. Howell and his few dozen followers, half of whom were children, obtained property in the Texas community of Palestine, about one hundred miles from Waco. They constructed crude structures and eked out a precarious existence.

In 1986 Lois Roden died. However, only two or three dozen residents remained at Mt. Carmel and Vernon Howell now had the loyalty of most of the community. The Branch Davidians' financial position deteriorated to the point that they were unable to pay school and property taxes on Mt. Carmel. The 1979 injunction Lois Roden had obtained against George remained in effect, so the Vernon Howell faction started proceedings to have George Roden found in contempt of court and displace him at Mt. Carmel. In retaliation, George Roden filed a series of legal motions and suits against Vernon Howell that were filled with such profanities that the justices issued contempt citations against Roden.

George Roden, in an effort to assert spiritual supremacy over Howell, proposed a spiritual contest to see which of the two men could raise a woman who had died twenty years earlier at Mt. Carmel from the dead. Vernon Howell declined the challenge. Instead, on November 3, 1987, Vernon Howell and a group of followers infiltrated the Mt. Carmel center seeking a photograph of the remains of the woman that would serve as evidence to prosecute Roden. A gun battle ensued between George Roden and Vernon Howell in which Roden was slightly wounded. Roden filed charges of attempted murder against Vernon Howell, but they were dismissed. Roden, however, was imprisoned for violating earlier restraining orders and for continuing to file profanity-filled legal suits and motions. The day after George's incarceration, Vernon Howell and his followers reoccupied Mt. Carmel. Shortly thereafter, Howell convinced a well-to-do Branch Davidian family to pay the back taxes on the property.

In 1987, Vernon Howell began taking "spiritual wives" from among the young, unmarried women in the group. In most cases, Koresh received the blessing of the parents either before or after the relationship commenced. For example, Howell received permission from Australian Branch Davidians Bruce and Lisa Gent to begin a sexual relationship with their nineteen-year-old daughter Nicole. Howell later expanded these relationships to include the wives of male Branch Davidian adherents. He requested permission to initiate sexual relations with Lisa Gent, and Bruce and Lisa both assented after considerable deliberation. Some members felt unable to go along with Howell's demands in this area and left the group.

Vernon Howell enunciated his controversial "New Light" doctrine in 1989. He asserted that as a messiah, he became the perfect mate of all the female adherents. Part of his mission was to create a new lineage of God's children from his own seed. These children would ultimately rule the world. The New Light Doctrine made all female Branch Davidians spiritual wives to Koresh. Koresh said that male adherents would be united with their perfect mates in heaven. The doctrine had the effect of annulling the spousal sexual exclusivity of all marriages within the church.

In 1990 Vernon Howell legally adopted the name David Koresh. "Koresh" is Hebrew for Cyrus, the Persian king who defeated the Babylonians five hundred years before the birth of Jesus. In biblical language, Koresh is *a* (not *the*) messiah, one appointed to carry out a special mission for God. By taking the first name David, he asserted his spiritual descendency from the biblical King David. By 1992, Koresh increasingly concluded that the apocalypse would occur in America rather than Israel, and the group began adopting a survivalist outlook, stockpiling large amounts of food, weapons, ammunition, and fuel. Koresh renamed the Mt. Carmel community "Ranch Apocalypse."

By 1993 more than one-third of the population at Ranch Apocalypse was children due to the concentration of the adult population in the twenty- to forty-five-year-old range. Black, Mexicans, and Asians comprised half of the community. Most were Americans but there were also British, Australian, Canadian, Jamaican, and Filipino members. Some of the men held paying jobs in the local manufacturing plants and several of the women worked as nurses in local hospitals. Members who worked outside the community contributed their wages and older members turned over their food stamps and Social Security checks. Well-to-do members gave money and sometimes property to the group. Members attempted to be as self-sufficient as possible, growing their own food and even making some of their own clothing. The community also operated an automobile repair/renovation enterprise. Member Paul Fatta operated a weapons business which purchased guns and hunting-related products by mail and sold them at gun shows.

On an average day at the Waco community, members rose around 6 A.M. and congregated in the communal dining room for breakfast. During the day men and women devoted their energy to paid work and activities necessary to sustain the community such as building, gardening, and child rearing. At times children were educated in local schools; at others they were home-schooled within the community. Following dinner there were regular Bible study periods that sometimes lasted well into the night. Morning and afternoon study sessions were sometimes held as well. Devotional activity was at the center of community life. Living conditions were primitive. The buildings lacked central heating and air conditioning and most indoor plumbing. Members were forced to pump water from a well on the grounds and remove waste from the buildings on a daily basis.

The Branch Davidians retained a biblical base for teachings, but the Bible was supplemented, and in certain respects supplanted, by revelations of the living prophet. They observed a Saturday sabbath and eschewed meat, alcohol, caffeine, and tobacco. They rejected ostentatious dress and grooming, birthday celebrations and television viewing. Koresh taught that Christ had died only for those who lived prior to his crucifixion. Koresh's mission was to permit the salvation of all subsequent generations. In contrast to Christ, who was sinless and therefore an impossible role model, Koresh was a "sinful messiah." Koresh taught that human sinfulness does not prevent humans from attaining salvation. Koresh informed his followers that Armageddon would begin in the United States with an attack on the Branch Davidians.

Accusations of misbehavior on the part of Koresh and some other residents of the Branch Davidian headquarters began to circulate among anticultists and others. The accusations were those frequently used against many unconventional religions by their opponents. The most frequent accusations alleged child abuse and possession of firearms. Local authorities investigated the child abuse allegations and found them groundless. The federal Bureau of Alcohol, Tobacco, and Firearms (ATF) of the Department of the Treasury obtained search and arrest warrants on the weapons charges.

On February 28, 1993, a force of seventy-six ATF agents raided the Branch Davidian compound. The raid turned into a shoot-out between federal agents and Branch Davidians who chose to defend themselves. The resulting standoff turned into a fifty-one-day siege that ended on April 19 when federal agents launched a new attack on the Davidian complex. Agents of the federal government used military equipment to batter holes in buildings through which they injected noxious gas in an attempt to force the Davidians outside. A fire ignited in the buildings and over eighty members died. Some of the surviving members of the group were tried for the murder of the four federal agents who were shot in the original raid. They were found innocent of the most serious charges.

The surviving Branch Davidians for the most part continue to adhere to their faith, although they have not at this writing regrouped into a single organization. Other groups of the Davidian movement, resulting from schisms previously mentioned, continue their work also. The largest is the Davidian Seventh-day Adventist Association, which was established following Florence Houteff's failed prophecy of 1959 and was never related to the leadership of David Koresh. This group is headquartered near Exeter, Missouri, and numbers several thousand.

The Davidian Seventh-day Adventist Association accepts all of the fundamental beliefs of the Seventh-day Adventist church. The association is dedicated to the work of announcing and bringing forth the restoration of the Kingdom of David. Most of the members also hold membership in the Seventh-day Adventist church and a separate census of Davidian Seventh-day Adventist Association members is not kept.

# 5    CONTROVERSIAL CHRISTIAN GROUPS

**A**LAMO  CHRISTIAN  FOUNDATION  (THE MUSIC SUARE CHURCH). The Alamo (pronounced ah-LAH-mo) Christian Foundation was opened in 1969 in Hollywood, California, by Tony and Susan Alamo. It is a Pentecostal church with doctrine similar to the Assemblies of God. It accepts the authority of the King James Version of the Bible and places its emphasis upon the preaching of Jesus Christ as the son of the Living God who died for humanity. The church adheres to a strict moral code and members condemn drugs, homosexuality, adultery, and abortions.

Susan Alamo was born Edith Opal Horn. She was raised as a Jew and grew up in Alma, Arkansas, but became an independent Pentecostal minister. She converted Tony Alamo (born Bernie Lazar Hoffman, also formerly Jewish) and married him. In the 1960s Susan and Tony Alamo began a ministry in Hollywood. They opened the Tony and Susan Alamo Christian Foundation there in 1969. The church became known as one segment of the Jesus People movement.

In the early 1970s the Alamo Christian Foundation became quite controversial and was heavily criticized because of the format its ministry had developed. Church members generally worked the streets of Hollywood inviting potential converts to evening services. The church had by this time been established at Saugus, a rural community approximately an hour's distance from Hollywood. The mostly young recruits were taken by bus to Saugus for an evangelistic meeting and meal. Many of those who did convert remained in Saugus to be taught the Bible and become lay ministers.

The church moved its headquarters in 1976 to Alma, Arkansas, where Susan Alamo had grown up. There it developed a community of several hundred members and established printing facilities, a school, and a large tabernacle. As part of its rehabilitation program it began to develop several businesses in which members, many of whom were former drug addicts, could begin a process of reintegration into society. As the organization expanded further, churches were opened in cities around the country, including Nashville, Chicago, Brooklyn, and Miami Beach.

The church has developed as an ordered community of people dedicated to evangelism. Converts who wish to receive the church's training and participate in its ministry take a vow of poverty, agreeing to turn over all their real property to the church. In return, the church agrees to provide the necessities of life (housing, clothes, food, medical assistance) and the education of children through high school. The church is headed by a three-person board presided over by the pastor. The church's first pastor was Susan Alamo. Upon her death in 1982, she was succeeded by Tony Alamo. The board sets the policy and direction for the ministry.

Approximately half of the members of the church reside on church property near Alma. Others reside at the several church centers around the United States. The headquarters complex includes housing for the members, a Christian school for grades one through twelve, a large community dining hall and offices. Periodically members are sent out on evangelistic tours around the United States, frequently using the established church centers as bases of operation. Services are held daily at each of the church centers and generally free meals are served.

The church publishes a variety of evangelistic tracts which are passed out in the street and are mailed out as requested. The church also distributes numerous tapes of sermons by Susan and Tony Alamo. Members include a number of talented musicians and the church has produced a set of records and tapes featuring Tony Alamo and other members. A national television ministry was begun in the 1970s but has been largely discontinued.

In 1981 Music Square Church was incorporated. It superseded the foundation in 1982. To support itself, the communal-style church developed a number of businesses. A number of former members who later aligned themselves with the anticult movement complained that they should have been paid at least minimum wage for their work hours while members. These complaints led to a series of lawsuits.

In 1985 the IRS stripped the Music Square Church of its tax-exempt status. The church went to court to fight this decision. In 1988 Tony Alamo was accused of beating the eleven-year-old son of a member. Charges were filed and Alamo disappeared. During the next three years, while a series of court battles were being carried out in various jurisdictions, Alamo became a fugitive from justice. During this time, he moved about the country, frequently making calls to talk shows and even dropping into public offices for visits. Meanwhile, the church's property in Arkansas was seized to pay off court judgements against the organization. Tony Alamo was arrested in July of 1991. The current status of the church, whose membership as of 1988 was approximately four hundred, is questionable.

**BODY OF CHRIST.** The Body of Christ was founded by former Marine Jimmie T. Roberts in 1970. Roberts was the son of a Pentecostal minister who came to believe that the mainline churches had become too worldly. Following Bible passages which called on believers to separate themselves from worldliness, Roberts wished to create a following similar to the disciples who moved around the countryside with Jesus, who traveled as he preached. He began to recruit members for his group in 1970 in Denver, Colorado, and in California.

Members of the group referred to Roberts as Brother Evangelist. The church had a heirarchy of brothers based on their length of time with the group. Women cared for the children and assisted the male members. The group wore a monk-like garb which made them highly visible. The group would gather periodically, divide into groups of two or three, and travel by separate routes to the next designated gathering place. While on the road, the members would witness and preach to any who would listen. During gatherings members would listen to Brother Evangelist preach, sing, and welcome new members. The group had a practice of raiding garbage bins behind restaurants and grocery stores to find free food, which earned them the label "Garbage Eaters." The members bathed infrequently and refused medical treatment.

In 1975, several members of the group were kidnapped in Fayetteville, Arkansas, and deprogrammed. In 1979, the story of a former member, Rachel Martin, was published. The group has since dropped out of sight and its present whereabouts and status are unknown.

**INTERNATIONAL CHURCH OF CHRIST.** International Church of Christ (originally referred to as the Boston Church of Christ) is the name given to a religious movement that began with a single congregation of the larger Church of Christ denomination. It has also been referred to as the Crossroads Movement (actually a distinct movement from which the Boston Movement developed), Multiplying Ministries, the Discipling Movement, and the International Church of Christ.

The Crossroads Movement was begun by Charles H. Lucas, who came to Gainesville, Florida, in 1967 to serve as campus minister for what was then the Fourteenth Street Church of Christ. Campus Advance, as the new campus ministry was called, grew quickly. Two practices were characteristic of the ministry: "soul talks" and "prayer partners." Soul talks were evangelistic group Bible studies with prayer and sharing which were held in student residences. Prayer partners was the practice of pairing up a new Christian with a more mature Christian so that the new Christian could be given one-on-one direction. Both practices emphasized in-depth involvement of members in one another's lives. In 1970 Lucas became pastor of the Fourteenth Street Church of Christ; in 1973 he moved it into new facilities and changed its name to Crossroads Church of Christ.

In 1972, a freshman at the University of Florida, Kip McKean, was converted through Campus Advance. McKean trained at Crossroads while finishing his education at the University of Florida. He left Crossroads and served as campus minister at other mainline Churches of Christ. In 1979, he accepted an invitation to take over as the pulpit and campus ministry of a struggling thirty-member church in a Boston suburb, the Lexington Church of Christ. The church was soon renamed the Boston Church of Christ. Later, it was renamed yet again as the International Church of Christ. Within two years the thirty-member church had grown to a membership of three hundred.

Kip McKean had a vision to establish churches in key metropolitan centers of the world that could in turn evangelize the cities around them. In 1982 the International Church of Christ established churches in Chicago and London and in 1983 in New York City. By 1993 the movement had grown to 42,855 members in 130 congregations worldwide, with 27,055 members and 48 congregations in the United States. The New York and Boston congregations currently have a Sunday morning attendance over 5,000 while the Los Angeles congregation has an attendance of over 4,000. The church believes that it is unscriptural to have more than one congregation per city. Usually a church affiliated with the movement will take the name of the city as its name, such as the Los Angeles Church of Christ or the Chicago Church of Christ.

A typical Sunday morning service of the International Church of Christ consists of singing, praying, preaching, and the Lord's Supper. Members accept the inspiration of the Bible, the virgin birth, the substitutionary atonement, the bodily resurrection of Jesus, the Trinity, and the Second Coming. The movement is exclusivistic, believing that it is virtually impossible to be among the elect outside their ranks. Movement leaders have a vision for converting the entire world by training individual members to be highly evangelistic and submissive to the leadership of the church.

Baptism is by immersion. Members believe that one must first be a disciple first for baptism to be valid. A person baptized in any other religious group is almost always rebaptized upon joining the movement. Often a member who has been previously baptized in the International Church of Christ will decide he or she did not have a proper understanding of baptism at the time of his baptism or that he was not a true disciple at the time of the earlier baptism and will be baptized a second time.

Discipleship is very important to the movement. In the movement, a disciple is one who is faithfully following Christ and has taken on the lifestyle and purpose of making disciples of all nations. Every single member of every congregation is supposed to be committed to making disciples. Any who are not so committed are not disciples themselves and will not be going to heaven.

While the Crossroads members chose their own prayer partners, in the International Church of Christ, the leaders of the congregation arrange for older, stronger Christians to give direction to each of the younger, weaker ones. These partners are always of the same sex and are to have daily contact and weekly meetings. These partnerships are not considered optional. Everyone in the congregation has a partner.

"Soul talks" as started in the Crossroads movement became "Bible talks" in the International Movement. They are held weekly at regular times and places. They are attended by an average of six to ten members. "Bible talks" may be for men or women only, or mixed. Each Bible talk has a leader and assistants who see that the leadership's expectations are met by the members of the group. Members are expected to bring visitors with them.

There is a definite hierarchy in the International Church of Christ, both internationally and within each congregation. There are nine world sectors, each headed by a world sector leader and a World Sector Administrator, who oversees the administration and finances of each world sector. Each individual congregation is usually divided geographically into sectors or quadrants, each with a sector or quadrant leader. Each sector or quadrant is further subdivided into geographical zones and the sector leader oversees the zone leaders. The zone leader oversees the individual Bible talks and Bible talk leaders. Anyone in the position of zone leader or higher is a paid employee of the church.

Very rarely will a congregation affiliated with the movement own a church building. A congregation will typically rent a facility in which to meet on Sunday morning. The money that would have gone toward a church mortgage is funneled into paid staff, the majority of whom are involved directly or indirectly in evangelistic efforts. The Crossroads Church of Christ and the International Church of Christ have severed all ties with each other. The mainline Churches of Christ disavowed the International movement in the mid-1980s and are now ardent opponents of it.

The movement has become the subject of considerable controversy. The controversy mainly centers on the level of commitment that is expected of church members and the authority the church exercises in members' lives. The church's manual for training potential converts, *Making Disciples*, makes it clear that members are expected to put the church above all else, including job, friends, and family. Each week the average member attends at least four or five meetings for worship and/or

Bible study. Numerous universities around the country either restrict or bar movement activities on their campuses. The movement has experienced a few cases of forcible deprogramming of members. A few ex-members have portrayed the movement in a negative light to the media, and two have produced books denouncing the movement. The leadership of the International movement has recognized that abuses of authority have occurred, and it has retracted some of its earlier teachings on authority and submission. Despite the controversy, more people have come into the movement than leave it. The movement is thus far untainted by sexual scandal or financial impropriety.

**MARANATHA CHRISTIAN CHURCHES.** Maranatha Christian Churches began in 1972 as a campus ministry under the direction of Bob Weiner, formerly a youth pastor for the Assemblies of God, and his wife, Ruth Weiner. Bob Weiner dropped out of the Evangelical Free Church's Trinity College at Deerfield, Illinois, and joined the U.S. Air Force. While in the Air Force he encountered Albie Pearson, a former baseball player turned evangelist-pastor, and received the baptism of the Holy Spirit.

Following his discharge from the Air Force, Weiner joined with Bob Cording to form Sound Mind, Inc. to evangelize youth. In 1971 he began to tour college campuses as an evangelist. As a campus minister, Weiner sought to convert students and train them in the fundamentals of the Christian faith.

In 1972 he moved to Paducah, Kentucky, where his wife's father was minister in the United Methodist Church, and began a campus ministry at Murray State University. While focusing on Murray State, he continued to travel as an evangelist and develop other ministries. By 1980 Weiner had established thirty Maranatha Campus Ministries. As members graduated from college, Maranatha Campus Ministries became part of the larger work which was named Maranatha Christian Churches.

In Maranatha's early years, each center had a dorm in which converts could live while attending college, but this is no longer the case. Maranatha's work is still focused in the campus ministry and all of the congregations are adjacent to a college or university. During the early 1980s, a variety of accusations were made against Maranatha Campus Ministries concerning their intense program for training new members. Many of these accusations proved to be unfounded. In other cases program adjustments were made which have ended any controversies. A program of parent-student contact was broadly implemented which reduced the problems which had arisen because of lack of knowledge by parents of Maranatha and the life shared by its new student members.

General meetings of the fellowship are held weekly and most members also participate in small group fellowships. Maranatha Christian Churches are Pentecostal in doctrine. Prophecy is an important practice and is seen as ongoing confirmation of God's present activity in the church. Bob and Rose Weiner have written a series of books published by Maranatha Publications which are used as textbooks in the discipleship training work.

Maranatha Leadership Institute in Gainesville, Florida, offers more advanced training for people on a national basis. It often features a variety of charismatic leaders not otherwise associated with Maranatha. A world leadership conference is held every two years. In 1985, Maranatha began a satellite TV network show as a televised prayer meeting in which sixty churches tied together for the broadcast pray for specific requests phoned in by viewers. There are 7,000 members worldwide and 150 churches in the United States.

THE TWELVE TRIBES. The Twelve Tribes is a communal, utopian society that emerged from the Jesus People Revival in 1972 under the leadership of Elbert Eugene ("Gene") Spriggs, whom the community members consider an apostle, and his wife, Marsha, in Chattanooga, Tennessee. It has gone by a number of different names in the past, including the Messianic Communities and the Northeast Kingdom Community Church. It has also been referred to as the Island Pond Community. Members adopt Hebrew names and consider themselves as part of the Commonwealth of Israel forming in the last days, bound by the New Covenant in Messiah's Blood, as mentioned in Ephesians 2:12. The communities have evolved into a distinct culture emphasizing craftsmanship and handiwork; they have evolved their own devotional music and dance forms and unique, neoconservative patterns of marriage and childrearing. The group condemns abortion and homosexuality and upholds monogamy, premarital chastity, and home schooling.

Spriggs, the son of a factory quiller and scoutmaster, was born in Chattanooga, Tennessee, and was brought up Methodist. In 1971 he became involved in the Jesus movement through Marineth Chapel and Center Theater in Glendale, California. By 1972 he and his wife opened up their residence in East Ridge, a suburb of Chattanooga, to young spiritual seekers and the poor and homeless and held coffee house meetings, which attracted "Jesus freaks" and hippies as well as "straight" Christian youth. Emulating the early Christians in sharing all things in common, after Acts 2:37–47, the group bought and renovated five old Victorian houses on Vine Street and opened up the Yellow Deli, a health food bakery and sandwich restaurant. Its menus stated, "Our specialty is the fruit of the spirit. Why not ask?" Around this time they began baking and serving wholegrain bread, which symbolized the Gospel of Jesus—real spiritual food as opposed to the lifeless "White Bread Jesus" found in mainline churches. Originally the group attended the Sunday services of different denominations, but when they arrived at church one Sunday to find the service cancelled because of the Superbowl, they turned their backs on conventional religion and began developing their own worship, gathering on Friday evening to welcome the Sabbath and on Saturday to break bread and celebrate the Messiah's resurrection.

Receiving an invitation from a Christian fellowship in Island Pond, Vermont, which wished to emulate their communal life, and discouraged by the declining response in Chattanooga, the group sold all their property and moved to Island Pond in 1979. In Chattanooga the households were centralized with "one big business, one office, one set of needs," but on moving to Island Pond they formed independent communes, each household specializing in its own cottage industry: A cobbler shop, printshop, candle-making factory, and a futon shop. Many members left after the first winter, discouraged by the cold and financial hardship, but the group opened up the Common Sense Restaurant and attracted new members. The Basin Farm Community, near Bellows Falls, Vermont, cultivates vegetables, grains, and strawberries to supply its sister communities in New England.

The belief system is compatible with evangelical Protestantism, but contains certain theological innovations in their views on communal living, marriage, and eschatology. Ongoing collective revelations continue to unveil the community's unique role in their postmillenialist vision of the last days, their relationship to Yahshua, and levels of salvation after Judgment. The communities define themselves as the lost and scattered tribes of the ancient Jews undergoing restoration in preparation for eternal life. They believe their community is undergoing a process of purification as the "pure and Spotless Bride" awaiting her Bridegroom, and that it will probably take three generations to be ready for the Second Coming. By increasing their ranks through conversions and childbearing, they are "raising up a people" in preparation for the Jubilee horn that heralds the return of Yahshua.

Since relocating in Island Pond, the group has developed an elaborate ritual life. Public "gatherings" are held on Friday and Saturday night (the Jewish Sabbath and the eve of the First Day), which feature circle dancing, devotional songs, spontaneous speaking and stories for the children. The public is also invited to their weddings, which dramatize the community's millenarian expectations: the Bride, representing the community, prepares herself for the call of the groom, her "King."

The church numbers around 1,500, and roughly half of the members are children. Communities have been established in Parana, Brazil; Navarreaux, France; Auckland, New Zealand; and Winnipeg, Canada, but the majority of members live in New England, mainly in Vermont or in Boston, Massachusetts. In 1993, the community in Island Pond, Vermont, numbered fifteen households. By 1994 it had shrunk to five, as families moved to Bellows Falls, Rutland, Burlington, Vermont, to Rhode Island, and to Hyannis, Massachusetts, in order to set up new communities.

Each local community is "covered" by a council of male elders (one from each household) and decision-making appears to be a collective process based on hearing from the brothers and sisters "what's on their heart," then consulting the Bible and group prayer. Under the elders an informal hierarchy of teachers, deacons, deaconesses, and shepherds is formed. Women wear head scarves "in church" or at the "gatherings" and meetings to demonstrate their submission to their husbands and the male elders who, in turn, are "covered" by "Our Master." The Spriggs, childless with no fixed abode, travel among the Communities offering counsel and inspiration and tend to maintain a low-key presence which fosters local self-sufficiency.

The community distributes the *Freepaper* to disseminate its religious message and invite the reader to become part of the "body of the Messiah." Evangelical efforts are organized for the Grateful Dead's concerts, the Billy Graham Crusade and the Rainbow Gathering, as well as county fairs and flea markets. Husband and wife teams will drive up in the community's famous double-decker bus, distribute *Freepapers*, perform Israeli dances to the rhythm of hand-made celtic instruments, and offer home-baked bread and cookies. "Walkers" are sent out on hitchhiking preaching tours. A recent trend has been for several married couples to move to a new city, get odd jobs and set up Way Out Houses—temporary communal homes— in order to model "a small demonstration of the life" to potential converts.

Church members have been the target of deprogrammers ever since the founding of communes in Chattanooga, but the most severe and widely publicized conflicts with secular authorities have involved child-beating allegations and child custody disputes. In 1984 the Vermont State Police, armed with a court order and accompanied by fifty Social Services workers, raided the Island Pond Community homes and took 112 children into custody. District Judge Frank Mahady ruled that the search warrant issued by the state was unconstitutional, and all the children were returned to their parents without undergoing examinations. Child custody disputes and investigations by Social Services continue, partly due to the influence of the anticult movement and disillusioned apostates. The group's commitment to their biblically based disciplinary practices are the primary focus of concern. Parents are instructed to discipline children who do not obey upon "first command" with a thin, flexible "reed-like" rod (as mentioned in Proverbs 23:13) so as to inflict pain but not injury.

Since their "deliverance" from the "raid" the group has emphasized cooperation with state authorities and has reached out to neighbors in trying to foster a better understanding. In August 1993 the Island Pond members joined search parties to find the missing pilot whose plane had crashed in Essex County. On June 25, 1994, the church held a ten-year anniversary celebration "to commemorate [our] deliverance from the 1984 Island Pond Raid." Many of those 112 children, now in their teens and twenties, shared their traumatic memories of the raid, denied allegations of abuse and declared their allegiance toward their parents and their community.

*—Susan J. Palmer*

**THE LOCAL CHURCH.** The Local Church, also known as the Little Flock, was founded in the 1920s in China by Ni Shu-tsu, popularly known as Watchman Nee (1903–1972). The group affirms the unity of the church, the corporate nature of church life, and the direct headship of Christ over the church. It sees itself as simply "the Church," since Nee's movement took no name by which to be denominated, and the term "local church" is a convenient designation rather than a name.

Born into a Chinese Christian family, Nee changed his name Ni Shu-tsu into To-Sheng, meaning that he was a bell-ringer with the purpose of raising up people for God. After being converted by Dora Yu, a Methodist evangelist, he began working with the independent missionary Margaret E. Barber, who introduced him to the writings of John Nelson Darby and the exclusive Plymouth Brethren. He became the leader of a small group of evangelical Christians, which soon spread throughout China. During the 1930s, he traveled to a number of cities where he founded congregations. He was convinced that there should be only one local church—only one congregation—in each city as the basic expression of the unity of Christianity. Nee's view of the church can be found in his numerous books on Christian life and church life, the most famous of which is *The Normal Christian Church Life*. Among other books is *The Spiritual Man*, in which Nee described his view of the tripartite nature of human beings as body, soul, and spirit.

Upon the rise of the new People's Republic of China to power in 1949, Nee was accused of being a spy for the Americans and the Nationalist government. After being exiled from Shanghai, in 1952 he was sent to prison, where he died in 1972. Among Nee's followers was the former Protestant minister Witness Lee, founder and elder of the church at Chefoo. He had joined Nee in the ministry in 1932, and after a three-year absence fighting tuberculosis, he rejoined Nee in full time work in 1948. He was eventually sent to Taiwan, where the church flourished.

The movement spread around the Pacific Basin, and was brought to the West Coast of the United States by migrating members. Lee himself moved to the United States, where he founded Living Stream Ministry, and has led the spread of the Local Church.

The writings of Watchman Nee and Witness Lee are summarized in a booklet titled "Beliefs and Practices of the Local Churches." The Local

Church believes in fundamental Christianity, similar to that of the Plymouth Brethren, affirming its faith in the Trinity, the deity of Christ, the virgin birth of Jesus, His second coming, as well as the verbal inspiration of the Bible. It emphasizes the unity of the church—the Body of Christ—and the oneness of all believers, whereas it rejects sectarianism, denominationalism, and interdenominationalism. The Local Church considers itself part of a history of recovery of the biblical church, a history of the restoration of the life and unity of the church that began with Martin Luther and the Protestant Reformation. This recovery continued through Count Zinzendorf and the Moravians, John Wesley and the Methodists, the Plymouth Brethren, and finally through the local churches, in which the practice of church life according to the Scripture is being finally and fully restored.

Among the practices of the Local Church is the so-called burning, denoting a close contact with God, since a person impressed by another with the message of the Gospel is seen as having been "burned." By this practice objects symbolic of a person's pre-Christian life or of a phase of lesser commitment are destroyed in a fire. "Burying," on the other hand, means rebaptism, through which a newer level of Christian commitment is achieved. Members of the Local Church may be baptized more than once.

Lee brought innovation to the church by introducing a number of theological emphases as well as new practices such as "pray reading," and "calling upon the name of the Lord." "Pray reading" is a devotional practice using the words of Scripture as the words of prayer. During this practice, which is supposed to allow the Scripture to impart an experience of the presence of God in the person praying, people repeat words and phrases from the Scripture over and over, often interjecting words of praise and thanksgiving. "Calling upon the name of the Lord," on the other hand, represents an invocation of God by the repetition of phrases such as "O Lord Jesus." Both these practices have been subjects of controversy.

A controversy emerged in the 1970s between the Local Church and some members of the larger Evangelical Christian community who regarded the theological innovations of Lee as departing from acceptable Evangelical thought. This controversy culminated in a series of legal actions in the mid-1980s. A number of anticult writers accused the Local Church of heresy and attacked its unique forms of Christian piety. The lawsuits instituted by the Local Church brought retractions and apologies from all organizations except the Spiritual Counterfeits Project, which had published the book *The God-Men*, attacking the church. This case went to trial, and in 1985 a financial settlement was ordered against the Spiritual Counterfeits Project.

The Local Church, which is organized as a fellowship of autonomous congregations, stresses the importance of church life, meeting together, and the responsibility of each member to keep alive his or her relationship with God and to share the duties of congregational life. Each congregation is led by a small group of elders, who teach, preach, and administer the church's temporal affairs. A small number of men have an apostolic function and start new congregations in those cities where the Local Church has not yet arrived. The largest number of congregations is found in the Pacific rim countries, although there are also churches in Europe, Africa, Australia, and New Zealand. It has initiated evangelical work in Eastern Europe and Russia, and congregations have survived intense persecutions in China, where the church has spread over the last decades.

**JESUS PEOPLE USA.** Jesus People USA (also known as JPUSA, pronounced Je-POO-sa) is an evangelical Christian communitarian group centered in Chicago. Originating within the Jesus Movement of the early 1970s, the group has continued to play a dynamic role in Christian youth and alternative/underground cultures through its music, magazine, Jesus festivals, and lifestyle; the group also maintains a sizable inner city ministry.

Jesus People USA began as part of Jesus People Milwaukee, a communal Jesus People group founded by Jim Palosaari in 1971. The following year this original group temporarily divided into three subministries: Jesus People Europe, led by Palosaari, which traveled to Europe to do youth ministry abroad; Jesus People USA, led by John and Dawn Herrin, which traveled the United States; and the original Milwaukee commune. The proposed reunion never occurred, however; the Milwaukee commune disbanded, and Jesus People Europe returned to the United States to form the basis for the Highway Missionaries and, later, the Servant Community (both now defunct).

The U.S. branch, after traveling to Florida and back, eventually settled in Chicago where they continued carrying out youth revivals, sponsoring a Christian rock group called the Rez Band, doing street theater and mime work, and publishing a well-produced street paper, *Cornerstone*. During the mid-1970s the community went through a number of changes; several business ventures were started, including moving, painting, contracting, roofing, music recording, and graphics. Founder John Herrin was ejected from the group and plurality of leadership instituted in the form of a council of elders assisted by Dawn Herrin, the ex-wife of the former leader. In addition, the community merged with a communal African American Bible study group, resulting in an interracial presence often lacking in other Jesus People groups.

In 1976 the group was chartered as a church by the Full Gospel Church in Christ, a small California-based Pentecostal body; this continued to 1990, when the group became a part of the Evangelical Covenant Church, a moderately conservative denomination of about 100,000 rooted in Swedish Pietism.

Members hold a Trinitarian evangelical Christian theology, worshipping a personal God having thoughts and emotions. The group professes to believe in the inspiration and inerrancy of the Bible, accepting the Chicago Statement of Biblical Inerrancy, and strongly affirms the doctrines of the Trinity, the historic Fall in the Garden of Eden, and literal views of the virgin birth of Jesus, his death and resurrection, substitutionary atonement, the imminent second coming of Jesus, heaven, hell, Satan, and the Last Judgment. The group also emphasizes individual free will and personal sanctification.

Baptism by immersion is practiced, along with the Lord's Supper, though they are viewed more as ordinances than sacraments. Emphasis is placed instead upon personal holiness and the individual's relationship with God. JPUSA affirms the existence and practice of the supernatural "gifts of the spirit," such as healing and tongue-speaking/glossolalia, though within the group these gifts tend to be employed privately rather than publicly.

In spite of the seemingly exclusivist theological beliefs, the group admits a certain latitude by affirming the spiritual unity of all true believers in Christ; Christian humanist strains are also present due to the community's encouragement of both individual and collective forms of musical, literary, and visual artistic expression.

Presently, Jesus People USA is led by a council of nine mutually accountable pastor/elders. While each is in charge of a particular aspect of the community's ministry, major policy decisions require unanimity among all nine. While the group notes that it is not a democracy, the community in engaged in so many ministries and enterprises that it appears that most members, except for the newest, occupy positions of some responsibility. Members tend to come from all segments of society, especially the counterculture, though presently it appears that the percentage of persons coming from Christian colleges is increasing with time. Presently the group has about five hundred members. About a third of these are young singles, a third married couples, and a third children. The community runs its own private school.

Over the years the group's street paper, *Cornerstone*, has evolved from a tabloid into a glossy four-color magazine with a circulation of about forty thousand. The publication carries articles on a variety of topics, including church history (both Protestant and Catholic), philosophy, Christian apologetics, sexual abuse, and other issues rarely found in material aimed at Christian youth. The magazine is also noteworthy for its exposes of Lauren Stratford and Mike Warnke, each of whom claimed to be participants and victims in a large nationwide underground Satanic conspiracy. Additional JPUSA publications include a small Christian punk magazine, the *Ma-Grr-Zine*, and a series of poetry chapbooks and books on Christian apologetics produced by a small publishing division, Cornerstone Press.

Other Jesus People USA outreaches include Streetlight Theater, a drama group; the Rez Band, a Christian heavy metal rock group; Crashdog, a Christian punk group; a Christian coffeehouse; and a music, art, and teaching festival—also named Cornerstone—attracting about ten thousand participants annually. Presently the community is experimenting with a new ministry, a mobile coffeehouse made out of a converted school bus. In addition to youth-oriented outreaches, the group runs an urban shelter for homeless women and children, a storefront church, and a Crisis Pregnancy Center. The community encourages visitors and provides unpaid internships for those considering careers in Christian magazine production, urban, and youth ministries.

Perhaps in part due to its socially remote location in a run-down region of urban Chicago, its traditional theology, and its openness to visitors, Jesus People USA has generally not been the subject of a great deal of hostile attention; establishmentarian critics such as Lowell Streiker have generally accused the group of having poor artistic taste and a supercilious attitude, but little else. The group has generally enjoyed good relations with local officials, who appear to support the group's efforts at inner-city mission work. The group was instrumental in voting one local alderman out of office when he attempted to convert the region into a local historic district, a move which the community felt would hurt the low-income residents of the area. There was also one case in which a parent accused the community of brainwashing a youth, but the case was decided in favor of the community.

At the time of this writing, however, it appears that the community may be entering into a period of controversy. Within the past three years former members of the community have begun to hold annual reunions; some of these individuals do not recall their time in the community and/or their departure with favor. Some have accused the group's leaders of excessive control of individuals, mismanagement, and nepotism. Others have complained that long-time members who choose to leave should be financially compensated for their time and effort spent on behalf of the community. Many of these complaints are expected to be publicized in a forthcoming book, *Recovering from Churches that Abuse*. The Jesus People USA community has responded by opening their community to even greater public scrutiny, including making public the correspondence dealing with the allegations; the community also dedicated a double issue of its magazine to examining the book's claims.

—*John Bozeman*

**THE WAY INTERNATIONAL, INC.** The Way International, Inc., a Pentecostal, ultradispensational Christian group, was founded in 1942 as a radio ministry under the name "Vesper Chimes." It assumed its present name in 1974, after being renamed the Chimes Hour in 1944, and the Chimes Hour Youth Caravan in 1947.

The Way International was founded by Victor Paul Wierwille (1916–1985), a minister in the Evangelical and Reformed Church. While a student at Mission House College, he decided to enter the ministry. He earned his B.D. at Mission House Seminary, in Minnesota, and did graduate work at the University of Chicago and Princeton Theological Seminary, earning a M.Th. in 1941. After being ordained in 1942, he became pastor of the Church at Paine, from which he moved to Van Wert, Ohio, two years later, to become pastor of St. Peter's E. & R. Church.

During his stay in Van Wert he became an avid student of the Bible, concentrating upon the doctrine of the Holy Spirit. In 1948, he was awarded a Ph.D. by the Pikes Peak Bible College and Seminary, in Manitou Spring, Colorado, and in 1951 he manifested the reception of God's holy spirit and spoke in tongues for the first time.

The first "Power for Abundant Living" (PFAL) class, given in 1953, contained the initial results of his research on biblical truth. After one year, he began to study Aramaic under the influence of Dr. George M. Lamsa, translator of the Lamsa Bible, and began to accept a view of Biblical doctrine which departed more and more from that of his denomination. In 1957 he resigned his ministry from the Evangelical and Reformed Church in order to devote himself full-time to his work. He led his ministry, which was chartered as the Way, Inc. in 1955, and then changed to the Way International in 1975. The headquarters of the Way was established on the family farm outside New Knoxville, Ohio. He retired from leading the ministry full time in 1983.

The Way grew steadily during the 1950s through the initiation of the PFAL classes and *The Way Magazine* (1954). After experiencing a slow growth in the 1960s, the Way underwent a spurt of growth in the 1970s as the ministry suddenly burgeoned at the time of the national Jesus People revival across the United States. In 1971, the Way expanded its facilities at New Knoxville, which hosted the first national Rock of Ages Festival, an annual gathering of Way members.

The Way Corps, a four-year leadership training program, was established, and in 1974 the Way purchased the former Emporia College in Emporia, Kansas, which became The Way College, the home of the Corps. The Word Over the World Ambassador, program which was initiated by Wierwille in 1971, began to send young people affiliated with the Way across the country for a year of witnessing activity.

Wierwille was succeeded as president of the Way by L. Craig Martindale (b. 1948) in 1983, at the fortieth anniversary of The Way's founding. A former football player at the University of Kansas, and president of the Fellowship of Christian Athletes, Martindale joined the Way while in college. He became involved in the work full time after he graduated, and served as the Way state coordinator for Oklahoma (1973–74), international director of the Way Corps (1975–77), and president of the Way College (1977–80). Among the activities of The Way, which considers itself a biblical research, teaching, and household fellowship ministry, have been the establishment of a large Aramaic facility and the training of a group of scholars in the Aramaic language.

An eleven-point statement summarizes the beliefs of the Way, which can be considered both Arian and Pentecostal. It rejects the Trinitarian orthodoxy of most Western Christianity and denies the divinity of Jesus, as emphasized in Wierwille's *Jesus Christ Is Not God* (1975). While believing in the divine conception of Jesus by God, the Way believes that he is the Son of God but not God the Son. The Way also believes in receiving the fullness of the Holy Spirit, the power of God, even though its personality is denied. This view corresponds to Arianism, which has been considered a heretical theology since the condemnation of Arius by the Council of Nicea in 325 C.E. According to the Way, the receiving of the fullness of God's power may be evidenced by the nine manifestations of the Spirit, that is to say speaking in tongues, interpretation of tongues, prophecy, word of knowledge, word of wisdom, discerning of spirits, faith, miracles, and healing.

The Way, like other Grace Gospel churches, teaches a form of dispensationalism known as ultradispensationalism, an approach which views the Scripture as a product of progressive "dispensations" or periods of different administrations of God's relationship to humanity. The Bible story is divided by dispensationalism into seven dispensations: Innocence, Conscience, Government, Promise, Law, Grace, and the Personal Reign of Christ. According to the Way, present believers live under the Church administration that began at Pentecost, a dispensation of grace that will continue until Christ's Second Coming. However, ultradispensationalism believes that there was another dispensation, a period of transition between Easter and the New Testament Church, which was characterized by John's water baptism, whose story is primarily told in the Book of Acts.

The Old Testament, the Four Gospels, the epistles of Hebrews and James, and Acts are regarded as pre-Pentecost scripture, and the Gospels belong to the previous Christ Administration. Paul's later epistles are seen by ultradispensationalism as the prime documents of the dispensation or administration of grace. The Way believes in one baptism, that of the holy spirit, and rejects water baptism.

Aramaic is seen as the language spoken by Jesus, and it is believed to be the language in which the New Testament was originally written, whereas most scholars believe it was written in Greek. The work of George M. Lamsa is particularly emphasized by the Way, especially his *The Holy Bible from Ancient Eastern Manuscripts* (1959), as well as the books of independent Indian Bishop K. C. Pillai, *The Orientalisms of the Bible*, and *Light through an Eastern Window*.

The organization of The Way International is based on the model of a tree: From the roots—represented by five educational and administrative centers that serve the organization as international headquarters located at New Knoxville, Ohio; the Way College of Emporia at Emporia, Kansas; the Way College of Biblical Research, Indiana Campus, at Rome, Indiana; Camp Gunnison (The Way Family Ranch at Gunnison, Colorado); and Lead Outdoor Academy at Tinnie, New Mexico; to trunks—represented by the national organizations; to limbs—represented by the state and province organizations; to branches—represented by the organizations in cities and towns; to twigs—represented by the numerous local community fellowships. Individual participants are likened to leaves. The ministry is administered by a three-member board of trustees, which appoints the cabinet overseeing the headquarters complex, and the staff of the other root locations.

The Way presents its teachings in the basic twelve-session course called "Power for Abundant Living" (PFAL). New members affiliate by attending it. Graduates of the course can either continue to attend twig fellowships, or become more involved by attending the Way College, in Emporia, Kansas; by joining the Way Corps; or by Becoming a "Word over the World Ambassador" for one year.

In 1983 the membership of the Way counted 2,657 twigs in the United States with approximately 30,000 people involved. The average was of ten members per twig. The Rock of Ages Festival, which was held in 1983, hosted over 17,000 people. Also, in 1983 PFAl classes were conducted abroad, namely in Zaire, Chile, Argentina, Venezuela, and Colombia. Intermediate PFAL, Christian Family and Sex, Renewed Mind, Witnessing, and Undershepherding were among the subjects offered by the advanced courses.

*The Way Magazine* is published by the American Christian Press, which is located within the International Headquarters complex at New Knoxville. Among other publications are Wierwille's books such as *The New Dynamic Church* (1971), *Receiving the Holy Spirit Today* (1972), *God's Magnified Word* (1977), and *Jesus Christ: Our Promised Seed* (1982).

The Way International provides its basic programs and training in its perspective on the Bible and its application to daily life through the activities of the Way Corps, headquartered at the Way College of Emporia, the Way Family Corps, and the Sunset Corps, both headquartered at the Way College of Biblical Research, Indiana Campus. The leadership in developing the arts according to Biblical principles is provided by Way Productions, based at the Way International's Cultural Center at New Bremen, Ohio, whereas the Way International Fine Arts and Historical Center at Sidney, Ohio, houses the historical records of the organization.

The Way International is one of the largest groups to have been labeled a "cult." It has also been the target of deprogramming, reporting in the early 1980s the most deprogramming attempts among its members. It has often been accused by anticult groups of brainwashing and mind control. Additionally, there have been two serious charges that have often been repeated in anti-Way literature: The first charge, in the 1970s, refers to the accusations of training members in the use of deadly weapons for possible future use against enemies of the organization. These accusations originated from the adoption at the College at Emporia of a State of Kansas program in gun safety, which was primarily directed to hunters. Although all the students at the college could attend the course, not all of them were required to enroll. The second charge came to the fore in the 1980s, as Christian anticultists attacked the Way for its radical departure from orthodox Christianity, its adoption of Arianism, and the denial of the divinity of Jesus and the Trinity.

The Way experienced a period of turmoil after Wierwille's death. Charges of improperties by Wierwille and many of his close friends resulted in the defection by several leaders, a few of whom established rival groups. As a result, the Way lost considerable support, although it recovered by 1990 when the attendance to the annual Rock of Ages festival began to return to its former level. The Internal Revenue Service questioned the Way's alleged partisan political involvement and its business activities at New Knoxville. Although its tax-exempt was revoked in 1985, that ruling was reversed by the Supreme Court in 1990.

**CHURCH OF JESUS CHRIST AT ARMAGEDDON.** The Church of Jesus Christ at Armageddon was founded by Love Israel in Seattle, Washington, in 1968. It was established "to fulfill the New Testament as revealed to Love Israel in the form of visions, dreams, and revelations received by members of the Church." All members of the church have had heavenly visions which explained their purpose on earth and the members' relationships with each other. The name of the church comes from the Book of Revelation, which mentions Armageddon as the gathering place of the end time.

The members of the church refer to themselves as the Love Family. They believe that their relationships are eternal and that through their love and commitment to each other they create the opportunity for Christ to express his personality in them. New members contribute all their possessions upon joining and begin a new life with a new name. Israel is the surname of all members of the church as it is the name of God's people. A biblical name such as "Abishai" or a virtue name such as "Honesty" is assumed as a first name. Members live in traditional family units or expanded households, but consider themselves married to one another in the universal marriage of Jesus Christ and are not bound by worldly traditions of matrimony. The father is respected as the head of each household and represents his household in the family government. The larger family is governed through frequent meetings.

Members of the church see themselves as God's chosen people and therefore as the beneficiaries of the Old Testament promises to Israel. They are committed to practicing the beliefs and lifestyle of the New Testament. Rules have been replaced by love, agreement, moderation, and common sense. Eating and drinking are considered sacramental, with all food and drink held to be the body and blood of Jesus Christ. Another sacrament is water baptism which frees members from the past and allows them to become a new personality with an eternal place within the Body of Christ.

The church enjoyed steady growth in the 1970s and reached a resident population of about three hundred members by 1983. The original headquarters were a handmade mansion on Seattle's Queen Anne Hill, surrounded by a small "village" of residences, gardens, and shops. The church maintained a twenty-four-hour inn where guests were housed and fed at no charge. Members distributed food from their farms and fishing boat to needy neighbors. The church also operated many small businesses. The unorthodox lifestyle of members made them a target of anticultists and deprogrammers and the object of much controversy.

In 1984 a former member filed a suit against the church which disrupted the community and resulted in the relocation of the headquarters and core members to a three hundred-acre ranch near Arlington, Washington. The ranch provides a cultural center for those members who remain dispersed throughout the region. Members continue to live at the ranch and in other small satellite communities and work together to fulfill their original vision of harmonious interdependence.

**ISRAELITE HOUSE OF DAVID AND ISRAELITE HOUSE OF DAVID AS REORGANIZED BY MARY PURNELL.** The Israelite House of David was founded in 1903 by Benjamin and Mary Purnell in Benton Harbor, Michigan. The Israelite House of David as Reorganized by Mary Purnell was incorporated in Benton Harbor in 1930, following the death of Benjamin Purnell, by his widow. The Mary Purnell group is often referred to as the City of David to distinguish it from the House of David. The Israelite House of David and the Israelite House of David as Reorganized by Mary Purnell are two surviving American groups of Southcottians, an Adventist movement which flowered in England throughout the nineteenth century.

Joanna Southcott was born in England in 1750. In the 1790s Joanna Southcott began to profess visions, to write them down in both prose and verse, and to gather a following. She was convinced that she was a prophetess. Several predictions, including France's conquest of Italy under the unknown general Bonaparte, created some attention. Southcott's message centered upon the imminent return of Christ. Joanna identified herself as the "woman clothed with the sun" (Rev. 12:1) who would bring forth the male child who would rule the nations with a rod of iron. She published her prophecies beginning in 1801 in several booklets.

In 1814, the age of sixty-four, Joanna Southcott had a climactic revelation. Having identified herself with the woman in Revelation 12, she was always concerned with the child the woman was to bear. Joanna's voice told her to prepare for the birth of a son. She began to show signs of pregnancy and was declared pregnant by seventeen out of twenty-two doctors. As the time of the delivery approached, she took an earthly husband. When the baby failed to arrive and the symptoms of the pregnancy left, Joanna's strength ebbed and she died in December.

Following these events, a man who called himself James Jershom Jezreel wrote a book, *The Flying Roll,* in which he asked himself if he was Shiloh, the son whom Joanna Southcott had awaited. He concluded that he was not Shiloh, but rather the sixth angel of the Book of Revelation. He identified Shiloh as the seventh angel of the Book of Revelation who was yet to come.

Jezreel and some of his followers made trips to America in 1878 and 1880 and won many followers there. Among these converts was Michael Keyfor Mills, a Detroit businessman and a Baptist up to the time of his conversion by Jezreel. Mills began a career selling *The Flying Roll* door to door. In 1891 Mills had a Spirit Baptism experience from which he concluded that it was his duty to gather the 144,000 who remained loyal to God and ready them for the battle of Armageddon mentioned in Revelation. He gathered the Jezreelites into a commune with himself as leader. Detroit was stirred by his power of healing and the miracles he produced. Among the many whom Mills introduced to the Jezreelite movement was Benjamin Purnell. For several years, Purnell and his wife Mary travelled around the Midwest before finally settling in Benton Harbor, Michigan, in 1903. There they purchased land and founded the Israelite House of David.

Joanna Southcott was considered by Benjamin Purnell and his followers to be the first messenger of Revelation (chapters 2, 9, and 3). The second messenger of Revelation was proclaimed by Purnell to be Richard Brothers. Richard Brothers was born in Canada in 1757, but moved to London in the 1780s. He was a psychic visionary who began to have revelations that identified him as a descendant of King David. When Brothers published these revelations and demanded the crown of England, he was found guilty of treason, but insane, and sent to an asylum. Despite this, Brothers's ideas caught on with some influential men and were developed into the British Israelite movement. The third and fourth messengers of Revelation 10:7 were George Turner and William Shaw. The fifth was John Wroe, founder of the Christian Israelite Church. The sixth was James Jershom Jezreel. Benjamin and Mary Purnell were believed to represent the two witnesses (11:3) announced by the seventh messenger of Revelation.

In 1904 the Israelite House of David received a cablegram from some members of the Christian Israelite Church (which was originally founded by John Wroe) in Melbourne, Australia. Having read some books by Purnell, they had accepted him as the seventh messenger spoken of in Revelation. They asked for instructions and in response, Purnell and several members of the House of David traveled to Melbourne and preached among the Christian Israelite Church centers. As a result, eighty-five Australians migrated to Benton Harbor and some members of the Israelite House of David stayed in Australia to become a permanent presence there.

The Israelite House of David purchased an additional thirty acres in Benton Harbor in 1907 on which it built an amusement park which opened in 1908. The park drew people for miles around for many years. In 1914 the church built an auditorium and began to hold regular lectures for visitors to the community.

The Israelite House of David holds to the King James Version of the Bible and the Apocrypha from which Jesus quoted (the Book of Enoch and the Books of Esdras). It is organized communally according to Acts 2. Members of the group are celibates, vegetarians, pacifists, and do not cut their hair.

Purnell taught that the true Israelites would be gathered from among both Jews and Gentiles. The elect are believed to be scattered among all of the Christian denominations, a fact which leads members of the House of David to have a high regard for other churches. Purnell asserted that it was possible to attain bodily immortality. Members of the church believe that salvation of the soul, as preached by most Christian groups, is a free gift of God, but by striving in this life it is possible to never taste death. Benjamin Purnell died in 1927. Following his death, members were divided in their loyalty between Benjamin's widow, Mary Purnell, and the prominent leader H. T. Dewhirst. After Mary was locked out of some of the group's facilities, she filed suit. In 1930, an out-of-court settlement awarded Mary Purnell some of the colony's farm property, with headquarters immediately east of the present House of David. With her followers, Purnell formed a new organization incorporated as the Israelite House of David as Reorganized by Mary Purnell. The beliefs of the newer church generally follow those of the Israelite House of David with the exception of the opinions held concerning Mary Purnell. The House of David as Reorganized by Mary Purnell considers Mary together with Benjamin to be the seventh messenger of Revelation. The City of David distributes Mary's books in addition to those of her husband. Mary Purnell died in 1953. Although the group once had over five hundred members, the Israelite House of David currently has less than sixty members and the Israelite House of David as Reorganized by Mary Purnell now has less than fifty.

**WORLDWIDE CHURCH OF GOD.** For most of its institutional life, the Worldwide Church of God taught a form of "Judaized" Christianity at variance with mainstream Evangelical Christianity. Recently (mid-1990s), however, this church made a dramatic turnabout. This upheaval was so thorough-going that by the spring of 1997 it had been admitted into the National Association of Eveanglicals.

The story of this church goes back to the Seventh Day Baptist Church that Stephen Mumford established in the New World 1671. In the following centuries several Adventist groups accepted the sabbatarian creed of Mumford's church and one of them gave life to the Church of God in Stanberry, Missouri; the group still exists under the name of General Conference of the Church of God.

Herbert W. Armstrong, founder of the Worldwide Church of God, was among those who chose to separate from the Stanberry church and create a small new congregation in Oregon in the late 1920s. Originally influenced by his wife's observance of the Sabbath, Herbert Armstrong became interested in the Bible, and in 1931 he was ordained in the Oregon Conference. He became a preacher and, in 1934, he started a radio ministry called "The World Tomorrow," and began publishing the periodical *The Plain Truth*. Disagreements about the observance of feast days and about the interpretation of the Old Testament caused a fracture within the Church of God. Armstrong followed the minority faction and was among the seventy members that formed the Church of God (Seventh Day) in Salem, Virginia, in 1933. The Salem congregation had chosen to observe the feast days, but in the following years disregarded the practice, which led Armstrong to withdraw and continue his ministry as Radio Church of God.

Armstrong's ministry expanded considerably after World War II; in 1947 he moved to Pasadena, California, where he opened Ambassador College. In 1953 he brought his work to Europe, and in the 1960s, his son, Garner Ted Armstrong, began a television ministry. The church acquired its present name in 1968, and continued its expansion through the 1970s, during which the circulation of *The Plain Truth* quadrupled. The Church's print and electronic ministries have been the most common way for new members to contact the church. In spite of its large membership, the hundreds of American congregations of the Worldwide Church of God are difficult to find. Most ceremonies are held in rented facilities, and are never advertised.

Issues like the prohibition of divorce and remarriage for the members, or the date of the Pentecost feast, though, were beginning to weaken the strength of the movement. General discontent caused the defection of a number of minor churches. Armstrong's son ended up being implied in a scandal and abandoned the church to create the Church of God, International. During the 1980s the situation returned to normality and the church again began to gain followers. Joseph W. Tkach Sr. succeeded Armstrong at his death in 1986.

While alive Armstrong led the church in an absolutely autocratic way, choosing and ordaining all of the church's ministers. He had always refused any form of election or selection of leaders and considered himself God's chosen messenger. The doctrine of the Worldwide Church of God follows the model of the Church of God movement, according to which the Bible is the fundamental text.

Shortly before his death in 1986, Herbert Armstrong confided in Tkach that he felt some of what he had taught—particularly about healing—was deficient, and asked that the church's teaching on this point be reexamined in light of the Scriptures. Beginning in 1987, Tkach prompted a review of the *Statement of Beliefs* to clarify the church's doctrine. Armstrong's admission that he could have been wrong combined with his instruction to reform his teaching by the measuring rod of Scripture set in motion an avalanche of change.

These changes reached a peak in an important Christmas Eve sermon which Joseph Tkach Sr. gave in 1994—a sermon which made it clear that the Worldwide Church of God had rejected its unique doctrines in favor of mainstream Evangelicalism. Not long afterwards, Joseph Tkach Sr. passed on. His son, Joseph Tkach Jr., assumed the leadership of the Worldwide Church of God in 1995. These radical changes prompted numerous schisms from the church. In 1992, 68,918 members were reported in the United States, while the membership reached 98,532 worldwide. After the dust had settled in 1997, the Worldwide Church of God had retained about seven hundred congregations with seventy-five thousand members worldwide. From the beginning of Herbert Armstrong's ministry to the present there have been over one hundred schisms from the church. These schisms are outlined in an appendix to Joseph Tkach's recent book, *Transformed by Truth*.

# 6 MORE CONTROVERSIAL CHRISTIAN GROUPS

**U**NIFICATION CHURCH ("MOONIES"). The Holy Spirit Association for the Unification of World Christianity (HSA-UWC), also known as the Unification Church (UC), refers to an important and highly controversial new religious movement led by the Reverend Sun Myung Moon (b. 1920). The church was founded to unite Christian denominations throughout the world, to bring unity among all major religions, and, on that basis, to build the Kingdom of Heaven on earth. However, the movement's efforts to achieve these objectives have been opposed vigorously. Derided offensively in the West as "the Moonies," the church has had to contend with intense and sustained reaction worldwide, rendering it quite possibly the most controversial new religious movement of the latter twentieth century.

The UC was formally established in Seoul, Korea, in May 1954. Having initially attempted to influence Korean Christianity, Rev. Moon was turned over to communist authorities in the North and rejected as a heretic in the South. He therefore founded the UC to fulfill his mandate of unifying worldwide Christianity in preparation for the Second Advent of Christ.

During the 1950s followers systematized church doctrine, evolved a cohesive organizational structure, and expanded membership through personal witnessing. University students and professors joined, especially at Ehwa Women's University in Seoul, which provoked intense hostility. Allegations swirled in Korean society that the UC was a "sex cult" and Rev. Moon was jailed on draft evasion charges but released soon after when no evidence was introduced. After 1961, the UC gained recognition for

---

having developed successful educational seminars and materials, particularly in opposition to communist ideology. Growth and expansion as well as the legalization of the movement by the Korean government in 1963 empowered congregants to succeed in their pursuits, notably in the areas of commerce, industry, politics, and the arts. This transformed the perception of the UC from a stigmatized sect into an expansive community.

The UC sent its first overseas missionaries to Japan and the United States in the late 1950s. The Japanese Church made inroads on college campuses and in Japanese society through its opposition to communism. However, development in the West was slow until Rev. Moon arrived in the United States in 1971. Seemingly out of nowhere, he catapulted into American consciousness via coast-to-coast evangelistic speaking tours, public advertisements in defense of the presidency during Watergate, and the conversion of college-age youth. These and other circumstances combined to foster suspicion and eventual hostility leading to a negative press and abusive involuntary "deprogrammings" of members. The 1982 conviction and subsequent incarceration of Rev. Moon on tax evasion charges is regarded by the church as the most singular instance of persecution in the West.

Despite these setbacks, Rev. Moon has been able to officiate over large international Blessing ceremonies involving at first hundreds and more recently thousands of couples. He and his wife have conducted several world speaking tours and met with numerous heads of state.

Core beliefs of the Unification Church are contained in its primary doctrinal and theological text, *Divine Principle* (1973), itself derived from two earlier Korean texts, *Woli Kang-ron* (1966) and *Woli Hae-sul* (1955). These texts express aspects of the "new truth" or "Principle" revealed through Sun Myung Moon. Utilizing familiar categories of Christian theology, key chapters include Creation, the Fall, Resurrection, Predestination, Christology, and History of Providence. While polemical opponents have identified departures from orthodoxy, the major novelty is the explicitness with which the text identifies the present as the time of the Christ's Second Advent. The family as the purpose of creation, the fall as misuse of sexual love, and the task of the Messiah to establish a model and salvific true family are cardinal doctrines.

An oral tradition consisting mainly of Rev. Moon's speeches exists alongside the official doctrinal texts. Many of these speeches are forthcoming about the Second Advent having arrived in the persons of Rev. and Mrs. Moon. Unificationists believe them to be the "True Parents" of humankind, ushering in the "Completed Testament Age." Since 1992, when this age is regarded to have begun, pronouncements of this nature have become increasingly public. Widespread and enhanced spiritual sensibility, the liberation of oppressed peoples, the emergence of global culture, and advanced technological development are all associated by the

Unification community with the Second Advent and Completed Testament Age. So, too, are ever greater numbers of couples participating in the joint weddings or "blessings" presided over by the True Parents.

Unificationists' spiritual practices and lifestyles are guided by their understanding of family which begins with the blessing. Through this ceremony, Unificationist couples understand themselves to have become part of the restored humanity inaugurated by the True Parents. Full-time missionaries typically follow a "formula course" of preparation for the blessing. This includes periods of fundraising and witnessing, usually in communal settings. Marriages personally arranged by Rev. Moon have been the norm, although interfaith blessings of previously married, non-UC couples are now a significant part of the blessing ceremonies. Interracial and intercultural unions are encouraged but by no means mandated. A degree of primacy is granted to Korea as the homeland of faith and members are encouraged to study Korean. Couples lead relatively conventional lives after the blessing although, on occasion, family separations in pursuit of particular church mission activities are undertaken.

Rev. Moon continues to exercise primary spiritual authority over the worldwide church. However, day-to-day activities are very much influenced by the nature of each indigenous church, its structure and organization. In general, deference is extended to elder Korean and Japanese couples, the early members of the church. These couples form a spiritual hierarchy extending from senior to more recent blessed couples. The UC has incorporated numerous national churches and maintains missions in more than one hundred twenty nations. Nevertheless, leadership is often rotated and missionaries dispersed in efforts to forestall premature institutionalization and, more importantly, in response to what are deemed providential requirements.

Although reliable UC membership totals are difficult to ascertain, the church claims some three million adherents worldwide. During the 1980s, some observers downplayed the movement's numbers in part due to a leveling-off of individual conversions in the West and differing definitions of membership. However, slower growth in the West was compensated for by rapid growth elsewhere. The number of blessing ceremony participants is another indicator of UC membership totals. The church claims that more than 400,000 thousand couples participated in its blessing ceremonies between 1960 and 1995. Not including an increasingly large percentage blessing participants who are not formally UC members, Rev. Moon "blessed" approximately 100,000 church marriages during that same period. This would indicate an adult UC membership population of 200,000. The UC appears poised to build on those totals given the favorable age, sex, and geographical distribution of its members.

The UC has invested considerable effort in publishing Rev. Moon's speeches and sermons. For the most part, the earliest speeches were delivered in Korean without notes and spontaneously translated for non-Korean speaking audiences. "Master Speaks" (1965–76) was an early collection of transcriptions which were minimally edited, paraphrased attempts to summarize the essence of Rev. Moon's discourses. The UC later declared these materials to be unreliable, a position which has been corroborated by linguistic experts. The church subsequently published the more carefully edited "Rev. Moon Speaks On" series (1977–). Currently, the UC is engaged in efforts to publish definitive translations of Rev. Moon's collected speeches, more than two hundred volumes in Korean, dating back to the mid-1950s.

Systematic and official published texts of Rev. Moon's teaching based on *Woli Kang-ron* (1966), the definitive Korean edition, have been translated into numerous languages and contain essential content taught in UC-sponsored workshops and seminars. *Unification News* (1980–) and *Today's World* (1982–) cover United States and international UC activity but are primarily for internal use as are works of spiritual instruction published by UC elders.

The UC's educational outreach includes Unification Theological Seminary (1975–) a graduate seminary in New York State, Sun Moon University, formerly Song Hwa University (1986–) in Korea, and the Little Angels School for the Performing Arts (1974–) in Korea. The UC runs primary schools in New Jersey; Washington, D.C.; Alabama; and the San Francisco Bay Area.

Although not subject to the apocalyptic conflagrations which have destroyed other movements, the scope and duration of reactions accompanying the UC's emergence, as stated, have rendered it quite possibly the most controversial new religious movement of the latter twentieth century. Negative reaction from the church's Korean mid-1950s origins has been mentioned. Although the UC gained a degree of credibility in Korea after 1961, relations have been tenuous and successive regimes have been embarrassed by UC initiatives, most recently by Rev. Moon's unauthorized visit to North Korea and Kim Il Sung in late 1991, which was repudiated by Seoul. Influential voices within the ranks of Korean Christianity have persisted in rejecting the UC as heretical.

Longstanding national animosities forced UC missionaries in Japan to conceal the church's Korean origins. Nevertheless, by 1967 the UC had become stigmatized as "Oya Nakase Genri Undo" ("the religion that makes parents weep"), family-based opposition groups coalesced, and in 1971 the practice of kidnapping and deprogrammings began. Opposition became ideological when the Japanese Communist Party (JCP) declared war on the UC and called on the entire party to "isolate and annihilate" it in 1978. Continued UC growth and in particular the business successes of Unificationists led to orchestrated attacks by the media, Japanese Bar Association, and Christian ministers after 1987. Departures of Japanese youth for overseas mission, intermarriage with Koreans and other nationals, and AUM

Shinriko—to which the media linked the UC—further escalated tensions after 1990. Similar, if less intense, responses have occurred elsewhere in the world, notably Europe, the Commonwealth of Independent States, Southeast Asia, and Latin America.

In the United States, as noted, the UC has faced widespread suspicion, hostility, and a negative press. Kidnapping and deprogrammings, a consequence of inflamed public opinion and the UC's public notoriety, were common in the mid-1970s. In 1977, a Gallup survey found that Sun Myung Moon "elicited one of the most overwhelmingly negative responses ever reported by a major poll." During the 1980s, the UC became a somewhat more acceptable part of the American religious landscape, largely through its diverse programs and projects. However, during this period, Rev. Moon was convicted and jailed on tax evasion charges for failure to pay a purported tax liability of $7,300 over a three-year period. This case was regarded by most jurists, civil libertarians, and religious leaders as biased and an intrusion on essential religious freedoms.

*—MICHAEL L. MICKLER*

**THE FAMILY (CHILDREN OF GOD).** The new religious movement known currently as the Family was founded in the late 1960s. It has undergone several transformations since that time and has been known variously as "Teens for Christ," "the Children of God," and "the Family of Love." Any discussion of the history and organization of the group must begin by looking at the movement's founder and spiritual leader, David Brandt Berg. Through the years he has been known by members of the Family as "Uncle Dave," "Moses David," "Mo," "Father David," and "Dad." David Berg has led the movement since its beginnings in Huntington Beach, California. Berg was born in 1919 to a family tradition of evangelical ministry. His mother spent much of her life as an evangelist and had ties to the Christian and Missionary Alliance Church. Berg followed this tradition and, for a brief time, served as pastor to a Christian and Missionary Alliance congregation in Valley Farms, Arizona. However, as early as 1952, Berg began to receive prophecies of the "end-time." This, coupled with a growing distrust of the "system" and "churchy" religion, led Berg to develop a more radical approach to missionary work. For several years up until 1967, he worked for TV evangelist Fred Jordon, booking his show across the United States.

In 1967, Berg moved his wife, Jane Miller (known in the Family as Mother Eve), and their children to Huntington Beach, California, after hearing his mother's description of the "hippies" who had begun moving into the area. The family began witnessing to the "dropouts" and "druggies" and soon had enough help to take over a beach coffeehouse that had been run by Teen Challenge. An iconoclast himself, Berg was ideally suited to his audience. He and his followers demonstrated their opposition to the "systemite" churches by visiting services and in some cases challenging the beliefs and behaviors of the local parishioners. Then, in 1969, the group left California and traveled around the United States in several missionary teams before finally regrouping in Canada.

It was in Canada that Berg revealed his Old Church/New Church doctrine. According to this pronouncement, the Old Church, represented by Berg's wife Jane, was hopelessly corrupt and must be replaced by the New Church, represented by Karen Zerby (known in the Family as Maria), a young woman who had, according to group leaders, joined the group in Tuscon, Arizona. After this announcement, the work of building the "new church" began in earnest. From 1970 to 1971, the group lived a very disciplined life at the Texas Soul Clinic Ranch (a property owned by Berg's former employer, Jordon) and developed a strict training program for new members. During this period, the group emphasized the boundary between the movement and the outside world. The goal of witnessing efforts was the total commitment of the "sheep." Joining required that the prospective member "forsake-all" worldly goods to the group and sever worldly ties. It was in reaction to this standard that the first anticult organization in the United States, FreeCOG, was formed. Despite the rigors of membership and the high level of dedication demanded, membership grew to about fifteen hundred during the three years after the move from California in 1969 when the group numbered less than one hundred.

In 1971, Berg and Maria left the United States and moved to Europe and, within one year, much of the membership followed. Prior to this time, the financial support for the movement had come from members "forsake-alls" and "provisioning," the solicitation of support from local businesses and organizations. After the move to Europe, Berg began to encourage members to sell samples of the groups' literature, or "litness," in order to fund the growing movement. Berg himself withdrew from an active leadership role and established a hierarchical structure to maintain the day-to-day operations. Much of the control was delegated to members of his immediate family who were known as the "Royal Family." Local control was in the hands of appointed leaders known as "Shepherds." Berg kept in touch with the membership and maintained authority over the movement through the "Mo Letters," which were by this time received as the "Word." "I am with you in spirit through these words that I speak unto you! They are my spirit & my life, by His spirit & His life—& if you will read them & study them, prayerfully & diligently, you will have more of me than you've ever had before."

The movement has undergone many organizational changes during its history. The most dramatic of these, the Reorganization and Nationalization Revolution (RNR), was effected by Berg at the end of the 1970s. The RNR involved the elimination of all intermediate leadership between Berg and the membership. "Which would you prefer? A low job or no job? Pretty soon you'll be surprised to discover that all the upper-crust offices & their bureaucracies have been totally wiped out along with the exalted staffs." The new regulations required that the leadership in local homes be elected and include citizens of the host nation. It was also at this time that Berg began encouraging the controversial practice of "flirty fishing" (FFing), a new approach to witnessing which allowed the use of sexual contact in order to save souls. Both "flirty fishing" and the increased emphasis on "litnessing" demonstrate a change in the movement's perception of group boundaries. Both techniques "won souls" and raised money for the group; however, especially in the case of "flirty fishing," the contacts made were not usually expected to "forsake all" and move into a Family home. In fact, since the early 1980s, the Family has had only limited recruitment success and children have accounted for almost all growth since that time.

At the end of the 1980s, members of the Family began returning to the United States. "All right! Things are tightening up & we've been forced out of country after country. . . . A lot of Westerners are going to be forced to go home." Currently, the use of "litnessing" has been largely supplanted as a money making technique by the distribution of videotapes. "Provisioning" continues to be an important means of support. At this time the Family claims a worldwide live-in membership of about nine thousand, two-thirds of which are teenage or younger. The current emphasis placed on child rearing and teen missionary work reflects these demographics. However, allegations of child abuse have placed the group at the center of a new controversy. The charges, stemming from selected quotes and art from old literature, as well as stories told by disaffected former members, have triggered a number of police raids on Family homes around the world. Investigations in a number of countries have all exonerated the Family of abuse charges. Nonetheless, the publicity has renewed earlier criticisms of the group's sexual morality, especially the practice of "flirty fishing," which was officially discontinued in 1987. The Family has responded with a major public relations campaign and an open-door policy.

The formal ideology of the Family may be described as antinomian and premillennial. It is produced by David Berg with the help of his close associates. All members are expected to read the Bible and "Mo Letters" daily and new members, or "babes," must memorize verses. The millennial nature of the Family's ideology has remained consistent throughout the group's history. However, the antinomian character of the group's beliefs was not expressed until after the early 1970s.

Berg's prophecies of the "end-time" predate the movement by a number of years and early witnessing efforts were aimed at the distribution of the "Warning Tract," a prophecy received by his mother. The Family predicts an imminent deterioration of world order which will enable the seizure of power by the Antichrist. Following the "Great Tribulation," Christ will return to defeat the forces of the Antichrist and reign on earth for one thousand years. After one thousand years, Satan will again attempt to defeat the forces of Christ. After the Battle of Gog and Magog the living and the dead shall be judged. Then, the heavenly city, New Jerusalem, will descend to earth to become the home of all those who have been saved.

The Family's interpretation of world events reflects their belief in the imminent rise of the Antichrist. Any disaster or crisis is viewed as a sign of the impending Tribulation and as an indication of the identity of the Antichrist and his forces. This outlook is well suited to conspiracy theory and the Family has incorporated some familiar examples. Notably, the Family has adopted portions of several anti-Semitic conspiracy theories. Berg states that "the Jewish world-Antichrist banking system has managed to loan out enough money to make the whole world its slaves." Berg also contends that the Holocaust, and indeed all of World War II, was staged by Jews in a bid for world domination. "Constantly talking about the Holocaust! They're still playing on the sympathy of the world to get what they want." In the same letter, Berg directs those who wish to know more about the way "they" operate to read "the famous 'Protocols of the Elders of Zion' and some of the other things about the World Jewish Conspiracy." The group has denied charges of anti-Semitism; Berg argues that "to be truly anti-Semitic you'd have to hate all the Orientals, be against them all." Ironically perhaps, Berg himself comes from Jewish heritage.

It is the sexual morality of the Family which demonstrates the antinomian character of their ideology. While there is a great deal of emphasis placed on "works" in other areas of Family theology, in this area, the Family has interpreted the doctrine of "salvation through grace" in a more radical way. Berg's letters have recommended "sexual sharing" and "Flirty Fishing," and questioned societal standards regarding the sexuality of children and the incest taboo. The main basis for such practices is the "Law of Love," the commandment to love one another which is believed to take precedence over all other laws. Berg also offers Old Testament support for his beliefs. "If you'll take a look at Bible history, you'll make the shocking discovery that most of God's greats had oodles of wives, women, mistresses, harlots & what have you, as well as multitudes of children!"

In other respects the Family's sexual morality is more in line with traditional fundamentalism. Homosexuality is condemned by the group and is an excommunicable offense. Birth control and abortion are seen as offenses to God and, consequently, most women have large numbers of children. And, in recent years, the group has moved away from some of the more controversial expressions of its sexual morality. The practice of FFing was officially discontinued in 1987 and any teenage-adult sex has been banned as well.

The Family's membership is quite different today than that of the "Teens for Christ" and the Children of God. The group has focused much of its attention on its younger members with home-schooling, teen missionary activities, and the inclusion of teens within group leadership. However, while group efforts have been focused on the retention of the second generation, the current controversy over the Family has centered around allegations of child abuse. Also, since the death of Berg in 1994, authority within the Family has become even more decentralized, though Maria is clearly the spiritual leader of the group. Despite Family reports that the more questionable of their practices have been discontinued, they continue to be accused of religious prostitution and child pornography, as well other forms of sexual child abuse. The controversy surrounding the Family burned white hot in the summer of 1993, but, following heavy-handed raids in several countries, the group was eventually declared innocent, all members were released, and the Family gradually faded from the headlines.

*—DAVID G. BROMLEY AND SIDNEY H. NEWTON*

**PEOPLE'S TEMPLE.** The central questions about People's Temple have always been: Why did the murders and mass suicide take place? And what is their cultural significance? People's Temple ended in an apocalypse without precedent in U.S. religious history. On November 18, 1978, in the South American country of Guyana, Jim Jones, the Temple's white charismatic leader, orchestrated a "revolutionary suicide" at the communal agricultural settlement called Jonestown. Over nine hundred people—mostly black, some white—died from drinking a deadly potion. Afterward, the body of Jim Jones was found with a gunshot to the head, consistent with suicide.

Like many other religious communal movements—both historical and contemporary—People's Temple practiced a way of life alien to mainstream America's ideology of individualism, capitalism, and the nuclear family. But Jones used prophetic religion in an especially political way. He insisted that followers give up their previous lives and become born again to a collective struggle against economic, social, and racial injustice that had no limits other than victory or death. This radical stance deepened the gulf between People's Temple and the wider society and set the stage for a protracted conflict with opponents that led to the mass suicide. How, then, did it develop?

Born poor in east central Indiana on May 13, 1931, James Warren Jones married Marceline Baldwin in 1949, moved to Indianapolis in 1951, and soon became a self-taught preacher who promoted racial integration and a veiled communist philosophy within a Pentecostal framework that emphasized faith healing. Over the years, Jones forged the mantle of a prophet who foresaw capitalist apocalypse and worked to establish a promised land for those who heeded his message.

Organizationally, People's Temple began as a small church. Jones increasingly modelled the Temple after the Peace Mission of American black preacher Father M. J. Divine, who, in the 1920s and 1930s, had established a racially integrated religious and economic community with himself at the center. Combining the Pentecostalist ethic of a caring community with the social gospel of liberal denominations, the Temple established care homes for the elderly, ran a free restaurant to feed the hungry, and maintained a social service center for the down-and-out. In 1960, the unconventional congregation became affiliated with the Christian Church (Disciples of Christ), which long had been committed to a social ministry.

People's Temple provoked controversy in Indianapolis by publicly challenging segregationist policies. In 1964, Jones laid the groundwork for a collective migration by his most committed followers. Tired of racial intolerance and citing fears of nuclear holocaust, they moved to the quiet northern California town of Ukiah. About seventy families, half white, half black, made the journey in the summer of 1965.

Jones's congregation became reestablished slowly, but by the late 1960s the church began to attract a wide range of people—blacks, hippies, progressive professionals, fundamentalist Christians, political activists and militants, street people, delinquents, and the elderly. By the early 1970s, the Temple was operating churches in San Francisco and Los Angeles, maintaining a fleet of buses to transport followers to church functions, running a "human services" ministry of "care" homes for juveniles and the elderly, and using the care homes as a nucleus for an increasingly communal organization. In comparison to both conventional churches and retreatist countercultural communal groups of its day, People's Temple was an anomaly— a relatively disciplined religiously and politically radical collective. By 1975, People's Temple was a formidable force in the left-liberal political surge in San Francisco, and the Temple began to reap political rewards.

Yet the status of People's Temple was precarious. Its success depended on using public relations techniques to create a facade that hid its more radical aspects. Because of the Temple's communal economy, its leadership began to be concerned in 1975 that the group would be charged by the U.S. Internal Revenue Service with tax evasion. More generally, People's Temple garnered considerable opposition—both from defectors and members' relatives, and from scandalized outsiders.

Beginning in Indianapolis, Jones had told his racially integrated group of followers that they would be persecuted, and they sometimes were subjected to racist incidents. Like Moses and the ancient Jews searching for a land of "milk and honey," like the Puritans who fled to North America from England to found a "city on a hill," Jones sought redemption for his followers in collective religious migration. During 1972 and 1973, Jones used internal defections and small incidents of external "persecution" as the warrant to establish People's Temple's "Promised Land"—an "agricultural mission" eventually called Jonestown—in a remote corner of Guyana, an ethnically diverse, socialist-governed South American country bordering the Caribbean.

In the summer of 1977, Jones finally ordered the collective migration for which the Temple had begun preparing four years earlier. At the time, it was widely believed that they left California because of press exposes, in which opponents raised the key issue of custody over children in People's Temple. Most notable of these was the child born to Grace Stoen, John Victor Stoen, who had been raised communally within the Temple, claimed as a biological son of Jim Jones. In July of 1976, Grace Stoen had defected from the Temple, leaving her husband—Temple attorney Tim Stoen—and her son behind. In the fall of 1976, Tim Stoen, as legal father, gave Jim Jones power of attorney over the four-and-a-half year old boy, who was taken to live at Jonestown. The ensuing struggle over John Stoen became the most celebrated among a series of custody battles that eventually extended to the question of whether adults at Jonestown were there of their own free will.

Although the migration took place during the press exposes, People's Temple actually undertook the migration because of concerns about U.S. government investigation of the Temple's tax status. By the standards of poor people, the Temple had created substantial collective wealth (between ten and fifteen million dollars). In early March 1977, the IRS notified the Temple that they had been denied tax-exempt status. Soon thereafter, the Temple leadership mistakenly concluded that they were the subject of an IRS investigation, and they initiated the migration of over nine hundred members to Jonestown.

There is no way of knowing how Jonestown would have developed as a communal settlement in the absence of its conflict with opponents. The migration did not cut the Temple off from its detractors; it simply shifted and amplified the struggle. After the 1977 migration, increasingly organized opponents initiated court proceedings to try to obtain legal custody of Jonestown children. The most famous case was the "child-god," John Stoen. In the summer of 1978, Tim Stoen, the legal father by California law, defected to the camp of Temple opponents. In September Grace Stoen's lawyer obtained a Guyanese court summons for Jim Jones and the child. At Jonestown, Jones reaffirmed his paternity of John Stoen and he threatened death: "I related to Grace, and out of that came a son. . . . They think that will suck me back or cause me to die before I'll give him up. And that's what we'll do, we'll die." Temple staff managed to vacate the court order (it had been made even though Grace Stoen had never revoked a standing grant of custody to a Temple member). The crisis abated. In the following months, the frustrated Temple opponents turned to political pressure and public relations campaigns. Calling themselves the "Concerned Relatives," they wrote to members of Congress, they met with State Department officials, and they organized human rights demonstrations. In reaction, the Temple hardened its siege mentality. A woman who defected from Jonestown in May, 1978, told an embassy official and the Concerned Relatives that plans were being developed for a mass suicide. In turn, the Concerned Relatives publicized the account to raise the alarm against Jonestown. Their efforts accomplished little. U.S. embassy officials in Guyana checked on relatives in Jonestown, but they did not find evidence for the opponents' charges of mass starvation and people living in bondage. One embassy consul later observed, "The Concerned Relatives had a credibility problem, since so many of their claims were untrue."

Frustrated, yet convinced that Jones had to be stopped, the Concerned Relatives increasingly pinned their hopes on Leo Ryan, a California congressman already sympathetic to the anticult movement. In response to a December 1977 inquiry from Ryan, the State Department described the situation as a legal controversy that did not warrant any "political action with justification." Ryan rejected this view. In May 1978, he wrote to People's Temple, "Please be advised that Tim Stoen does have my support in the effort to return his son from Guyana." Then Ryan and the Concerned Relatives began organizing an expedition to Jonestown.

With a congressman, Concerned Relatives, and newsmen planning on coming, the expedition confronted Jones with the choice of submitting to external scrutiny or precipitating further governmental inquiry and a flood of bad press. People's Temple staff sought to establish conditions for the proposed visit. But in November, 1978, without having reached any agreement about the visit, Ryan's group flew to the capital of Guyana, Georgetown. From there, after several fruitless days of negotiations, Ryan flew on with the reporters and four Concerned Relatives to Port Kaituma, a small settlement near Jonestown. Faced with a fait accompli, Jones acquiesced to the visit.

At Jonestown, on the evening of November 17, 1978, Jonestown offered the visitors an orchestrated welcome. But during the festivities a note was passed to a reporter. "Help us get out of Jonestown." The next day, embassy staff began to make arrangements for the note's two signers to leave. Then members of the Parks family also decided to leave with Ryan. "I have failed," Jones muttered to his lawyer, Charles Garry. "I live for my people because they need me. But whenever they leave, they tell lies about the place."

As a dump truck was loaded for departure, Ryan told Jones that he would give a basically positive report. Suddenly bystanders disarmed a man who had started to attack Ryan with a knife. Ryan was disheveled but unhurt. "Does this change everything?" Jones asked Ryan. "It doesn't change everything, but it changes things," Ryan replied. Then an embassy official led Ryan to the truck, and they piled in with the reporters, the four representatives of the Concerned Relatives, and sixteen people who had decided to leave Jonestown.

At the Port Kaituma airstrip, as the travelers started loading two planes, a Jonestown man posing as a defector pulled out a pistol in the smaller plane and started shooting. Simultaneously, a tractor came up pulling a flatbed; from it the Jonestown sharpshooters shot toward the other plane. Left dead were Congressman Leo Ryan, three newsmen, and defector Patricia Parks. At Jonestown, Jim Jones told the assembled community that they would no longer be able to survive as a community. With a tape recorder running, Jones argued, "If we can't live in peace, then let's die in peace." One woman spoke against the plan, but others argued in favor. Amidst low wails, sobbing, and the shrieks of children, people walked up to take the "potion" laced with cyanide, then moved out of the pavilion to huddle with their families and die. In the confusion, two black men slipped past the guards. The community's two American lawyers, Charles Garry and Mark Lane, sequestered at a perimeter house, plunged into the jungle. Everyone else died.

The proximate cause of the murders and mass suicide was the refusal of Jim Jones, his staff, and the loyalists among his followers to compromise with opponents whom they believed were out to destroy Jonestown. Rather than submit to external powers that they regarded as illegitimate, they chose to stage the airstrip murders as revenge and shut out their opponents by ending their own lives. With their community unraveling under the pressure of pitched opposition, they sought revolutionary immortality. In the popular mind, they achieved infamy instead. The stigma of the mass deaths carved this infamy into the narrative structure of myth. Specifically, a film, a television docudrama, and more than twenty books enshrined Jim Jones as the pop-culture image incarnate of the anti-Christ, the Temple, as the paragon of the religious "cult." But as Roland Barthes once observed, "The reader lives the myth as a story at once true and unreal." Put differently, history is much messier than any story about it. The popular accounts of People's Temple gradually have been supplanted with careful scholarly research. More is still needed. Particularly central is the question of the biological paternity of John Stoen. To date, the evidence is not yet definitive. If Jones was the father, then one of the Concerned Relatives' central atrocity contentions—that Jones amounted to a kidnapper—lacks any moral force, and one significant element of their campaign against People's Temple would turn out to be based on a public construction of reality that differed from privately held knowledge.

Whatever further research yields, the popular myth about People's Temple already has been substantially revised. Immediately after the mass suicides, popular accounts portrayed the Concerned Relatives, Leo Ryan, and the press that visited Jonestown as tragic heroes. Yet it is now evident that their own actions had devastating consequences. The murders and mass suicide cannot be adequately explained except as the outcome of an unfolding and interactive conflict between two diametrically opposed groups—Peoples Temple *and* the Concerned Relatives. In this conflict, the Concerned Relatives were able to marshall to their side significant allies within the established social order—the press, governmental investigators, a congressman. It is now possible to see what was once obscured by the popular myth. The apocalypse at Jonestown is an extreme case of a more general pattern of religious conflict. In this pattern (found in the Pilgrims and the Mormons, for example), collective religious migration is a strategy employed by the religious movement when conflict erupts between the movement and opponents who regard it as threatening to an established social and moral order.

People's Temple ended with the mass suicides. It made its historical mark not by success, but by dramatic failure. Yet this organization was infused with many of the contradictions of American culture, and its cultural legacy keeps changing. With the murders and mass suicide, Jonestown confirmed the anticult movement's most dire warnings. "Jonestown" became a template of popular culture, ready to be applied to subsequent religious movements, notably, the Branch Davidian followers of David Koresh, who were consumed in a fiery conflagration near Waco, Texas, during their standoff with the FBI in April of 1993. But the cultural significance of People's Temple also is deeply intertwined with other American social issues, most notably, the status of minorities within a racially divided society; the character of religion in an increasingly secular society, and in a society where Jones borrowed many of his most questionable practices from the wider culture; and ethical issues about social welfare, bureaucratic organization, social control, politics, and public relations. The connections between Jones's world and ours run deeper than is easy to admit.

—*John R. Hall*

**MOVEMENT FOR THE RESTORATION OF THE TEN COMMANDMENTS OF GOD.** The Movement for the Restoration of the Ten Commandments of God was a doomsday religious sect in Uganda that made headlines in the wake of what was initially thought to be a mass suicide in March 2000. The number of bodies increased daily until it exceeded 1,000. About 530 died in an intentionally set fire that gutted their church in Kanungu, Uganda on Friday, March 17, 2000. Police counted 330 skulls in the church; however, some bodies had been converted to ash. Almost all were burned beyond recognition. The dead included at least 78 children. The precise number of the dead will never be known. In the days following the tragedy, police discovered innumerable other bodies at different sites. All had been murdered prior to the group holocaust, apparently at the behest of the leadership.

Most of the deaths occurred in Kanungu, a small trading center, about 217 miles (360 km) southwest of Kampala, the capital of Uganda. While some still believe that the parishioners committed suicide, the current consensus is that the group leader, Joseph Kibweteere, murdered the members by luring them inside the church and then setting it on fire. The church's windows had been boarded up and its doors nailed shut with the members inside. They sang for a few hours. One witness said that they doused themselves with gasoline and set themselves ablaze. Other witnesses reported the smell of gasoline at the scene, an explosion that preceded the fire, and some screams from inside the building.

Fox News reported that the sect's leaders included three excommunicated priests and two excommunicated nuns. Some believe that the leadership all died along with the general membership; other suspect that a few of the leaders escaped. Some sources say that the members wore white, green, and black robes. The Associated Press said that the women wore white veils while men more black, green, or red shirts.

Before the tragedy, Kibweteere allegedly said that he overheard a conversation between Jesus Christ and the Virgin Mary. Mary had stated that the world would come to an end unless humans started to follow the Ten Commandments closely. The group initially believed that the end of the world would occur on December 31, 1999. During 1999, members sold their possessions, presumably in preparation for the end times when they would be transported to heaven. They slaughtered cattle and had a week-long feast. When the end did not come, Kibweteere changed the date to December 31, 2000. Later, he taught that the Virgin Mary would appear on March 17 and take the faithful to Heaven. Devastation would then descend upon the world and the remaining six billion people in the world would be exterminated. They believed that they would experience a life much like Adam and Eve enjoyed, with no clothes, no cultivating, and no work. In preparation for the event, members slaughtered three bulls, and had a great feast on the evening before the tragedy.

The movement was founded by excommunicated Roman Catholic priests: Joseph Kibweteere, Joseph Kasapurari, John Kamagara and Dominic Kataribabo; two excommunicated Roman Catholic nuns; and Credonia Mwerinde, an ex-prostitute. There are conflicting reports of the year in which the group was founded. Some say it was 1989, others say

1994. They were registered as a nongovernmental organization in 1994. Their school was shut down by the government in 1998 because of unsanitary conditions, their use of child labor, and allegations of kidnapping of children. Estimates of the membership before the murder/suicide range from 235 to about 650.

Most of the group's members were originally Roman Catholic. The group taught that the Catholic Church was an enemy, badly in need of reform. Their own rules came from the Virgin Mary, as channelled through Mwerinde. The leaders taught that the Ten Commandments needed to be restored to their original importance. Medical care was discouraged. Members rarely spoke. They used mostly gestures to communicate, out of fear of breaking the ninth commandment (the eighth commandment for Roman Catholics and some Lutherans): "Thou shalt not bear false witness against thy neighbour."

The group was located in southwest Uganda—one of the most unstable areas of the world. Two separate programs of mass murder have been conducted in the vicinity: In Rwanda, 800,000 lost their lives. Under Idi Amin, as many as 500,000 Ugandans lost their lives. A civil war currently rages in the Democratic Republic of the Congo, across the border from Uganda. A significant percent of the population had died or is dying from AIDS.

There is general agreement about some events leading up to the tragedy: The membership appears to have anticipated being taken to Heaven by the Virgin Mary on March 17, 2000. They expected the end of the world to occur at that time. They slaughtered a cow, and ordered seventy crates of soda for a feast on March 16. They said goodbye to friends and relatives.

There was one initial report, never confirmed, that the members had applied gasoline and paraffin to their skin before the explosion and fire. However, it is difficult to see how the observer could have witnessed these preparations if the windows and doors of the church had been nailed shut. If confirmed, this would be one indicator that the deaths might have been the result of mass suicide, similar to that of Heaven's Gate. The police investigation cast doubt on this sole witness; they found no signs of paraffin having been used at the church. Most of the world media initially emphasized the suicide theory, as did representatives of the anitcult movement.

It is now almost certain that the tragedy was a mass murder, not a mass suicide. Several news sources reported that the doors of the church were nailed shut from the inside. That might indicate that the leadership wanted to confine the full membership within the church in order to murder the entire group. The discovery of additional bodies which had been murdered and buried in latrines near the church gives weight to the mass murder theory. The discoveries of many hundreds of murder victims at other locations also point toward mass murder. Leader Kibweteere appears to have planned the tragedy in advance. He allegedly sent a letter to his wife before the tragedy, encouraging her to continue the religion "because the members of the cult were going to perish the next day."

Also, the group's membership are almost entirely ex-Roman Catholic—a faith that strongly forbids suicide. Traditional belief also very strongly forbids suicide. Finally, locally held belief is that if a person dies in a fire, not only is their body killed but their soul is as well. This is the reason why evil sorcerers were once burned alive: so that they would be completely annihilated. It is very unlikely that if a person in this area wanted to commit suicide that they would have chosen death by fire.

The deaths were precipitated by failed prophecy. When the end of the world did not occur on December 31, 1999, some members of the sect demanded their money and possessions back. This, in turn, may have triggered the mass murders.

*—BRUCE A. ROBINSON*

**CHURCH OF THE FIRST BORN OF THE FULLNESS OF TIMES; CHURCH OF THE FIRST BORN; CHURCH OF THE LAMB OF GOD.** The Church of the First Born of the Fullness of Times was incorporated in 1955 by brothers Joel, Ross Wesley, and Floren LeBaron. The Church of the First Born was founded by Ross Wesley LeBaron after he left his brothers' church. The Church of the Lamb of God was founded by another LeBaron brother, Ervil, after he was dismissed from the Church of the First Born of the Fullness of Times.

The LeBaron family and its patriarch, Alma Dayer LeBaron, were members of the Church of Jesus Christ of Latter-Day Saints. In 1934, one of Alma's sons, Benjamin LeBaron, claimed to be the One Mighty and Strong, the prophetic figure mentioned in Mormon writings, and several family members substantiated his claims as a prophet. In 1944, the LeBaron family was excommunicated from the Church of Jesus Christ of Latter-Day Saints. The family then associated with the "fundamentalist" Mormon colony in Mexico directed by Rulon C. Allred, leader of the Apostolic United Brethren.

In 1955, the LeBarons left Allred's Mexican colony. Benjamin's brothers, Joel, Ross Wesley, and Floren established the Church of the First Born of the Fullness of Times. Joel claimed to have the Patriarchal Priesthood and had a revelation directing Rulon C. Allred to become his councilor. Both Allred and Joel's brother Benjamin rejected Joel's claims.

Also rejecting Joel LeBaron's claim to Patriarchal Priesthood was his brother and co-founder of the Church of the First Born of the Fullness of Times, Ross Wesley LeBaron. Ross Wesley left his brother's church and formed the Church of the First Born. The doctrine of the Church of the

First Born states that the church was first established by Adam and restored in Joseph. It believes in One Mighty and Strong to come as presented in the Doctrine and Covenants. Ross Wesley LeBaron disincorporated the church in the early 1980s. Joel's claim to the "Patriarchal Priesthood" followed a line of succession through his father, Alma, to Alma's grandfather, Benjamin F. Johnson, who was secretly ordained by founder Joseph Smith.

In 1970, the Church of the First Born of the Fullness of Times dismissed Ervil LeBaron, its second-highest ranking officer and the brother of its leader Joel LeBaron. Ervil formed the Church of the Lamb of God and claimed full authority over all of the polygamy-practicing groups, even going so far as to claim an authority to execute anyone who would refuse to accept him as the representative of God. Beginning with the establishment of the Church of the Lamb of God, a series of murders and assaults on polygamy-practicing Mormons began.

On August 20, 1972, Joel LeBaron, leader of the Church of the First Born of the Fullness of Times, was shot to death in Ensenada, Mexico. On June 16, 1975, Dean Vest, an associate of Joel LeBaron, was killed near San Diego, California. On May 10, 1977, Dr. Rulon C. Allred, leader of the Apostolic United Brethren, was murdered in his chiropractic office in Salt Lake City while attending patients. On May 14, 1977, an attempt was made on the life of Merlin Kingston, another polygamy leader. Thirteen other polygamy-practicing Mormons were killed before Ervil LeBaron was arrested for the murder of Rulon Allred. Ervil LeBaron was tried, convicted, and sentenced to prison in 1980. He died in prison of natural causes in 1981.

Joel LeBaron headed the Church of the First Born of the Fullness of Times from 1955 until he was murdered in 1972. He was succeeded by his brother Verlan who led the church until his death in 1981. The current leader of the church is Siegfried Widmar. The Church of the First Born of the Fullness of Times has several hundred members, most of whom live in Mexico.

**CHURCH OF JESUS CHRIST CHRISTIAN, ARYAN NATIONS:** The Church of Jesus Christ Christian, Aryan Nations was founded in the late 1940s by Wesley A. Swift in Lancaster, California. It follows the Christian-Israel identity message which believes that modern Anglo-Saxons, Scandinavian, Germanic, Celtic, and related peoples are the physical descendants of ancient Israel, and hence heir to the promises of the Bible which refer to Israel as a whole. The church is adamantly pro-white.

Wesley Swift died in 1970 and his widow succeeded him as head of the congregation. After Swift's death, Richard Girnt Butler, a minister in the church, moved to Hayden Lake, Idaho, and began an independent branch of the church there in 1974. In 1979 Butler hosted the Pacific States National Identity Conference.

During the 1980s Butler and the church drew national attention because of his association with the Ku Klux Klan and the American Nazi movement. In 1982 Butler hosted the first World Aryan Congress, which brought together a wide variety of white-separatist groups and has called for the establishment of an all-white nation in the Pacific Northwest.

Some former members of the Church of Jesus Christ Christian, Aryan Nations formed group called The Order, which was blamed for the 1984 murder of Jewish radio talk-show host Alan Berg in Denver, and a number of crimes in the Seattle, Washington area. A manhunt for members of The Order resulted in the death of the leader, Robert Matthews, who was killed in a gun battle with police, and the arrest, trial, and conviction of eleven members on charges of racketeering. Richard Butler noted the former affiliation of The Order's leaders and sympathized with their frustrations but rejected their violent and illegal activities. In 1987 Butler was indicted by the federal government for sedition, but he was found innocent. The Church of Jesus Christ Christian, Aryan Nation has come under close scrutiny by the media and groups such as the Anti-Defamation league of B'nai B'rith because of The Order and the connections between the church and several Klan and Nazi organizations.

**COVENANT, THE SWORD AND THE ARM OF THE LORD:** The Covenant, the Sword and the Arm of the Lord was founded in the mid-1970s by James D. Ellison, a minister in San Antonio, Texas. Ellison had a vision of the coming collapse of the American society and decided to flee the city. He established a survivalist community on a 224-acre tract of land in the Ozark Mountains of Arkansas. The commune was seen as a purging place and given the Biblical name Zarephath-Horeb.

Ellison's teachings identified the white Anglo-Saxon race as the literal descendants of Ancient Israel and hence the heir to the covenants and promises God made to Israel. They believed that the Anglo-Saxons had been called to be the light of the world, and that black people were created for perpetual servitude. Ellison and his followers also believed that God's Spirit would be coming soon in judgment to the earth and that the Covenant, the Sword, and the Arm of the Lord would be the Arm of God that would administer that judgment.

The members of the Covenant, the Sword and the Arm of the Lord, in accordance with Ellison's vision, expected the imminent collapse of America and ensuing war. In that war (Armageddon), they believed that Anglo-Saxons would be set against Jews, blacks, homosexuals, witches, Satanists, and foreign enemies. At that point they held that the settlement in Arkansas would become a Christian haven. In preparation for the difficult times ahead, the community stored food and stockpiled weapons and ammunition.

The community was largely self-supporting. A farm produced most of the food. Educational and medical service were provided internally, and most families lived without electricity or plumbing. Beginning in 1978, the group began to acquire sophisticated weaponry adequate for modern warfare. In 1981, it opened a survival school and gave training to the public in the use of firearms and survivalism. In the winter of 1981–1982, the group splintered over the continuance of paramilitary training and those most in favor of it left the commune.

In 1984, a grand jury was investigating the murder of an Arkansas state trooper. A gun found in the possession of the person accused of the murder was registered to James Ellison. Ellison was ordered to appear before the grand jury and a warrant was issued for his arrest when he failed to appear. In April 1985, agents of the FBI surrounded Zarephath-Horeb and arrested Ellison and several members on federal racketeering charges. Following the raid, the Covenant, the Sword and the Arm of the Lord disbanded. Subsequently, James Ellison was sentenced to twenty years for racketeering. Three other members received lesser terms.

# 7

## JEWISH TRADITION

### JUDAISM

**J**udaism, though small for a world faith, has a significance beyond
its size as the "parent" of the world's two largest religions, Christianity and Islam. In contrast to its offspring, which tend to focus their
concerns on the other-worldly fate of individual souls, Judaism is built
around a this-worldly covenant relationship—which is both a contractual
agreement and a "marriage" of love—between God and his chosen
people, Israel. Because Judaism is built around a relationship involving
agreements and promises in *this* life, the afterlife is less essential for
Judaism than for other world religions. Although most contemporary
practicing Jews believe in the resurrection of the dead, it would be relatively easy to imagine Judaism *without any afterlife beliefs whatsoever.* In
marked contrast, the promise of a postmortem paradise—and salvation
from eternal damnation—lies at the very core of the believer's religious
life in Christianity and Islam.

As a tradition with ancient roots, Judaism has undergone a number of
important transformations. Of particular importance was Judaism's contact with Zoroastrianism during Persian rule of the Middle East for two
centuries following conquest of the Babylonian empire by Cyrus the Great
in 539 B.C.E. Zoroastrianism exercised a powerful influence, introducing
such ideas as a powerful evil god (the Devil) who is locked in conflict with
the good god, a final judgment, an apocalypse, hell, and the resurrection
of the dead. Zoroaster himself is often compared to the Hebrew prophets.

Like the prophets of Israel, he preached the rejection of ancient practices he regarded as barbaric in favor of an ethical monotheism.

The dynamic underlying the creation of new sects within Judaism in the last few centuries has been the tension between the desire to adhere to tradition and the equally powerful urge to adapt to the modern world. Orthodox Judaism is at the traditional end of the spectrum. Reformed Judaism, which was originally created in the nineteenth century, has adapted the most to modernity and the demands of secular society. Various other forms of Judaism, such as Conservative Judaism, fall somewhere between these two extremes. None of these various subdivisions of the Jewish faith are normally regarded as cults, sects, or new religions. The one possible exception is mystical Judaism, or Hasidism, which might appropriately be viewed as a reformist sect.

The most important contemporary manifestation of Judaism to be regarded as a "cult" is so-called Messianic Judaism. Messianic Jews are Jews who have converted to Christianity and yet wish to continue to adhere to certain aspects of Jewish tradition. On the other hand, there are a number of small Christian groups that have adopted certain Jewish practices from the Old Testament and become Judaized Christians. Until recently, the Worldwide Church of God was one of the more prominent contemporary Christian sects falling into this category. Also significant is Black Judaism— a movement that emerged among African Americans, who identified themselves as the original Israel.

One might finally note that, at various stages in the development of Judaism, the tradition underwent radical changes which, had they occurred in the late twentieth century, would have been labelled "cultic." Rather than viewing him through traditional eyes, one author chose to view a famous Hebrew leader in terms of our current stereotype of a "cult" leader:

> He claimed to have visions from God, so he led his people far away from the evils of the world and into the mountains. Then, to back up his claim of divine guidance, he seemed to perform miracles. He said he received spiritual laws that his followers were required to honor. He began writing down his story in the hope it would become law. What was this cult leader's name?
>
> Many people would be shocked to think that the life of a man who contributed so much to the Judaic, Christian, and Islamic religions could be compared to today's leaders of "cults." Nevertheless, the biblical Moses who led his followers out of Egypt, parted the Red Sea, received the Ten Commandments, and wrote part of the Old Testament, was the ultimate cult leader.

The author uses the life of Moses to illustrate the point that almost all mainstream religions have originated from movements that could at one time have been characterized as "cults."

The manner in which the Jewish tradition developed certain key notions has decisively influenced the process by which new sects form in the larger Judeo-Christian-Islamic family of religions. How, for example, does the founder of a new religious movement legitimate her or his new vision? The claim, quite often, is that the founder has received a direct revelation from divinity. The earliest models for this kind of authoritative claim are the various manifestations of Yahweh in which he sets forth the terms of the covenant, most dramatically and elaborately in the revelation to Moses at Mt. Sinai.

By stressing monotheism—one god to the exclusion of others—Judaism also influenced all succeeding religious manifestations in the Judeo-Christian-Islamic family to stress that only one revelation can be true. In other words, in a polytheistic religious system it is possible to have a multiplicity of revelations, all of which have equal standing and authority. In a monotheistic system, only one revelation—or, at least, only one revelation at any single time—can be true. As a corollary, all other revelations must be false. The problem with this understanding, as should be obvious, is what criterion does one utilize to distinguish between true and false revelations.

While the pattern is also associated with Zoroastrianism, Judaism is the most immediate source of the prophetic tradition by which religious change comes about in the name of reform. Many new Protestant sects, for example, begin as reformist splinters from older, more established religious bodies. In most, the ideal is to return to the original faith, as practiced by first-century Christians. The paradigm for this reformist impulse is the example of the Hebrew prophets who preached against the perceived corruptions of their day and urged their fellow Jews to return to a purer faith, though this reformism has only rarely led to the formation of distinctive sects within Judaism.

As a key to religious authority, the Jewish utilization of scripture contributed yet another method by which new sects form. In the Judeo-Christian-Islamic family, scripture contains a record of God's revelations to humanity. While people within that family rarely dispute the authority of scripture, there is enough ambiguity in such writings to permit a diversity of understandings of what the scriptures mean. Partially because it has emphasized the importance of practice over the details of belief, Judaism has traditionally tolerated a wide variety of interpretations of the Bible. Christianity, however, has been quite different. Disagreement over the meaning of a few aspects of scripture has often contributed to the formation of a new Christian sects.

**UNION OF MESSIANIC JEWISH CONGREGATIONS.** In a meeting held in the summer of 1979, the leaders of thirty-three Messianic congregations formed a congregational organization. Nineteen congregations accepted to join the union, and three years later the number had reached twenty-five. Daniel C. Juster was the first elected president.

The origins of Messianic Judaism date to the 1960s when it began among American Jewish who converted to Christianity. Its members believe that their conversion still allows them to be part of the Jewish religious culture and its religious rites. Rather than seeing a contrast between Judaism and Christianity, they consider the latter a completion of the former. After the establishment of a Messianic synagogue in Philadelphia in the 1960s, the movement became more diffused and found strong support in Chicago where the Hebrew Christian Alliance was formed in the 1970s.

The Messianists grew in number particularly within the Young Hebrew Christian Alliance which, in 1975, changed its name to that of Messianic Jewish Alliance of America. After the first meeting of 1979, the Union of Messianic Jewish Congregations began to establish Messianic synagogues, and to sponsor the training of Messianic leaders. The Union accepted the statement of faith of the National Association of Evangelicals in 1981; according to it, the Bible is the definitive authority with regard to the creed, Jesus is called by his Jewish name Yeshua, his divinity is accepted, and faith in his atonement guarantees salvation.

To be part of the Union a congregation must have at least ten Messianic Jewish members. The organization is not strict, and congregations are granted freedom as regards service days and the kind of worship. Fifty-seven congregations were part of the Union in 1987.

**RESEARCH CENTRE OF KABBALAH.** The Research Centre of Kaballah dates from 1922 and the work of Rabbi Yehuda Ashlag (1886–1955). Ashlag was a scholar seeking to move the Kaballah out of the realm of the esoteric and into the realm of avaliablility for anyone interested in studying it. He made the text (the *Zohar*) accessible by translating it from Aramaic to modern Hebrew and by dividing the text into chapters and paragraphs. He also supplied an explanatory text for the novice readers, *Ten Luminous Foundations*.

Following Ashlag's successor in this work was Dr. Philip S. Berg (formerly Gruberger), who opened the first office of the Research Centre in the United States in 1965 (in New York). There is also a thriving center in the Los Angeles area. Berg has been a prolific author, devoted to fulfilling Ahlag's dreams for the Research Centre.

Berg's organization, which has been successful at recruiting Jewish celebrities such as Roseanne, has often been criticized by mainstream American Jews. Although in practice extremely orthodox, Berg teaches astrology and reincarnation as part of the Kabbalistic tradition—subjects viewed askance by the more traditional. Berg's centers also open their classes, services, and other events to non-Jews.

## BLACK JUDAISM

Many African Americans have rejected the Christianity they associate with slaveowners in favor of religions with more distinctively black identities. Beginning in the early nineteenth century some individual African Americans became legends as regular worshipers at local synagogues. To this day, and in growing numbers, there are black members of predominantly white Jewish congregations.

A second source of black Judaism was the West Indies, where some blacks converted to Judaism under the influence of Jewish plantation owners. In the late nineteenth century, some of these Jamaican Jews migrated to the United States and became the source for the first all-black synagogues.

For centuries a legend existed that black Jews, descendants of the Queen of Sheba, had lived in Ethiopia but had long ago disappeared. The rediscovery in the late nineteenth century of the Falashas, the black Jews of Ethiopia, by French explorer Joseph Halevy, spurred some black people to elect Judaism as an alternative to Christianity.

The first African American Jewish denomination was started by William Saunders Crowdy, a black cook for the Santa Fe railroad. In 1893, Crowdy had a vision from God calling him to lead his people to the true religion. He started preaching on the streets of Lawrence, Kansas, in 1896. Crowdy preached that Africans were the descendants of the lost tribes of Israel and thus the true surviving Jews. By 1899, Crowdy had founded churches in twenty-nine Kansas towns. He called his denomination The Church of God and Saints of Christ, which, despite its Christian-sounding name, had from the start an identification with Judaism. The Christ of the church's name refers to the still-awaited Messiah. Crowdy purchased land in Belleville, Virginia, just after the turn of the century. For many years the core members of the church lived there communally. The headquarters of the church were moved to Belleville in 1917.

As it evolved, the doctrine of the Church of God and Saints of Christ became a mixture of Jewish, Christian, and black nationalist precepts. The Jewish elements include observance of the Jewish Sabbath and the use of Jewish terminology to describe leaders, buildings, and observances. A key theme is the Exodus, the liberation of people in bondage. The year culminates in Passover, a week-long homecoming in Belleville with a ceremonial Seder. There are an estimated thirty thousand to forty thousand members in over two hundred churches.

In 1900 charismatic black leader Warren Roberson founded the Temple of the Gospel of the Kingdom in Virginia. Members learned Yiddish and adopted Jewish cultural patterns. By 1917 the group had moved its headquarters to Harlem. There it established a communal household, called a kingdom, for members. Another kingdom near Atlantic City, New

Jersey, aroused controversy when media reports came out saying that it was actually a baby farm where women bore Roberson's children. Roberson was charged with transporting women across state lines for immoral purposes in 1926. He pleaded guilty and was sentenced to eighteen months in the Atlanta Penitentiary. The movement collapsed at that point.

In 1915, Prophet F. S. Cherry established the Church of God in Philadelphia, Pennsylvania. Cherry was influenced by both the Church of God and Saints of Christ and the Temple of the Gospel of the Kingdom. Cherry taught that God, who is black, originally created black humans, the descendants of Jacob. The first white person, Gehazi, became that way as the result of a curse. The church teaches that Jesus was a black man. Prophet Cherry's followers believe that they are the true Jews and that white Jews are impostors. The church does not use the term synagogue, the place of worship of the white Jews. Cherry read both Hebrew and Yiddish and based his teachings on the Old Testament and the Talmud. The church has a Saturday Sabbath and a liturgical year which focuses on Passover. The church has prohibitions against eating pork, divorce, taking photographs, and observing Christian holidays.

Arnold Josiah Ford was a self-proclaimed Ethiopian Jew and the choirmaster for Marcus Garvey, founder of the Universal Negro Improvement Association. Coming from the West Indies, Marcus Garvey instilled within his followers and admirers a dream of a Black nation where Black men would rule. Ford tried to get Garvey to accept Judaism, but he refused. Marcus Garvey expelled Ford in 1923 and Ford soon founded the Beth B'nai Abraham congregation. The Beth B'nai Abraham congregation suffered financial problems and collapsed in 1930, whereupon Ford turned the membership over to Rabbi Wentworth Matthew. Ford then went to Ethiopia where he spent the rest of his life.

Arthur Wentworth Mathew was born in Lagos, West Africa, and lived for a time in St. Kitts, British West Indies, before coming to New York. Matthew had been a minister in the Church of the Living God, the Pillar and Ground of Truth, a black pentecostal church which had endorsed the Universal Negro Improvement Association founded by Marcus Garvey. In 1919 Matthew and eight other men organized the Commandment Keepers: Holy Church of the Living God. In Harlem, he had met white Jews for the first time and in the 1920s came to know Arnold Josiah Ford. Matthew began to learn Orthodox Judaism and Hebrew and acquire ritual materials from Ford. Ford and Matthew learned of the Falashas, the black Jews of Ethiopia, and began to identify with them. When Ford's congregation ran into financial trouble in 1930, the membership was put into Matthew's care and Ford moved to Ethiopia. In 1935, when Haile Selassie was crowned emperor of Ethiopia, Matthew declared his group the Falashas in American and claimed credentials from Haile Selassie.

The Commandment Keepers believe that they are the lineal descendants of the ancient Hebrews by way of the Ethiopian Jews, who, although cut off from the rest of Judaism thousands of years ago, still used the Torah and claimed as their ancestors King Solomon and the Queen of Sheba. They believe the biblical patriarchs to have been black. Matthew taught that the temporary ascendancy of whites was nearly over and that the end of white domination and the restoration of the true Israelites would come with a devastating atomic war in the year 2000. The Commandment Keepers maintain some contact with the mainstream Jewish community in New York City and observe a version of the kosher diet. The group's program includes study of Hebrew. Services are held on the Jewish Sabbath. Men wear yarmulkes and prayer shawls. Jewish holidays are observed with Passover being the most important. Some elements of Christianity are retained, including footwashing, healing and the gospel hymns, but the loud emotionalism of the holiness groups is rejected.

The Original Hebrew Israelite Nation, or Black Israelites, emerged in Chicago in the 1960s around Ben Ammi Carter (born G. Parker) and Shaleah Ben-Israel. Carter and Ben-Israel were proponents of Black Zionism whose purpose was a return to the Holy Land by their members. Beginning in the late 1960s, they made attempts to migrate to Africa and then to Israel. The group moved first to Liberia. Soon after their arrival, they approached the Israeli ambassador about a further move to Israel, but were unable to successfully negotiate the move. In 1968, Carter and thirty-eight Black Israelites flew directly from Chicago to Israel. The group from Liberia was then given temporary sanction and work permits, and joined them in Israel. Over 300 members of the group had migrated to Israel by 1971, when strict immigration restrictions were imposed on them. Other members of the group continued to arrive using tourist visas. By 1980, between 1,500 and 2,000 had settled in four different colonies in Israel.

The Black Israelites feel they are descendants of the ten lost tribes of Israel and thus Jews by birth. They celebrate the Jewish rituals and keep the Sabbath. However, they are polygamous, with a maximum of seven wives allowed. In Israel, the group lives communally. Due to a lack of legal status, the group in Israel lives under harsh conditions and the continual threat of mass deportation. They have been unable obtain necessary additional housing for those members who immigrated illegally and the children are not allowed to attend public schools. There are approximately three thousand members of the Black Israelites remaining in the United States.

The House of Judah is a small Black Israelite group founded in 1965 by Prophet William A. Lewis. Lewis was converted to his black Jewish beliefs by a street preacher in Chicago in the 1960s. Lewis opened a small storefront on the southside and in 1971 moved his group to a twenty-two acre tract of land near Grand Junction, Michigan. The group lived quietly until 1983 when a young boy in the group was beaten to death and media attention resulted. The mother of the boy was sentenced to prison for manslaughter. By 1985 the group had moved to Alabama. The House of Judah teaches that Jacob, Judah, and their descendants were black. They believe that Jerusalem, not Africa, is the black man's land. They believe that the white Jew is the devil who occupies the black man's land but will soon be driven out. Adherents believe that God will send a deliverer, a second Moses, to lead his people, the blacks, from the United States to the promised land of Jerusalem. The group consists of about eighty people living communally.

The Nation of Yahweh, also called the Hebrew Israelites or the Followers of Yahweh, was founded in 1970s by Yahweh ben (son of) Yahweh, who was born Hulon Mitchell Jr. Yahweh ben Yahweh was the son of a Pentecostal minister and at one point joined the Nation of Islam. Yahweh ben Yahweh teaches that there is one God, whose name is Yahweh, and who is black with woolly hair. Yahweh ben Yahweh says that he is the son of God, who has been sent to save and deliver the black people of America. Black people are considered to be the true lost tribe of Judah. Members, upon joining, renounce their slave names and take the surname Israel. Many members wear white robes as commanded in the Bible. They believe that all people who oppose God are devils, regardless of race or color. The Nation of Yahweh sees itself as establishing a united moral power to benefit the total community of America. It supports voter registration, education, business opportunities, scholarships for children, health education, better housing, strong family ties, and harmony among people regardless of race, creed, or color. The corporate entity of the church is the Temple of Love, which has purchased several hotels and apartment buildings and more than forty-two businesses which are used to support the organization and its members. In 1991, Yahweh ben Yahweh and fifteen of his followers were arrested on a variety of charges including racketeering and conspiracy to commit murder. At a trial in the spring of 1992, Yahweh ben Yahweh and seven of his codefendants were convicted of the conspiracy charges, but were not convicted of racketeering. Yahweh ben Yahweh is in jail pending appeal.

The United Hebrew Congregation was a group of several congregations of black Jews which were centered upon the Ethiopian Hebrew Culture Center in Chicago in the mid-1970s. The group was headed by Rabbi Naphtali Ben Israel. These congregations adhered to the belief that Ham's sons, including the Hebrews of the Bible, were black. Sabbath services were held on Saturday. The group appears to be defunct. Other small black Jewish groups in the United States include the B'nai Zakin Sar Shalom, the Moorish Zionist Temple, and Rabbi Ishi Kaufman's Gospel of the Kingdom Temple.

**NATION OF YAHWEH.** (Hebrew Isrealites) The Nation of Yahweh was founded by Yahweh ben Yahweh. Yahweh ben Yahweh was born Hulon Mitchell Jr., the son of a Pentecostal minister. In the 1970s he began to call together the Followers of Yahweh.

The church believes in one God whose name is Yahweh. God is black with woolly hair (Daniel 7:9, Revelation 1:13–15, Dueteronomy 7:21) and has sent his son Yahweh ben Yahweh to the Savior and Deliverer of His people, the so-called black people of America. Black people are considered the true lost tribe of Judah. People who oppose God are devils, regardless of race or color. Any person of any race or color can be saved by faith in Yahweh ben Yahweh.

The Nation of Yahweh supports voter registration, education, self-help jobs, business opportunities, scholarships for children, health education, better housing strong family ties, and peace and harmony among people regardless of race.

The Church is headed by Yahweh ben Yahweh. The nation has purchased several hotels and apartment buildings. It owns the Temple of Love and more than forty-two (in 1988) businesses which are used to support the organization and its members.

**THE ANSAARU ALLAH COMMUNITY.** Best known as the Ansaaru Allah Community, this highly eclectic Black Hebrew communal movement has gone by many different names and since 1992 has adopted the new title of the Holy Tabernacle of the Most High. Its founder-prophet is Dwight York, born in Baltimore on June 26, 1945. As a youth growing up in Brooklyn, York was involved in drug-related crimes and spent some time in prison where he encountered the teachings of Elijah Muhammad and was converted to Islam. On his release, he adopted the name Isa Abdullah, preached a racialist interpretation of the Bible and the Koran, and formed his own community called Ansaar Pure Sufi. In 1969, borrowing concepts from Black Hebrew leaders Ben Ami and Clarke Jenkins, the group was renamed the Nubian Hebrew Mission. By 1973 the Ansaaru Allah Community was formed, its headquarters established in Brooklyn and its male evangelists highly visible in their white robes on the streets disseminating literature, while the women remained indoors, hidden behind veils.

York's authority is based on his claim to be the great grandson of Muhammed Ahmed Ibn Abdullah (1845–1885), the Sudanese Mahdi who led the holy war against the British colonialists in the 1880s, although York's pedigree has been challenged by the Mahdi's family. His title changes frequently and his charismatic role has gradually escalated from prophet to messiah. Currently titled "The Lamb," his whereabouts are unknown; Dwight York remains an enigma.

Ansaar literature conveys idealized portraits of Islamic family life and urges African-American women to adopt the veil and produce the 144,000 pure Nubian children who will "Rapture" their parents during the violent cataclysms of the year 2000, when the reign of Shaytan winds down and the leprous "paleman" is forced to retreat from the hot rays of the sun into underground caves.

The Ansaaru Allah Community does not release membership figures and exhibits a high turnover rate, attracting youthful defectors from other Black nationalist identity movements. Large congregations are visible in Brooklyn, New York; Washington, D.C.; Boston; and the Carribean where the community has established mosques, communal housing, bookstores, and boarding schools where their children study the Koran, Hebrew, Arabic, and Nubic. Their evangelical presence is felt in other cities like Toronto, London, and England, through study groups.

The Ansaar's literature can be ordered from The Tents of Kedar bookstore on Bushwick Avenue, Brooklyn, and is sold from crafts booths in Times Square and major subway exits in New York City and Washington, D.C. The books and pamphlets combine folk art illustrations of black Adams, Eves, Jesus, and other prophets with fundamentalist Muslim diatribes, Egyptian and UFO lore, and racialist interpretation of Genesis and Revelations.

—*Susan J. Palmer*

# 8 ISLAM AND SUFISM

## ISLAM

Islam is fundamentally a prophetic religion based on a series of revelations given to the prophet Muhammad through an angel during the latter part of his life, around 610 to 632 B.C.E., and contained in the Koran, the basic scripture of Islam. The Koran represents the revelation, and Muslims revere Muhammad for transmitting the revelation and for translating it into action, although they do not perceive him as an innovative founder or an author. The term Islam is formed from the infinitive of a verb meaning "to accept," "to submit," "to commit oneself," and means "submission" or "surrender." Thus, a Muslim is one who submits or one who commits himself to Islam, which is accepted as the absolute and final faith.

The religion in pre-Islamic Arabia was a development out of the primitive Semitic desert faith, that, in southern Arabia, resulted in an advanced astral cult, centered in the moon-god and reflecting Babylonian and Zoroastrian influences. In other regions the native converts of Judaism and Christianism abandoned their primitive faiths and became monotheists. Most Arabs worshipped local gods and goddesses, as well as certain astral deities. The three goddesses venerated in the city of Mecca were al-Lat, a mother-goddess, perhaps a representative of the sun; al-Manat, the goddess of faith; and al-'Uzza, the morning star. They were believed to be the daughters of Allah, who was conceived as the creator. Besides these divinities, there were lesser spirits, such as angels and various sorts of spirits (jinn), which were allegedly created from fire two thousand years before Adam, and could at will appear to human eyes. Some of them were friendly, whereas others were hostile and demonic. Among the demonic beings who were always evil were the ghouls.

The ancient faith of Arabia also seems to have venerated stones, particularly unusual stones such as the meteorite that was built into the corner of the Ka'ba (the cube), an ancient pilgrimage site that was to become the spiritual center of the new faith of Islam. The meteor has been worshipped by the inhabitants of Mecca since it fell in some far past, and it has been called "the black stone that fell from heaven in the days of Adam." The Meccans claimed that Abraham, while on a visit to his son Ishmael, had built the Ka'ba and embedded the Black Stone in it. Year after year the tribes of Arabia came on a pilgrimage to offer sacrifices and to run the circuit of the stone seven times and kiss it. Near the Ka'ba was the holy well Zamzam, whose water was sacred to the pilgrims who ran the circuit. Within the Ka'ba itself there were murals and a number of idols around the chief male deity, Hubal. Together with Allah, who was imageless, these deities constituted a sort of Pantheon, drawing people from every region to Mecca, which was regarded as sacred territory.

The Islamic creed presupposes a cosmology that includes an invisible world, consisting of heaven an hell, as well as the visible one, populated by humans and other life-forms. According to Islam, a purposeful force created and governs both worlds and will ultimately judge them. This force is only knowable through human mediaries, the prophets.

According to tradition, Muhammad was born in 570 B.C.E., the same year Mecca was attacked by the army of Abrahah, ruler of Yemen. His father, a Quraysh of the Hashimite clan, died before his birth and his mother when he was six years old. Muhammad grew up in poverty, sharing the religious beliefs of his community. However, as he came to maturity he more and more looked upon the Meccan religion with a critical eye. He was particularly dissatisfied with the perceived primitiveness of traditional Arabian religion, reflected in its polytheism and animism. Like the Jews and the Christians, he believed that there would be a last judgement and a punishment of idolaters by everlasting fire, and that the one true God could not be represented by any image but only by prophetic spokesmen.

Muhammad visited a cave near the base of Mt. Hira, a few miles north of Mecca, for days at a time to meditate and pray. Suddenly one night, during the holy month of Ramadan, he received the first revelation of the Koran. Belief in the revelation given to Muhammad by the angel Gabriel is a fundamental tenet of Islam. In the "Night of Power and Excellence" the angel Gabriel rose in vision before him crying, "Recite!" After this vision, a long period of self-questioning followed, and finally Muhammad came to the conclusion that he was a true prophet and apostle of Allah; that is, he was a messenger of the one and only God already known to the Jews and Christians. He believed that Allah was using him as a mouthpiece, and that the verses he recited, reflecting the power and final judgment of God, were real revelations.

After many years of preaching, Muhammad brought in to mediate an ongoing dispute in another Arabian town, Medina, where he erected the first mosque, which was both his house and a place of worship. He rapidly evolved a new cultus and a number of practices were soon established, such as weekly services on Friday, prostration during prayer in the direction of Mecca, a call to prayer from the mosque's roof, and the taking up of alms for the poor and for support of the cause.

After his death, his spiritual practices and the teachings revealed through him became the basis of the faith and practice of Islam. Most of Islam is subsumed by Muslim authorities under three heads:

1. *Articles of Faith.* These contain the most important article in Muslim theology: "(There is) no god but God." God stands alone and supreme, and exists before any other being or thing, is self-subsistent, omniscient, and omnipotent. God is the creator, and in the day of judgment he will save the believer and place him in paradise. Allah reveals his will and guides men in three distinct ways: through Muhammad, his messenger; through the Koran; and through the angels. Muslim prophecy distinguishes the prophets according to degree of visionary perception, from the sights and sounds of a dream to the suprasensible perception in the waking state. According to this classification, which is probably derived from criteria suggested in Hebrew Scriptures, there is the simple prophet, who sees or hears an angel in a dream. Then there is the envoy—to a more or less numerous group—who sees the angel while awake. Finally, among the envoys there are six great prophets who were charged to reveal the new law and who received the dictation of the law from an angel while in a waking state. These six prophets are Adam, Noah, Abraham, Moses, Jesus, and Muhammad. Muhammad is the Seal of the Prophets, meaning that his revelation closes the cycle of the six periods of prophecy.

2. *Right Conduct.* The Koran and the example of the Prophet supplies Muslims with guidance for everyday life. Islamic law prescribes a wide range of acts for Muslims from birth to death. They include the laws prohibiting wine and gambling, the regulations covering the relations of the sexes and granting a higher status to women.

3. *Religious Duty.* This is summed up in the "Five Pillars": (1) the repetition of the creed "There is no god but Allah, and Muhammad is the prophet of Allah"; (2) prayer, for which the good Muslim reserves five moments each day; (3) almsgiving, or Zakat, which consists of a free-will offering, represented by gifts to the poor, the needy, debtors, slaves, wayfarers, beggars, and charities of various kinds; (4) the fast during the sacred month of Ramadan; and (5) the pilgrimage that every Muslim is expected to make once in a lifetime during the sacred month.

Lines of divergent thought appeared early in Muslim tradition. The issues underlying the first Muslim controversies concerned sin, conflicts about faith and acts, an certain political conflicts. The Kharijites—separatists or secessionists—for example, claimed that the only sure way of getting the right caliph (secular and religious leader of the community) was to select the best qualified person, not necessarily a person from just the Prophet's family or tribe.

The position of the Murjites—the advocates of delayed judgement—was that only God can judge who is a true Muslim and who is not, and that believers should treat all practicing Muslisms as real Muslims, leaving to the final judgment the fixing of their final status.

The need to establish clear criteria for Muslim behavior led to the formulation of an orthodox majority position. This formulation, accepted by 90 percent of the Islamic world, is referred to as Sunni Islam. The Sunnis appeal to the sunna—behavior or practice—of Muhammad and the early Muslim community in Medina as the basis for their religious practices. Other sources of proper belief and practices are the hadith—traditions—that recorded the Prophet's spoken decisions or judgments. If an appeal to these sources proves inconclusive for determining proper conduct, analogies are drawn from the principles embodied in the Koran or in Medinan precedents, or from the consensus of opinion of the local Muslim community. This formulation of sources for determining proper behavior and practice is followed by the four schools of the law that arose during the first two centuries of Islam: the Hanifite, the Malikite, the Shafi'ite, and the Hanbalite.

The Mu'tazilites, on the other hand, who appeared first in Syria and Iraq during the Ummayad caliphate, were among the first Muslims to engage in what was called kalam, or reasoned argument in defense of the faith, which laid emphasis upon the free response of men to the moral demands of Allah, seeking men's rational assent.

The emergence of Islamic mysticism was encouraged by the popular yearning for the presence of unworldly men dedicated to God, asceticism, and holiness. These mystics, the Sufis, appeared in the eighth century and, although they based their mysticism on the Koran, sought philosophical aid from Neo-Platonism and Gnosticism, while Christian monasticism supplied them with organizational hints. Those Sufis who undertook a wandering life, dependent on charity, came to be called dervishes, from the Persian *darwish*, meaning poor.

The most significant disagreement within Islam led to the Shi'ah Schism, which focused on issues of spiritual perfection and political succession. It was motivated by the powerful desire to have the Islamic community directed by Muhammad's own descendants, specifically by descendants of his daughter Fatima, his cousin and son-in-law 'Ali, and his grandsons al-Hasan and al-Husayn. The Shi'ah declaration of faith is: "There is no God

but God; Muhammad is the Prophet of God, and 'Ali is the Saint of God."
The murder of 'Ali and the deaths of his two sons has haunted the lives of
the Shi'ites, much as the death of Jesus has conditioned Christian faith.
Shi'tes also believe in the expected return of a divinely guided Messianic per-
sonage, the Mahdi, who will be a descendant of the Prophet through 'Ali.
The descendants of 'Ali with special spiritual status are referred to as imams,
which is a confusing term because the people who lead the faithful in prayer
are also called imams. Disagreement over which descendant receives the
mantle of the "imam-ship" has led to divisions within the Shi'ite community.

Subjected to constant opposition and persecution by the Sunni, the
Shi'ites were able to survive as an underground movement in the areas where
their views were proscribed. (Modern Iran is the only contemporary country
in which Shi'ism predominant.) Underground sects have continued to form.
Some sects have built states within states, others have ruled large areas as
outlaw kingdoms, and a violent minority has conspired secretly to annihilate
its enemies. The three general groups that form the Shi'ite sects are:

1. The Zaidites, who approximate most closely the traditionalist position. They consider Zaid as the fifth imam instead of Muhammad
   al-Baqir, the fifth imam of the other sects.
2. The Twelvers, who claim the great majority of the Shi'ites as members, and get their name from reckoning from the twelfth imam,
   Muhammad al-Muntazar.
3. The Isma'ilites or Seveners and their Offshots. Found chiefly in
   India, Pakistan and East Africa, they are so called because they have
   remained loyal to Isma'il, the first son of the sixth imam.

Various movements originated from the Isma'ilites, such as the Qarma-
tians, a secret society organized along communistic lines, and the mysterious Assassins, who perfected the terrorist art of worming one's way in
disguise into the presence of Muslim rulers and officials and striking them
down with a poisoned dagger.

*—Michela Zonta*

**BLACK MUSLIMS.** Africans south of the Sahara had developed
Islamic centers prior to the time of the slave trade and Muslims were
among the first slaves in the United States. Muslim slaves tended to be
viewed as superior by both themselves and other slaves, as they were often
educated. They resisted acculturation and assimilation, thus retaining
their faith longer. Some Muslim slaves, under pressure from Christianizing
forces, would try to accommodate to the new faith by equating God with

Allah and Jesus with Mohammed. While no definite connection can be made between twentieth-century Black Muslims and those who might have survived the slave era, it is possible that some American Muslim groups had their roots in the descendants of Muslim slaves.

For many African Americans, Islam has provided an alternative to Christianity, which failed to establish a truly racially inclusive society. The growth of Islam among African Americans is related to the idea that Islam is a religious faith that has affirmed their African heritage. Most of the non-immigrant Muslims in America are African American converts to Islam.

The Black Muslim movement began when Timothy Drew, who became known as Noble Drew Ali, founded the Moorish Science Temple in Newark, New Jersey, in 1913. Drew Ali stated that black Americans were racially not Africans but Asians, descended from the Moors who settled the northern and western coasts of Africa. He claimed that he had been commissioned by the King of Morocco to teach Islam to black Americans. Drew Ali was exposed to black nationalist leader Marcus Garvey's ideas after Garvey arrived in the United States in 1917, and these became central to the movement's ideology. Drew Ali published a book called *The Holy Koran*, which, rather than being a translation of the Koran, was put together from a mixture of American occult literature and Islamic, Christian, and black nationalist ideas. The Moorish Science Temple came to real prominence in Chicago in the 1920s. Temple members wore bright red fezzes and converted their slave names into new ones by adding to them the suffixes "el" or "bey." After Marcus Garvey was deported in 1927, the Moorish American Science Temple wooed, and to a great extent won over, Garvey's followers. Noble Drew Ali died in 1929 and was succeeded by a younger colleague.

The original Nation of Islam arose in Detroit in 1930. In that year a peddler appeared with goods and stories from the black homelands. He became increasingly strident in denouncing the white race. The stranger was called W. D. Fard or Wali Farrad Muhammad. He was a former member of the Moorish Science Temple of America who claimed to be Noble Drew Ali reincarnated. He asserted that he had been sent from Mecca to secure freedom, justice, and equality for African Americans. He established a temple in Detroit. Fard disappeared in 1934 and his top lieutenant, Elijah Muhammad (formerly Elijah Poole), became leader of the movement.

Under the leadership of Elijah Muhammad, the Nation of Islam grew into a strong, cohesive unit. Muhammad moved the headquarters to Chicago and opened temples, mosques, schools, housing projects, stores, restaurants, and farms. Some themes taught in the Nation of Islam reflect traditional Islamic teachings: submission to Allah, and the repudiation of alcohol, sex outside of marriage, the eating of pork, and gambling. However, some teachings run counter to traditional Islam: The white man as devil, the identification of W. D. Fard as Allah and Elijah Muhammad as a prophet, and the quasi-scientific theory of human history and purpose. Elijah Muhammad's creation myth helped explain the present-day oppression of blacks. Muhammad taught that blacks were the original humans, but a rebellious scientist produced and released genetically weakened pale stock. The whites that he created were given six thousand years to rule, ending in 1914. In the meantime, most Muslims were to use "X" as a surname, indicating that their original African names were lost in slavery. The Black Muslims looked to the establishment of a black nation to be owned and operated by blacks. Whites were excluded from the movement and food, dress, and behavior patterns were regulated.

In the mid-1950s, a former nightclub singer named Louis Eugene Wolcott joined the Nation of Islam. He dropped his last name and became known as Minister Louis X. His oratorical and musical skills carried him to a position in charge of the Boston Mosque.

Malcolm X, the most famous member of the Nation of Islam, was the charismatic leader of the New York Temple. He was expelled from the Nation of Islam, either for speaking approvingly of the assassination of John F. Kennedy or for publicizing to other members the sexual improprieties of Elijah Muhammad. Upon Malcolm X's expulsion, Louis X was made the leader of the large Harlem center and designated as official spokesperson for Elijah Muhammad. After his expulsion from the Nation of Islam, Malcolm X made a pilgrimage to Mecca, during which he experienced true interracial harmony for the first time. He then abandoned the theme of black racism and formed a more traditional Islamic group, the Muslim Mosque, Inc. Malcolm X's teachings following his trip to Mecca influenced many African Americans, including Elijah Muhammad's son, Wallace (also known as Warith) D. Muhammad, to move toward orthodox Islamic traditions. Malcolm X was shortly thereafter killed by members of the Nation of Islam.

When Nation of Islam leader Elijah Muhammad died in 1975, many members thought that Louis X, who was by then known by the name of Abdul Haleem Farrakhan, would become the new leader of the Nation of Islam. However, Elijah Muhammad's son, Wallace, was chosen instead. During his first three years as leader of the Nation of Islam, Wallace Muhammad brought the organization into mainstream Islamic belief and practice and away from the racial and black national policies of his father. The group began to admit white people to membership. The organization went through a series of name changes and is now known as the American Muslim Mission. The organization has since been decentralized and the approximately two hundred centers now function as independent mosques.

A notable contribution made by the Nation of Islam and the American Muslim Mission is its nationwide system of over sixty schools, the Clara Muhammad Schools. The teachers tend to be immigrants with advanced degrees from their native countries. Islamic studies are emphasized along with English, history, and science. Arabic is taught from kindergarten. The philosophy of the schools is racially inclusive and religiously tolerant.

The abandonment by Wallace Muhammad of his father's antiwhite rhetoric and identification of Elijah Muhammad as prophet was not accepted by all members. At least four splinter groups left the American Muslim Mission and formed their own congregations which adhered to Elijah Muhammad's original doctrines.

Silis Muhammad was the first to leave the American Muslim Mission in 1977, in order to reestablish the Nation of Islam as intended by Elijah Muhammad. Silis Muhammad had joined the Nation of Islam in the 1960s and become the national circulation manager for the Nation's tabloid, *Muhammad Speaks.* He became a close confidant of Elijah Muhammad and eventually assumed a role as his spiritual son, although there was no biological relationship. Silis Muhammad rejected the changes instituted by the Nation of Islam's new leader, Warith D. Muhammad, charged Warith with being a false prophet, and demanded that the property of the Nation of Islam be returned to Elijah Muhammad's true followers. Silis Muhammad established the headquarters of the new Nation of Islam in Atlanta, Georgia. The group believes that Allah appeared in the person of W. D. Fard in 1930 and that he spoke face to face with Elijah Muhammad from 1931 through 1933. Elijah Muhammad is therefore considered to be Moses, the Bible being considered a prophetic and symbolic history of black America today.

In 1978, Louis Farrakhan and several thousand followers left the American Muslim Mission and reestablished the Nation of Islam as instituted by Elijah Muhammad. Louis Farrakhan and Silis Muhammad did not agree on the role of Elijah Muhammad in regard to Jesus. Farrakhan had interpreted some of Elijah Muhammad's statements as meaning that he claimed to be the fulfillment of some of Jesus' prophecies. Silis rejected this interpretation. Because of their disagreement on this point, the two were unable to join together to create one Nation of Islam. Membership of Farrakhan's Nation of Islam is estimated between five thousand and ten thousand members.

John Muhammad, the brother of Nation of Islam founder Elijah Muhammad, also left the American Muslim Mission in 1978 and formed a new Nation of Islam temple in Detroit to perpetuate the programs outlined in Elijah Muhammad's two books, *Message to the Blackman* and *Our Saviour Has Arrived.* John Muhammad believes that Minister Elijah Muhammad was the last Messenger of Allah and was sent to teach the black man a New Islam. The periodical of the congregation is *Minister John Muhammad Speaks.*

A fourth Nation of Islam was formed following Wallace Muhammad's shift to a more orthodox form of Islam. Emmanuel Abdullah Muhammad claimed to be the Caliph of Islam raised up to guide the people in the absence of Allah (W. D. Fard) and his Messenger (Elijah Muhammad). There is an Islamic tradition that says that a caliph always follows a messenger. Mosques were set up in Baltimore and Chicago.

Many years before Wallace Muhammad moved the Nation of Islam toward Orthodox Islam, there was another movement to do so. The Hanafi Madh-hab Center was set up in the United States by Dr. Tasibur Uddein Rahman, a Pakistani Muslim, in the late 1920s. The Hanafi Muslims have taken a special interest in presenting Islam to African Americans and informing them that Islam is a religion that does not recognize distinctions of race or color. In 1947, Rahman met Ernest Timothy McGee, gave him a new name of Khalifa Hammas Abdul Khaalis and taught him the traditions and practice of the Prophet Muhammad. In 1950, Dr. Rahman sent Khalifa Hamaas Abdul Khaalis into the Nation of Islam to guide the members into Sunni Islam, the faith and practice recognized by the great majority of Muslims. By 1956, Khaalis was the national secretary of the Nation of Islam. He left the Nation of Islam in 1958, after unsuccessfully trying to convince Elijah Muhammad to change the direction of the movement. At the beginning of 1973, Khaalis wrote letters to the members and leaders of the Nation of Islam, again asking them to change to Sunni Muslim belief and practice. On January 18, 1973, members of the Nation of Islam came into the Hanafi Madh-hab Center in Washington, D.C. (which also served as Khaalis' home), and murdered six of his children and his stepson and wounded his wife. Five members of the Philadelphia Nation of Islam were convicted of the murders and given relatively light sentences. In 1977, Khalifa Hamaas Abdul Khaalis and other members of his group took action against the showing of a motion picture due to be released in American theaters, *Mohammad, Messenger of God,* which they considered to be sacriligious. They took over three buildings in Washington, D.C., and held the people inside hostage for thirty-eight hours. One man was killed. Khaalis was sentenced to spend from 41 to 120 years in prison; eleven of his followers were also convicted and sentenced. Since there were no Muslims on the jury, Khaalis considers the jury to have lacked impartiality.

Separate from the mainstream of the Black Muslim movement in the United States is the Ahmadiyya Movement in Islam, which was brought to the United States in 1921 by Dr. Mufti Muhammad Sadiq. The movement originated in India in 1889 as a Muslim reform movement. It differs from orthodox Islam in that it believes that Hazrat Mirza Ghulam Ahmad (1835–1908) was both the expected returning savior of Muslims and the promised Messiah of Christians. Ahmad said that Jesus had not died on the cross, but had come to Kashmir in his later life and died there. The divinity of Jesus is denied in line with the assertion that Allah is the one true God.

Ahmadiyya has the most aggressive missionary movement in Islam. Dr. Sadiq opened the first American Ahmadiyya center in Chicago. He began to publish a periodical, *Muslim Sunrise*. While Sadiq did not have the intention that Ahmadiyya become a black man's religion, it turned out that the overwhelming majority of Dr. Sadiq's converts were black. The movement currently has about ten thousand American members in thirty-seven cities.

—*KAY HOLZINGER*

## SUFISM

Sufism (Arabic, *tasawwuf*) is the mystical dimension of Islam. It refers to a variety of modes of spirituality that developed in the Islamic world, including ascetic-social-critical movements, esoteric and poetic interpretations of the Koran, and spiritual confraternities. The goals of traditional Sufism include purity of devotion and the interiorization of the *shahada*, the most fundamental tenet of Islamic faith: "*La ilaha illa Allah.*" "There is no God but God," or in the classic Sufi formulation, "There is no reality but The Reality." Sufis have been major transmitters of Islamic piety to geographic regions beyond the Middle Eastern "heartland" of Islam. Sufism came to North America with the arrival of the Indian teacher, Hazrat Inayat Khan (see Sufi Order) in the early twentieth century, and since then a number of Sufi groups have emerged with different understandings as to their relationship to the Islamic tradition. Sufism in America today includes groups whose members see themselves as "Muslims first," groups that see Sufism as a universal call to unity and peace that is not inherently connected to Islam, and groups that have individuals of both perspectives.

Sufism in the Islamic world has its origins in the inspired preachers and teachers of the early period of Islam, who called the faithful to constant remembrance of God and to a life based on the virtues exemplified in the life of Muhammad, the Prophet of Islam. Teachers such as Hasan al-Basri of Iraq (d. 728 C.E.), Rabia, the woman saint from Iraq (d. 801), and Dhu'l-Nun, the Egyptian of Nubian descent (d. 859) are known, respectively, for their teachings on the need for constant struggle (*jihad*) with the lower self (*nafs*), the way of pure love of God, and the way of intuitive knowledge of God (*ma'rifa*). Al-Tustari (d. 896) began discussions on the human heart (*qalb*) as locus of union and knowledge of God and on "the light of Muhammad" as primal cosmic origin of the human race. Al-Hallaj (d. 922) represents those Islamic mystics whose ecstatic utterances brought criticism and sometimes persecution from the juridical or theological authorities of Islam. Hallaj was executed for declaring "*Ana al-Haqq*," "I am the Truth," as an expression of what "remains" when the individual ego has been annihilated (*fana*) in God. Most Sufis were more "sober" in their expressions of spiritual realization. Theosophical and poetic expressions of Sufism developed, the most well-known representatives being Ibn Arabi and Rumi. They share the Sufi doctrine referred to as *wahdat al-wujud*, or "Unity of Being," which maintains that ultimately all of reality is not other than God. Outer forms of difference and distinction between God and creatures, between individuals, and even between religions are in a sense illusory; at the heart of all beings is Being itself (God). The fundamental human problem is forgetting the primordial unity human beings share with God.

By the twelfth century, formal religious orders (*tariqas*) began to crystalize around revered teachers, and certain institutions developed. Each order was headed by a spiritual master (*shaykh*, or *murid*) whose function was to inculcate spiritual doctrines, practices, and virtues to the disciples (dervishes), who in turn, vowed absolute obedience to their teacher. The Sufi path, with its various "states and stations," was seen as a journey toward union with God. Disciples could marry and were expected to participate in their ordinary professions, but they would meet in lodges (*khanaqahs*) for prayer, rituals, and counsel with the shaykh. Emphasized were the virtues of trust, repentance, patience, contentment, gratitude, poverty, love, and absolute surrender ("islam") to God. Noble conduct also included modesty, loyalty, hospitality, and generosity.

Sufi orders developed their own particular communal rituals and practices, based on the teachings of the shaykh, to complement and deepen the understanding of the requirements of faith. There were initiation rituals, night vigils, litanies of prayer, times of retreat, and seclusion. The most central practice was the *dhikr* (or *zikr*), the ritual (as the term indicates) of "remembrance" of God, which always included the invocation of the name of God, usually in the form of the creedal statement, "*La ilaha illa Allah.*" Some groups developed a "silent dhikr," silent repetition of the *La ilaha* as an aid toward surrender of the ego. Other groups utilized a spoken *dhikr* in which blessings on the prophets and saints and the "ninety-nine most beautiful names of Allah" were repeated hundreds of times. Many groups came to utilize both kinds of *dhikr*. The *sama*, or spiritual concert, described as "listening with the ear of the heart to music" became an important part of Sufi gatherings in many parts of the Islamic world, and "dance" was utilized in some orders, such as the Mevlevis (the Whirling Dervishes). Inspired poetry recital and musical compositions were intended to express and cultivate spiritual states. Popular Sufi piety came to include pilgrimages to the shrines of Sufi saints, although this practice has been criticized or disallowed where the influence of modernist puritanical movements prevailed (such as the Wahabis of Saudi Arabia).

Some of the important traditional orders of Islam, with their historic locations of activity, are: the Qadiri order (the largest order in the world, with members from West Africa to Indonesia); the Naqshbandi order (Central Asia and India); the Chisti order (India); the Shadhili order (North Africa); the Mawlawi (the "Mevlevis"), Khalwati, and Bektashi orders of Turkey; the Nimatullahi order (Iran); and the Tijani order (West Africa). All of these traditional orders are represented in America today, as Sufi teachers arrived by way of immigration patterns or by way of invitations from Westerners searching for alternative sources of wisdom. These teachers, following in the pattern of the historical Sufis, continue to be transmitters of traditional Islamic mystical teachings and values, now to the West. Of course, Sufism itself has been shaped by the cultures that have received it, and Sufism in the Euro-American context is no exception.

The Sufi Order established by Hazrat Inayat Khan in 1910 is the oldest of Sufi groups in America. Hazrat Khan was initiated in India by a traditional Chisti master, yet for his western audiences he taught Sufism as a universal path to unity with God and attunement to underlying cosmic structures. The order has tended to attract members from the middle classes (a phenomenon generally true for Sufism in America), and utilizes Sufi teachings as well as other "alternative" approaches to spiritual development.

The Khalwati-Jerrahi Sufi order is (at least in its Spring Valley, New York branch) an example of the more traditional form of Sufism, where Islamic religion coupled with and, from the point of view of the dervishes, deepened by practice of the "interior" dimension of their religion.

The Bawa Muhaiyaddeen Fellowship is an example of a group whose community life came to include more traditional Islamic practices as time passed. Established in Philadelphia in 1971 by a teacher/"holy man" well known in Sri Lanka since the 1940s, Bawa Muhaiyaddeen utilized both Hindu and Sufi wisdom stories and cosmology, but his building of a mosque in 1982 became an invitation to closer involvement with the larger Islamic community. Bawa emphasized "Islam" as a state of unity "beyond" distinction of religion, race, or caste, but many of Bawa's original followers also perform normative Islamic religious duties. The mosque has also become a magnet for non-Sufi Muslim immigrants and African American Muslims to join the community.

A number of Sufi groups are involved in publication, either of their own shaykh's teachings (such as the Bawa Muhaiyaddeen Fellowship and the Khaniqahi-Nimaltullahis) or of translations of classical Sufi expositors (e.g., Coleman Barks's translations of Rumi). A major inspiration for the academic study of Sufism in both the United States and abroad has been the writings of Seyyed Hossein Nasr and others connected with the "perennialist school" of Frithjof Schuon. Sufism, through past interpreters such as Idries Shah and present interpreters such as Kabir Helminski, has been an important influence in a number of human potential and transpersonal psychology movements. The most complete listing of Sufi materials—classical, contemporary, popular, and academic—has been the periodical, *Sufi Review*, published by Pir Publications in Westport, Connecticut.

—*GISELA WEBB*

**THE SUFI ORDER.** The Sufi order represents the earliest phase of Sufi activity in the United States. It was founded in 1910 by the Indian teacher, Hazrat Inayat Khan, who believed that his "Sufi message" of the modern era could unite East and West through its teachings of universal brotherhood and "attunement" to cosmic structures of unity. The Sufi Order has continued its work under Hazrat Khan's son, Pir Vilayat Khan, since the late 1960s, and it is perhaps best known for the "Sufi Dances" created by Hazrat's disciple, Sam Lewis in the late 1960s.

Hazrat Inayat Khan was an accomplished musician trained in classical Indian music and initiated into the Chisti order, well known for its use of music. Hazrat Khan's musical concerts and spiritual talks found a receptive audience among wealthy and artistic elites in America and Europe who were drawn to the conciliatory message of spiritual unity taught by Hazrat Khan during the period of social and political tumult surrounding Indian independence and World War I. He initiated a number of disciples during his visits to the United States between 1910 and 1925, with Fairfax, California, being the site of the first Sufi *khanaqah* (lodge) in America. After Hazrat Khan's death in 1927, an important early disciple of Hazrat, Rabia Martin, turned over Sufi properties to Meher Baba, who adapted Sufi order teachings and began the "Sufism Reoriented" movement.

A new wave of interest in Hazrat Khan's teachings took place in the 1960s and 1970s, and the Sufi Order grew rapidly under leadership of Hazrat Khan's European-educated son Pir Vilayat Khan. Pir Vilayat began giving lectures and conducting meditations in New York for the "flower children" generation. Samuel L. Lewis, a west coast disciple of Hazrat Khan, introduced thousands of people to the "Message" through Sufi dancing, with Shahabuddin Less leading Sufi dancing (now known as Dances of Universal Peace) at the cathedral of St. John the Divine in New York. A *khanaqah* was opened in New York during this time, but it was closed in 1982 as a decline in energy and changes in leadership took place. Land had been purchased in the Berkshire hills of New England during the 1970s to be the site of the "Abode of the Message," and it continues to be used for the many activities sponsored by the Sufi Order. It is also the site of a small community of Sufi Order families.

Hazrat Khan's teachings embody characteristics of Chisti Sufism, especially in the belief that sacred music could help elevate and "attune" the soul. The Chisti orientation also blends Hindu Advaita Vendanta ("nondu-alistic") thought with the "unity of being" philosophy of traditional Sufism, maintaining that in reality "Truth is one," and that "Moslem" and "Hindu" and Christian" are only outer distinctions. Hazrat also taught that Sufism was not essentially tied to historical Islam but, rather, consisted of timeless universal teachings related to peace, harmony, and the essential unity of all being(s). Thus, his teachings carry the imprint of traditional Sufism (especially Ibn Arabi and Rumi) as well as the "untraditional" conviction that new universal forms of worship should be created to affirm the integrity and common truth of different religions. "Universal worship" as well as forms of *dhikr*, meditation, meditative dancing, retreat, counseling, and studies of Hazrat Khan's teachings led by Pir Vilayat form some of the activities of the Sufi Order today. However, the activities have expanded beyond Hazrat Khan's teachings to include lectures and workshops in a wide variety of holistic areas (e.g., ecological, psychotherapeutic, Chinese medicine).

The Sufi Order is led by Pir Vilayat, and the order utilizes the traditional teacher/disciple (*murshid/murid*) structure. However, membership includes differing levels of participation from very active, to occasional attenders of workshops, to mere subscribers to periodicals.

The organization's quarterly publication is *Hearts and Wings*, but Omega Press in New Lebanon, New York, is the main publication arm, serving as distributor of Hazrat Khan/Pir Vilayat literature as well as other Sufi and non-Sufi New Age literature.

Differences of opinion over Pir Vilayt's authority led to a splintering of some west coast members and the formation of the Sufi Islamia Ruhaniat Society. Many were Samuel Lewis's followers.

*—GISELA WEBB*

**SUFI ISLAMIA RUHANIAT SOCIETY.** Sufi Islamia Ruhaniat (SIRS) is an offshoot of the Sufi Order founded by Hazrat Khan. Its members are mainly followers of Samuel L. Lewis, (also known as "Sufi Sam" and his formal title, Sufi Ahmed Murad Chisti), the early west coast disciple of Hazrat Khan responsible for developing "sufi dancing."

As early as the late sixties, there were discussions between Pir Vilayat, Hazrat Khan's son and now leader of the Sufi Order, and Sam Lewis as to the relationship between their contingencies of followers. Sam Lewis's diary, 1970, indicates talk of "separation" from Pir Vilayat. By 1977 (six years after Sam Lewis's death) the San Francisco group separated from Pir Vilayat, disagreeing with Pir Vilayat's rejection of homosexuals in the membership, his forbidding of the use of mind-altering drugs, and his demand for acceptance as prime spiritual guide. The Sufi Islamia Ruhaniat continues to use Sam Lewis's teachings and inspiration. Sam Lewis represents an important phase, not only of Sufism, but of contemporary American religious history, when a tide of universalist-oriented religious leaders, eastern and western, traditional and nontraditional, participated in global cross-fertilization of world spiritualities (and not without its often eclectic results).

Samuel Lewis's work reflects Hazrat Khan's approach to Sufism with its emphasis on spiritual development *toward* peace and unity and with its belief in the power of sacred music to elevate the soul. Out of his work with American dancer/choreographer, Ruth St. Denis, his visits to traditional Sufi orders in the east who used music and dance (he mentions the Chisti, Mevlevi, Rufai, and Bedawi orders), and his own mystical visions, he created "Spiritual Dance" and "Spiritual Walk," with their goals including cosmic attunement, moral development and psychic purification. Activities of SIRS include Spiritual Walk and Dance, zikr, and other practices associated with Sufism. Different levels of instruction are available through the Center for the Study of Spiritual Dance and Walk in San Francisco.

Leaders of the organization are Murshid (guide) Moineddin Jablonski and Masheikh Wali Ali Meyer. Headquarters are in San Francisco, with centers in other cities in California. Interaction between SIRS and other Sufi groups exists, with SIRS leader Wali Ali Meyer, for example, conducting workshops at the "Abode of the Message" in New Lebanon, New York.

*Bismillah* is the quarterly journal. The SIRS publishing arm is Sufi Islamia/Prophecy Publications of San Francisco; they provide Sufi literature by Samuel Lewis and Hazrat Khan as well as recorded music used in Dances of Universal Peace and zikr. A most helpful source on the historical period, vision, and activities of Samuel Lewis is *Sufi Vision and Initiation*, a compilation of diary entries by SIRS member, Neil Douglas-Klotz.

—*GISELA WEBB*


**BAWA MUHAIYADDEEN FELLOWSHIP.** Bawa Muhaiyaddeeen Fellowship was founded in 1971 by followers of Shaikh Muhaiyaddeen M. R. Guru Bawa, a Ceylonese Sufi teacher said to be over one hundred years old. Bawa established the Serendib Study Group in Colombo, Sri Lanka, in the 1930s. He was first brought to Philadelphia, Pennsylvania, in 1971 by a disciple. Since the establishment of the Bawa Muhaiyaddeen Fellowship, Bawa has spent his time traveling between Philadelphia and Sri Lanka.

Bawa does not see himself as the teacher of a new religion, but as dealing with the essence of all religion. He teaches the unity of God and human unity in God. As a Sufi, Bawa has lost the self in the Solitary Oneness that is God. God-realization is achieved by the constant affirmation that nothing but God exists, the continual elimination of evil from one's

life, and the conscious effort to acquire God's qualities of patience, tolerance, peacefulness, compassion, and the assumption that all lives should
be treated as one's own. In addition to the United States headquarters in
Philadelphia, groups of the Bawa Muhaiyyaddeen Fellowship have been
established around the United States and Canada.

GURDJIEFF FOUNDATION. The Gurdjieff Foundation was
founded by Jeanne de Salzmann in Paris following the death of spiritual
teacher Georges Ivanovitch Gurdjieff in 1949. This foundation became the
model for similar structures around the world. A foundation was established in New York in 1953 and in San Francisco in 1955.

Georges Ivanovitch Gurdjieff was born in 1872 in a small town on the
Armenian-Turkish border. He studied the mysticism of Greek Orthodoxy
and developed an interest in science and the occult prior to leaving home
as a young man. As a member of the Seekers of the Truth he wandered
from Tibet to Ethiopia in quest of esoteric wisdom. He claimed to have
met representatives of a Hidden Brotherhood (probably Sufi) in central
Asia which preserved an occult tradition.

In 1911, Gurdjieff surfaced in Russia, where he frequented the major
cities. During the First World War, Thomas de Hartmann, who would
become one of Gurdjieff's most loyal followers, first met with Gurdjieff in
what was then Petrograd (now Leningrad). De Hartmann was an aristrocrat,
an officer, and a promising composer. He felt conspicuous in the disrep-
utable cafe in which Gurdjieff required that they meet. Gurdjieff appeared,
a small man with a bushy mustache wearing a black coat. De Hartmann was
impressed with Gurdjieff's deep, penetrating eyes. By the end of this brief
meeting, de Hartmann was determined to study with Mr. Gurdjieff.

In 1915, Pyotr Demianovitch Ouspensky, who would become Gurdjieff's most important disciple, first met his teacher and observed Gurdjieff
groups. Ouspensky asked the members questions about the nature of their
work but they gave him no direct answers. They spoke a terminology that
was unintelligible to him. They spoke of "work on oneself" but failed to
explain what that work consisted of. Ouspensky described Gurdjieff as a
man of an oriental type who was no longer young. He had a black mustache and piercing eyes and wore a black overcoat with a velvet collar and
a black bowler hat.

Gurdjieff and a small band of followers in 1920 emigrated to Tiflis (capital of the Georgian Republic) and then to Constantinople where they stayed
for about a year. From Constantinople they went to Berlin. Finally, in 1922
Gurdjieff and his followers moved to Fontainebleau, south of Paris. There they
bought a manor, the Chateau du Prieure, and started the Institute for the Harmonious Development of Man. Gurdjieff devloped a variety of techniques to
assist the awakening of his followers to contact with higher forces. The most

famous of these techniques were the Gurdjieff movements or Sacred Gymnastics, a series of dancelike exercises. Residents of the Chateau du Prieure included Alexander and Jeanne de Salzmann, writer/editor Alfred R. Orage, and the New Zealand novelist Katherine Mansfield, who died there. A bell woke everyone at six. Breakfast was coffee and bread after which members went straight to work. Outside work, interrupted only for a simple lunch, continued until darkness. Residents would dress for the evening meal, which would occasionally be a banquet in the grand style. After supper, Gurdjieff would sometimes speak and the "Sacred Gymnastics" would take place.

Gurdjieff generated considerable controversy by placing students in situations of tension and conflict designed to force self-conscious awareness. Gurdjieff would order a project begun and then abandoned or shout harshly at people for stupidity, or demand work be done at top speed. At other times he would explain the reasons for these episodes. In the 1920s Gurdjieff worked with composer Thomas de Hartmann to compose the Gurdjieff/de Hartmann music. In 1923 Gurdjieff's entourage presented their "Sacred Gymnastics" with music arranged by de Hartmann in Paris.

Gurdjieff and forty of his pupils first traveled to the United States in early 1924. He presented public demonstrations of his movements in New York and laid the groundwork for the opening of the first branch of his institute. He left the former London editor Alfred R. Orage in New York as his representative. In mid-1924, shortly after he returned to France, he suffered a nearly fatal automobile accident. Due to the long period necessary for his recovery Gurdjieff was forced to scale back the activities of the institute and his plans for opening the New York branch were delayed. During his convalescence, Gurdjieff dedicated himself to writing books to communicate his ideas. Gurdjieff dictated many of his writings to Olga de Hartmann, the aristocratic wife of the composer.

Gurdjieff felt that pupils should remain with him only for a limited period of time and then go back into the world. Some could not break the spell of his fascination and failed to go. He made more and more intolerable demands on those students. Gurdjieff made life so intolerable for Ouspensky that he was forced to leave Fontainebleau in 1924 and move to London. There he expounded on Gurdjieff's teachings to new students. Among these was Henry John Sinclair (Lord Pentland) who studied under P. D. and Sophia Ouspensky in the 1930s and 1940s.

Jane Heap first visited Gurdjieff's Institute in 1925 and was at the center of a group of women that included Gertrude Stein. Ten years later, Jane Heap moved to London at Gurdjieff's request and directed Gurdjieff groups there for many years. By the early 1930s there were very few followers left at the Institute in Fontainebleau and the property was sold in 1933. Gurdjieff continued to travel and groups based on his principles were organized by former students of the Institute around the world.

During World War II, P. D. and Sophia Ouspensky took refuge in the United States and spread Gurdjieff's ideas there. Sophia lived in the United States until her death in the early 1960s, but P. D. Ouspensky returned to England at the end of the war and died there in 1947. Upon Ouspensky's death, many of his students journeyed to Paris to study directly with Gurdjieff. One of these was Henry John Sinclair (Lord Pentland), the Ouspenskys' longstanding pupil. He was in contact with Gurdjieff during the last two years of Gurdjieff's life. Ouspensky's book *In Search of the Miraculous* was published posthumously with Gurdjieff's authorization, and recounted his years with Gurdjieff from 1915 to 1924.

In 1949, Gurdjieff died, but his teaching was carried on by others. Jeanne de Salzmann founded the Gurdjieff Foundation in Paris. In 1950, the first volume of Gurdjieff's proposed three-volume work, *All and Everything*, was published. The second volume, *Meetings with Remarkable Men*, was published later, but the third was never published and presumably lost. Written in the format of an epic science fiction novel, the book is meant to upset the worldview of the reader and in the end to evoke feelings of compassion and hope.

John Pentland founded the Gurdjieff Foundation of New York in 1953. The New York foundation owns a building on 63rd Street which contains meeting rooms, a dance studio, a library, a workshop, and a music room. Some five hundred people are involved in activities such as academic studies of initiatory traditions, music, dance, and work projects. In 1955 Gurdjieff Foundation was started by John Pentland in San Francisco. Pentland was president until his death in 1984. The film *Meetings with Remarkable Men* was released in 1979. It was conceived by Jeanne de Salzmann and completed under director Peter Brook. The film effectively conveys the energy of Gurdjieff's early spiritual quest.

Gurdjieff taught that humans are asleep and that they are operated like puppets by forces of which they are unaware. He sought students who were or could become aware of the other forces of their environment. Gurdjieff's system requires an individual teacher-student relationship. It became known as the "fourth way," the way of encounter with ordinary life, as opposed to the ways of the yogi, monk, or fakir. The fourth way is symbolized by a nine-pointed design in a circle, called the enneagram. The Gurdjieff Foundation has centers in New York, San Francisco, Los Angeles, and most major cities.

**INSTITUTE FOR THE DEVELOPMENT OF THE HARMONIOUS HUMAN BEING.** The Institute for the Development of the Harmonious Human Being was established in the early 1960s with the purpose of presenting the teachings of E. J. Gold on voluntary evolution as preparation for service to the Absolute. Gold's doctrine drew upon the teachings of George Gurdjieff, whose inspiration is evident in Gold's choice of a name for his work, his use of the enneagram in his Institute's logo, and his picturing of a Gurdjieff look-alike on the cover of a number of publications.

Gold emphasized the representation of the being or Essential Self as neither awake nor asleep, but rather identified with the body, emotions, and psyche. These are collectively named "the machine," which is described as asleep, and which has a transformational role in relation to the Essential self, but only if it is led to an awakened state. The awakened state can be produced through practices as well as special living conditions. The lifestyle of the individual is supposed to be based on the adequate consideration of the machine's Psycho-physical activities. Gold claimed that long-term, gradual erosion—the so-called wind-and-water method—is fundamental to achieve the awakening of the machine, the activation of its transformational functions, as well as the eventual transformation of the Essential Self according to its true purpose. In his numerous books, Gold stressed the importance of the clearsightedness of the waking state, the use of indirect methods to defeat the fixed habits of the machine, and the study of the individual's "chronic," a defense mechanism against the waking state acquired by everyone during early childhood.

Gold's teachings have been developed by his students over the years through intensive research and their wide application in such fields as architecture, psychotherapy, early childhood education, and computer programming. Members of the Institute for the Development of the Harmonious Human Being can be found in the United States and Canada, as well as in Australia, Great Britain, Germany, and Norway. *Talk of the Month* is the periodical of the institute.

**S U B U D .** Subud is a spiritual movement that began in Indonesia in the 1920s with the inner revelatory experiences of a Javanese Muslim, Muhammad Subuh, who believed that his "contact" with the divine power, the universal "life force," was to be transmitted to anyone who desired it without distinction as to nationality, race, or religion; that it would move the person to a life lived in accordance with one's true nature and the will of God; and that it simply required the attitude of surrender, patience, and sincerity. Subud is an acronym for the Sanskrit words *Susila Budhi Dharma*, which denote character and conduct that is "truly human." Subud has approximately five thousand members in seventy countries around the world, with about two thousand in the United States.

Muhammad Subuh, referred to by members as Bapak (Indonesian for elder, father), was a civil servant acquainted with, but apparently not initiated in, Sufi groups in Indonesia. He had an initial revelatory experience lasting "1,001 nights" which he understood to be an awakening of the deepest part of the self, an intense purification, and a form of guidance from God. The experience involved spontaneous bodily movements, visions, and noises. Bapak described his experience, his "*latihan kedjiwaan*" (Indonesian for spiritual exercise) as a contact with the power of God (God's spirit, the *ruh al-qudus*, and vibration). He came to understand that the experience was to be passed on, not as a new religion, but as an inner training and source of guidance for everyday life. Bapak proceeded to "open" people—the term for the initial "contact" latihan—and practiced the latihan with Indonesians in Semarang during the 1940s. Subud came to be known internationally through the writings of journalist and linguist, Hussein Rofe, who met (and was opened by) Bapak while researching Sufism in Indonesia, and especially through the work of John Bennett, a major teacher of Gurdjieff's and Ouspensky's "Fourth Way" teachings. Bennett invited Bapak to Coombe Springs, England, in 1957, was opened, and became a major ambassador for Bapak. (Bennett eventually left Subud.) Subud activity in the United States began with Bennett's visit to America in 1958 and Bapak's in 1959. Since its early surge in membership, the rate of growth has been matched by the same rate of attrition. Grown children of early Subud members constitute a rising population of new openings.

The core activity of Subud groups is the practice of the latihan, which generally consists of group meetings twice a week to "latihan" for about thirty minutes. Men and women latihan separately. Members are encouraged to do a latihan by oneself at home during the week. The latihan is considered to be a purifying of the self of its negative qualities and a receiving of guidance. While the latihan itself is different for each person, it is usually characterized by spontaneously arising bodily movement, sounds, and feelings that correspond to "inner work" being effected by God's power. One is not to try to influence the latihan through the will, the mind, or the feelings. Effects of the latihan can be immediate; more often they are gradual. Although Bapak used Sufi concepts to describe the various inner forces at work in the individual, he rejected the title of teacher as well as the identification of Subud with Sufism. He said that Subud would have no teachings or dogma, and that one should not accept Bapak's words unless one received it for oneself. Members must be at least eighteen years old. Subud members tend to describe their attraction to Subud in terms of its emphasis on autonomous personal experience and inner guidance without mediation of belief or institution as well as the active sense of release and surrender of negative and nonhelpful aspects of the self experienced in the latihan.

Subud is extremely heterogeneous in terms of cultures and religions represented. Groups tend not to be communal in nature; members meet, do latihan, occasionally socialize, and go back to home or work. The organization is divided in terms of functions. Members more experienced in the latihan may function as "helpers," assisting new or prospective members, being supportive to members as needed, but not claiming authority. Each group also has an administrative side which handles meeting space, communications, and financial matters. Funds are obtained on a voluntary donation basis only. Some Subud members have joined together in cooperative business ventures, and there is a social welfare arm which supports a number of social projects around the world (medical care and supplies, schools, supporting shelters for the homeless) and has United Nations NGO (nongovernmental organization) status. Every four or five years the World Subud Association holds a World Congress to review activities and formulate future plans.

Subud publications are few and hard to find because there has been a tradition that proselytizing and advertising were not correct. Nevertheless, one can obtain a list of Subud literature from Subud U.S.A. national headquarters, 14019 N.E. 8th Street, Suite A, Bellevue, Washington, 98007.

Members speak of the early seventies as a time when there was felt pressure to join or support business enterprises which would in turn support the social welfare arm. Many of the ventures failed; some continue; there is still disagreement on the issue of Subud enterprises. More current dilemmas include the issue of responsibilities and limits of helpers given the goal of a "nonhierarchical" organization and the issue of whether Subud literature can or should be amended in light of changing cultural norms regarding gender roles and patriarchal language.

—*GISELA WEBB*

# 9    HINDU TRADITION

**H**induism is a blanket term for the indigenous religious tradition of the Indian subcontinent. To be considered "within the fold," one must nominally acknowledge the authority of the four Vedas. These are ancient religious texts that express concepts and values bearing little resemblance to current Hinduism, much as the first five books of the Old Testament express a religious ideology at variance, on many points, from that of current Christianity. Indian religions that reject the authority of the Vedas—particularly Jainism, Buddhism, and Sikhism—are regarded as non-Hindu. However, what is left over even after these other religions are subtracted is a broad diversity of beliefs and practices that, at their extremes, bear little resemblance to one other. A villager sacrificing a goat during a Kali festival in Bengal is as much a Hindu as the office worker engaged in quiet meditation in his suburban Bombay home.

Hinduism's sometimes mind-boggling diversity is at least partially a result of India's complex history. Over the millennia, the Indian subcontinent has been subjected to innumerable influxes of different peoples. Rather than serving as a "melting pot" in which various ethnicities are completely submerged into the preexisting culture, India has tended to allow each new group of migrants to maintain at least some of their distinctiveness. A new social grouping (subcaste) was created for each group, a social institution that simultaneously incorporates and draws a boundary around intruders. Thus, new ideas, practices, and gods could be at least partially retained within the invaders' communities, thereby contributing to Hinduism's complexity.

Another trait of the Hindu tradition is that earlier strands of spiritual expression tend to be retained rather than discarded as new religious forms emerge. Thus, in the wake of a devotional reform movement, for example, certain segments of the population might be persuaded to abandon older practices and ideas in favor of something new, but other members of the community will continue in the old ways. As a result of this characteristic, ideas and practices that are very ancient—sometimes thousands of years old—are still practiced by at least some contemporary Hindus.

The reader may recall from her or his early education the notion that humanity made the transition from tribal lifestyles to the more complex forms of social organization we call "civilization" along four great river basins—in China, India, Egypt, and what is today Iraq. A civilization that thousands of years ago existed along the Indus River in Western India left ruins of sophisticated cities. One of the bodies of ruins was uncovered near Harappa; hence this civilization is sometimes referred to as the "Harappan" civilization. Because their written records were apparently composed on perishable materials, we know very little about them or about their religious beliefs. Scholars have, however, surmised that some of the basic beliefs of classical Hinduism, such as the doctrines of reincarnation and karma, are probably Harappan in origin.

One of the reasons we know so little about the Harappans is that around 1000 to 1500 B.C.E. (some would say much earlier) a group of aggressive pastoral peoples from central Asia invaded India through the northern mountain passes, conquered the Harappans, and destroyed whatever records might have remained from the original civilization. These peoples, who called themselves Aryans ("nobles"), originated from around the Caspian Sea. For unknown reasons, groups of Aryans took off in every direction, subjugating indigenous peoples in every area of the world from India to Ireland ("Iran," "Ireland," and "Aryan" all derive from the same root). The Indo-European family of languages is one of the legacies of this expansion.

The worldview of the Aryan invaders of India was preserved in the Vedas. The religious vision of the Vedas, unlike that of classical Hinduism, focused very much on this world. The gods were ritually invoked to improve one's situation in this life, so that priests became something approaching magicians. After settling down in the Indian subcontinent, the Aryans became more introspective, started asking questions about the ultimate meaning of life, and developed an ideology centered around release or liberation (moksha) from the cycle of death and rebirth (samsara). The various disciplines that are collectively referred to as yoga developed out of this introspective turn. A new vision of reality that was first expressed in the Upanishads superseded the Vedic worldview. Because some of the figures that survive from the Harappan period appear to be human beings in yogic meditation poses, it is likely that the Aryans picked up these practices from the indigenous peoples. Classical Hinduism culminated in innumerable devotional movements that swept across the subcontinent, and which shaped the face of contemporary popular Hinduism.

While there are many other ways of organizing Hindu religious history, for the purpose of discussing beliefs and practices we will distinguish only the three "layers" of the Hindu tradition outlined above, namely Vedic ritualism, Upanishadic mysticism, and devotional salvation. Around 800 B.C.E. and afterward, Vedic Hinduism, with its heavy dependence on ritualistically knowledgeable priests, was challenged by a more individualistic form of spiritual expression that rejected many of the basic views and values of Vedism. This emergent view was expressed in a set of religious texts collectively referred to as the Upanishads. The differences between Vedic and Upanishadic Hinduism are quite marked. For example, in contrast to the risky, tenuous afterlife body that it was the function of certain Vedic rituals to create and maintain, the Upanishads postulated an eternal, changeless core of the self that was referred to as the *Atman.* Atman appears to have originally referred to the "breath." (As the invisible part of the person that stopped once life had departed, the breath was often associated with—and sometimes even identified with—the soul in many different world cultures.) This soul or deep self was viewed as being identical with the unchanging godhead, referred to as *Brahman* (the unitary ground of being that transcends particular gods and goddesses). The equation of the deep self with the ultimate is expressed in innumerable ways, such as in the Upanishadic formula *Tat tvam asi* ("Thou art that!"), meaning that the essential "you" is the same as that indescribable ("Wherefrom words turn back") essence of everything:

> He who, dwelling in all things, yet is other than all things, whom all things do not known, whose body all things are, who controls all things from within—He is your soul, the Controller, the Immortal.

Untouched by the variations of time and circumstance, the Atman was nevertheless entrapped in the world of samsara. Samsara is the South Asian term for the world we experience in our everyday lives. This constantly changing, unstable world is contrasted with the spiritual realm of Atman/Brahman, which by contrast is stable and unchanging. Samsara also refers to the process of death and rebirth (reincarnation) through which we are "trapped" in this world. Unlike many Western treatments of reincarnation, which make the idea of coming back into body after body seem exotic, desirable, and even romantic, Hinduism, Buddhism, and other South Asian religions portray the samsaric process as unhappy: Life in this world is suffering.

What keeps us trapped in the samsaric cycle is the law of karma. In its simplest form, this law operates impersonally like a natural law, ensuring that every good or bad deed eventually returns to the individual in the form of reward or punishment commensurate with the original deed. It is the necessity of "reaping one's karma" that compels human beings to take rebirth (to reincarnate) in successive lifetimes. In other words, if one dies before reaping the effects of one's actions (as most people do), the karmic process demands that one come back in a future life. Coming back into another lifetime also allows karmic forces to reward or punish one through the circumstance in which one is born. Hence, for example, an individual who was generous in one lifetime might be reborn as a wealthy person in her or his next incarnation.

Moksha is the traditional Sanskrit term for release or liberation from the endless chain of deaths and rebirths. In the South Asian religious tradition, it represents the supreme goal of human strivings. Reflecting the diversity of Hinduism, liberation can be attained in a variety of different ways, from the proper performance of certain rituals to highly disciplined forms of yoga. In the Upanishads, it is proper knowledge, in the sense of insight into the nature of reality, that enables the aspiring seeker to achieve liberation from the wheel of rebirth.

What happens to the individual after reaching moksha? In Upanishadic Hinduism, the individual Atman is conceived of as merging into the cosmic Brahman. A traditional image is that of a drop of water which, when dropped into the ocean, loses its individuality and becomes one with the ocean. While this metaphor is widespread, it does not quite capture the significance of this "merger." Rather than *losing* one's individuality, the Upanishadic understanding is that the Atman is *never* separate from Brahman; hence individuality is illusory, and moksha is simply waking up from the dream of separateness.

The most that the classical texts of Hinduism say about the state of one who has merged with the godhead is that she or he has become one with pure "beingness," consciousness, and bliss. From the perspective of world-affirming Western society, the results of this awakening appears distinctly undesirable. This largely static conception cannot, however, even be said to have wide appeal among ordinary Hindus. The third "layer" of the Hindu tradition introduced a devotional approach to the divine, in which the nature of the human/divine relationship—as well as Hindu vision of the afterlife—was reconceived.

Beginning at least several centuries B.C.E., devotionalism rejected the impersonalism of both the ritual strategy of Vedism and the intellectual emphasis of the Upanishads. Instead, god was approached as a personal, supremely loving deity who would respond to devotional worship. The gods of the Vedic pantheon, like the deities of ancient Greece and Rome, were not particularly concerned with human affairs. And, while the Upan-ishadic sages accepted the existence of the Vedic gods, the focus of their reflections was the godhead—the abstract ground of being that tran-scended the gods.

By way of contrast, the foci of devotional theism were the great gods/goddesses of classical Hinduism. In the wake of the devotional move-ments that swept across the subcontinent, various strands of "sectarianism" developed, focussed on the worship of Vishnu/Krishna, Shiva, Durga/Kali, or some other form of the divine. The deity of one's sect was portrayed as *the* supreme god or goddess, and the other divinities envi-sioned as demigods or demigoddesses, inferior to the supreme. This high god/goddess deity was also seen as being the creator, a creator concerned with her or his creation, and particularly concerned with the fate of human beings. In the words of one scholar:

> The world is thus not an impersonal or unreal realm, but the arena of divine activity and divine encounter. Vishnu incarnates himself in the world as Rama and Krishna to save the world from unrighteousness, Shiva manifests himself in the world in theophanies to save his devotees, and the goddess enters the world to defeat demons who threaten its security. (Hopkins, p. 153)

Despite these modifications, the samsaric cycle of death and rebirth was still viewed as attractive, and the goal was still to achieve release from the cycle. By the time of Buddha (approximately 600 B.C.E.), the Indian consensus was that it was desire (passion, attachment, want, craving) that kept one involved in the karmic process, and hence desire that kept one bound to the death/rebirth process. Consequently, the goal of getting off the ferris wheel of reincarnation necessarily involved freeing oneself from desire.

To reduce the possibility of karma-producing actions, the Upanishadic tradition had tended to view asceticism/monasticism as the mode of life best suited achieving the goal of release from samsara. However, by the time of the Bhagavad Gita, the earliest important work of devotional theism, another possibility had been thought through. Because it was the craving associated with activity that set the karmic process in motion rather than the activity itself, the author(s) of the Bhagavad Gita developed the alternative approach of remaining in the everyday world while performing one's deeds with an attitude of dispassionate detachment. In the Gita, this detachment is discussed in terms of detachment from the "fruits of actions," meaning that actions are not undertaken for personal gain. Difficult though this may be, Krishna, who in the Gita is the principal spokesperson for this point of view, asserts that such a frame of mind is indeed possible if the individual will con-stantly maintain an attitude of devotion to god. When successful, one can even engage in such activities as war (as long as one is fighting because it is one's duty) and avoid the negative karma that normally results from such actions. In the words of the Gita:

> Set thy heart upon thy work, but never on its reward. Work not for a reward; but never cease to do thy work. Do thy work in the peace of Yoga and, free from selfish desires, be not moved in success or in failure. Yoga is evenness of mind—a peace that is ever the same. . . . Seers in union with wisdom forsake the rewards of their work, and free from the bonds of birth they go to the abode of salvation. (2:47–48, 51)

The "abode of salvation" in devotional theism is not the static, abstract bliss of merging into the ocean of Brahman. Rather, the devotional tradition views the state of the liberated soul as participating in a blissful round of devotional activities in a heaven world that is comparable, in certain respects, to the heaven of Western religions.

**VEDANTA SOCIETY.** Established in New York in 1894, the Vedanta Society is the oldest Hindu group in the United States. Its doctrine has attracted a variety of people, including intellectuals such as Aldous Huxley, Christopher Isherwood, and Gerald Heard. The society has a worldwide diffusion, and, in the United States, it numbered 1,500 members in thirteen centers in 1984.

Sri Ramakrishna (1836–1886), a Calcutta priest, is the main figure of the group; some of his disciples considered him an avatar even prior to his death. Through meditation he achieved the state of God-consciousness, called samadhi, and elaborated a doctrine according to which all religions are a means to one single goal. His mission was to help humanity raise its spirituality. He assigned to his disciple Swami Vivekananda the task of creating a brotherhood of monks among the younger disciples, with the mission of assisting suffering people.

Vivekananda came to the United States in 1893, where he is best remembered for his stirring speech at the World Parliament of Religions in Chicago. Besides creating the Vedanta Society in New York, he founded two more centers in San Francisco and Boston. Each center is independent and is linked to the Ramakrishna Order. Vivekananda returned to India in 1897 where he founded the Ramakrishna Mission.

According to the teachings of the Vedanta Society, the goal of each individual is to realize the divinity within the self and in the others. Individual separateness is an illusion caused by prejudices and fears, and can be overcome through purification of the mind. Vivekananda has codified four kinds of yoga that can lead to purification: intellectual discrimination, devotion, psychic control, and unselfish work. Each follower is free to worship any prophet or personality, since the Society, unlike other Hindu groups, disregards the cult of personality. The importance of a guide is nevertheless stressed. *Prabuddha Bharata or Awakened India* and *Vedanta in the West* are the two publications available through the Vedanta Society.

**VEDANTA CENTRE AND ANANDA ASHRAMA.** The Vedanta Centre of Boston was established in 1909 by Swami Paramananda, a monk of the Ramakrishna Order of India. In 1923, he founded the Ananda Ashrama in La Crescenta, California, as an extension of the Boston center. In 1929, Swami Paramananda dedicated the Ananda Ashrama in Cohasset, Massachusetts. In 1952, the Boston center was moved to Cohasset. It is the permanent headquarters of the Vedanta Centre.

Paramananda was born Suresh Chandra Guha Thakurta in 1884 in India. He was initiated into Sannyas at the age of seventeen by Swami Vivekananda, becoming his youngest monastic disciple. He came to the United States in 1906 to assist Swami Abhedananda at the New York Vedanta Society, the first U.S. center. In 1909 Paramananda opened the Vedanta Centre in Boston, as well as establishing a monastic community of American women. Like his teacher, he believed in the equality of men and women. He ordained Sister Devamata to teach Vedanta from the platform in 1910. During his lifetime, women monastics carried major responsibility in every area of the work.

In 1931, Swami Paramananda founded work in India for destitute women and children. Two ashramas, which include schools, an orphanage, shelter, and training for women in need, continue to flourish in Calcutta.

Until his death in 1940, all of the centers founded by Swami Paramananda were part of the Ramakrishna Math (monastery) and Mission whose headquarters were at Belur, Calcutta, India. At his death, his centers were excommunicated from Ramakrishna Math and Mission because he left as his designated spiritual successor Srimata Gayatri Devi, an Indian woman of his monastic community. The beliefs, traditions, and practices of the Vedanta Centre and Ananda Ashrama remain identical with those of the Ramakrishna Order, the break between the two being purely administrative. Those beliefs include the view that the true nature of each individual is divine and that the purpose of human life is to realize the divine within one's own soul. Srimata Gayatri Devi (1906–1995) was the spiritual leader of the communities for fifty-five years until her death in 1995. She chose an American woman monastic member of her community, Srimata Sudha Puri Devi (Dr. Susan Schranger) as her spiritual successor.

Vedanta Centre and Ananda Ashrama teach Vedanta. The two centers are home to a monastic community, householder residents, and people of all religions who attend the weekly public services, classes, and retreats.

**SELF-REALIZATION FELLOWSHIP.** The Self-Realization Fellowship was founded by Paramahansa Yogananda (1893–1952), who was of the lineage of Swami Babaji of India. Yogananda brought his teachings on India's ancient philosophy of Yoga and its time-honored science of meditation to the West. He first came to the United States in 1920 when he was invited to serve as a delegate to the International Congress of Religious Liberals convening in Boston. That same year, he established Self-Realization Fellowship and opened a center in Boston, which became his base for travels in the United States. Following tours of America in the early 1920s, he opened an international headquarters in Los Angeles to facilitate his work. He remained in America for the remaining thirty-two years of his life, attracting many followers.

Along with the original center in Boston and the international headquarters in Los Angeles, Yogananda established centers in countries around the world for the dissemination of his teachings. Unlike many other movements, Self-Realization Fellowship survived the passing of its founder and today has grown to include nearly five hundred temples, ashrams, retreats, and meditation centers worldwide.

Self-Realization Fellowship brings together the philosophy and practice of the *Yoga Sutras* of Patanjali with an emphasis on raja yoga. It includes techniques for concentration and meditation, including the sacred technique of Kriya Yoga, which seeks to envigorate the psychic centers (chakras) located along the spinal column. Kriya Yoga is an advanced raja yoga technique, in which practitioners redirect energy from external sensations toward inner awareness of their true soul nature.

SRF also maintains that Eastern and Western religions are essentially the same. To that end some of SRF's writings engage in such exercises as examining passages of the New Testament and the Bhagavad Gita that are believed to be parallel passages. Key to worship in the SRF is the process of meditation to focus cosmic energy and attain the presence of the Divine.

Paramahansa Yogananda is perhaps best known as the author of *Autobiography of a Yogi*. He passed away in 1952 and was succeeded by Rajasi Janakananda (aka James J. Lynn), who died in 1955. Lynn was succeeded by the current president and spiritual leader of SRF, Sri Daya Mata.

**HARE KRISHNA MOVEMENT (INTERNATIONAL SOCIETY FOR KRISHNA CONSCIOUSNESS).** The International Society for Krishna Consciousness (ISKCON), better known as the Hare Krishna movement, is a transplanted form of conservative Hinduism, representing one of the most conspicuous religious groups in America since the 1960s. Its followers practice ecstatic worship, and those dedicated to monastic life live in close-knit communalism. They are usually noticeable for wearing their orange or white robes. The last dozen years have seen a dramatic increase in the lay community, chiefly composed of married devotees who raise children, pursue outside professions, and contriute funds and expertise to the mission. They are often the target of humor and satire.

While the Hare Krishna movement traces its ultimate roots to the ancient Vedic scriptures, ISKCON's immediate parent tradition of Krishna devotionalism originated in the sixteenth-century movement of Chaitanya (sometimes Romanized as Caitanya) Mahaprabhu (1486–1534?), a Bengali saint. After a pilgrimage changed his life at about the age of twenty-one, Lord Chaitanya decided to spend the rest of his life pursuing the mystical path, with intense devotional activities focused upon chanting the names of Krishna. He moved to Puri Orissa, near the Jagannatha Temple, where he established a strong movement among the Vaishnava Hindus. The movement declined after Chaitanya disappeared in 1534, when he allegedly merged into the Deity of Jagannatha (Krishna) at the great temple in Puri. Revivals of the movement occured in the seventeenth and mid-nineteenth centuries. The leader of the movement in the nineteenth century, Swami Bhaktivinode Thakur, founded the Gaudiya Vaishnava Mission in 1886, and, after his death, his son, Sri Srimad Bhakti Siddhanta Goswami, continued his work. He founded the Gaudiya Math Institute and about sixty-four missions.

He was the guru of A. C. Bhaktivedanta Swami Prabhupada, born Abhay Charan De (1896–1977), the founder of the International Society for Krishna Consciousness. Swami Prabhupada was born in Calcutta, where he graduated in 1920 with majors in English, philosophy, and economics. Asked by the Swami to write about Krishna Consciousness in English, he authored a commentary on the Bhagavad Gita, and was formally initiated into the Gaudiya Mission. The Swami gave him a charge to carry Krishna Consciousness to the West, a charge that he did not take seriously at first. He continued to produce material for the Mission in English, and he began a magazine, *Back to Godhead*, during World War II, although it lasted only a few issues due to a paper shortage.

When he retired in 1950, he began to give thought to the charge his guru had set for him, and, after moving to Virndavana and the Vamsigopalaji Temple, he began to translate the *Srimad-Bhagavatam*, a central scripture of Krishna devotionalism, and wrote a small work, *Easy Journey to Other Planets*. In 1959 he decided to go to the West after he had a vision of his guru telling him to do so. He also took the vows of sannyasin, the renounced life.

Family obligations were a primary barrier keeping him from moving, but in 1959, at the age of sixty-three, he separated from his wife and family to take up his mission, and he left for the United States in 1965. He was able to exchange his tourist visa for a residency visa when the Oriental Exclusion Act was rescinded. He was then able to begin his missionary work in New York City on the Lower East Side, where he was chosen by a few hippies as their guru. Within a short time a center had been opened, his magazine *Back to Godhead* revived, and the movement started to grow, with the opening of a center in San Francisco in 1967.

Meanwhile, Swami Prabhupada continued to write and translate, working on the *Srimad-Bhagavatam* and on the *Caitanya-Caritamrta*. In 1968 a copy of his translation of the Bhagavad Gita, *As It Is*, appeared. By 1972 over sixty 400-page volumes of his work had been published by the Bhaktivedanta Book Trust. When Swami Prabhupada died in 1977, the twenty-two-person Governing Board Commission, which included eleven people empowered to initiate new disciples, began to lead the international movement. Many senior disciples of Shrila Prabhupada were dissatisfied with the new leadership, particularly when the eleven initiators declared themselves gurus. By the mid-eighties, this internal dissatisfaction had evoked a reform movement which, eventually, overturned the "guru system," resulting in the decentralization of spiritual authority within ISKCON.

Although the movement has maintained a high profile in American life, in the past it was frequently attacked for threatening common family patterns with its ascetic, communal, and separatist lifestyle. At present, the majority of its current membership today lives outside its communal temples. Most members now have families, own property, and pursue normal professions, while continuing to practice the basic principles of Krishna Consciousness and serving the mission in various ways. Members of the movement were early the target of deprogramming, such as the one of Ed Shapiro by Ted Patrick in the early 1970s. Other anticult activities included the arousing of the public opinion against the group, the imposing of some restrictions to the group's public soliciting at the airports, the efforts to require building permits for the establishment of Krishna temples, and parade permits.

Beginning in the mid-1970s, a number of Krishnas were arrested for soliciting without permit in Santa Claus outfits, although the Krishnas do not celebrate Christmas. In spite of their pacifist stance, they were reported to be stockpiling weapons. These accusations seemed to have substance when the local guru in the Bay Area was discovered to have a car trunk full of guns. He was severely disciplined by the Society, who renounced him.

Despite attacks from anticult groups and the media, the Society received a favorable welcome from religious scholars, such as J. Stillson Judah, Harvey Cox, Larry Shinn, and Thomas Hopkins, who praised Swami Prabhupada's translations, and defended the group against distorted media images and anticult misrepresentations. The American Academy of Religion also welcomed various members of the Society.

During the 1980s, the Hare Krishna movement was shaken by a reform movement focused on a number of concerns, including the issue of the authority of the new initiating gurus, who were believed to have taken Prabhupada's place—with related power, prestige, and privilege—after his death. Although the gurus' authority to receive *guru puja*, a worship in which the guru is venerated, was confirmed by the GBC in 1979, some of the gurus did not live up to the purity of their role. The gurus Hansadutta (in Berkeley) and Jayatirtha (in London) were disciplined. In 1983 three new gurus were appointed. In 1985 the GBC voted to lower the seats of the new gurus below that of Prabhupada's in each temple. Also, the majority of initiating gurus began to be appointed by the GBC, while the practice of guru puja was discouraged and began to be abandoned.

The movement maintains that the Vedas, the Bhagavad Gita, and the canonical lives of Krishna are literally true, and that Krishna is the supreme personal Lord and lives in a paradisal world. It also believes that the souls of all individuals are eternal, and are trapped in a series of material bodies (reincarnation) owing to ignorance and sensory illusion. The soul overcomes this identification with the temporary body and lives outside of karma, by love for Krishna.

Conversion to Krishna Consciousness has obvious cultural dimensions, since devotees become culturally Indian to a significant degree, through a process of initiation constituted by a rite of passage in which persons de-identify themselves not only with their bodies but with their past life history and culture, and acquire a new identification. Further, one undertakes to de-identify oneself with the body and adopts an entirely new attitude toward it. A strictly regulated life is adopted, as well as a number of Indian ways of doing things, including such areas as eating, sleeping, and bathing. Diet is strictly vegetarian, and food is prepared for and offered to Krishna before eating. On the eleventh day after the full and new moons, a partial fast is observed.

A male devotee shaves his head except for a single lock, the sikha, a sign of surrender to the spiritual master, and dons the dhoti, a simple Indian-style garment. Women retain their hair but dress in saris. Devotees wear a string of small beads around their necks, and place a clay marking called the tilaka on their forehead and nose, indicating that the body is a temple of the Supreme Lord. The International Society for Krishna Consciousness is centered upon the practice of *bhakti yoga*, a path of devotional service. Among a number of different practices, the devotional service is based on the repetition of the Hare Krishna mantra, during which a set of japa beads are utilized as a kind of rosary.

For most devotees, the main activity of the day is sankirtan, during which they chant the holy names of God. This usually occurs in the temple setting, though public chanting can also be a regular feature of devotee life. Most activities are done together, since a member senses himself and his companions as highly distinct from the outside world. The close company of nondevotees is given up, as is common with all monastics.

A Governing Board Commission consisting of twenty-four senior disciples was appointed by Swami Prabhupada to administer the Society internationally. Eleven of the commissioners were each responsible for a particular area of the world, assuming full authority. The GBC has gradually assumed authority to both depose several of the initiating gurus, disfellowship another, and appoint new gurus as the organization has expanded.

International headquarters of the movement are Sridhama Mayapur and West Bengal, India. There is no official headquarters in the United States, since the movement has decentralized, but a public information ministry is located in San Diego. The Bhaktivedanta Book Trust is located in Los Angeles.

The movement's primary magazine, *Back to Godhead*, ceased publication in the mid-1980s, but was revived in 1991, and is currently published in Alachua, Florida. The movement, which founded more than fifty centers in the United States, and more than 175 centers throughout Canada, the British Isles, Europe, and on other continents, claims 3,000 initiated members and 500,000 lay members who regularly visit a temple at least once a month.

**ADIDAM.** The religion of Adidam—also called the "Way of the Heart" by followers—was founded by the American-born spiritual teacher, Avatar Adi Da Samraj. One of the central teachings of Adidam is what Adi Da calls the "Lesson of Life": "You cannot *become* happy. You can only *be* happy." By this, he means that no form of seeking for happiness is ever permanently successful because the means of *becoming* happy—money, food, sex, relationships, knowledge, religious belief, or any other kind of seemingly fulfilling experience—are always temporary and changing. In fact, Adi Da points out that seeking is the constant activity that *prevents* the conscious realization of that which is always prior to seeking: a changeless state of being that he calls "Self-Existing and Self-Radiant Consciousness," and which is "Most Perfect Happiness."

In his writings, Adi Da asserts that he has realized this Most Perfect Happiness—God, Truth, or Reality—and has the power to transmit that divine self-realization to others. The Way of the Heart, then, consists of a devotional relationship with Adi Da—the traditional Guru-devotee relationship—who his devotees assert is the source of divine self-realization. The devotee is involved in a sequential process of first "listening" to Adi Da's teaching on the Lesson of Life; then "hearing" that teaching, so that the devotee becomes fully committed to Perfect Happiness rather than temporary fulfillment; then "seeing" Adi Da, or fully receiving His Spiritual Blessing; and—in the "Perfect Practice" of the Way of the Heart—awakening fully to the Most Perfect Happiness of Radiant Divine Consciousness.

Adi Da, whose original name was Franklin Jones, was born in Long

Island in 1939. In his autobiography, *The Knee of Listening*, he says that he was born in a state of perfect freedom and awareness of ultimate reality, or what he calls the "Bright." He further asserts that he sacrificed that reality at the age of two, so that he could completely identify with the limitations and mortality of suffering humanity, and thereby discover a way for every human being to awaken to the unlimited and deathless happiness of the Heart. According to *The Knee of Listening*, Jones spent his college and subsequent years intensely pursuing ultimate truth through many experiential means, and this search led him to spiritual practice under the tutelage of well-known gurus in India, such as Swami Muktananda. Finally, in 1970, Jones says that he "re-Awakened" to the "Bright," and also "understood" (a technical term in his teaching) that all seeking actually *prevents* the realization of the Divine.

Adi Da began to teach this "radical understanding"—a combination of discriminative self-observation and guru-devotion—in 1972, opening a small ashram in Los Angeles. His method of working with his students was initially simple and traditional: He would sit formally with a small group in the meditation hall in his ashram, and simply transmit his state of perfect Happiness to them. As time passed, Adi Da introduced traditional religious disciplines related to money, food, sexuality, and community living. But, over time, it became clear that none of his devotees were capable of a simple and fruitful approach to self-discipline and "radical" understanding. Thus began Adi Da's "Crazy-Wise" work—with many precedents in the Hindu, Zen, and Tibetan Buddhist traditions—characterized, in those early years, by an intimate, informal teaching style in which lessons of every kind were generated for the sake of breaking the spell of the ego.

In 1974, his growing spiritual community purchased property in northern California, and established an ashram there (now called the Mountain of Attention Sanctuary of Adidam). In 1979, Adi Da took the name Da Free John ("Da" meaning "the One Who Gives"), signifying to his devotees the Divine nature of his revelation as guru. He also established a second ashram in Hawaii, now called Da Love-Ananda Mahal. In 1984, he moved to the country of Fiji, and established a third ashram on the remote island of Naitauba. In 1986—after an event he called his "Divine Emergence," in which Adi Da says that his body-mind became a perfect vehicle for his "Divine Self-Nature"—he changed his name to "Swami Da Love-Ananda," and called his devotees to "true renunciation," or the constant choice of the perfect Happiness of unconditional Divine Consciousness, rather than choosing to let attention wander in temporary, conditional states. He changed his name again during the late 1980s and early 1990s, and was known as Da Avabhasa (the "Bright"). In 1995, he became Adi Da ("Adi" is a Sanskrit word meaning "primal source"). This last change, says Adi Da, signaled the completion of his Revelation Work, and he renewed his call to his devotees to seriously and wholeheartedly engage in the God-Realizing practice of the fully revealed Way of the Heart.

In Adidam, all the traditional means of religious life are employed as a means of "radical understanding" and devotional communion with Adi Da—meditation; study; ceremonial worship; community living; ethical observances; disciplines related to diet, health, and sexuality; money; and so on. The specific, or technical, practice of this sacred relationship to Adi Da is called Ruchira Avatar-Bhakti Yoga—or the God-Realizing practice ("Yoga") of devotion ("Bhakti") to the Spiritual Master ("Ruchira Avatar") who is the chosen Beloved ("Ishta") of your heart. According to Adidam, Ishta-Guru-Bhakti Yoga is the turning of every faculty of the body-mind to Adi Da—always bringing attention, feeling, body, and breath into contemplative communion with him.

The religion of Adidam has a culture, community, mission, and institution. The institution of Adidam exists (1) to protect and preserve the spiritual "treasures" of Adidam, its founder and guru, the formal renunciate order of which he is a member, and the retreat sanctuaries that have been established; (2) to disseminate the teaching of Adi Da, both to the devotees of Adi Da and to the general public; and (3) to provide access to Adi Da and the retreat sanctuaries of Adidam. In addition to the sanctuaries, which are staffed by devotees, there are community centers throughout the world where devotees live cooperatively with one another and offer retreats and educational programs.

There are many possible levels of involvement, depending on the individual's interest and seriousness. In addition, there are four distinct "congregations" of devotees of Adi Da. The first and second congregations are comprised of individuals who are "impulsed" to God-Realization and who are therefore moved to grow in religious and spiritual terms through the formal stages of practice in the Way of the Heart.

Third congregation members are associated with Adi Da primarily through their service and patronage, and are periodically invited into his company to receive his blessing. Their practice of devotion is not developed and elaborated through formal stages, but is very simple, revolving around loving remembrance and service of the Divine in the person of Adi Da.

The fourth congregation is comprised of individuals who were born into traditional (or nonindustrialized) cultures, and who are not highly educated in the formal, Western sense of that word. They may be involved in the traditional religion of their culture while acknowledging Adi Da as a source of blessing and spiritual help in their lives. There are approximately two thousand individuals throughout the world formally associated with Adidam.

The institution of Adidam has an educational organization, called the Laughing Man Institute, which is responsible for conducting courses all over the world to familiarize people with the teaching and the person of Adi Da. Additionally, the institution has a publishing mission, the Dawn Horse Press, which publishes books by and about Adi Da; since 1972, over fifty volumes have been published. The institution also runs educational courses for people who want to become devotees. Adi Da's books have been translated into Dutch, German, and French. Adidam also maintains the Adidam Web site at http://www.adidam.org called "the Adidam Sacred City."

Adidam became the subject of media attention for a time in the mid-1980s following the filing of a lawsuit by a disaffected former member who alleged that she had been mistreated in various ways while a member. In response to media interest, several other disaffected former members then publicly expressed their own complaints and questions about Adi Da and his way of teaching during the early years of Adidam. Members of Adidam responded by saying that the disaffected former members had simply misunderstood Adi Da's "Crazy-Wise" way of teaching. The media soon lost interest in the story, Adidam settled its differences with the former members, and the legal conflict was resolved.

**S.A.I. FOUNDATION.** The S.A.I. Foundation grew up around the miraculous works of Satya Sai Baba, born in India in 1926. From his childhood Sai Baba has performed miracles and related miraculous visions to the astonishment and praise of his audiences and followers. His followers identify Sai Baba as the Lord of Serpents, Sheshiasa.

In 1940, Sai Baba emerged from a two-month coma, proclaiming himself the reincarnation of an earlier Indian holy man, Sai Baba of Shridi. Sai Baba of Shridi died in 1918, but many in India continued to follow his teachings and a following remained in 1940. Satya Sai Baba impressed and convinced many of the older followers of Sai Baba of Shridi by recalling specific conversations that had taken place before the younger Sai Baba was even born.

The Foundation combines the telling of Sai Baba's miracles with standard Hindu teachings. The Hindu elements of the movement rely on four specific emphases: firmly grounding the faith (*Dharma Sthapana*), promoting scholarship (*Vidwathposhana*), preserving the Vedas (*Vedasamrakshana*), and protecting followers from the debilitating effects of materialsm and secularism (*Bhaktirakshana*).

The focal point of the movement is in Prasanthi Nidayan, or the Home of Supreme Peace. There the devout gather on Thursdays for a *darshan*, a vision of Sai Baba. Particularly significant are the *darshans* during October (the Dasara holidays) and November (the month of Sai Baba's birth). Following lectures and a film series at the University of California at Santa Barbara in 1967, the movement spread across the United States. Teachings of the Foundation are promoted in the periodical, *Sathya Sai Newsletter*, published in West Covina, California.

**SAIVA SIDDHANTA CHURCH.** In 1949 a native Californian—who would later become Master Subramuniya—traveled to Sri Lanka, then known as Ceylon. While there he received initiation from Siva Yogaswami. After returning to the United States, Subramuniya practiced the spiritual disciplines (*sadhana*) given to him by his guru. In 1957 he organized a yoga church in San Francisco and founded the Subramuniya Yoga Order. Centers were opened in Redwood City, California; Reno, Nevada; and Virginia City, Nevada.

Subramuniya emphasized Saivite Hinduism as he learned it from his Sri Lankan guru. His order underwent three name changes, becoming first the Wailua University of the Contemplative Arts. In 1973 it became known as the Saiva Siddhanta Yoga Order. Later in the 1970s Subramuniya adopted the present name, Saiva Siddhanta Church.

The teachings derive from the ancient Vedas and Agamas, the scriptures of Saivite Hinduism. Subramuniya also makes use of the *Saiva Agamas* and the *Tirumantiram* that explain and summarize Saivite beliefs. Subramuniya received the teachings from Yogaswami, who received them from his predecessors in a long succession of teachers.

Human beings are believed to have immortal souls, but, because of our ignorance (anava), the consequences of our prior thoughts and actions (karma), and by virtue of illusions created by materiality (maya), our immortality is hidden from us. The soul, however, evolves continually, primarily by means of reincarnation. The duty of every human being is faithfully to follow the pattern (dharma) in his or her life. Individuals are encouraged to practice good behavior as defined in classical yoga (the yamas and niyamas). Ultimately, under the guidance of an awakened guru, every soul attains self-realization and moksha.

The Temples of Siva, regarded as the residence of the deity, house the communal life of Saivites. *Puja* is offered at temples each day. Puja is an invocation of Siva and other deities, but it also serves as an expression of love for Siva. Many devout also have home shrines where the deity can be invoked.

The leadership of the church is shared by Subramuniya with a priesthood of swamis, the Saiva Swami Sangam. Joining the order of priests requires twelve years of training prior to taking the necessary vows of poverty, purity, obedience, and chastity.

Headquarters for the church moved from California to Hawaii. In 1970 the church bought sufficient acreage on Kauai to for a temple, administrative offices, and a seminary. The Himalayan Academy, also based on Kauai, produces a correspondence course and issues a monthly magazine, *Hinduism Today*.

Subramuniyaswami is the hereditary guru of 2.5 Sri Lankan Hindus. He oversees some fifty temples worldwide and is the author of over thirty books. In 1986, New Delhi's World Religious Parliament named him one of the five modern Jagadacharyas, or world teachers, for this international efforts in promoting a renaissance of Hinduism, and in 1995 bestowed the title of Dharmachakra on him for his publishing activities. Subramuniyaswami was one of three Hindu representatives to the core group of the centenary Parliament of World Religions in 1993, and, on August 25, 2000, received the United Nations' prestigious U Thant Peace Award.

### OSHO (RAJNEESH) FOUNDATION INTERNATIONAL.

Bhagwan Rajnessh (December 11, 1931–January 19, 1990), founder of the Rajneesh Foundation International and the Osho Commune International, was born Rajneesh Chandra Mohan in Kuchwada, India. On March 21, 1953, during his early college days, he announced an experience of samadhi, or enlightenment. He went on to receive his M.A. in philosophy in 1957 and took a professorship at Jabalpur University. Over the following years the tensions between his work as scholar and his position as unorthodox spiritual teacher became too great and he resigned from the university in 1966.

In 1970 he founded a congregation in Bombay and the next year adopted the title Bhagwan, or God. He intended this to signify his method of direct, soul-to-soul teaching, rather than an intellectualized experience. In 1974 his following had grown sufficiently to support the purchase of six acres in Poona, which became his headquarters. Drawing from sources as diverse as humanistic psychology and Sufism, he believed that releasing emotions and developing self-expression in freedom were key elements in the process toward enlightenment. He taught "dynamic meditation," which activated the body through various means, including regulated breathing, chanting, and screaming. He encouraged indulgence in sex as liberating and consciousness-raising. Initiates took vows, not to renounce life, but to embrace it with abandon.

His following became almost entirely European and American as Indians abandoned his teachings as immoral. Seeking a more conducive environment, Rajneesh moved to the United States in 1981 and moved to a 64,000-acre ranch near Antelope, Oregon. As his unusual teachings and lavish lifestyle (93 Rolls-Royces) became known in the area, and particularly after he proposed building a communal village to be called Rajneeshpuram, opposition became as intense there as in India. In 1985 he was charged with immigration fraud and deported back to India, where he reactivated the Poona compound. In 1988 he dropped "Bhagwan" from his name in favor of "Osho," meaning "one upon whom the heavens shower flowers," and the organization was renamed Osho Commune International. On January 19, 1990, he died suddenly without having appointed a successor. The organization continues under the leadership of some of his close disciples.

# 10 MORE CONTROVERSIAL HINDU GROUPS (YOGA GROUPS)

**Y**oga, a Sanskrit term meaning "union" that is related to the English word "yoke," refers to a complex variety of practices, all of which "unite" the individual with the godhead. In the Industrialized West, the widespread popularity of hatha yoga has led the term to be associated with an exotic set of physical exercises. However, in its original South Asian setting, "yoga" referred to everything from devotional love of the divine (Bhakti Yoga) to the study of metaphysical ideas (Jnana Yoga).

In common with other forms of South Asian spirituality, the ultimate goal of yoga is moksha, release from the endless chain of deaths and rebirths (samsara). While many contemporary, Western forms of "metaphysical" and New Age religion embrace the same basic notion of reincarnation, one gets the sense from reading metaphysical discussions of reincarnation that the prospect of returning to earth in some future incarnation is distinctly desireable. This stands in marked contrast to the South Asian attitude—embodied in Hinduism, Buddhism, Sikhism, and Jainism—that views life in this world as distinctly *un*pleasant, and thus something to be avoided if at all possible. Yoga, rather than being a technique for enhancing enjoyment of this life, was originally a technique for escaping this life.

Because certain of the figures found in the ruins of pre-Aryan India seemed to be striking yoga postures (referred to as asanas), scholars speculate that yoga practices antedated the Aryan period. After settling down in the Indian subcontinent, the originally world-affirming Aryans became more introspective. They started asking questions about the ultimate meaning of life, and developed an ideology centered around liberation from this life. The various disciplines that are collectively referred to as yoga developed out of this introspective turn, presumably with the guidance of aboriginal Indians.

The oldest technique to be termed yoga was the meditation system codified in the *Yoga-sutras* (yoga aphorisms) of Patanjali. This yoga system, referred to as Raja Yoga (meaning the "kingly" or "royal" yoga) was regarded as one of the six orthodox philosophical systems of classical Hindu philosophy. Patanjali defined the goal of yoga as the restraint of the modifications of the mind, meaning that Raja Yoga aims to bring the field of human consciousness under the direct control of the will. Patanjali prescribes an exacting discipline that aims to train the awareness until it can be focused on one point without wavering. Once one is able to maintain this one-pointedness of mind for extended periods of time, one attains samadhi, the superconscious state of mind in which liberation is acheived.

At a later stage in the development of Hinduism, Raja Yoga came to be viewed as one of the four "classical" yogas, along with Jnana Yoga, Karma Yoga, and Bhakti Yoga. Jnana refers to knowledge, but the stress in jnana yoga is less on acquiring information than on developing the mind's power of analysis, with the goal of activating the power of the discrination (termed "buddhi" in Vedanta philosophy). The enlightenment gained from this insight enables one to escape the cycle of death and rebirth.

Karma Yoga means the path to liberation through activity or action (the root meaning of the word "karma"). In the Hindu stradition, it originally referred to someone who sought liberation through the correct performance of ritual action. The meaning of Karma Yoga expanded over time to include moral action. The contemporary understanding of Karma Yoga has been shaped by the Bhagavad Gita, an important Hindu scripture that portrays the detached, selfless performance of one's duty as the ultimate path to God.

Bhaki Yoga refers to the path of union with God through devotion. Bhakti represents a form of Indian spirituality that is similar to Christianity in its emphasis on devotion to God. During the period of Indian history that corresponds roughly with Europe's middle ages, devotional movements swept across the subcontinent and decisively reshaped Hinduism so that contemporary South Asian religion has become predominantly bhaktic in flavor. With the expection of the Hare Krishna Movement, this devotional emphasis was not evident in most of the Hindu-inspired yoga groups that emerged in the West in the 1960s and 1970s, which tended to present the more intellectual side of the Hindu tradition to Westerners.

Hatha Yoga is the form of yoga emphasizing body postures (asanas) that has become "yoga" in the Western mind. "Ha" and "Tha" mean sun and moon, and refer to the balancing of positive and negative energies in the body that is accomplished through the practice of yoga. One of the more important aspects of traditional Hatha Yoga is a system of breathing exercises (Pranayama), conceptualized as controlling the flow of a subtle form of energy that flows into the body during breathing. In the original Indian context, Hatha Yoga could be practiced as an adjunct to meditation practices, or as part of traditional Indian medicine (Ayurveda).

After U.S. immigration barriers were lowered in 1965, many Hindu spiritual teachers moved to the West. Some of these people, particularly those who were disciples of Swami Sivananda, began their ministries by teaching Hatha Yoga as a path to physical health and "inner peace." Students who stayed with these teachers, particularly those with an unfulfilled spiritual hunger, were gradually introduced to other, more explicitly religious yoga practices. Many of these loosely organized yoga movements later evolved into more structured spiritual groups.

A number of other new religious groups have emerged that were centered around the practice of other forms of yoga. The Hare Krishna movement, which practices a form of Bhakti Yoga centered on devotion to Krishna, has already been mentioned. Another well-known yoga group is Yogi Bhajan's organization, 3HO. Yogi Bhajan teaches a form of Kundalini Yoga, a type of yoga related to Hatha Yoga that focuses on the activation of a normally dormant energy said to be "sleeping" at the base of the spine (the kundalini energy). Once "awakened," the kundalini is drawn up the spine and into the head where it activates the chakra associated with higher states of consciousness, and the yoga practitioner experiences enlightenment.

Another well-known yoga group is Yogananda's Self Realization Fellowship. Yogananda is best known as the author of *Autobiography of a Yogi*. He came to the United States in the early 1920s, and taught a form of yoga called Kriya Yoga. In common with Kundalini Yoga, Kriya Yoga sees the key to liberation in the arousal of the kundalini energy. The core of Kriya Yoga is a meditation in which the mind imaginatively moves the subtle energy up and down the spine. This movement is coordinated with the breath and with a specific mantra. This process prepares the way for, and eventually activates, the kundalini.

**SIDDHA YOGA DHAM ASSOCIATES (SYDA).** Siddha Yoga Dham is a spiritual tradition originating in India and brought to the West by Swami Muktananda (1908–1982) at the command of his guru, Bhagawan Nityananda of Ganeshpuri. Muktananda left home at the age of fifteen and began wandering throughout India, studying philosophy and practicing the various branches of yoga. In 1947, he received shaktipat initiation from Bhagawan Nityananda. After nine years of intense spiritual practice he attained full self-realization. He succeeded Nityananda in the siddha lineage, and established an ashram, Gurudev Siddha Peeth, near the town of Ganeshpuri, where the first American seekers began to arrive in the 1960s. In the wake of a world tour in 1970, large centers were established in South Fallsburg, New York, and Oakland, California, and several hundred smaller centers were founded throughout the world.

Siddha Yoga meditation teaches that each individual has an inner transformative energy that is dormant within; the Siddha Guru is the one who awakens that spiritual energy through an initiation known as shaktipat. This initiation enables the seeker to transform his or her life through the practices of meditation, chanting, and selfless service.

Swami Muktananda—or Baba, as he is widely known—first left the mother ashram of Siddha Yoga in Ganeshpuri, India, for a three-month world tour in 1970; in the mid-1970s, the SYDA (Siddha Yoga Dham Associates) Foundation was formally established. Shree Muktananda Ashram in the Catskill Mountains of New York State quickly became the organization's international headquarters, while many hundreds of smaller meditation centers sprung up around the world.

Baba Muktananda took mahasamadhi (left his body) in October 1982. His chosen successors were Swami Chidvilasananda and her brother, Swami Nityananda. After three years, Nityananda retired from his position and Swami Chidvilasananda—known as Gurumayi—continues on today as the Siddha Guru and the living master of the Siddha Yoga lineage.

**SELF-REALIZATION FELLOWSHIP.** The Self-Realization Fellowship was founded by Paramahansa Yogananda (1893–1952), who was of the lineage of Swami Babaji of India. Yogananda brought his teachings on India's ancient philosophy of Yoga and its time-honored science of meditation to the West. He first came to the United States in 1920 when he was invited to serve as a delegate to the International Congress of Religious Liberals convening in Boston. That same year, he established the Self-Realization Fellowship and opened a center in Boston, which became his base for travels in the United States. Following tours of America in the early 1920s, he opened an international headquarters in Los Angeles to facilitate his work. He remained in America for the remaining thirty-two years of his life, attracting many followers.

Along with the original center in Boston and the international headquarters in Los Angeles, Yogananda established centers in countries around the world for the dissemination of his teachings. Unlike many other movements, Self-Realization Fellowship survived the passing of its founder and today has grown to include nearly five hundred temples, ashrams, retreats, and meditation centers worldwide.

Self-Realization Fellowship brings together the philosophy and practice of the *Yoga Sutras* of Patanjali with an emphasis on raja yoga. It includes techniques for concentration and meditation, including the sacred technique of Kriya Yoga, which seeks to envigorate the psychic centers (chakras) located along the spinal column. Kriya Yoga is an advanced raja yoga technique, in which practitioners redirect energy from external sensations toward inner awareness of their true soul nature.

SRF also maintains that Eastern and Western religions are essentially the same. To that end some of SRF's writings engage in such exercises as examining passages of the New Testament and the Bhagavad Gita that are believed to be parallel passages. The key to worship in the SRF is the process of meditation to focus cosmic energy and attain the presence of the Divine.

Paramahansa Yogananda is perhaps best known as the author of *Autobiography of a Yogi*. He died in 1952 and was succeeded by Rajasi Janakananda (aka James J. Lynn), who died in 1955. Lynn was succeeded by the current president and spiritual leader of SRF, Sri Daya Mata.

**ANANDA VILLAGE.** Ananda Village was founded by Swami Kriyananda (J. Donald Walters) in Nevada City, California, in 1968. J. Donald Walters was born of American parents in Rumania in 1926. He was educated in Rumania, Switzerland, England, and the United States. In 1948, at the age of twenty-two, he became a disciple of Paramhansa Yogananda. He lived with Yogananda until the master's death in 1952. He took the name Kriyananda in 1955.

During the years 1948–1961, Kriyananda lived at Mt. Washington, the headquarters of the Self Realization Fellowship (SRF, the organization founded by Yogananda), where he served as a minister, as director of center activities, as vice president of the organization, as a lecturer and was directed, by Yogananda, to give kriya initiation. In his role as an SRF official, he traveled and taught extensively in many countries. While lecturing in India, he sought to establish an ashram where Yogananda's teachings could be disseminated. His actions were misinterpreted by the head of the organization, who called him back to New York. When they met, he was told to sign papers of resignation from SRF, which he did as an act of obedience. Left on his own, he struggled to find a way to serve the work of his guru, to whom he had givien his life. From this separation was born the Ananda World Brotherhood Village, thirty-two years old as of this writing.

In 1968, Kriyananda founded Ananda Village near Nevada City, California, in response to Yogananda's plea to "cover the earth with world brotherhood colonies, demonstrating that simplicity of living plus high thinking lead to the greatest happiness." Ananda Village is situated at a 2,600 foot elevation on 750 acres of wood- and meadowland in the Sierra foothills of northern California. Many members support themselves through a variety of businesses, some of which are privately owned and some of which are owned and operated by the community. Other members work in the greater Nevada County community.

Most of the resident children attend the Ananda's Living Wisdom School, K through 8th grades, located at the village. There are also Living Wisdom schools at the Ananda communities in Palo Alto and Sacramento, California; and in Portland, Oregon. These schools are attended by children who are residents and nonresidents of the Ananda communities.

Ananda operates a guest facility called the Expanding Light, which is open year-round for personal retreats, one-week and four-week training courses, special events and holiday programs. Ananda members practice regular daily meditation using the techniques of Kriya Yoga as taught by Paramhansa Yogananda. Resident members are all disciples of Yogananda. The group is directly involved in a worldwide outreach to those interested in the teachings of Paramhansa Yogananda and his line of gurus.

Ananda has five branch residential communities in Seattle, Washington; Portland, Oregon; Sacramento, California; Palo Alto, California; Rhode Island; and Assisi, Italy. Each community is separately incorporated and operates with the freedom to serve its members and greater community in ways deemed appropriate by its own community and spiritual directors. There are, additionally, some seventy centers and meditation groups throughout the world. Ananda's church congregation was established in 1990; Ananda's sangha members and regular participants number around three thousand. The church is open for membership to those who find inspiration in the teachings offered by Ananda, including those of Paramhansa Yogananda and Swami Kriyananda. There are about 140 ordained ministers as of this writing. The goal of the church is to provide fellowship and inspiration for those who want to find God through the practice of the ancient Raja Yoga techniques brought to the west by Paramhansa Yogananda.

Kriyananda has given his life to writing and lecturing to help people apply Yogananda's teachings in their everyday lives. He spent some time as a householder and was married in 1985. He was released from his sannyasi vows by SRF at this time to become a householder. He was divorced in the early 1990s and renewed his monastic vows. He is now known as Swami Kriyananda, though those close to him have always called him *Swami*, a title both familiar and respectful.

Kriyananda has published more than sixty books in sixteen languages and in twenty-one countries, including *Superconsciousness,* formerly published by Warner Books, now published as *Awaken to Superconsciousness: Secrets of Life; Secrets of Life,* published by Warner Books, now out of print; *The Rubaiyat of Omar Khayyam, Explained; The Promise of Immortality in the Bible and the Bhagavad Gita,* a comparative work of the two sacred texts; the *Secrets* gift book series; *The Path: One Man's Quset on the Only Path There Is;*

*Intentional Communities: How to Start Them and Why; Crises in Modern Thought; The Art of Supportive Leadership; Education for Life;* and *Art as a Hidden Message.* He is a gifted composer and lyricist, having created more than four hundred choral and instrumental pieces, including a stringed quartet; the oratorio *Christ Lives;* albums of devotional singing; and several albums of Irish music as well as Indian music. He lectures in English, Italian, German, French, Bengali, and Hindi.

In recent years, Ananda has been involved in ongoing conflict with the Self-Realization Fellowship, the organization in which Kriyananda formerly served. In particular, SRF sued Ananda over the use of the trademarked expression "self-realization." In 1997, after seven years of litigation, the court entered a final judgment in Ananda's favor. The SRF have aggressively fought to appeal a very narrow copyright issue that was a small part of the case. They have pressed the court to allow a trial on these minor points pertaining to a few works of Yogananda; as of this writing, there is a trial set for August of 2001.

TRANSCENDENTAL MEDITATION AND THE WORLD PLAN EXECUTIVE COUNCIL. The Transcendental Meditation movement, at one time a widespread fad, is now institutionalized in the World Plan Executive Council, founded by Maharishi Mehesh Yogi. It consists primarily of a simple system of daily meditation through the use of a mantra, a word which is repeated over and over again as one sits in silence.

This type of meditation derives from an old and honored Hindu technique. Maharishi advocated the use of a single mantra, given to each student at the time of their taking the basic TM course. Each mantra is supposed to suit the nature and way of life of the particular individual. These mantras are given out only at puja ceremonies, that is to say at simple Hindu devotional services venerating the lineage of gurus. Maharishi claimed his authority from these gurus.

The World Plan Executive Council has asserted that the practice of TM has extraordinary effects, the validity of which has been tested by scientists who were among the individuals who took the basic TM course. Among the claims made by the Council is that the regular practice of TM can produce changes in the body, leading to increased intelligence, improved academic performance, higher job prouctivity, improved resistance to disease, and better psychological health. TM is generally claimed to transform a person's life.

The scientific findings have been published in several scientific journals, and in many Council publications such as *Fundamentals in Progress* (1975). They provide the basis for a total worldview, the Science of Creative Intelligence, defined as the experience and knowledge of the nature, range, growth, and application of what is called creative intelligence. This concept approaches what others have called the Absolute, in common parlance, the Divine.

The knowledge and experience of creative intelligence is expanded through attacking problems in the seven basic areas of human life: individual, governmental, educational, sociai, environmental, economic, and spiritual. The creative intelligence has a specific goal in each different area: to develop the full potential of the individual, to improve government achievements, to realize the highest ideal of education, to eliminate the age-old problem of crime and all behavior that brings unhappiness to the family of man, to maximize the intelligent use of the environment, to bring fulfillment to the economic aspirations of individuals and society, and to achieve the spiritual goals of mankind in this generation.

The spread of TM among the population is considered fundamental in order to achieve these goals, although additional steps have been taken by Maharishi, who has declared the presence of the World Government of the Age of Enlightenment, a government which has sovereignity over the domain of consciousness. In 1978, Maharishi inaugurated a world peace campaign, during which he sent over one hundred "World Governors" to each of five sites of major global tension: Iran, Lebanon, Zimbabwe, Central America, and Thailand.

In addition, in 1983 he invited government leaders to make contact with the World Government, which he claimed was ready to solve the problems of any existing government. At the end of the same year a huge collective meditation involving some seven thousand TM siddhas took place at Maharishi International University in Iowa for a two-week period of peace, during which the goal was the purification of world consciousness.

It is believed that during the practice of TM the body produces a particular substance which is referred to as soma in the Vedas, the Hindu holy books. Soma is considered the food of the Gods, who are nourished by this substance in the dark age. This age will be followed by the coming age of Enlightment.

Maharishi was a yogi, though he was very different from Paramahansa Yogananda of the Self Realization Fellowship who had preceded him by thirty-five years. According to some testimonies, he was born Mehesh Prasad Varma in Utter Kashi on October 18, 1911 (other sources say 1918), the son of a local tax official (some sources say forest ranger) of the Kshatriya (warrior) caste.

However, it is only in 1940 that his confirmed biography begins. After having studied physics at Allahabad University, he turned to religion, becoming a student of the yoga master Swami Brahmananda Saraswati who, popularly known as Guru Dev, was the spiritual leader of the Math (monastery). He studied at Joytir Math in Baarinath, where he became Guru Dev's favored student, and stayed with him until his death in 1953.

After three years, Maharishi emerged from a period of seclusion, and began to teach transcendental meditation in India. He toured India, speaking and lecturing, and organized the Spiritual Development Movement in 1957. In December of the same year, Maharishi held a large meditation conference at Madras, and on January 1, 1958, he introduced a "spiritual regeneration" movement to spread the teachings of Guru Dev around the world.

He then traveled to Burma, Singapore, and Hong Kong before arriving in Hawaii in the spring of 1959. He continued his travel to San Francisco, Los Angeles, and London, and, after establishing the International Meditation Society, developed a three-year plan to spread Transcendental Meditation around the world. He returned to India, where he decided to concentrate on teacher training. Beulah Smith, who became the first teacher in America, was among the first teachers who graduated in 1961.

For several years, Maharishi made an annual world tour, including the United States, during which he visited a variety of centers and followers. Among them was Jerome Jarvis, who convinced him to begin speaking on university campuses, out of which the Student International Meditation Society originated.

In 1967 the Beatles, the popular rock group, became followers of Maharishi. In particular, George Harrison, who was later connected with the Hare Krishna movement, after having taken lessons from Indian musician Ravi Shankar and having learned of Maharishi's presence in London, persuaded the other Beatles to attend his meetings. In January 1968, they went to Maharishi's center in India with actress Mia Farrow, becoming the first of a number of celebrities who became meditators and who helped make Maharishi a celebrity among older teens and young adults.

During the early 1970s, the movement had a considerable growth in Europe and the United States and, by the end of the decade, almost a million people had taken the basic TM course. The goal of the World Plan, which was announced in 1972, is to share the Movement's comprehensive understanding of life and knowledge (Science of Creative Intelligence), with the whole world. Some 3,600 World Plan Centers were established, one for each million people on earth, with a constant ratio of one teacher per 1,000 persons in the general population.

However, the World Plan suffered several major reverses in the mid-1970s, and around 1976 the number of new people taking the basic TM course in North America dropped drastically. As a response to the decline, the Council announced an advanced siddha program, which included the teaching of levitation to meditators. Since the evidence of these claims was not validated, the program was attacked and the organization suffered a credibility gap.

In 1978 a federal ruling, asserting that TM was a religious practice, denied access to public funds with which teachers were supported. As a result, progress slowed dramatically in the United States, although growth proceeded in other areas of the world, where new programs were introduced during the 1980s, such as the Ayurvedic Medicacl Program, a comprehensive science of natural health care. Through this program the organization is sponsoring the distribution of Maharishi Amrit Kalash, an herbal compound, designed to balance the body and protect it from harmful influences. Among further plans is the establishment of the Maharishi Center for Perfect Health and World Plan Peace in Fairfield, Iowa.

Maharishi and the World Plan, besides their success, have often been the target of criticism and controversy centering mainly on three issues: TM's claims to scientific verification have often been challenged, particularly those related to the physical effects of TM which, according to the psychologists studying yoga and meditation, could be produced from a wider variety of practices. Also, other scientists pointed out that positive results could only be obtained from special samples of meditators.

Critics interested in the separation of church and state, supported by evangelical Christians who opposed TM, challenged the use of state funds to spread the practice, arguing that the World Plan Executive Council was in fact a Hindu religious organization and TM a practice essentially religious in nature. TM critics have also charged the movement with an element of deception, claiming that Maharishi, in his effort to bring TM to America, created a new image, in part based upon the early scientific papers, denying the religious elements and arguing that the practice of TM led to reduced dependence on drugs.

During the 1970s, TM was attacked by Bob Kropinski, who took the organization to court charging fraud and psychological damage from the practice of the siddha program. According to Kropinski, while the advertisements promised to teach students the ability to levitate, in fact they taught only a form of hopping while sitting in a cross-legged position. As a response to his attack, TM proponents have answered with testimonies of TM's healthful effect upon their life, although the organization has yet to produce generally verifiable evidence of the siddha program involving the ability to levitate, walk through walls, or become invisible.

The international headquarters of the World Plan Executive Council are at the World Plan Administrative Center in Seelisberg, Switzerland. American headquarters are in Washington, D.C. There are over three hundred World Plan Centers in the United States, and the active meditators are estimated to number in tens of thousands. *Modern Science and Vedic Science* represents the Plan's journal since 1987, focusing on the dialogue between Maharishi's teachings and modern Western Science.

—*MICHELA ZONTA*

**SIVANANDA YOGA VEDANTA CENTERS.** Swami Vishnu Devananda, the North American representative of Swami Sivananda Saraswati, set up the Sivananda Yoga Vedanta Centers to further the work of Sivananda. Sivananda was initiated in the 1920s, having devoted his life to the service of humanity. Sivananda merged traditional forms of yoga (Hatha, Karan, Jnana, Raja) and added a fifth (Japa, or repetition of a mantra). His motto, "serve, love, meditate, realize," evokes the lives Sivananda intended for his students. He set them on a path to enlightenment (*sadhana*), which included the practice of love for others (*bhakti*) and the constant effort to cause no pain or harm (*ahimsa*).

Sivananda never came to North America, but he dispatched many initiates to further his work. Eventually he sent Swami Vishnu Devananda to Canada and the United States. Other followers of Sivananda have come to North America since, but Vishnu Devananda is the only teacher acknowledged by the Divine Life Society of India.

Vishnu Devananda became a disciple of Sivananda in 1947 and was initiated in 1949. His talents as a pupil and his rigorous devotion to spiritual disciplines made him a trusted lieutenant. Sivananda's appraisal of Vishnu Devananda is best reflected by his choice in 1957 of Vishnu Devananda to propagate his teachings in North America. Initially Devananda established centers in the United States, but the permanent headquarters was placed in Montreal in 1958. He follows the teaching of integral yoga as developed by Sivananda, emphasizing in addition the value of intense spiritual discipline and hatha yoga. By 1988 there were eighteen centers and three ashrams in the United States and Canada.

Two unique centers set up by Devananda include the Sivananda Ashram Yoga Camp in Quebec and the Sivananda Ashram Yoga Retreat in the Bahamas. Each provides intense yoga training, but the atmosphere is that of a resort. In 1969 Vishnu Devananda founded the True World Order, an organization devoted to peace and brotherhood. Through this organization, Vishnu Devananda has conducted peace mission around the world, the best known of which was a mission to Belfast in the 1970s. A characteristic method employed by True World Order is to airdrop leaflets and flowers at the world's trouble spots.

The work of the Sivananda Yoga Vedanta Center is worldwide, but membership records as such are not kept. One indicator of the strength of the movement is the fact that Devananda's book, *The Complete Illustrated Book of Yoga*, has sold more than three million copies since its publication in 1960. The Centers also publish a periodical, *Yoga Life*.

**INTEGRAL YOGA INTERNATIONAL.** The first Integral Yoga Institute was founded in New York City in 1966 by Sri Swami Satchidananda. Swami Satchidananda was born in southern India on December 22, 1914. He married and started a family at the age of twenty-three. However, a mere five years later his wife died, leaving Satchidananda with two young sons. Placing his sons in the care of his parents, in 1946 Satchidananda entered the Ramakrishna Mission and was initiated into the life of intentional celibacy, study, and service. In May 1949, Satchidananda met Swami Sivananda at his ashram in Rishikesh on the banks of the Ganges River. Two months later, Swami Sivananda initiated Satchidananda into the Holy Order of Annyas (a sannyasin being one who leads a life of total renunciation and service). Swami Sivananda gave him the name Satchidananda, along with the title of Yogiraj, Master of Yoga. Thus, Satchidananda began seventeen years of work with Sivananda's Divine Life Society.

In 1953 Sivananda instructed Satchidananda to go to Sri Lanka and serve that island's people by opening a branch of the Divine Life Society. Satchidananda found Sri Lanka to be divided by differences in caste, language, and religion. He transformed the traditional July festival in honor of the guru into an All Prophets Day that honored masters from all religions. He worked for peace and interreligious understanding between the Tamil and Singhalese populations. Satchidananda and his followers built temples and conducted services for those in prison. He became one of the best-known people in Sri Lanka and was asked to travel around the island in a regular circuit in order to be available to all who needed him.

In 1959 Satchidananda gave public lectures and yoga demonstrations in Hong Kong for the Divine Life Society. He made a more extensive teaching tour to the Philippines, Malaysia, Hong Kong, and Japan in 1961. On the invitation of artist Peter Max, Satchidananda came to New York city in 1966. Within two months, his following had grown from a few friends of Max to the founding membership of the Integral Yoga Institute. Due to the extraordinary interest in his teaching in America, Satchidananda decided to work in the United States. He returned to Sri Lanka to reorganize the religious center under new leadership before making his final move to the West.

On July 25, 1968, Satchidananda received the first permanent resident visa ever issued for the entry of a "Minister of Divine Words" into the United States. Swami Satchidananda was present at the opening of the Woodstock festival in 1969. In 1975 Swami Satchidananda initiated twenty-eight disciples into the Holy Order of Sannyas. Sannyasins take vows of renunciation and service. They also vow to practice nonviolence toward all living beings. Swami Satchidananda became a citizen of the United States in 1976.

Integral Yoga International purchased 750 acres of land along the James River in Virginia in 1979 as a permanent home for the Satchidananda Ashram and an extended residential community called Yogaville. In order to live at the Ashram, one must become acquainted with its values and rules, feel that they are helpful for guiding one's life, participate in the daily program, which includes meditation and service, and above all want to be there. Members voluntarily contribute their time and material resources to help meet human needs in the surrounding county, too. The food is strictly vegetarian. There is a community school, the Yogaville Vidyalayam, for children up to age twelve. In addition to residents of the ashram, about thirty-five families have homes in the community. A few commute from nearby towns and cities.

The Integral Yoga Ministry was established in 1980. Integral Yoga ministers may be married or single. They take vows to live in the spirit of nonattachment, physical and mental purity, and dedicated service. The ministers form one category of people at the ashram and Yogaville, another being the sannyasins who have taken vows to enter a service-oriented monastic life. In addition to monks and ministers, there are three other categories of people at Yogaville. A third category is made up of people who are not seeking to be ministers or monks but who find the practice of yoga meaningful, who are devoted to Swami Satchidananda and who want to participate in a community based on spiritual values. A fourth category is that of short-term visitors who come to attend a course, take a workshop, or see what it is like to follow that way of life. Finally there are day visitors who come to see what the Ashram is like and has to offer.

Officers in the ashram include a president, vice president for finance, and vice-president for administration, each of whom is a monk or minister. Community meetings are held regularly so that questions of mutual concern can be discussed and resolved. Swami Satchidananda is the final authority.

In 1986 the Light of Truth Universal Shrine (LOTUS) was dedicated to honor all the world religions at the Virginia ashram. The outer shape of the building is based on the lotus flower, which is an ancient symbol of higher truth because the flower grows from mud through brackish water to emerge in the light with surprising beauty. The opening petals of the flower are also a symbol of the process of transformation by which every individual's spiritual nature becomes evident. Inside the LOTUS building the central point of interest is a column of moving light which moves upward to the ceiling and then radiates outward to several altars that represent all the religious traditions located around the perimeter of the circular shrine. People of all faiths can come to honor their own and all other religions and contemplate the one Truth, or God, that is the source of all religions. The LOTUS symbolizes the unity in diversity of all religions and reflects Satchidananda's teaching that "Truth is One—Paths are Many."

In addition to the LOTUS, Yogaville has another symbol of Integral Yoga's ideals for living—attention, balance, courage, skillful movement, surpassing of limitations, and compassion for all. It is a bronze image of Siva Nataraja, the Lord of the Dance, which stands at the top of a hill. It was presented to Yogaville by Sri Karan Singh, former Indian ambassador to the United States. There are thirty centers of Integral Yoga in the United States, four in Canada, and twelve in other countries.

**ANANDA MARGA YOGA SOCIETY.** The Ananda Marga Yoga Society was founded in 1955 in Bihar, India, by Prabhat Ranjan Sarkar, known to his followers as Shrii Shrii Anandamurti, which translates as "one upon seeing him falls into bliss." Prabhat Ranjan Sarkar was born in India in 1921. He was an accomplished yogi at the age of four and initiated his first devotees at the age of six. Sarkar worked as a railway clerk until he took the vows of the renounced life and founded Ananda Marga Yoga Society in 1955. Sarkar combined a strong orientation to social service with his yogic philosophy. In 1958 he organized Renaissance Universal to mobilize intellectuals and others for the improvement of humanity's condition.

Ananda Marga was a political as well as a religious movement. Sarkar articulated his political ideals as the Progressive Utilization Theory, abbreviated as "Prout." According to Prout theories, Sarkar began to organize the lower classes in opposition to both the Communists and the ruling government. In 1967 and 1969, the Proutist Bloc ran candidates for office in India.

In 1969 Anandamurti sent Acharya Vimalananda to the United States to establish the Ananda Marga Yoga Society. Within four years there were more than one hundred centers and three thousand members in the United States. Ananda Marga brought its social idealism to the United States. Renaissance Universal was organized in America, sponsored directly by Ananda Marga. It organizes Renaissance Universal Clubs on college campuses, the Renaissance Artists and Writers Association, and publishes the *Renaissance Universal* magazine. Proutist Universal, which advocates Sankar's political ideals, is officially independent of Ananda Marga, but informally associated. Acharya Vimalananda, who founded Ananda Marga in the United States, left the organization to found the Yoga House Ashram.

In 1971, Sarkar was accused by a former follower of having conspired to murder some ex-members. Sarkar was arrested and jailed. In 1975, Prime Minister Indira Ghandi proclaimed a national emergency in India and, among other actions, banned Ananda Marga which had been involved in a number of incidents, some aimed at protesting Sarkar's imprisonment. Sarkar was finally brought to trial. Under the conditions of the emergency he was unable to call witnesses on his behalf and was convicted. In 1978, Sarkar was retried and found not guilty. The number of reported incidents by Ananda Marga decreased markedly. While still a large movement in India, Ananda Marga has not regained its pre-1975 size.

Upon initiation into the Ananda Marga Yoga Society, the devotee is privately instructed by a guru. He is then taught the negative discipline of yama (abstention from violence, falsehood, theft, incontinence, and acquisitiveness) and the positive observance of niyama (purity, contentment, austerities, study and dedicated activity). He then learns meditation. The initiate is required to learn by heart the "supreme command," which instructs him or her to practice twice-daily meditation, observe yama and niyama, and the obligation to bring all into the path of perfection.

# 11

# SIKHISM AND THE SOUND CURRENT TRADITION

## SIKHISM

Sikhism is a monotheistic religion founded in the sixteenth century. The founder of Sikhism was Guru Nanak, born to a Hindu family in Punjab, North India, in 1469. He took instruction in Hindu lore from a village teacher and also attended a Muslim school, where he acquired a knowledge of Islamic teaching and some instruction in the Arabic and Persian languages. In northern India in Nanak's youth, two social systems lived side by side. The Hindus had a tolerant religion but a closed social system based on caste. The Muslims had a more open social system but a less tolerant religious ideology.

At about the age of sixteen, Nanak became an accountant in the household of an important Muslim official in the town of Sultanapur. He gathered about him a group of followers who bathed together in a river before dawn every day and met in his home in the evening to sing religious songs he had composed. One day he failed to return from his morning swim. His friends found his clothes on the banks of the river and dragged the waters in an unsuccessful attempt to recover his body. Three days later Nanak reappeared. He said, "There is neither Hindu nor Muslim, so whose path should I choose? I shall follow God's path. God is neither Hindu nor Muslim and the path which I follow is God." Later he said that during the time he was missing he had been carried into God's presence, where he had received a cup of nectar and a message from God to go forth into the world to teach the repetition of the name of God and the practices of charity, meditation, and worship.

Nanak traveled widely to spread his religious message. According to tradition he made four journeys, visiting Assam in the east, Sri Lanka in the south, Ladakh and Tibet in the north, and Mecca, Medina, and Baghdad in the west. Nanak's followers began to call themselves sikhs, or disciples.

In 1504 India was invaded by a Muslim conqueror from central Asia. By 1525, the sultan of Delhi had been deposed and the Mogul Empire established in its place. During this time of upheaval, Nanak looked for a place of refuge and stability. He and his family established a religious center at Kartarpur, a village built on land donated by a wealthy member of the new faith.

Nanak stressed that there was but one creator God. Although he regarded his revelation as transcending both Islam and Hinduism, his teachings embodied certain traditional South Asian ideas, such as karma, reincarnation, and the ultimate unreality of the world. He emphasized the unique role of the guru as necessary to lead people to God. He urged his followers to meditate, worship God, and sing hymns.

According to Sikhism, the ultimate purpose of religion is union with God through his indwelling in the human soul. Receiving divine grace in this way, human beings are freed from the cycle of birth and rebirth and then pass beyond death into a realm of infinite and eternal bliss. Nanak's teaching offered a clear and simple path to salvation. By meditating on the divine name, human beings were cleansed of their impurities and were enabled to ascend higher and higher until they achieved union with the eternal one. Sikhs hold that suffering in the world arises as a result of humanity's separation from God.

Toward the end of his life, Nanak ensured that his teaching would not die but survive and become a new religion. He appointed a successor, Lehna, passing over his own two sons whom he did not regard as suitable. Nanak gave Lehna a new name, Angad, meaning "limb." Lehna would become a "limb" or a part of Nanak. After Guru Nanak's death in 1539, Angad became the second of the ten Sikh gurus. He compiled a hymnal of Guru Nanak's compositions to which he added his own.

The third guru, Amar Das, served from 1552 to 1574. He dug a well with eighty-four steps at Goindwal which became a place of pilgrimage and a focus of special rites and festivals. Amar Das nominated his son-in-law Ram Das Sodhi as the fourth guru. Thereafter the guruship remained in the Sodhi family.

The fourth guru, Ram Das, began the Golden Temple of Amritsar, the present headquarters of the world Sikh community. He nominated his son Arjan as the fifth guru.

The fifth guru, Arjan, completed the Golden Temple with four doors on four sides to indicate that it was open to all castes, and installed the *Adi Granth*, the collected writings of Nanak and the other gurus, within it. Arjan was eventually tortured and executed by the Mogul Emperor for refusing to delete from the *Adi Granth* all passages opposing Hindu and Islamic orthodoxy. His martyrdom created a gulf between Sikhs and Muslims and ended the first phase of Sikhism. Before his imprisonment, Arjan had nominated his son Hargobind as the sixth guru and girded him with two swords symbolizing spiritual and temporal power. He ordered, "Let him sit armed upon the throne and maintain an army to the best of his ability."

The sixth guru, Hargobind, established a group of horse and foot soldiers. He was imprisoned by the Mogul emperor for several years, but upon his release he regrouped his armed followers and fought against the Moguls.

The seventh guru was Hargobind's grandson Har Rai. The eighth guru was Har Rai's son Harikrishan, who died as a child. Upon the death of the young eighth guru, the Mogul emperor nominated a successor. The Sikhs, however, acclaimed Tegh Bahadur as their ninth guru. Guru Tegh Bahadur traveled through the Punjab preaching. His popularity annoyed the Mogul emperor, who had him arrested and beheaded in 1675.

The tenth guru, Gobind Singh, completed the *Adi Granth* and militarized the Sikhs by forming the Khalsa, the Community of the Pure. Members of the Khalsa were initiated by a baptism in which they drank and were sprinkled with sweetened water stirred with a sword. They changed their name to Singh (Lion) and adopted the five Ks: Kesh, long hair, a sign of saintliness; Kangh, a comb for keeping the hair neat; Kach, short pants for quick movement in battle; Kara, a steel bracelet signifying sternness and restraint; and Kirpan, a sword of defense. The Khalsa was open to men and women of all castes. Members were admitted only after an initiation ceremony at which they pledged themselves to an austere code of conduct. Each morning they were to bathe at dawn and spend some time in meditation. Liquor, tobacco, and narcotics were forbidden. They pledged loyalty to the teachings of the gurus. Sikhs who did not accept baptism into the Khalsa fraternity came to be known as Sahajdhari. Those once baptized into the Khalsa who later cut their hair or beards were rejected as renegades or apostates.

When all four of his sons died in fighting the Moguls, Guru Gobind Singh proclaimed that the line of the gurus would come to an end with himself. After Gobind Singh was killed by two hired assassins, the *Adi Granth* (subsequently referred to as the *Guru Granth Sahib*) became the guru and no further human gurus were allowed.

Following Gobind Singh's death, the Khalsa became a military and political power in Punjab. Conflict between the Sikhs and the Mogul Empire continued. In 1799 the Sikhs captured Lahore and made it the capital of the Sikh kingdom of Ranjit Singh which dominated the Punjab and other areas of northwest India. This kingdom granted religious freedom to the Hindus and Muslims. During the rule of Maharajah Ranjit Singh from 1799 to 1839, large numbers of Hindu peasants converted to the Khalsa.

During the nineteenth century the Sikhs fought valiantly against the British invaders. The army of Ranjit's successor was defeated in 1849 and the Sikh realm was annexed to British India. The British built a system of canals in the Punjab which benefited the whole state. Because the British administration was generally fair and even-handed, the Sikhs remained loyal to the British during the Great Mutiny of 1857 and became welcome recruits in the British army. The Sikhs continued to increase in numbers during British rule, largely because of the special favors accorded to the Khalsa in the army and the civil services.

At the turn of the century Sikhs began to arrive in Canada and the United States. By 1915, there were approximately seven thousand Indians in America. The first gurdwara, or Sikh temple, was opened in Vancouver, British Columbia, in 1908. In 1912 a gurdwara was opened in Stockton, California. Others soon followed. In 1917, the United States stopped almost all immigration from Asia. After that time, the mostly male Sikh population in the United States found wives among their non-Indian neighbors, many of whom were Mexican.

In 1931 leading Sikh authorities and associations in India held a meeting at Amritsar and drew up a document called the *Rehat Maryada* (Guide to the Sikh way of life) which all Sikhs are expected to follow. In this document, a Sikh is defined as anyone who believes in one God, the ten gurus and their teaching, and the *Guru Granth*. Every Sikh is expected to serve the community of the faithful, lead a life of prayer and meditation, and recite or read a prescribed number of hymns each day.

The British withdrew from the Indian subcontinent in 1947. When the British decided to partition the Punjab, all Sikhs were bitterly disappointed as many places sacred to them, such as the birthplace of Nanak, were in the western section of Punjab which was given to Pakistan. East Punjab remained in India. Sikhs and Hindus subsequently joined in fighting against the Muslims that resulted in over a million deaths. Eventually two and a half million Sikhs were forced to immigrate to East Punjab. The Sikhs demanded a separate state, but were denied one by the Indian government. They have, however, been allowed a fair amount of autonomy within the Indian state of Punjab.

In the Indian census of 1971, the number of Sikhs (both Khalsa and Sahajdhari) was over ten million, which was still less than two percent of the population of India. About 85 percent of the world's Sikhs live in Punjab, northern India.

There are several Sikh sects. The Udasi, or "detached," are followers of Sri Chand, the ascetic elder son of Guru Nanak. They did not convert to the Khalsa started by Guru Gobind Singh. During the period of Sikh persecution by the Muslim rulers, the Udasi took over the management of several Sikh Shrines and introduced Hindu idols and ritual into Sikh temples.

This met with the disapproval of orthodox Sikhs who divested the Udasi of their control of the temples in the 1920s. Most Udasi today observe Hindu customs and pay nominal homage to the *Adi Granth.*

The Nirmala, or "unsullied," are a sect of theologians started by Guru Gobind Singh. The guru had a group of scholars study Sanskrit and the Vedas to be better equipped to interpret the writings of the gurus, which make frequent allusions to Hindu mythology and sacred texts. Nirmala wear white clothes and are vegetarians.

The Nihangi, or "crocodiles," are a militant order of Khalsa. They wear blue clothes and always carry arms on their person. Today they live mostly on alms and are notorious for their addiction to hashish.

The Namdhari, or "adopters of the name," are a sect founded by Balak Singh, who criticized the rich lifestyle of the Sikh aristocracy and preached the virtues of poverty. He exhorted the Sikhs to practice no ritual except repeating God's name. The Namdhari dress in white handspun cloth, abstain from liquor, and are vegetarians. Their gurdwaras are unostentatious and their wedding ceremonies are performed in austere simplicity.

The Nirankari believe in the succession of gurus continuing after Guru Gobind Singh and pay homage to a living guru. They include persons of all religions without requiring conversion to Sikhism.

Immigration of Sikhs into the United States began to flow again after a 1965 change in immigration laws, and the American Sikh community has grown considerably. Gurdwaras have been established from coast to coast.

**SIKH DHARMA (HEALTHY, HAPPY, HOLY ORGANIZATION).** Yogi Bhajan (b. 1929), a well-educated Sikh from Delhi, India, moved to Toronto in 1968. From Toronto he moved to Los Angeles in December 1968, and in 1969 he founded an ashram and the Healthy, Happy, Holy Organization (3HO) to teach kundalini yoga. Corporately, 3HO was later supplanted by Sikh Dharma, and 3HO retained as Sikh Dharma's educational wing.

Individuals associated with Bhajan's Sikh Dharma are usually Westerners rather than Punjabis. They are encouraged to seek formal initiation and join the Khalsa, the Brotherhood of the Pure Ones, a fellowship begun by Guru Gobind Singh. Members of the Khalsa are required to keep the traditional practices introduced by Guru Gobind Singh that became the distinguishing marks of the Sikh community, known popularly as the five "k's."

3HO Sikhs are vegetarian, usually preferring natural foods. Fish, meat, alcohol, and drugs are prohibited. Several members have opened vegetarian restaurants and groceries. They also prefer natural methods of healing. The traditional holidays of Sikhism are observed by 3HO Sikhs, such as Balsakhi Day, the birthday of Khalsa (April); the Martyrdom days of Guru Tegh Bahadur (November); and Guru Arjun Dev (May); and the birthdays of the ten gurus.

The first controversy involving the Sikh Dharma regarded its relationship to the older Punjabi Sikh community. American Sikhs criticized criticized Punjabi Sikhs for becoming lax in their discipline, especially in their adherence to the five "k's." An attack followed on Yogi Bhajan by Dr. Narinder Singh Kapany, editor of the *Sikh Sangar*, the magazine of the Sikh Foundation, who condemned Bhajan's emphasis on yoga and diet. Other Sikh leaders echoed Kapany's criticisms in the United States, as well as in India. Although these issues were never resolved, Bhajan's emphasis on orthodoxy was supported by the center of Sikh authority in Amritsar.

Sikh Dharma has received relatively little attention from the anticult movement. Few deprogramming attempts took place. In the early 1980s, militant Sikhs announced a policy of actively opposing any attempts by deprogrammers to attack their organization. No further attempts have been reported.

Yogi Bhajan was accused by one ex-member of sexual involvement with several of his staff members, but there was no verification of the charges. In 1984 a number of high ranking leaders in the Sikh Dharma left the organization, complaining of the intense discipline and being cut off from the Sikh community as a whole and middle American culture.

Controversy has mainly been focused in other issues, such as members' dress, especially the turban, as in the case of Thomas Costello who, in 1971, faced a military court-martial for refusing to either cut his hair or remove his turban.

Although this case led to a change in Army regulations granting permission for Sikhs to wear turbans, in 1983 Gurusant Singh Khalsa was not allowed to enlist in the Army because he was a Sikh. In 1984 Karta Kaur Khalsa was threatened with losing her teaching certificate because she refused to take off her turban during classes, but in 1985 the Oregon Court of Appeals declared the law under which she was suspended to be unconstitutional.

## THE RADHASOAMI TRADITION

The Radhasoami movement was founded by Shiv Dayal Singh (1818–1878) in the mid-nineteenth century in Agra, India. "Radhasoami" (defined as "Lord of the Soul") has many branches, each of which has a presiding guru or master who is believed to have traversed all of the higher regions of consciousness and become one with the Supreme Lord. It is estimated that there are over thirty different Radhasoami groups in the world. Outstanding among these are: Radhasoami Satsang Beas (the largest of all the groups); Dayal Bagh, Agra; Soami Bagh, Agra; Peepal Mandi, Agra; Manavta Mandir, Hoshiarpur; Pabna Satsang; Radha Swami Association, Tarn

Taran; and Sarai Rohilla, Delhi. There are also several genealogically related movements which are directly linked with Radhasoami, but have identified themselves under different names, including Sawan-Kirpal Mission, Delhi; Sant Bani, Rajasthan; Kirpal Light Satsang, Delhi; and Ruhani Satsant Inc. Furthermore, there are other shabd yoga related movements which have associations with Radhasoami but have tried to distance themselves. Such groups include Eckankar, MSIA (the Movement for Spiritual Inner Awareness), and the Divine Light Mission. The total number of followers with some connection with Radhasoami and its many branches is estimated to be well over two million worldwide.

Surat shabd yoga is designed to enable the soul or consciousness to ascend beyond the physical body to higher spiritual regions by means of an internal sound or life current, known variously in the literature as shabd, nad, logos, audible life stream, or ringing radiance. It is through this union of the soul with the primordial music of the universe that the practice derives its name: surat, soul/attention; shabd, sound current; and yoga, union.

The masters of this path (honorifically given titles such as Satguru, Param Sant, and Perfect Master) describe a number of subtle planes through which a neophyte must pass to reach the highest realm, Anami Lok, "Nameless Abode," where all sound, light, and creation have their transcendental source.

It appears that surat shabd yoga in one form or another was prevalent in the Upanishadic period of India. However, the yogic practice has become clearly articulated and well known only in the last five hundred years. This is primarily due to a distinctive school of nirguna bhakti poets (mystical lyricists) who sang of One Supreme and Unfathomable God. Known today as Sants (saints), the chief exponents of nirguna bhakti, such as Kabir, Nanak, Dadu, and Paltu Sahib, have written in detail about the path of surat shabd yoga. These Sants, whose eclectic tradition is now popularly called Sant Mat (the doctrine or way of the saints) were instrumental in paving the way for such movements as Sikhism, the Kabir-panthis, the Sat-namis, and the Radhasoamis.

Central to the teachings of Radhasoami and surat shabd yoga is the necessity of a living human master who is competent in initiating disciples into the practice and technique of listening to the inner sound (bhajan), contemplating the inner light (dhyan), and leaving the physical body at will (dying while living). Although there are theological differences and some minor technical variances in the different Radhasoami groups, the basic tenets of the tradition are as follows:

1. The practice of surat shabd yoga (between two and three hours of meditation daily).
2. Obedience to the living master who initiates the disciple into the path.

3. A pure moral life which includes abstinence from meat, fish, eggs, alcohol, drugs, and sex outside of marriage.
4. The firm conviction that jivan mukti (liberation while living) is possible under the guidance of a realized saint or mystic.

The tremendous importance given to a living master in the Radhasoami tradition has led to several bitter successorship controversies. In fact, the first succession controversy occurred right after the death of Shiv Dayal Singh, the acknowledged founder of the Radha Soami. Several followers (and not just one) acted as gurus which resulted in a proliferation of satsangs. This in turn led to further schisms; the net result is that there are a number of groups which identify themselves as Radhasoami satsangs. The following is a brief history of the major Radhasoami centers now operating in America, including an outline of those groups which have splintered off and founded their own traditions.

The largest of all Radhasoami related movements in the world, the Radhasoami Satsang in the Beas, Punjab, India, was founded by Jaimal Singh, who was initiated by Shiv Dayal Singh in the latter part of the 1850s. Jaimal Singh was a celibate who attracted several thousand disciples before his death in 1903. He was succeeded by Sawan Singh, popularly known as the "Great Master," a military engineer who developed the Beas satsang into a major religious center in India. He initiated over 125,000 people, including hundreds of Europeans and Americans. After his death in 1948, he was succeeded by Jagat Singh, a retired chemistry professor, who had one of the shortest reigns of any guru in Radhasoami history. Before his death in 1951, he appointed Charan Singh, a grandson of Sawan Singh, to assume the Mastership at the Beas colony (also known as Dera Baba Jaimal Singh in honor of its original founder). Charan Singh (1916–1990) commanded the largest following of any guru in Radhasoami history, initiating over 1.25 million seekers. Moreover, he was instrumental in making Radhasoami a transnational religious movement with centers in countries around the world. Two days before his death on June 1, 1990, he appointed his nephew, Gurinder Singh Dhillon, to succeed him. Today the Radhasoami Satsang Beas has more followers than all of the other groups combined.

When Jagat Singh was appointed via a registered will by Sawan Singh to assume mantleship of the Radhasoami Satsang Beas, some disciples broke off and started their own separate ministries. Outstanding among these was Kirpal Singh (1894–1974), who founded Ruhani Satsang in Delhi, India. He wrote a number of well-received books, including *Crown of Life*, and attracted a significant American following. Before his death, he initiated 80,000-plus disciples. However, after his death there followed a severe succession dispute, which eventually led to several disciples claiming mastership. The most popular and most widely accepted successor was Kirpal Singh's eldest son, Darshan Singh, who established *Sawan-Kirpal Mission* in Vijay Nagar, Delhi.

Before Darshan Singh died in 1989, he appointed via a will his eldest son, Rajinder Singh. Other followers of Kirpal Singh who claimed succession were Thakar Singh, who founded Kirpal Light Satsang and Ajaib Singh who established Sant Bani in Rajasthan. It is estimated that there are around 200,000 followers of Kirpal Singh related groups in India and abroad.

There are several Radhasoami groups in Agra, India, the birthplace of its founder, Shiv Dayal Singh. The three most popular ones are Soami Bagh, Dayal Bagh, and Peepal Mandi. All three groups trace their lineage back to Shiv Dayal Singh through Rai Salig Ram, who was instrumental in organizing (or altering, depending upon one's satsang affiliation) his guru's teachings into an incarnational religion. Salig Ram also published Shiv Dayal Singh's poetry and prose writings, as well as publishing a number of articles and books on his own. After Salig Ram's death in 1898, there was again a succession dispute over who was the rightful heir. Eventually Brahm Shankar Misra assumed control and during his tenure he established the Central Administrative Council, which attempted to control the various Radhasoami branches that had developed after Shiv Dayal Singh's death. Although the Council was a political disaster, it did pave the way for Misra's successors to establish their own unbending orthodoxy. Following Misra's death there was a split between two camps, which later became more popularly known as Soami Bagh and Dayal Bagh. These two groups, though occupying property right across the street from each other, are extremely antagonistic to each other (there was a disputed lawsuit between both camps over worship rights that ran over forty years in the courts). Though both Dayal Bagh and Soami Bagh are similar in terms of doctrines, they disagree over who properly succeeded Brahm Shankar Misra. Dayal Bagh recognized Kamata Prasad Sinha, whereas Soami Bagh recognized Misra's sister, Maheshwari Devi. Today Dayal Bagh follows Dr. Lal Sahab; Soami Bagh does not recognize any living guru, as such, and is in a state of "interregnum" following the death of their last living guru, Madhav Prasad Sinha in 1949. The Peepal Mandi group is a family dynasty, apparently started by Rai Salig Ram and continued by his son, grandson, and great grandson. The current leader is Agam Prasad Mathur, the well-known author of the book, *The Radhasoami Faith*.

There are a number of smaller Radhasoami groups in India and America which have splintered off (usually after the death of a guru). One which has drawn increasing attention is Manavta Mandir, founded by Fagir Chand (1886–1981), a disciple of Shiv Brat Lal, who was a student of Rai Salig Ram. Fagir Chand was perhaps the most radical guru in the first hundred years of Radhasoami history because he has categorically denied the powers and miracles usually attributed to Sant mat masters. Indeed, Fagir

Chand has gone to great lengths to argue that almost all gurus, more or less, have deceived their followers into believing that such teachers have omnipotence and omnipresence, when in fact they have neither. Fagir Chand was succeeded in 1981 by Dr. I. C. Sharma, a philosophy professor who taught in the United States for two decades.

Of the groups affiliated with Radhasoami, the two most controversial ones are Eckankar, founded by Paul Twitchell (a one-time disciple of Kirpal Singh and L. Ron Hubbard), and MSIA (Movement for Spiritual Inner Awareness), established by John-Roger Hinkins, a one-time follower of Paul Twitchell and Eckankar, who claims to have been given part of his spiritual authority by Sawan Singh on the inner planes. In both groups, however, there has been a concerted attempt to dissociate themselves with their genealogical heritages and to emphasize their own unique callings.

In the past one hundred years Radhasoami has emerged from its origins as a tiny guru satsang in Agra into one of the fastest growing religious movements in the world, with a total membership exceeding two million. With the increasing factionalization of the movement into tens of distinct sublineages, it appears that Radhasoami will have a significant impact on the development of new religions around the world. Already new groups, related with Radhasoami, have cropped up in such diverse places as Taiwan, Nigeria, and Arizona. Individuals such as Chiang Hai, a one-time follower of Thakar Singh, have established large groups which appear to have drawn a large number of recruits. Still others are in the beginning stages, like Sri Michael Turner's satsang classes in Tucson, Arizona. What is more likely to occur is that the older, more established Radhasoami groups (particular Beas) will continue to expand at a steady rate, whereas other newly emerging groups (like Eckankar and Chiang Hai's ministry) will reach new markets not necessarily open to the more Indianized and traditional Radhasoami and Sant Mat related groups and gurus.

—*David Christopher Lane*

**RADHA SOAMI SATSANG, BEAS.** The Radha Soami Satsang, Beas is one of a number of movements flowing from the teachings of Param Sant Soami Ji Maharaj (Soami Ji). Soami's successors quarreled and split over succession to leadership of the movement he created. Radha Soami Satsang, Beas developed from the teachings of Baba Jaimal Singh, who had been charged by Soami to spread his (Soami Ji's) teachings into the Punjab. The successor to Baba Jaimal Singh, Maharaj Sawan Singh, spread the teachings thoughout the Punjab and, eventually, into the United States.

The latter occurred when a follower of Sawan Singh, Kehar Singh Sasmus, visited Port Angeles, Washington, in 1911. While there, he initiated Dr. H. M. Brock and his wife into the movement. After the Brocks received the authorization to initiate others, they attracted a number of followers, including one Julian Johnson. Johnson's book, *The Path of the Masters*, published in the 1930s, helped to further disseminate Sawan Singh's teachings to American audiences. Under the leadership of Sawan Singh's grandson, Charan Singh, the Radha Soami Satsung, Beas is now the largest of all of the Sant Mat groups in the world.

The teachings of the group are strikingly parallel to those of the ancient Manicheans. The Supreme Spiritual Being, Radha Soami Dayal, produced emanations from which the created order emerged. The emanations of the Supreme Being became imprisoned in matter to the extent that the emanations cannot escape without assistance. Therefore, the Supreme Being incarnated Masters (sant satgurus) to teach humans the techniques for freeing the emanations.

The path to freeing the divine is surat shabad yoga, a three-fold methodology. The first step, surat shab yoga, entails the repetition of the five divine names (the simram). Next, the seeker contemplates the form of the master (dhayar). Finally, the seeker listens to the divine melody. That process permits the individual to perceive the sound and the divine light that emanates from it. The Master's guidance is indispensable to the process since it is the Master who assists the seeker in perceiving the divine sound and following the sound back to the source from which it emanated (the Supreme Being). Those who follow the system must live according to a code of behavior requiring vegetarianism, abstinence from alcohol, and moral character. Two and a half hours per day are to be set aside for meditation.

Charan Singh is the recognized Master of the group. He is also known as the Patron of Radha Soami Stasang, Beas. The central organization for the group is in India. There are four initiating masters in the United States at the present time with two more in Canada. There are in excess of one hundred meeting places in the United States and seven in Canada. The teachings are also disseminated in the periodical, *Radha Soami Greetings*.

**ECKANKAR.** Eckankar is known as the Religion of the Light and Sound of God. Founded by Paul Twitchell in 1965, it claims ancient roots. From humble beginnings it has grown to an international organization head-quartered in Minneapolis, Minnesota, with tens of thousands of members.

Eckankar's modern-day founder was the pioneer of soul travel today. Twitchell's complex background as a spiritual seeker leaves much of his biography unclear—including the exact year of his birth. He was born in Kentucky, probably between 1908 and 1912. During the 1950s he explored many avenues of esoteric spirituality and philosophy. He later studied with L. Ron Hubbard's Scientology for a while. He also served on the staff of Swami Premananda's Self-Revelation Church of Absolute Monism. Sometime during the nineteen-fifties he was accepted into the Ruhani Satsang version of the Indian Radhasoami sect by its founder Kirpal Singh.

Twitchell repudiated all of these affiliations and began holding lectures and publishing esoteric newsletters. He asserted that in 1956 he experienced "God-realization" after being trained by a group of spiritual masters known as the Order of the Vairagi Masters. Eckankar teaches that these beings have quietly given out the teachings of Eck to humanity throughout history. Twitchell claimed that he was assigned the role of bringing these teachings to the modern world as the "971st Living Eck Master" by these higher spiritual beings—a role similar to world teacher in theosophical lore.

After Twitchell founded Eckankar in 1965, he established its headquarters in Las Vegas, Nevada. For the next few years he wrote and published several key books of Eckankar theology, including *Eckankar: The Key to Secret Worlds* (1969), which served as a basic introductory text to Eckankar for many years. Twitchell's biography, written by Brad Steiger and entitled *In My Soul I Am Free,* was also published in the nineteen sixties and helped to bring Twitchell and Eckankar to public attention.

Paul Twitchell died in 1971. His wife, Gail, announced his successor as the 972d Living Eck Master—Darwin Gross. Gross and Gail married shortly afterward. Eckankar continued to grow and flourish. In the mid-1970s, its new headquarters was established at Menlo Park, California. In 1981, Gross announced that he had been succeeded by the 973d Living Eck Master, Harold Klemp.

Inspired by a "spiritual vision," Klemp led Eckankar to move its headquarters to a suburb of Minneapolis, Minnesota, where its spiritual home, the Temple of Eck, was opened in 1990. Under Klemp and Skelskey Eckankar has continued to grow and change. With Klemp's leadership as the Mahanta, the living Eck master, Eckankar has continued to grow and change. The primary body of Eckankar writings have now been authored by Klemp, with over thirty books by him in print. While retaining its original doctrine of "soul travel," it has been at the forefront of today's emphasis on spirituality in everyday life. This has made it attractive to people from all walks of life.

Eckankar, the Religion of Light and Sound of God, has also been known as "the ancient science of soul travel." These beliefs and practices appear to share common ground with Rosicrucian teachings as well. To scholars of new religions, Eckankar appears to be one of the most eclectic and syncretistic spiritual movements in America.

Eckankar teaches that God is "Sugmad"—the transcendant source of all being. Everything that exists is an emanation of this divine Spirit. More attention is given to "Eck," than to God, however. "Eck," the Light and Sound of God, is the life current, which emanates from Sugmad. It has various levels and on these levels takes different forms including various intelligences. Eck can be experienced through chanting the mantra "HU," a special name for God in Eckankar. Chanting HU is the central spiritual practices of Eckankar. It is alleged to help lift one to spiritual self-realization, and ultimately God-realization.

Eckankar teaches reincarnation and karma in the Western mode. That is, once one has attained the level of human there is nowhere to go but "up." Eckists believe that the core of each person is an individual soul, a divine spark of God that lives throughout eternity. They also believe that each of us progresses through many lifetimes to reach a full realization of our innate divine qualities. Eckankar does not teach transmigration of souls.

Eckankar holds the Living Eck Master in high esteem. He is the living oracle of God and the "Dream Master" on the spiritual (inner) plane. Eck "chelas" (members) are encouraged to learn the spiritual significance of their dreams as out-of-body experiences in which Eck masters, including the Living Eck Master, show them the deeper meaning behind daily life events and those in the heavenly worlds.

The Eckankar organization is operated by a board of trustees with Harold Klemp as the spiritual leader. The headquarters are located in offices in the western suburbs of Minneapolis and at the Temple of Eck, which stands on beautiful land between the exurb of Chanhassen and farmlands.

Eckankar sponsors centers and study groups around the world. It holds major conferences throughout the year, including the Eck Worldwide Seminar held near the time of Eckankar's spiritual new year on October 22. The Mahanta, the Living Eck Master, Sri Harold Klemp, traditionally speaks at international conferences every year. Eckankar does not divulge exact statistics, but claims to have "tens of thousands" of dedicated chelas, most of whom reside in North America, Europe, and Africa.

Eckankar operates a publishing house known as Illuminated Way Press. It is located in Crystal, Minnesota, and publishes numerous books by Twitchell, Klemp, and other lower "higher initiates" of Eckankar. It also distributes correspondence courses, video tapes, brochures, and paintings of higher worlds.

Eckankar considers itself largely an educational organization. That is, its primary mission is to disseminate knowledge of "soul" to people ready to experience God-realization and become "coworkers with God." To this end it sponsors various levels of courses in dream interpretation, soul travel, and practical lifestyle for creating good karma. So far it has not established any institutions of higher learning such as college or seminary—at least not on the physical plane. It teaches that there are libraries, research centers, and educational opportunities in monasteries run by the Vairagi Masters in secret locations on a spiritual plane of reality which can be reached through spiritual exercises.

Eckankar has studiously avoided controversy in the media. The only time this has happened was during the initial phase of moving its headquarters and building its Temple of Eck in Minnesota. Some citizens of the city of Chanhassen attempted to prevent the city council from permitting it. Articles were written about this controversy in the Twin Cities press and this was the first time most people outside California had heard of Eckankar.

Within Eckankar there was controversy when Twitchell died and was succeeded by Gross and again when Gross was replaced by Klemp. There was lengthy and complicated litigation between Gross and Eckankar over use of the term itself as well as other related terms used by the organization which it has trademarked.

*—Roger E. Olson*

**Elan Vital (Divine Light Mission).** Elan Vital grew out of Sant Mat (literally, the way of the saints), a nineteenth-century spiritual tradition which developed out of the Sikh religion in northern India. One of the goals of the movement was the instruction of the world in a type of yogic meditation technique that was said to connect the devotee to the universal primordial force through meditation on the Holy Name (Word) and on the divine light and which pervades everything.

Initiation into the yoga occurs through a process referred to in Elan Vital as *giving Knowledge,* during which an instructor, called a mahatma, introduces new members to four yogic techniques which reveal the means of experiencing the divine light, sound, word, and nectar. Once the initiates learn these techniques, they practice them every day, often under a blanket in order to block outside disturbances. Among the goals of the original mission were the promotion of human unity, world peace, improved education for all, and relief from the distress caused by ill health and natural calamities.

The Divine Light Mission was founded by the Hindu Shri Hans Maharaj Ji. Disciple of the guru Sarupanand Ji, Hans Maharaj Ji diffused the teachings of the Sant Mat tradition in Sind and Lahore, and in 1930 he established a mission in Delhi. Shortly after the declaration of Indian independence, he authorized the initiation and propagation activities of the first mahatmas, followers who committed their own lives to the teaching of Hans Maharaj's doctrine. Hans Maharaj founded the monthly magazine *Hansadesh,* and by 1960 the need to organize the numerous followers who could be found across Northern India led to the founding of the Divine Light Mission.

When Hans Maharaj died (1966), he was succeeded by his youngest son, Prem Pal Singh Rawat, who was initiated at the age of six and who, two years later, was recognized as the new "Perfect Master," an embodiment of

God on earth and hence an object of worship and veneration, assuming the title of Maharaj Ji. When his father died, he was commissioned as the one to take the knowledge to the world, and although he became officially the autocratic leader of the mission, his whole family shared the authority because of his young age.

In 1971, Maharaj Ji made his first visit to the West, after having been invited by some Americans who became initiates while in India to search for spiritual guidance. Against his mother's wishes he went to Colorado, where a large crowd heard his first set of discourses given in America. A considerable number of people were initiated, and the American headquarters of the mission was established in Denver. By the end of 1973 several hundred centers and over twenty ashrams had emerged. Two periodicals, *And It Is Divine* and *Divine Times,* were also begun. However, in November 1973, the mission suffered a major reverse because of the failure of "Millennium '73," an event organized to celebrate the birthday of Maharaj Ji's father and the beginning of a thousand years of peace and prosperity. The event had been scheduled to take place at the Houston Astrodome, and all of the movement's resources were invested into the event. When the anticipated large crowds of people failed to manifest, the movement fell into deep debt which effectively crippled it.

After the Millennium 1973 fiasco, the mission gradually withdrew from the public scene. Many followers left the movement, many ashrams were discontinued, and Maharaj Ji began to replace his Indian image with a Western one by wearing business suits instead of his all-white attire. A number of ex-members became critics of the movement, attacking it with charges of brainwashing and mind control. Maharaj Ji himself was described by anticultists as immature and unfit to be a religious leader, and his teachings were condemned as lacking in substance.

The movement also suffered from internal problems within Maharaj Ji's family. Mataji, Maharaj Ji's mother, disapproved of his lifestyle and of his marriage with his secretary Marolyn Johnson, whom he declared to be the incarnation of the goddess Durga. After accusing her son of breaking his spiritual disciplines, she took control of the mission in India by replacing him with his oldest brother. In 1975 Maharaj Ji took his family to court. He received control of the movement everywhere but in India, where his brother remained the leader. By the end of the 1970s, an estimated 80 percent of the followers had left the Mission. In the early 1980s Maharaj Ji ordered all of the ashrams disbanded, and declared that he was no longer to be venerated as God.

When the Divine Light Mission was disbanded, the organization Elan Vital was created in order to relate Maharaj Ji to his students on a one-to-one basis and to support his travels in thirty-four countries worldwide, where he could speak to his followers, the number of whom is very difficult to estimate. With the transformation of the mission into Elan Vital, the emphasis on making provision for the future establishment of hospitals, maternity homes, and residences has been lost.

### THE MOVEMENT OF SPIRITUAL INNER AWARENESS (MSIA).

The Movement of Spiritual Inner Awareness (MSIA) is a contemporary religious movement that was founded by John-Roger Hinkins in 1971. While MSIA has often been characterized as New Age, and while it participates in the larger metaphysical subculture, MSIA's core spiritual practices lie squarely in the Sant Mat (Radhasoami) tradition.

MSIA was founded by John-Roger Hinkins, generally called Sri John-Roger, or, more informally, "J-R." John-Roger was born Roger Hinkins in 1934 to a Mormon family in Rains, Utah. He completed a degree in psychology at the University of Utah, moved to southern California in 1958, and eventually took a job teaching English at Rosemead High School. In 1963, while undergoing surgery for a kidney stone, he fell into a nine-day coma. Upon awakening, he found himself aware of a new spiritual personality—"John"—who had superseded or merged with his old personality. After the operation, Hinkins began to refer to himself as "John-Roger," in recognition of his transformed self.

Hinkins soon left Eckankar, a Sant Mat-inspired group with which he had been affiliated, and began holding gatherings as an independent spiritual teacher. In 1971 he formally incorporated the church of the Movement of Spiritual Inner Awareness. Other organizations founded by John-Roger and/or MSIA members were Prana (now Peace) Theological Seminary (1974), Baraka Holistic Center (1976), and Insight Training Seminars (1978). The John-Roger Foundation was created in 1982 in order to coordinate the various programs initiated by MSIA, as well as to celebrate the Integrity Day, through which the Foundation could promote global transformation by the enrichment and uplift of individuals. An annual Integrity Award banquet has been held since 1983: during this event awards were given to individuals for their achievement along with checks which could be donated to their favorite charities. In 1988, the John-Roger Foundation was divided into the Foundation for the Study of the Individual and World Peace and the International Integrity Foundation.

The basic MSIA worldview is similar to that of the religious traditions that have originated on the South Asian subcontinent—Hinduism, Buddhism, and Sikhism (particularly the latter). In common with these religions, MSIA accepts the notion that the individual soul is trapped in the material world, which is viewed as a realm of suffering. Because of the related processes of reincarnation and karma, the death of the physical body does not free a person from suffering. Only through the practice of certain spiritual techniques, such as the practice of yogic meditation, can individuals liberate themselves from the cycle of death and rebirth.

In common with other Sant Mat groups, MSIA pictures the cosmos as composed of many different levels or "planes." At the point of creation, these levels sequentially emerged from God along a vibratory "stream" until creation reached its terminus in the physical plane. The Sant Mat tradition teaches that individuals can be linked to God's creative energy, and that this stream of energy will carry their consciousness back to God. The Mystical Traveler Consciousness—which formerly manifested through John-Roger (it has since been anchored in John Morton)—accomplished this link up during initiation, although the individual still had to appropriate and utilize the link through the practice of special meditation techniques (referred to as spiritual exercises), particularly meditation on the mantra "Hu."

According to MSIA, each individual is involved in a movement of spiritual inner awareness, of which the Movement of Spiritual Inner Awareness is an outward reflection. Individuals who wish to develop a total awareness, and free themselves from the necessity of reincarnation can seek the assistance of the Mystical Traveler, who exists simultaneously on all levels of consciousness in total awareness. He can teach them how to reach this awareness as well as assist them in understanding and releasing themselves from their karmic responsibilities, by reading the karmic records of each individual. One of the main goals of MSIA consists in helping individuals adjust to the rapid changes and resultant stresses, so they are not distracted in their spiritual search.

Some of the several New Age healing techniques dealing with different aspects of the self have been adopted by MSIA, such as "aura balancing," which is a technique for clearing the auric (magnetic) field that exists around each individual; "inner-phasings," a technique through which the individual can reach into the subconscious and bring to consciousness and remove the dysfunctional patterns learned early in life; and "polarity balancing," which releases blocks in the physical body. A major emphasis upon holistic healing originated from these early techniques, and resulted in the development of the Baraka Holistic Center for Therapy and Research in Santa Monica, California.

There are many levels of involvement in MSIA. A useful criterion of membership is whether or not one is actively enrolled in a series of monthly lessons referred to as "discourses." After specified periods of time "on discourses," one may apply for the initiation. There are four formal initiations, each of which indicates progressively deeper involvement in the spiritual path which is at the core of MSIA's various practices.

Independently of the initiation structure, one may become an MSIA minister. The basic MSIA gathering is the home seminar. Thus, MSIA ministers do not normally minister to congregations. Rather, MSIA ministers are involved in some type of service work, which constitutes their "ministry."

For many years, MSIA published a popular periodical, the *Movement*

*Newspaper*, that reported on a wide variety of topics in the New Age/metaphysical subculture. In the late 1980s, the *Movement Newspaper* was supplanted by the *New Day Herald*, an insider publication focused on MSIA-related events.

In the late 1970s, MSIA developed its own training seminars—Insight Training Seminars—in order to provide an intense transformational experience. These seminars can be compared to est (Erhard Seminar Trainings) and Lifespring, although MSIA's emphases is on the ability to move beyond self-imposed limitations. Insight has since developed into a separate organization, independent of MSIA.

MSIA also gave birth to the University of Santa Monica which, like Insight, has since developed into a separate institution. A second educational institution, Peace Theological Seminary (PTS), was formed later, and has become an integral part of MSIA's outreach. The majority of MSIA seminars and workshops are held under the auspices of the Seminary. At the time of this writing, PTS's relatively new master's program has been vigorously expanded to reach students across the United States.

As a low-intensity group that does not make excessive demands upon either the time or the resources of most members, MSIA largely escaped the attention of the anticult movement until the late 1980s. In 1988, the *Los Angeles Times* published a highly critical article on MSIA. A similar article appeared in *People* magazine. Both pieces dwelt on charges by ex-staff members that Hinkins had sexually exploited them. Depending significantly upon the testimony of disgruntled ex-members and drawing heavily on the "cult" stereotype, MSIA was portrayed as an organization that was created for no other purpose than to serve the financial, sexual, and ego needs of John-Roger Hinkins. After a brief moment in the spotlight, reporters turned their attention to other stories, and MSIA disappeared from the pages of the mass media.

Two events occurred in 1994 that once again brought MSIA to the attention of the media circus. First was Michael Huffington's campaign to become a California senator. Arianna Huffington, Michael Huffington's wife, is a member of MSIA. When someone in the media discovered this fact, the link became a focus of a number of sensationalistic articles in which all of the earlier accusations against John-Roger and MSIA were dragged out and uncritically repeated. In the same year as the campaign, Peter McWilliams, an MSIA minister who had coauthored a series of popular books with John-Roger, dropped out of the movement and authored a bitter anti-MSIA book, *LIFE 102: What To Do When Your Guru Sues You*, which attracted some media attention.

# 12 BUDDHIST TRADITION

**B**uddhism is a major world religion that was founded by Gautama Buddha in the Indian subcontinent around 600 B.C.E. Like many other religious leaders, Buddha saw himself as being more of a reformer than an innovator, and early Buddhism is clearly in the same religious "family" as Buddhism's parent religious tradition, Hinduism. However, to be considered within the Hindu fold, one must nominally acknowledge the authority of the four Vedas, Hinduism's most ancient religious texts. Buddha rejected the authority of the Vedas, and hence, despite its close relationship with Hinduism, Buddhism is technically non-Hindu. Interestingly, Buddhism almost completely disappeared from the land of its birth. Rather, it was transplanted and bore fruit in other parts of Asia, to the North, South, and East of India.

For many years, Buddha studied under spiritual teachers in the Upanishadic tradition. The religious texts collectively referred to as the Upanishads articulate a worldview centered around release or liberation (moksha) from the cycle of death and rebirth (from the ongoing cycle of reincarnation). The Upanishads also postulated an eternal, changeless core of the self that was referred to as the Atman. This soul or deep self was viewed as being identical with the unchanging godhead, referred to as "Brahman" (the unitary ground of being that transcends particular gods and goddesses). Untouched by the variations of time and circumstance, the Atman was nevertheless entrapped in the world of samsara. Samsara is the South Asian term for the world we experience in our everyday lives. This constantly changing, unstable world is contrasted with the spiritual realm of Atman/Brahman, which by contrast is stable and unchanging. Samsara also refers to the process of death and rebirth (reincarnation) through which we are "trapped" in this world.

What keeps us trapped in the samsaric cycle is the law of karma. Karma operates impersonally like a natural law, ensuring that every good or bad deed eventually returns to the individual in the form of reward or punishment commensurate with the original deed. It is karma that compels human beings to reincarnate in successive lifetimes. In other words, if one dies before reaping the effects of one's actions, the karmic process demands that one come back in a future life. Moksha is the traditional Hindu term for release or liberation from the endless chain of deaths and rebirths. According to the Upanishadic view, what happens at the point of moksha is that the individual Atman merges into the cosmic Brahman, much like a drop of water which, when dropped into the ocean, loses its individuality and becomes one with the ocean.

Buddha accepted the basic Hindu doctrines of reincarnation and karma, as well as the notion, common to most South Asian religions, that the ultimate goal of the religious life was to escape the cycle of death and rebirth (samsara). Buddha asserted that what kept us bound to the death/rebirth process was desire, desire in the generic sense of wanting or craving anything in the world of samsara. Hence the goal of getting off the ferris wheel of reincarnation necessarily involves freeing oneself from desire. Nibbana—or, in later Buddhism, nirvana—is the Buddhist equivalent of moksha. Nirvana literally means "extinction," and it refers to the extinction of all craving, an extinction that allows one to break out of samsara.

Where Buddha departed most radically from Upanishadic Hinduism was in his doctrine of anatta, the notion that individuals do not possess eternal souls. Instead of eternal souls, individuals consist of a "bundle" of habits, memories, sensations, desires, and so forth, which together delude one into thinking that he or she consists of a stable, lasting self. Despite its transitory nature, this false self hangs together as a unit, and even reincarnates in body after body. In Buddhism as well as in Hinduism life in a corporeal body is viewed negatively, as the source of all suffering. Hence the goal is to obtain release from the samsaric process. In Buddhism, this means abandoning the false sense of self so that the bundle of memories and impulses disintegrates, leaving nothing to reincarnate and hence nothing to experience pain.

From the perspective of the present-day, world-affirming Western society, the Buddhist vision appears distinctly unappealing: Not only is this life portrayed in an unattractive manner, but the prospect of nirvana, in which one dissolves into nothingness, seems even less desirable. A modern-day Buddha might respond, however, that our reaction to being confronted with the dark side of life merely shows how insulated we are from the pain and suffering that is so fundamental to human existence.

But, someone might respond, why not just try to live life, despite its many flaws, as best one can, avoiding pain and seeking pleasure? Because, Buddha would respond, while we might be able to exercise a certain amount of control over this incarnation, we cannot foresee the circumstances in which our karma would compel us to incarnate in future lives, which might be as a starving child in a war-torn area of the third world. Also, the Buddha would point out, if we closely examine our life, we can see that even the things that seem to bring us our greatest enjoyments also bring us the greatest pain. This aspect of Buddhist thought was embodied in that part of Buddha's system referred to as the Three Marks of Being.

In the first place, Buddha points out, we have to contend with the experiences everyone recognizes as painful—illness, accidents, disappointments, and so forth. Secondly, the world is in a constant state of change, so even the things we experience as pleasurable do not last, and ultimately lead to pain. (Romantic relationships, for example, initially bring us great happiness, but usually end in greater suffering.) And thirdly, because we ourselves are in a constant process of change, we ultimately lose everything we have gained, particularly in the transition we call death.

Buddha, as it should be clear by this point, was less inclined to speculative metaphysics, and was more a practical psychologist. Someone once asked him about the nature of ultimate reality, and Buddha responded that this question was insignificant. The human condition is comparable to someone who has been shot by an arrow, and metaphysical questions are like the wounded person asking about the type of wood out of which the arrow was made, the kind of bird from which the feathers came, and the name and occupation of the person who shot the arrow. If one insisted on knowing the answers to all of these queries before having the arrow extracted, one would surely die. Buddha concluded this discourse by saying that what concerned him was extracting arrows and healing wounds; everything else was unimportant. For similar reasons, he refused to speculate on the nature of the afterlife state of one who had experienced nirvana. The practical, no nonsense approach of the Buddha is particularly evident in the Four Noble Truths, which constitute the core of his teaching:

1. Life is Suffering—the original word Buddha used for suffering was *dukkha,* which means "out of joint." Dukkha is a comprehensive term which covers everything from physical pain to vague psychological dissatisfactions.
2. The Cause of Suffering is Desire—the word for desire here is *Tanha* (literally "thirst"), which refers to any craving, from sexual desire to even mild desires to help humanity.
3. To eliminate Suffering, one must eliminate Desire—a logical corollary to the second Noble Truth.

4. To eliminate Desire, one must following the Eight-fold Path—Buddha outlined the process of overcoming one's cravings under eight principal headings; everything from proper meditation procedure to following a proper career that did not interfere with the goal of reaching nirvana.

As befits Buddha's practical emphasis, these four points present a one-to-one correspondence with medical practice. In other words, the first noble truth corresponds with symptoms, the second with diagnosis, the third with prognosis, and the fourth with prescription.

While Buddha himself was profoundly antispeculative and antimetaphysical, many of his later followers were not. Particularly after Buddhism split into Theravada (southern Buddhism, found today in Sri Lanka and Southeast Asia) and Mahayana (northern Buddhism, found today in Korea, Japan, and Taiwan), metaphysical speculation flowered in Mahayana Buddhism. Various forms of devotional Buddhism also developed within the Mahayana fold. Devotional Buddhism focused on different Bodhisattvas (enlightened souls who delayed the final stages of their nirvana so that they could stay around and help ordinary mortals) who, like the great gods and goddesses of later Hinduism, could help their devotees. The notion of heaven-worlds was also developed in these forms of Buddhism, heaven-worlds where the earnest devotee would find her or himself after death, and where she or he could continue the quest for enlightenment, less hindered by the demands of this world.

In these developments, it is clear that popular theism has reemerged in the worship of godlike Bodhisattvas. The development of heaven-realms is also interesting. While devotees continue to express an ideology of regarding such realms as temporary way stations on the journey to nirvana, de facto such realms occupy the foreground in devotees' contemplation of the afterlife, and nirvana is pushed to the background. Pure-land Buddhism is perhaps the widely known form of popular Buddhism. When a Pure-land Buddhist is on the edge of death, a scroll depicting the Pure-land is unrolled and placed in the dying person's field of vision so that it will be easier for her or him to make it to the Pure-land after death.

Tibetan Buddhism is the most prominent living school of Tantric Buddhism. Tantric Buddhism is a difficult strand of the Buddhist tradition to explain briefly. Sometimes it is viewed as a form of Mahayana Buddhism, at others as a third form of Buddhism. However it is classified, Tantric Buddhism is characterized by an elaborately developed mythology and exotic spiritual practices.

Wherever Buddhism was carried, it tended to merge with, or at least to pick up elements of, the local, indigenous religion. Tibet's indigenous Bön religion was, or included, a rather elaborate form of shamanism.

Shamanism is a form of spiritual expression that involves, among other elements, ecstatic journeys to other realms—including the realm of the dead—by a religious specialist known in the disciplines of anthropology and religious studies as a shaman.

**VAJRADHATU (SHAMBHALA INTERNATIONAL).** The Movement Vajradhatu, literally "the realm of the indestructible," has diffused the growth of Tibetan Buddhism in the United States. It was found by Chogyam Trungpa Rinpoche (1939–1987), who emphasized Buddhism as a practice to awaken the mind through three aspects: (1) meditation, the state of being in the present moment which consists of training the mind to exist in the here and now; (2) study, which sharpens the understanding of the experience of meditation and the communication of the experience to others; and (3) work, which allows the meditator to share what has been learned with others.

Trungpa was born in the village of Geje in northeast Tibet, and was identified as the reborn tenth Trungpa tulku by the monks of the Buddhist sect Karmapa Kargyupa. He was trained at Dudtsi-til Monastery, and received his degrees when he was a teenager. He became a monk and, after the invasion of Tibet by China in 1959, he went to India where he learned English. He then traveled to the West, and in 1963 he went to Oxford, where he studied art, psychology, and comparative religion.

During his stay in Oxford, he discovered the Buddhist contemplative center Johnstone House in Scotland. After a severe injury in 1969, he decided to become a layman in order to better communicate to Western people the complicated and sophisticated Tibetan tradition. *Cutting Through Spiritual Materialism* is the title of one of Trungpa's early books as well as a major theme of his teaching, according to which the primary mistake of Western followers of a spiritual discipline was their conversion of what they had learned to egoistical uses.

After his marriage with Diana Judith Pybus in 1970, he immigrated to the United States. In Vermont, some of his followers built Tail of the Tiger Monastery. He gave several lectures around the country and established many centers, such as the Rocky Mountain Dharma Center at Ft. Collins, a small facility used primarily for meditative retreats and other short-term programs. In 1973 he established his organization, Vajradhatu.

In 1974, he held the first seminar which led to the formation of Naropa Institute, which has received the support of Buddhist leaders and scholars throughout North America. During the same year he received the visit of Gyalwa Karmapa, the international leader of the Kargyupa Buddhists, who performed the famous black hat ceremony and recognized Trungpa as a Vajracarya (a spiritual master).

In 1976, Trungpa named Thomas Rich, an American disciple, as his

Dharma successor. Rich, who took the name Osel Tendzin, assumed administrative leadership of the community when Trungpa died. In 1989 the *Los Angeles Times* broke the story that Tendzin had AIDS, and it was also reported that for three years he had known of his infection and had continued to have sexual relations with others withouth telling them of the risk. He was then asked by Vajradhatu's board to take a permanent leave of absence. Tendzin died in 1990. Trungpa's son, Sawang Osel Rangdrol Mukpo succeeded him, returning some stability to the organization. He established Shambhala International as an umbrella organization to encompass a number of his father's organizations, including Vajradhata.

Since its formation, Vajradhatu has grown consistently, although it was early the center of controversy because of Trungpa's un-monk-like personal habits, such as eating meat and using both alcohol and tobacco. Among the few episodes of controversy is the one which occurred in the fall of 1975, when a pacifist student attending the classes for advanced students at Naropa Institute was disturbed by the bloody images in some of the Tibetan material used during the sessions. The same student, who was an outstanding poet, was stripped of his clothes after being ordered by Trungpa to return to a Halloween party at Naropa that he had left earlier in the evening with a friend. The incident became subject of articles in a national magazine and a book.

**SOKA GAKKAI INTERNATIONAL.** Soka Gakkai International (SGI) is a Japanese Buddhist group with a comparatively large following in the United States and other Western countries. Founded in the 1930s, Soka Gakkai has grown to become Japan's largest and most controversial new religion. Although classified as a new religion, SGI's roots lie in thirteenth century Japan.

Like most other Japanese Buddhist groups, SGI belongs to the Mahayana school. Mahayana developed out of the older Theravada school, some six centuries or so after the time of the historical Buddha. At the time of their emergence, Mahayanists presented the world with "new" scriptures that legitimated their interpretation of the Buddhist tradition. The claim was that these newly revealed texts represented Gautama's higher teachings, but that Shakyamuni (one name for the historical Buddha)—seeing that his contemporaries were too dense to comprehend such profundities—kept the more advanced scriptures secret until a generation would come along that could grasp them.

Due to their historically prior position, the Theravadins controlled most of Buddhism's sacred real estate—meaning, in particular, that they owned the pilgrimage sites constituted by the stupas that were built up around Buddhist relics (e.g., one of Gautama Buddha's teeth). Control over the real estate was important because making pilgrimages to holy sites was the chief means by which ordinary lay (nonmonastic) Buddhists accumulated spiritual merit (thus ensuring future rebirths into fortunate circumstances). Perhaps as a way of compensating for their lack of stupas, the emergent Mahayanist movement proposed an alternative method for gaining merit—the reading, recitation, studying, and making copies of sacred scripture (specifically, the new scriptures). The spiritual potency of the Mahayanist scriptures was extolled within the text of each one—in such a way as to assure the reader that the merit gained by studying the newly revealed scripture far outweighed the merit gained by visiting holy places (i.e., Theravadin holy places).

A later generation of Mahayana Buddhists—reading these claims found in their scriptures independent of the original context—were led to ask a somewhat different question, namely, Which text was the most of potent? This question was the subject of debate in thirteenth-century Japan, when the Buddhist reformer Nichiren Daishonin concluded that the *Saddharmapundarika* (the Lotus of the True Law), better known simply as the Lotus Sutra, was the most important of all Buddhist books. In fact, the Lotus Sutra was so powerful that all one had to do was to chant Namu-myoho-renge-kyo (which can be translated in various ways, including "I bow to the Lotus Sutra") to gain the merit promised in its pages.

Nichiren and his teachings gave rise to a monastic movement, which eventually splintered into different sects. Soka Gakkai began as a movement of lay practicioners attached to the Nichiren Shoshu (Orthodox Nichiren Sect). The founder, Tsunesaburo Makiguchi (1871–1944), was an educator who died in prison during the Second World War. After the war, Josei Toda (1900–1958) took over as president and built Soka Gakkai into a major religion. This period of rapid growth was accompanied by negative media attention. The group matured under the presidency of Daisaku Ikeda, who became the third president of Soka Gakkai after the passing of Toda.

Soka Gakkai later spread to the United States, where it aroused controversy as a result of its intensive proselytizing activities. Although never as controversial as groups like the Hare Krishna Movement or the Unification Church, Soka Gakkai (which in the United States went under the name Nichiren Shoshu of America until recently) was not infrequently stereotyped as a brainwashing cult, particularly by anticult authors. Soka Gakkai has often been attacked in Japan because of its support of reformist political activity.

—*MICHELA ZONTA*

**AUM SHINRIKYO (AUM SUPREME TRUTH).** On March 20, 1995, a poison gas attack occurred in a Tokyo subway that killed twelve people and injured many others. Within a few days of the attack, AUM

Shinrikyo, a controversial Japanese religious group, was fingered as the most likely suspect. The leadership was eventually arrested and the organization disbanded.

AUM Shinrikyo was founded by Master Shoko Asahara in Tokyo in 1987. A form of Tantric Buddhism, AUM Shinrikyo's teachings emphasized yoga practices and spiritual experiences. Master Asahara, whose original name was Chizuo Matsumoto (b. 1955), had traveled to India seeking enlightenment. Before returning to Japan, he sought out the Dalai Lama and received what he believed to be a commission to revive true Buddhism in the land of his birth. By the time of the subway incident, AUM Shinrikyo had acquired a large communal facility near Mt. Fuji and a following of approximately ten thousand members in Japan (with an estimated thirty thousand followers in Russia).

In addition to the usual teachings that go hand in hand with mainline Buddhism, Master Asahara was also fascinated with seeing into the future. His preoccupation with divination may have grown out of the weakness of his physical senses, as he was born blind in one eye, with only partial use of the other. Before undertaking yoga and meditation practices, Asahara pursued the study of such divinatory practices as astrology. Like many other Japanese spiritualists, he was fascinated by Western biblical prophecies as well as by the prophecies of Nostradamus. Perhaps influenced by the apocalyptic flavor of these predictions, Asahara himself began preaching an apocalyptic message to his followers. In particular, he prophesied a confrontation between Japan and the United States before the end of the century that would in all likelihood decimate his home country.

As one of the few leaders warning the Japanese about what he thought was certain disaster, Asahara came to feel that the United States was "out to get" him and his followers. For example, because U.S. military jets sometimes flew over AUM installations, he became convinced that something sinister must be happening. Depending on what piece of AUM literature one reads, these aircraft were accused of dropping poison, disease, or both on AUM communities. When the subway gassing occurred, Asahara responded by asserting that the CIA had carried out the attack as a plot to defame AUM Shinrikyo.

While there were many suspicious aspects of this attack, in retrospect it is clear that at least some highly placed AUM members were involved in the subway attack. The attack was said to have been motivated by increased police scrutiny of the AUM Shinrikyo, with the idea of distracting police attention away from the movement—an explanation that has struck many observers as rather odd.

In the end, it was Asahara's own pronouncements that led the police to the door of AUM Shinrikyo. In particular, Master Asahara had predicted that gas attacks by terrorists would occur in the not-too-distant future. This made him an obvious target of suspicion. Hence the subway attack, far from diverting attention away from AUM Shinrikyo, actually had the opposite effect.

In addition to throwing the organization's leadership in jail, AUM Shinrikyo was dissolved as a corporate entity and its assets dissolved to pay victims of the subway gassing—despite the fact that the criminal trials of Asahara and certain other leaders are still in process (i.e., convictions had not yet been handed down). During Ministry of Justice hearings in 1996, Asahara declared himself no longer head of AUM Shinrikyo. From this in combination with certain earlier remarks, followers eventually deduced that he had passed the mantle of guruship to his children. In January 1997, the Ministry of Justice declared that AUM Shinrikyo was no longer a threat to society.

Over the next two years, a remnant of the AUM followers who had been driven off the group's former properties and scattered across the country came back together to form a much smaller group of approximately 1,500 members. Although there were a few conflicts prior to 1999, AUM Shinrikyo came back into the headlines in the spring of that year. Newspeople more interested in sensationalistic stories than in accuracy portrayed the group as growing and prosperous, and, further, as posing a new threat to Japanese society. The police began raiding AUM facilities in June, but found no evidence of wrongdoing. Despite the innocence of the remaining followers, public opinion was so strongly anti-AUM at the time of this writing that it appeared almost inevitable that Japanese authorities would crush the group.

**SAN FRANCISCO ZEN CENTER.** After his 1959 arrival in San Francisco as the new head of the Sokoji Temple, Shunryu Suzuki Roshi began to attract American students in addition to the Japanese congregation he originally came to serve. Together with his American students he founded San Francisco Zen Center in 1967 and purchased a hot springs resort near Carmel Valley, California, where he established Tassajara Zen Mountain Center, the first Zen Buddhist monastery outside Asia. From September through April, Tassajara's gates are closed to the public and two monastic training periods are observed. Admission is by application. In May the gates open and visitors from all over the world arrive to enjoy the natural beauty of the surrounding wilderness and summer guest season. Guest accommodations are by reservation only.

In 1969 the SFZC group purchased a large building on San Francisco's Page Street to serve as its administrative headquarters, Beginners' Mind Temple, and a residence for guests. In 1972, the group acquired Green Gulch Farm/Green Dragon Temple located on the Pacific Ocean just north of San Francisco. The farm grows organic produce and operates a guest and conference center.

SFZC offers classes, workshops, meditation instruction and many diverse opportunities for practice. Today official membership is approximately one thousand. The current abbots of SFZC are Zoketsu Norman Fisher and Zenkei Blance Hartman. The founder and former abbots of Zen Center have written and published the following books: *Zen Mind, Beginners' Mind* by Shunryu Suzuki, *Returning to Silence* by Dainin Katagiri, and *Warm Smiles from Cold Mountains: A Collection of Talks on Zen Meditation* by Tenshin Reb Anderson. SFZC teacher Edward Espe Brown is the author of many cook books including the *Tassajara Cook Book* and most recently *Tomato Blessings and Radish Teachings.* San Francisco Zen Center is also well known for its gourmet vegetarian restaurant Green at Fort Mason located on San Francisco Bay.

**IMPERSONAL    ENLIGHTENMENT    FOUNDATION (MOKSHA FOUNDATION).** The Impersonal Enlightenment Foundation (formerly the Moksha Foundation) is a spiritual group founded by Andrew Cohen. Cohen has been a teacher of Enlightenment since the mid-1980s. He was born in New York City in 1955, where he spent his childhood and early adolescence, traveling abroad to complete his education before returning again in his early twenties. Unable to forget a spontaneous spiritual experience that occurred when he was sixteen, Cohen decided to abandon all other aspirations and at the age of twenty-two became a serious spiritual seeker. His meeting with Swami Hariharananda Giri led him to the practice of martial arts and Zen meditation. After pursing many different spiritual teachers and paths, his seeking led him to India where in 1986 he met a little known spiritual teacher named H. W. L. Punja. This meeting was a catalyst for a spiritual awakening that completely transformed his life. Cohen's natural gift for communicating the understanding of awakening drew people to him almost immediately, and his teaching was born.

Since that time Cohen has continued to travel and teach extensively around the world. In addition to giving over one hundred public talks each year, he holds lengthy retreats and many shorter intensives. In 1988 he returned to the United Sates and estabished a group in Cambridge, Massachusetts. A year later he moved to Marin County, California, to join a communal group founded by some of his followers. In the mid-1990s, the group moved its headquarters once again to Lenox, Massachusetts, in western Massachusetts. Communities of students dedicated to living his teachings have also formed in New York, Boston, Europe, and Australia. Cohen devotes much time and energy to these communities, bringing people together in a common vision of unity and the dedicated pursuit of living life not for oneself, but for the sake of the whole.

Cohen's constant investigation into the nature of spiritual understanding and the spiritual pursuit has led him to initiate meetings with teachers, scholars, and leaders in many different fields of inquiry in order to explore and elucidate the fundamental truths at the heart of human life. He is also the founder and editor of *What is Enlightenment?* magazine, a biannual publication devoted solely to the purpose of conducting and promoting significant spiritual inquiry. Cohen is the author of a number of books, including *An Unconditional Relationship to Life, Autobiography of an Awakening, My Master Is My Self,* and *Enlightenment is a Secret.* In 1997 he established a worldwide retreat center in western Massachusetts where he currently resides.

**FALUN GONG.** Qi Gong is the generic name of a complex of techniques for physical and spiritual well-being, with a tradition in China predating the Christian era. It is often referred to as Chinese yoga. Although spiritual and religious activities in general are viewed with suspicion in Communist China, Qi Gong has been tolerated as a traditional set of physical exercises. A semiofficial National Qi Gong Federation has never been seriously disturbed by the regime. The situation is different, however, with respect to Qi Gong groups who strongly claim the primacy of the spiritual element, and who recognize a charismatic living leader.

The largest (but by no means the only) such Qi Gong group is Falun Gong. Its founder, Li Hongzi, was probably born in 1951 (the question of his precise birth date has been the source of controversy) and established his peculiar brand of Qi Gong in 1992, after having left the semiofficial Federation. In 1998, Li moved permanently to New York City, from where he oversees the expansion of Falun Gong internationally. Small groups exist in the main metropolitan areas of the United States and Canada, and in some thirty other countries.

In 1999, the Chinese regime launched a new campaign against spiritual and religious groups, and Falun Gong was targeted as a superstitious and reactionary group by a press campaign. Unlike other groups, Falun Gong reacted with an unauthorised demonstration of more than ten thousand followers outside Beijing's Zhongnanhai, the residence of China's top leaders, the largest such demonstration in recent Chinese history.

The regime was particularly scared by the failure of its intelligence service to prevent the demonstration, and by membership in Falun Gong of some medium-level political and military leaders. The authorities started an unprecedented public campaign against the movement with the help of tracts and comics, and hundreds of local leaders and members were arrested. China also asked the United States to arrest and extradite Li, a request the United States quickly turned down, inviting the Chinese instead to stop what the outside world perceived as an obvious instance of religious persecution.

Although the persecution has scared many followers and driven them underground, millions remain in China and several thousand abroad. Exactly how many "members" Falun Gong has is a matter of dispute (the government uses a figure of two million; Li claims one hundred million), and "membership" may not be an entirely applicable concept. In fact, although the movement recommends a nine-day introduction course and frequent contacts with local centers, it also states that everybody can simply start practicing Falun Gong by following the instructions from one of the many books, cassettes and Web sites (the principal of the latter being http://falundafa.org/) quickly available in a variety of languages. The possibility of such a self-initiation, without a master and a lengthy discipline, is at the core of the criticism by other Qi Gong groups against Li and his movement.

Falun Gong is, basically, a form of Qi Gong. Its main differences with other Qi Gong groups are the unique authority of Master Li as the only living person authorized to define what exactly techniques are to be used, and the claim that all previously secret teachings should now be disclosed. It also emphasizes, contrary to what groups tolerated by the Chinese regime claim, that it is essential to add to the practice of the exercises (the Xiu Lian), a spiritual discipline called "cultivation of the Xinxing." This is a simple path based on Buddhism and Confucianism, and aimed at promoting the three key values of Zhen (truthfulness), Shan (benevolence) and Rhen (forbearance), both at the individual and societal level. Falun Gong also teaches the law of karma and reincarnation, the need for "tribulations" in order to test the disciple and to pay off karmic debts, and the existence of both benign deities and demonic forces (the aliens interfering with Planet Earth in this century may be manifestations of the latter). The Xiu Lian practiced without the cultivation of the Xinxing, according to Master Li, will not generate any result and may even be counterproductive, if not "demonic."

Falun Gong emphasizes the Qi Gong concept of Falun, the center of spiritual and physical energy believed to be situated in the lower abdomen. Master Li describes the Falun in terms derived from both Buddhism and Taoism as a microcosm containing all the secrets of the universe. Its symbol, and the symbol of Falun Gong, is a (Buddhist) swastika in a disk, surrounded by four (Taoist) rotating yin-yang symbols. The aim of Xiu Lian is to awaken the universal energy of the Falun, so that it may flow harmoniously through the body, thus guaranteeing well-being and, at the end of the training, even supernatural powers.

Although Falun Gong does not reject all forms of modern medicine, it teaches that many ailments may be cured through its techniques. There are five key exercises—"Buddha showing the thousand hands"; "Standing stance exercise"; "Penetrating the two cosmic extremes"; "Falun heavenly circulation"; "Strengthening supernormal powers"—involving, in particular, movements of the hands, the legs, and the tongue, in ways reminiscent of certain yoga practices. Falun Gong is an easy way for the Chinese to connect with their spiritual roots through a basic set of simple ideas and exercises. It may also appeal to Westerners, increasingly fascinated by all things Chinese. While the Chinese regime may be able to eradicate, or at least drive underground, any Falun Gong "organization," Falun Gong as a diffuse and unorganized practice will probably remain popular despite opposition from the government.

—*MASSIMO INTROVIGNE*

# 13 THEOSOPHY AND THE THEOSOPHICAL SOCIETIES

*James Santucci*

T he modern theosophical movement is represented today in the United States primarily through six organizations: the Theosophical Society, headquartered in Adyar, Madras, India; the Theosophical Society, headquartered in Pasadena, California; the United Lodge of Theosophists, formed in Los Angeles, California; the Temple of the People, with headquarters at Halcyon, near Pismo Beach, California; the Word Foundation of Dallas, Texas; and Point Loma Publications in San Diego, California. Of these groups, the Adyar Theosophical Society is considered by most (though not by all) theosophists to be the parent organization. All claim to disseminate Theosophy, a term popularized and defined by Helena Petrovna Blavatsky (1831–1891) to denote the Wisdom of the Ages, embodying "higher esoteric knowledge"—hence, a "Secret Doctrine"—partially recoverable in imperfect and incomplete form in those portions of the scriptures of the world's great religions that express mystical teachings and in those philosophies that display a monistic or pantheistic bent.

## HISTORY

The Theosophical Society was founded in New York City in 1875 with Henry Steel Olcott (1832–1907) becoming its first president, H. P. Blavatsky becoming its first corresponding secretary, George Henry Felt and Seth Pancoast the vice presidents, and William Quan Judge (1851–1896) the counsel for the Society. First proposed on September 7 by Colonel Olcott, the society—entitled "The Theosophical Society" on September 13—was inaugurated on November 17. Less than three years later, in May 1878, the Theosophical Society affiliated with a reformist Hindu organization known as the Arya Samaj under the leadership of Swami Dayananda Sarasvati (1824–1883), whose promotion of the Vedas—the ancient compositions of the north Indian Aryan tribes composed between 1600 and 500 B.C.E.—as the font of truth served as the basis of his attempt to return Hinduism to a more pristine form devoid of later corruptive teachings and practices such as polygamy, child-marriage, caste, sati, and polytheism. Due to differences that arose within a few months of affiliation—one of which was the Swami's adoption of a personal Supreme God, a position that was not acceptable to many members of the Theosophical Society—it was decided to modify the association by distinguishing three bodies: (1) the Theosophical Society; (2) The Theosophical Society of the Arya Samaj of Aryavarta, that is, a "link society"; and (3) The Arya Samaj. Separate diplomas existed for each, with only members of (2) belonging to both (1) and (3). By 1882, all affiliations were broken due to Swami Dayananda's attacks on the theosophists for their leaders Olcott and Blavatsky associating with Buddhists and Parsis and for their formally converting to Buddhism in Ceylon (Sri Lanka) by taking pansil "the Five Precepts" in May 1880. Around this period of time, the headquarters of the Theosophical Society in the persons of H. S. Olcott and H. P. Blavatsky, moved first to Bombay in early 1879 and then to Adyar, Madras, in December 1882.

During the 1880s, four significant events occurred in theosophical history: the Coulomb affair (1884); the formation of the Esoteric Section of the Theosophical Society under Mme. Blavatsky on October 9, 1881; the publishing of the *Secret Doctrine*—the seminal work of the Theosophical Movement—in 1888; and the joining of the Theosophical Society in May 1889 of Annie Besant (1847–1933), the second president of the Theosophical Society (Adyar) and certainly the most prominent Adyar Theosophist in the twentieth century. Regarding the Coulomb affair, Emma Coulomb, a housekeeper at the Adyar headquarters, charged that Blavatsky had produced fraudulent psychic phenomena and was responsible for writing letters in the name of her Masters or Mahatmas. She was investigated by Richard Hodgson for the Society for Psychical Research (S.P.R.), whose well-known 1885 report (this was the second report issued by the S.P.R.; the 1884 preliminary report of the S.P.R. was more neutral) charged that she committed these misdeeds, thus calling to question her claim that Masters or Adepts actually existed. Though the Hodgson Report was accepted by the S.P.R. at its general meeting held on June 26, 1885, it was never the official or corporate opinion of that organization. As such, it could not withdraw a report that it has never issued. What it has done was to "make amends for whatever offence we [the S.P.R.] may have given." The damage was done, however. Ill at the time, Mme. Blavatsky departed from Adyar. She eventually settled in London, where she instituted at the suggestion of Mr. Judge the formation of the Esoteric Section under her leadership as Outer Head (the Inner Heads being the Mahatmas). It was an organization designed to "promote the esoteric interests of the Theosophical Society by the deeper study of esoteric philosophy" (Notice of "The Esoteric Section of the Theosophical Society," October 9, 1888). Although it had no institutional connection with the Theosophical Society, it was only open to its membership; furthermore, all teachings and activities were conducted in secret.

With the death of H. P. Blavatsky on May 8, 1891, the leadership of the Esoteric Section (by this time called the Eastern School of Theosophy) passed to William Q. Judge and Annie Besant. A few short years later, charges were brought against Judge that he was "misusing the Mahatmas' names and handwriting"—in other words, claiming that he received messages from the Master, or, as Mrs. Besant put it, "giving a misleading material form to messages received psychically from the Master." Although the charges were dropped in July, 1894, by Mrs. Besant and Colonel Olcott, they were reopened toward the end of 1894 by Mrs. Besant, who proposed a resolution during the December 1894 convention of the Theosophical Society at Adyar that President Olcott "at once call upon Mr. W. Q. Judge to resign" his vice presidency of the society. The resolution having been passed, Judge refused to resign. Later, at the Convention of the American Section of the Theosophical Society in Boston (April 28–29, 1895), delegates voted for autonomy of the American Section from the Theosophical Society at Adyar with Mr. Judge elected president for life, calling itself the "Theosophical Society in America." Whether this separation is to be interpreted as a schism (the position of the Adyar Theosophical Society) or simply the recognition that there was never any legal connection between the Adyar Theosophical Society and the original New York Theosophical Society in the first place (according to the interpretation of the "Theosophical Society in America") is a matter of opinion. The vote on the part of the American Section was followed by the expulsion by Colonel Olcott of Judge and all who followed him. This included over five thousand members in the United States and affiliated societies elsewhere, including lodges in England and Australia.

After W. Q. Judge's death in March 21, 1896, Ernest Temple Hargrove (d. 1939) was elected president of Judge's Theosophical Society in America. The Eastern School of Theosophy (the new name of the Esoteric Section as of 1890) had also "split" on November 3, 1894: one group remaining in the Adyar Society with Annie Besant as Outer Head, and one within Judge's Society under an Outer Head whose name was to have been kept secret until 1897, but in May 1896 it was revealed (in the *New York Sun* [May 27-28] and *Theosophy* [June 1896]) that it was Katherine Tingley (1847–1929) who was to be Judge's successor. Tingley followed and further developed the direction that Mr. Judge pursued in the latter years of his life, emphasizing less theoretical and more practical applications of theosophical teachings in the area of social and educational reform. In February 1897, she laid the cornerstone of a community in Point Loma, San Diego, which was to become the new international headquarters of the Theosophical Society in America (the old headquarters being in New York). In the same year she founded the International Brotherhood League with herself as president, which was designed to carry on a number of humanitarian functions ranging from educational to philanthropical. Furthermore, all of the lodges of her society were closed to the public in 1904.

By the latter part of 1897, Hargrove became disenchanted with Tingley's activities and also perhaps with her unwillingness to share her power with him or with anyone else. He resigned the presidency and attempted to gain control of the 1898 convention held in Chicago but was unsuccessful both at the convention and in subsequent court action. As a consequence of Hargrove's intense opposition at the convention over the contents of the new constitution composed by Madame Tingley (about which he knew nothing until its introduction at the convention), Hargrove left the society and formed his own organization with about two hundred former members of Tingley's Theosophical Society in America. Hargrove's New York-based reformed Theosophical Society in America, later renaming itself the Theosophical Society in 1908, with A. H. Spencer becoming the Acting President. It remained a viable organization for many years until the Society, and possibly its own Esoteric School of Theosophy, entered a period of "indrawal" from active work. The direction of Mrs. Tingley's leadership and her forceful leadership led to two dissenting bodies: the Temple of the People, founded in 1898, and the United Lodge of Theosophists, established in 1909, by Robert Crosbie and others in Los Angeles.

In 1898, Mrs. Tingley renamed the Theosophical Society in America the Universal Brotherhood and Theosophical Society, and as its "Leader and Official Head" she pursued her activities in applied Theosophy, including an ambitious educational program called Raja Yoga that was initiated in 1900, which emphasized an integration of physical, mental, spiritual training, and education. From the earliest student population of five, the number quickly jumped to one hundred by 1902, two-thirds of whom were Cuban, owing to her abiding interest in Cuba arising from the Spanish-American War in 1898 and the support by Mayor Bacardi of Santiago of Mrs. Tingley's objectives. In 1919 the educational program was expanded with the establishment of the Theosophical University. With the closing of the lodges in 1903, most of the committed and talented members were now at Point Loma engaging not only in this formal educational experiment but also in related activities such as agriculture and horticulture, writing, researching, publishing, dramatic, and musical productions.

By the 1920s, however, these activities began to taper off due mainly to financial problems. With the death of Mrs. Tingley in 1929, the direction under its more intellectual and scholarly leader, Gottfried de Purucker, moved once again in the direction of theoretical Theosophy, with emphasis on the teaching and study of the core theosophical works. Renaming the Universal Brotherhood and Theosophical Society the Theosophical Society, Dr. de Purucker embarked on a Fraternization Movement—partly owing to the hundredth anniversary of the birth of H. P. Blavatsky in 1831 approaching—with the ultimate aim of reuniting all the societies. Unification, however, was not possible but conventions and other cooperative activities between Adyar and Point Loma were held throughout the 1930s. Toward the close of Dr. de Purucker's tenure, he made the practical decision of selling the community holdings at Point Loma, called Lomaland, and moving the Society to Covina, a small community east of Los Angeles. In that same year (1942), de Purucker died, and the society was led by a cabinet for the next three years until a new leader, Colonel Arthur Conger, was elected in 1945. According to one dissident account, shortly after his election, those members of the cabinet who did not acknowledge Colonel Conger's esoteric status as "mouthpiece for the Masters"—thereby claiming the same status of H. P. Blavatsky—were stripped of all responsibilities in the Theosophical Society. These former officers and several other individuals in the United States and Europe eventually left the Theosophical Society headquarters: some voluntarily resigning their memberships, others having their memberships involuntarily canceled. The work of the Point Loma tradition established by Mrs. Tingley was continued by an organized number of groups in the United States and Europe, one such group being Point Loma Publications, which was chartered in 1971 as a nonprofit religious and educational corporation.

In the meantime, the Theosophical Society in Covina remained under the leadership of Colonel Conger until his death in early 1951. William Hartley (1879–1955), a long-time resident member of the society, was the chosen successor of Conger, but James A. Long (1898–1971) was accepted by the cabinet of the Theosophical Society instead, the argument for his appointment being that the original document containing Colonel Conger's designated appointee was not produced, only a photostatic copy. Hartley, together with his followers, left Covina and established their own Theosophical Society, now headquartered in the Hague, Netherlands.

James Long continued to head the Theosophical Society. A number of significant events took place during his leadership. The Theosophical University and all the lodges (chartered during the tenure of Dr. de Purucker) were closed; the National Sections (including the Swedish property in Visings) were also closed; the printing and publishing activities, headquarters, and library were moved to Altadena and Pasadena in 1951; and *Sunrise*, a monthly magazine, was established. Mr. Long also went on extensive lecture tours overseas and set about visiting the membership outside the United States. Upon his death in 1971, Miss Grace F. Knoche became the Leader of the Theosophical Society.

During the eventful year of 1898, another Theosophical organization came into existence with the founding of the Temple of the People by Dr. William H. Dower (1866–1937) and Mrs. Francia LaDue (1849–1922), who believed that they were following the instructions of the "Master" to separate from the Tingley-led Universal Brotherhood and Theosophical Society and, according to its own declaration, to lay the "mental, physical, and spiritual foundations of the coming sixth race." Arising out of the Syracuse (New York) Lodge of the Universal Brotherhood and Theosophical Society, they and their group moved to California in 1903, where they settled on land east of Oceano, establishing the headquarters known as Halcyon. By 1904, Dr. Dower opened the Halcyon Hotel and Sanitorium in order to continue his medical practice, treating such maladies as tuberculosis, nervous disorders, alcoholism, and drug addiction. The following year (1905), the Temple Home Association was incorporated, which laid out a town plan and sold or leased house sites, thus organizing a cooperative colony with Mrs. LaDue, also known as Blue Star, becoming the first head—Guardian in Chief—of the Temple. In 1908, the Temple was incorporated under the title "The Guardian in Chief of the Temple of the People, a Corporation Sole." After Mrs. LaDue's death in 1922, Dr. Dower became the second head of the Temple, supervising the construction of the Blue Star Memorial Temple. Begun in 1923 and completed in 1924, the Blue Star Memorial Temple was built in accordance with mathematical and geometrical symbolism illustrating the Unity of all Life, or the Higher Self. Upon Dr. Dower's death in 1937, Mrs. Pearl Dower became the third Guardian in Chief, who organized the property according to its present specifications, a ninety-five-acre property consisting of fifty-two homes, thirty of which are owned by the Temple, aznd the William Quan Judge Library, which also houses the Temple offices and an apartment for visitors. The successor to Mrs. Dower in 1968 was Harold Forgostein, who painted twenty-two pictures in the early 1930s at the request of Dr. Dower depicting the Native Americans' contributions to understanding the balance in nature and scenes from the life of Hiawatha, both important in Temple teachings. These paintings are now in the Temple's University Center. Mr. Forgostein remained head of the Temple until 1990; the present Guardian in Chief is Eleanor L. Shumway.

Another association, the United Lodge of Theosophists, was organized by a former member of the Universal Brotherhood and Theosophical

Society at Point Loma and Hargrove's Theosophical Society. Robert Crosbie (1849–1919), a Canadian living in Boston who became a theosophist under the influence of W. Q. Judge, originally lent his support to Mrs. Tingley as Judge's successor. Around 1900, he moved to Point Loma to help in the work she initiated there. In 1904, losing confidence in her leadership and methods for private reasons, he left Point Loma and moved to Los Angeles, where he associated for a time with Hargrove's Theosophical Society and with a number of theosophists who were later to support the U.L.T., John Garrigues among them. In 1909, Crosbie, with these same interested acquaintances who shared his view that only the Source Theosophy of Blavatsky and Judge carried the teachings of Theosophy as it was intended to be delivered in modern times (i.e., in the latter decades of the nineteenth century and beyond), formed the United Lodge of Theosophists in Los Angeles. What set this group apart from other theosophical societies was (and continues to be) its stress only on Source Theosophy and such writings as are in accord philosophically with those of Blavatsky and Judge (but excluding the letters of the Masters K. H. and M. written between 1880 and 1886 to the prominent theosophical writer, vice president of the Theosophical Society, and rival to H. P. Blavatsky, A. P. Sinnett, the reason being that private letters were no substitute for the actual theosophical teachings), the rejection of leaders and teachers (all associates in the U.L.T. are described as students), and the stress on anonymity for those writings on behalf of the U.L.T. Even Crosbie himself claimed no special status, although he is held in high esteem by associates. After Crosbie's death, the Lodge in Los Angeles established the Theosophy Company in 1925 to serve as fiduciary agent for the associates. No leader was recognized but John Garrigues was acknowledged as a major figure in the Los Angeles U.L.T. until his death in 1944, along with Mrs. Grace Clough and Mr. Henry Geiger, but students in the U.L.T. insist that the principle of anonymity outweighs its disadvantages. The U.L.T. developed into an international association of study groups through the efforts of another important figure in the Theosophical Movement, the Indian Parsi B. P. Wadia (1881–1958). Originally a member of the Adyar Theosophical Society, which he joined in 1903 and where he served in a number of capacities—including that of Annie Besant's secretary—he resigned in 1922 because of his perception that the Theosophical Society "strayed away from the 'Original Programme.'" From 1922 to 1928 he remained in the United States and assisted in founding U.L.T. lodges in New York, Washington, D.C., and Philadelphia. Following his departure for India via Europe, he encouraged local students to found U.L.T. lodges, including those in Antwerp, Amsterdam, London, Paris, Bangalore, and Bombay. At present, U.L.T. lodges and study groups are located throughout the United States and in Belgium, Canada, England, France, India, Italy, Mexico, the Netherlands, Nigeria,

Sweden, and Trinidad (West Indies). Because of the considerable contributions of Mr. Wadia, he is the only person, with the exception of Mr. Crosbie, within the U.L.T. who is identified by name.

Turning now to the Theosophical Society (Adyar), the largest society by far (despite the loss of most of the original American Section in 1895), the work that was conducted primarily by Colonel Olcott, and also to a lesser extent by Mme. Blavatsky during her abbreviated stay in India, adopted an activist stance with their championing of Hinduism and Buddhism upon their arrival in India in 1879. Colonel Olcott was especially active in helping to initiate a Buddhist revival in India and Sri Lanka and to upgrade the position of the outcasts in India. As the first American to convert to Buddhism overseas in 1880, he worked with great enthusiasm for the cause of Buddhism not only in Sri Lanka but also in other Buddhist nations: promoting the foundation of Buddhist schools, writing the Buddhist Catechism (which attempted to unite both Northern and Southern Buddhists), helping to design a Buddhist flag that all Buddhist nations could adopt as their universal emblem symbolizing Buddhist unity. In India, Colonel Olcott established "Pariah schools" for the uplift of the depressed classes. One such school, known today as the Olcott Memorial School in the vicinity of Adyar, celebrated its one hundredth anniversary. The purpose was to offer free education for the children of these classes in skills that would provide self-sufficiency, such as tailoring, gardening, carpentry, and printing. One further contribution made by Colonel Olcott was the establishment of the Oriental Library in order to preserve Indian manuscripts from neglect and to keep them in India. The manuscripts were housed in the newly built Adyar Library building, formally opened in December, 1886.

His activist role was continued by the second president of the Theosophical Society, Annie Besant, who became involved in numerous activities both within and outside the society, including such diverse activities as occult investigations, education, politics, social reform, and the introduction of ritual within the society. Among her numerous contributions, Mrs. Besant was instrumental in founding the Central Hindu College in Benares in 1898 and became active in Indian politics serving as president of the Indian National Congress, forming the Home Rule League and later drafting the Home Rule Bill (1925). Within the Theosophical Society, she founded the Theosophical Order of Service in 1908, which is intended to carry out the first object of the Society—to form a nucleus of the universal brotherhood of humanity—by carrying out works of compassion and alleviating suffering, including such activities as the giving of goods, medicine, clothes, and so on to the needy, and the abolition of the cruelty of animals. Mrs. Besant's activities within the society during her presidency are closely associated with another prominent though controversial theosophist,

Charles Webster Leadbeater (1854–1934). In large part, under his influence, theosophical teachings were introduced in the Theosophical Society
that are considered by Blavatskyites to have deviated from the original
teachings of Blavatsky and her Masters. Derisively called "Neo-Theosophy"
by F. T. Brooks, a theosophical writer and the tutor of Jawaharlal Nehru in
the early years of the twentieth century, these teachings were considered by
those who limited themselves to the writings of Blavatsky and Judge to be
heretical, judging from the opinions that appeared in theosophical literature of the 1920s. "Neo-Theosophy" included two highly significant and
innovative actions: Leadbeater's discovery, in 1909, of the physical vehicle
for the coming World Teacher—known as Maitreya or the Christ—Jiddu
Krishnamurti (1895–1986), and the alliance with the Old (later, Liberal)
Catholic Church from 1917 under the direction of Bishops Leadbeater and
James Wedgwood. As if this were not controversial enough for many within
the Theosophical Movement, the man behind these innovations, Leadbeater, was himself under a cloud of scandal. In 1906, charges were raised
by the secretary of the Esoteric Section in America, Helen Dennis, that he
was teaching her young son and other boys masturbation as a form of occult
practice. This charge, which raised the specter of pederasty in the eyes of
his accuser, led to Leadbeater's resignation from the society. Upon his rein-
statement in 1908, with the help of Mrs. Besant, Leadbeater soon thereafter
discovered J. Krishnamurti, a young Hindu boy who he said was to be the
vehicle for the coming World Teacher. Much of the work of the society
revolved around the training of the boy and preparing the way for the
World Teacher's coming. In 1911, another organization known as the
Order of the Star in the East (O.S.E.) was founded in Benares by George
Arundale—which soon became a worldwide organization with the help of
Mrs. Besant—specifically for this purpose. Not long thereafter, the General
Secretary of the German Section, Rudolf Steiner, disenchanted with the
O.S.E. and his displeasure with the Mrs. Besant's Presidency, caused the
General Council of the Theosophical Society to advise the president to
cancel the German Sectional Charter and to issue a new Sectional Charter
to the German Lodges. Fifty-five out of sixty-nine German lodges followed
Dr. Steiner, who soon organized a new society, the Anthroposophical
Society, in early 1913. Despite the defections of Steiner and others, however, the Theosophical Society gained more members than it had lost. The
promise of the imminent coming of the World Teacher in the vehicle of
Krishnamurti contributed to both unprecedented controversy within, and
popularity of, the Theosophical Society until 1929, when Krishnamurti
renounced his role and left the society. Thereafter, the society never
regained the popularity that it had in the 1920s.

The second event that generated controversy was the promotion of
the Old Catholic, later Liberal Catholic, Church by members of the society.

This promotion was primarily the brainchild of C. W. Leadbeater, who, with James Ingall Wedgwood (1883–1951), helped to establish the Church. Theosophists, especially those belonging to non-Adyar groups, viewed the L.C.C. ritual and the acceptance of the apostolic succession, on which the bishopric is authenticated, as having no place in theosophical teaching. As the 1920s progressed, there was an attempt to combine the claims centering on the World Teacher with the ritual of the L.C.C., including the selection of twelve "apostles" for Krishnamurti, but ultimately the whole plan dissolved with Krishnamurti's rejection of that role.

After 1929, the Theosophical Society retrenched and returned more to those teachings generally associated with Theosophy. After the death of Mrs. Besant in 1933, the presidency passed on to George Arundale (1934–1945), who continued the activism that was so typical of Mrs. Besant's term. During his tenure, his wife, Srimati Rukmini Devi (1904–1986), established the International Academy of Arts on January 6, 1936 (later known as Klakshetra "the Field or Holy place of Arts"), having as its objects (1) "to emphasise the essential unity of all true Art"; (2) "to work for the recognition of the arts as vital to individual, national, religious and international growth"'; and (3) to provide for such activities as may be incidental to the above objects." Associated with the second purpose of Klakshetra was to revive and develop the ancient culture of India. To Dr. Arundale, Indian dance revealed occult ritual, in his words "the occultism of beauty."

Following him was a protege of Leadbeater's, C. Jinaradasa (1946–1953), who, among his many contributions to the society, displayed an active interest in publishing many documents relating to the history of the Society from the early years of the Theosophical Society. As one of the foremost theosophical authors, Mr. Jinarajadasa displayed a distinctly scholarly bent in his published works, and, in order to carry out the third object of the society, inaugurated in 1949 the School of the Wisdom at the International Headquarters of the Theosophical Society at Adyar on the anniversary of the Theosophical Society's own inauguration, November 17. In his inaugural address, Mr. Jinarjadsa stated that the school's purpose is "to equip its students to become, each according to his temperament and aptitude, philosophers, scientists, ethical teachers, artists, givers of economic law, statesmen, educators, town planners and every other possible type of server of humanity."

Following Mr. Jinarajadasa were N. Sri Ram (1953–1973), responsible for building the current Adyar Library building, John S. Coats (1973–1979), and the present international president of the Theosophical Society, Radha Burnier (1980).

## BELIEFS AND PRACTICES

The teachings promulgated by the theosophical societies are ultimately those that have secured the attention of its members as well as what individuals understand Theosophy to be. As a rule, most theosophists associate the basic teachings with the "three fundamental propositions" contained in the proem of H. P. Blavatsky's magnum opus, *The Secret Doctrine.* An overview of the development of Blavatsky's and other theosophists' understanding of Theosophy reveal a variety of interpretations. In fact, the term "Theosophy," chosen to represent the aspirations and objects of the society, had little to do with its later development. Theosophy was accepted as the name of the society in accordance with the definition found in the American edition of Webster's unabridged dictionary (published ca. 1875), which is given as follows:

> Supposed intercourse with God and superior spirits, and consequent attainment of superhuman knowledge by physical processes as by the theurgic operations of ancient Platonists, or by the chemical processes of the German fire philosophers.

In a gathering held on September 7, 1875, a lecture given by one George H. Felt entitled "The Lost Canon of Proportion of the Egyptians" echoed this definition. The future president of the Theosophical Society, Henry S. Olcott, proposed the formation of a society for the purpose of obtaining "knowledge of the nature and attributes of the Supreme Power and of the higher spirits by the aid of physical processes." Such was the statement in the Society's "Preamble and By-Laws" (October 30, 1875) as well as in Colonel Olcott's inaugural address as president of the society:

> How can we expect that as a society we can have any very remarkable illustrations of the control of the adept theurgist over the subtle powers of nature?
> But here is where Mr. Felt's alleged discoveries will come into play. Without claiming to be a theurgist, a mesmerist, or a spiritualist, our Vice-President promises, by simple chemical appliances, to exhibit to us, as he has to others before, the races of beings which, invisible to our eyes, people the elements. . . . Fancy the consequences of the practical demonstration of its truth, for which Mr. Felt is now preparing the requisite apparatus!

In other words, the original purpose of the Theosophical Society was—in the words of the minutes taken on September 8, 1875—"for the study and elucidation of Occultism, the Cabala &c"; or, perhaps to use a term that more directly reflects the remarks given by Olcott above, to demonstrate, by what passed as "scientific" means, the existence of a hidden world, replete with occult forces and beings therein. Taken in this light, the society's original 1875 objects ("to collect and diffuse a knowledge of the laws which govern the universe") take on enhanced meaning. Over the ensuing years, however, the term took on different connotations, with most theosophists viewing it as the Wisdom that has existed from the dawn of humanity, preserved and transmitted by great teachers such as Pythagoras, Buddha, Krishna, and Jesus from its inception to the present and ascertained in the myths, legends, and doctrines of the historical religious traditions, such as Christianity, Judaism, Hinduism, Buddhism, and Islam, and lesser known mystery cults. The first book-length expression of this wisdom and of the Theosophical Society's original (1875) objects was Mme. Blavatsky's *Isis Unveiled,* published in 1877. In the ensuing two years, over ten thousand copies were sold, making it one of the most popular books of its kind in the nineteenth century. It continues to have considerable influence in theosophical circles, with over 150,000 sold since its publication. The wisdom described in *Isis Unveiled* was given a more "Oriental" (i.e., Indian) flavor in the 1888 publication of H. P. Blavatsky's *The Secret Doctrine.* Therein, three propositions serve as the starting point for most Theosophists: (1) the existence of an Absolute, Infinite, Reality, or Principle; (2) the cyclic nature or periodicity of the universe and all therein; and (3) the fundamental identity of the soul with the Universal Oversoul and the pilgrimage of all souls through the cycle of incarnation in accordance with Karmic law. Theosophy, in this sense, took on a nondualistic or monistic view of ultimate reality, manifested or emanated in a dynamic complementarity and evolutionary progressionism. These general "propositions" presented by Blavatsky were restated in more specific teachings in *The Secret Doctrine* and elsewhere, some of which may be summarized in the following statements:

1. the evolution of the immortal individual continues through innumerable lives, such continuity made possible through reincarnation: the entrance of Self—the trinity of Spirit, Soul, and Mind—into another (human) body;

2. the complement of reincarnation is that force, known as the "Law of Cause and Effect (Karma)," that fuels future rebirths and determines the quality of the experience therein;

3. the structure of the manifested universe, humanity included, may be viewed as septenary in composition, and cooperative in all relationships;

4. humanity evolves through seven major groups or periods called Root Races, each of which is divided into seven subraces. At the present time, we humans belong to the fifth Root Race, known as the

Aryan (Sanskrit "Noble") Race. The term, however, is not limited here to "Indo-European" peoples; it has a much broader meaning;

5. the individual is in actuality but a miniature copy or microcosm of the macrocosm;

6. the universe—and humanity—is guided and animated by a cosmic hierarchy of sentient beings, each having a specific mission to fulfill.

Although most Theosophists would subscribe to all or part of the above statements, one should keep in mind that the above statements may take on various interpretations depending on the understanding of each Theosophist. Furthermore, although some commentators emphasize the presence of Eastern (Hindu and Buddhist) philosophy in Theosophical teaching after 1880 when Blavatsky and Olcott arrived in India, this does not preclude the presence of important Western (Kabbalistic, Christian, Masonic, and pre-Christian) teachings, myths, and doctrines after 1880 or the presence of Eastern thought prior to 1880 as evidenced in *Isis Unveiled.*

## ORGANIZATION AND MEMBERSHIP

The Theosophical Society, with international headquarters in Adyar, Madras, India, as of the end of 1993 has a worldwide membership of about 31,044 distributed in almost seventy countries; the Theosophical Society in America, one of its sections, has a national membership of 4,623. It considers itself to be the parent Theosophical Society and thus goes back to its New York origins in 1875 although the Theosophical Society (Pasadena) takes the position that the original Theosophical Society divided in 1895, with each Theosophical Society having equal claim to the 1875 New York origins.

The Theosophical Society (Adyar), incorporated at Madras in 1905, is currently under the presidency of Mrs. Radha Burnier. It is comprised of forty-seven national societies or sections, the oldest being the American Section (the Theosophical Society in America as it is now known), formed in 1886 and the British Section (chartered in 1888), and the most recent being the Regional Association in Slovenia formed in 1992. The sections are composed of lodges. The governing body of the Theosophical Society is the general council consisting of the president, vice president, secretary, and treasurer, all elected general secretaries of the national sections, and up to twelve additional members nominated by the president and elected by the general council. The international president is elected by popular vote every seven years. The national president of the American Section is similarly elected every three years. An international convention is held annually usually at Adyar. The society boasts a magnificent library on the grounds of the headquarters that houses original manuscripts in Sanskrit and other Asian languages, books and journals on Theosophy, philosophy, and religion. The archives of the society are currently housed in the head-quarters building and contains many thousands of documents, including the important scrapbooks of Blavatsky and the Olcott diaries. The theo-sophical publishing house also functions in Adyar and produces a number of pamphlets and books, written primarily by its members, and continues to issue the oldest theosophical periodical, *The Theosophist.* In addition, the quarterly *Adyar Newsletter* is published by the society as is also the respected Adyar Library Bulletin, a scholarly journal specializing in oriental research. The Theosophical Society in America is headquartered in Wheaton, Illinois, which is also the site of a rather extensive lending and research library. It also publishes a number of works, including Quest Books, through the Theosophical Publishing House (Wheaton). The Theosophical Society in America also publishes *The American Theosophist* for its members and *Quest* magazine for the general readership. Although organizationally not a part of the Theosophical Society, the Esoteric Sec-tion is closely associated with the Theosophical Society. Its headquarters in the United States is in Ojai, California, at the Krotona Institute. On its grounds is also the Krotona School of Theosophy, whose principal purpose is to serve as an educational arm of the society, to promote its work, and to implement the three objects of the Theosophical Society. These objects (according to the international society's wording) are:

1. To form a nucleus of the universal brotherhood of humanity, without distinction of race, creed, sex, caste, or color.
2. To encourage the study of comparative religion, philosophy and science [the Theosophical Society in America has "comparative study of religion"].
3. To investigate unexplained laws of nature and the powers latent in man [the Theosophical Society in America substitutes "humanity" for "man"].

Members of the Theosophical Society are expected to approve and pro-mote these objects. They are also expected to search for truth through study, service, and devotion to high ideals. As the society states: "All in sym-pathy with the Objects of The Theosophical Society are welcomed as mem-bers, and it rests with the member to bcome a true Theosophist."

The Theosophical Society, now headquartered in Pasadena, is the direct descendant of the Theosophical Society in America, of which W. Q. Judge was the first president, followed by Mrs. Tingley's Universal Brother-hood and Theosophical Society. It is currently described as a worldwide association of members "dedicated to the uplifting of humanity through a better understanding of the oneness of life and the practical application of this principle." Membership figures are not given out; the number, however, is low, perhaps a few thousand. Members are known as Fellows of The Theosophical Society (F.T.S.); their only obligation is the acceptance of the principle of universal brotherhood and a willingness to try to live it. Fellows are received as probationary Fellows; full Fellowship is implemented with the issuance of a diploma, signed by the leader and secretary general, which is issued by the International Theosophical Headquarters. Other groups within the Theosophical Society include Branches, formed by three or more F.T.S. who apply for a charter, and National Sections, the latter headed by a National Secretary. The head of the Theosophical Society is designated as leader—at present it is Grace F. Knoche—who serves for life and who is also responsible for appointing a successor. The general officers include the members of the cabinet, the secretary general, treasurer general, and the national secretaries, all of whom are appointed by the leader. The leader has the power to remove from office any officer of the society. The publishing arm of the Theosophical Society is the Theosophical University Press, which publishes the bimonthly *Sunrise: Theosophic Perspectives*, and over forty book titles authored by H. P. Blavatsky, Katherine Tingley, G. de Purucker, A. Trevor Barker, William Q. Judge, James A. Long, Charles J. Ryan, and others. The Theosophical Society (Pasadena) has initiated correspondence courses, library centers, public meetings and study groups, and overseas translation and publishing agencies in the Netherlands, United Kingdom, Sweden, Australia, Germany, South Africa, and Finland. The objects of the Theosophical Society are as follows:

1. To diffuse among men a knowledge of the laws inherent in the Universe.
2. To promulgate the knowledge of the essential unity of all that is, and to demonstrate that this unity is fundamental in Nature.
3. To form an active brotherhood among men.
4. To study ancient and modern religion, science, and philosophy.
5. To investigate the powers innate in man.

The United Lodge of Theosophists is "a voluntary association of students of Theosophy" founded in 1909 by Robert Crosbie and others, having as its main purpose the study of Theosophy using the writings of Blavatsky and Judge as their guide. Because personality or ego is considered to have negative effects, "associates" pursue anonymity in their theosophical work. Regarding this work, the U.L.T. Declaration, the only document that unites associates, states that its purpose "is the dissemination of the Fundamental Principles of the philosophy of Theosophy and the exemplification in practice of those principles, through a truer realization of the SELF; a profounder conviction of Universal Brotherhood." It regards as theosophists all "who are engaged in the true service of Humanity, without distinction of race, creed, sex, condition or organization." The work of the U.L.T. is mainly practical and educational, conducting meetings and classes on various theosophical subjects, and publishing books, pamphlets, and magazines. Lodges and study groups exist, with lodges typically consisting of between twenty and one hundred associates, and study groups from five to thirty associates. Associates can voluntarily participate in the work of a study group or lodge, ranging from attending or teaching classes in the public dissemination of theosophical teachings. All activities are voluntary. In addition, there are associates who do not belong to any lodge because they live in countries and regions that have no proximate U.L.T. center. No leader exists in the U.L.T., nor is there any formal organization, although the Theosophy Company serves as fiduciary agent for the U.L.T. and its publications. All lodges and study groups are independent of one another but are united in a common goal, the individual goal of pursuing the three objects of the U.L.T., which are nearly identical to the objects of the Adyar Theosophical Society (the first object is "to form the nucleus of a Universal Brotherhood of Humanity, without distinction of race, creed, sex, caste, or color"; the second is "The study of ancient and modern religions, philosophies and sciences, and the demonstration of the importance of such study; and the third is the investigation of the unexplained laws of Nature and the psychical powers latent in man"). The work of the lodges focuses on the dissemination of source Theosophy. Those who are in accord with the U.L.T. Declaration are considered "associates." They express their sympathy with the work of the U.L.T. in the following manner:

> Being in sympathy with the purposes of this Lodge, as set forth in its "Declaration," I hereby record my desire to be enrolled as an Associate, it being understood that such association calls for no obligation on my part, other than that which I, myself, determine.

The number of associates is uncertain because renewable or "sustaining" memberships do not exist, nor is there a published list of associates. The only figure supplied by an associate in Los Angeles is that "many thousands of associates" have belonged to the U.L.T. since 1909, but the figure today is not more than a few thousand worldwide. Lodges and study groups exist in Los Angeles but also in other parts of the United States, Canada, Belgium, England, France, India, Italy, Mexico, The Netherlands, and Sweden. Publications include the works of Blavatsky and Judge, compilations of articles, letters, and talks by Robert Crosbie, entitled *The Friendly Philosopher*, his commentary and discussion on Judge's *The Ocean of Theosophy* entitled *Answers to Questions on the Ocean of Theosophy*, and a small book,

Universal Theosophy. The Theosophy Company also publishes works that are associated with ancient Theosophy (such as the Bhagavad Gita, Patanjali's *Yoga Sutras*, and *The Dhammapada*), and the magazines *Theosophy*, the *Theosophical Movement* (Bombay), and *Vidya* (Santa Barbara, California).

The Temple of the People as a religious society and the village of Halcyon are both currently under the leadership (known as guardian in chief) of Eleanor L. Shumway, who was selected by her predecessor. Besides this office, there is a seven member board of officers, selected each year by the guardian in chief. On the board is an inner guard and treasurer, both reserved for women, an outer guard and a scribe, both reserved for men, and three delegates at large, selected from members not living in Halcyon. Membership of the temple is neither solicited nor closed to any individual; the only responsibility of the member is his or her own development. Of the total of some 250 members worldwide, about eighty reside at Halcyon. An annual convention that lasts about a week begins on the first Sunday of August. The objects of the temple are:

1. To formulate the truths of religion as the fundamental factor in the evolution of the human race. And this does not mean the formulation of a creed.
2. To set forth a philosophy of life that is in accord with natural and divine law.
3. To promote the study of the sciences and the fundamental facts and laws upon which the sciences are based which will permit us to extend our belief and knowledge from what is known to the unknown.
4. To promote the study and practice of art on fundamental lines, showing that art is in reality the application of knowledge to human good and welfare, and that the Christos can speak to humanity through art as well as through any other fundamental line of manifestation.
5. The promotion of a knowledge of true social science based on immutable law, showing the relationship between one human being and another, and between human beings, God, and nature. When these relationships are understood we will instinctively formulate and follow the law of true brotherhood: the unity of ALL life.

The Word Foundation, Inc. was established in 1950 "to make known to the people of the world all books written by Harold Waldwin Percival, and to ensure the perpetuation of his legacy to humanity." The books of Mr. Percival include *Thinking and Destiny; Adepts, Masters, and Mahatmas; Masonry and its Symbols; Man and Woman and Child;* and *Democracy is Self-Government.* Percival (1868–1953) was born in Bridgetown, Barbados, British West Indies. He came first to Boston, then to New York City with his mother after the death of his father. There, he joined the Theosophical Society in 1892, eventually established the Theosophical Society Independent, which emphasized the study of the writings of H. P. Blavatsky and Eastern "scriptures" and from 1904 to 1917 published *The Word* magazine. In addition, he established the Theosophical Publishing Company of New York. In 1946, the Word Publishing Co., Inc. was constituted and it was under this aegis that Percival's books were first published and distributed. The foundation is directed by a board of directors consisting of the president, vice president, treasurer, and secretary. Mr. Arnold E. Menze is the current president. In addition to publishing the works of Percival, it also has introduced in 1986 a new series of *The Word* magazine, published quarterly. The foundation claims a worldwide membership of about one thousand as of 1994. The purpose of membership is to support the foundation's publishing activities and to facilitate "student-to-student" study groups.

Point Loma Publications, Inc. is not a society but an independent publishing firm whose aim is to carry on the literary legacy of members of the Point Loma Theosophical Society (now the Theosophical Society, Pasadena). It was established on January 22, 1971, by former members of the cabinet of the Theosophical Society who refused to acknowledge the esoteric status of Colonel Conger, the new leader of the Theosophical Society, in 1945. The former chairman of the cabinet of the Theosophical Society, Iverson L. Harris, became the president and chairman of the board of directors. In the 1950s, disaffected members started to organize and give public lectures in San Diego, California. The importance of the name "Point Loma" in the history of the Theosophical Movement, however, led eventually to the establishment of P.L.P. in San Diego as is evident in the Articles of Incorporation:

> To publish and disseminate literature of a philosophical, scientific, religious, historical and cultural character, faithful to the traditions and high standards maintained by the Theosophical Society with International Headquarters formerly at Point Loma, California, under the leadership of Katherine Tingley from 1900 to 1929, and of Gottfried de Purucker, from 1929 to 1942: to pursue and perpetuate the aims of the original Theosophical Society, founded in New York City by Helena Petrovna Blavatsky, Col. H.S. Olcott, Wm. Q. Judge and others, as enunciated by them on October 30, 1875.

P.L.P. remained under the leadership of Mr. Harris until his death in 1979. W. Emmett Small became the new president that year and remained so until his retirement in 1993. The current president is Carmen H. Small. Branches of P.L.P. are in the Hague, Netherlands, and Costa Rica. There are no members belonging to P.L.P., only associates or "friends" who support the work of the corporation. As a side note, other organizations based on the original work of Point Loma Theosophical Society arose in Europe. One group is the Theosophical Society-HPB, which was founded by William Hartley after Mr. James Long was elected leader (see above). This society now functions in the Hague, the site of its International Headquarters, under the presidency of Mr. Herman C. Vermeulen. England and Germany also have small groups following the Point Loma tradition.

## PUBLICATIONS AND EDUCATIONAL OUTREACH

The first magazine of the Theosophical Society, *The Theosophist*, was initiated with the October 1879 issue in Bombay under the editorship of H. P. Blavatsky. The periodical, published at the international headquarters in Adyar, Madras, continues to this day and is the official organ of the international president of the Theosophical Society (Adyar). Also published are the *Adyar Newsletter* and *Adyar Library Bulletin. The American Theosophist* and *The Quest* are both published by the Theosophical Society in America, and journals are published by each of the forty-seven national sections of the Society. In addition to periodical literature, the Theosophical Society also carries on an active publishing program through the Theosophical Publishing House in both Adyar, India, and Wheaton, Illinois, the headquarters of the Theosophical Society in America. The Theosophical Publishing House of the Theosophical Society in America also publishes Quest Books, books devoted to a variety of subjects that reflect the theosophical viewpoint in its broadest perspective.

The Theosophical Society (Pasadena) publishes the magazine *Sunrise.* Its publishing arm, Theosophical University Press, features the source literature and classics of Theosophy, including the works of H. P. Blavatsky, W. Q. Judge, Katherine Tingley, G. de Purucker, and others.

The Theosophy Company, the fiduciary agent of the United Lodge of Theosophists, publishes the journal *Theosophy.* In addition, *Vidya* is published by students at the Santa Barbara Lodge U.L.T., California, and the Theosophical Movement, founded by B. P. Wadia, is published in Bombay, India. Both the Theosophical Society (Pasadena) (through its Theosophical University Press) and U.L.T. (through the Theosophy Company) publish the major works of Blavatsky *(The Secret Doctrine* and *Isis Unveiled)* and Judge *(The Ocean of Theosophy)* as well as a variety of other works. The Temple of the People publishes the quarterly *The Temple Artisan at Halcyon* as well as several works unique to its organization, *Theogenesis, Temple Messages, Teachings of the Temple,* and *From the Mountain Top.*

The Word Foundation publishes *The Word,* revived in 1986, as well as the works of Harold W. Percival mentioned above.

Point Loma Publications published *The Eclectic Theosophist,* at first a bimonthly journal, later a quarterly, under the joint editorship of W. Emmett Small and Helen Todd (until her death in 1992). The present editor (since 1993), Kenneth Small, has announced in the winter 1994 issue (published in late 1995) a broadening of the magazine's focus and a change of its name to *The Path,* Point Loma Publications also publishes a variety of works that were originally issued during the Point Loma years of the Universal Brotherhood and Theosophical Society as well as a number of original works, including *The Buddhism of H.P.Blavatsky* by H. J. Spierenburg, *The Way to the Mysteries* by L. Gordon Plummer, and *Introduction to Sanskrit* by Thomas Egenes.

# 14 OTHER ESOTERIC GROUPS

**A** NTHROPOSOPHICAL SOCIETY IN AMERICA. The Anthroposophical Society in America is the counterpart of the Anthroposophical Society of Dornach, Switzerland, which was formed in Germany in 1912 by Rudolf Steiner (1861–1925), who had formerly been the leader of the German Theosophical Society. Rudolf Steiner was a distinguished scholar, having edited Goethe's scientific writings for the critical edition of Goethe's work. His writing, editing, and teaching led him into mystic Christian philosophy. Steiner was invited to address an audience of theosophists in the winter of 1901–1902. The thesis of his lecture was that the ancient mystics had served to prepare the way for Christ on earth and that Christ was the focus of earth's evolution. Theosophists had generally been taught to regard Jesus as just another avatar. Despite this difference in viewpoint, the theosophists were impressed with Steiner's intellect and charisma. In 1902, when the German Theosophical Society was chartered, the forty-one-year-old Steiner was elected to lead it. As the theosophists were those most interested in his work, Steiner accepted the leadership role, with the proviso that he maintain his independence as a philosopher and writer.

Annie Besant became president of the Theosophical Society in 1907. In 1909, Steiner published *Spiritual Hierarchies*, which presented his teachings on the centrality of Christ and underscored his differences with Annie Besant. Under Besant's leadership, the Theosophical Society was becoming more and more involved with Eastern mystical occult practices. It practiced a system of withdrawal from the manifest material world and centered on meditative yogic disciplines. It regarded Christ as just another God-embodied teacher and Christianity as just another religion. Steiner, on the other hand, saw Eastern religion as a way of the past, replaced by Christianity. In Steiner's opinion, Christ summed up the Eastern search and launched the new era of finding the spiritual in the material (science).

The disagreements between Steiner and Besant came to a head when Besant announced the return of Christ in Jiddu Krishnamurti. She formed the Order of the Star of the East to prepare for the coming of a new Christ in Krishnamurti, then still a youth. Steiner declared no one could be a member of the German Theosophical Society and the Order of the Star of the East. Besant revoked the charter of the German Theosophical Society in 1912. Steiner then took fifty-five of the sixty-five German theosophical lodges and formed the Anthroposophical Society.

Anthroposophy holds that reality has a spiritual basis; that is, matter is real, but is derivative from spirit. It believes in reincarnation and the possibility of initiatory experiences which expand consciousness of the spiritual realm. Steiner taught that humanity had originally shared the spiritual consciousness of the cosmos. Humanity's present knowledge is only a vestige of primordial cognition. Human beings have, however, a latent capacity for horizonless vision and there are certain disciplines by which it can be recovered. Steiner did not limit the recovery of vision to mere techniques, but held that initiatory openings might come through study, music, art, and the informed use of imagination. Steiner saw his work as the organization of a science of initiation. Jesus Christ was viewed by Steiner as both the one fully initiated person in human history, the one with full supersensory perception, and as the Christ being.

As the Anthroposophical Society developed, Christian pastors and theological students began to press Steiner for a system of worship that was in keeping with the new relationship to the Christ of which Steiner had spoken. In 1922, the Christian Community Church was formed as a separate entity, not formally connected with the Anthroposophical Society.

The headquarters of the Anthroposophical Society was established in Dornach, Switzerland, where a huge center was designed by Steiner and built. The architecturally unique, wooden building was built by volunteers from dozens of countries during World War I and was named the *Goetheanum*. This building was burned to the ground by an arsonist in 1923. Following this, a little more than two years before his death on March 30, 1925, Steiner reformed the Anthroposophical Society and began work on a second Goetheanum building which was one of the first structures of its size to be made from preformed concrete.

Even up to a few days before his death in 1925, Steiner continued lecturing and working. He delivered more than six thousand lectures which are available in more than three hundred volumes. In addition, he published more than four hundred books.

After World War I, Steiner's ideas on social reform, published in *The Threefold Commonwealth*, were seriously considered as one of the plans for the restructuring of post-war Germany. This prominence led to the spread of Anthroposophy in Europe and England. It was brought to the United States in 1925. The Anthroposophical Society in America was legally formed in 1930. It spread initially among German immigrants but was soon to be found in urban centers throughout the United States and Canada. After World War II, Steiner's books were translated into English and a publishing venture was formed. The Anthroposophic Press, now located in upstate New York, is part of a worldwide publishing effort to translate Steiner's works.

Work arising from Steiner's world-affirming approach has continued to flourish in both arts and sciences. In addition to his efforts to manifest the spiritual in architecture, Steiner worked in many art forms. He wrote plays—a series of modern mystery dramas. He developed Eurythmy, which translates the sounds, phrases, and rhythms of speech, or the dynamic elements of music into movement and gesture. It has been called "visible speech" or "visible song" and the "movement language of the soul." In painting, Steiner encouraged exploration of the laws of color and form not bound by matter. The colors themselves speak, which opens the doors to an art that embodies the spirit. He was a sculptor and sought to influence this art with "living forms"

Steiner's insights into science has been actively taken up in the more than seventy years since his death. In 1923, Steiner founded Biodynamics, the first nonchemical ("organic") agricultural movement which relates to the earth as a living organism. There is a Biodynamic association in the United States which reports more than thirty thousand acres under Biodynamic management in the United States. In the 1980s, Biodynamic gardeners launched the Community Supported Agricultural (CSA) movement. The Demeter Association certified Biodynamic farms in the United States, Mexico, and the Dominican Republic. Since the 1950s, soil scientists working with spiritual insights have successfully composted TNT and managed organic composting projects for the cities of New York and Los Angeles. A Physicians Association for Anthroposophically Extended Medicine (PAAM) and the Artemesia association of therapies, work with Steiner's insights into health and healing in 130 private practices and clinics throughout the United States. Companies such as Weleda, and others in the United States and Europe, research and develop pharmaceuticals and personal care products based on anthroposophical insights. In 1997, an anthroposophical cancer therapy based on mistletoe extract was named to the National Institute of Health (NIH) short-list of alternative therapies worthy of further study.

The Camphill Association is dedicated to working with handicapped adults and children in what is called "curative education and social therapy" which sees developmental disabilities and mental retardation not as illnesses, but as part of the fabric of human experience. Camphill Villages are dedicated to caring for individuals in the context of healthy home and community life. Groups such as the fellowship community in New York have formed intergenerational communities focusing on the care for the aging. In such places, coworkers and their families live and work together, learning and nurturing the old and young alike.

New forms of finance and banking have been founded. The Rudolf Steiner Foundation (NY) receives deposits and lends funds to worthwhile nonprofit ventures. In addition, a federally chartered bank was founded in 1997 which seeks to promote a new consciousness regarding money and community life. Independently working management consultants have taken Steiner's insights in social life into large and small organizations. Small presses and independent, special interest magazines are published in addition to the society's quarterly newsletter and the *Journal of Anthroposophy*.

The Waldorf Schools were begun in 1919 to show how a new education system based on Steiner's understanding of human nature could be applied. Waldorf education is the fastest growing independent school movement in the world with more than six hundred Waldorf Schools worldwide, and more than 230 Waldorf schools and kindergartens in the United States and Canada. It places as much emphasis on creativity and moral judgment as it does on intellectual growth. The curriculum integrates academics, artistic activity, and a unique teacher-student relationship to awaken a student's reverence for beauty and goodness as well as truth.

Adult education centers provide learning and practice for those interested in taking up a field of work arising from Anthroposophy. Adult learning centers are in Los Angeles, Toronto, and Detroit. Masters Degree programs in Waldorf Education are offered by Rudolf Steiner College (CA), Sunbridge College (NY), and the Waldorf Teacher Training Institute (NH). The Rudolf Steiner Institute is a three-week intensive summer seminar which takes place in Maine each year.

The Anthroposophical Society in America is organized into "branches" throughout the country which sponsor lectures, cultural events and study groups discussing Steiner's writings. The Rudolf Steiner Library in New York houses a collection of more than twenty thousand volumes which include Steiner's work and anthroposophical titles in German and English as well as books covering the full spectrum of western spirituality. There are independent national Societies for Mexico, Canada, and Hawaii.

**THE "I AM" RELIGIOUS ACTIVITY.** The "I AM" Religious Activity is a popularized form of Theosophy, reformulated to appeal to a broader audience than earlier theosophical organizations. The founder of the movement was Guy Ballard (1878–1939), who was born in Kansas. He had long been interested in occultism, and had studied theosophical teachings. He married Edna Wheeler (1886–1971) in 1916 and three years later their son Donald was born.

Ballard was engaged in mining exploration and promotion. In 1930, while he was working near Mt. Shasta—a giant volcanic cone in northern California where strange occult events had been said to occur—he had his initiatory contact with the hidden world. While hiking in the woods around the mountain, Ballard reports in his first book, *Unveiled Mysteries* (1934), he encountered another hiker, who gave him a marvellous drink and introduced himself as the Ascended Master Saint-Germain. The Compte de Saint-Germain was one of the most famous occultists of modern times.

Ballard was chosen as a messenger to restore to humankind the truths of reembodiment. Saint-Germain showed him many of his former lives which he had shared with his wife Edna and their son Donald. During these tours, the master imparted information about karma; the inner reality of the divine, or "Mighty I AM Presence"; the occult world history; and the creative power of thought.

Ballard returned to Chicago in 1931 to propagate Saint-Germain's message. Saint-Germain's teachings had certain distinctive characteristics which contributed to the remarkable spread of the I AM. Among its tenets are the American setting and nationalistic overtones. According to I AM, the Masters are found in the romantic American West—Mt. Shasta, the Grand Tetons, and Yellowstone.

It is believed that humanity began in America, and that this is the seventh and last cycle of history, under the Lord of the Seventh Ray, Saint-Germain. The history of this epoch will also end in America, which will be the vessel of light to bring the world into new and paradisal times.

I AM makes rich use of vivid colors, which characterize the rays of the masters and the spiritual characteristics of people. In addition, the I AM bookshops and centers are bright with color diagrams and lights. Ballard's writing is packed with color words. Ballard, who was fascinated by mines and gold, loved to depict the masters' retreats as underground.

It has been confirmed by a leader in the movement that color is very important because of the vibratory action of each color. Everything is constituted by energy and electrons, which manifest in different qualities through various colors. Also, sound-talking can be considered energy, which can be largely destructive, and, as a matter of fact, has done much to get humanity into its current troubles. I AM followers believe that constructive activity can be brought forth by surrounding oneself with harmonious colors.

These revelations were spread during the lectures of the three Ballards, who traveled in the 1930s as "Accredited Messengers" of the masters. Further messages from the ascended masters, especially from Saint-Germain and the master Jesus, were sometimes produced in public or private. The main teaching is that the "Mighty I AM Presence" is God-in-action, which is immediately available. It is also said that one's "individualized presence" is a pure reservoir of energy, from which power can be drawn at will.

Saint-Germain and Jesus are considered the mediators between the "I AM Presence" and humans. The ascended masters, at one time, were all human beings who became able to tramscend the physical world through purification of their lives. The goal of human life is represented by ascension.

The deeds and desires of a person are reflected by each individual's karma-made aura, which is generally both dark and light. When it is dark, it reaches a point where the person can no longer be of much service, or make much progress. Thus, the person dies physically to begin another life. Through purification of thought and feeling, the causal (higher spiritual) body becomes fully luminous, and draws the individual into the ascension, acting like a magnet. Through the ascension, the person joins the ascended masters, with whom he shares their unconditioned state of joy and freedom.

In 1938, the I AM Activity was given a dispensation according to which persons who had devoted themselves so much to the movement that they had not given all they might to personal purification, could upon normal death ascend from the after-earth state without reembodiment. It is believed that manifestation of constructive activities can be brought forth through one's acknowledgment and use of the power of qualification and visualization through music and contemplation. This can be done also through decrees, which are affirmations or prayers used only for constructive purposes. It is said that all that is destructive comes from human beings, and that records of past karmic debts can be consumed by the use of the "Violet Consuming Flame," which is like the grace of the New Testament. Through the use of this "Sacred Fire," humans can be liberated from the toils of what has gone before.

The "I AM" Activity worked publicly from 1937 to 1940 to establish a group of devoted followers numbering over one million. With the death of Guy Ballard on December 29, 1939, the movement began to decline. Edna Ballard claimed that her husband had become an Ascended Master. However, the fact that Guy Ballard had experienced a physical death rather than bodily ascension threatened the movement's credibility. The following year a sensational trial of the leaders of the movement took place, after some members of Ballard's personal staff accused the Ballards of obtaining money under fraudulent pretenses. The indictment was voided in 1944 by the Supreme Court with a landmark decision on religious liberty. The case was finally dismissed after Justice Douglas, in stating the prevailing opinion, asserted, "Men may believe what they cannot prove. They may not be put to the proof of their religious doctrines or beliefs."

The "I AM" Activity experienced a new growth in the 1980s, and is still alive today in a number of cities, where it has temples, reading rooms, and radio programs. The "I AM" Activity was directed by Edna Ballard until her death in 1971. The current board of directors is formed by Mr. and Mrs. Gerald Craig, who are the "Appointed Messengers," and Mt. Shasta is a major center. Every summer, in an ampitheater on the spotless grounds of the Saint-Germain Foundation, the "I AM" Activity of the Saint-Germain Foundation stages a pageant on the life of the "Beloved Master Jesus." In this version, the crucifixion is left out, whereas the ascension is what is believed to be important.

The Saint-Germain Foundation owns the large Shasta Springs resort near the town of Mt. Shasta. There youth and adult conclaves are held every summer. When the "I AM" Activity began to establish work at their sacred mountain in the 1940s, there was considerable local antagonism between the movement and the community of Mt. Shasta. The movement was accused of weird and fantastic practices, and slander followed its members. Full acceptance did not come until 1955 when three thousand people came to attend the pageant on the life of Christ for the first time.

**CHURCH UNIVERSAL AND TRIUMPHANT:** The Church Universal and Triumphant (C.U.T.) is a theosophically inspired, Montana-based New Age Church led by Elizabeth Clare Prophet. A successor movement to the "I AM" Religious Activity, it began as Mark L. Prophet's Summit Lighthouse. In terms of negative media coverage, by the late 1980s it had become *the* most controversial new religion in North America.

The "I AM" Religious Activity, founded by Guy Warren Ballard and his wife Edna W. Ballard, is a popularized form of Theosophy that views the ascended masters, especially the Comte de Saint-Germain, as leading the world toward a New Age of light and truth. These fairly standard theosophical teachings are mixed with patriotism, derived in part from Guy Ballard's association with William Dudley Pelley, the controversial originator of Soulcraft philosophy and the practice of "decreeing," a modified version of New Thought affirmations.

Mark L. Prophet had been active in two "I AM" splinter groups, the Bridge to Freedom (now the New Age Church of Truth) and the Lighthouse of Freedom. He eventually founded his own group, the Summit Lighthouse, in Washington, D.C., in 1958. The orientation of Prophet's new group was the publication and dissemination of the Masters' teachings. In the theosophical tradition, the spiritual evolution of the planet is conceived of as being in the hands of a group of divinely illuminated beings—Jesus, Gautama Buddha, and other advanced souls. In the tradition of earlier theosophical leaders, Mark Prophet viewed himself as serving as the mouthpiece for these ascended masters.

Elizabeth Clare Wulf joined the group in 1961, eventually marrying Mark

Prophet. Over the course of their marriage, Elizabeth Prophet also became a messenger. After Mark's death in 1973, Elizabeth took over his role as the primary mouthpiece for the masters, as well as leadership of the organization.

The headquarters of Summit Lighthouse moved to Colorado Springs in 1966. In 1974, Church Universal and Triumphant (C.U.T.) was incorporated, taking over ministerial and liturgical activities, while Summit Lighthouse remained the publishing wing of the organization. During the seventies, the work of C.U.T. expanded tremendously. New departments were steadily added, and study groups were established throughout the world. After several moves within southern California, church headquarters was finally established on the Royal Teton Ranch, in Montana just north of Yellowstone Park in 1986. In addition to its teaching and publishing activity, the church has also established an intentional community of several thousand people in the surrounding area. The community now boasts a number of businesses, schools, and an extensive farm.

The core beliefs of Church Universal and Triumphant are held in common with other branches of the theosophical tradition. These include the notion of ascended masters guiding the spiritual evolution of the planet, and certain basic ideas from the South Asian tradition, such as the belief in reincarnation and karma. The church views itself as being part of the larger Judeo-Christian tradition, although conservative Christians would not thus classify it.

The individual soul is viewed as a spark of the divine, bound to the material world and to the necessity of incarnating in a physical body because of prior mistakes and misdeeds. God is always present in the individual in the form of the "I AM" presence, a miniature replica of the divine. The goal of life is to purify oneself through service and through certain spiritual practices until one is free from the cycle of death and rebirth. At that point, the soul is able to return to God (in C.U.T. parlance, the soul "ascends").

The spiritual practices of Church Universal and Triumphant are based on the science of the spoken word. Through such concrete activities as decreeing, the soul is purified and transformed by becoming attuned to divine vibrations. Decrees also bring the power of the divine to bear on earthly matters, and can be utilized to invoke protection. For example,

> Let the light flow into my being,
> Let the light expand in the center of my heart,
> Let the light expand in the center of the earth,
> And let the earth be transformed into the new day!
>
> (Vesta, "The New Day")

For maximum effect, these poetic invocations are repeated as rapidly as possible. These practices often strike outsiders as quite strange.

Church Universal and Triumphant views itself as being under the spiritual guidance of the Great White Brotherhood (i.e., the body of ascended masters; "White" refers to their purity, not their race) which speaks through Elizabeth Clare Prophet. When not serving as a messenger, Prophet is regarded as an ordinary person. Church members who treat her as more than human are regarded as being guilty of idolatry. As a corporation, Church Universal and Triumphant is run by a board of directors.

Membership in the church is flexible. Church outreach around the globe is primarily accomplished through study groups—groups with which spiritual seekers can become informally affiliated. They may also received the weekly publication *Pearls of Wisdom* (started by Mark Prophet in 1958) which contains messages from the masters. In 1962, the Keepers of the Flame Fraternity was established. Keepers vow to keep the flame of life and liberty alive, and receive monthly graded instruction dictated through Elizabeth Prophet by the masters. After they have advanced to a certain stage, Keepers of the Flame may choose to become communicants. These full members are formally baptized, subscribe to certain church tenets, and tithe. Members may also choose to become part of the church's staff, serving in local teaching centers or as part of the Royal Teton Ranch.

It is against the policy of the church to report membership figures. About five thousand people attend the annual summer conference, and it has been estimated that communicant membership is approximately twice that figure. Because of the range of possible memberships, it is difficult to judge the size of membership beyond communicant level.

Through its educational wing the Summit Lighthouse, Church Universal and Triumphant produces innumerable books and other teaching materials. The publishing facility in Livingston, Montana, employs about a hundred people. Summit Lighthouse also employs its own distributors, who distribute the church's publications to bookstores across the country.

In addition to *Pearls of Wisdom*, the church also publishes the *Royal Teton Ranch News* on a regular basis. Summit University, founded in Santa Barbara in 1971, provides instruction to individuals who want more intensive exposure to the Masters' teachings. Summit University sessions are currently held at the Royal Teton Ranch in the form of twelve-week retreats. The church also established a Montesorri preschool in 1970 to provide education for members' children. This program eventually grew to include a complete elementary and high school program.

When "cults" became a public issue in the mid-1970s, Church Universal and Triumphant was not particularly prominent. While still in southern California, several members were kidnapped and deprogrammed. One major lawsuit, brought against the church by ex-member

Gregory Mull, cost C.U.T. several million dollars. Despite these struggles and some media attacks, the group remained a relatively minor player in the cult wars until it moved its headquarters to Montana.

As could have been anticipated, the intrusion of a large number of exotic outsiders evoked intense curiosity and antagonism. A significant component in Church Universal and Triumphant's troubles after moving to the mountains was a local newspaper that took particular offense to the church. A close study of the negative reviews the church has received in the national press since the early eighties reveals that most of the negative information was ultimately taken from articles generated by this single source, the *Livingston Enterprise*, based just down the road in Livingston, Montana.

Much of the church's negative media derives from incidents clustered around its extensive fallout shelters and its preparations for the possibility of a nuclear attack against the United States. At one point in the construction, for instance, fuel stored in several underground tanks (which were sold to the church in defective condition) ruptured and spilled gas and diesel oil into the water table. In 1990, members from around the world gathered in Montana because of the predicted possibility of an atomic holocaust—a gathering that would have gone all but unnoticed had not the *Livingston Enterprise* painted it in sinister colors and broadcast the news through the AP wire service to the world. This AP story made the front page of the *New York Times* of December 15, 1990, as a result of which Montana was flooded by reporters from around the world eager for sensationalist stories on a "doomsday cult." Most of the visitors supplemented the information they gathered at the Royal Teton Ranch with information from the *Livingston Enterprise*'s clipping file.

Finally, in 1989, two church members—without the knowledge or approval of Elizabeth Clare Prophet—attempted to acquire otherwise legal weapons in a nonpublic, illegal manner (to be stored in the underground shelters). The motivation was to avoid the negative media exposure that would have resulted if members had purchased guns in Montana. Needless to say, the plan backfired and resulted in a public relations disaster. This series of incidents, particularly the gun purchase fiasco, was the basis for subsequent accusations that Church Universal and Triumphant was a potential Waco. In the wake of the initial government attack on the Branch Davidians the *Enterprise* began running articles comparing the Waco community with Church Universal and Triumphant. The publicity generated by this activity led to many similar articles in papers throughout the country and, eventually, to a CBS special, *The Standoff in Waco* (a special edition of the TV tabloid *48 Hours* that was aired on March 17, 1993), that pushed the comparison to an absurd extreme. In the late summer of 1993, officials of both the Bureau of Alcohol, Tobacco, and Firearms and the Federal Bureau of Investigation visited the Royal Teton Ranch to assure the community that neither agency viewed Church Universal and Triumphant as a threat. Needless to say, the unsensational results of these visits were not newsworthy enough to make either the national or the local papers.

Following the events of 1993, Church Universal and Triumphant seemed to rebound, and then went into a decline. Part of the problem was that Elizabeth Prophet was suffering from a debilitating illness that was making her a progressively less effective organizational leader. She eventually stepped down from her role as the corporate head of the church to assume a more purely spiritual role. The church was then able to reorganize, sold off some of its holdings, and effectively stopped what had threatened to be a gradual dissolution.

**HOLY ORDER OF MANS.** The Holy Order of MANS was a nondenominational, nonsectarian, service and teaching order founded by Earl W. Blighton in 1968. The group represented itself as a kind of "New Age Mystery School" that trained its members in the doctrines of "Esoteric Christianity" and spiritual alchemy. After experiencing rapid growth between 1968 and 1977, the movement declined in the late 1970s and early 1980s. Blighton's successor, Vincent Rossi, decided to merge the brotherhood with an autocephalous Eastern Orthodox jurisdiction during the late 1980s. In time, the order wholly rejected its Rosicrucian, New Age roots, and proclaimed its new mission as the defender of Christian Orthodoxy in an "age of apostasy." It now calls itself Christ the Savior Brotherhood. The brotherhood's evolution provides an interesting case study of the radical processes of conventionalization, accommodation, and identity distortion that new religious movements can undergo during their founding generation.

The order emerged in the counterculture milieu of mid-1960s San Francisco. Earl W. Blighton was a retired electrical engineer and social worker who had studied with the Freemasons, the Ancient and Mystical Order of the Rosae Crucis (AMORC), the Subramuniya Yoga order, the New Thought movement, and various spiritualist churches. At the height of the hippie explosion in 1966, he set up a small office/chapel on Market Street to provide young runaways with food, shelter, employment counseling, and spiritual direction. His early students decided they wanted to live together as a kind of monastic brotherhood dedicated to charitable service and spiritual transformation. The Holy Order of MANS, modeled on Roman Catholic religious orders like the Jesuits, emerged from their deliberations and was incorporated on July 24, 1968.

The order spread rapidly throughout the United States and Europe. It elaborated its organizational outreach by creating a lay order of discipleship and a Christian Community movement. Lay disciples studied the order's esoteric teachings through a graded correspondence course called the "Tree of Life" lessons, yet remained financially independent. Christian

Communities were organized by lay families and single people who wished to create a chapel for daily sacraments and a center for classes and social activities. These communities were chartered by the order, which sent a priest to provide initiatory training and spiritual counseling. Blighton also created two celibate suborders to train renunciate members in service work and Marian devotional practices. The suborders were called the Immaculate Heart Sisters of Mary and the Brown Brothers of the Holy Light. By 1977 there were about three thousand participants in all of these order-affiliated organizations. These members were spread throughout sixty-seven "brotherhouses," mission centers, and Christian Communities in the United States, Canada, Western Europe, South America, and Japan.

After Blighton's sudden death in 1974, the brotherhood was torn apart by internal power struggles. Several years of interim leadership left the group disunited, confused as to its mission and identity, and in danger of collapse. Coupled with these developments was the growing influence of the anticult movement, which began placing the order on its list of dangerous "cults." Vincent Rossi, one Blighton's early disciples, was given the task of solving these problems in 1978 by the group's collective membership. The new director general began to craft a more "user-friendly" public face for the brotherhood, one that at first made it appear like a conventional evangelical Christian movement. Following the anticult hysteria generated by the Jonestown mass suicide, however, Rossi began an earnest search for a more traditional form of Christianity within which to plant the order. In Eastern Orthodoxy he found a tradition that was compatible with the order's mystical orientation, its valorization of the monastic ideal, and its elaborate ceremonialism. With the aid of Father Herman Podmoshensky of the Russian Orthodox St. Herman of Alaska Brotherhood, Rossi gradually replaced every element of the order's teachings and rituals with Orthodox dogmas and liturgies.

This process was completed in 1988, when the order changed its name to Christ the Savior Brotherhood and came under the protection of Pangratios Vrionis, the metropolitan of an independent Orthodox archdiocese headquartered in Queens, New York. Since this final break with its past the brotherhood has steadily lost members and vitality. The causes of this gradual dissolution are twofold: (1) the loss of a cohesive sense of community that occurred when the renunciate brotherhood disbanded and merged with movement's lay organizations, and (2) the continuing questions concerning the legitimacy of Metropolitan Pangratios's episcopal consecration and thus of the brotherhood's priestly ordinations. Many former members have joined established Orthodox parishes around the United States. Those members who have remained affiliated with the brotherhood are now being encouraged to set up small Orthodox missions throughout the country. These missions sell the movement's books and periodicals and hold small-scale Orthodox liturgies.

The Holy Order of MANS taught an original synthesis of Rosicrucian cosmology, Tantric initiatory philosophy, Freemasonic ritualism, dispensational millenarianism, and theosophical light mysticism. Members believed that Blighton received revelations (while in a trance state) from the "Master Jesus" and other members of the "Great White Brotherhood." This august body of advanced initiates was said to be responsible for humankind's long term spiritual evolution. Blighton claimed that this brotherhood had commissioned him to call together the reincarnated followers of Jesus of Nazareth and to create a New Age mystery school wherein these souls could be retrained in the "ancient Christian mysteries." He also claimed that his spiritual "shock troops" would bring humankind into the "higher solar initiations" so that it would be prepared when the earth underwent its imminent planetary "illumination." This great "lift in vibration" would be accompanied by chaos and confusion, Blighton taught, and only those who had themselves experienced the illumination would be able to function effectively in the earth's transformed atmosphere.

Order members underwent a rigorous training in meditation, concentration, spiritual healing, intercessory prayer, visualization, and the creative use of the spoken word. They also learned to intervene in crisis situations on the street and to help and counsel the homeless and victims of domestic violence. Like Roman Catholic monastic orders, the brothers and sisters of the order attended a daily eucharistic celebration and engaged in regular periods of prayer, scriptural study, and work. Unlike traditional Catholic monasteries, however, the order accepted both men and women, ordained women priests, and was located in largely urban environments. In addition, the order embraced an assortment of initiatory practices, "Temple" rituals, and mystical teachings from outside the Christian tradition. Once the movement became Christ the Savior Brotherhood, all of its early teachings, rituals, and spiritual practices were replaced with those of traditional Eastern Orthodoxy.

The order published several books on esoteric Christianity, astrology, and tarot symbolism during the Blighton era. In the late 1970s it published *Epiphany*, an ecumenical Christian journal, *Sonflowers*, a magazine for its lay disciples, and *Tree of Life*, for all lay members. Christ the Savior Brotherhood copublishes (with the Saint Herman of Alaska Brotherhood) a number of works on traditional Russian Orthodox monasticism.

The Holy Order of MANS pioneered several practices and activities that have since become commonplace in late twentieth-century America. For example, they were among the first organizations in the country to establish emergency shelters for battered women and children. These "Raphael Houses," as they were called, provided a temporary sanctuary for victims of domestic violence as well as counseling, advocacy with governmental relief agencies, and long-term child care and housing. In another instance, the order's Eleventh Commandment Fellowship was instrumental in the creation of the North American Conference on Christianity and Ecology. This ecumenical organization is dedicated to raising ecological awareness among mainstream Christians. Such consciousness-raising groups are now springing up within most mainline denominations. A final example is the group's early advocacy of spiritual equality for women and its ordination of women to its priesthood. Women are now routinely ordained to the ministry in a number of mainstream denominations and appear to have overcome their traditional stigma as unworthy of sacerdotal authority (Roman Catholics and fundamentalists notwithstanding). Ironically, Christ the Savior Brotherhood has now adopted Eastern Orthodoxy's traditional proscription of women priests.

*—PHILLIP C. LUCAS*

**SOLAR TEMPLE.** On October 4 and 5, 1994, fifty-three people died in Switzerland and in Canada. Their bodies—some showing signs of violence suffered before the fires—were found in the incinerated centers of a neo-Templar movement called originally International Order of Chivalry Solar Tradition or, for short, Solar Tradition, and after 1990–1991 Order of the Solar Temple. The movement is part of one of several currents which as a whole compose the universe of the contemporary occult-esoteric movements, the neo-Templar tradition.

The founder/leader of the Solar Temple, Luc Jouret (1947–1994) was born on October 18, 1947. Trained as a medical doctor, Jouret became an accomplished practitioner of homeopathy. He also lectured on naturopathy and ecological topics, active in the wider circuit of the French-speaking New Age movement. About 1981, he established the Amenta Club, an organization managing his conferences (the name was later changed into Amenta— without "Club"—and then into Atlanta). He spoke in New Age bookstores (in France, Switzerland, Belgium, and Canada) and in eclectic esoteric groups such as the Golden Way Foundation of Geneva (previously called La Pyramide, which had as its leader Joseph Di Mambro [1924–1994] who later became the cofounder—and largely the real leader—of the Solar Temple, while the Golden Way became for all purposes the parent organization of the Atlanta, Amenta, and later Archédia clubs and groups). In 1987, Jouret was able to be received as a paid "motivational speaker" by two district offices of Hydro-Québec, the public hydroelectric utility of the Province of Québec. Besides getting paid 5,400 Canadian dollars for his conferences in the period of 1987 to 1989, he also recruited fifteen executives and managers who later followed him to the end.

Amenta was the outer shell of an esoteric organization. Those who most faithfully attended Jouret's homeopathic practices and conferences were given the invitation to join a more confidential, although not entirely secret, "inner circle": the Archédia Clubs, established in 1984, in which one could already find a definite ritual and an actual initiation ceremony, with a set of symbols taken from the Masonic-Templar teachings of Jacques Breyer. According to Canadian reporter Bill Marsden, Breyer personally attended OICTS meetings in Geneva in 1985: An ex-member described Julien Origas, Breyer, and Di Mambro as having been earlier "the three chums who spoke of esoteric things" in the first Templar meetings he had attended in Geneva.

The Archédia Clubs were not yet the truly inner part of Jouret's organization. Their most trusted members were invited to join an even more "inner" circle, this one truly a secret organization: the International Order of Chivalry Solar Tradition (OICST), Solar Tradition for short, later to be called Order of the Solar Temple (although it is not impossible that an Order of the Solar Temple had originally existed as an inner circle of OICST). OICST can be considered both a schism and a continuation of Julien Origas's ORT (Renewed Order of the Temple), which Jouret had joined in 1981 with the knowledge of only a few friends. Apparently former Communist Luc Jouret and neo-Nazi Julien Origas understood each other very well, at least for a few months. After Origas's death, Luc Jouret tried unsuccessfully to be recognized as ORT's leader, facing opposition from the founder's daughter, Catherine Origas: hence the 1984 schism and the establishment of OICTS. On the other hand, some of Luc Jouret's coworkers in the Archédia Clubs, such as Joseph Di Mambro, co-founder of OICTS, and Geneva businessman Albert Giacobino, had been members, according to press sources, of Alfred Zappelli's Sovereign and Military Order of the Temple of Jerusalem (18) and possibly of AMORC. But according to Jouret's most secret teachings, the schism that had given birth to OICTS was not only the mere fruit of disagreements, but was rather according to the will of the ascended masters of the Grand Lodge of Agartha, who had revealed themselves in 1981, before Julien Origas's death, disclosing a "plan" that was supposed to last thirteen years, until the end of the world, predicted for the year 1994.

Luc Jouret's OICTS teachings stressed the occult-apocalyptic themes of Jacques Breyer's OSTS and Julien Origas's ORT, connecting together three traditions on the end of the world: (a) the idea found in some (but by no means all) New Age groups of an impending ecological catastrophe (for instance, Jouret was very insistent about the lethal nature of modern diets and food); (b) some neo-Templar movements' theory of a cosmic "renovatio" revealed by the ascended masters of the Grand Lodge of Agartha; (c) the political ideas of a final international *bagarre* propagated by survivalist groups both on the extreme right and on the extreme left of the political spectrum, with which Jouret had contacts in different countries. It seems that, in the years 1986 to 1993, Luc Jouret kept receiving "revelations," following Julien Origas's tradition, especially of four "sacred objects": the Grail, the Excalibur Sword, the Menorah, and the Ark of the Covenant, until it was revealed to him that between the end of 1993 and the beginning of 1994 the Earth would have been forsaken by its last "guardians": at first six "entities" hidden in the Great Pyramid of Egypt, and later—but this could have been a metaphor used for a spiritual experience of three leaders of the Temple—three ascended masters who had received a revelation on the end of this cycle near Ayers Rock Mountain, Australia (a country in which the Temple had in the meantime established itself).

Luc Jouret was able to keep up his speaking engagements in the New Age circuit as long as the existence of a secret order with peculiar ideas on the end of the world was well hidden behind the different Amenta, Atlanta, and Archédia groups and clubs. When some curious journalists and the unavoidable disgruntled ex-members started to talk about the Solar Temple, the doors shut. The Archédia Clubs dissolved in 1991, and various European New Age bookstores had by this time begun refusing to host Luc Jouret's conferences. There remained, however, a solid operation in Canada, where Jouret and Joseph Di Mambro spent a great deal of their time since 1986, and where they had founded a Club Archédia de Science et Tradition International. Under the Atlanta and Archédia Clubs labels, Luc Jouret could thus keep up his conferences—on topics such as *The Sphinx, Christ, and the New Man*—in Québec (and it seems even at the University of Québec at Montreal) in the years 1991 and 1992. Motivational classes were offered to companies under the aegis of an Académie pour la Recherche et la Connaissance des Haute Sciences (ARCHS, whose literature was printed by Éditions Atlanta).

On March 8, 1993, a crucial episode in the history of the Solar Temple occurred in Canada. Two Temple members, Jean Pierre Vinet, fifty-four, engineer and project-manager for Hydro-Quebéc and Herman Delorme, forty-five, insurance broker, were arrested as they were attempting to buy three semiautomatic guns with silencers, illegal weapons in Canada. Daniel Tougas, a police officer of Cowansville and a Temple member, was temporarily suspended from office on charges of having helped the two. On March 9, judge François Doyon of Montreal committed them to trial, freeing them on parole. Luc Jouret—who according to police reports asked the two to buy the weapons—was also committed to trial, and an arrest warrant was issued against him. (The Temple leader could not be found, as he was in Europe at the time.) The event drew the attention of the Canadian press on what newspapers called "the cult of the end of the world."

The separated wife of one of the members, Rose-Marie Klaus, a Swiss citizen, took advantage of the situation, calling for a press conference on March 10, in which she denounced sex magic practices and economical

exploitation of members. On the same day, March 10, another press conference was held in Sainte-Anne-de-la-Pérade. Sitting beside Jean-Marie Horn,
president of the Association pour l'Étude et la Recherche en Science de Vie
Québec, and Didier Quèze, Solar Temple spokesman, was the town's Mayor,
Gilles Devault, who declared that the Temple "never caused any trouble"
but, on the contrary, "contributed to the development of the community."

Even the reporters most bent to sensationalism could not find any hostility between this Québec town and the Solar Temple, and recounted that
"residents of Sainte-Anne-de-la-Pérade met yesterday [March 10, 1993] do
not seem to have any grievances towards members of the Order." Rose-Marie
Klaus was considered an unreliable fanatic, and even the local parish priest,
Father Maurice Cossette, admitted that, true, they were not Catholics, but he
let them advertise their conferences on nutrition and health on the church
bulletin as long as they didn't "talk about Apocalypse." Later the Solar
Temple's lawyer, Jacques Rochelle, hinted at a "schism" that would have happened "more or less" in 1990, during which the Canadian members supposedly left Luc Jouret. Allegedly also Herman Delorme and Jean-Pierre Vinet
had left the order several months before their arrest. It is unclear whether
this information represented a simple attempt of sidetracking the investigations, or if tension within the Order of the Solar Temple actually existed. In
any case, the official leader of the Canadian Branch in March 1993, Robert
Falardeau, head of a Department at Quebéc Ministry of Finance, died in
October 1994 with Luc Jouret and Joseph Di Mambro.

Three institutions were concerned about connections their officers
and employees had with a "cult": the police (which had agent Daniel
Tougas condemned—with parole—and expelled him from its ranks),
Hydro-Québec (which nominated an investigation commission that veri-
fied how twenty-two employees had participated in the activities of the
Solar Temple and fifteen were actual members of it, advising Hydro-
Québec to refrain in the future from hosting occult-religious "motiva-
tional" conferences), and the Ministry of Finances (which sent Chief of
Department Robert Falardeau on leave for one week, then let him slip qui-
etly back into office). The tempest seemed to end smoothly, even if on
March 17, 1994, a letter signed "Order of the Solar Temple" was found in
Montréal, in which the order claimed responsibility for an attack against a
Hydro-Québec tower in Saint-Basile-Le-Grand on February 24. The police
questioned the authenticity of the letter as it mentioned only the Saint-
Basile-Le-Grand attack and not another one committed the same day
against a Hydro-Quebec installation in the Native American reserve of
Kahnawake but kept secret by the authorities (which, however, had to obviously be known to the attackers). The Canadian incident later appeared to
be extremely significant in the final crisis of the Solar Temple.

It will take years to find out exactly how the events developed during the first week of October 1994. The most essential information has been extensively covered in the world media. On September 30, nine people, including Luc Jouret, had dinner at the Bonivard Hotel in Veytaux (in the Vaud Canton, Switzerland). On October 3, Joseph Di Mambro was seen having lunch with others at the Saint-Christophe Restaurant in Bex (same canton). On October 4, a fire destroyed Joseph Di Mambro's villa in Morin Heights, Canada. Among the ruins, the police found five charred bodies, one of which was a child's. At least three of these people seemed to have been stabbed to death before the fire. In Salvan (Valais Canton, Switzerland), Luc Jouret and Joseph Di Mambro asked a blacksmith to change the lock in their chalet, and bought several plastic bags. On October 5, at 1:00 A.M., a fire started in one of the centers of the Solar Temple in Switzerland, the Ferme des Rochettes, near Cheiry, in the Canton of Fribourg—which was also a center for natural agriculture—owned by Albert Giacobino, who as mentioned earlier was as an associate of Joseph Di Mambro in several esoteric and neo-Templar activities. The police found twenty-three bodies, one of which was a child's, in a room converted into a temple. Among the corpses was Albert Giacobino's, the farm's owner. Some of the victims were killed by gunshots, while many others were found with their heads inside plastic bags. The same day, at 3:00 A.M., three chalets, inhabited by members of the Solar Temple, caught fire almost simultaneously at Les Granges sur Salvan, in the Valais Canton. In the charred remains were found twenty-five bodies, along with remainders of devices programmed to start the fires (such devices were also found at Morin Heights and at Cheiry), and the pistol which shot the fifty-two bullets destined for the people found dead in Cheiry. On October 6, Swiss historian Jean-François Mayer, secretary of the International Committee of CESNUR (Center for Studies on New Religions)—a scholar who in 1987 had conducted a participant observation of the Clubs Archédia—received a package mailed from Geneva on October 5 (in the space for the sender it said simply "D.part," meaning "departure" in French). The package included four documents summing up the ideology of the Solar Temple and explaining what had happened that night, together with an article extracted from the American *Executive Intelligence Review* as republished in *Nexus* on the Randy Weaver incident. Other copies of the package or parts of it were sent also to some Swiss newspapers.

On October 8, in Aubignan, France, the police discovered in a building owned by a member of the Solar Temple a deactivated device which could have burned down the house, similar to the ones found in Switzerland and in Canada. On October 9, the French Minister of the Interior, Charles Pasqua, received in Paris the passports of Joseph Di Mambro and his wife Jocelyne (both already identified among the victims of the Swiss fire). The sender's name on the envelope is that of a "Tran Sit Corp" in Zurich. The

Canadian television announced the same day that, according to their investigations, Joseph Di Mambro used the Solar Temple as a cover for weapon
smuggling and for money-laundering, and had huge bank funds in Australia. The figures allegedly involved in this traffic (millions of dollars),
which supposedly corresponded with those of the Australian bank account,
were however drastically reduced by the Swiss prosecutors. On October 13,
the Swiss police stated to have identified without a doubt among the
charred bodies that of Luc Jouret (whom many thought had escaped), and
to have recognized as Patrick Vuarnet (a young member of the Solar
Temple, son of former olympic ski champion and president of a multina-
tional firm of eyeglasses, Jean Vuarnet) the "mailman" who had sent the
documents to Jean-François Mayer and the passports to French Minister
Charles Pasqua following instructions by Joseph Di Mambro.

Suicide and/or murder? We can find some answers—if we know how
to search for them beyond the esoteric jargon and without barring the possibility that they could also include some information aimed at sidetracking—in the four documents sent to Jean-François Mayer (whom we
thank for passing them on to the CESNUR network promptly). The explanation includes a suicide and two types of murder. According to the documents, some especially advanced members of the order are able to understand that—as the cycle started by the Grand Lodge of Sirius or of Agartha
in 1981 is completed—it is time to move on to a superior stage of life. It is
"not a suicide in the human sense of the term," but a deposition of their
human bodies to immediately receive new invisible, glorious and "solar"
ones. With these new bodies, they now operate in another dimension,
unknown to the uninitiated, presiding over the dissolution of the world
and waiting for an esoteric "redintegratio." There is also another class of
less advanced members of the Solar Temple who cannot understand that
in order to take on the "solar body" one must "depose" of the mortal one.
The documents state that these members must be helped to perform their
"transition" (in other words, must be "helped" to die) in the least violent
way possible. Lastly, the documents state that within the Temple's membership were also found backsliders and traitors, actively helping the arch-
enemies of the Solar Temple: the government of Québec and Opus Dei.
To them the documents promise "just retribution" (in other words,
murder, without the cautions used with the less advanced members).
According to a survivor, Thierry Huguenin—whose last-minute escape was
apparently responsible for reducing the casualties to fifty-three—Jouret
and Di Mambro had planned that exactly fifty-four victims should die in
order to secure an immediate magical contact with the spirits of fifty-four
Templars burned at stake in the fourteenth century.

—*Massimo Introvigne*

**AGNI YOGA SOCIETY.** The Agni Yoga Society began in the mid-1920s as a group of students who gathered to study a book published in 1924, *The Leaves from M's Garden.* This was the first of a series of books received from the Master Morya by Helena Roerich. Helena Roerich and her husband, Nicolas, left Russia at the time of the Revolution and came to the United States in 1920 on the invitation of the Art Institute of Chicago (Nicolas was an outstanding artist). Soon after coming to America, the Roerichs joined the Theosophical Society. Helena Roerich translated *The Secret Doctrine,* the major work of Theosophical Society Founder Helena Petrovna Blavatsky, into Russian. Helena Roerich began to receive regular communications from one of the masters originally contacted by Blavatsky, the Master Morya. Helena produced thirteen volumes of material from the Master Morya, the first of which was *The Leaves from M's Garden.* These thirteen volumes have become the prime teaching material of the Agni Yoga Society. Membership in the Agni Yoga Society, which is currently estimated at five hundred, is open to those who have studied the books for one to three years. Study groups meet semimonthly at various locations around the country.

**ARCANE SCHOOL.** The Arcane School was founded by Alice and Foster Bailey in 1923 and continues the work and thought of former Theosophist Alice Bailey. It is the largest of the full moon meditation groups. Correspondence lessons, which are based on Alice Bailey's books and lead the student through various degrees, are mailed out to students internationally. The school has headquarters in New York, London, and Geneva. Since the school's founding, several subsidiary programs have been created to implement Alice Bailey's program. "World Goodwill" was established in 1932 as an accredited nongovernmental organization with the United Nations in New York and Geneva to establish right human relations in the world. "Triangles" was created in 1937 to build groups of three people who would unite daily in a mental chain radiating energy into the world.

# 15 NEOPAGANISM

*Aidan A. Kelly*

**N**eopaganism as a religious concept is based on a desire to recreate the pagan religions of antiquity, usually not as they actually were, but as they have been idealized by romantics ever since the Renaissance. The gap between the ancient reality and the modern reconstructions is exhibited most clearly by the fact that all classical paganism—like first-temple Judaism—was based squarely on animal sacrifice, which is avoided with something like horror by all modern neopagans. (Animal sacrifice is still central to several African American religions, such as Vodoun (Voodoo), Santeria, or Macumba, but that is an entirely different religious movement.)

The concept of recreating the lost pagan religions of antiquity appeared early in the Renaissance. Such Italian scholars as Pico della Mirandola and Marsilio Ficino were neopagans (as well as occultists and magicians) in precisely the current sense of desiring to recreate the lost religions of the past in order to participate in them, and this desire has remained a thread in Western occultism ever since. Fascination with the classics was a major theme of Romanticism, and the idea of reviving some sort of classical religion gained strength and became programmatic during the late nineteenth century, at which time attention was divided between Greco-Roman and Norse paganism. It was further strengthened as the new discipline of classical archaeology revealed the existence of civilizations in the Middle East that predated the Greeks by millennia, and turned up pagan religious texts that had been baked in clay as palaces burned down around them.

There were many attempts at recreating pagan religions in the late nineteenth and early twentieth centuries, most of which left only literary results, as in the poetry of Swinburne and the magnificent paintings of the "Pre-Raphaelite Brotherhood" and their colleagues. Other types of paganism emerged into the light during this period also, as Celtic and Near Eastern studies revealed more and more about the cultures that had existed before biblical, Roman, or Christian times.

Attempts to recreate paganism began to succeed only in the 1960s, apparently because the new magical and theological technology of Wicca lent these neopagan experiments a crucial and previously lacking ingredient. The typical pattern here was for a neopagan group to be founded—typically by college students—and to remain in existence as a very small group until the late 1960s or early 1970s, at which time the group leaders would run into some Gardnerian-style Witches (descendants of Gerald B. Gardner), begin learning the religion of Wicca, and adapting various aspects of Wicca to the needs of their neopagan group. At this stage the synergism of the eclectic enterprise would inspire new enthusiasm in all members of the group, and the group would begin to expand very rapidly, both in recruiting new members and in multiplying the frequency and variety of its activities.

Because of the other neopagan's habit of coopting the best traits of Wicca, until the mid-1970s Wicca appeared to be just one among many equally important neopagan religions. During the next decade this situation changed remarkably. In the mid-1980s, Margot Adler, in her *Drawing Down the Moon* observed, "Wiccan organizations have come to the foreground as the primary form of neopaganism in America, and these organizations now dominate the discussion." Well over 50 percent of all the neopagans in America had become neopagan witches. This apparently came about for several reasons: (1) the witches were growing in numbers, and continue to grow, faster than any of the other neopagan religions (and, in fact, faster than any other religion in the history of the New World); (2) many neopagans came to realize that Wicca provided everything they had been hoping to gain from the other neopagan religions, and so shifted their focus more exclusively onto Wicca.

Wicca is therefore the most important of the neopagan religions, and the witches always form the backbone of neopagan voluntary associations. However, there are other neopagan religions with substantial followings, as well as theologies quite distinct from that of Wicca.

It is difficult to get hold of accurate demographic data for the neopagan movement, since its members range between extremely closed-mouthed and grandiose in discussing the numbers of members in each coven, the number of covens, and so on; but several independent methods for estimating the size of the movement, based on circulation of national periodicals, sales of specialized books, attendance at national festivals, and size of contact lists, arrive at figures of somewhere between 50,000 and 300,000 for its somewhat serious adherents.

There is also a women's spirituality movement that overlaps the neopagan movement; the overlap began in 1971, when many women at a Women's Rights conference in Los Angeles dropped in on the World Science Fiction Convention, and heard an address by Julia Carter Zell on the craft. This event led to the foundation of "Dianic" covens, which were for women only; whereas all other neopagan covens had been mixed in gender. Soon afterward covens for men only—some gay, some straight— were also founded.

**WICCA.** The word "wicca" was originally the Saxon term for a male witch, and was pronounced "witch-ah"; the female "wicce" was pronounced "witch-ay." However, the term was adopted by Gerald Gardner as a general name for the witchcraft religion he had helped to found and/or revive in the 1930s, and is now used mainly in that sense, being pronounced "wickah." A member of the religion is therefore a Wiccan, pronounced "wickun." The religion is also referred to as "the Craft"; Gardner began using this term, originally a Masonic term for Freemasonry, as a name for the movement in the late 1950s.

There have been a great many descriptions of this religion published by now, and there is no need to repeat all of those descriptions here. However, for the sake of precision, let us define Wicca as having the following characteristics:

1. Worship is polytheistic, and always includes an exalted concept of a goddess as being close to the ultimate level of divinity.
2. Worship occurs in the small group known as a coven (which may consist of anywhere from three to around twenty members) according to the phases of the moon. These monthly meetings for worship (and the working of practical magic) are referred to as esbats. Worship also occurs in larger groups, which may be two covens meeting together or several hundred people, some coming from long distances, for the sabbats, of which there are eight in each year.
3. In addition to worship, coven activity focuses on the working of magic, which includes both the practical kind of folk magic and a much more abstract magical system, based essentially on the system of the Hermetic Order of the Golden Dawn, which is highly psychologized, eclectic, and variegated, since the magical training procedures used in any one coven will depend on what training in magic, psychic abilities, psychology, or other disciplines the coven's leaders have had in academia, New Age groups, or other Western occult tradition groups.
4. Despite the anarchism of neopagan witches, and their freedom to innovate within their covens and their lives, they are just as clear as

members of other religions are about which individuals and groups belong to their religion and which do not. The distinguishing criteria might be hard for an outsider to learn to perceive, but a Wiccan coven always knows whether another group is in fact also Wiccan, or whether it is instead a Ceremonial Magick lodge, a New Age group, or some other sort of Western occult tradition group. This clear intuitive awareness of membership boundaries is one of the distinguishing characteristics of religions.

All religions also seem to have both foundation myths—which almost always claim to be historical, in order to propose a meaning for the history of the religion—as well as actual histories, and the Gardnerian movement is no exception to this general rule. Like all the other religions that have come into existence during the last five thousand years of documented history, Gardnerian witchcraft began as a new religion at a specific time and place: in England, in the late 1930s.

The foundation myth of Wicca has grown around Gardner's claim that in the late 1930s he was initiated into one of the very last of the English covens, and that he later built up its system of worship and magic into the Gardnerian system that has formed the basis for almost all of modern witchcraft. The myth proposes that modern witchcraft therefore can claim continuity with the witches who were persecuted during the "Burning Times" (that is, during the witch hunts of the sixteenth and seventeenth centuries), as well as with pre-Christian pagan religions going back to the Stone Age. One of the best-known forms of this myth is woven into the second and third editions of Robert Graves's *The White Goddess.*

The publication of Margaret Murray's *The Witch Cult in Western Europe* (Oxford University Press, 1921) set off a new burst of interest in paganism, since Murray proposed that the witch-hunters of medieval and early modern times were actually finding the remnants of the pagan religions of northern Europe. The idea of recreating the kind of witch cult described by Murray was discussed by English occultists during the 1920s and 1930s, and some work on this may have been done by a student group called the Pentangle Club at Cambridge in the 1930s. However, the first successful attempt to recreate Murray's "witch cult" was apparently actually carried out by Gerald B. Gardner, a retired British civil servant, and his colleagues among the New Forest occultists, under the leadership of one Dorothy Clutterbuck, a locally prominent homeowner and socialite, during World War II. The founding members probably included Dolores North, later known for her regular column in a British occult magazine similar to *Fate,* as well as others in the occult circles of London and southern England. They had begun their work on this project by the time the war broke out in September 1939; by August 1940 they were well-organized enough to try "raising a cone of power" as a spell to prevent Hitler from invading England, an event reported by several English occultists of the period.

The New Forest coven continued working through the 1940s. Gardner took over leadership of the group, perhaps by default, around the end of World War II, and began developing it in a direction that was more to his liking. He began writing and publishing in the late 1940s and 1950s, and his books have been primary documents of the movement ever since.

When Dorothy Clutterbuck died in 1951, Gardner was free to begin building up the "witch cult" into something even more to his liking. He began to claim that he had been initiated in 1939 into a coven that had survived in England into modern times, and he began actively recruiting and initiating new members. In 1953 he initiated Doreen Valiente, who soon became the High Priestess of the central coven, and who rewrote the coven's *Book of Shadows* (liturgical manual) into the form in which it is still used in the movement. She has described her contributions modestly but accurately in her recent *The Rebirth of Witchcraft*. The *Book of Shadows* contains rituals for the coven's full moon esbats; for the eight "sabbats" at the solstices, equinoxes, and cross-quarter days; and for various rites of passage, as well as some basic magical techniques. The central coven fissioned in two in 1957, with Gardner and Valiente each taking a half; but Gardner soon went off on his own again, initiating new priestesses and founding new covens at a fairly rapid pace until his death in 1964, and these have carried on the craft enthusiastically.

Raymond Buckland, after a long correspondence with Gardner, was initiated in 1963 in Perth, Scotland, by Lady Olwen. Buckland then brought the Craft back to the United States and, with his wife Rosemary as High Priestess, founded the New York coven in Bayside, Long Island, which became the center of the Gardnerian movement and the neopagan movement in America for the next twenty years.

Almost all the "official" Gardnerians in America are descendants of the New York coven, and they maintain their identity by maintaining a strict apostolic succession of High Priestesses who can trace their initiation back to Lady Theos, Lady Rowen (Rosemary Buckland), and Lady Olwen (Monique Wilson). However, these "official" Gardnerians are now a very small fraction of Gardnerian witchcraft, and of the neopagan witchcraft movement in general, largely because they adhere to a fairly strict interpretation of the rules gradually established by the New York coven in its steadily expanding text of the *Book of Shadows*. Most American witches, being spiritually akin to anarchists, libertarians, and other proponents of radical theories, regard the Gardnerian concept of "orthodox witchcraft" as an oxymoron, and practice the Craft much more flexibly, using whatever they like from the Gardnerian repertoire, and creating whatever else they need from whatever looks useful in past or present religions.

Almost all other traditions of neopagan witchcraft in America began as an imitation of the Gardnerians. Some of the imitators (such as the New, Reformed, Orthodox Order of the Golden Dawn, still perhaps the largest neopagan witchcraft organization in California) admitted their dependence on the Gardnerians openly from their beginning in 1967. Other imitators have claimed an ancestry that goes back to European witchcraft independent of the Gardnerians, but these claims have always proved to lack substance. The very few witches in America whose traditions seem to predate Gardner (and which differed radically from the Gardnerian theology) have enthusiastically adopted the Gardnerian "reforms" because of their popularity and usefulness; the most important of these is certainly Victor Anderson, founder of the Fairy tradition, and, along with Sara Cunningham, a major teacher of Starhawk.

All neopagan witches believe themselves to be practicing the same religion, and so have been able to form local, regional, and national churches and networking organizations. One of the largest of these is the Covenant of the Goddess (COG), a California nonprofit corporation established on Hallowe'en 1975 to serve the Craft movement as a legal church; however, only a small minority (in the range of 1 to 5 percent) of all the covens in America have yet become members of the covenant.

**CHURCH AND SCHOOL OF WICCA.** The Church and School of Wicca was founded by Gavin and Yvonne Frost in 1965. Initially located near St. Louis, Missouri, it was moved to North Carolina in the late 1970s. In late 1996, it moved to West Virginia. It practices and teaches a form of neopagan witchcraft, but operated originally with a theology derived directly from an aristocratic British tradition into which Gavin was initiated in 1948. This instead of the Gardnerian system based on Margaret Murray and Robert Graves; the differences led to some unfortunate misunderstandings with other neopagans in the early 1970s. In recent years CSW has evolved a more eclectic theology that is more compatible with the beliefs of other neopagan witches, and have also developed a uniquely Western form of Tantric Yoga.

Gavin Frost was born in 1930 in Staffordshire, England, to a Welsh family. In 1948 he was initiated into an aristocratic coven that apparently went back to a group called the Pentangle Society (or Pentacle Club, among other names), a student group at Cambridge which in the mid-1930s began trying to reconstruct the pagan witchcraft religion proposed by Margaret Murray in her *The Witch Cult in Western Europe* (1921). It is possible that this group was also connected with the New Forest coven that Gerald Gardner was initiated into in 1939. From 1949 to 1952, Gavin attended London University, graduating with a B.S. in mathematics; he went on to earn a doctorate in physics and mathematics. While working for an aerospace company on the Salisbury Plain, he became curious about Stonehenge, and his investigation of it deepened his knowledge of the Craft.

Yvonne Frost was born Yvonne Wilson in 1931 in Los Angeles, into a Baptist family. Married in 1950, divorced in 1960, she earned an A.A. degree in secretarial skills, and went to work for an aerospace firm in Anaheim. In its halls, she met Gavin, who had arrived there from Canada. She was involved with the Spiritual Frontiers Fellowship, and together they studied psychic development. Another career move took them to St. Louis, where they pursued the Craft. Together Gavin and Yvonne have authored more than twenty books that are now available in five languages. They are proud to describe themselves as "spiritual libertarians."

They now began to work on founding the Church and School of Wicca, and wrote *The Witch's Bible*, based on the correspondence courses they were teaching. It was published in 1971, and caused much controversy among neopagan witches, almost none of whom were able to perceive that the Frosts' tradition went back to eighteenth-century Druidic concepts along a pathway different from that of Gardnerianism. Over the years, the Frosts have been able to negotiate a theological interface that allows them to get along with the neopagan witches, who in term have generally learned that there is more than one variety of witchcraft in the world.

The Church and School of Wicca is one of the largest and most accessible of the current witchcraft groups, and sponsors some of the largest festivals. Its Samhain Seminar has been held, usually in Atlantic Beach, North Carolina, every year since 1972, and was one of the models on which the current system of festivals was based. Over the years, it has chartered twenty-eight independent CSW-Tradition churches. A milestone of which the church is very proud is the Federal Appeals Court's recognition in 1985 of the church as equal to any other church.

More than 50,000 students have enrolled in the CSW correspondence courses since its inception, and roughly 250 students graduate from them each year, so that the CSW Tradition has become one of the most widespread. Its journal, *Survival*, is available by subscription and to students enrolled in the school, at Box 297, Hinton, WV 25951; www.wicca.org.

**CHURCH OF ALL WORLDS.** The Church of All Worlds (CAW) is an organization of individuals who regard the Earth and all life on it as sacred. CAW considers living in harmony and understanding with life's myriad forms a religious act. While the community prescribes no particular dogma or creed, the commonality of the members lies in their reverence and connection with nature and with Mother Earth, seeing her as a living entity. Human beings are not only her children, but evolving cells in her vast, organic body. Indeed, in 1970, it was CAW's founder who first formulated and published the theology of deep ecology that has come to be known as the "Gaia Thesis."

CAW embraces philosophical concepts of immanent divinity and emergent evolution. CAW is also a self-described neopagan group, implying an eclectic reconstruction of ancient nature religions, and combining archetypes of many cultures with other mystic, environmental, and spiritual disciplines. CAW views its mission as being

> to evolve a network of information, mythology and experience to awaken the divine within and to provide a context and stimulus for reawakening Gaia and reuniting her children through tribal community dedicated to responsible stewardship and the evolution of consciousness.

The Church of All Worlds grew out of a "water-brotherhood" called "Atl" formed by Tim (now Oberon) Zell, Lance Christie, and their wives at Westminster College, Fulton, Missouri, in 1962. The group continued at the University of Oklahoma, Norman, Oklahoma, in the mid-1960s. After Zell moved to St. Louis, Missouri, in 1968, it was incorporated as the Church of All Worlds, a name derived, along with some central theological concepts, from Robert Heinlein's novel *Stranger in a Strange Land*; in that year Zell also began *Green Egg* as the church's newsletter. In 1971, it became the first neopagan religion to win federal tax-exempt status, the state ruling against it being overturned as unconstitutional.

The results of this social experiment will not be in for many years to come, of course, but its seriousness and ingenuity cannot be doubted. Still, one can observe that during the initial years, when CAW was based strictly on a science-fictional theology, it hovered on the edge of existence. Then, in about 1970, Zell and the other members of the group ran into Bobbie Kennedy, Carolyn Clark, and perhaps a few other Gardnerian-style witches as well. They began learning the Craft system, being initiated as witches, and combining the theology of Wicca with Heinlein's libertarian philosophy; the resulting synergism catapulted the Nest's newsletter, *Green Egg*, into national prominence as the major communication channel for the neopagan movement between about 1971 and 1976. CAW's spiritual pathway is organized into nine circles, which are subdivided into three rings. The first ring is of laypersons, the second ring is of scions (who are somewhat parallel to deacons), and the third ring is of the ordained clergy.

CAW and its journal *Green Egg* continued to be a major force in the neopagan movement until 1976, when Zell and his new wife, Morning Glory, moved to northern California, leaving administration and magazine editing in the hands of others. CAW became virtually moribund within a few months. However, several subsidiary or affiliated organizations (including Nemeton, Forever Forests, and several neopagan covens) kept going during the late 1970s and early 1980s. In 1978, CAW merged with Nemeton, which had been founded by Alison Harlow and Thomas

DeLong, on whose land the Zells were living, and Nemeton became the publishing arm of CAW. In 1987, five years after DeLong's death, CAW, which had inherited his land, also absorbed Forever Forests, which had been overseen by several stewards, including Anodea Judith.

In 1988, with desktop publishing changing publishing realities, Zell decided to revive *Green Egg*, whose niche in the neopagan scene had never been filled by any of the hundreds of periodicals that had come and gone over the intervening year. This was a timely move: the magazine began growing rapidly; as a result, CAW has reemerged as a major force in the neopagan movement, and *Green Egg*, under the aggressive editorship of Diana Darling, has become one of the major national neopagan journals. The available membership statistics confirm the existence of this pattern. In 1988, CAW reported one hundred members in six "nests" (local chapters). In 1993, membership was around five hundred dues-paying members nationally, in several dozen nests and protonests.

The church is governed by a board of directors elected by the general membership at CAW's annual meeting. The scions elect a special representative, and the presidency must be held by a member of CAW's ordained clergy, which numbered ten persons in 1994. The presidency has been held in recent years by Anodea Judith and by Tom Williams. There is an uneasy balance between the secular aspects of the organization and the processes that lead to ordination of clergy; much thought is going into finding creative ways to resolve this tension.

**CIRCLE.** Circle was founded in 1974 by Selena Fox and Jim Alan in Madison, Wisconsin. The central concept, logo, and name were received in meditation by Fox. Shortly thereafter, she and Alan began to host informal gatherings of people interested in Wicca, magic, and mysticism at their home in Madison. Fox and Alan moved to a farm near Sun Prairie, Wisconsin, which they named Circle Farm in June 1975. Circle Farm became the meeting place of the Circle's first coven and later for its first community, which included several covens. In 1977 they published a songbook and a tape of their spiritual music. Through their writings and music, Fox and Alan began to meet and correspond with pagans around the United States and in Great Britain. Fox founded Circle Network in 1977. In 1978 Fox began to devote herself full time to the Circle ministry which was incorporated as the Church of Circle Wicca. In May 1979, Fox compiled a networking directory and source book which contributed to the growth of the pagan movement. The Church of Circle Wicca began to get national media attention.

In November 1979 Fox and Alan were evicted from their farm near Sun Prairie because of their religion. Circle moved first to a farm near Middleton, Wisconsin, and then to a farm outside of Black Earth. Circle began publishing *Circle Network News*, a quarterly newspaper, in 1980. In 1983 Circle Sanctuary Nature Preserve was purchased near Barneveld, Wisconsin, and Circle changed it corporate name to Circle Sanctuary. The preserve includes an indoor temple, outdoor ritual sites and meditation places, a stone circle, and outdoor shrines. In 1985, Circle expanded its Wiccan-pagan religious freedom work through its leadership in a nationwide action. In 1988, after a two-year legal battle, Circle Sanctuary won local zoning as a church. It began to be listed alongside churches of other faiths in the worship directory of Madison area newspapers. In 1991, Circle began its School for Ministers, a leadership training program for women and men, which includes teaching by priestesses and priests from a variety of pagan groups affiliated with Circle Network.

The doctrine of Circle is a synthesis of Wiccan spirituality, nature mysticism, multicultural shamanism, and humanistic and transpersonal psychology. The faith emphasizes communion with the divine in nature and honoring the goddess as Mother Earth. Rituals involve elements of ecofeminism, animism, shamanic healing, and Native American land spirit wisdom. Circle characterizes its spiritual focus as "Nature Spirituality," a term coined by Selena Fox in 1981. Circle states its purpose as encouraging the growth and well-being of nature spirituality.

Circle has become one of the most visible and public centers for witchcraft and neopaganism in the United States. Selena Fox is frequently called upon by the media, government, and other churches to represent and speak for the larger neopagan community.

Circle is currently headed by Selena Fox and her husband, Dennis Carpenter, who function as high priestess and priest respectively. Both are professionally trained psychotherapists. Fox does spiritual healing and counseling and heads the School for Priestesses, a ministerial training program for women in Goddess-oriented spirituality. Carpenter concentrates on scholarly research and writing.

**SUSAN B. ANTHONY COVEN.** After what she has called a lifetime of preparation, Zsusanna Budapest in 1971 collected six friends and began holding sabbats for women only in Los Angeles. A coven was born on the winter solstice 1971, named the Susan B. Anthony Coven, after the leader of the women's suffrage movement.

Word-of-mouth quickly drew more participants, and the expanding group was moved to the beach, a location that drew too many onlookers, and then to a mountaintop in Malibu. For ten years, Budapest led sabbats and full-moon circles, initiating priestesses and teaching women to bless each other and connect with the goddess through Mother Nature. One of Budapest's pupils was Starhawk. In addition, Budapest opened a shop, the Feminist Wicca, in Venice, and self-published a book that became a basic text of Dianic Wicca, *The Feminist Book of Light and Shadows*, which is based on the parts of the Gardnerian *Book of Shadows* that were publicly available by 1971; it rewrites them to eliminate all mention of males, both mortal and immortal, and then adds some other rituals, spells, and lore. The book was later expanded published as the two-volume *The Holy Book of Women's Mysteries.*

During the 1970s, the Dianic Wicca movement grew to be a major force both in witchcraft and feminism. Cerridwen Fallingstar, now known as a novelist, was a member of Susan B. Anthony #1. The very concept of a form of witchcraft that was for women only was controversial in the Craft movement, and was strongly rejected by many conservative Gardnerians. The issue is no longer controversial in any way.

By 1976 the core of the Susan B. Anthony Coven consisted of twenty to forty women; up to three hundred participated in some of the activities. Related covens were formed in at least five other states. In the early 1980s, Budapest closed her shop, turned the Susan B. Anthony Coven over to another leader, and moved to Oakland, where she formed a new coven, the Laughing Goddess. When the original Susan B. Anthony Coven disbanded in Los Angeles, she formed a new one of that name in Oakland.

**SATANISM.** Satanism, the worship of the Chistian devil, has traditionally been associated with a number of practices which parody Roman Catholic Christianity. Among its rituals is the black mass, which usually includes the profaning of the central acts of worship, the repeating of the Lord's Prayer backwards, the use of a host which has been dyed black, the slaughter of an animal, and so forth. The worship usually culminates with the invocation of Satan for the working of malevolent magic.

Satanism, as described above, appeared in the fifteenth century, when its practitioners became subject to the Inquisition's action. The first well-documented case of a devil-worshipping group refers to the courtiers around Louis XIV, who used black magic in the attempt to remain in favor with the king. The governmemt was almost brought down when the practice was discovered.

Although Satanist groups were quite rare prior to the 1960s, Satanism has provided a rich variety of imaginative material for novels and horror movies. Among the most famous are those by British novelist Dennis Wheatley, who developed the theme of an ancient worldwide secret and powerful Satanic society which regularly gathered its conspiratorial forces to attack the structures of order and goodness. However, such novels do not reflect an existing social phenomenon; no large organized Satanist movement or group exists, as an examination of all evidence shows.

Although Satanists produced almost no literature prior to the 1970s, their tradition was created and sustained by generation after generation of anti-Satanist writers, above all conservative Christians, who authored a

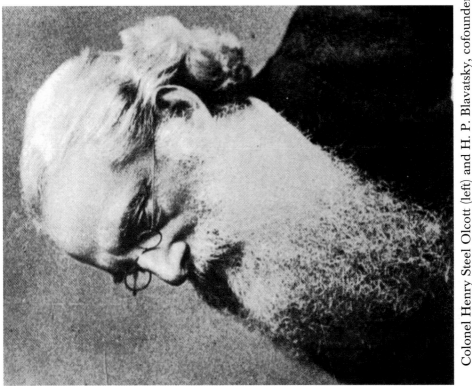

Colonel Henry Steel Olcott (left) and H. P. Blavatsky, cofounders of the Theosophical Society. (*Courtesy American Religion Collection*)

Annie Besant, influential theosophist who led the Theosophical Society after Blavatsky's death. (*Courtesy American Religion Collection*)

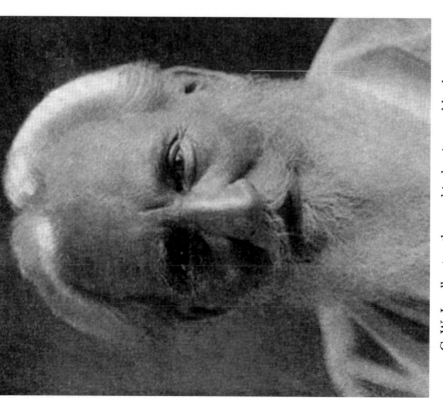

C. W. Leadbeater, theosophical writer and leader. (*Courtesy American Religion Collection*)

Rudolf Steiner, founder of the Anthroposophical Society.
*(Courtesy American Religion Collection)*

William Q. Judge, founder of the Theosophical Society in
America. *(Courtesy American Religion Collection)*

Mark Prophet, founder of Church Universal Triumphant. (*Courtesy Church Universal and Triumphant*)

Elizabeth Clare Prophet, long-time leader of Church Universal Triumphant. (*Courtesy Church Universal and Triumphant*)

Yvonne Frost (left) and Gavin Frost, cofounders of the Church and School of Wicca. (*Courtesy Church and School of Wicca*)

J. Z. Knight, channeling Ramtha. It is a convention among Rathma students that when Knight wears a cap, her personality is being overshadowed by the spirit of Ramtha. (*Courtesy J. Z. Knight*)

Rael, founder of the Raelian Movement. (*Courtesy Raelian Movement*)

Cosmic Space Cadillac at the future landing site for the "vehicles of light." Unarius purchased sixty-seven acres to serve as a landing site for the Space Brothers, who will initiate a new golden age in 2001. (*Courtesy Unarius Academy of Science*)

Chen Tao leaders announcing God's return in a UFO (Garland, Texas).
(*Courtesy Ryan J. Cook*)

L. Ron Hubbard, founder of the Church of Scientology.
*(Courtesy Church of Scientology)*

Dianetics counseling, one of the core techniques of Scientology, uses an E-meter as
part of the procedure of "auditing." (*Courtesy Church of Scientology*)

number of books about Satanism, describing its practices in great detail, although none had ever seen a Satanist ritual or met a real Satanist. The Satanism portrayed in the Christian literature has been reproduced by groups and individuals over the last two centuries.

An increase in the number of ritual remains found in graveyards, church break-ins, and vandalism, and mutilated bodies of animals has been reported since the early 1970s, showing a rise of Satanic activities. During the 1980s, the emphasis shifted to the New Satanism and the emergence of the accounts by several hundred women who claimed to have been survivors of Satanic ritual abuse.

The forms of Satanism characterizing the 1990s include a traditional Satanism consisting of ephemeral groups of teenagers and young adults; a new form of Satanism was initiated by Anton LaVey and developed in various directions by the several groups which split off from his Church of Satan. The Church of Satan originated from an attempt to reorganize modern occult and magical teachings around a Satanic motif. The church preaches a philosophy of individual pragmatism and hedonism, rather than emphasizing the worship of Satan. It promotes the development of strong individuals who seek gratification out of life, and practice the selfish virtues as long as they do not harm others.

All of the formal trappings of an organized religion were given to the movement by its founder, Anton LaVey (1930–1997), who began to read occult books as a teenager. He developed a deep fascination for real magic, such as the practice of creating change in the world through the use of cosmic powers controlled by the individual's will. He worked in the circus, and in the 1960s he began to hold informal meetings on magic. Finally, on April 30, 1966, he announced the formation of the Church of Satan, with some members of the magic groups among his first members.

In 1967 the church received the attention of the media, when LaVey performed the first Satanic wedding and a funeral for a sailor. Membership grew rapidly, though the active membership was rarely over one thousand. In 1969 LaVey published the first of three books, *The Satanic Bible*, containing the perspective of the Church of Satan. It was followed by *The Compleat Witch* (1970) and *The Satanic Rituals* (1972). He also began to work as a consultant for the movie industry, becoming the occult advisor on several films, such as *Rosemary's Baby*, in which he appears briefly as the Devil.

The most important date on the Church of Satan calendar is an individual's birthday. By the 1970s, the Church of Satan had a national membership and groups in many cities around the United States. At one time it was considered the largest occult organization in America. However, it always counted its active membership in the hundreds. The *Cloven Hoof*, edited by LaVey, was the newsletter of the church.

The Church of Satan was a rich source of splinter groups. In 1973 the

Church of Satanic Brotherhood was formed by group leaders in Michigan, Ohio, and Florida. The church lasted only until 1974, when one of the founders announced his conversion to Christianity in a dramatic incident staged for the press in St. Petersburg. Other members of the Church of Satan in Kentucky and Indiana left to form the Ordo Templi Satanis, also short lived.

As more schisms occured, LaVey disbanded the remaining grottos, the local units of the Church of Satan, and decided to reorganize the church as a fellowship of individuals. The active membership has not grown beyond the level reached in the 1970s. There are many presently existing groups which derive from the Church of Satan, the most important of which are the Temple of Set, the Church of Satanic Liberation founded in 1986 by Paul Douglas Valentine, and the Temple of Nepthys founded in the late 1980s.

At the present time, the most active group of organized Satanists is the Temple of Set. The Temple was established by Michael A. Aquino, a Magister Templi with the Church of Satan, and Lilith Sinclair, head of the largest of the grottos, in Spottswood, New Jersey. The Temple of Set is a group dedicated to the ancient Egyptian deity believed to have become the model for the Christian Satan. The group affirms that Satan is a real being.

In 1975 Aquino (b. 1946) invoked Satan to receive a new mandate for continuing the Church of Satan apart from LaVey. According to Aquino, Satan appeared to him as Set, giving him the content of a book, *The Book of Coming Forth by Night.* Aquino holds a Ph.D. from the University of California at Santa Barbara and is a lieutenant colonel in the U.S. Army.

The main purpose of the temple is to awaken the divine power of the individual through the deliberate exercise of will and intelligence. Its members believe that over the centuries Set has manipulated human evolution in order to create a new species possessing a nonnatural intelligence. Its program is directed to an intellectual elite, which is supposed to undertake the reading of a lenghty list of required material.

The temple, which includes approximately five hundred members in North America and some additional members in Europe, is headed by a Council of Nine which appoints a High Priest of Set and an executive director. Aquino became well known as a Satanist and the subject of a variety of media coverage by the end of the 1970s. In 1987 to 1988 he was briefly charged with sexually molesting a young girl at the army base in San Francisco, but was later exonerated of all charges.

**SHAMANISM.** Shamans are the religious specialists of hunter and gatherer cultures. They are particularly associated with the aboriginal peoples of central Asia and the Americas, and are perhaps most familiar as the "medicine men" of traditional Native American cultures. Contemporary neopagan witches often associate themselves with shamanism, identifying contemporary witchcraft as the lineal descendant of pre-Christian European shamans.

Although the terms *shaman* and *shamanism* have come to be used quite loosely, in the disciplines of anthropology and comparative religion shamanism refers to a fairly specific set of ideas and practices that can be found in many, but not all, world cultures. Characteristically, the shaman is a healer, a psychopomp (someone who guides the souls of the dead to their home in the afterlife), and more generally a mediator between her or his community and the world of spirits (most often animal spirits and the spirits of the forces of nature).

For smaller-scale societies, especially for hunting and gathering groups, shamans perform all of the functions that doctors, priests, and therapists (and sometimes mystics and artists as well) perform in contemporary Western societies. The religious specialists of traditional American Indian societies that people sometimes refer to as "medicine men" are examples of shamans. True shamans are more characteristic of hunting societies than pastoral or farming societies, although one can often find segments of the shamanic pattern in nonhunting cultures. Shamanism in the strict sense is not found in certain culture areas, such as in Africa, although there are religious specialists that fill the same "slot" in traditional African societies.

As a system, shamanism frequently emphasizes contact and communication with spirits in the other world, healing practices in which the shamans search for lost souls of the living, and rituals in which shamans guide the spirits of the deceased to the realm of the dead. Shamanism thus has certain parallels with spiritualism. The word "shaman" comes from the Tungusic term for this religious specialist, *saman*. The term was originally coined by an earlier generation of scholars who were studying societies in Siberia and Central Asia, and was later extended to similar religious complexes found elsewhere in the world. Depending on how one interprets the archeological evidence, shamanism is many thousands of years old.

Within the past decade or so, shamanism has become somewhat of a fad in the West's occult-metaphysical subculture due to the recent development of interest in American Indian religions. While there is a long tradition romanticizing Native Americans and their spiritual traditions, Anglos have rarely been prompted to engage in actual Indian religious practices. This changed in the 1960s when certain groups of counter-culturists made an effort to adopt what they conceived of as "tribal" lifestyles. In the late 1980s, the occult-metaphysical subculture began focussing attention on Native American religion when shamanism—and, more particularly, the phenomenon which has come to be known as "neoshamanism"—became popular.

Neoshamanism has clearly impacted certain aspects of modern neopagans. For example, some neopagans have reconceptualized the idea of familiars in the light of neoshamanic thinkings about "power animals" (the anthropological concept of "totems"). In terms of this line of interpretation, the witch's familiar—which can be imaginal, in that one need not actually keep a living animal around as a kind of pet—embodies certain traits and powers which one taps by asking for help from a specific animal in one's imagination.

# 16 CHRISTIAN SCIENCE AND THE NEW THOUGHT TRADITION

## CHRISTIAN SCIENCE

Popularly known as Christian Science, the First Church of Christ, Scientist, has been one of the most important of the nonconventional religions in America because of its influential espousal of spiritual healing and its affirmation that Christian Science is incompatible with reliance upon *materia medica*.

The Church of Christ, Scientist, was founded in Lynn, Massachusetts, in 1879 by Mary Baker Eddy (1821–1910). She had always been troubled with poor health, which worsened during the 1860s. She tried a number of different alternative treatments, until she finally placed herself under the care of Dr. Phineas Parkhurst Quimby, a mental healer in Portland, Maine. She soon experienced some relief, and became his student. However, she was periodically disturbed by the return of her illness, and by the conflicts between his ideas and those she found in the Bible.

Shortly after Quimby's death in 1866, she was severely injured in a fall on icy pavement. While a doctor and friends feared for her life, she asked for her Bible. Reading the account of one of Jesus' healings, she was immediately restored to health. This marked the beginning of the discovery of Christian Science and the abandonment of Quimby's mental and magnetic teachings. She claimed that there was no healing agent, either magnetic force or mind, other than God, and that God was the only life, which was the only reality of being. In the next few years she began teaching and writing her first book, *The Science of Man*, and the presentation of her teaching, entitled *Science and Health with Key to the Scriptures* (the first edition appeared in 1875).

The Christian Scientist Association, a fellowship of her personal students, was formed in 1876 and three years later the Church of Christ, Scientist, was organized. In 1881 she was ordained as pastor of the church, in 1883 the first issue of the *Journal of Christian Science* appeared, and in 1886 the National Christian Scientists Association was established. However, Eddy soon began to doubt the soundness of the structures she had created, and in 1889 she dissolved the church, the college, and the Christian Scientist Association. The church was restored in 1892.

In 1882, two former students of Quimby, Julius and Annetta Dresser, with former Eddy student Edward Arens, began teaching mental healing in Boston, following a combination of Quimby's and Eddy's teachings. Arens was accused of plagiarizing some of Eddy's writings, and was defended by Julius Dresser, who accused Eddy of plagiarizing Quimby's ideas and of distorting Quimby's teachings. This case began a long controversy between Christian Science and New Thought, which was developed in the late 1880s by Emma Curtis Hopkins, one of Eddy's former students.

Eddy spent the rest of her life clarifying her understanding of Christian Science. Her books, *Science and Health with Key to the Scriptures* and the *Church Manual*, which contain her work and insights, are regarded as authoritative documents for the church. At her death, leadership passed to the five-person board of directors of the Mother Church in Boston, Massachusetts.

The beliefs of Christian Science are contained in the authorized edition of *Science and Health with Key to the Scriptures*. Christian Scientists accept the Bible as their guide to eternal life. They believe in God, in the Christ, in the Holy Ghost, and in human beings' true identity as the image and likeness of God. They believe in God's forgiveness of sin through the destruction of belief in sin. They believe that Jesus' atonement illustrated humanity's unity with God, and that his crucifixion and resurrection demonstrated the power of God, Spirit, and the nothingness of matter.

Christian Science departs from orthodox Christianity in that it teaches what it terms the "allness of God" and hence the unreality of disease, sin, and death. Christ does not defeat evil, but demonstrates its lack of reality beyond our belief in it. The impersonal aspect of God as Principle, Mind, Life, Truth, and Love is emphasized by Christian Science. The church also distinguishes between the man Jesus and the eternal spiritual selfhood, Christ, Son of God, which is regarded as having been expressed most fully by Jesus. Throughout the centuries, spiritually minded individuals have expressed the Christ idea to a lesser degree.

The church's healing activity most concretely represents its beliefs and practices. Healing is regarded as one of the natural by-products of growing closer to God. The *Christian Science Journal* includes a directory of Christian

Science practitioners—individuals who devote their full time to the public practice of spiritual healing through prayer. The *Journal* also lists Christian Science nurses who give nonmedical nursing care either in the home or in independently owned Christian Science nursing facilities.

Although the authority for the theology of Christian Science is derived from the Bible, the authority for the government of the church organization is the *Church Manual* by Mary Baker Eddy and is vested in the Christian Science board of directors. The board has direct oversight of the mother church, the various church agencies, teachers, lecturers, and practitioners. It does not have direct oversight over the congregations.

Headquarters of the Church of Christ, Scientist, is located at the Christian Science Church Center, in Boston's Back Bay, where the Publishing Society is also located. Among the several periodicals published by the Church are the *Christian Science Journal,* the *Christian Science Sentinel,* the *Christian Science Quarterly,* and the *Herald of Christian Science.* The *Christian Science Monitor* represents the church's prominent newspaper. A Board of Lectureship provides free lectures on Christian Science worldwide. In the 1997–1998 lecture year, sixty-five members were serving on the Board of Lectureship. The Church has approximately 2,300 branches and societies in some 70 countries around the world. Membership figures are not published.

Christian Science has been attacked since the beginning. Critics of Christian Science have frequently adopted the Dresser perspective, which sees it as merely an extreme and somewhat distorted form of a movement begun in the middle of the nineteenth century by Quimby. However, the major challenges to Christian Science came from a medical profession that, at the time of the founding of the Church, was just consolidating its position as the normative authority in the treatment of illness in the United States. Numerous court cases were fought over the rights of Christian Scientists to refrain from the use of doctors and the rights of Christian Science practitioners to treat the sick.

The medical attacks have had inconclusive results. Church periodicals report the accounts of people, many unhelped by visits to doctors, who found health through Christian Science. However, during the past thirty years, there have been several highly publicized cases of criminal prosecutions of Christian Science parents whose children have died while receiving Christian Science treatment through prayer instead of medical treatment. Such cases forced judge and jury to consider as possibly criminal the behavior of loving parents who held deep religious beliefs. In the Sheridan case, which arose in Massachusetts in 1967, a mother was convicted of manslaughter for failing to provide "proper physical care" for her daughter because the child had received Christian Science treatment instead of medical treatment and subsequently died.

In the 1980s, seven child deaths under Christian Science treatment resulted in the prosecutions of Christian Scientist parents. Of these, three occurred in California and one each in Massachusetts, Minnesota, Arizona, and Florida. Although in most of these cases parents were convicted of crimes ranging from manslaughter to child endangerment, almost all of the convictions have been subsequently overturned by the courts.

Christian Science has often been accused of heresy by some orthodox Christian churches. Others see it as outside the mainstream of Christian denominations or as a minority religion. How it is described depends upon the religious viewpoint of the observer. Several groups of former Christian Scientists still exist and continue to actively criticize the church. A network of independent Christian Science practitioners has always existed, and its first generation created the New Thought movement. Independents such as the United Christian Scientists, whose headquarters is in San Jose, California, and the independent Christian Science Church in Plainfield, New Jersey, were active in their opposition to the Church of Christ, Scientist, in the 1970s and 1980s.

## NEW THOUGHT

New Thought is not so much a religion as a type of teaching which has influenced a number of groups. It includes such churches as the Church of Religious Science, the Church of Divine Science, and Unity. Major New Thought writers include Phineas Quimby (*Immanuel*), Ralph Waldo Trine (*In Tune with the Infinite*), Horatio Dresser (*A History of the New Thought Movement, Spiritual Health and Healing, The Quimby Manuscripts*), and Ernest Holmes (*Creative Mind, The Science of Mind*). Belief in the supreme reality and power of mind is fundamental to New Thought.

Like Theosophy, New Thought holds the inner reality of the universe to be mind and idea. However, it differs from Theosophy in that it does not point to masters as the minds which make things happen, but to the mental potential of every individual. New Thought teachers strive to show how thoughts of health, wholeness, and success can create their corresponding material realities.

The "mind cure" movement of Phineas Parkhurst Quimby (1802–1866) of Belfast, Maine, set down roots which would later evolve into New Thought. Quimby had been exposed to hypnosis at a lecture-demonstration by mesmerist Dr. Collyer in 1838. He began to experiment with mesmerism. One of Quimby's subjects would, while hypnotized, frequently diagnose and prescribe for illnesses of people brought before him. Quimby noted on several occasions that people were healed by taking a prescribed medicine that had no real medicinal value. He began to believe that sickness was the result of erroneous thinking and that a cure would consist of changing one's belief system. He eventually dropped hypnosis as a therapeutic tool and began speaking directly with the patient about linking the individual's spiritual nature with divine spirit. Quimby felt that priests and doctors were benefactors of human misery who had wicked and unethical holds on the minds of people. Rather than healers, he considered priests and doctors to be the major sources of error and therefore the major sources of illness. Quimby's students included Warren Felt Evans, Annetta and Julius Dresser, and Mary Baker Eddy, all of whom influenced the New Thought movement.

Warren Felt Evans (1817–1887) had been a devotee of Emanuel Swedenborg. Evans was a former Methodist minister who forsook his Methodist training and became a minister in the church of the New Jerusalem. In 1863 Evans became a client of Phineas P. Quimby and was healed by Quimby's methods. After Quimby's death, Evans moved to a Boston suburb and opened a healing practice. Evans brought his Swedenborgian thinking to his practice. He wrote prolifically from 1869 onward about spiritual healing methods. Evans stressed that disease is a result of a disturbance in the human spiritual body which adversely affects the physical body.

As noted earlier, Quimby also exercised considerable influence over Mary Baker Eddy, founder of Christian Science. Christian Science, in turn, helped shape the New Thought movement.

On October 23, 1881, eight students resigned from the Christian Scientist Association, among them Elizabeth Stuart. Stuart continued to practice what she had been taught throughout New England and is most remembered as the teacher of some of the most prominent of the New Thought leaders, including Charles Brodie Patterson, who influenced the founders of the Christ Truth League.

In 1885, Mary Baker Eddy excommunicated Emma Curtis Hopkins, who then went on to found the New Thought Movement. Hopkins had studied with Mary Baker Eddy and had edited the *Christian Science Journal* in 1884 and 1885. After her break with Eddy, Hopkins founded the Emma Curtis Hopkins College of Christian Science in 1886.

In the mid-1880s there was an array of healers in some manner related to Christian Science throughout the United States. Many of them interacted with other nonconventional healers such as spiritualists, theosophists, and Christian healers. As word about her work spread, students began to travel to Chicago to study with her and she began to travel to other places to teach. By the end of 1887 she was organizing the independent Christian Science practitioners and her students into associated centers across the country.

In 1888 she transformed her Emma Hopkins College of Metaphysical Science into the Christian Science Theological Seminary and offered advanced training for students planning to enter the Christian Science ministry. (This had never been possible within the Church of Christ, Scientist because Eddy was the only person ordained, and since her death the church has been led by lay people.) In January 1889 Hopkins held the first graduation ceremonies from the seminary and, assuming the office of bishop, she became the first woman to ordain others to the ministry in modern times. Her first graduating class consisted of twenty women and two men, both of whom were husbands of other members of the graduating class. Hopkins had added an innovation to Christian Science in the form of the identification of the Holy Spirit as female, an idea which was originated by Joachim of Flore (1145–1202). After ordaining her students, she sent them to create new churches and ministries throughout the country.

In 1895, after ordaining more than one hundred ministers, Hopkins retired, closed the seminary and moved to New York City. She spent the rest of her life teaching students on a one-on-one basis.

As Hopkins's students established their own centers, they began to differentiate themselves from Christian Science. Myrtle and Charles Fillmore in Kansas City, Missouri, adopted the name Unity. Melinda Cramer and Nona E. Brooks in Denver named their work Divine Science. Faculty member Helen Van Anderson moved to Boston after the seminary closed and formed the Church of the Higher Life. Annie Rix Militz, another faculty member, established the Homes of Truth on the West Coast. George and Mary Burnell formed the Burnell Foundation in Los Angeles. Albert C. Grier founded the Church of the Truth. Ernest S. Holmes, one of Hopkins's last students, founded the Institute of Religious Science, later called the Church of Religious Science. These were all New Thought churches.

Thomas Troward was a retired judge who developed a second career as a New Thought lecturer. He introduced new psychological concepts into the movement in the early twentieth century. He argued for the differentiation of the mind into its objective (waking consciousness) and its subjective (unconscious) aspects. In doing so he opened the movement to the new concept of the dynamic subconscious, a concept missing from the theology of both Eddy and Hopkins. Ernest S. Holmes would take Troward's main insights and use them in creating Religious Science.

The International New Thought Alliance was formed in 1914. It produced a statement of agreement, which became its first declaration of principles. It affirmed the belief in God as Universal Wisdom, Love, Life, Truth, Power, Peace, Beauty, and Joy; that the universe is the body of God and that the human is an invisible spiritual dweller inhabiting a body, and that human beings continue, grow and change after death. An important feature of the INTA has been its ability to allow individualism among its members.

New Thought distinguishes itself from the Christian Science from which it developed in the following ways:

1. It comes under the leadership of an ordained ministry, although there are many lay teacher-writers.

2. It developed a decentralized movement which celebrates its diversity of opinion.
3. It developed an emphasis on prosperity. New Thought leaders reason that poverty is as unreal as disease and teaches students to live out of the abundance of God.
4. Rather than retaining an exclusively Christian emphasis, the movement as a whole has moved to what it sees as a more universal position that acknowledges all religious traditions as of value.

New Thought, like Christian Science, looks to a manifestation of the truth they teach in the individual's life. That manifestation is usually referred to as demonstration. To move from sickness to health is to demonstrate healing. To move from poverty to wealth is to demonstrate abundance. The role of the practitioner is to aid in demonstration. The practitioner is a professional who has been trained in the arts of healing prayer. Each church trains its practitioners in slightly different ways and advocates slightly different techniques by which they are to work, but all New Thought churches provide their membership with the assistance of healing prayer specialists.

**UNITY SCHOOL OF CHRISTIANITY.** The Unity movement, founded in the 1880s, represents the largest of the several metaphysical churches which are generally grouped together under the name New Thought. Two visible aspects of the movement are constituted by the Unity School of Christianity, and the Association of Unity Churches.

The Unity School of Christianity, which was founded in 1887 by Charles S. Fillmore (1854–1948), and his wife Myrtle Fillmore (1845–1931), was among the first organizations to be developed from the movement begun by Emma Curtis Hopkins (1849–1925), the founder of New Thought. Hopkins, who had been student of Mary Baker Eddy, became editor of the *Christian Science Journal* in 1884, and eventually resigned her position in Boston in 1885, because of a disagreement with her teacher. She moved to Chicago, where in 1886 she opened her own office and school, and began teaching her modified version of Christian Science. Many of her students opened centers across the country, and her teachings arrived to Kansas City, Missouri, where the Fillmores lived.

Unity School of Christianity originated in 1886 with the attendance of the Fillmores at a lecture by Eugene Weeks, a student of the Illinois Metaphysical College, headed by independent Christian Scientist George B. Charles, whose words, "I am a child of God and therefore do not inherit sickness," had profoundly affected her. At the time, Myrtle had developed tuberculosis, which forced her to leave Weeks's lecture. However, over a period of months, she recovered through the techniques learned during the lecture, and she soon decided to use her experience to bring health to other people. In 1890 she founded the Society of Silent Help, in order to offer prayer for those in need.

Charles Fillmore, who had been skeptical at first, began to attend the lectures offered by various teachers and slowly accepted the new metaphysical ideas. In 1889, after leaving the real estate business, he decided to devote full time to the pursuit and promulgation of those ideas, and began to publish *Modern Thought,* a magazine devoted to the discussion of all of the new religious impulses emerging in America at the time. Also, he began to lead gatherings of interested students in Kansas City, and to teach some classes for supporters of his magazine, and he opened a lending library of mataphysical books.

When the Fillmores heard of Emma Curtis Hopkins, they arranged her visit to Kansas City, sponsoring her lectures. While in Chicago, where they traveled to take classes at Hopkins's school, they decided upon the name "Unity," and the symbol of the winged sphere for their work. Charles renamed his magazine *Christian Science Thought,* and in 1891 the Fillmores were ordained by Hopkins. At about the same time they published the first issue of a new magazine, *Unity.*

Over the next few years, the Society of Silent Help became Silent Unity, by which name it is known today. Silent Unity had thousands of members, and its publishing activity was placed under the Unity Book Company. A student of Hopkins's in New York City, H. Emilie Cady, began to write for Unity, authoring a series of lessons later reprinted as Lessons in Truth. A children's magazine, *Wee Wisdom,* issued in 1893 and discontinued in 1893, was the oldest children's magazine in America. Another one of Hopkins's students, Annie Rix Militz, began to write a Bible column commenting upon the weekly International Sunday School Lessons, and wrote articles that became important Unity textbooks, *Primary Lessons in Christian Living and Healing,* and *Both Riches and Honor.*

As Unity developed, expanding its organization around the country, the Fillmores instituted a free-will offering plan for those in need. This plan set them apart from many other metaphysical groups, whose practitioners used to charge a fee for their healing assistance work. In 1896, a general meeting of other New Thought groups, which named themselves "Divine Scientists," took place in Kansas City.

In 1905, Charles Fillmore began to publish his own lessons in a magazine which became his first book, *Christian Healing,* and soon afterward he turned to writing a Unity correspondence course. In 1906, the Fillmores and seven other students were ordained as Unity ministers.

In 1914, the Unity Tract Society and Silent Unity were incorporated together as the Unity School of Christianity, and the following year a field department was organized in order to link the school and the teachers and healers around the country, and as a coordinating center for Unity groups. A training school for teachers and preachers developed, as well as the Unity School of Religious Studies, which had formerly been a two week summer intensive course.

The first annual Unity convention was held in 1923, and at the third annual meeting in 1925, a Unity Annual Conference was formed in order to provide some organization for people who used the Unity name, since some teachers had begun to offer students ideas not in agreement with those of the Fillmores. The conference became the Unity Minister's Conference in 1946, and in 1966 it emerged as a separate organization, the Association of Unity Churches, headquartered in nearby Lee's Summit, Missouri. It is now in charge of the training of all Unity ministers, and the servicing of all churches in the United States. Two years after Myrtle's death (1931), Charles married Cora G. Dedrick. He eventually died in 1948.

Unity is considered a noncreedal church whose purpose is helping people to acquire the practical benefits of Christianity. It offers a liberal degree of freedom of belief among its members. Based on prayer and healing, the movement teaches "practical Christianity," a return to the primitive Christianity of Jesus and the Apostles. Its members believe in one God, best understood as Mind, and in Christ, the Son of God, made manifest in Jesus of Nazareth. Humanity is the expression of God. Although Jesus is believed to be divine, divinity is not confined to Jesus, whereas all people are potentially divine, since they all are created in the image of God. Jesus is considered as the great example in the regeneration of each person. He created an "at-one-ment" between God and men who, through Jesus, can regain their estate as sons of God. All of the problems of life, such as sin, sickness, and poverty, can be overcome through the atonement between God and humanity.

Unity accepts the authority of the Bible, even though it follows a metaphysical interpretation offering a somewhat allegorical approach to Scripture. For instance, the Twelve Apostles are regarded as twelve powers in humans which can be used for the salvation of the world, and the kingdom of God is regarded as the harmony within each individual. Unity has dropped traditional rituals and sacraments, even though some rituals have been created to mark special occasions, such as Christmas, and the birth of a baby.

Reincarnation is taught as a step toward immortality. Vegetarianism and chastity are recommended as helpful means to reach physical immortality which, according to Charles Fillmore, can occur through union with Jesus. Fillmore saw a process of purification and spiritualization in various incarnations, which eventually led to a form of perfection allowing for the transformation of the body. Through the possession of a transformed body, the individual would gain eternal life.

The teachings of Unity find their standard presentation in *Lessons in*

*Truth,* and other books written by Charles Fillmore, as well as several recent textbooks, such as *Foundations of Unity,* and *Metaphysics.* An attempt to summarize such teachings was made in what was termed "Unity's Statement of Faith," which remains one of the better succinct presentations of Unity's perspective although it is not in use today.

Among Unity's teachings is what is called prosperity consciousness, a belief according to which just as a relationship with God handles the problems of sin and sickness, so it can handle the problem of poverty, which is a matter of consciousness and success manifesting itself when one realizes that God is all abundance.

Unity emphasizes the form of prayer termed "entering into the silence," beginning in a quiet inwardness and establishment of a state of receptivity, and underlines the use of affirmations, that is the repetition of positive statements affirming the presence of a condition hoped but not yet visible.

Unity's headquarters moved permanently in 1949 to Unity Village, nearby Lee's Summit, Missouri, and it is currently headed by Connie Fillmore, the great-granddaughter of Charles and Myrtle Fillmore. Upon Unity Village are centered the various activities of the Unity School of Christianity, and of the Association of Unity Churches. Located at Unity Village are also Silent Unity, the Unity School for Religious Studies, the Village Chapel, the Unity School Library and Heritage Rooms, Unity Inn, and a publishing concern which produces several publications a year, as well as cassette tapes, and radio and television programs.

Unity's two major magazines are *Unity,* which contains inspirational articles aimed at effective spiritually based living, and *Daily World,* a daily devotional magazine which is now printed in 10 languages and circulated in 153 countries. Although it is part of the largest New Thought movement, Unity has had only nominal relations with it, as well as with the International New Thought Alliance, of which it was a member for a few years.

Unity has established several congregations in every section of the United States. In 1992, the Association of Unity Churches counted approximately 70,000 members, with 547 congregations and 116 study groups in North America, and an additional 55 congregations and 50 study groups in 15 different countries, most being in Europe.

Although Unity has successfully escaped the anticult attacks of the 1970s and 1980s, it has been consistently accused by Evangelical Christians to be a cult and to improperly use Christian words and symbols while interpreting them in an unorthodox manner. An example is often represented by Unity's metaphysical interpretation of the Twenty-third Psalm. Unity has also been charged with denying basic Christian affirmations of the distinction between the Omnipotent God and His creatures, the reality of sin, and the nature of salvation.

A special attack has involved Unity's extensive literature ministry. Since most of the readers of Unity's publications are not directly associated with a Unity congregation, Unity has been accused by Evangelical Christians of infiltration of literature, which is seen as an act of deception because it parades as normal Christian devotional and inspirational material while denying fundamental teachings. Unity has rarely replied to its critics, although in the 1980s it answered charges that Unity was a cult with an article in *Unity* magazine. The charges were eventually dismissed as religious bigotry.

**UNITED CHURCH OF RELIGIOUS SCIENCE.** The metaphysical teaching of Ernest S. Holmes (1887–1960) originated this church in the early 1920s. His education was influenced by Mary Baker Eddy, who founded the Church of Christ, Scientist, and by such thinkers as Christian D. Larson, and Ralph Waldo Emerson.

He moved from the East Coast to California to join his brother in 1912. There he discovered the writings of the New Thought writer Thomas Troward, under whose influence he created the Metaphysical Institute in 1916. He began lecturing, and was ordained by the Divine Science Church in Denver, Colorado. The Metaphysical Institute became affiliated with the International New Thought Alliance (INTA), of which it remains a major supporter.

In 1925 Holmes published his fundamental book *The Science of Mind*, which offers a systematic presentation of Religious Science. The Religious Science and School of Philosophy was founded in 1927 and underwent several reorganizations and a major division in 1953; the present name dates to 1967.

As of 1992 the church numbered about ninety thousand members in five continents. A board of trustees establishes the mission and the activities of the church at the national level; the trustees also choose a president and a chief executive officer, ordain ministers, and charter new churches. Local member churches are granted authority and ownership of their property.

The teachings of the United Church of Religious Science aim at satisfying the aspirations and needs of mankind through tools provided by philosophy, science, and religion. Holmes has developed a particular way of praying called spiritual mind treatment. It is a five-step process that leads the individuals to solve their personal problems through the acceptance of divine reality.

**ADVENTURES IN ENLIGHTENMENT, A FOUNDATION.** Adventures in Enlightenment, a Foundation, was organized in 1985 by Terry Cole-Whitaker, formerly of Terry Cole-Whitaker Ministries. Adventures in Enlightenment is a spiritual educational organization dedicated to the study, development and implementation of methods by which people can live and work in harmony with mutual respect, freedom and creativity.

Terry Cole-Whitaker was ordained as a minister of the United Church of Religious Science in 1975. She became the pastor of the La Jolla, California, congregation of that church in 1977. This church's membership grew significantly under her leadership, and in 1979 she began a television show which at its peak was shown on fifteen stations nationwide. In 1982, Cole-Whitaker left the United Church of Religious Science and organized Terry Cole-Whitaker Ministries, an independent church, in San Diego, California. Cole-Whitaker drew an attendance of more than four thousand to her Sunday services and traveled widely as a lecturer and workshop leader. In 1985, Cole-Whitaker disbanded her church and stopped the television show due to financial difficulties. It was at this time that she established Adventures in Enlightenment, a Foundation.

# 17 SPIRITUALISM AND CHANNELING

## SPIRITUALISM

**S**piritualism is usually referred to as a religious movement emphasizing the belief in survival after death, a belief spiritualists claim
is based upon scientific proof, and upon communication with the surviving personalities of deceased human beings by means of mediumship.

The continuity of the personality after death through a new birth into a
spiritual body (not a new physical body) represents the central important
tenet of spiritualism. According to spiritualists, at death the soul, which is
composed of a sort of subtle matter, withdraws itself and remains near the
earth plane for a longer or shorter period of time. After this, it advances in
knowledge and moral qualities and proceeds to higher planes, until it eventually reaches the sphere of pure spirit. The rapidity at which the soul advances is in direct proportion to the mental and moral faculties acquired in
earth life. Spiritualists originally conceived of planes as spheres encircling the
earth, one above the other, whereas now they are more commonly supposed
to interpenetrate each other and to coexist at different rates of vibration.

Bliss, hell, and eternal damnation are not part of spiritualist belief, nor
are the last judgment and the resurrection of the physical body. Communication with the dead, through the agency of mediums, represents the
other central belief of spiritualism. Spirits contacted by mediums are traditionally asked first of all to prove their identities by giving correct information about their earthly lives and concerns. Spiritualism is regarded by
its adherents as a religion based on a science, combining elements from

other religions and creeds. Sir Arthur Conan Doyle wrote that "spiritualism is a religion for those who find themselves outside all religions; while on the contrary it greatly strengthens the faith of those who already possess religious beliefs."

The phenomena of spiritualism fall into three main groups, which include physical mediumship, spiritual healing, and mental mediumship. Among the physical phenomena are acoustic phenomena, such as raps and blows; apports, passing of matter through matter, transportation of the human body; chemical phenomena such as psychic photography; electric and magnetic phenomena; fire immunity; levitation of the human body and materialization; telekinesis, the movement of objects without contact; psycho-physiological phenomena such as elongation, transfiguration, stigmata, trance, ectoplasm, aura, and emanations; thermodynamic effects, such as psychic winds.

Spiritual healing includes contact healing, which is a laying on of hands, and absent healing, in which the medium, working with spirit doctors, has no direct contact with the patient and effects healing at a distance. Mental phenomena include clairvoyance, clairaudience, crystal gazing, divination, premonition, monition, dowsing, healing, personation, psychometry, trance speaking, telepathy, and xenoglossis. Many of these phenomena have been explained as the result of unknown mental processes of the medium, although the more common interpretation involves the role of an extraneous factor, which can be the will of some other, living person, a disembodied human consciousness (a spirit), or something unknown of nonhuman origin.

The most obvious explanation and the one with the greatest appeal is the spirit hypothesis. This theory has been adopted by many well-known, nonspiritualist psychical researchers, according to whom a human spirit which has survived death is able to cause such phenomena. Both spiritualist and alternative explanations must deal with the validation of paranormal phenomena, as the history of mediumship has too often been plagued by fraud and tricks by fake mediums.

The belief in the possibility of communication with the spirit world has been held in most of the societies of which we have records. Spiritualism has many parallels and predecessors among so-called primitive people, in the miracles of world religions, and in the phenomena associated with witchcraft, poltergeist activity, and possession. These manifestations were not always associated with the spirits of deceased people, but they were traditionally associated with angelic or diabolic possession, most frequently with the latter.

In ancient times, mediumship was the craft of oracles, seers, shamans, and prophets—that is, of those individuals who were the intermediaries between this world and the spirit realm. Ancient Egyptian priests and priestesses, Chinese emperors, Shinto shamans, Greek oracles, and the founders of many major religions claimed to have communicated with disembodied souls and to have received instructions from them. Among the best known mediums in recorded history is the oracle of Delphi, in Greece, where people would travel to seek advice from the god Apollo, who was believed to communicate through the medium Pythia. Contact with the spirit world became suspect with the rise of monotheism, which admitted only communication from the one God through prophets. The New Testament also contains many accounts of glossolalia, visions, apparitions, and disembodied voices.

The significance of the doctrine of Animal Magnetism, described in Franz Antoine Mesmer's *De Planetarum Influxu* in 1766, was very considerable from the Spiritualist point of view. Mesmerism, with Swedenborgianism, began in Europe in the late eighteenth century, and was later exported to the United States. Its transition to spiritualism was effected by Andrew Jackson Davis, a student of Swedenborg who practiced the psychic diagnosis of illness. Davis wrote a number of books, including *The Harmonial Philosophy*, which deals with the origins and nature of the universe and the afterlife.

What is generally regarded as the origin of modern spiritualism, however, took place in America in 1848, when the sisters Maggie and Katie Fox started communicating with spirits through rappings in their house at Hydesville, New York. The Fox sisters discovered that if they clapped their hands, they received a response from a spirit who claimed to have been killed by a former occupant of the house. Their older sister Leah took charge of them, and eventually took them on tour, during which they made money with their increasingly elaborate seances, despite accusations of fraud. At the same time other mediums appeared, inspired by the success of the Fox sisters, and by about the mid-1850s spiritualism had achieved a considerable popularity.

Mediums are usually distinguished as being either mental mediums, whose communications with deceased persons occur by means of extrasensory perception, and physical mediums, who act as channels for physical manifestations initiated by disembodied spirits. Physical mediumship usually involves rappings, table-turning, levitation, the passage of matter through matter, materializations, apports, ghostly music, spirit lights, and strange scents. Mental mediumship, which is claimed to offer the best evidence of survival after death, is characterized by such manifestations as inner visions, clairaudience, and mental "impressions."

Mediumistic sensitivity is often present early in life, although it can begin at any age. Sometimes it is initiated spontaneously following a trauma, a near-death experience, an extreme emotional shock or profound grief. Among mediumistic practices are the diagnosis and cure of diseases, some of which have been pronounced incurable. There is some debate as to whether mediumship is an inborn ability or whether it may be acquired. It is, of course, an open question as to whether or not mediums interact with deceased persons. Most parapsychologists claim that some mediums possess striking psychical abilities, whereas most spiritualists hold the belief that all individuals are mediums, although in varying degrees.

Among the most common physical phenomena were cases of telekinesis, such as those occurred in the presence of the famous medium D. D. Home, while the most common mental phenomena, which had already attained some prominence in the mesmeric movement of the preceding half-century, included that of clairvoyance. Trance mediums, such as Mrs. Gladys Osborne Leonard and Mrs. Leonora E. Piper, would sometimes assert having been in the other world and having spoken with its inhabitants. In other cases the medium's body was purportedly controlled by spirits who, through automatic writing and automatic speaking, gave information about their earthly lives, and transmitted detailed and often lengthy accounts of the next world and its inhabitants. Sometimes they communicated ethical and theological teachings, like those of the British clergyman Reverend W. Stainton Moses, whose *Spirit Teachings* (1883) is considered the bible of Anglo-American spiritualism.

Many publications reputedly authored by spirits through mediums appeared during the later decades of the nineteenth century, such as the 900-page book entitled *Oahspe*, Frederick S. Oliver's *A Dweller on Two Planets*, and Mme Blavatsky's books *Isis Unveiled* and *The Secret Doctrine*. One of the most famous investigations into this area was Frederic Myers's *Human Personality and Its Survival of Bodily Death*, in which the author postulated that cross-correspondences represented a valid proof of the survival of human consciousness after bodily death.

Although a considerable number of people began to discover and practice mediumistic powers, the spiritualist movement soon began to come under attack. It was condemned by official religions, and suffered negative publicity as a result of the many investigations of mediums that exposed frauds. After enjoying a resurgence of popularity during and after World War I, the heyday of mediumship was over by 1920, though interest in spiritualism continued in various parts of the world, such as America, Britain, Brazil, and other countries where spiritualist churches continue to exist.

After 1900, interest in mediumship declined, due to the numerous frauds which were exposed by investigators such as those belonging to the Society for Psychical Research, founded in England in 1882, and the American Society for Psychical Research, established in 1884. A number of physical mediums were caught using stage magic tricks, or impersonating the spirits which they were supposed to be materializing. Fraud also existed in mental mediumship, particularly around the mid-twentieth century, although fraud never explained all of the phenomena.

In Britain spiritualism enjoys a larger following than in the United States, even though its growth was difficult because habit and tradition were more firmly settled, due especially to the great influence of the well-established Church of England. Efforts to organize spiritualist groups began in 1865, and one of the key figures in British spiritualism was the medium Maurice Barbanell, who founded *Psychic News,* a leading spiritualist newspaper. The British National Association of Spiritualists was founded in 1884, and in 1890 Emma Hardinge Britten, founder of the spiritualist journal *Two Worlds,* established the National Federation of Spiritualist Churches, which reorganized in 1901 as the Spiritualist National Union, in order to unite spiritualist churches and promote research on mediumship and healing. In the United States, in response to fraud and other issues within the movement, the National Spiritualist Association of Churches (NSAC) was established in Chicago in 1893.

**NATIONAL SPIRITUALIST ASSOCIATION OF CHURCHES.** The spiritualist phenomenon of the nineteenth century was not immediately one that lent itself to a great deal of structure. After the beginning of the movement with the mediumship of the Fox sisters in 1848, spiritualism spread quickly as individuals discovered their own psychic abilities and became professional mediums, attracting crowds with public exhibitions or giving private sessions. Local spiritualist churches were formed around various leaders, but for many years the only kind of larger organization was that of summer spiritualist camps, held in numerous places throughout the country, which provided a comfortable meeting/training place for both professional and lay spiritualists and a vacationlike atmosphere for proselytizing the public through lectures and demonstrations.

Over time, however, spiritualism came under attack from without with charges of fraud leveled against several mediums. Henry Slade, a famous slate medium (one who received messages on a slate board), was caught in trickery several times, and in 1888 the Fox sisters themselves confessed to fraud. Spiritualism also experienced controversy from within because of differing interpretations of the meaning of spiritualism. In response to these issues, the National Spiritualist Association of Churches (NSAC) was created in 1893 in Chicago, led by two former Unitarian clergy, Harrison D. Barrett and James M. Peebles, and a well-known medium and author, Cora L. Richmond. They put together a structure, presbyterial in form, with various state associations of member congregations and an annual national convention.

The NSAC immediately set about establishing standards for spiritualist ministry and investigating reports of fraud. Even today, with several other spiritualist organizations in existence, the NSAC maintains the highest standards for ordination. The NSAC has also spent a great deal of time and energy on establishing a common statement of spiritualist beliefs. In 1899 it adopted a "Declaration of Principles" with six articles; three other articles were added at a later time. The full nine articles are as follows:

1. We believe in Infinite Intelligence.
2. We believe that the phenomena of Nature, both physical and spiritual, are the expression of Infinite Intelligence.
3. We affirm that a correct understanding of such expression and living in accordance therewith constitute true religion.
4. We affirm that the existence and personal identity of the individual continue after the change called death.
5. We affirm that communication with the so-called dead is a fact, scientifically proven by the phenomena of Spiritualism.
6. We believe that the highest morality is contained in the Golden Rule: "Whatsoever ye would that others should do unto you, do ye also unto them."
7. We affirm the moral responsibility of the individual, and that he makes his own happiness or unhappiness as he obeys or disobeys Nature's physical and spiritual laws.
8. We affirm that the doorway to reformation is never closed against any human soul here or hereafter.
9. We affirm that the precept of Prophecy and Healing contained in the Bible is a divine attribute proven through Mediumship.

The last three articles reflect the later move away from an emphasis on remarkable phenomena and toward an emphasis on philosophical development. Besides these nine articles, the NSAC has also established common definitions of spiritualist terms and practices. The two major definitional controversies of the twentieth century have centered on the questions of whether spiritualists are also Christians and whether spiritualists believe in reincarnation. In 1930 the NSAC specifically condemned belief in reincarnation, but not without repercussions in the form of diminished membership. The controversy over Christian identity has not been as clearcut. Spiritualism in general has historically drawn most of its membership from the Christian denominations, and most spiritualists identify with some form of original Christian practice in the sense that they might say that Jesus was a master medium and spiritualist healer. If, however, they are asked to identify as a Christian in a more traditional sense, in the context of denominations and historic creeds, most spiritualists are reluctant to do so. The NSAC has generally taken the position that spiritualists are not also Christians. Those who wish to identify as Christians have tended to gravitate to other spiritualist organizations.

## CHANNELING MOVEMENT

Channeling is a more recent term for what spiritualists traditionally termed mediumship—an event or process in which an individual "channel" is able to transmit information from a nonordinary source, most often from a nonembodied spirit. The term *channeling* was popularized in UFO circles as the name for psychic communications from "space brothers," and was only later applied to New Age mediums. While some channels retain full consciousness during their transmissions, most of the prominent New Age channels are what spiritualists refer to as trance mediums—mediums who lose consciousness while a disembodied spirit takes over the channel's body and communicates through it. These spirits frequently claim to be spiritually advanced souls whose communications consist of metaphysical teachings. The teaching function of this communication contrasts with traditional, nineteenth-century mediums who were more concerned with transmitting messages from departed relatives and with demonstrating the reality of life after death.

As vehicles for communications from the other world, channels are merely the most recent manifestations of a phenomenon that can be traced back at least as far as archaic shamanism. Ancient shamans mediated the relationship between their communities and the other world, often transmitting messages from the deceased. Modern channels also sometimes view themselves as being in the tradition of ancient prophets, transmitting messages from more elevated sources. Unlike the prophets, however, New Age channels rarely claim to be delivering messages directly from God, nor do they usually rail against the sins of society as did the Hebrew prophets. Most often their communications consist of some form of New Age philosophy, which they explain to their listeners. With respect to this teaching function, contemporary channels can be placed in the tradition of Western Theosophy. Although neither movement would claim them, New Age channels can be understood as representing a blend of spiritualism and Theosophy.

Important precursors to modern channeling were Edgar Cayce, Jane Roberts, and Ruth Montgomery. At the time the New Age became a popular topic in 1987, the most publicized channel was J. Z. Knight. She made frequent media appearances, even channeling for TV audiences, before the general public's interest in the New Age waned. Knight channeled an entity named Ramtha, who claimed to be the spirit of an ancient Atlantean warlord. When channeling Ramtha, Knight appeared to take on a more masculine demeanor, and spoke in an indecipherable accent that many less famous channels imitated. Ramtha taught a variation on New Age philosophy build around standard metaphysical teachings. Channeling began a gradual but steady decline in popularity following the media blitz of the late eighties.

A number of popular new age books have been produced by automatic or inspired writing, including those authored by Ken Carey and Ruth Shick Montgomery. Other than Montgomery's books, the most well-known "channeled" book is probably *A Course in Miracles*, which claims to be the New Age teachings of the historical Jesus. Some channelers are primarily psychics who give private readings to individual clients. Others conduct workshops and lectures for large groups, and have become quite well-known in New Age circles, such as Jach Pursel (Lazaris) and Penny Torres (Mafu).

**ASSOCIATION FOR RESEARCH AND ENLIGHTENMENT (A.R.E.).** The Association for Research and Enlightenment is a nonprofit corporation whose chief mission is to preserve and spread the clairvoyant "readings" of the famed psychic, Edgar Cayce. The organization has become an influential proponent of New Age Spirituality since the early 1970s.

The Association was incorporated in Virginia Beach, Virginia, in 1931 by followers of the "sleeping prophet" Edgar Cayce. Cayce was a native of Kentucky who learned how to put himself in a hypnotic trance and deliver readings that diagnosed the illnesses of people he had never met. These readings also discussed his patients' past lives, karmic problems, and spiritual needs. A secretary was hired to record the readings verbatim, and soon a considerable archive of material had been gathered. The A.R.E. was created to catalogue these readings so that they could be used for medical and psychical research.

Following Cayce's death in 1945, the association nearly disbanded. Under the leadership of Cayce's son, Hugh Lynn Cayce, however, the organization survived this crisis and began to establish itself around the world as a purveyor of esoteric Christianity and psychical research. Cayce made annual lecture tours around the United States, created the Edgar Cayce Foundation to secure his family's legal rights to his father's readings, promoted scientific studies that correlated the readings with psychological and archaeological discoveries, and crafted a self-representation for A.R.E. that stressed its non-religious nature and its compatibility with mainstream Christian values.

The association found ways to attract young counterculture seekers during the late 1960s and began to grow rapidly. Whereas in the early 1960s the organization had supported 2,500 members and 90 study groups, by 1970 this number had grown to 12,000 members and 1,023 study groups. The A.R.E. Press expanded its publication of Cayce-related materials during this period as well, printing nine million books and pamphlets between 1956 and 1974.

During the 1970s the movement began to sponsor workshops and seminars that focused on the theme of a coming New Age (or Aquarian Age) of spiritual illumination. This millenarian theme complemented Cayce's earlier prophecies of cataclysmic earth changes during the late twentieth century. As the decade progressed, A.R.E. wedded itself to the developing New Age movement and became a major promoter of New Age-related health therapies, spiritual practices, and trance-channeling. General membership increased to thirty-two thousand by 1981 and extended to Canada, Western Europe, Australia, and New Zealand.

The A.R.E. also expanded its institutional presence during this period. It reactivated the charter of Atlantic University (a liberal arts school that offered courses and licenses in such fields as meditation, holistic health, dream interpretation, and humanistic psychology) in 1972 and completed the Edgar Cayce Memorial Library in Virginia Beach in 1975. The library became the home of A.R.E.'s large collection of books on psychic phenomena and spiritual growth and the archive of the readings' transcripts. The facility also provided seminar rooms, an auditorium, study areas, and offices for the association's varied educational activities. Over the past decade the association has branched into television and film, health research at major universities, and a huge New Age mail-order business that sells books, tapes, and health products. Hugh Lynn Cayce's son, Charles Cayce, has taken over as president of the A.R.E. and chairman of the Edgar Cayce Foundation. From its beginnings during the Depression, the Association for Research and Enlightenment has developed into a major promoter of New Age psychism and esoterism in the Western world.

The A.R.E. embraces an eclectic variety of teachings and practices. These include meditation, aura cleansing, astrology, numerology, past-life regression, reincarnation, psychic archaeology, creative visualization, and mental healing. The association's study groups use two small books of specialized Cayce readings called *A Search for God*. These readings include teachings on such topics as prayer, healing, faith, and meditation. Members read and discuss these teachings in a small group setting and attempt to implement them in their personal spiritual journeys.

*—Phillip C. Lucas*

**R A M T H A ' S   S C H O O L   O F   E N L I G H T E N M E N T .** Ramtha is a Gnostic esoteric organization founded and headed by J. Z. Knight who channels Ramtha, a spiritual entity believed to have lived on earth approximately thirty-five thousand years ago. Knight was born Judith Darlene Hampton in Roswell, New Mexico, on March 16, 1946. Following high school, she married and became the mother of two, but was soon divorced as her husband's alcoholic and abusive manner became evident. She moved to California where she became a successful businesswoman. Here she also picked up her nickname "J. Z." Feeling some sense of guidance, she eventually settled in the Pacific Northwest where she remarried.

Living in Tacoma, Washington, in 1977, Knight had her first encounter with Ramtha one Sunday afternoon. She and her husband had been playing with pyramids, then a rage within the New Age community, when, without prior warning, Ramtha appeared to the startled housewife as she was working alone in her kitchen. He was almost seven feet in height and his body glowed with a beautiful light. His angelic beauty calmed her initial fear. He told her simply, "I am Ramtha, the Enlightened One. I have come to help you over the ditch." She did not understand, and he continued, "It is the ditch of limitation and fear I will help you over." Ramtha began to speak through her and over the next few years she emerged as a channel. During her channeling, she is in a full trance and Ramtha operates as a second complete personality. Upon awakening, Knight has no memory of what has been said.

Ramtha has described himself as a person born among a group of survivors of ancient Lemuria. He grew up in the despised refugee community of Lemurians at Onai, the port city of Atlatia (more popularly known as Atlantis). He grew to hate the Atlatians, and during his teen years, following his mother's death, he left the city and eventually led a successful revolution. He emerged as a warrior conqueror and after a number of military victories he became a powerful despot. He was attacked by an assassin and was almost killed from a sword plunged into his back.

During his lengthy recovery period he had time to contemplate the unknown god to be found in the life force all around him and wandered what it would be like to be this unknown god. He was led to consider the wind, that powerful unseen force—on-going, free-moving, and without boundaries, limits, or form. After several years of contemplation of the wind, he had an out-of-body experience, his consciousness separating from his body and soaring high in the air from which he could look on the land below. Further concentration on his ideal eventually led to his change and the transformation of his body into a body of light. For a time, he was able to change at will, but eventually he ascended with his transformed body.

Ramtha did not again incarnate into a body, and only in the 1970s did he begin to relate to embodied existence when he started to teach using Knight as his channel. Through her he has told numerous stories of his earthly existence, all of which appear as parables for the guidance of his present students. While his biographical story has been challenged by critics, and there is little confirmatory evidence from mundane historical and archeological studies, students of Ramtha generally accept his account of his earthly life at face value based in large part upon their adoption of his teachings and acceptance of his status as a separate entity now speaking through Knight.

Knight first publicly operated as a channel in November 1978 to a small group in Tacoma, and found an immediate public response. During 1979 she began to travel to gatherings in different parts of the country and allowed Ramtha to speak through her. The number of these events, termed Dialogues, increased dramatically in 1980, and through the early 1980s she expanded the amount of time she could stay in trance. By the mid 1980s she was regularly holding two-day weekend Dialogues drawing from three thousand to seven thousand people.

Ramtha's coming forth occurred concurrently with the development of the New Age movement, and the spread of channeling as one of its major activities. Based in large part on the success of the many-channeled volumes of the entity Seth who spoke through channel Jane Roberts (1929–1984), literally hundreds of channels arose. Knight, among the first of the new generation, was the most prominent, and the books, cassettes, and video-tapes drawn from Ramtha's teachings could be found in metaphysical book-stores across North America. Several celebrities found their way to Ramtha's door, and the size of his audiences jumped after author Jess Stern included a chapter on him in his book *Soul Mates* (1984) and Shirley MacLaine spoken glowingly of Ramtha in her book *Dancing in the Light* (1985). While Ramtha always reminded MacLaine that she already knew all of the answers to her questions, his advice to her to turn down a lucrative offer for a movie and wait for a later film part was notable. The film she later accepted was *Terms of Endearment,* one of her more notable career successes.

Knight enjoyed great success through the mid 1980s, and culminated her first decade as Ramtha's channel in 1987 with the publication of her autobi-ography, *A State of Mind.* While outwardly prosperous, however, she recog-nized the manner in which the format that made Ramtha a New Age super-star was limiting the progress of his work. Through the Dialogues and the resultant books and tapes, he was able to engage students only with ideas, and not with the substance of the work they must do if they were to manifest the mastery of their lives about which Ramtha spoke and which they professed an intense desire to possess. Thus, it was in 1988 that Knight commenced a process of withdrawal from public appearances and made a significant change in direction by founding of Ramtha's School of Enlightenment.

The school, formally initiated in May 1988, would become the place of the students' learning and practice of the spiritual disciplines required if they were to leave behind their limited existence and assume the essential godlike mastery which was their real goal and purpose in life. Knight's ranch in rural Yelm, Washington, became the school's campus, and almost all of the classes have been held in the barn/arena on the ranch originally built as a showplace for Arabian horses.

*Teachings at the School.* Through the mid-1980s, the keystone of Ramtha's message could be summarized as the calling of people to remember their divinity. They grew up living a limited existence having forgotten their origin, but it was possible to manifest the divine unlimited life in the world. At the school, Ramtha expanded the ideas of his early

Dialogues into a systematic theology and developed a program of spiritual disciplines. The theological/philosophical perspective was gnostic and one can see its kinship to the earlier gnosticism of ancient teachers such as Valentinus and Plotinus and its more modern forms in Rosicrucianism, Freemasonry, and Theosophy.

According to Ramtha, what we know as the universe originated in the void, a sea of pure potentiality. It was the nothingness, in which nothing existed, but out of which everything that exists derived. In the timeless past, the void contemplated itself and as a result an original point of consciousness, generally referred to as Point Zero, appeared. Point Zero had one important attribute, momentum, and received from the void one creative thought, "Make of me what you will." The void (potentiality) invited consciousness to actualize the potential. Point Zero then turned inward and contemplated itself and as a result a second point of awareness appeared in the void. Between the two points appeared space and time. In the atmosphere resulting from the separation between the two points a flux emerged filled with particles of energy.

Actually, not only did one new point of awareness emerge, but many new points emerged. And from the particles of energy which existed in the flux between the points, the creation of the universe, the actualizing of the void's potential, began. Existence was characterized by the very high frequency at which points of awareness and the particles of energy vibrated. At some point, also in the primeval past, the points of awareness desired to expand their exploration of the void. To accomplish this goal, they oriented themselves on Point Zero, momentarily merged with it, and then moved further out into the void. That movement led to the formation of a new level of existence characterized by the slowing of the frequency at which the points of awareness, now spoken of as "entities," and the particles of energy which were dragged down to this new level as the entities moved away from Point Zero. In a similar fashion, four additional levels were formed, each characterized by an increasingly slower rate of frequency at which those entities who chose to go exploring at the next level, and the particles of energy pulled along in the process of that level's establishment, moved.

The universe which resulted from the entities following their original directive to "make known the unknown" can be pictured as a triangle (called the triad) with Point Zero at the top. We presently exist at the first level along the bottom, the slowest level of frequency. Above our world, at the second is the astral world, and above that at the third level is the light world. Between the third and fourth level is a significant barrier. The moment of the original movement of entities from the fourth to the third level billions of years ago was identical with what is now termed the Big Bang by contemporary cosmologists. That moment was characterized by energy taking on a polarized quality as light and electricity and of the entities differentiating into male and female. Once some entities ventured to the seventh level, they began the process of creation and evolution which has resulted over the millions of year in our present existence as human beings on planet Earth.

The discussion of the creation of the world, the evolution of humanity, and the analysis of where humanity's present state (largely asleep and forgetful of the origin, purpose, and destiny which has brought it here), constitute the "philosophy" of the school. The adoption of that philosophy is seen as a precondition of the transformation of the individual students into awakened aware masters who can assert their divine identity. But the actual work of making that transformation is accomplished in the practice of the several spiritual disciplines taught at the school. As the student begins his or her work, the triad which pictures the physical structure of the universe also serves as a map to the inner esoteric structure of the individual. Through the disciplines, once one is aware of the map, the map guides the individual entity in the exploration of their inner world and leads them into the experience of the truth of what is taught in the philosophy. It is only in the direct experience of truth as one in engaged in transformation that knowledge is gained and mastery begins. In the accomplishment of extraordinary things as a result of performing the disciplines, the student comes to accept a new self-definition as a master and is able to integrate the teachings into daily life.

The basic spiritual practice at the school is termed Consciousness & Energy (C&E). It combines Kundalini Yoga with focused concentration. Once mastered, students are asked to choose images (symbolic of desires) upon which they concentrate while evoking the kundalini energy as a means of empowering them. The various advanced disciplines of the school provide a means of practicing C&E in a gamelike setting with specific goals to be accomplished as a means of training the self in the new reality being proposed by Ramtha. In one such exercise, for example, students work in an open field bounded by a fence. Each draws an image upon a card which is then taped to the fence face down at some unknown point. Blindfolded, the student practices C&E and attempts to mentally merge their consciousness with the image on the card.

*Organization of the School.* Ramtha's School of Enlightenment is organized as an esoteric academy. New students are invited to an introductory beginning weekend at which they are introduced to Ramtha's philosophy and to the practice of C&E. Should they choose to continue, they attend several additional events over the next year at which they are given the more complete and detailed overview of the school's teachings and introduced one-by-one to the various disciplines. Upon completing that series of classes, they have the option of joining the larger student body as a student. To retain their status as current students, individual students must attend two mandatory events a year, each a seven-day retreat, one in the spring and one in the fall. There are also a number of additional classes which students may attend; many do, especially those who reside near the school.

As of the beginning of the new century, there are slightly more than three thousand students, approximately half of the population of the northwest corner of the state of Washington. The others are scattered across North America, Europe, Australia, and New Zealand. Given the instability of society, seen most clearly in the fluctuating economic climate and frequently symbolized in various natural environmental disasters (earthquakes, floods, tornadoes, and so forth), Ramtha has advised the students to choose their place of residence carefully and to develop a lifestyle that would allow them to survive in case of unplanned catastrophes. Also, as students develop, he has encouraged them to find employment in ways which offer expression to their creative urges. Association with the school tends to make students more aware of suppressed wishes and dreams and more dissatisfied with jobs that prevent the exercise of their creative impulses. These themes of mastering life and expressing creativity have tended to give the students a distinctive lifestyle, have led many to alter careers, and have begun to manifest in a developing cultural life amid the student body.

During the late 1980s and early 1990s, Knight went through a period of intense criticism, much of it concurrent with the major challenge to channeling posed by critics of the New Age, many of whom considered channeling a fraudulent activity. However, even within the New Age movement following the founding of the school, Knight was criticized for abandoning her previous format of public appearances, the suggestion being made that the move to center her activities on a relatively small number of students in the school was a sign of a dark trend, a paranoid focus upon apocalyptic warnings.

Also in the 1980s, Knight's love of horses led her to begin a business of raising and selling Arabian horses. While the business prospered for several years, at one point in the mid 1980s, the bottom fell out of the Arabian horse market, her business went bankrupt, and Knight was plunged into debt. At the same time a number of students who had invested in the business lost their investments. Many had done so with an understanding that Ramtha had approved and sanctioned their investment. However as Knight recovered financially, she offered to pay back all of the students (as well as the other investors) any money they lost. While some refused her offer, she eventually returned the investment to all who accepted it.

During the period of the school's founding while Knight said little to the media and few understood what was occurring in the school, the popular New Age assessment of her work was rarely contradicted. However, as she has again become relatively public, that image has been gradually dissipated. From 1988 to 1995, the Ramtha School issued no publications for circulation to the general public, but beginning in 1996 a number of new books, cassette tapes, and videos have appeared.

In 1996, a team of scholars conducted a study of the school. Their work, the subject of a conference in 1997, included psychologists who had conducted a variety of tests on Knight and some of her students, and concluded that Knight was neither a fake nor suffering from any pathological state. Their report has dramatically altered her image in the media.

At the end of the 1990s, Knight also began to shift her schedule. She turned over duties for the beginning events at the school to some senior students and for the first time in over a decade made appearances at events outside of Yelm. In 1999 she staged an initial round-the-world tour, and has subsequently continued to spread Ramtha's message with selected appearances in such diverse places as Australia, South Africa, and Eastern Europe.

—*J. Gordon Melton*

# 18 UFO RELIGIONS

The great psychologist Carl Jung postulated a drive toward self-realization and self-integration which he referred to as the individuation process. The goal of this process was represented by the self archetype, an archetype characterized by wholeness and completeness. One of the concrete symbols of this archetype can be a circle, and it was various forms of the circle that Jung referred to as mandalas. According to Jung, mandala symbols emerge in dreams when the individual is seeking harmony and wholeness, which frequently occurs during periods of crisis and insecurity. Jung interpreted the phenomenon of flying saucers—which often appear in the form of circular disks—as mandala symbols, reflecting the human mind's desire for stability in a confused world.

Another line of thought regarding religious interpretations of the UFO phenomenon is that the Western tradition's marked tendency to imagine God as somehow residing in the sky gives us a predisposition to view unusual *flying* objects as well as beings from outer space in spiritual terms. In other words, the god of the Bible is, in a certain sense, an extraterrestrial being. Not all spiritual beings are, however, beneficent. A more negative interpretation of UFOs is evident in recent claims of abduction by aliens.

If in the earlier literature flying saucers were technological angels, in abductee literature ufonauts are technological demons. Abductees, most of whom appear to have been genuinely traumatized by their experience, report being treated coldly and inhumanely by their alien captors—much like animals are treated when captured, tagged, and released by human zoologists. During their brief captivity, frightened abductees also often report having been tortured, usually in the form of a painful examination. If such reports are to be taken seriously, it appears that many alien scientists involved in kidnapping human beings are proctologists.

A careful reading of abduction narratives indicates that the patterns alleged to have been discovered by abduction investigators often have religious overtones or similarities with more traditional types of religious experience—similarities often ignored by UFO researchers. Hypnosis, which is generally used to explore the abduction experience, allows access to a subconscious level of an individual's psyche. This enables the hypnotic subject to recall repressed memories of actual events, but also makes it possible to derive "memories" of things which have never happened.

As Jung argued, the subconscious is a storehouse of religious ideas and symbols. Such symbols can become exteriorized through anxiety or stress. Thus, the crypto-religious imagery brought out by hypnosis—in this case torment by demonic beings, which is an initiatory motif—could be a confabulation of the subject's subconscious, perhaps worked into a UFO narrative in an effort to please the hypnotist. More literal demonologies have been proffered by conservative Christian observers of the UFO scene, many of whom view ufonauts as demons-in-disguise.

Inverted images of "friendly aliens" are reflected in the many portrayals of hostile aliens found in film and literature. The ugly, octopuslike extraterrestrials of H.G. Wells's imagination have their counterparts in innumerable invasion narratives, from straight horror movies like *The Blob* (which dropped to earth inside a meteorite) to such recent offerings as the box office record-breaker *Independence Day* and the short-lived TV series, *Dark Skies*. While friendly aliens appear to be projections of our hopes of being rescued from ourselves, hostile aliens seem to embody our worst fears.

**THE UFO CONTACTEE MOVEMENT.** In 1946 the phrases "flying saucers," "unidentified flying objects," and "contactees" existed in no one's vocabulary, though sightings of unusual aerial phenomena had been reported for at least the previous century and a half. Charles Fort's *The Book of the Damned* (1919), the first book on what would be called UFOs, had linked such oddities to visitors from space. Fort even speculated, perhaps facetiously, that certain individuals were in contact with their pilots. If so, no one owned up to it till the evening of October 9, 1946, when the Kareeta flew over San Diego.

It came in the shape of a long, bullet-shaped structure with large wings which looked to witnesses like a giant bat's. Those who saw it said it was dark except for two red lights along the side. Visible for an hour and a half and moving at speeds varying from slow to very fast, it periodically swept a searchlight along the ground.

Not till the following summer, following private pilot Kenneth Arnold's widely publicized June 24, 1947, encounter with nine shiny discs over Mount Rainier, Washington, would things like this get to be called flying saucers. Even in 1946, however, San Diegans did not have to be told that this object was something decidedly out of the ordinary.

Just how out of the ordinary, however, was left to local medium Mark Probert to say. Probert had been channeling messages from a variety of discarnates who discoursed at stultifying length on cosmic philosophical issues for the recently formed, San Diego-based Borderland Sciences Research Associates (BSRA), directed by occult theorist N. Meade Layne.

As it happened, Probert was among the many San Diegans who, their eyes raised skyward in anticipation of a meteor shower, observed the passage of the mysterious structure. While it was still in view, Probert phoned Layne, who urged his associate to attempt telepathic communication with the craft's presumed occupants. The attempt succeeded, Probert would assert, telling a newspaper reporter:

> The strange machine is called the Kareeta. . . . It is attracted at this time because the earth is emitting a column of light which makes it easier of approach. The machine is powered by people possessing a very advanced knowledge of anti-gravity forces. It has 10,000 parts, a small but very powerful motor operating by electricity, and moving the wings, and an outer structure of light balsam wood, coated with an alloy. The people are nonaggressive and have been trying to contact the earth for many years. They have very light bodies. They fear to land, but would be willing to meet a committee of scientists at an isolated spot, or on a mountain top.

So Probert would distinguish himself as the first of what soon would be called "contactees." Not at first a term of endearment, in time it became merely descriptive, a way of characterizing the worldwide host of human beings who would profess to believe themselves to be recipients of messages from friendly extraterrestrials looking out for our best interests.

The heretofore scattered contactee subculture coalesced into a movement in January 1952, when aircraft mechanic George W. Van Tassel initiated a series of public gatherings in the high desert country of southern California. Van Tassel channeled elaborate messages from starship ("ventla") commanders, soon introducing the first metaphysical superstar of the flying-saucer age, Ashtar, "commandant quadra sector, patrol section Schare, all projections, all waves"—an extraterrestrial/interdimensional being who even today communes with a small army of mediums and automatic writers.

On November 20, 1952, George Adamski entered occult history through his claimed meeting with Orthon, a golden-haired Venusian, near Desert Center, California. In no time at all others were alleging physical encounters with benevolently intentioned "Space Brothers," here to rescue the human race from imminent nuclear war. As if to up the ante, contactees soon recounted rides in flying saucers into outer space or to neighboring planets.

One figure who quickly rose to prominence in the new movement was occultist and maverick anthropologist George Hunt Williamson, who first heard from extraterrestrials in mid-1952 when a Martian named Nah-9 psychically warned him and his associates that evil space people were conspiring with evil earthlings to wreak havoc. As the messages grew ever more ominous, a frightened Williamson wrote a friend in Guatemala that "time is *very, very short*! . . . Disaster will come before Dec. 1st, *this year*! So only a few weeks remain!" He went on:

> We have been told that a man will contact us soon, when all is in readiness! And there will be a landing in this vicinity by special ship direct from Mars within two or three weeks from now! . . . The landing will be near here.

Nonetheless, Williamson was able to pull himself together enough to be in Desert Center on November 20, when he served as one of the six "witnesses"—albeit at some considerable distance—to the epocal Adamski/Orthon rendezvous.

Most contactees believe that the "Space Brothers" are representatives of a galaxywide civilization, here to guide humanity. Many believe there will be some physical cataclysm on Earth, during which many will die, and the survivors will be rescued by the Space Brothers; this appears to be an interpretation influenced by concepts derived from the Revelation to John in the Christian Bible.

Contactees differ from abductees in being essentially volunteers, with a positive attitude toward the ETs they communicate with, and usually with a strong background in metaphysical religion. Abductees, in contrast, believe themselves to have been victims of a kidnapping that was at best traumatic by humanoid aliens, and do not tend to have beliefs different from those of the general population. Ufologists tend to regard abductees as part of UFO phenomena as such, but contactees as part of a religious movement based on a theology about UFO phenomena. Whitley Strieber's books, beginning with *Communion*, attempted to persuade the public that the humanoids also have benevolent intentions. Strieber was not very successful in doing so, although his books have generated a following of their own.

Contactees are often thought to be typified by George Adamski, who claimed to have had rides in flying saucers. Aside from a few devoted followers, most people consider Adamski to have been a fraud. Current contactees, in contrast, rarely claim physical contact. Far more often, their contact is mental, via the media of channeling, automatic writing, visions, dreams, and voices heard in the mind. Some of these mental phenomena can be symptoms of mental illness, but among contactees they appear to be aspects of spiritual experience, as they might be in any other religious movement.

In the 1960, John Alva Keel reported on the growing number of "silent contactees," that is, members of a growing religious movement; he believed they were dealing with "ultraterrestrials," beings intent on harming them, a notion quickly taken up by the Christian right wing. In the 1970s, Brad Steiger's writings chronicled the growing phenomenon of channeling, and began offering new interpretations of its significance. The seventies also saw the emergence of the idea of extraterrestrials being reincarnated as Earthlings, either at birth or as "walk-ins"—that is, alien humans who take over a human body when the ordinary human personality is about to depart (i.e., die). This latter experience has been described by many contactees; it may be a way of describing a conversion experience. In any event, religious scholars have been observing the growth of the contactee movement since the 1970s as a new type of metaphysical religion.

In 1980 R. Leo Sprinkle, a psychologist, organized the first Rocky Mountain Conference on UFO Investigation in Laramie, Wyoming; it has ever since been an annual event, usually with entirely new attendees. It is not a gathering of ufologists, but of contactees, who are thus enabled to become a support group for one another, sharing and validating their similar experiences. Sprinkle and other psychologists have also used this as an opportunity to investigate the psychological makeup of contactees. They turn out to be no different from the general population in any significant way.

A complete list of contactees who channel messages from the Space Brothers would be extensive. Among the more prominent are Michael and Aurora El-Legion of Malibu, California, who channel the Space Brothers known as the Ashtar Command. It is sometimes not clear whether the intelligences whom clairvoyants channel are "Space Brothers" or not; some seem to reject ordinary concepts of time and space. As a result, the boundaries of the contactee movement are sometimes difficult to define.

Truman Bethurum also joined the swelling contactee ranks with his own tale of friendly space people. He met them one night in July 1952, he said, while employed as a heavy-equipment operator in the Nevada desert. A between-shifts nap was interrupted by eight little men with "Latin" features. They guided him to a nearby flying saucer and its captain, "a gorgeous woman, shorter than any of the men, neatly attired, and also having a Latin appearance: coal black hair and olive complexion. She appeared to be about 42 years old." Her name, she told him, was Aura Rhanes. She and the crew of the "scow" (spaceship) hailed from the planet Clarion, a world never visible to us because it is always on the other side of the moon. As Bethurum would learn in subsequent contacts, Clarion is an idyllic world devoid of conflict or disease. Clarionites had come here out of concern that human beings might blow up their planet in a nuclear war.

In August 1953 the first major contactee gathering, the Interplanetary Spacecraft Convention, brought more than ten thousand space communicants, true believers, and curiosity-seekers to Van Tassel's residence at Giant Rock (literally a giant rock), between Lucerne Valley and Twenty-nine Palms, California. The Giant Rock meetings, which were held every year through 1977, provided a forum in which contactees could exchange information and ideas. In the process they borrowed names and concepts from one another, even as the meaning and context changed from telling to telling. Though contactees agreed on a general cosmology, no two of them described a precisely similar one.

Believers either ignored these disparities or dismissed them as meaningless, much to the exasperation of skeptics. One of them, ufologist Isabel L. Davis, wrote in the science-fiction magazine *Fantastic Universe* (November 1957):

> Where was Clarion . . . during the night of August 23–24, 1954? On that night, Adamski claims, he was shown both sides of the Moon by Ramu of Saturn, through an instrument on the Venusian carrier ship. . . . As the ship goes around from the familiar toward the unfamiliar side, ahead of it in the sky should have been Captain Aura Rhanes' Clarion. But neither Ramu nor Adamski mention[s] it. Adamski certainly knew about Clarion—for Bethurum had visited Palomar Gardens [Adamski's residence] during the summer of 1953, and Adamski had then accepted Bethurum's story. But with a whole planet missing from where it should be, Adamski is neither surprised nor curious.

Some contactees have gone so far as to actually form religions based on messages they received from extraterrestrials. The Cosmic Circle of Fellowship, for instance, was formed in Chicago, Illinois, in 1954 by William A. Ferguson. Ferguson was a mail carrier who learned the techniques of absolute relaxation and became adept at relaxing his body, mind, and conscious spirit. In 1937, Ferguson wrote *Relax First* and then began to teach relaxation techniques to others.

On July 9, 1938, while lying in a state of absolute relaxation, Ferguson's body was charged with energy and he was carried away to the Seventh Dimension. He stayed there two hours and his soul became illuminated. When he returned to normal waking consciousness, he found that his physical body was no longer where he had left it and he could not be seen nor heard by his wife and his friend. He placed his noncorporal being back where his body and been had soon regained physical three-dimensional form.

One week later, Ferguson was carried away to the "center of creation" and experienced the sixth dimension. He saw creation in action: Rays of pure intelligent energy of all forms and colors were flowing throughout a cube of pure universal substance. In the 1940s Ferguson began to gather a group primarily related to cosmic healing techniques, especially the "clarified water device" taught to Ferguson by Khauga. This device, thought to impart healing properties to water, got Ferguson in trouble with the American Medical Association. In 1947 Ferguson was convicted of fraud in relation to the clarified water device and served a year in prison.

Also in 1947, a being named Khauga (also identified as the Spirit of Truth, the angel who gave the Book of Revelation to St. John and a perfected being from the Holy Triune) took Ferguson on a trip to Mars. Upon his return, family and friends could not see or hear him until he went into the next room, lay on a cot and was rematerialized. He delivered a message that the Martians were sending an expedition to Earth. Within a few months, many UFOs were reported and several people claimed to have made personal contacts with their inhabitants.

In 1954 Ferguson was taken aboard a Venusian spacecraft where he learned that spacecraft normally function in four dimensions and are therefore invisible to us, but they can also function in three dimensions. When they disappear suddenly, they have merely changed back into the fourth dimension. Ferguson joined with Edward A. Surine and Edna I. Valverde and in 1954 formed the Cosmic Circle of Fellowship. The group was incorporated in the state of Illinois in 1955. In 1958 Ferguson started traveling around the country, founding circles in other cities including Washington, Philadelphia, New York, and San Francisco. Since Ferguson's death in 1967, the Chicago group has continued to publish his writings.

Eduard Albert Meier is the most prominent contemporary Adamski-style contactee. Born February 3, 1937, in Bulach, Switzerland, he acquired the nickname "Billy" as a result of his interest in classic American cowboy figures like Billy the Kid, Wild Bill Hickok, and Buffalo Bill. Meir had a troubled childhood, running away from home several times. As an adult, he held a number of odd jobs, served briefly in the Foreign Legion, and did time for theft.

Meier claims to have been in contact with ufonauts since the age of five. The space people, who are human in appearance and who are from the Pleiades star system, eventually selected him as a "truth offerer." To prove their existence, they permitted Meier to take innumerable pictures of their "beamships." Though rejected by most ufologists, Meier acquired prominence as an occult celebrity by the mid-1970s due to coverage in European periodicals. In the late seventies, he entered into an agreement with a group of Americans who promoted his books and other materials to the UFO/New Age community. Meier has also attracted a number of critics who accuse him and his associated of exploiting the credulous.

*—JEROME CLARK*

**A E T H E R I U S   S O C I E T Y .**  The Aetherius Society is probably the most
well-known and organized flying-saucer religion. It was founded by George
King who, in May 1954, received a command from interplanetary sources
to become "the Voice of Interplanetary Parliament." Until his death in
1997, he has continually received trance messages and/or telepathic communications from various beings, mainly from different planets in the
solar system. His eminence Dr. George King, as the members of the society
usually addressed him, had been lavished with innumerable titles, academic degrees, and honors. He authored many books and, because of his
teachings and works, was recognized as a charismatic leader by the
society's members. Roy Wallis described him in classical Weberian terms,
namely, as a mystagogue who "offers a largely magical means of salvation."
Members of the society, however, see salvation in terms of the laws of
karma and understood Dr. King's role as that of a teacher who conveyed
messages and instructions from extraterrestrial beings, rather than that of
a miracle worker or a dispenser of magical rites.

The Aetherius Society, which gets its name from the pseudonym of a
being from the planet Venus who first contacted Dr. King, is a structured
organization founded by King and run by a board of directors. Some
internal hierarchy exists with several degrees of initiation and merit awards
being available to its members. Headquartered in Hollywood, California,
the society has centers and branches on several continents, including North
America, Europe, (West) Africa, and Australia. Its membership, though not
very large, is thus varied. In the United States, members are more likely to
be adult, middle-class, and white. One must add, however, that in some
cities, white members actually form a minority. Further, many of its ministers and priests are women and black. These factors, plus the society's presence on several continents, makes its overall membership cosmopolitan.

The society publishes Dr. King's books and taped lectures, a newsletter,
the *Cosmic Voice*, which has been in print since 1956, and a quarterly *Journal
of Spiritual and Natural Healing*, which, a number of years ago, was replaced
with the *Aetherius Society Newsletter*. This newsletter covers many topics,
including information from the society's headquarters and various
branches, activities of members, and columns on the cosmic teachings.

Among the many aims of the Aetherius Society are the spreading of
the teachings (or transmissions) of the cosmic masters, the preparation
for the coming of the next master, the administration of spiritual
healing, the creation of the right conditions necessary for contacts and
ultimate meetings with beings from other planets, and the conduct of
various missions and operations.

The beliefs of the Aetherius Society are rather complex. Reference to
God is common in its prayers, though the planetary beings appear to
occupy the central stage in the members' spiritual lives. Among its teach-

ings are included those on the chakras, the aura, kundalini, karma, and reincarnation. Yoga and meditation are considered to be very important. George King was also said to have been a master of yoga, a well-advanced stage that he achieved at an early age and later enhanced by practices given by a master who resides on Earth. Meditation or Samadhi is, according to the society, the experiential state of adeptship "when the soul is bathed in the Light of pure Spirit and one becomes a knower of truth." Mantras are also frequently repeated during services.

A common theme that runs through all the teachings of the Aetherius Society is "spiritual service." The greatest yoga and the greatest religion is service to humankind. Many of the operations and missions upon which the society has embarked should be understood primarily as acts of service to the human race which has at times placed itself on the edge of destruction.

Some of the teachings of the Aetherius Society has led one scholar, Robert Ellwood, to place the society within the theosophical tradition. The literature of the Aetherius Society in the late 1950s and early 1960s exhibits both great concern for the dangers of atomic warfare and fallout as well as excitement about UFO sightings. These features, plus accounts that the earth is under attack by evil cosmic forces and the interest in the coming of the next cosmic master, have led Ellwood to conclude that "like the Adamski teachings, Aetherius can be thought of as apocalyptic Theosophy." In the regular prayer services, however, such apocalyptic concern is not prominent.

One of the Aetherius Society's central beliefs is the existence of a kind of pantheon of beings largely from other planets in the solar system. These beings live in a kind of paradise and are, scientifically and spiritually, millions of years ahead of the human race here on Earth. In the society's literature there is mention of four interplanetary beings (Shri Krishna, the Lord Buddha, the master Jesus, and Lao Tsu) who descended to earth as teachers. The Great White Brotherhood, made up of masters from all races, is, according to the society, the spiritual hierarchy on Earth and is made up of adepts, masters, and ascended masters. The function of these beings is mainly to preserve and develop spirituality upon earth.

Detailed descriptions of several "Cosmic Intelligences," of their planetary habitats, and of the major types of space craft they use were provided by George King. Mother ships, scout patrol vessels, and special-purpose vessels are among those accounted for in the Aetherius Society's literature. The reason why these beings cannot land openly is because of the negative karmic effects created by human beings by their neglect of God's laws and the teachings of the masters.

There has been little attempt by the Society's members to embark on an evangelization campaign and, consequently, the Aetherius Society does not fit into the popular image of a new religion that indulges in heavy-handed recruiting tactics. In practice much of the work of the society is dedicated to conducting and/or maintaining several operations and/or missions among which are: (1) Operation Starlight, a mission, carried out between 1958 and 1961, during which nineteen select mountains were charged with spiritual energy that can be radiated to uplift our world by anyone who prays unselfishly on them; (2) Operation Space Power, which involves the cooperation of the Aetherius Society with Interplanetary Beings to radiate spiritual power to Earth during "Spiritual Pushes"; (3) Operation Bluewater, which alleviated the effects of a warp in the earth's magnetic field, a warp produced by atomic experiments, and the negative thoughts and actions of human beings that interfere with the natural flow of spiritual energies to Earth; (4) Operation Sunbeam, through which spiritual energy is restored to the Earth as a token repayment for all the energy humanity has taken from it; (5) Operation Prayer Power, which involves the storing of spiritual energy through prayer and mantra, an energy that can be released to relief suffering anywhere on Earth; and (6) several missions that saved the Earth from evil extraterrestrial intelligences or entities (the Alien Mission and Operation Karmalight). These two missions were almost entirely performed by interplanetary beings and are not being conducted or maintained by the society.

Probably one of the most interesting aspects of these missions is their technical aspect. Some of them required the designing and building of special equipment. Thus, for instance, Operation Power needs unique batteries and transmission systems that were designed by George King to respectively store spiritual energy safely and beam it effectively to trouble spots on Earth.

The ritual of the Aetherius Society, which can be rather elaborate, is carried out on a weekly basis and on special commemorative occasions. The temple (often a small room) where the services are held is usually decorated with religious symbols that include a photograph of George King and a portrait of the Master Jesus. Every week the following services are held: (1) a prayer meeting that includes a short meditation period, the recitation of the Twelve Blessings of Jesus, and petitions for the healing at a distance for anyone who has requested to be placed on the healing list; (2) a service dedicated to Operation Prayer Power; (3) a private healing service; and (4) a regular Sunday service, during which taped instructions or lectures of Dr. King and messages from various planetary beings might be played. On a yearly basis the start and/or completion of several of the missions and operations are commemorated. Pilgrimages to the Holy Mountains, charged with spiritual power during Operation Starlight, are periodically made by devoted members of the society.

Since the death of its founder in 1997, the Aetherius Society has been run by a board of directors. Otherwise, it has continued to function with little change in its rituals and beliefs. The charisma of its deceased leader seems to be in the process of institutionalization, a development which, from a sociological point of view, is not surprising since the society has a well-structured organization and a well-defined religious agenda. The society has, so far, continued to operate as a small religious movement or organization where belief in extraterrestrials who help humankind is central and spiritual healing is regularly practiced. Whether George King will be replaced by another cosmic master and if so, when, are not pressing issues in the minds of its members. The society's literature published since King's death has not dealt with the question of succession. The more common belief appears to be that George King will not be succeeded in the near future by another master who will act as the primary mental channel. In the unspecified future, however, a cosmic intelligence could come on Earth and be the next master.

—*John A. Saliba*

**Raelian Movement International.** The Raelian Movement was founded in 1973 by French race car driver and journalist Claude Vorilhon (known as Rael to his followers), born to a Catholic farm girl in 1946 in Vichy, France. The movement originated as a result Rael's alleged encounter with space aliens during a walking tour of the Clermont-Ferrand volcanic mountains in France. These beings, whom Rael describes in his book *The True Face of God*, entrusted him with a message for humanity. This message concerns our true identity: We were "implanted" on earth by a team of extraterrestrial scientists, the "Elohim," who created us scientifically with DNA in laboratories. Rael's mission, as the last of forty prophets (crossbred between Elohim and mortal women) is to warn humankind that since 1945 and Hiroshima, we have entered the "Age of Apocalypse" in which we have the choice of destroying ourselves with nuclear weapons or making the leap into planetary consciousness which will qualify us to inherit the scientific knowledge of our space forefathers. Science will enable 4 percent of our species in the future to clone themselves and travel through space and create life on virgin planets "in our own image."

Denying the existence of God or the soul, Rael presents as the only hope of immortality a regeneration through science (cloning), and to this end members participate in four annual festivals so that the Elohim can fly overhead and register the Raelians' DNA codes on their machines. This initiation ritual, called "the transmission of the cellular plan," promises a kind of immortality through cloning. New initiates are required to send a letter of apostasy to the church they were baptized in.

The movement currently claims around fifty thousand members worldwide, distributed mainly throughout French-speaking Europe, Japan,

Korea, the United States, and Quebec. The members can be divided into two levels of commitment. The great majority are the loosely affiliated "Raelians"—those who have acknowledged the Elohim as their fathers through the initiation or "baptism," sent a "letter of apostasy" to the church they were baptized in at birth, and made funeral arrangements for being cloned. The more committed members join the "Structure." They work on a voluntary basis to further the two goals of the movement: To spread the message to mankind and to build an intergalactic space embassy in Jerusalem by the year 2025 to receive the Elohim when they descend. From the bottom up, the seven levels in the Structure range from trainee, probationer, assistant animator, animator, assistant guide, priest guide, bishop guide, to planetary guide (who is Rael himself). All members are expected to pay a tithing of 10 percent of their income, but there is no disciplinary action to enforce this rule.

Members are encouraged through summer courses to achieve worldly success in their careers, to have better health through avoiding all recreational drugs and stimulants, and to enlarge their capacity to experience pleasure which, Rael claims, will strengthen their immune system and enhance their intelligence and telepathic abilities. Rael advises Raelians not to marry or exacerbate the planetary overpopulation problem, but to commune with the wonder of the universe by exploring their sexuality with the opposite sex, the same sex, or with biological robots. To this end, Raelians participate annually in the Sensual Meditation Seminar in a rural setting which features fasting, nudity, sensory deprivation/awareness exercises, and sexual experimentation (which is not part of the seminar itself), the ultimate goal being to experience the "cosmic orgasm."

Raelians have always captured the interest of journalists who tended to portray them as delightful, harmless nuts until comparatively recently. The Raelians aroused some controversy in 1992 by distributing free condoms in front of the playground of the major high schools of Quebec in protest of the Catholic school board's decision not to have condom machines installed. Anticult groups have portrayed Rael as a sexual libertine enjoying a luxurious life. Rael is the founder of CLONAID, and, according to the Raelian Movement International, was the first to announce that human cloning was inevitable twenty-seven years ago. He was also the first to instruct his followers to have one of their bones preserved after death, forseeing the time when it could be possible to recreate human beings using a single cell. As Rael wrote in *The True Face of God*, "now is no longer a time to believe, it's a time to understand."

—*SUSAN J. PALMER*

**UNARIUS ACADEMY OF SCIENCE.** Located in El Cajon, California, the Unarius Academy of Science uses channeling techniques to contact beings in outer space, referred to as the "non-atomic spiritual worlds." These beings, collectively named the Space Brothers, guide Unarius members in their cosmic "fourth-dimensional science." Unarius predicts a landing of one spacecraft in the year 2001, followed by thirty-two starships at the appropriate spiritual time. While communicating with extraterrestrials remains an important practice, Unarius also focuses on healing and spirituality. As a benefit of the spiritual science, followers believe they can heal themselves of all mental, physical, and emotional maladies. The study of the Unarian science is believed to bring about rebirth on an ascendant planet or return to a higher dimension. Until her death, the charismatic Ruth Norman (1900-1993) led the group. Most Unarius beliefs and practices come from their oral tradition that developed over the years. The practice of channeling is considered the best way to bring forth "infinite intelligence." The teachings say that the Unarius Science of Life expressed itself through master teachers who spoke in the idioms of the cultures they lived in, such as the discourses of Buddhism, Taoism, Theosophy, Swedenborgianism, and the true teachings of Jesus of Nazareth. These ascended masters, among others, speak in channeling sessions, also called "transmissions." Ruth Norman's higher self is called Uriel, a spiritual presence that figures prominently in the group's history.

In 1954 Ernest L. Norman (1904–1971) met his future wife, Ruth at a psychic convention. Mr. Norman, who had worked with spiritualist churches, did a psychic reading for Ruth that revealed her past-life connection to him. In Unarian lore, this earthly meeting of the two ascended beings inaugurated the Unarius mission. According to the group, the Unarian mission brings peace and love to earth through the celestial science of logic and reason. Originally the Unarius Science of Life, the organization went through several major transitions. Throughout the fifties Ernest channeled various books; the most widely read is *The Voice of Venus* (1954). Ruth typed manuscripts and letters while Ernest received enlightened teachings. Until Ernest's death, they held classes in their home and gave psychic readings through the mail to help students of the "Science." During this time, they discovered their many past lives together, including one cycle when Ernest was Jesus of Nazareth and Ruth lived as Mary of Bethany. When Ernest (also called the Moderator) died, Ruth took responsibility for the organization. With the help of two of her students known by the spiritual names of Cosmon and Antares (Charles Spaegel), Ruth channeled many more messages from the Brothers. In 1973, Mrs. Norman received a vision from the planet Eros where she was renamed Queen Uriel, Queen of the Archangels. By the mid-seventies Unarius incorporated as the Unarius Educational Foundation, permanently establishing their center in El Cajon, California.

By 1973 to 1974, the channeling of messages from outer space began to rapidly increase. Mrs. Norman received messages from scientists and ascended masters on "higher" planets. She also established contact with beings (called polarities) on thirty-two unknown planets, and she proclaimed that an Interplanetary Confederation had been formed to help earth with its positive progressive evolution. Thirty-two planets in this confederation were preparing themselves to send their starships to earth. Around this time Ruth purchased sixty-seven acres of land in the mountains in order to establish a landing site for the "vehicles of light." The prophecy of the massive spacefleet landing went through several revisions. Since 1984, Unarians have known that one spaceship would arrive in 2001; subsequently the other ships would come when the people of earth were receptive.

Ruth's contact with the Space Brothers became only part of her legacy. In all respects her charismatic authority was absolute in the organization. Throughout the years her past lives revealed themselves to all Unarians. Only a few are cited here. According to Unarius, she had been the inspiration for the Mona Lisa. In ancient times as the goddess Isis, she brought the fourth-dimensional science to her followers in Egypt. Long ago she reigned as Ioshanna, the peacock princess of Atlantis. Some 800,000 years ago, she came as the scientist Dalos to the planet Orion. In 1975, she received knowledge from the inner worlds that she lived in the spiritual dimensions as the "Spirit of Beauty, Goddess of Love." In this form she holds aloft the "Sword of Truth" while projecting healing rays from her eyes. In 1979, Mrs. Norman received a mental transmission that she, as Uriel, was crowned "Prince of the Realm," a higher status than her previous title of archangel. As such she would rule as one of the "Lords of the Universe" on the planet Aries. Much of Unarius cosmology and lore revolves around the past lives of Uriel. While Ruth Norman was alive, her pupils treated her with the greatest of deference. As Uriel, she appeared costumed in long capes and high collars. Wielding a royal scepter, she also acted out her charismatic persona crowned in a tiara of glistening stars. Her students immortalized her in their paintings that adorn the Unarius Academy. Uriel is believed to be closer than ever now, because she is now free from the bonds of earthly energy.

Currently, Unarius is passing through a transitional period. Mrs. Norman was supposed to greet the Space Brothers at the end of the millennium. Until 1991, members believed that she would live to be well over one hundred years old. However, in that year she suffered so many health problems that she longed for release from her physical body. The first transitional problems were solved by Mrs. Norman herself. About two years before she died, she began to prepare her students with dissertations from the Space Brothers. Her student, Antares, channeled the messages from "Interplanetary Ambassador, Alta of the planet Vixall." Her mission according to the Space Brother was accomplished. She was free to leave her body. In the interim students rededicated themselves to the Unarius mission. They adjusted to the fact that Antares would be left in charge. Mrs. Norman died quietly in her sleep on July 12, 1993. In December 1999, shortly before the new millennium began, Antares passed away. Now the board of directors composed of long-time students manages the center.

At the academy the course of study remains the Unarian science and its branches, the psychology of consciousness, reincarnation physics, and past-life therapy. Art therapy classes are also held regularly. The academy is open to everyone. Members call themselves "students." Women slightly outnumber men, but their numbers do not predominate. Two times a week the students attend classes at the center. The most adept pupils will learn to channel higher intelligence and transmit messages from the Space Brothers. Few actually acquire this ability, although Unarius reports that these numbers are increasing. In October the students annually celebrate the formation of the Interplanetary Confederation under leadership of Uriel. Members accept that they have always been students of Uriel when they lived on other planets with her or when they resided in different civilizations throughout time and space. The core group of students call themselves "the nucleus." Although Unarius has gained thousands of members throughout the world, their nucleus averages forty-five to fifty people per year. Smaller satellite centers exist in North Carolina, Canada, Austria, and one in Nigeria. Those who live too far away from El Cajon engage in home study and correspond with the group.

While waiting for the starships to arrive, Unarius serves the express function of spiritual growth and healing. Most dedicated students "get healings" from recognizing past lives. If needed, they usually adopt lifestyle changes such as giving up promiscuity, drugs, alcohol, and cigarettes. Unarians distinguish themselves from similar groups by profuse cultural productions in the areas of book publishing, art, and film-making. They have produced hundreds of books and films that explain their teachings. Creating books, art, and films are at the heart of Unarian projects. Many Unarian films record psychodramas wherein students act out the recovered memories of past lives, while others record student testimonials of healings. Often the films celebrate stories about the "accomplishments" of Uriel, while other videos herald the prophesied landing or depict legends of colonization from outer space. One of the most easily understood films is called The Arrival. In this film a student acts out his past life as Zan, a primitive man of Lemuria. The Space Brothers visit Zan in their dazzling spaceship. The Brothers enlighten him and help him to remember his previous life on the planet Tyron where he had commanded a battle cruiser that destroyed civilizations. Finally Uriel appears to Zan out of a vortex of stars, healing him and setting him on the path of progressive evolution.

These programs regularly air on television via public access channels around the country.

—*DIANA TUMMINIA*

**MARK-AGE, INC.** Charles Boyd Gentzel channeled messages from the "Hierarchical Board," which governs the solar system, since the late 1950s. Together with Pauline Sharpe, a channel also known as Nada-Yolanda, Gentzel organized a communiction plan that spans through the last forty years of the twentieth century. Such period is considered a transition phase from the Piscean to the Aquarian Age.

The Mark-Age Meta Center was established in Miami, Florida, in 1962, but subsequently changed its name to Mark-Age, Inc. It regards itself as a chosen point of contact with higher spiritual beings, and is devoted to channel and diffuse their messages through telepathy and automatic writing. Gloria Lee, who founded the Cosmom Research Fundation, the theosophical master El Morya, and John F. Kennedy have provided messages to Mark-Age.

Communication with the Hierarchical Board takes place also through spaceships; Jesus is believed to have been orbiting in an ethereal earth orbit since 1885, and is expected to materialize after the cleansing of the planet.

Messages channeled and the beliefs of the organization are published in a number of books, the most fundamental of which is *Mark-Age Period and Program*. In 1979 the organization settled in its new headquarters in Ft. Lauderdale, Florida.

**HEAVEN'S GATE.** The story of Heaven's Gate was recounted in the first chapter.

Most ordinary people recoil in incomprehension at the transparent absurdity of Bo (Marshall Herff Applewhite) and Peep's (Bonnie Lu Nettles) teachings—how could any sane human being buy into such silliness? In view of the group's dramatic end, it will repay our efforts if we examine the larger spiritual subculture out of which Heaven's Gate emerged and attempt to reconstruct the ideological system within which such a prophecy might sound plausible rather than absurd.

Since at least the nineteenth century, the industrialized West has been home to a strand of alternative religiosity that has been variously referred to as "occult," "metaphysical," or, more recently, as "New Age." Despite the existence of formal organizational structures, the core of this ambiguous subculture is constituted by a largely unaffiliated population of "seekers" who drift promiscuously from one spiritual group to another, never committing themselves to any single vision of truth. Heaven's Gate derived its basic ideology as well as its members from the New Age subculture.

One of the ideas that Applewhite and Nettles took from the New Age movement was the walk-in notion. A walk-in is an entity who occupies a body that has been vacated by its original soul. An extraterrestrial walk-in is a walk-in who is supposedly from another planet. Walk-ins are somewhat similar to possessing spirits, although in possession the original soul is merely over-shadowed—rather than completely supplanted—by the possessing entity. The contemporary notion of walk-ins was popularized by Ruth Montgomery in her 1979 book, *Strangers Among Us*. According to Montgomery, walk-ins are usually highly evolved souls here to help humanity. In order to avoid the delay of incarnating as a baby, and thus having to spend two decades maturing to adulthood, they contact living people who, because of the frustrating circumstances of life or for some other reason, no longer desire to remain in the body. The discarnate entity finds such people, persuades them to hand over their body, and then begins life as a walk-in.

In a later book, *Aliens Among Us* (1985), Montgomery developed the notion of extra-terrestrial walk-ins—the idea that souls from other planets have come to earth to take over the bodies of human beings. This notion dovetailed with popular interest in UFOs, which had already been incorporated into New Age thinking. Following Montgomery, the New Age movement viewed extraterrestrial walk-ins as part of the larger community of advanced souls that have come to earth to shepherd humanity through a period of crisis. It is easy to see how this basic notion could fit nicely into the Two's ideology, explaining away their human personal histories as the histories of the souls who formerly occupied the bodies of Applewhite and Nettles.

It should also be noted that the walk-in idea—a notion implying a radical disjunction between soul and body—would have provided Applewhite with an essential ideological component in his rethinking of the ascension scenario. In other words, after the death of Nettles, Applewhite had to come to grips with the fact that—under the physical ascension scenario which had been a cornerstone of their teachings for almost two decades—his spiritual partner would miss the chance to escape the planet with the rest of the group. This option was, however, unimaginable to Applewhite. Hence, by the time of the mass suicide, Applewhite had reconceptualized the ascension as an event in which Heaven's Gate members let go of their physical containers and ascended *spiritually* to the waiting saucers. Once on board, they would consciously "walk-into" a new physical body and join the crew of the next level spacecraft. This scenario is related in one of the group's Internet statements:

> Their final separation is the willful separation from their human body,
> when they have changed enough to identify as the spirit/mind/soul—
> ready to put on a biological body belonging to the Kingdom of Heaven.
> (This entering into their "glorified" or heavenly body takes place aboard
> a Next Level spacecraft, above the Earth's surface.)

Presumably, these new physical bodies would be supplied to Heaven's Gate members out of some sort of "cloning bank" kept aboard the spaceships.

Yet another theme Applewhite and Nettles absorbed from the metaphysical subculture was the view that the spiritual life is a series of learning experiences culminating—in the case of Heaven's Gate—in a "graduation" to the next evolutionary kingdom. Members of the group thought of themselves as "students," their fellows as "classmates," and Applewhite as their "tutor." These educational metaphors would have been particularly comfortable and natural for a man who had been a popular university teacher during the first part of his adult life.

As is evident from even the most casual perusal of the group's writings, Heaven's Gate was dominated by the educational imagery. Their spiritual process was likened to an educational process (in their "metamorphic classroom"), and their ultimate goal was frequently referred to as a graduation. In the group's internet postings, they discussed how their "teachers" on the next level had an "extremely detailed lesson plan" designed for their personal growth. Then, toward the end, they received signals that their "classroom time" was over and that they were ready to graduate to the next level.

Thus, with the exceptions of (1) suicide being the means by which the transition to the next evolutionary sphere is to take place and (2) the next sphere being a literal, physical realm (a spacecraft), the basic concepts informing Heaven's Gate's thought world would be recognizable to any serious metaphysical seeker. However, even the notion of a physical spaceship being a quasi-heavenly realm is already implicit in the marked tendency of the New Age movement to portray ufonauts as spiritual beings. Furthermore, the widely accepted walk-in notion provides a readily understandable mechanism by which such a transition could be accomplished.

This leaves only suicide as the one anomalous component of Applewhite's synthesis. We should note, however, that there are many phases of the New Age movement that portray death—if not suicide—in a positive light. For example, the basic metaphysical/New Age afterlife notion is reincarnation. This process is regarded somewhat differently by the New Age than by the Asian religions from which the notion is derived. Whereas in a tradition like Buddhism reincarnation is viewed negatively, as a process that brings one back into the world to suffer, in the metaphysical subculture reincarnation is viewed as part of an extended education program stretched across many lifetimes, and is thus part of an ultimately positive process.

The New Age movement is also home to advocates of conscious dying. The term "conscious dying" refers to an approach to dying in which death is regarded as a means of liberation of one's own consciousness—as a means of achieving enlightenment. This approach, ultimately inspired by Tibetan Buddhism, was popularized in the New Age subculture through the work of Baba Ram Das and Stephen Levine. In line with the New Age emphasis on spiritual-unfoldment-as-education, dying thus acquires a positive valence as part of the larger learning process.

Finally, it is within the metaphysical subculture that one finds the most interest in the near-death experience. The expression near-death experience (NDE) refers to the seemingly supernatural experiences often undergone by individuals who have suffered apparent death, and have been restored to life. The near-death experience has attracted extensive public interest because of its seeming support for the notion of life after death. The main impetus for modern studies on NDEs was the publication in 1975 of the book *Life After Life* by psychiatrist Raymond A. Moody.

Moody outlined nine elements that seemed to occur generally (but not universally) during NDEs. The fifth component of this process was described as:

> **Rising rapidly into the heavens.** Some NDEers report an experience of rising suddenly into the heavens, and seeing the earth and the celestial sphere as if they were astronauts in space.

This trait almost sounds like it could have been the source of Applewhite's idea that his group would "drop their bodies" and ascend to a waiting spacecraft. As reflected in the work of Moody and others, it is clear that the overall picture of the dying process to emerge from NDE studies is quite positive, even attractive.

In another one of his books, Moody mentions a ecstatic vision the famous psychologist Carl Jung experienced during an apparent NDE. Following a heart attack, Jung found himself a thousand miles above the surface of the earth, on the threshold of entering a floating temple in which he would finally discover the answers to all of his questions. In this vision, Jung vividly describes the terrestrial globe, his sense of letting go of everything associated with earthly life, and his sense of anticipation of the glories awaiting him upon his entrance into the temple.

Again, with only a little interpretation (e.g., floating temple = spacecraft), the whole experience could be taken as almost a blueprint for what Heaven's Gate members believed would happened after their deaths. This is not, of course, to assert that either NDE research or the writings of Carl Jung encourage people to take their own lives. It is, however, clear that, if taken seriously, reports of near-death experiences paint a positive enough portrait of dying to take the sting out of death. Thus, far from being crazy or irrational, even the final dramatic exit of Heaven's Gate becomes understandable in terms of the thought world of the metaphysical subculture from which Applewhite drew his theological synthesis.

**CHEN TAO.** The Taiwanese religious movement known as Chen Tao was briefly in the news when its leader announced that God would appear on television on March 25, 1998, and then in person on March 31, 1998. In Chinese, chen (zhen) means right or true, and tao (dao) means way.

The history of Chen Tao goes back roughly four decades to a spiritual self-improvement association based in urban southern Taiwan, called the Association for Research on Soul Light. The group sought to locate, quantify, and cultivate spiritual light energy using technological devices and traditional Chinese practices like qigong; its mixture of Buddhist-Taoism and high technology attracted a good number of students, academics, and white collar professionals several thousand by one account.

Among them was sociology professor Hon-ming Chen, who joined the Association in the early 1990s. In it he found an explanation for his reportedly lifelong visions of spheres of golden light. Through these golden spheres God the Heavenly Father wished to communicate several things to him: First, that he had a special role to play as spiritual teacher and critic of degraded popular religion; and second, that he was to deliver messages about the end of the world and the return of Christ.

Chen succeeded to prophetic leadership of the group in 1995, refashioning Chen Tao's steady-state cosmology by coupling the Buddhist conception of reincarnation according to merit with a cyclical model of history, bringing in a biblical apocalypse as an exclamation point. According to Chen, the End Times are brought about by the collective negative karma of all living beings. God, as a loving father, creates and recreates the cosmos, and sends Christ and Buddha, first to teach us, and then, at the end of each cycle, to save those who have followed the Right Way and attempted to rebalance their karmic books. But God also grants His children complete free will, allowing souls to take on bodies, to be seduced by the lusts of corporeality, and thus to create negative karma for themselves, to injure other living beings, and ultimately to propel the material cosmos to repeated destructions. Evidence provided by the damage to our natural environment and the degradation of our civilization is cited by Chen to bolster his claim that ours are the last days and that Christ will soon arrive in God's space aircrafts.

He proclaimed that the Kingdom of God descended first on the group's headquarters in Taiwan in 1995, and then on the North American continent. One site in particular, Garland, Texas, was singled out by Chen as the location of the repeated creations and salvations of humanity. Chen moved to this Dallas suburb in the spring of 1997, and was followed by up to 160 Chen Tao members that fall. In Garland, Chen made public his prophecies concerning the two televised theophanies, statements which for several weeks in the spring of 1998 earned his group headlines around the world. The news media of their own accord, but also at Chen's earnest invitation, came in droves, hyping Chen Tao as the next Heaven's Gate.

When events failed to take place exactly as predicted on March 25, Chen held a press conference at his Garland home at which he stated that the news media and audience worldwide could consider the prophecy nonsense. However, he and his followers hung on until God's appearance of March 31. When the Heavenly Father once again did not appear as promised, press interest dissolved almost entirely and many followers returned to Taiwan. A small remnant of the group moved to upstate New York in April, 1998 to await the prophesied saucer salvation set for late 1999.

—*RYAN J. COOK*

# 19

# OTHER GROUPS AND MOVEMENTS

## NEW AGE

The New Age can be viewed as a revivalist movement within a pre-existing metaphysical-occult community. As such, the New Age can be compared with Christian revivals, particularly with such phenomena as the early Pentecostal movement (i.e., a movement that simultaneously revived and altered a segment of Protestant Christianity). Comparable to the to the influence of Pentecostalism on Christianity, the New Age had an impact on some but not all segments of the occult community. Also like Pentecostalism, the New Age revival left a host of new organizations/denominations in its wake without substantially affecting the teachings of pre-existing organizations/denominations.

From another angle the New Age can be viewed as a successor movement to the counterculture of the 1960s. As observers of the New Age vision have pointed out, a significant portion of New Agers are baby-boomers, people who two decades earlier were probably participating, at some level, in the phenomenon known as the counterculture. As the counterculture faded away in the early 1970s, many former "hippies" found themselves embarking on a spiritual quest—one that, in many cases, departed from the Judeo-Christian mainstream. Thus, one of the possible ways to date the beginnings of the New Age movement is from the period of the rather sudden appearance of large numbers of unconventional spiritual seekers in the decade following the sixties.

Narrowly considered, as a social movement held together by specific ideas, the New Age can be traced to England in the late 1950s. At that time, the leaders of certain independent occult groups heavily influenced by the reading of many theosophists, especially Alice Bailey, began to meet to discuss the possible changes coming during the last quarter of the twentieth century. Those meetings continued through the 1960s and, as they grew, came to include their most well-known participants—the founders of the Findhorn Community in Scotland. By the 1970s a vision of the New Age had been clarified, and the movement was ready to reach out to like-minded people around the globe. The process of spreading was greatly assisted by the work of Anthony Brooke and the Universal Foundation. Brooke toured the world contacting occult and metaphysical groups, and created the first international networks of New Age believers. David Spangler, a student of the Alice Bailey writings, traveled to England in 1970 and stayed at Findhorn for three years. Upon his return to the United States, he began to author a series of books which laid out the hopes and aspirations of the New Age. One can pinpoint four essential ideas which came to distinguish the movement. None are particularly new ideas, their distinctiveness being in their being brought together in a new gestalt.

1. *The possibility of personal transformation.* The New Age movement offers the possibility of a personal transformation in the immediate future. While personal transformation is a common offering of some occult and New Thought groups, it is usually presented as the end result of a long-term process of alteration through extensive training and indoctrination into the occult life (in conscious contrast to the immediate transformation offered by revivalist Christianity). Thus, the New Age, without radically changing traditional occultism, offered a new immediacy which had been lacking in metaphysical teachings.

The transformative process is most clearly seen in the healing process, and transformation often is first encountered as a healing of the individual, either of a chronic physical problem or of a significant psychological problem. Healing has become a metaphor of transformation and the adopting of a healthy lifestyle a prominent way of being a New Ager.

2. *The coming of broad cultural transformation.* The New Age movement offered the hope that the world, which many people, especially those on the edges of the dominant culture, experience in negative terms, would in the next generation be swept aside and replaced with a golden era. As articulated by Spangler, the hoped for changes are placed in a sophisticated framework of gradual change relying upon human acceptance of the new resources and their creating a new culture. According to Spangler, a watershed in human history has been reached with the advent of modern technology and its possibilities for good and evil. At the same time, because of unique changes in the spiritual world, symbolized and heralded (but not

caused) by the astrological change into the Aquarian Age, this generation has a unique bonus of spiritual power available to it. It is this additional spiritual energy operating on the world and its peoples that make possible the personal and cultural transformation that will bring in a New Age.

It is, of course, the millennial hope of the coming of a golden age of peace and light that gave the New Age movement its name. The millennialism also provided a basis for a social consciousness which has been notably lacking in most occult metaphysics. Once articulated, the New Age vision could be and was grounded in various endeavors designed to assist the transition to the New Age. The New Age movement wedded itself to environmentalism, lay peace movements, animal rights, women's rights, and cooperative forms of social organization.

3. *The transformation of occult arts and processes.* Within the New Age movement one encounters such familiar occult practices as astrology, tarot, mediumship, and psychic healing. However, in the New Age movement the significance of these practices have been significantly altered. Astrology and tarot are no longer fortune telling devices, but have become tools utilized for self transformation. Mediumship has become channelling, in which the primary role of the medium is to expound metaphysical truth, rather than to prove the continuance of life after death. Spiritual healing launches and undergirds a healing relationship to life.

The number of practitioners of astrology, tarot, mediumship, and psychic healing had been growing steadily throughout the twentieth century. Thus, the New Age movement did not have to create its own professionals de novo; rather, it had merely to transform and bring into visibility the large army of practitioners of the occult arts already in existence.

Possibly the most widely practiced New Age transformative tool is meditation (in its many varied forms) and related tools of inner development. In its utilization of meditation, the New Age movement borrowed insights from the findings of the human potentials movement and transpersonal psychology, both of which, in isolating various practices for study, demonstrated that techniques of meditation and inner development could be detached from the metaphysical teaching in which they were traditionally embedded. Thus, one could practice Zen meditation without being a Buddhist and yoga without being a Hindu. That insight made all of the Eastern, occult, and metaphysical techniques immediately available to everyone without the necessity of their changing self-identifying labels prior to their use.

4. *The self as divine.* Within the New Age, one theological affirmation has found popular support—the identification of the individual as a one in essence with the divine. Underlying this notion, which finds a wide variety of forms, is a monistic world in which the only reality is "God," usually thought of in predominantly impersonal terms as mind or energy.

However, as it is expressed, the New Age offers a decisive alternative to traditional Christian theological approaches which draw a sharp separation between God as Creator and humans as God's creation. It is most clearly seen in New Thought and Christian Science, which see the basic healing-transformative process occurring as one discovers the truth of their oneness with the Divine.

Thus, the New Age movement, narrowly defined, can best be seen as an occult-metaphysical revival movement generated among independent British theosophists in the post–World War II generation which spread through the well-established occult-metaphysical community in the 1970s. Through the 1980s it became a popular movement which enlivened the older occult-metaphysical community and which both drew many new adherents to it and greatly assisted the spread of occult practices (such as astrology and meditation) and ideas (such as reincarnation) into the general population far beyond the boundaries of the New Age movement proper.

The New Age movement is comparable to the Civil Rights movement of the 1960s. The Civil Rights movement drew upon century-long efforts to bring some equity to the culture's treatment of black people. That effort drew new strength and vitality from a new program and a new, somewhat millennial, hope of a society that could do away with racism. While building on older efforts, it articulated a new program (which some of the older groups could not accept) and both drew many new supporters to the cause of destroying racism and spread its goals through the population to many never directly involved in the movement. And like the Civil Rights movement, the New Age movement is destined to have a short life span, the signs of its disintegration already before us as the millennial hope of cultural transformation has faded dramatically. That fading would have occurred in any case, but it has been hastened by negative media treatment. Unlike the Civil Rights movement, the New Age movement was rarely taken seriously, and frequently held up to ridicule by writers who combined a theological hostility to it with an inability to perceive its importance as an agent of change in culture. Like the Civil Rights movement, however, as the New Age movement fades, its effects upon the culture (in drawing many new people to the occult-metaphysical community and its making some of the community's key ideas acceptable to the middle class) remain.

The effects of the New Age movement on the occult community were not uniform. Many of the older denominations, such as the National Spiritualist Association of Churches, never really participated in the New Age, and those that did, such as Unity, eventually rejected certain New Age innovations in favor of the "orthodoxy" of their tradition. In the wake of the movement (viewing the New Age as a revivalist movement that has already peaked), it is clear that most of the older occult-metaphysical bodies have grown and certain new organizations have been formed. The occult has become more "respectable," and has penetrated the mainstream to greater extent than even during the "occult explosion" of the late sixties.

—*J. GORDON MELTON*

**AUMISM.** Founded in 1969 by His Holiness Lord Hamsah Manarah, Aumism is considered a religion of unity, representing a synthesis of all the religions and spiritual movements of the planet. Its headquarters are located in the Holy City of Mandarom Shambhasalem in the Alps of Haute-Provence in France.

Born in a French family practicing traditional catholicism, Lord Hamsah Manarah was attracted by mysticism and occult sciences in his youth. He later studied law, philosophy, economy, and medicine while he dedicated his nights to esoteric research, following all of the Western initiatory paths (Kabbala, Alchemy, etc.). Traveling to India, he stayed at Swami Sivananda's spiritual center, receiving the initiation of "Sannyasin" (renouncing person consecrated to God) from him on February 13, 1961, at Rishikesh in the Hymalayas. At that time, he was given the name Hamasananda Sarasvati. During his numerous trips, Lord Hamsah Manarah was initiated into Jainism, Sufism, different branches of Hinduism, Theravada, Mahayana, and Vajrayana Buddhism, Japanese Shingon, and certain African religions. The titles of Acharya and Mahacharaya—teacher who preaches what he himself accomplished—were given to him in stages by Jainist and Hindi Masters. He also received the title of Adinath, First Master or Patriarch, a title that is unusual for Western people to receive, and is reserved to certain fulfilled beings regarded as divine incarnations.

It was after this long initiatory journey, which led him to the holy places of the earth, that Lord Hamsah Manarah, known under the name of Shri Mahacharya Hamsananda Sarasvati, settled on a desert mountain over the small village of Castellane in the Alps of Haute-Provence. This place corresponded to one he had seen in a dream. He knew it was there that he must settle, which he did in 1969. Soon many curious people, as well as many people who were spiritually oriented, arrived and wanted to meet him. They had heard about him as an exceptional person. Gradually what began as a simple camp was transformed into an ashram. Many men and women went to live close to the holy man and began to build a city around him. Today the Holy City of Mandarom Shambhasalem is a spiritual museum. Temples and statues from every religion—including the biggest Buddha in the West (twenty-one meters), a giant Christ (seventeen meters), and the Cosmoplanetary Messiah (thirty-three meters)—were erected there. In 1990, Lord Hamsah Manarah announced to the world that he was the Cosmoplanetary Messiah, that is a messiah whom all the traditions wait for. Today Lord Hamsah Manarah is dedicated to prayer, to writing his books (twenty-two at present), and to the spiritual direction of his disciples.

Aumism, the Unity of Religions, is said to synthesize all the religions and spiritual movements of the planet. Thus, Aumists pray to Buddha as well as to Allah, Christ, and Mother Nature. One does not have to give up one's faith in order to become Aumist. One becomes an Aumist and integrates it with the faith of other people.

The name Aumism is derived from the Hindu mantra OM, said to be the root of all the sounds found in every tradition (Amen, Amin, etc.). The benefits brought about by the repetition of the sound Om are supposedly countless, assuring inner peace, elevating and protecting the soul, and so on. Aumists also repeat various other mantras (sanskrit holy formulas).

Aumists believe in reincarnation according to the Law of the Evolution of the Souls. A vegetarian diet is recommended for a better spiritual journey, although it is not imposed. Aumism is opposed to drugs, suicide, and sexual "deviations" (e.g., polygamy and homosexuality).

The Aumist Religion has its headquarters at the Holy City of Mandarom Shambhasalem in the Alps of Haute-Provence, in southern France. About fifty monks and nuns live there permanently. Aumism is organized into a Church, with priests and priestesses (in the hundreds), and bishops (108). Priests and priestesses can provide five sacraments: baptism, confirmation, rennovation, marriage, and transition.

Anyone who receives the baptism or the transmission of the sound OM is regarded Aumist. If one decides to go further in one's spiritual search, the Aumist may enter the Initiatory Order of Triumphant Vajra and become a knight. The Initiatory Order contains twenty-two degrees. Every degree corresponds to a spiritual journey of prayer and study. The knights who wish to continue and devote themselves to the diffusion of the Aumist message can ask for their admission into the prelate. Both men and women have unfettered access to the prelate. Aumist priests can marry. There also exists a monastic branch for those who decide to become renunciates and live in the Holy City.

The Centroms are the places for prayer (churches) where Aumists from the same town or region gather. It is possible to find Centroms in France (about one hundred), but also in most European countries, in Africa, in Oceania, and around the Indian Ocean. An Ashram also exists in Canada, where the Aumist religion has a considerable following.

Aumists and Knights from all over the world gather together at the Holy City for seminars. There are about one thousand Knights and thousands of Aumists in the world. The Holy City is open to the public for guided tours. It is open every day during the summer, and on the weekend during the other seasons. Thousands of tourists visit Mandarom Shambhasalem every summer.

Lord Hamsah Manarah is the author of twenty-two books divided into three collections: "Les Yogas Pratiques" (The Practical Yogas), a series of nine works written while he was an accomplished Yogi; "Les Livres Saints de la Révélation" (The Holy Books of Revelation), a series of four works published in 1990 to 1991 upon his revelation to the world of his status as the Cosmoplanetary Messiah (this series explains Aumist religion, the Unity of Religions, and the return of the Messiah); "Les Nouvelles Lois" (The New laws), a series of five works that appeared in 1993 and that present the Law of Evolution of the Souls and the Codes of Life of the New Age; "Le Livre des Sacrements de l'Aumisme" (The Book of the Sacraments of Aumism) (1994), which reveals the holy rites that characterize the existence of each Aumist; and "Périple d'un Yogi et Initié d'Occident" (Vicissitudes of a Yogi and Initiated in the West), which appeared on June 30, 1995, in order to answer the accusations against Lord Hamsah Manarah (he was said to have abused female disciples, among other accusations).

The first attacks began in 1990 when Lord Hamsah Manarah revealed himself to the world as the Cosmoplanetary Messiah. The international media, which gathered together for the occasion, spread the news all over the world. Since then the police, the government, ecologists, and the anticult movement became interested in Lord Hamsah Manarah, in the Holy City of Mandarom Shambhasalem, and in Aumism. Critical articles and reports appeared. The pyramidal Temple that was supposed to attract pilgrims from all over the world was never built—the building permit that had already been obtained was withdrawn before the beginning of the work. Today Aumists are harrassed at their workplaces, and some have lost their employment. In the summer of 1995 Lord Hamsah Manarah served eighteen days in prison, but was later found innocent and released.

**SCIENTOLOGY (THE CHURCH OF SCIENTOLOGY).** Scientology, one of the genuinely new religions to originate in the United States in the twentieth century, was founded by L. Ron Hubbard (1911–1986). Hubbard's extensive writings and taped lectures constitute the beliefs and the basis for the religion's practices. The aims of Scientology are "a civilization without insanity, without criminals and without war, where the able can prosper and honest beings can have rights, and where man is free to rise to greater heights."

L. Ron Hubbard grew up mostly in Montana, but also lived in Nebraska; Seattle, Washington; and Washington, D.C. As a child he read extensively, and by the age of twelve was studying the theories of Freud. As a teenager Hubbard travelled throughout Asia and the East, continuing his studies of philosophy, religion, and human nature. In 1929 he returned to the United States and in 1930 enrolled in George Washington University, studying mathematics, engineering, and nuclear physics. Hubbard wanted to answer the basic questions relating to the human being's nature, and decided to do further research on his own. In order to finance this, he began a literary career in the early 1930s, publishing numerous stories and screenplays in various genres, including adventure, mystery, and science fiction. Hubbard continued his travels, and then served in the United States Navy during World War II. He was injured during the war, and used some of his own theories concerning the human mind to assist in his healing.

By 1950 Hubbard had completed enough of his research to write *Dianetics: The Modern Science of Mental Health.* This book described mental techniques designed to clear the mind of unwanted sensations, irrational fears, and psychosomatic illnesses. *Dianetics* quickly became a bestseller and generated a large following. Groups were soon formed so that individuals could assist each other in the application of the techniques described in *Dianetics,* called "auditing." Hubbard lectured extensively, continued his research and wrote numerous volumes covering his discoveries. His research soon led him into a spiritual realm, and in 1952 the "applied religous philosophy" of Scientology was born. It was described as a subject separate from Dianetics, as it dealt not only with the mind, but also with one's spiritual nature. The goal of Scientology would be to fully rehabilitate the spiritual nature of an individual, including rehabilitating all abilities and realizing one's full potential.

In 1954, the first Church of Scientology was established in Los Angeles, California. In 1959 Hubbard moved to Saint Hill Manor, in Sussex, England, to continue his research and the worldwide headquarters of Scientology relocated there. The religion continued to grow during the 1950s and 1960s, and many more churches were founded around the world. In 1966, Hubbard resigned his position as executive director of the Church in order to devote himself to researches into higher levels of spirituality. In August of 1967, he formed the "Sea Organization," a group of dedicated members of the church and continued his travels and research on-board various ships acquired by the church. In 1975 the activities outgrew the ships, and were moved onto land in Clearwater, Florida. From this time on until his death in 1986, Hubbard wrote and published materials on the subjects of Dianetics and Scientology, as well as a number of works of science fiction. The Church of Scientology now has more than three thousand churches, missions, and groups worldwide.

The Church of Scientology believes "that Man is basically good, that he is seeking to survive, [and] that his survival depends on himself and upon his fellows and his attainment of brotherhood with the universe." This is achieved in Scientology by two methods, referred to as "auditing" and "training." Dianetics and Scientology auditing (counselling of one individual by another) consists of an "auditor" guiding someone through various mental processes in order to first free the individual of the effects of the "reactive mind" and then to fully realize the spiritual nature of the person. The "reactive mind" is said to be that part of the mind that operates on a stimulus-response basis, and is composed of residual memories of painful and unpleasant mental incidents (called engrams) which exert unwilling and unknowing control over the individual. When the individual is freed from these undesired effects, he is said to have achieved the state of "clear," which is the goal of Dianetics counselling. An individual then goes on to higher levels of counselling dealing with his nature as an immortal spiritual being (referred to in Scientolgy as a "thetan"). Scientologists believe that a "thetan" has lived many lifetimes before this one and will again live more lifetimes after the death of their current body (the doctrine of reincarnation).

Scientology "training" consists of many levels of courses about (1) improving the daily life of individuals by giving them various tools (i.e., concerning communication) and (2) learning the techniques of auditing so that one can counsel others. Scientologists refer to the presence of a supreme being as representing infinity, but do not worship any deity as such, instead spending their time on the application of Scientology principles to daily activities. Regular church services are held, however, and concern themselves with dicussing the principles of Scientology and their application.

Internationally, the Scientology religion consists of over one thousand separate churches, missions, and groups, spread over 139 countries. Its membership includes people from a wide variety of ages and backgrounds, and is said to encompass eight million members, including over ten thousand staff members. The church sponsors more than one thousand community action and social reform groups that concern themselves with human rights, education, and drug rehabilitation, among other issues. There is an elaborate management structure in the church, with many different levels of types of activities needed to run all the various acitivites of the church.

L. Ron Hubbard's publications number in the hundreds. They cover a wide variety of subjects from communication, the problems of work and how to solve them, to past lives. *Dianetics: The Modern Science of Mental Health* has continued over the years to be a best seller. There are numerous church magazines published on a regular basis, the principal ones being *Source, Advance, Auditor,* and *Freedom.* These serve to inform the membership of current events, progress made, the activities of celebrity and other Scientologists, and the availability of classes and Scientology materials.

The Church of Scientology has been involved in a considerable number of controversial episodes since 1958, such as battles concerning tax issues, a ten-year battle with the Food and Drug Administration regarding the Electro-meters used to assist auditing, and a conflict with Australian government. In addition, the "cult" controversies of the 1970s led to a number of civil lawsuits.

The most notorious series of events in the church began in July 1977, when the FBI conducted a raid on the Washington, D.C., and Los Angeles churches and seized many files of documents. The raid was declared illegal, but the documents remained in government possession and were open to public scrutiny. According to these documents, the church was keeping files on people it considered unfriendly, and there had been various attempts to infiltrate anticult organizations.

As a result of the FBI's raid, some members were indicted and convicted for theft of government documents. The convicted members were released from their offices in the church, which began a reorganization and closing of the Guardian Office.

Problems with the IRS continued through the 1980s and 1990s, and the IRS often moved against the church in ways that questioned its tax-exempt status. These problems terminated in a landmark decision in 1993, when the IRS ceased all litigation and recognized Scientology as a legitimate religious organization. The church has also been attacked in Europe. One of the most significant battles took place in Italy, where a number of officials were charged with both tax evasion and various criminal acts, but were acquitted and Scientology recived judicial recogniton as a religion.

In 1991, *Time* magazine published a front-page attacking Scientology, which responded with a massive public relations campaign and with a lengthy series of full-page ads in *USA Today*. Early in 1992 the church filed a major lawsuit against *Time*, after discovering that the maker of prozac— a psychiatric drug that Scientology had been active in opposing—had been the ultimate prompter of *Time*'s assault on the church. Despite the controversies, the church has been able to grow and expand its membership.

*—JENNIFER ROBINSON*

**ERHARD SEMINARS TRAINING (EST) AND THE FORUM.** Erhard Seminars Training, more commonly known as est, was begun in 1971 by Werner Erhard. While not a church or religion, est is included here because it has often been accused of being a cult. In 1985, est was discontinued and replaced by a program called The Forum, which is very similar to est.

Werner Erhard was born John Paul "Jack" Rosenberg on September 5, 1935, in Pennsylvania. Within a few months of graduating from high school, he married his girlfriend, Patricia Fry. Rosenberg took a series of jobs that included working in an employment office, a meat packing plant, a restaurant, and a construction company. Rosenberg discovered he had a talent for salesmanship when he began selling cars.

On May 25, 1960 Rosenberg left his wife and four small children and flew to Indianapolis with a young woman named June Bryde. En route they changed their names to Werner Hans and Ellen Virginia Erhard. From Indianapolis the Erhards took a train to St. Louis, where Werner got a job as a car salesman. Rosenberg's abandoned wife and four children survived on welfare and the largess of family and friends until Pat found work as a seamstress and then a housekeeper. Five years after Jack left, having heard nothing from or about her husband, Pat Rosenberg obtained a divorce on the grounds of desertion and remarried.

While he was in St. Louis, Werner Erhard read *Think and Grow Rich* (1937) by Napoleon Hill and *Psycho-Cybernetics* (1960) by Maxwell Maltz, both of which greatly influenced him. These books were mass market publications which stressed success, individualism, self-reliance, and imagination. During the next few years he worked selling correspondence courses and books. He and his wife moved to San Francisco where Erhard was in charge of *Parents Magazine*'s child development operations for California, Nevada, and Arizona. He was introduced by one of his employees to the ideas of Abraham Maslow and Carl Rogers, the founders of the "human potential movement," and shifted his orientation from success to fulfillment and satisfaction.

Erhard had read some books and heard radio talks by Alan Watts, the former Episcopalian minister and leading Western interpreter of Zen Buddhism. He attended seminars that Watts held on his houseboat in Sausalito, and credits Watts with pointing him toward the distinction between self and mind. In late 1967, he took the Dale Carnegie course. He was impressed by the course and arranged for his employees to take it. The techniques and format of the Dale Carnegie course interested him and he was beginning to think of starting a course of his own.

Erhard investigated one discipline after another, including Encounter and Transactional Analysis. He took an "Enlightenment Intensive" with H. Charles Berner, founder of Abilitism. He received instruction in martial arts. For nearly a year he participated in Subud. In 1968 he started to receive Scientology auditing or counseling. He and some of his sales staff took a Scientology communications course. He read many Scientology books, including *Problems of Work, A New Slant on Life*, and *Dianetics: The Original Thesis*. He later stated, "I have a lot of respect for L. Ron Hubbard and I consider him to be a genius and perhaps less acknowledged than he ought to be." Erhard acknowledges that est and The Forum use variations on some of the Scientology charts and that the est and Forum terminology is partially taken from Scientology.

In November 1970 he enrolled in a two-weekend course called Mind Dynamics held at San Rafael's Holiday Inn. Mind Dynamics was drawn on techniques cultivated by the famous psychic Edgar Cayce and by Jose Silva, founder of Silva Mind Control, as well as Rosicrucianism and Theosophy. It featured demonstrations and training in memory feats, enhancement of psychic powers, ESP, precognition, psychic diagnosis, and healing. Erhard was so impressed with Mind Dynamics that he immediately signed up to take instructor training from Mind Dynamics founder Alexander Everett. Upon completing the instructor training, he was given the Mind Dynamics San Francisco franchise. He taught his first class to thirty-two students at the Holiday Inn near Fisherman's Wharf a month later. Erhard was soon filling his classes with sixty to one hundred people. By June he was also giving classes in Los Angeles.

After a short time, he began to feel restricted by the confines of the Mind Dynamics program. Alexander Everett and William Penn Patrick, the heads of Mind Dynamics, invited Erhard to become partners with them. He refused, preferring to set up a program of his own. (William Penn Patrick died in a plane crash in 1972 and without his financial backing, Mind Dynamics collapsed in 1973.)

Erhard became a client of eminent and controversial tax attorney Harry Margolis, who had become famous for sheltering the income of middle-class people by applying tax laws and international trust arrangements that had been passed by Congress in order to aid the very rich. Erhard Seminars Training was incorporated as a profit-making educational corporation. The training was aimed at the broad public with the fee initially set at $150 for a two-weekend course.

Erhard officially announced est on September 13, 1971, at his last Mind Dynamics lecture in a ballroom at the Mark Hopkins Hotel on San Francisco's Nob Hill. After finishing his obligatory remarks about Mind Dynamics, he announced that he was quitting Mind Dynamics to begin his own self-awareness program. He had decided to call it Erhard Seminars Training and preferred that it be known only as est. Within three years he had sold $3.4 million of est training sessions.

Est was known for its intensive workshops that promote communications skills and self-empowerment. The purpose of est was to transform one's ability to experience living so that the situations one had been trying to change or had been putting up with, clear up just in the process of life itself. The first two hours of est training were devoted to the rules: No one could move from his seat unless told to do so. No smoking, eating, or drinking were allowed in the room. One meal break was scheduled during the day. The sessions began a 9:00 A.M. and went to somewhere between midnight and 4:00 A.M. No one could go to the bathroom except during short breaks announced by the trainer. Note taking was prohibited. Wristwatches had to be turned over to an assistant. No one could talk unless called on and they had to wait until an assistant came over with a microphone. Students were commonly called "assholes" during the training.

By the end of the second day, students underwent the danger process, an exercise Erhard had adapted from the Scientology communications course. A row of the audience at a time would go on stage and be confronted by est staff. One person would "bullbait" all of them, saying and doing things in order to get them to react. Other volunteers would be body catchers for those who fell, a common occurrence. Later the participants would lie on the floor and imagine that they were afraid of everyone else and then that everyone else was afraid of them.

The third and fourth days were taken up with lectures on what was real and what was unreal and the anatomy of the mind. The lecturer concluded that "what is, is and what ain't, ain't," and that "true enlightenment is knowing you are a machine." The trainer finally told them they were perfect just the way they were. Going around the room, the trainer asked for a show of hands from everyone who had "gotten it," the underlying message of est.

Erhard led all the est training himself for the first year or so. After awhile several others were trained in his exact methods and style and they began to lead training also. There were ten est trainers other than Erhard by the mid 1970s. After est became a success, he recontacted his family in Philadelphia. His ex-wife Pat and his younger brothers and sister began working for him in the est organization. A second est center was opened in Los Angeles in June 1972 and a third in Aspen where John Denver was enlightened. A Honolulu branch opened in November 1973. A few months later one was opened in New York.

In the early 1970s, Erhard traveled to Asia in search of spiritual leaders from whom he could learn. He went to Ganeshpuri, India, where he met Swami Muktananda. In Tibet, he met His Holiness the Gyalwa Karmapa, one of the chief religious leaders of Tibet. Erhard sponsored visits to America by both of these gurus. Est has enjoyed the endorsements of several celebrities. In the mid-1970s John Denver dedicated one of his albums, *Back Home Again*, to est. Denver also wrote a song, "Looking For Space," about est. In 1975 actress Valerie Harper, while accepting an Emmy for her TV show *Rhoda*, thanked "Werner Erhard who changed my life."

Along with its tremendous success, est has generated inevitable controversy. One facet of the controversy centered upon Erhard's financial and tax manager and attorney, Harry Margolis, who was twice indicted by federal grand juries in San Francisco on federal criminal tax fraud charges. One of the counts alleged that Margolis had filed a fraudulent tax return in 1972 for Erhard Seminars Training, Inc. Margolis was acquitted of all charges.

In 1975, a state board in Hawaii decided that est amounted to a form of psychology and, as a result, had to comply with a state law requiring that either a certified psychologist or a physician supervise every training taking place there. Est wrote to the board, stating that it would not comply with the board's decision. Two months later the matter was turned over to the state's Office of Consumer Protection for enforcement.

In 1977, two articles appeared in the *American Journal of Psychiatry* that described five patients who had developed psychotic symptoms, including paranoia, uncontrollable mood swings, and delusions, in the wake of taking the est training. The following year, a Berkeley psychiatrist, who himself had taken the est training in 1973, published in the *American Journal of Psychiatry* his account of sixty-seven of his patients who had taken the est training. The article reported that five of his patients had suffered a regressive episode during or shortly after going through est, but these episodes were short-term and reversible. Aside from this, the response of his patients was positive.

In 1978 Erhard vowed to end hunger in two decades and started the Hunger Project. The project was accused by *Mother Jones* magazine of collecting several million dollars and donating only a few thousand dollars to a San Francisco church that operated a soup kitchen at Christmas and to OXFAM, a prominent hunger organization. The author of the article concluded that Erhard was using the Hunger Project for self-aggrandizement and for promoting est, a profit-making corporation. In late 1990 Erhard formally broke all ties to the Hunger Project.

Several suits were filed against est by trainees and their families. In 1980 a suit was filed which claimed that a trainee's hospitalization and emotional injuries resulted directly from her est training seven months earlier. The psychiatrist who treated this woman for her mental breakdown immediately following her first weekend at est claimed that est broke down her defenses and concept of reality and left her to put herself back together again, which she was unable to do. The case was settled out of court and the terms of the settlement were confidential.

In 1984, a $5 million suit was filed against Erhard by the family of a seemingly healthy twenty-six-year-old man who had dropped dead during est training. In 1992 the jury in the case ruled that Werner Erhard and his company had been negligent and were responsible for inflicting severe emotional distress on the trainee, but found that the est training itself did not proximately cause his death. No money was awarded to the plaintiffs.

In December 1988 a $2 million civil lawsuit was filed against Werner Erhard and Associates claiming that a woman had been wrongfully terminated from her position as an est and Forum leader. The jury determined that neither Erhard nor anyone else at the company had acted improperly in dismissing the employee. They awarded her $28,400 in damages after deciding that Werner Erhard & Associates interfered with her attempt to start a relationships seminar of her own after her firing.

The name of the movement was changed to the Forum in 1985. The Forum runs two-weekend self awareness seminars, advanced six-day courses, a program for those interested in becoming Forum leaders themselves, a Sales Course and a More Time Workshop. In January 1991 Erhard sold the assets of Werner Erhard & Associates to his brother Harry Rosenberg and some other loyal employees.

On March 3, 1991, CBS aired a segment of *60 Minutes* which accused Erhard of beating his wife and children and raping his daughters. One year Erhard filed a lawsuit against CBS, claiming that the broadcast contained false, misleading and defamatory statements. The lawsuit was dropped before a court decision was reached. Erhard left the United States in 1991, beginning a self-imposed exile.

*—KAY HOLZINGER*

**SUKYO MAHIKARI.** Mahikari is the Japanese word for divine true light, believed to be a spiritual and purifying energy. Mahikari began in 1959 when Kotama Okada (1901–1974), received a revelation from god concerning how the use of the Divine Light of the Creator could produce health, harmony, and prosperity. Mahikari is viewed as a cleansing energy sent by Sushin, the Creator of Heaven and Earth, that both spiritually awakens and tunes the soul to its divine purpose. In 1963, he organized what became known as the Sekai Mahikari Bunmei Kyodan (Church of World True Light Civilization). Okada soon became known as Sukui-nushisama (Master of Salvation).

God also revealed to Okada the existence of a divine plan. According to his teachings, all of the phenomena of the universe have been controlled by the plan of the creator. Under this plan, human souls are dispatched to the earth for the specific purpose of learning to utilize its material resources in order to establish a highly evolved civilization governed by spiritual wisdom. These revelations and teachings are to be found in *Goseigen* (The Holy Words), the Mahikari scriptures, and English-language edition of which was published in 1982.

Okada dedicated his life to teaching the art of the divine light to anyone desiring to be of service to the Creator. Today it is taught in a three-day session at which attendees may learn to radiate the Light through the palm of the hand, a process known as *Mahikari no Waza*. At the time of initiation, new members receive an *Omitama*, a pendant used to focus the light.

In 1974, following a divine revelation just prior to his death, Okada passed the mission to his daughter, Seishu Okada, the present leader. In 1978, subsequent to another revelation, Seishu Okada changed the name of the organization to Sukyo Mahikari (*Sukyo* means universal laws). Under her guidance, a new international headquarters was established in Takayama, Japan. In 1984, she completed the mission to construct a World Main Shrine (Suza) in Takayama.

It is said that there are approximately 800,000 members worldwide and 5,000 members in the North American region (United States, Puerto Rico, and Canada). There are sixteen centers in the United States, two centers in Puerto Rico, and two centers in Canada. There are associated centers in over seventy-five countries.

**RAMA SEMINARS.** Rama Seminars were a succesor to Lakshmi, an organization formed in the 1970s by Frederick Lenz, now known as Tantric Zen Master Rama. The Rama Seminars began in 1985 after a series of extraordinary occurrences (levitation, disappearance, and the like) during sessions of group meditation. After such experiences, Lenz told as assembled class of about one hundred students that he had been renamed "Rama" by eternity. Thereafter, the Rama Seminars began.

Humanity is at the end of a cycle, in this case a dark age immediately preceeding an incarnation of Vishnu. Rama is one of the names given a prior incarnation of Vishnu. While Lenz does not claim to be the same as that prior incarnation, he does claim to be an embodiment of a portion of that prior incarnation.

When the Rama Seminars began, the membership of its predecessor, Lakshmi, had reached about eight hundred. Rama Seminars then took up the task of enlightening those individuals who began with Lakshmi. The teachings of the Seminar are styled by Rama as Tantric Zen, a formless Zen that incorporates Chan, Vajrayana Buddhism, Taoism, and jnana yoga.

In 1995 Rama closed down his teaching activities, dissolved his organization, and turned his full attention to the highly successful businesses in which he was engaged with some of his students. However, the later success of his book, *Surfing the Himalayas,* once again propelled him into public view and stirred up old controversies. He died in a drowning accident near his home in 1998.

**THE SYNANON CHURCH.** The Synanon Church was begun in 1958 by Charles E. Dederich in Ocean Park, California, as Synanon Foundation, Inc., a therapeutic group for alcoholics and drug addicts. The group, which within a year grew and moved to Santa Monica, gained a considerable reputation for reeducating drug addicts. During the 1960s, Synanon communities began to appear along the West Coast, as well as in the East, Midwest, and Puerto Rico. In 1968, Dederich settled in Marin County, where three rural Synanon communities were established near the town of Marshall.

Although its religious nature had been tacitly recognized since the beginning of its existence, Synanon was never formally called a religion because many of the people assisted by it had rejected organized religion, while many others outside Synanon regarded it as a therapeutic community. However, as its community life developed, Synanon's religious nature could no longer be denied. The Articles of Incorporation signed in January 1975 designated the Synanon Foundation as the organization through which the Synanon religion and church is manifest, and in November 1980 the name Synanon Church was formally adopted.

Synanon's theological perspective derives from Buddhism and Taoism, as well as from such Western mystics as Ralph Waldo Emerson and Aldous Huxley. Members of the Synanon community seek to manifest the basic principles of oneness in themselves and in their relations with each other. The "Synanon Game" represents the group's central sacrament, and the principal means for the search for unity. It is "played" by a small group of members who meet together as equals in a circle to share in an intense and emotionally expressive context. The outcome of a successful game consists of mutual confession, repentance, and absolution, while offering complete pastoral care. Synanon members follow the golden rule and help each other, believing that the most effective way to redeem humanity from alienation is to form religious communities based upon the beliefs and practices of the Synanon religion and church.

Synanon has been subject of controversy since its inception, and during the last several years over forty people associated with it have been indicted on various charges by grand juries. In December 1961, Dederich went to jail on a zoning code violation. Synanon's practices and techniques have been attacked by the *San Francisco Examiner*, against which Synanon filed a libel suit that ended with a large settlement. However, the most controversial event occurred in 1978 when an attorney suing Synanon was bitten by a rattlesnake. In the following year, Dederich suffered three strokes, and as the trial date approached, he found himself unable to pursue the defense of the case. Thus, those charged settled the case by pleading no contest.

# 20

# CONCLUDING REMARKS:

# THE FUTURE OF NEW RELIGIONS

Since at least the time of the Enlightenment, there have been groups of individuals in Western societies who have looked forward to the day when the ongoing process of secularization would finally sweep away religion entirely. Contrary to these expectations, however, religion has continued to be a vital force in contemporary society. If anything, the revival of conservative Christianity and the explosion of new religions that took place in the latter half of the twentieth century have positioned religion to be a significant player in the twenty-first century. The influential sociologist Max Weber, who was the early twentieth-century's chief analyst of the secularization process, would not have been surprised.

In the concluding paragraphs of his classic study, *The Protestant Ethic and the Spirit of Capitalism*, Weber painted a grim picture of a future in which the last drops of humanness would be squeezed out of the social order by the "iron cage" of modern industrial capitalism:

> Specialists without spirit, sensualists without heart, this nullity imagines that it has attained a level of civilization never before achieved.

This empty world would be brought about by a process he referred to as "rationalization," by which he meant the increasing regimentation, bureaucratization, and "disenchantment" of life that characterizes modernization. However, Weber also speculated that toward the end of this process there was a slim possibility humanity might break free of its cage, either by returning to older ideals of human culture or by embracing new visions of what it means to be human:

> No one knows who will live in this cage in the future, or whether at the end of this tremendous development entirely new prophets will arise, or there will be a great rebirth of old ideas and ideals, or, if neither, mechanized petrification.

Some scholars have called attention to this passage as having been prophetic of our present situation, in which so many new religions have come into being. These academic observers have not, however, generally given this statement its proper Weberian significance. The tendency has been to interpret Weber's brief mention of "new prophets" as predicting that new religions would arise in protest against the inevitable dehumanization of the world. In other words, this religious creativity would be a helpless railing against the machine—a last desperate gasping for air before the whirlpool of rationalization sucked us all beneath the surface forever. It is unlikely, however, that this was Weber's view of the matter.

The primary thesis of *The Protestant Ethic and the Spirit of Capitalism* was that rationalizing capitalism—the dominant force shaping modern society—was given birth within and nurtured at the bosom of emergent Protestantism. Although its innovativeness has been obscured by five centuries of rhetoric about the Reformation recovering and restoring original Christianity (which had supposedly been corrupted by Roman Catholicism), it is now clear in retrospect that Protestantism was the "new religion" of its day. Thus, Weber's fleeting mention of "new prophets" was not meant to assert that the appearance of new religions would necessarily represent humanity's last gasp before the iron cage closed in for the final kill. Rather what he meant to suggest was that perhaps an alternative social force might arise out of some future new religion, just as rationalistic capitalism had arisen out of the Reformation. Furthermore, Weber seemed to imply that this new force might even have the power to throw open the cage door and save humanity from an otherwise dismal fate.

Weber could cast new religions in this role because the subcultures created by youthful religious communities are perfect laboratories within which to experiment with new forms of social organization. Members of such groups are open to this kind of experimentation for two reasons: First, they are frequently adverse to at least some features of modern society. Second, they are often inclined to accept the insights of their religion's leadership as being on par with—and, in many cases, more legitimate than—the norms of the surrounding social order. Thus, new religions promote an environment within which alternative ideals and social arrangements can be entertained, legitimated, and practiced. Once established, these new patterns of human life then have the potential for breaking through the boundaries of their original subcultures and influencing the larger society.

To point this out is not, of course, the same as asserting that the world of the future will emerge out of some exotic new religion. Weber did, however, seem to indicate this scenario as a possibility. And who knows? Perhaps like Protestantism, one or more of the religious movements we have examined in the preceding pages might indeed emerge to set the tone for the future—for good or for ill.

# BIBLIOGRAPHY

"The Acid Test of Accountability." *Cornerstone* 22 (1994):102–103

Adamski, George. *Pioneers of Space: A Trip to the Moon, Mars, and Venus.* Los Angeles: Leonard-Freefield Co., 1949.

———. *Questions and Answers by the Royal Order of Tibet.* N.p.: Royal Order of Tibet, 1936.

Adkin, Clare E. *Brother Benjamin: A History of the Israelite House of David.* Berrien Springs, Mich.: Andrews University Press, 1990.

Adler, Felix. *Creed and Deed: A Series of Discourses.* New York: Putnam, 1877.

Adler, Jacob, and Robert M. Kamins. *The Fantastic Life of Walter Murray Gibson: Hawaii's Minister of Everything.* Honolulu: University of Hawaii Press, 1986.

Adler, Margot. *Drawing Down the Moon: Witches, Druids, Goddess-Worshippers, and Other Pagans in America Today.* 2d ed. Boston: Beacon Press, 1989.

*Adolph Ernst Knoch, 1874–1965.* Saugus, Calif.: Concordant Publishing Concern, 1965.

Aetherius Society. *Temple Degree Study Courses.* Hollywood, Calif.: The Aetherius Society, 1982.

Age, Mark. *How to Do All Things: Your Use of Divine Power.* Ft. Lauderdale, Fla.: Mark-Age, 1988.

Ahmad, Hazrat Mirza Bashiruddin Mahmud. *Ahmadiyyat or the True Islam.* Washington, D.C.: American Fazl Mosque. 1951.

———. *Invitation.* Rabwah, Pakistan: Ahmadiyya Muslim Foreign Missions Office, 1968.

Ahmad, Mirza Ghulam Hazrat. *Our Teaching.* Rabwah, West Pakistan: Ahmadiyya Muslim Foreign Missions Office, 1962.

Aho, James. *The Politics of Righteousness: Idaho Christian Patriotism.* Seattle, Wash.: University of Washington Press, 1990.

Ahrens, Frank. "A Krishna Clan's Chants for Survival." *Washington Post,* 8 September 1991, F1.

Aitken, Robert. *A Zen Wave*. New York: Weatherhill, 1978.

———. *The Mind of Clover*. San Francisco: North Point Press, 1984.

al-'Arabi, Ibn. *Sufis of Andalucia*. Berkeley and Los Angeles: University of California Press, 1971.

———. *The Bezels of Wisdom*. New York: Paulist Press, 1980.

Alan, Jim, and Selena Fox. *Circle Magick Songs*. Madison, Wis.: Circle Publications, 1977.

Ali, Nobel Drew. *Moorish Literature*. The Author, 1928.

———. *Timothy Drew: The Holy Koran of the Moorish Science Temple of America*. Baltimore, Md.: Moorish Science Temple of America, 1978.

Allen, A. A., and Walter Wagner. *Born to Loose, Bound to Win*. Garden City, N.Y.: Doubleday, 1970.

———. *My Cross*. Miracle Valley, Ariz.: A. A. Allen Revivals, n.d.

Allen, James B., and Glen M. Leonard. *The Story of the Latter-day Saints*. Salt Lake City: Deseret Book Company, 1992.

Allen, Paul M., ed. *A Christian Rosenkreutz Anthology*. Blauvelt, New York: Rudolph Steiner Publications, 1968.

Allred, Rulon C. *Treasures of Knowledge*. 2 vols. Hamilton, Mont.: Bitteroot Publishing Co., 1982.

Alper, Frank. *Exploring Atlantis*. Farmingdale, N.Y.: Coleman Publishing, 1982.

Althma, Leh Rheadia. *The Garden of the Soul*. Newberry Springs, Calif.: AUM Temple of Universal Truth, 1943.

*The American Buddhist Directory*. New York: American Buddhist Movement, 1985.

Amipa, Lama Sherab Gyaltsen. *The Opening of the Lotus*. London: Wisdom Publications, 1987.

Amma. *Swami Muktananda Paramahansa*. Ganeshpuri, India: Shree Gurudev Ashram, 1969.

Amrit Desai, *Guru and Disciple* Sumneytown, Pa.: Kripalu Yoga Ashram (1975).

*An Account of the Conflagration of the Ursuline Convent*. Boston: "Printed for the Publisher," 1834.

Anandamurti, Shrii Shrii. *Baba's Grace*. Denver, Colo.: Amrit Publications, 1973.

———. *Baba's Grace*. Los Altos Hills, Calif.: Ananda Marga Publications, 1973.

———. *The Great Universe: Discourses on Society*. Los Altos Hills, Calif.: Ananda Marga publications, 1973.

———. *The Spiritual Philosophy of Shrii Shrii Anandamurti*. Denver, Colo.: Ananda Marga Publications, 1981.

*The Ancient Wisdom School: A Collection of Teachings from Ramtha*. Edited by Diane Munoz. Yelm, Wash.: Diane Munoz, 1992.

Anderson, Alan. "Horatio W. Dresser and the Philosophy of New Thought." Ph.D. diss., Boston University, 1963.

Anderson, Arthur M., ed. *For the Defense of the Gospel*. New York: Church of Christ Pub. Co., 1972.

Anderson, C. LeRoy. *For Christ Will Come Tomorrow: The Saga of the Morrisites*. Logan, Utah: Utah State University Press, 1981.

Anderson, Max J. *The Polygamy Story: Fiction or Fact*. Salt Lake City: Publishers Press, 1979.

Andrews, Sherry. "Maranatha Ministries." *Charisma* 7, no. 9 (May 1982).

Anderson, Victor H. *Thorns of the Blood Rose*. 1960; reprint, Redwood Valley, Calif.: Nemeton, 1970.

Anka, Darryl. *Orion and the Black League*. Encino, Calif.: Interplanetary Connections, 1978.

*Apocalypse* (magazine). Bulletin de Liaison du Mouvement Raelian.

*The Aquarian Academy*. Eureka, Calif.: Sirius Books, 1978.

Aquino, Michael A. *The Church of Satan*. N.p.: The Author, 1989.

Arbaugh, George Bartholemew. *Revelation in Mormonism*. Chicago: University of Chicago Press, 1932.

*Arcana: Inner Dimensions of Spirituality* 1:1. Bryn Athyn, Pa.: Swedenborg Association, 1994.

Arguelles, Jose. *The Transformative Vision: Reflections on the Nature and History of Human Expression*. Berkeley, Calif.: Shambhala, 1988.

Armor, Reginald. *Ernest Holmes, the Man*. Los Angeles: Science of Mind Publications, 1977.

Armstrong, Herbert W. *The United States and the British Commonwealth in Prophecy*. Pasadena,Calif.: Worldwide Church of God, 1980.

Arnold, Eberhard. *Why We Live in Community*. Rifton, N.Y.: Plough Publishing House, 1967.

Arnold, Emmy. *Torches Together*. Rifton, N.Y.: Plough Publishing House, 1971.

Asch, Solomon E. "Studies of Independence and Conformity: A Minority of One Against a Unanimous Majority." *Psychological Monographs* (1956).

Ashlag, Yehuda. *Kabbalah: A Gift of the Bible*. Jerusalem, Israel: Research Centre of Kabbalah, 1994.

Atkinson, William Walker. *The Law of the New Thought*. Chicago: The Psychic Research Co., 1902.

*Atlantis: Fact or Fiction*. Virginia Beach: ARE Press, 1962.

Avenell, Bruce. *A Reason for Being*. La Grange, Tex.: Eureka Society, 1983.

*The Awakened*. Los Angeles: Awakened, 1933.

Awbrey, Scott. *Path of Discovery*. Los Angeles: United Church of Religious Science, 1987.

Bach, Marcus. *He Talked With God*. Portland, Oreg.: Metropolitan Press, 1951.

Bach, Richard. *The Bridge Across Forever*. New York: Dell, 1984.

Baer, Hans A. "Black Spiritual Israelites in a Small Southern City." *Southern Quarterly* 23 (1985): 103–24.

———. *The Black Spiritual Movement: A Religious Response to Racism*. Knoxville, Tenn.: University of Tennessee Press, 1984.

Bailey, Alice A. *The Unfinished Autobiography*. New York: Lucis Publishing Company, 1951.

Bailey, Dorothy A. *The Light of Ivah Bergh Whitten*. Southampton: A.M.I.C.A., n.d.

"Baker Roshi Forms New Group." *Vajradhatu Sun* (March 1985): 4.

Ball, John. *Ananda: Where Yoga Lives*. Bowling Green, Ohio: Bowling Green University Popular Press, 1982.

Ballard, Guy W. *The "I AM" Discourses*. 4th ed. Chicago: St. Germain Press, 1935, 1982.

———. *Unveiled Mysteries*. 4th ed. Chicago: St. Germain Press, 1934, 1982.

Balsekar, Ramesh S. *Experiencing the Teachings*. Redondo Beach, Calif.: Advaita Press, 1988.

Balsekar, Ramesh S. *From Consciousness to Consciousness*. Redondo Beach, Calif.: Advaita Press, 1989.

Balyoz, Harold. *Three Remarkable Women*. Flagstaff, Ariz.: Altai Publishers, 1986.

Banerjee, H. N. and W. C. Oursler. *Lives Unlimited: Reincarnation East and West*. New York: Doubleday, 1974.

Barker, Eileen. *New Religious Movements*. London: Her Majesty's Stationary Office, 1989.

———. *The Making of a Moonie: Choice or Brainwashing?* New York: Basil Blackwell, 1984.

Barkun, Michael. *Religion and the Racist Right: The Origins of the Christian Identity Movement*. Chapel Hill, N.C.: University of North Carolina Press, 1994.

Barnouw, Victor. "Siberian Shamanism and Western Spiritualism." Journal of the Society of Psychical Research 36 (1942): 140–68.

Bartley, William Warren III. *Werner Erhard: The Transformation of a Man, the Founding of est*. New York: Clarkson N. Potter, Inc., 1978.

Basham, Don. *A Handbook on Holy Spirit Baptism*. Monroeville, Pa.: Whitaker Books, 1969.

———. *Ministering the Baptism of the Holy Spirit*. Monroeville, Pa.: Whitaker Books, 1971.

*A Basic Introduction of the Teachings and Practices of the Hohm Community*. Prescott Valley, Ariz.: Hohm Community, n.d.

Bayard, Jean-Pierre. *La Guide des sociétés secrètes*. Paris: Philippe Lebaud. 1989.

Beacham, A. D., Jr. *A Brief History of the Pentecostal Holiness Church*. Franklin Springs, Ga.: Advocate Press, 1983.

Bear, Robert. *Delivered Unto Satan*. Carlisle, Penn.: The Author, 1974.

Beckford, James. "The Media and New Religious Movements." In *From the Ashes: Making Sense of Waco*. Edited by James R. Lewis. Lanham, Md.: Rowman & Littlefield, 1994.

Bednaroski, Mary Farrell. 1989. *New Religions and the Theological Imagination in America*. Bloomington: Indiana University Press.

Beebe, Charles S. *Spirits in Rebellion*. Dallas: Southern Methodist University Press, 1977.

Beecher, Lyman. *Plea for the West*. Cincinnati: Truman and Smith, 1835.

Begg, W. D. *The Holy biography of Hazrat Khwaja Muinuddin Chishti*. Tucson, Ariz.: Chishti Mission of America, 1977.

*The Beliefs and Practices of the Local Church*. Anaheim, Calif.: Living Stream Ministry, 1978.

Bell, Alfreda Eva. *Boadicea: The Mormon Wife*. Baltimore: Arthur R. Orton, 1855.

Bell, Jessie W. *The Grimoire of Lady Sheba*. Llewellyn, 1972.

Benner, Joseph S. *The Impersonal Life*. San Gabriel, Calif.: Willing Publishing Company, 1971.

Bennett, John G. *Gurdjieff: Making a New World*. New York: Harper & Row, 1973.

———. *Is There "Life" on Earth?* New York: Stonehill Publishing Company, 1973.

Bennett, John. *Witness: The Autobiography of John Bennett*. London: Turnstone Books, 1974.

Berg, Philip, ed. *An Entrance to the Zohar*. Jerusalem, Israel: Research Centre of Kabbalah, 1994.

———. *Kabbalah for the Layman*. 3 vols. Jerusalem, Israel: Research Centre of Kabbalah.

———. *The Wheel of the Soul*. Jerusalem, Israel: Research Centre of Kabbalah, 1984.

Berger, Peter L. *The Social Construction of Reality*. Garden City, New Jersey: Doubleday, 1966.

Bergesen, Albert. *The Sacred and the Subversive.* Storrs, Conn.: SSSR Monograph Series, 1984.

Bernard, Pierre. "In Re Fifth Veda." *International Journal of the Tantrik Order.* New York: Tantrik Order in America, 1909.

Besant, Annie. *Autobiographical Sketches.* London: Freethought Publishing Co., 1885.

Beskow, Per. *Strange Tales About Jesus.* Philadelphia: Fortress Press, 1983.

Bestor, Arthur. *Backwoods Utopias.* Philadelphia: University of Pennsylvania Press, 1950.

Bethards, Betty. *There Is No Death.* Novato, Calif.: Inner Light Foundation, 1975.

Bhagavad Gita. Translated by Juan Mascaro. Baltimore, Md.: Penguin, 1970.

Billington, Ray Allen. *The Protestant Crusade 1800–1860: A Study of the Origins of American Nativism.* New York: Macmillan, 1938.

Bjorling, Joel. *The Churches of God, Seventh Day: A Bibliography.* New York: Garland Publishing, 1987.

Blavatsky, Helena Petrovna. *Collected Writings.* 16 vols. Wheaton, Ill.: Theosophical Publishing House, 1950–1987.

———. *Isis Unveiled.* Wheaton, Ill.: Theosophical Publishing House, 1972.

———. *The Secret Doctrine.* 1889.

———. *Some Unpublished Letters of Helena Petrovna Blavatsky.* Introduction and commentary by Eugene Rollin Corson. London: Rider and Co., n.d.

Bletzer, June G. The Donning International Encyclopedic Psychic Dictionary. Norfolk, Va.: Donning, 1986.

Bliss, Sylvester. *Memoirs of William Miller.* Boston: Joshua V. Himes, 1853.

Block, Marguerita Beck. *The New Church in the New World.* New York: Henry Holt and Company, 1932.

Blofeld, John. *Taoism: The Road to Immortality.* Boulder: Shambhala, 1978.

Blumhofer, Edith. "The Finished Work of Calvary." *Assemblies of God Heritage* 3 (fall 1983): 9–11.

Bolen, Jean Shinoda. *Goddesses in Everywoman: A New Psychology of Women.* Harper and Row, 1984.

———. *Gods in Everyman: A New Psychology of Men's Lives and Loves.* Harper and Row, 1989.

Bonewits, Isaac. *Authentic Thaumaturgy.* Albany, Calif.: The CHAOSium, 1978.

Bonewits, P. E. I. *Real Magic.* Weiser, 3d ed., 1988.

*The Book of Books.* East Rutherford, N.J.: Dawn Bible Students Association, 1962.

*A Book of Commandments for the Government of the Church of Christ.* Independence, Mo.: Church of Christ (Temple Lot), 1960.

*Book of Doctrines, 1903–1970.* Huntsville, Ala.: Church of God Publishing House, 1970.

*The Book of Yahweh.* Abilene, Tex.: House of Yahweh, 1987.

Bosbeke (van), André, with Jean-Pierre de Staercke. *Chevaliers du vingtième siècle. Enquête sur les sociétés occultes et les ordres de chevalerie contemporains.* Anvers: EPO, 1988.

Boswell, Charles. "The Great Fume and Fuss Over the Omnipotent Oom." *True* (January 1965): 31–33, 86–91.

Bouchard, Alain. "Mouvement Raelian." In *Nouvel Age . . . Nouvelles Croyances*. Montreal: Editions Paulines & Mediaspaul, 1989.

Bowden, Henry Warner. *Dictionary of American Religious Biography*. Westport, Connecticut: Greenwood Press, 1977.

Bozeman, John. "A Preliminary Assessment of Women's Conversion Narratives at New Vrindaban." *Syzygy* 3 (1994).

———. "Jesus People USA after Twenty Years: Balancing Sectarianism and Assimilation." Paper read before the Communal Studies Society, New Harmony, Indiana, 16 October 1993.

———. "Jesus People USA: An Examination of an Urban Communitarian Religious Group." M.A. thesis, Florida State University, fall, 1990.

———. "The Interfaith Mission of New Vrindaban." Paper read before the Communal Studies Association, Nauvoo, Illinois, 16 October 1992.

Bracelin, J. L. *Gerald Gardner: Witch*. London: Octagon Press, 1960.

Braden, Charles S. "Gestefeld, Ursula Newell." In *Notable American Women*. Edited by Edward T. James, Janet Wilson James, and Paul S. Boyer. Vol. 2. Cambridge, Mass.: The Belknap Press of Harvard University Press, 1971, pp. 27–28.

———. "Hopkins, Emma Curtis." In *Notable American Women*. Edited by Edward T. James, Janet Wilson James, and Paul S. Boyer. Vol. 2. Cambridge, Mass.: The Belknap Press of Harvard University Press, 1971, pp. 219–20.

———. *Spirits in Rebellion*. Dallas: Southern Methodist University Press, 1963.

———. *These Also Believe*. New York: Macmillan, 1949.

*Brahma Baba—The Corporeal Medium of Shiva Baba*. Mount Abu, India: Prajapita Brahma Kumaris Ishwariya Vishwa Vidyalaya, n.d.

Brahmavidya, Swami. *Transcendent-Science or the Science of Self Knowledge*. Chicago: Transcendent-Science Society, 1922.

Brandon, Ruth. *The Spiritualists*. New York: Alfred A. Knopf, 1983.

Branham, William Marrion. *Conduct, Order, Doctrine of the Church*. Jeffersonville, Ind.: Spoken Word Publications, 1974.

———. *Footprints on the Sands of Time*. Jeffersonville, Ind.: Spoken Word Publications, n.d.

Braude, Ann. *Radical Spirits*. Boston: Beacon Press, 1989.

*A Brief Biography of Darshan Singh*. Bowling Green, Va.: Sawan Kirpal Publications, [1983].

*Brief Life Sketch of Param Sant Kirpal Singh Ji Maharaj*. Wembly, England: Kirpal Bhavan, 1976.

Britten, Emma Hardinge. *Modern American Spiritualism*. 1870; reprint, New Hyde Park, N.Y.: University Books, 1970.

———. *Nineteenth Century Miracles*. New York: William Britten, 1884.

Brock, Peter. *The Quaker Peace Testimony, 1660–1914*. York: Sessions, 1991.

Bromage, Bernard. *Tibetan Yoga*. Wellingborough, Northamptonshire, England: The Aquarian Press, 1979. First published 1952.

Bromley, David G., and James T. Richardson. *The Brainwashing/Deprogramming Controversy*. New York: Edwin Mellen, 1983.

Bromley, David G., and Anson D. Shupe Jr. *Moonies in America: Cult, Church, Crusade*. Beverly Hills, Calif.: Sage, 1979.

———. *Strange Gods: The Great American Cult Scare*. Boston: Beacon Press, 1981.

Brooke, Anthony. *The Universal Link Revelations.* London: Universal Foundation, 1967.

Brooks, Louise McNamara. *Early History of Divine Science.* Denver, Colo.: First Divine Science Church, 1963.

Brooks, Nona L. *Short Lessons in Divine Science.* Denver: The Author, 1928.

———. *The Prayer That Never Fails.* Denver: Divine Science Church and College, 1935.

Brotz, Howard M. *The Black Jews of Harlem.* New York: Schocken Books, 1970.

Brown, Charles E. *When the Trumpet Sounded.* Anderson, Ind.: 1951.

Brown, Gordon. *Christian Science Nonsectarian.* Haslemere, Surrey, England: Gordon and Estelle Brown 1966.

Brown, Kingdon L. *The Metaphysical Lessons of Saint Timothy's Abbey Church.* Grosse Pointe, Mich.: St. Timothy's Abbey Church, 1966.

Browne, Robert T. *Introduction to Hermetic Science and Philosophy.* Hermetic Society, n.d.

Brown, Slater. *The Heyday of Spiritualism.* New York: Hawthorn Books, 1970.

Bryan, Gerald B. *Psychic Dictatorship in America.* Burbank, Calif.: The New Era Press, 1940.

Buckland, Raymond. *Buckland's Complete Book of Witchcraft.* St. Paul, Minn.: Llewellyn Publications, 1986.

———. *The Tree: The Book of Shadows of Seax-Wica.* Samuel Weiser, 1974.

Buckley, Tim. "History of the Zen Meditation Center of Rochester." *Wind Bell* 8 (fall 1969): 51–53.

Buczynski, Edmund M. *Witchcraft Fact Book.* New York: Magickal Childe, 1969.

Budapest, Zsuzsanna E. *The Feminist Book of Lights and Shadows.* Venice, Calif.: Luna Publications, 1976.

———. *The Holy Book of Women's Mysteries.* Berkeley: Wingbow Press, 1989.

*Buddhist Churches of America, 75 Year History, 1899–1974.* 2 vols. Chicago: Norbert, 1974.

Buehrens, John A., and F. Forrester Church. *Our Chosen Faith.* Boston: Beacon Press, 1989.

Burgess, Stanley M., and Gary B. McGee, eds. *Dictionary of Pentecostal and Charismatic Movements.* Grand Rapids, Mich.: Zondervan Publishing House, 1988.

Burgoyne, Thomas H. *Celestial Dynamics.* Denver, Colo.: Astro-Philosophical Publishing Co., 1896.

———. *The Light of Egypt.* 2 vols. Albuquerque, N.Mex.: Sun Publishing Company, 1980.

Burham, Kenneth E. *God Comes to America.* Boston: Lambeth Press, 1979.

Burkett, R. K. *Garveyism as a Religious Movement:The Institutionalization of a Black Civil Religion.* London: Scarecrow, Press, 1878.

Burkett, Randall. *Garveyism as a Religious Movement.* Metuchen, N.J.: Scarecrow Press, 1978.

Bussell, D. J. *First Steps in Metaphysics.* Los Angeles: National Academy of Metaphysics, n.d.

Butler, Hiram E. *The Goal of Life.* Applegate, Calif.: Esoteric Publishing Company, 1908.

————. *The Narrow Way of Attainment.* Applegate, Calif.: Esoteric Publishing Company, 1901.

————. *The Seven Creative Principles.* Applegate, Calif.: Esoteric Publishing Company, 1950.

————. *Special Instructions for Women.* Applegate, Calif.: Esoteric Fraternity, 1942.

Buzzard, Anthony. *The Kingdom of God—When and Whence?* Oregon, Ill.: Restoration Fellowship, 1980.

Byers, Andrew L. *Birth of a Reformation.* Anderson, Ind.: 1921.

Cabot, Laurie. *Power of the Witch: The Earth, the Moon, and the Magical Path to Enlightenment.* New York: Delacorte Press, 1989.

*Cambridge Buddhist Assocation.* Cambridge, Mass.: Cambridge Buddhist Association, 1960.

Cameron, Charles, ed. *Who Is Guru Maharaj Ji?* New York: Bantam Books, 1973.

Cammell, C. R. *Aleister Crowley.* London: New English Library, 1969.

Campbell, Bruce F. *Ancient Wisdom Revived: A History of the Theosophical Movement.* Berkeley: University of California Press, 1980.

Carden, Karen W., and Robert W. Pelton. *The Persecuted Prophets.* New York: A. S. Barnes, 1976.

Carter, Ben Ammi. *God, the Black Man, and Truth.* Chicago: Communicators Press, 1982.

Carus, Paul. *The Dawn of a New Religious Era.* Chicago: Open Court Publishing Co., 1913.

————. *The Gospel of Buddha.* Chicago: Open Court Publishing Co., 1894.

Case, Paul Foster. *The True and Invisible Rosicrucian Order.* The Author, 1928.

*Cat's Yawn.* New York: First Zen Institute in America, 1947.

Cavendish, Richard, ed. *Encyclopedia of The Unexplained: Magic, Occultism, and Parapsychology.* London: Arkana Penguin Books, 1989.

Cavendish, Richard. *A History of Magic.* London: Weidenfeld and Nicolson, 1977.

Cayce, Edgar. *What I Believe* (Virginia Beach: Edgar Cayce Publishing Company, 1946).

Cayce, Hugh Lynn. *Venture Inward* (New York: Harper and Row, 1964).

Chadda, H. C., ed. *Seeing Is Above All: Sant Darshan's First Indian Tour.* Bowling Green, Va.: Sawan Kirpal Publications, 1978.

Chaffanjon, Arnaud, and Bertrand Galimard Flavigny. *Ordres & contre-ordres de chevalerie,* Paris: Mercure de France, 1982.

Chainey, George. *Deus Homo.* Boston, Mass.: Christopher Publishing House, 1927.

————. *The Unsealed Bible.* London: Kegan Paul, Trench, Truebner & Co., 1902.

Chaney, Earlyne, and William L. Messick. *Kundalini and the Third Eye.* Upland, Calif.: Astara's Library of Mystical Classics, 1980.

Chaney, Robert G. *The Inner Way.* Los Angeles: DeVorss & Co., 1962.

————. *Mediums and the Development of Mediumship.* Freeport, N.Y.: Books for Libraries Press, 1972.

————. *Mysticism, the Journey Within.* Upland, Calif.: Astra's Library of Mystical Classics, 1979.

Chapman, A. H. *What TM Can and Cannot Do for You.* New York: Berkeley Publishing Corporation, 1976.

*The Charlestown Convent; Its Destruction by a Mob on the Night of August 11, 1834.*
    Boston: Patrick Donahoe, 1870.

Chen, James. *Meet Brother Nee.* Hong Kong: The Christian Publishers, 1976.

Chia, Mantak, and Maneewan Chia. *Healing Love Through the Tao: Cultivating Female
    Sexual Energy.* Huntington, N.Y.: Healing Tao Books, 1986.

Chinmayananda, Swami. *Kindle Life.* Madra: Chinmaya Publications Trust, n.d.

———. *A Manual for Self-Unfoldment.* Napa, Calif.: Chinmaya Publications (West),
    1975.

———. *Meditation (Hasten Slowly).* Napa, Calif.: Family Press, 1974.

———. *The Way to Self-Perfection.* Napa, Calif.: Chinmaya Publications (West), 1976.

Chryssides, George D. *The Advent of Sun Myung Moon: The Origins, Beliefs, and Prac-
    tices of the Unification Church.* New York: St. Martin's, 1991

Church, Connie. *Crystal Clear.* New York: Villard Books, 1987.

"Church of Aphrodite, Goddess of Love is chartered in New York." *Life,* 4
    December 1939.

"Church of Christ Restored." *Restoration* 4, no. 3 (July 1985): 7.

*Circle Guide to Pagan Resources.* Mt. Horeb, Wis.: Circle, 1987.

"*Clarion Call,* a Classy New Journal from S. F. Gaudiyas." *Hinduism Today* 10, no. 9
    (September 1988): 1, 17.

Clark, Jerome. "Life in a Pyramid." *Fate* 36, no. 6 (June 1983): 33–44.

———. "UFOs in the 1980s." In *The UFO Encyclopedia.* Vol. 1. Detroit, Mich.:
    Apogee Books, 1990.

Clymer, R. Swinburne. *The Rosicrucian Fraternity in America.* 2 vols. Quakertown, Pa.:
    Rosicrucian Foundation, 1935.

Coates, James. *Armed and Dangerous.* New York: Hill and Wang, 1987.

Cohen, Andrew. *Autobiography of an Awakening.* Corte Madera, Calif.: Moksha
    Foundation, 1992.

———. *My Master is Myself.* Moksha Foundation, 1989.

Cohn, Norman. *Cosmos, Chaos, and the World to Come: The Ancient Roots of Apocalyptic
    Faith.* New Haven: Yale University Press, 1993.

———. *The Pursuit of the Millennium.* London: Oxford University Press, 1957.

Cole, W. Owen, and Piara Singh Sambhi. *The Sikhs.* London: Routledge & Kegan
    Paul, 1978.

Cole-Whitaker, Terry. *How to Have More in a Have-Not World.* New York: Fawcett
    Crest, 1983.

———. *Love and Power in a World Without Limits: A Woman's Guide to the Goddess
    Within.* San Francisco: Harper & Row, 1989.

Collier, Sophia. *Soul Rush: The Odyssey of a Young Woman in the '70s.* New York:
    William Morrow and Co., 1978.

Coloquhoun, Ithell. *Sword of Wisdom: MacGregor Mathers and the Golden Dawn.* New
    York: G. P. Putnam's Sons, 1975.

*Communities of the Past and Present.* Newllano, La.: Llano Cooperative Colony, 1924.

*The Constitution: Abiding Laws or Empty Words?* Island Pond, Vt.: Island Pond Freep-
    aper, 1987.

Conway, Flo, and Jim Siegelman. "Information Disease: Have Cults Created a New
    Mental Illness?" *Science Digest* (1982).

————. *Snapping: America's Epidemic of Sudden Personality Change.* New York: Lippincott, 1978.

Conze, Edward. *Buddhist Thought in India.* 1962; reprint, Ann Arbor: University of Michigan Press, 1967.

Cook, Philip L. *Zion City, Illinois: John Alexander Dowie's Theocracy.* Zion, Ill.: Zion Historical Society, 1970.

Cooper, John. "The Esoteric School Within the Hargrove Theosophical Society." *Theosophical History* 4, no. 7–8 (April/July 1993): 178–86.

*A Course in Miracles.* 3 vols., New York: Foundation for Inner Peace, 1975.

*Covenant of the Goddess Newsletter* (published eight times a year, available by subscription from Covenant of the Goddess, Box 1226, Berkeley, Calif. 94704).

Cranston, Sylvia. *HPB: The Extraordinary Life and Influence of Helena Blavatsky, Founder of the Modern Theosophical Movement.* New York: Jeremy P. Tarcher/Putnam Book/G. P. Putnam's Sons, 1993.

*The Creator's Grand Design.* East Rutherford, N.J.: Dawn Bible Students Association, 1969.

*The Creed.* London: Christian Community Press, 1962.

Crenshaw, James. *Telephone Between Two Worlds.* Los Angeles: DeVorss & Co., 1950.

Crim, Keith, ed. *The Perennial Dictionary of World Religions.* 1981; reprint, New York: Harper & Row, 1989.

Cronon, Edmund David. *Black Moses: The Story of Marcus Garvey and the U.N.I.A.* Madison, Wis.: University of Wisconsin Press, 1969.

Crowley, Aleister Edward. *Confessions.* New York: Hill and Wang, 1969.

Cryer, Newman. "Laboratory for Tomorrow"s Church." *Together* 10, no. 3 (March 1966).

Culpepper, Emily. "The Spiritual Movement of Radical Feminist Consciousness." In *Understanding the New Religions.* Edited by Jacob Needleman and George Baker. New York: Seabury, 1978, pp. 220–34.

Cushing, Margaret. "Emma Curtis Hopkins: The Teacher of Teachers." *New Thought Bulletin* 28 (spring 1945): 5–7.

D'Andrade, Hugh. *Charles Fillmore.* New York: Harper & Row, 1974.

Dahl, Mikkel. *The Coming New Society.* Windsor, Ont.: Dawn of Truth, n.d.

————. *God's Master Plan of Love for Man.* Windsor, Ont.: Dawn of Truth, 1961.

————. *Have You Heard, the Great Pyramid Speaks.* Fulton, Mo.: Shepherdsfield, 1986.

Dallimore, Arnold. *Forerunner of the Charismatic Movement: The Life of Edward Irving.* Chicago: Moody Press, 1983.

Darby, John Nelson. *The Collected Works.* 34 vols. Oak Park, Ill.: 1971.

Dass, Baba Ram. *The Only Dance There Is.* New York: Jason Aaronson, 1976.

————. *Remember, Be Here Now.* San Christobal, N.Mex.: Lama Foundation, 1971.

Davis, Andrew Jackson. *The Magic Staff.* New York: J. S. Brown & Co., 1857.

Dayton, Donald W. *Theological Roots of Pentecostalism* (Grand Rapids: Zondervan Publishing House, 1987).

De Leon, Victor. *The Silent Pentecostals.* Taylor, S.C.: Faith Printing Co., 1979.

DeCharms, George. *The Distinctiveness of the New Church.* Bryn Athyn, Pa.: Academy Book Room, 1962.

————. *The Holy Supper.* Bryn Athyn, Pa.: General Church Publication Committee, 1961.

Dederich, Charles E. *The Tao Trip Sermon.* Marshall, Calif.: Synanon Publishing House, 1978

Delaforge, Gaetan. *The Templar Tradition in the Age of Aquarius.* Putney, Vt.: Threshold Books, 1987.

Demos, John Putnam. *Entertaining Satan.* New York: Oxford University Press, 1982.

Dennon, Jim. *Dr. Newbrough and Oahspe.* Kingman, Arizona: Faithist Journal, 1975.

DeSmet, Kate. "Return to the House of Judah." *Michigan, the Magazine of the Detroit News,* 21 July, 1985).

Desroche, Henri. *The American Shakers.* Amherst: University of Massachusetts Press, 1971.

*Directory of Sabbath-Observing Groups.* Fairview, Okla.: Bible Sabbath Association, 1980.

*Divine Science, Its Principle and Practice.* Denver, Colo.: Divine Science Church and College, 1957.

Downton, James V., Jr. *Sacred Journeys.* New York: Columbia University Press, 1979.

Doyle, Sir Arthur Conan. *The History of Spiritualism, Vol. I and II.* New York: Arno Press, 1975.

Dresser, Horatio W. *History of the New Thought Movement.* New York: T. Y. Crowell, 1919.

Dresser, Horatio W., ed. *The Quimby Manuscripts.* New York: T. Y. Crowell, 1921.

Drew, Richard, ed. *Revelation to the Priesthood.* Voree, Wisc.: Church of Jesus Christ of Latter Day Saints, 1986.

———. *Word of Wisdom.* Voree, Wisc.: Church of Jesus Christ of Latter Day Saints, 1986.

Driscoll, J. Walter. *Gurdjieff: An Annotated Bibliography.* New York: Garland Publishing, 1985.

Duffield, Guy P., and Nathaniel M. Van Cleave. *Foundations of Pentecostal Theology.* Los Angeles: L.I.F.E. Bible College, 1983.

Duffy, Joseph. "The Church of bible Understanding: A Critical Expose." *Alternatives* (New York) 4, no. 6 (April/May 1977).

DuPree, Sherry Sherrod. *African American Holiness Pentecostal Charismatic: Annotated Bibliography.* New York: Garland Publishing, 1992.

DuQuette, Lon Milo, and Christopher S. Hyatt. *Aleister Crowley's Illustrated Goetia: Sexual Evocation.* Phoenix, Ariz.: Falcon Press, 1992.

Durnbaugh, Donald F., ed. *The Brethren Encyclopedia.* 3 vols. Philadelphia, Pa.: Brethren Encyclopedia, 1983.

Ebon, Martin, ed. *The Devil's Bride, Exorcism: Past and Present.* New York: Harper & Row, 1974.

———. *Maharishi, the Guru.* New York: New American Library, 1968.

Eddy, Mary Baker. *Science and Health with Key to the Scriptures.* Boston: Trustees under the Will of Mary Baker G. Eddy, 1906.

*Edgar Cayce on Atlantis.* New York: Paperback Library, 1968.

Edwards, Chris. *Crazy for God.* Englewood Cliffs, N. J.: Prentice-Hall, 1979.

Edwards, F. Henry. *Fundamentals, Enduring Convictions of the Restoration.* Independence, Mo.: Herald Publishing House, n.d.

Eek, Sven, and Boris de Zirkoff. *William Quan Judge, 1851–1896.* Wheaton, Ill.: Theosophical Publishing House, 1969.

Ehrman, Albert. "The Commandment Keepers: A Negro Jewish Cult in America Today." *Judaism* 8, no. 3 (summer 1959): 266–70.

Ehrmann, Naftali Hertz. *The Rav.* New York: Feldheim Publishers, 1977.

Eikerenkoetter, Frederik. *Health, Happiness, and Prosperity for You!* New York: Science of Living Publications, 1982.

Eklund, Christopher. "Witches Jim Alan and Selena Fox Let Their Cauldron Bubble with Minimal Toil and Trouble." *People* (November 5, 1979): 47, 50.

Eliade, Mircea. *Shamanism: Archaic Techniques of Ecstasy.* Princeton, N.J.: Princeton University Press, 1964.

Eliade, Mircea, ed. *Encyclopedia of Religion.* New York: Macmillan, 1987.

Eller, Cynthia. *Living in the Lap of the Goddess: The Feminist Spirituality Movement in America.* New York: Crossroad, 1993.

Elliott, Errol T. *Quakers on the American Frontier.* Richmond, Ind.: Friends United Press, 1969.

Ellwood, Robert S., and Harry B. Partin. *Religious and Spiritual Groups in Modern America.* Englewood Cliffs, N.J.: Prentice-Hall, 1988.

Ellwood, Robert S., Jr. *Mysticism and Religion.* Englewood Cliffs, N.J.: Prentice-Hall, 1980.

———. *One Way.* Englewood Cliffs, N.J.: Prentice-Hall, 1973.

Ellwood, Robert. *Theosophy.* Wheaton, Ill.: Theosophical Publishing House, 1986.

Evans, Warren Felt. *The Divine Law of Cure.* Boston: H. H. Carter & Co., 1884.

Fabre des Essarts, Léonce. *Les Hiérophantes. Études sur les fondateurs de religions depuis la Révolution jusqu'à nos jours.* Paris: Chacornac, 1905.

Farajaje-Jones, Elias. *In Search of Zion: The Spiritual Significance of Africa in Black Religious Movements.* New York: P. Long, 1991.

Farkas, Mary. "Footsteps in the Invisible World." *Wind Bell* 8 (fall 1969): 15–19.

Farquhar, J. N. *Modern Religious Movements in India* New York: Macmillan (1915).

Farrar, Janet, and Stewart Farrar. *The Witches' God: Lord of the Dance.* London, Robert Hale, 1988. Custer, Wash.: Phoenix Publishing, 1989.

———. *The Witches' Goddess: The Feminine Principle of Divinity.* London: Robert Hale, 1987. Custer, Wash.: Phoenix Publishing, 1988.

Farrar, Stewart, and Janet Farrar. *Eight Sabbats for Witches.* London: Robert Hale, 1981.

———. *The Life and Times of a Modern Witch.* London: Robert Hale: 1987. Custer, Wash.: Phoenix Publishing, 1988.

———. *The Witches' Way.* London: Robert Hale, 1985.

Farrar, Stewart. *What Witches Do: The Modern Coven Revealed.* Coward, McCann, 1971.

Fauset, Arthur H. *Black Gods in the Metropolis.* Philadelphia, Pa.: University of Pennsylvania Press, 1971.

Ferguson, Marilyn. *The Aquarian Conspiracy.* Los Angeles, Calif.: Jeremy Tarcher, 1980.

Fessier, Michael, Jr. "Ervil LeBaron, the Man Who Would Be God." *New West* (January 1981): 80–84, 112–17.

Festinger, Leon, Henry W. Riecken, and Stanley Schachter. *When Prophecy Fails.* New York: Harper & Row, 1956.

Fields, Rick. *How the Swans Came to the Lake.* Boulder, Colo.: Shambhala, 1986.

Fillmore, Charles S. *Metaphysical Bible Dictionary.* Kansas City, Mo.: Unity School of Christianity, 1931.

———. *Prosperity.* Kansas City, Mo.: Unity School of Christianity, 1938.

Fillmore, Myrtle. *The Letters of Myrtle Fillmore.* Kansas City, Mo.: Unity School of Christianity, 1936. Reprinted as *Myrtle Fillmore's Healing Letters.* Unity Village, Mo.: Unity Books, n.d.

Findhorn Community. *The Findhorn Garden.* New York: Harper & Row, 1975.

Fiore, Edith. *The Unquiet Dead: A Psychologist Treats Spirit Possession.* Garden City, N.Y.: Dolphin/Doubleday & Co., 1987.

Flanders, Robert Bruce. *Nauvoo: Kingdom on the Mississippi.* Urbana: University of Illinois Press, 1965.

Fletcher, Rupert J. and Daisy Whiting Fletcher. *Alpheus Cutler and the Church of Jesus Christ.* Independence, Mo.: Church of Jesus Christ, 1975.

Fletcher, Rupert J. *The Scattered Children of Zion.* Independence, Mo.: The Author, 1959.

———. *The Way of Deliverance.* Independence, Mo.: The Author, 1969.

Flint, B. C. *An Outline History of the Church of Christ (Temple Lot).* Independence, Mo.: Board of Publication, church of Christ (Temple Lot), 1967.

———. *Autobiography.* Independence, Mo.: Privately printed, n.d.

———. *What About Israel?* Independence, Mo.: Board of Publication, Church of Christ (Temple Lot), 1967.

Fodor, Nandor. *An Encyclopaedia of Psychic Science.* 1933; reprint, Secaucus, N.J.: The Citadel Press, 1966.

Fogarty, Robert S. "Utopian Themes with Variation: John Murray Spear and His Kiantone Domain." *Pennsylvania History* (April 1962).

———. *Dictionary of American Communal and Utopian History* (Westport, Conn.: Greenwood Press, 1980).

Forfreedom, Ann, and Julie Ann, eds. *Book of the Goddess.* Sacramento: Temple of the Goddess Within, 1980.

———. *Mythology, Religion, and Woman's Heritage.* Sacramento: Sacramento City Unified School District, 1981.

Foster, Fred J. *Their Story: Twentieth Century Pentecostals.* Hazelwood, Mo.: World Aflame Press, 1981.

Fox, Selena. *Circle Guide to Pagan Resources.* Mt. Horeb, Wis.: Circle, 1987.

Frazer, James George. *The Golden Bough: A Study in Magic and Religion.* New York: Macmillan, 1922.

Freeman, James D. *The Story of Unity.* Unity Village, Mo.: Unity Books, 1978.

Fripp, Peter. *The Mystic Philosophy of Sant Mat.* London: Neville, Spearman, 1964.

Frisby, Neal. *The Book of Revelation Scrolls.* Phoenix: The Author, n.d.

Froom, Leroy Edwin. *The Prophetic Faith of Our Fathers.* Washington, D.C., 1954.

Frost, Gavin, and Yvonne Frost. *The Magic Power of Witchcraft.* West Nyack, New York: Parker Publishing Co., 1976.

———. *The Witch's Bible.* New York: Berkley Publishing Co., 1975.

———. *Who Speaks for the Witch.* New Bern, N.C.: Godolphin House, 1991.

Fulton, Gilbert A., Jr. *That Manifesto.* Kearns, Utah: Deseret Publishing Co., 1974.

*Fundamental Beliefs and Directory of the Davidian Seventh-Day Adventists.* Waco, Tex.: Universal Publishing Association, 1943.

Furst, Jeffrey. *Edgar Cayce's Story of Jesus.* New York: Coward-McCann, Inc., 1970.

*The Gabriel Papers,* Nevada City, Calif.: IDHHB, 1981.

Gale, William P. *Racial and National Identity.* Glendale, Calif.: Ministry of Christ Church, n.d.

Gambhrananda, Swami. *History of the Ramakrishna Math and Mission.* Calcutta: Advaita Ashrama, 1957.

Gardner, Gerald B. *Witchcraft Today.* London: Jerrolds, 1954.

Gayer, M. H. *The Heritage of the Anglo-Saxon Race.* Haverhill, Mass.: Destiny Publishers, 1941.

Gelberg, Steven J. "The Fading of Utopia: ISKCON in Transition." *Bulletin of the John Rylands Library of Manchester* 7 (Autumn 1988): 171–83.

Gelberg, Steven, ed. *Hare Krishna, Hare Krishna.* New York: Grove Press, 1983.

*The General Church of the New Jerusalem: A Handbook of General Information.* Bryn Athyn, Pa.: General Church Publication Committee, 1965.

Gerstel, David U. *Paradise Incorporated: Synanon.* Novato, Calif.: Presidio Press, 1982.

Gilbert, R. A. *The Golden Dawn, Twilight of the Magicians.* Wellingborough, Northamptonshire, England: Aquarian Press, 1983.

Goff, James R., Jr. *Fields White Unto Harvest: Charles F. Parham and the Missionary Origins of Pentecostalism.* Fayetteville, Arkansas: University of Arkansas Press, 1988.

Gold, E. J. *Autobiography of a Sufi.* Crestline, Calif.: IDHHB Publications, 1976.

Gomes, Michael. *The Dawning of the Theosophical Movement.* Wheaton, Ill.: The Theosophical Publishing House, 1987.

———. *Theosophy in the Nineteenth Century: An Annotated Bibliography.* New York & London: Garland Publishing, Inc., 1994.

Gonzalez-Wippler, Migene. *Santeria, the Religion.* New York: Harmony Books, 1989.

Gordon, James S. *The Golden Guru.* Lexington, Mass.: Stephen Greene Press, 1987.

Greenwalt, Emmett A. *California Utopia: Point Loma: 1897–1942.* 2d. ed. San Diego, Calif.: Point Loma Publications, 1978.

Grim, John A. *The Shaman: Patterns of Siberian and Ojibway Healing.* Norman, Okla.: University of Oklahoma Press, 1983.

Gross, Darwin. *From Heaven to the Prairie: The Story of the 972nd Living ECK Master.* Menlo Park, Calif.: IWP Publishing, 1980.

———. *Your Right to Know.* Menlo Park, Calif.: IWP Publishing, 1979.

Gurdjieff, Georges I. *Beelzebub's Tales to His Grandson.* 3 vols. New York: E. P. Dutton, 1978.

———. *Life is Only Then, when "I Am."* New York: E. P. Dutton, 1982.

———. *Meetings with Remarkable Men.* New York: E. P. Dutton, 1963.

Haberman, Frederick. *Tracing Our White Ancestors.* Phoenix, Ariz.: Lord's Covenant Church, 1979.

Hall, John R. Afterward to "The Apocalypse at Jonestown." In *In Gods We Trust.* Edited by Thomas Robbins and Dick Anthony. New Brunswick, N.J.: Transaction, 1988, pp. 290–93.

———. *Gone from the Promised Land: Jonestown in American Cultural History.* New Brunswick, N.J.: Transaction, 1987.

———. "Public Narratives and the Apocalyptic Sect: From Jonestown to Mount Carmel." *Armageddon in Mount Carmel.* Edited by Stuart A. Wright. Chicago: The University Chicago Press, forthcoming.

Hall, Manly Palmer. *Reincarnation: The Cycle of Necessity*. Los Angeles: The Philosophical Research Society, 1956.

Hancock, Pauline. *Whence Came the Book of Mormon?* Independence, Mo.: Church of Christ, [1958].

Harrington, Walt. "The Devil in Anton LaVey." *The Washington Post Magazine*, 23 February 1986, pp. 6–9, 12–17.

Harrison, Vernon. "J'Accuse: An Examination of the Hodgson Report of 1885." *Journal of the Society for Psychical Research*. 53, no. 803 (April 1986): 286–310.

Harris, Iverson L. *Mme. Blavatsky Defended*. San Diego, Calif.: Point Loma Publications, 1971.

Harrison, J. F. C. *The Second Coming, Popular Millenarianism 1780–1850*. London, 1979.

*Hate Groups in America*. New York: Anti-Defamation League of B'nai B'rith, 1982.

Hawken, Paul. *The Magic of Findhorn*. New York: Harper & Row, 1985.

Heindel, Max. *Rosicrucian Cosmo-Conception*. Seattle, Wash.: Rosicrucian Fellowship, 1909.

Heindel, Mrs. Max [Augusta Foss]. *The Birth of the Rosicrucian Fellowship*. Oceanside, Calif.: Rosicrucian Fellowship, n.d.

Hemleben, Johannes. *Rudolf Steiner*. East Grimstead, Sussex, United Kingdom: Henry Goulden, 1975.

Herbert, David Robinson. *Armstrong's Tangled Web*. Tulsa, Okla.: John Hadden Publishers, 1980.

Herr, John. *Complete Works*. Buffalo, New York: 1890.

Hollenweger, Walter J. *The Pentecostals*. Minneapolis: Augsberg Press, 1972.

Holloway, Mark. *Heavens on Earth: Utopian Communities in America, 1680–1880* (London: Turnstile Press, 1951).

Holmes, Ernest. *The Science of Mind*. New York: Dodd, Mead, and Company, 1944.

Holmes, Fenwicke L. *Ernest Holmes, His Life and Times*. New York: Dodd, Mead and Company, 1970.

Holt, Simma. *Terror in the Name of God*. New York: Crown Publishers, 1965.

Homer, Michael W. "Protection of Religion Under the First Amendment: Church Universal and Triumphant." In *Church Universal and Triumphant in Scholarly Perspective*. Edited by James R. Lewis and J. Gordon Melton. Stanford, Calif.: Center for Academic Publishing, 1994.

———. "New Religions and Child Custody Cases: Comparisons Between the American and European Experience." In *Sex, Slander and Salvation: Investigating The Family/Children of God*. Edited by James R. Lewis and J. Gordon Melton. Stanford, Calif.: Center for Academic Publishing, 1994.

Hopkins, Thomas. "Hindu Views of Death and Afterlife." In Hiroshi Obayashi, ed., *Death and Afterlife: Perspectives of World Religions*. Westport, Conn.: Greenwood Press, 1992, pp. 149–64.

Hoshor, John. *God Drives a Rolls Royce*. Philadelphia, Pa.: Hillman-Curl, 1936.

Houteff, V. T. *The Great Controversy Over "The Shepherd's Rod."* Waco, Tex.: Universal Publishing Association, 1954.

———. *The Shepherd's Rod Series*. Salem, S.C.: General Association of the Davidian Seventh-day Adventists, 1990.

———. *The Shepherd's Rod*. Vol. 1. Waco, Tex.: Universal Publishing Association, 1945.

Hubbard, L. Ron. *Dianetics: The Modern Science of Mental Health* (New York: Hermitage House, 1950).

Hultkrantz, Ake. "A Definition of Shamanism." *Temenos* 9 (1973): 25–37.

"I Am That." *Hinduism Today* 11, no. 3 (March 1989): 1, 5.

Ichazo, Oscar. *The Human Process for Enlightenment and Freedom*. New York: Arica Institute, 1976.

*The International Theosophical Year Book: 1938*. Adyar: The Theosophical Publishing House, 1938.

"Interview with Penny Torres." *Life Times* 1 (1987): 94–98.

*Interviews with Oscar Ichazo*. New York: Arica Institute Press, 1982.

*Introduction to Apostles' Doctrine*. Cleveland, Tenn.: Church Publishing Company, 1984.

Introvigne, Massimo, ed. *Massoneria e religioni*. Leumann (Torino): Elle Di Ci, 1994.

———. *Il cappello del mago. I nuovi movimenti magici dallo spiritismo al satanismo*, Milan: SugarCo, 1990.

———. *Il ritorno dello gnosticismo*, Carnago (Varese): SugarCo, 1993.

Isherwood, Christopher. *Ramakrishna and His Disciples*. New York: Simon and Schuster, 1965.

Israel, Love. *Love*. Seattle: Church of Armageddon, 1971.

Jacques-Garvey, A., ed. *The Philosophy and Opinions of Marcus Garvey* (1924–1926). Vols. 1, 2. New York: Arno Press, 1967, 1969.

Jefferson, William. *The Story of the Maharishi*. New York: Pocket Books, 1976.

Jinarajadasa, C., ed. *The Golden Book of the Theosophical Society: A Brief History of the Society's Growth from 1875–1925*. Adyar, Madras: Theosophical Publishing House, 1925.

———. "The School of the Wisdom: Inaugural Address Delivered on November 17, 1949." *The Theosophist* vol. 71, no. 3 (December 1949): 153–60.

Johns, June. *King of the Witches: The World of Alex Sanders*. Coward McCann, 1969.

Johnson, Julian P. *With a Great Master in India*. Beas, India: Radha Soami Sat Sang, Dera Baba Jaimal Singh, 1953.

Jones, Franklin *The Knee of Listening*. Los Angeles: Dawn Horse Press, 1972.

Jones, Franklin [Heart-Master Da Free John]. *The Dawn Horse Testament*. San Rafael, Calif.: Dawn Horse Press, 1985.

Jones, Jerry. *What Does the Boston Movement Teach?* Vols. 1–3. Bridgeton, Mo.: The author, 1990–93.

Jouret, Luc, *Médecine et conscience*, Montreal: Louise Courteau, 1992.

Judah, J. Stillson. *Hare Krishna and the Counterculture*. New York: John Wiley & Sons, 1974.

———. *The History and Philosophy of the Metaphysical Movements in America*. Philadelphia: Westminster Press, 1967.

Judge, W. Q. "The Theosophical Soceity." *The Path* X (May 1895): 55–60. Reprinted in *Echoes of the Orient: The Writings of William Qan Judge*. Compiled by Dara Eklund. Vol. 2. San Diego: Point Loma Publications, 1980, 197–202.

Juergensmeyer, Mark. *Radhasoami Reality*. 1st edition. Princeton University Press, 1991.

Jung, Carl Gustav. *Flying Saucers.* Princeton: Princeton University Press, 1958.

———. *Memories, Dreams, Reflections.* New York: Vintage Books, 1965.

Kagan, Paul. *New World Utopias.* Baltimore: Penguin Books, 1975.

Kaplan, Jeffrey. "The Context of American Millenarian Revolutionary Theology: The Case of the 'Identity Christian' Church of Israel." *Terrorism and Political Violence* 5 (1993): 30–82.

Kapleau, Philip. *The Three Pillars of Zen.* Boston: Beacon Press, 1965. Rev. ed., Garden City, New York: Doubleday & Co., 1980.

Kaur, Sardarni Premka. *Guru for the Aquarian Age.* Albuquerque, N.Mex.: Brother-hood of Life Books, 1972.

Kell, Wane. *B. P. Wadia: A Life of Service to Mankind* (unpublished).

Kelly, Aidan A. "An Update on Neopagan Witchcraft in America." *Perspectives on the New Age.* Edited by James R. Lewis. State University of New York Press, 1993.

———. *Crafting the Art of Magic, Book I: A History of Modern Witchcraft, 1939–1964.* St. Paul, MN: Llewellyn Publications, 1991.

Khaalis, Hamaas Abdul. *Look and See.* Washington, D.C.: Hanafi Madh-hab Center Islam Faith, 1972.

Khan, Hazrat Inayat. *Biography of Pir-O-Murshid Inayat Khan.* London: East-West Publications, 1979.

Khan, Pir Vilayat Inayat. *The Call of the Dervish.* New Lebanon: Omega Press, 1992.

King, Francis. *The Magical World of Aleister Crowley.* New York: Coward, McCann & Goeghegan, 1978.

———. *Ritual Magic In England, 1887 to the Present.* Spearman, 1970.

———. *Tantra: The Way of Action: A Practical Guide to Its Teachings and Techniques.* Rochester, Vt.: Destiny Books, 1990.

King, George. *A Book of Sacred Prayers.* Hollywood, Calif.: Aetherius Society, 1966.

———. *The Nine Freedoms.* Los Angeles: Aetherius Society, 1963.

———. *The Practices of Aetherius.* Hollywood, Calif.: Aetherius Society, 1964.

———. *You Are Responsible.* London: Aetherius Press, 1961.

King, Godfre Ray [Guy Ballard]. *The Magic Presence.* Chicago: Saint Germain Press, 1935.

———. *Unveiled Mysteries.* Mount Shasta, Calif.: Ascended Master Teaching Foun-dation, 1986.

Kinney, Jay. "Sufism Comes to America." *Gnosis Magazine* 30 (winter 1994): 18–23.

Kirkpatrick, R. George, and Diana Tumminia. "Space Magic, Techno-Animism, and the Cult of the Goddess in a Southern Californian UFO Contactee Group: A Case Study in Millenarianism." *Syzygy: Journal of Alternative Religion and Culture.* 1, no. 2 (1992): 159–72.

———. "California Space Goddess: The Mystagogue in a Flying Saucer Cult." In *Twentieth Century World Religious Movements in Weberian Perspective.* Edited by William H. Swatos Jr. Lewiston, N.Y.: The Edwin Mellen Press, 1992, pp. 299–311.

Klassen, Ben. *Building a Whiter and Brighter World.* Otto, N.C.: Church of the Cre-ator, 1986.

Klimo, Jon. *Channeling.* Los Angeles: Jeremy P. Tarcher, Inc., 1987.

Knight, J. Z. *A State of Mind: My Story.* New York: Warner Books, 1987.

Knoch, Adolph Ernst. *Spirit, Spirits, and Spirituality.* Canyon Country, Calif.: 1977.

Kokoszka, Larry. "Time Mellows Communities Caught in Raid." *The Caledonian Record* 156, no. 268 (June 22, 1994).

Kornfield, Jack. *Living Buddhist Masters.* Santa Cruz, Calif.: Unity Press, 1977.

Koszegi, Michael M. "The Sufi Order in the West: Sufism's Encounter with the New Age." In *Islam in North America: A Sourcebook.* Edited by J. Gordon Melton. New York: Grayland, 1992.

Krishnamurt, J., ed. *The Herald of the Star.* Vol. 1, no. 1 (January 11, 1912), and 6, no. 3 (March 1917).

Kriyananda, Swami. *Cooperative Communities, How to Start Them and Why.* Nevada City, Calif.: Ananda publications, 1968.

———. *Crises in Modern Thought.* Nevada City, Calif.: Ananda Publications, 1972.

———. *The Path: A Spiritual Autobiography.* Nevada City, Calif.: Ananda Publications, 1977.

Land, Gary, ed. *Adventism in America: A History.* Grand Rapids, Mich.: Eerdmans Publishing Company, 1986.

Landau, Ron. *The Philosophy of Ibn 'Arabi.* London: Allen and Unwin, 1959.

Lane, David Christopher. *The Making of a Spiritual Movement: The Untold Story of Paul Twitchell and ECKANKAR* (Garland Press, 1993).

———. *The Radhasoami Tradition: A Critical History of Guru Successorship.* 1st ed. New York and London:Garland Publishing, 1992.

Larson, Martin A. *New Thought: A Modern Religious Approach.* New York: Philosophical Library, 1939.

Lattin, Don. 1990. "Journey to the East." *New Age Journal* (December 1992): 70–76.

———. "'New Age' Mysticism Strong in Bay Area." *The San Francisco Chronicle,* 24–25 April, 1990.

LaVey, Anton Szandor. *The Compleat Witch.* New York: Lancer Books, 1971.

———. *The Satanic Bible.* New York: Avon, 1969.

———. *The Satanic Rituals.* Secaucus, N.J.: University Books, 1972.

Layman, Emma McCloy. *Buddhism in America.* Chicago: Nelson-Hall, 1976.

Lazaris [Jach Pursel]. *The Sacred Journey: You and Your Higher Self.* Beverly Hills, Calif.: Synergy Publishing, 1987.

———. *A Spark of Love.* Beverly Hills, Calif.: Synergy Publishing, 1987.

LeBaron, Ervil. *An Open Letter to a Former Presiding Bishop.* San Diego, Calif.: The Author, 1972.

———. *Priesthood Expounded.* Buenaventura, Mexico: Mexican Mission of the Church of the Firstborn of the Fullness of Times, 1956.

LeBaron, Ross W. *The Redemption of Zion.* Colonia LeBaron, Chihuahua, Mexico: Church of the First-Born, 1962.

LeBaron, Verlan M. *Economic Democracy Under Eternal Law.* El Paso, Tex.: Church of the Firstbron of the Fullness of Time, 1963.

———. *The LeBaron Family.* Lubbock, Tex.: The Author, 1981.

———. *The LeBaron Story.* Lubbock, Tex.: The Author, 1981.

Leland, Charles Godfrey. *Aradia: The Gospel of the Witches of Tuscany.* New York: Scribner's, 1897. Reprint, London: Buckland Museum, 1964.

Lenore Friedman, *Meetings with Remarkable Women: Buddhist Teachers in America* Boston: Shambhala (1987).

Lenz, Frederick [Rama]. *The Last Incarnation: Experiences with Rama in California.* Malibu, Calif.: Lakshmi, 1983.

———. *Life-Times: True Accounts of Reincarnation.* Indianapolis, Ind.: The Bobbs-Merrill Co., 1979.

Levine, Saul. *Radical Departures: Desperate Detours to Growing Up.* New York: Harcourt Brace Javanovich, 1984.

Lewis, H. Spencer. *Cosmic Mission Fulfilled.* San Jose, Calif.: Supreme Gran Lodge of AMORC, 1973.

———. *The Mystical Life of Jesus.* San Jose, Calif.: Rosicrucian Press, 1941.

———. *Rosicrucian Manual.* San Jose, Calif.: Rosicrucian Press, 1941.

———. *Rosicrucian Questions and Answers.* San Jose, Calif.: Supreme Grand Lodge of AMORC, 1969.

———. *Yesterday Has Much to Tell.* San Jose, Calif.: Supreme Grand Lodge of AMORC, 1973.

Lewis, Harvey S. *Mansions of the Soul.* San Jose, Calif.: Rosicrucian Press, 1930.

Lewis, James R. "Apostates and the Legitimation of Repression: Some Historical and Empirical Perspectives on the Cult Controversy." *Sociological Analysis* 49, no. 4 (winter 1989).

———. "Edgar Cayce." In the *American National Biography.* New York: Oxford University Press, 1999.

———. *From the Ashes: Making Sense of Waco.* Lanham, Md.: Rowman & Littlefield, 1994.

———. "L. Ron Hubbard." In *American National Biography.* New York: Oxford University Press, 1999.

———. *Seeking the Light.* Los Angeles: Mandeville Press, 1997.

Lewis, James R., ed. *The Gods Have Landed: New Religions from Other Worlds.* Albany, N. Y.: State University of New York Press, 1995.

Lewis, James R., and J. Gordon Melton, eds. *Church Universal and Triumphant in Scholarly Perspective* (special issue of *Syzygy: Journal of Alternative Religion and Culture,* 1994).

———. *Perspectives on the New Age.* Albany: State University of New York Press, 1992.

———. *Sex, Slander, and Salvation: Investigating The Family/Children of God.* Stanford, Calif.: Center for Academic Publication, 1994.

Lewis, James R., and David G. Bromley. "The Cult Withdrawal Syndrome: A Case of Misattribution of Cause?" *Journal for the Scientific Study of Religion* 26, no. 4 (December 1987).

Lewis, Samuel L. *Sufi Vision and Initiation.* San Francisco: Sufi Islamia/Prophecy Publications, 1986.

Lindsey, Gordon. *William Branham: A Man Sent From God.* Jeffersonville, Ind.: William Branham, 1950.

Lucas, Phillip C. "From Holy Order of MANS to Christ the Savior Brotherhood: The Radical Transformation of an Esoteric Christian Order." In *America's Alternative Religions.* Edited by Timothy Miller. Albany: State University of New York Press, 1995.

———. "The Association for Research and Enlightenment: Saved by the New Age." In *America's Alternative Religions.* Edited by Timothy Miller. Albany: State University of New York Press, 1995.

————. *The Odyssey of a New Religion: The Holy Order of MANS from New Age to Orthodoxy.* Bloomington: Indiana University Press, 1995.

Luhrmann, T. M. *Persuasions of the Witch's Craft: Ritual Magic in Contemporary England.* Cambridge, Mass.: Harvard University Press, 1989

Lyons, Arthur. *Satan Wants You.* New York: The Mysterious Press, 1988.

Ma Jaya Sati Bhagavati. *Bones and Ash.* Sebastian, Fla.: Jaya Press, 1995.

————. *The River.* Roseland, Fla.: Ganga Press, 1994. 85 pp.

MacGregor, Geddes. *Angels: Ministers of Grace.* New York: Paragon House, 1988.

————. *Images of Afterlife: Beliefs from Antiquity to Modern Times.* New York: Paragon House, 1992.

MacLaine, Shirley. *Out on a Limb.* New York: Bantam Books, 1983.

Mafu [Penny Torres]. *And What Be God?* Vacaville, Calif.: Mafu Seminars, 1989.

————. *Reflections on Yeshua Ben Joseph.* Vacaville, Calif.: Mafu Seminars, 1989.

Maharaj Ji, Guru. *The Living Master.* Denver, Colo.: Divine Light Mission, 1978.

*The Mahatma Letters to A. P. Sinnett from the Mahatmas M. & K.H.* Transcribed, compiled, and with an introduction by A.T. Barker. London: Rider and Company, 1926.

Maharishi Mahesh Yogi. *The Science of Being and Art of Living.* London: International SRM Publications, 1963. Rev. ed. 1967.

Martello, Leo Louis. *Weird Ways of Witchcraft.* New York: HC Publishers, 1969.

————. *What It Means to Be a Witch.* New York:The Author, 1975.

Martin, Edward. "The Boston Movement as a 'Revitalization Movement.' " D.Min. thesis, Harding Graduate School of Religion, 1990.

Martin, Rachel, as told to Bonnie Palmer Young. *Escape.* Denver, Colo.: Accent Books, 1979.

Martin, Tony. *Marcus Garvey, Hero: A First Biography.* Dover, Mass.: Majority Press, 1984.

Martin, Walter. *The New Cults.* Santa Ana, Calif.: Vision House, 1980.

Mathison, Richard. *Faiths, Cults, and Sects of America.* Indianapolis, Ind.: Bobbs-Merrill, 1960.

May, Hal, ed. *Contemporary Authors.* Vol. 114. Detroit: Gale Research, Inc., 1985.

Mayer, François. "Des Templiers pour l'Ere du Verseau: les Clubs Archédia (1984–1991) et l'Ordre International Chevaleresque Tradition Solaire." *Mouvements Religieux* 14, no. 153 (January 1993), pp. 2–10.

McKean, Kim. "Revolution Through Restoration," *UpsideDown* 1 (April 1991): 6.

McKnight, Floyd. *Rudolf Steiner and Anthroposophy.* New York: Anthroposophical Society in America, 1967.

*Meet Our Family.* Chicago: Jesus People USA, n.d.

Meiers, Michael. *Was Jonestown a CIA Medical Experiment?* Lewiston, N.Y.: Edwin Mellen Press, 1988.

Melton, J. Gordon. *Biographical Dictionary of American Cults and Sect Leaders* (New York: Garland, 1986).

————. *Encyclopedia of American Religions.* 4th ed. Detroit: Gale Research, 1993.

————. *Encyclopedic Handbook of Cults in America.* Rev. ed. New York & London: Garland Publishing, Inc., 1992.

————. *Religious Leaders of America.* Detroit: Gale Research, 1992.

Melton, J. Gordon, ed. *The Peoples Temple and Jim Jones.* New York: Garland Publishing Co., 1990.

Melton, J. Gordon, Jerome Clark, and Aidan A. Kelly. *New Age Encyclopedia.* Detroit, Mich.: Gale Research, 1990.

Meredith, George. *Bhagwan: The Most Godless Yet the Most Godly Man.* Poona, India: Rebel Publishing House, 1987.

Michael, R. Blake. "Heaven, West Virginia: Legitimation Techniques of the New Vrindaban Community." In *Krishna Consciousness in the West.* Edited by David Bromley and Larry Shinn. Lewisburg: Bucknell University Press, 1989.

Mickler, Michael L. *The Unification Church in America: A Bibliography and Research Guide.* New York: Garland, 1987.

Milgram, Stanley. *Obedience to Authority.* New York: Harper & Row, 1974.

Milne, Hugh. *Bhagwan: The God That Failed.* New York: St. Martin's Press, 1986.

Montgomery, Ruth. *Aliens Among Us* (New York: Putnam's, 1985).

Moody, Raymond A. *Life After Life.* New York: Bantam, 1976.

Moon, Elmer Louis. *The Pentecostal Church.* New York: Carleton Press, 1966.

Moon, Sun Myung. *God's Warning to the World.* 2 vols. New York: HSA-UWC, 1985.

———. *The New Future of Christianity.* Washington, D.C.: Unification Church International, 1974.

Morgan, Richard E. *The Supreme Court and Religion.* New York: Free Press, 1972.

Moses, Wilson J. *Black Messiahs and Uncle Toms: Social and Literary Manipulations of a Religious Myth.* University Park and London: Pennsylvania State University Press, 1982.

Muhammad, Elijah. *Message to the Blackman in America.* Chicago: Muhammad Mosque of Islam no. 2, 1965.

———. *Our Savior Has Arrived.* Chicago: Muhammad's Temple of Islam no. 2, 1974.

Muhammad, Silis. *In the Wake of the Nation of Islam.* College Park, Ga.: The Author, 1985.

Muhammad, Wallace D. *Lectures of Elam Muhammad.* Chicago: Zakat Propagation Fund Publications, 1978.

Muktananda, Swami. *Guru.* New York: Harper & Row, 1981.

———. *I Have Become Alive.* South Fallsburg, N.Y.: SYDA Foundation, 1985.

Murphy, Joseph M. "Santeria and Vodou in the United States." In *America's Alternative Religions.* Albany: State University of New York Press, 1995.

Murphy, Larry G., J. Gordon Melton, and Gary L. Ward, eds. *Encyclopedia of African American Religions.* New York and London: Garland Publishing Co., 1993.

Musser, Joseph W. *Celestial or Plural Marriage.* Salt Lake City: Truth Publishing Co., 1944.

Nada-Yolanda [Pauline Sharpe]. *Mark-Age Period and Program.* Miami, Fla.: Mark-Age, 1970.

———. *Visitors from Other Planets.* Miami, Fla.: Mark-Age, 1974.

Nanji, Azim. "The Nizari Ismaili Muslim Community in North America; Background and Development." In *The Muslim Community in North America.* Edited by Earle H. Waugh, Baha Abu-Laban, and Regula B. Qureshi. Edmonton, Alberta: University of Alberta Press, 1983.

Nee, Watchman. *The Normal Christian Church Life.* Washington, D.C.: International Students Press, 1969.

Nelson, Robert. *Understanding the Crossroads Controversy.* Fort Worth, Tex.: Star Bible Publications, 1986.

Nethercott, Arthur H. *The First Five Lives of Annie Besant.* Chicago: University of Chicago Press, 1960.

———. *The Last Four Lives of Annie Besant.* Chicago: University of Chicago Press, 1963.

*New Catholic Encyclopedia.* San Francisco: McGraw-Hill, 1967.

*New Golden Dawn: Flying Roll.* Parts 1–15. Phoenix, Ariz.: Thelemic Order and Temple of Golden Dawn, 1990–91.

Nichol, John Thomas. *Pentecostalism: The Story of the Growth and Development of a Vital New Force in American Protestantism.* New York: Harper & Row, 1966.

Nickels, Richard D. *A History of the Seventh Day Church of God.* The Author, 1977.

Nielsen, Niels C., Norvin Hein, Frank E. Reynolds, Alan L. Miller, Samuel E. Karff, Alice C. Cochran, and Paul McLean. *Religions of the World.* New York: St. Martins, 1983.

Nikhilananda, Swami. *Ramakrishna: Prophet of New India.* New York: Harper & Brothers, 1948.

———. *Vivekananda: A Biography.* Calcutta: Advaita Ashrama, 1975.

Nordhoff, Charles. *The Communistic Societies of the United States.* Reprint, New York: Schrocken Books, 1965.

Nordquist, Ted A. *Ananda Cooperative Village.* Upsala, Sweden: Borgstroms Tryckeri Ab, 1978.

Nori, Don. "Persecution at Island Pond." *Charisma* 10, no. 4 (November 1984).

O'Gorman, Edith. *Convent Life Unveiled.* London: Lile & Fawcett, circa 1881 (originally published in the United States circa 1871).

Obayashi, Hiroshi, ed. *Death and Afterlife: Perspectives of World Religions.* Westport, Conn.: Greenwood Press, 1992, pp. 49–64.

Olcott, Henry Steel. *Old Diary Leaves.* 6 vols. Adyar, India: 1972–75.

*One Hundredth Anniversary of Modern American Spiritualism.* Chicago: National Spiritualist Association of Churches, 1948.

Orrmont, Arthur. *Love Cults and Faith Healers.* New York: Ballantine, 1961.

Osterhaven, M. Eugene. *The Spirit of the Reformed Tradition.* Grand Rapids, Mich.: William B. Eerdmans Publishing Company, 1971.

Owens, J. 1976. *Dread: The Rastafarians of Jamaica.* London: Heinemann.

Palmer, Susan J. "Woman as Playmate in the Raelian Movement:Power and Pantagamy in a New Religion." *SYZYGY: Journal of Religion and Culture* 1, no. 3 (1992): 227–45.

———. *Moon Sisters, Krishna Mothers, Rajneesh Lovers: Women's Roles in New Religions.* Syracuse: Syracuse University Press, 1995.

———. "The Ansaaru Allah Community: Postmodernist Narrative and the Black Narrative." In *New Islamic Movements in the West.* Edited by Peter Clarke. London, England: Curzon Press.

Parker, Gail Thain. *Mind Cure in New England.* Hanover, N.H.: University Press of New England, 1973.

Pastor, David Horowitz. *Charles Taze Russell, an Early American Christian Zionist.* New York: Philosophical Library, 1986.

Patrick, Ted with Tom Dulack. *Let Our Children Go!* New York: E. P. Dutton, 1976.

Peel, Robert. *Mary Baker Eddy: The Years of Authority.* New York: Holt, Rinehart and Winston, 1977.

———. *Mary Baker Eddy: The Years of Discovery.* New York: Holt, Rinehart and Winston, 1966.

———. *Mary Baker Eddy: The Years of Trial.* New York: Holt, Rinehart and Winston, 1971.

Pelley, William. *The Door to Revelation.* Asheville, N.C.: The Foundation Fellowship, 1936.

———. *Road to Sunrise.* Noblesville, Ind.: Soulcraft Press, 1950.

Pernoud, Régine. *Les Templiers,* Paris: Presses Universitaires de France, 1988.

Peterson, Joe V. *Jesus People: Christ, Communes, and the Counterculture of the late Twentieth Century in the Pacific Northwest.* Eugene, Oreg.: M.A. Thesis, Northwest Christian College, 1990.

Pfeifer, Jeffrey E. "The Psychological Framing of Cults: Schematic Representations and Cult Evaluations." *Journal of Applied Social Psychology* 22, no. 7 (1992): 531–44.

Philips, Abu Ameenah Bilal. (1988) *The Ansar Cult in America.* Sudan: Tawheed Publications.

Pitts, Bill. "Davidians and Branch Davidians: 1929–1987." In *Armageddon in Mount Carmel.* Edited by Stuart A. Wright. Chicago: University of Chicago Press, 1995.

———. "The Davidian Tradition." *Council of Societies for the Study of Religion Bulletin.* 22, no. 4 (November 1993): 99–101.

———. "The Mount Carmel Davidians: Adventist Reformers, 1935–1959." *Syzygy* 2, no. 1–2 (1993): 39–54.

Power, Mary Elizabeth. "A Study of the Seventh-Day Adventist Community, Mount Carmel Center, Waco, Texas," M.A. thesis, 1940.

Prabhupada, A. C. Bhaktivedanta Swami. *Bhagavad-Gita As It Is.* New York: Bhaktivedanta Book Trust, 1972.

"Preamble and By-Laws of the Theosophical Society." 30 October 1875.

Pressman, Steven. *Outrageous Betrayal: The Dark Journey of Werner Erhard from est to Exile.* New York: St. Martin's Press, 1993.

Prophet, Elizabeth Clare. *The Great White Brotherhood in the Culture, History, and Religion of America.* Los Angeles: Summit University Press, 1976.

———. *The Great White Brotherhood.* Malibu, Calif.: Summit University Press, 1983.

———. *The Lost Teachings of Jesus.* 2 vols. Livingstone, Mont.: Summit University Press, 1986, 1988.

Prophet, Mark L., and Elizabeth Clare Prophet. *Climb the Highest Mountain.* Colorado Springs, Colo.: Summit Lighthouse, 1972.

———. *The Science of the Spoken Word.* Colorado Springs, Colo.: Summit Lighthouse, 1974.

Prophet, Mark L. *The Overcoming of Fear Through Decrees.* Colorado Springs, Colo.: Summit Lighthouse, 1966.

———. *Understanding Yourself: Doorway to the Superconscious.* Los Angeles: Summit University Press, 1981.

Purnell, Benjamin. *The Book of Dialogues.* 3 vols. Benton Harbor, Mich.: Israelite House of David, 1912.

————. *The Book of Wisdom.* 7 vols. Benton Harbor, Mich.: Israelite House of David, n.d.

Purnell, Mary. *The Comforter, The Mother's Book.* 4 vols. Benton Harbor, Mich.: Israelite House of David, 1926.

Rahula, Walpola. *What the Buddha Taught.* 2d. ed. New York: Evergreen, 1974.

Rajneesh, Bhagwan Shree. *Meditation: The Art of Ecstasy.* New York: Harper and Row, 1976.

————. *Tantra, Spirituality, and Sex.* San Francisco: Rainbow Bridge, 1977.

Ram Dass, Baba. *Be Here Now.* San Christobal, New Mexico: Lama Foundation, 1971.

————. *The Only Dance There Is.* New York: Aronson, 1976.

Ramakrishna, Sri. *The Gospel of Ramakrishna.* Boston: Beacon Press, 1947.

Randolph, Paschal Beverly. *P. B. Randolph . . . His Curious Life, Works, and Career.* Boston: The Author, 1872.

Ransom, Josephine, compiler. *A Short History of the Theosophical Society: 1875–1937.* Adyar, Madras: The Theosophical Publishing House, 1938.

Reed, Rebecca Theresa. *Six Months in a Convent.* Boston: Russel, Odiorne & Metcalf, 1835.

Regardie, Israel. *The Golden Dawn.* St. Paul, Minn.: Llewellyn Publications, 1969.

————. *The Golden Dawn: An Account of the Teachings, Rites, and Ceremonies of the Order of the Golden Dawn, 1937–1940.* 2d ed. Hazel Hills, 1969.

————. *What Every One Should Know About the Golden Dawn.* Phoenix, Arizona: Falcon Press, 1983.

Regardie, Israel, ed. *Gems from the Equinox: Selected Writings of Aleister Crowley.* Llewellyn, 1974.

*Report of a Meeting Between a Group of Shepherd's Rod Leaders and a Group of General Conference Ministers.* Washington, D.C.: The Research Committee of the General Conference of Seventh-Day Adventists, 1960.

Resnick, Rosalind. "To One City It's Cruelty. To Cultists It's Religion." *National Law Journal,* 11 September, 1989.

Reston, James. *Our Father Who Art in Hell: The Life and Death of Jim Jones.* New York: Times Books, 1981.

*The Revelations of James J. Strang.* Church of Jesus Christ of Latter Day Saints, 1939.

Richards, Henry W. *A Reply to "The Church of the Firstborn of the Fullness of Times."* Salt Lake City: The Author, 1965.

Richards, M. C. *Toward Wholeness: Rudolf Steiner Education in America.* Middletown, Conn.: Wesleyan University Press, 1980.

Ring, Kenneth. *The Omega Project.* New York: William Morrow and Company, 1992.

Robbins, Thomas and Dick Anthony, eds. *In Gods We Trust: New Patterns of Religious Pluralism in America.* New Brunswick: Transaction, 1981.

Roberts, Dana. *Understanding Watchman Nee.* Plainfield, N.J.: Haven Books, 1980.

Roberts, David L. *The Angel Nephi Appears to David L. Roberts.* Independence, Mo.: The True Church of Jesus Christ Restored, 1974.

Roberts, Jane. *The Coming of Seth.* New York: Frederick Hall Publishers, 1966.

Robertson, Constance Noyes. *Oneida Community: An Autobiography, 1851–1876.* Syracuse, N.Y.: 1970.

Robertson, George. "Island Pond Raid Begins New Pattern." In *Sex, Slander and Salvation.* Edited by James R. Lewis and J. Gordon Melton. Stanford, Calif.: Center for Academic Publishing, 1994.

Ross, Joseph E. *Krotona of Old Hollywood: Volume 1, 1866–1913.* Montecito, Calif.: El Montecito Oaks Press, Inc., 1989.

Rothenberg, Paula. "The Prison of Race and Gender: Stereotypes, Ideology, Language, and Social Control." In *Racism and Sexism.* Edited by Paula Rothenberg. New York: St. Martins, 1988.

Rudolf Steiner. *An Autobiography.* Blauvelt, N.Y.: Rudolf Steiner Publications, 1977.

Ryan, Charles J. *H. P. Blavatsky and the Theosophical Movement.* San Diego, Calif.: Point Loma Publications, Inc., 1975. Also published as a second edition edited by Grace F. Knoche. Pasadena, Calif.: Theosophical University Press, 1975.

Saliba, John A., "Religious Dimensions of UFO Phenomena." In *The Gods Have Landed.* Edited by James R. Lewis. Albany: State University of New York Press, 1995, pp. 15–64.

———. *Understanding New Religions.* Grand Rapids, Mich.: Wm. B. Eerdmans, 1995.

Sananda, as recorded by sister Thedra. *I, the Lord God Say Unto Them.* Mt. Shasta, Calif.: Association of Sananda and Sanat Kumara, [1954].

*Sant Thakar Singh: A Brief Life Sketch.* N.p., n.d.

Sarkar, P. R. *Idea and Ideology.* Calcutta: Acarya Pranavananda Avadhuta, 1978.

Sasaki, Ruth Fuller. *Zen, A Method for Religious Awakening.* Kyoto, Japan: First Zen Institute of America in Japan, 1959.

Schwartz, Alan M., and Gail L. Gans. *The Identity Churches: a Theology of Hate.* In *ADL Facts* 28, no. 1 (spring 1983).

Scientology, Church of. *L. Ron Hubbard: The Man and His Work.* Los Angeles: Church of Scientology, 1986.

Scott, Gini Graham. *Cult and Countercult.* Westport, Conn.: Greenwood Press, 1980.

Sebald, Hans. "New-Age Romanticism: The Quest for an Alternative Lifestyle as a Force of Social Change." *Humboldt Journal of Social Relations* 11, no. 2 (1984).

*Seventh-Day Adventist Encyclopedia,* Washington, D.C.: 1976.

Seymour, William J. *The Doctrine and Discipline of the Azusa Street Apostolic Faith Mission of Los Angeles.* Los Angeles: Apostolic Faith Mission, n.d.

Shaku, Soyen. *Sermons of a Zen Buddhist Abbot.* Chicago: Open Court Publishing Co., 1906. Reprinted as *Zen for Americans.* LaSalle, Ill.: Open Court Publishing Co., 1974.

Sharma, Indrajit. *Sivananda: Twentieth Century Saint.* Rishikish, India: Yoga-Vedanta Forest Academy, 1954.

Shaw, David. "From Headline to Prime Time." *TV Guide.* 1993.

Shearman, Hugh. *Charles Webster Leadbeater, A Biography.* Sydney, Australia: St. Alban Press, 1982.

Sheng-Yen, Ch'an Master. *Faith in Mind: A Guide to Ch'an Practice.* Elmhurst, N.Y.: Dharma Drum Publications, 1987.

———. *Getting the Buddha Mind: On the Practice of Ch'an Retreat.* Elmhurst, N.Y.: Ch'an Meditation Center, 1982.

———. *Ox Herding at Morgan's Bay.* Elmhurst, N.Y.: Institute of Chung-Hwa Buddhist Culture, 1988.

Shepard, Leslie A., ed. *Encyclopedia of Occultism & Parapsychology.* Detroit: Gale Research, 1991.

Shepherd, William C. *To Secure the Blessings of Liberty.* Chico, Calif.: Scholars Press, 1985.

Shields, Steven L. *Divergent Paths of the Restoration.* Los Angeles: Restoration Research, 1990.

———. *The Latter Day Saint Churches: An Annotated Bibliography.* New York: Garland Publishing, Inc., 1987.

Shumway, Eleanor L. "The Temple of the People: A History" (a pamphlet distributed by the Temple of the People, P.O. Box 7100, Halcyon, Calif. 93421).

Sinclair, John R. *The Alice Bailey Inheritance.* Wellingsborough, Northamptonshire: Turnstone Press, 1984.

Singh, Darshan. *The Cry of the Soul.* Bowling Green, Va.: Sawan Kirpal Publications, 1977.

———. *The Secret of Secrets.* Bowling Green, Va.: Sawan Kirpal Publications, 1978.

Singh, Huzur Maharaj Sawan. *Philosophy of the Masters.* 5 vols. Beas, India: Radhasoami Satsang, Beas, 1963–1967.

Singh, Kirpal. *Surat Shabd Yoga.* Berkeley, Calif.: Images Press, 1975.

———. *The Way of the Saints.* Sanbornton, N.H.: Sant Bani Ashram, 1976.

Singh, Sawan. *Tales from the Mystic East.* Beas, India: Radha Soami Satsang Beas, 1961.

Singh, Thakar. *Gospel of Love.* Delhi, India: Ruhani Satsang, Sawan Ashram, 1984.

Sitchin, Zecharia. *The 12th Planet.* 1976; New York: Avon, 1978.

Sivananda, Swami. *Practical Lessons in Yoga.* Sivanandanagar, India: Divine Life Society, 1978.

Snyder, Mark. "Self-Fulfilling Stereotypes." In Paula Rothenberg. *Racism and Sexism.* New York: St. Martin's, 1988, pp. 263–69.

*Songs for the Old Religion.* Oakland, Calif.: Nemeton, 1972.

Sontag, Frederick. *Sun Myung Moon and the Unification Church.* Nashville: Abingdon Press, 1977.

Sowards, Bruce A., Michael J. Walser and Rick H. Hoyle. "Personality and Intelligence Measurement of the Church Universal and Triumphant." In *Church Universal and Triumphant in Scholarly Perspective.* Edited by James R. Lewis and J. Gordon Melton. Stanford, Calif.: Center for Academic Publishing, 1994.

Spalding, John Howard. *Introduction to Swedenborg's Religious Thought.* New York: Swedenborg Publishing Association, 1977.

Spangler, David. *Emergence, the Rebirth of the Sacred.* New York: Delta, 1984.

Spangler, David, ed. *Conversations with John.* Elgin, Ill.: Lorian Press, 1980.

———. *Towards a Planetary Vision.* Forres, Scotland: Findhorn Publications, 1977.

Speeth, Kathleen Riordan. *The Gurdjieff Work.* Berkeley, Calif.: And/Or Press, 1976.

Speeth, Kathleen Riordan, and Ira Friedlander. *Gurdjieff, Seeker of Truth.* New York: Harper & Row, 1980.

*The Spinner of Tales: A Collection of Stories as Told by Ramtha.* Ed. by Deborah Kerins. Yelm, Wash.: New Horizon Publishing Co., 1991.

Starhawk. *Dreaming the Dark.* Boston, Mass.: Beacon Press, 1982.

———. *The Spiral Dance:A Rebirth of the Ancient Religion of the Great Goddess,* 2d ed. San Francisco: Harper and Row, 1989.

Stevenson, Ian. *Twenty Cases Suggestive of Reincarnation.* 2d ed. Charlottesville, Va.: University Press of Virginia, 1974.

*The Story of the Aetherius Society.* Hollywood, Calif.: Aetherius Society, n.d.

Strang, James J. *The Prophetic Controversy.* Lansing, Mich.: n.p., 1969.

Strang, Mark A., ed. *The Diary of James J. Strang.* East Lansing: Michigan State University Press, 1961.

Strieber, Whitley. *Communion.* New York: Morrow/Beech Tree Books, 1987.

Sullivan, Matthew. *Living Religion in Subud.* East Sussex, England: Humanus, Ltd., 1991.

Suster, Gerald. *Crowley's Apprentice.* London: Rider, 1989.

———. *The Legacy of the Beast: The Life, Work, and Influence of Aleister Crowley.* York Beach, Maine: Samuel Wizer, 1989.

Sutphen, Dick. *You Were Born Again to Be Together.* New York: Pocket Books, 1976.

Suzuki, Daisetz Teitaro. *On Indian Mahayana Buddhism.* New York: Harper & Row, 1968.

Suzuki, Shunryu. *Zen Mind, Beginner's Mind.* New York: Weatherhill, 1970.

Swihart, Altma K. *Since Mrs. Eddy.* New York: Henry Holt and Company, 1931.

Switzer, A. Irwin III. *D. T. Suzuki: A Biography.* London: The Buddhist Society, 1985.

Taizan, Maezumi Hakuyu, and Bernard Tetsugen Glassman, eds. *The Hazy Moon of Enlightenment.* Los Angeles: Zen Center of Los Angeles, 1977.

Taylor, Anne. *Annie Besant: A Biography* (Oxford: Oxford University Press, 1992).

*Teachings of the Temple.* 3 vols. Halcyon, Calif.: Temple of the People, 1947–85.

Thedra, Sister. *Mine Intercome Messages from the Realms of Light.* Sedona, Ariz.: Association of Sananda and Sanat Kumara, 1990.

Thedra. *Excerpts of Prophecies from Other Planets Concerning Our Earth.* Mt. Shasta, Calif.: Association of Sananda and Sanat Kumara, 1956.

"Theosophical Endowment Corporation" (a nonprofit corporation chartered by the state of California, 16 September 1942).

"Theosophical Endowment Corporation" (Certificate of Amendment of the Articles of Incorporation, 23 July 1953).

*The Theosophical Movement: 1875–1950.* Los Angeles: The Cunningham Press, 1951.

"The Theosophical Society: Inaugural Address of the President Delivered Before the Soceity November 17th, 1875."

The Theosophical Society Constitution (as amended August 27, 1971).

Thomas, Wendell. *Hinduism Invades America.* New York: Beacon Press, 1930.

Tiryakian, Edward, ed. *On the Margin of the Visible.* New York: John Wiley and Sons, 1974.

Trine, Ralph Waldo. *The Greatest Thing Ever Known.* New York: Thomas Y. Crowell, 1899.

Trungpa, Chögyam. *Born in Tibet.* Boulder, Colo.: Shambhala, 1976.

———. *Shambhala: Sacred Path of the Warrior.* Boulder, Colo.: Shambhala, 1985.

Tumminia, Diana and R. George Kirkpatrick. "Unarius: Emergent Aspects of a Flying Saucer Group." In *The Gods Have Landed: New Religions from Other Worlds.* Edited by James R. Lewis. Albany: State University of New York Press, 1995.

Twitchell, Paul. *Difficulties of Becoming the Living ECK Master.* Menlo Park, Calif.: IWP Publishing, 1980.

————. *ECKANKAR: The Key to Secret Worlds* (Crystal, Minn.: Illuminated Way Press, 1969).

United Lodge of Theosophists (U.L.T.) Biochronology of Robert Crosbie (unpublished)

————. *The Theosophical Movement: 1875–1950.* Los Angeles: The Cunningham Press, 1951.

————. "The United Lodge of Theosophists: Its Mission and Its Future." Los Angeles: Theosophy Comany, n.d.

Valiente, Doreen. *The Rebirth of Witchcraft.* London: Robert Hale, 1989.

Van Der Leeuw, G. *Religion in Essence and Manifestaton. Vol. 1.* (Gloucester, Mass.: Peter Smith, 1967.

Van Tassel, George. *I Rode a Flying Saucer* (Los Angeles: New Age Publishing Co., 1956).

————. *When Stars Look Down* (Los Angeles: Kruckeberg Press, 1976).

Versluis, Arthur. *Theosophia: Hidden Dimensions of Christianity.* Hudson, N.Y.: Lindisfarne Press, 1994.

Vincent, T. G. 1976. *Black Power and the Garvey Movement.* Berkeley: Ramparts Press.

Vivekananda, Swami. *The Complete Works of Swami Vivekananda.* 12 vols. Calcutta: Advaita Ashrama, 1965.

Von Däniken, Erich. *Chariots of the Gods? Unsolved Mysteries of the Past.* New York: G. P. Putnam's Sons, 1970.

Vorilhon, Claude [Rael]. *Extraterrestrial Took Me to their Planet.* Brantome:l'Edition du Message, 1986.

Wach Joachim. *Sociology of Religion.* Chicago: University of Chicago Press, 1944.

Wachsmuth, Guenther. *The Life and Work of Rudolf Steiner.* New York: Whittier Books, 1955.

Wadia, B. P. *To All Fellow Theosophists and Members of the Theosophical Society.* Los Angeles, 1922.

Wallis, Roy. "The Aetherius Society: A Case Study in the Formation of a Mystagogic Congregation." *Sociological Review* 22, no. 9 (1974): 27–44.

Walters, J. Donald. *Cities of Light.* Nevada City, Calif.: Crystal Clarity Publishers, 1987.

————. *The Path.* Nevada City, Calif.: Ananda Publications, 1977.

Ward, Maria. *Female Life Among the Mormons.* New York: J. C. Derby, 1855.

*We're Your Neighbor.* Alma, Ark.: Holy Alamo Christian church Consecrated, 1987.

Weaver, C. Douglas. *The Healer-Prophet, William Marrion Branham: A Study in the Prophetic in American Pentecostalism.* Macon, Ga.: Mercer University Press, 1987.

Webb, Gisela. "Subud." In *America's Alternative Religions.* Edited by Timothy Miller. Albany: State University of New York Press, 1995.

————. "Sufism in America." In *America's Alternative Religions.* Edited by Timothy Miller. Albany: State University of New York Press, 1995.

Weisbrot, Robert. *Father Divine and the Struggle for Racial Equality.* Urbana, Ill.: University of Illinois Press, 1983.

Wentz, Abdel Ross. *A Basic History of Lutheranism in America.* Philadelphia: Muhlenberg Press, 1964.

White, James. *Sketches of the Christian Life and Public Labors of William Miller.* Battle Creek, Mich.: Steam Press, 1875.

White, Joseph. *Musser Celestial or Plural Marriage*. Salt Lake City: Truth Publishing Co., 1944.

White, Philip. "Island Pond Raid 10 Years Later: State Versus Church." *The Sunday Rutland Herald and the Sunday Times Argus*. 19 June 1994.

Whitney, Louise Goddard. *The Burning of the Convent*. New York: Arno Pr., 1969; rpt. of 1877.

Williams, Raymond Brady. *Religions of Immigrants from India and Pakistan: New Threads of the American Tapestry*. New York: Cambridge University Press, 1988.

Williamson, George Hunt. *The Saucers Speak*. London: Neville Spearman, 1963.

Winberg, Steven L., ed. *Ramtha*. Eastsound, Washington: Sovereignty, 1986.

Yehuda, Shaleak Ben. *Black Hebrew Israelites from America to the Promised Land*. New York: Vantage Press, 1975.

Yinger, J. Milton. *Religion, Society, and the Individual*. New York: Macmillan, 1957.

Yogananda, Swami Paramahansa. *Autobiography of a Yogi*. 11th ed. Los Angeles: Self-Realization Fellowship, 1971.

————. *The Science of Religion*. Los Angeles: Yogoda Sat-Sanga Society of America, 1928.

Zablocki, Benjamin. *The Joyful Community*. Baltimore, Md.: Penguin Books, 1971.

Zalman, Aryeh Hilsenrad. *The Baal Shem Tov*. Brooklyn, New York: 1967.

Zell, Timothy [Otter]. *Cataclysm and Consciousness: From the Golden Age to the Age of Iron*. Redwood Valley, Calif.: The Author, 1977.

Zimmer, Heinrich. *Philosophies of India*. New York: Bollingen, 1951. Macmillan, 1987.

Zinsstag, Lou. *George Adamski: Their Man on Earth*. Tucson, Ariz.: UFO Photo Archives, 1990.

# INDEX